BUSINESS AND GOVERNMENT IN AMERICA SINCE 1870

A *Twelve-Volume Anthology of Scholarly Articles*

T0298628

Series Editor

ROBERT F. HIMMELBERG

Fordham University

SERIES CONTENTS

VOLUME

2

THE MONOPOLY ISSUE AND ANTITRUST 1900–1917

Edited with introductions by

ROBERT F. HIMMELBERG

Routledge
Taylor & Francis Group

LONDON AND NEW YORK

First published 1994 by Garland Publishing Inc.

2 Park Square, Milton Park, Abingdon, Oxfordshire OX14 4RN
52 Vanderbilt Avenue, New York, NY 10017

Routledge is an imprint of the Taylor & Francis Group, an informa business

First issued in paperback 2019

Introductions copyright © 1994 Robert F. Himmelberg

Library of Congress Cataloging-in-Publication Data

The Monopoly issue and antitrust, 1900–1917 / edited with introductions by Robert F. Himmelberg.
    p.   cm. — (Business and government in America since 1870 ; v. 2)
    Journal articles previously published 1958–1990.
    Includes bibliographical references.
    ISBN 0–8153–1404–3 (alk. paper)
    1. Trade regulation—United States—History. 2. Monopolies—United States—History. 3. Antitrust law—United States—History. 4. Progressivism (United States politics). 5. Business and politics—United States—History.   I. Himmelberg, Robert F. II. Series.
HD3616.U46M66 1994
338.8'2'0973—dc20   93–44788
                                               CIP

ISBN 13: 978-0-8153-1404-2 (hbk)
ISBN 13: 978-1-138-86558-7 (pbk)

CONTENTS

SERIES INTRODUCTION

This compilation of articles provides a very broad and representative selection of the scholarly literature found in learned journals on the subject of government-business relations in the age of industry, the period since 1870. The scope of this collection is wide, covering all the arenas of business-government interaction. Sectorially, the focus is on manufacturing and transportation, upon whose rapid expansion after the Civil War the modern industrial economy was founded.

For the volumes covering the years from 1870 to 1965 (Volumes I through IX) it has been possible, while exercising selectivity, to include a very high proportion of everything published within the past thirty years. This literature is found largely in historical journals. More selectivity had to be employed for Volumes X through XII, which cover the period since 1965. Historians have not yet trodden much on the ground of the very recent past but social scientists and legal scholars have offered abundant materials, so abundant as to require a relatively severe selectivity. By choosing articles that appear to have a long-term analytical value and by excluding those too narrow in scope, too preoccupied with methodological questions or otherwise unsuitable for a non-specialized audience, an extensive and accessible body of writing has, however, been assembled for the post-1965 period, mainly from economics and legal periodicals.

The volumes are designed to contain articles relating to a particular period and to one or more topics within a period. The literature of business-government relations has four logically distinct major topics: antitrust, regulation, promotion, and cooperation. These topics define distinctive aspects of the relationship. Yet, the distinctions sometimes in practice blur, the ostensible, publicly proclaimed purposes of policy sometimes differing from the actually intended purposes or the actual outcomes.

Antitrust policy emerges in Volume I, which covers the era 1870–1900 when big business appeared, and figures prominently throughout the series. Several volumes are devoted entirely to it. Uniquely American, at least until relatively recently, antitrust policy has a complex history and much of what scholars have discovered about its origin and evolution is recorded only in the articles gathered in this collection. The literature reproduced here makes clear that the intent and impact of antitrust policy has varied enormously during its one-hundred-year history, which dates from the Sherman Act of 1890. Tension between competing objectives has existed from the outset. Should the "trusts" be broken up on the grounds that super-corporations inevitably conflict with democratic government and entrepreneurial opportunity? Or should only "bad trusts", those guilty of crushing competitors through unfair methods, suffer dissolution? Is cartelistic behavior always an illegal restraint of trade, or should it sometimes be tolerated if it helps small business to survive? Put most broadly, should the aim of antitrust policy be simply promoting competition, or should other conflicting social and economic values be recognized?

Business regulation also arose during the early stages of industrialization, appearing at the federal level with the enactment of the Interstate Commerce Act in 1887. The term "regulation" is used here to denote government policies intended, not to promote or restore competition, but to require specific behavior from business. The classic justification for regulation was the argument that in some situations the public interest could be served only through governmental prescription, that in some instances a remedy simply could not be obtained through the workings of the marketplace. Theoretically there are two such instances. The first occurs in the case of "natural monopoly," market situations in which competition would be wasteful and competing firms do not and should not exist. Railroads and public utilities were early identified as industries of this sort and were the first targets of government regulation. Would-be regulators early discovered a second justification for applying the regulatory approach, the situation in which competition fails to provide rival firms with incentives to avoid methods that may injure public health or well being. The argument found early expression in regulation of the meat-packing industry and has over the course of the twentieth century created a remarkable body of federal regulatory practices. The history of regulation, however, has not unfolded, any more than the history of antitrust, according to the logic of theory. It has been determined by the interplay between many factors, including the ideas of reformers, the complaints of those who have felt injured, policy rivalries among businessmen themselves, and the capacity or incapacity of government to execute planned reform. A major focus of recent literature on regulation, and to an extent on antitrust also, is the thesis of capture, the notion that regulatory efforts have often fallen captive to the interests they were intended to oppose.

The third theme of relations between government and business, promotion and encouragement, also emerged during the initial stages of the industrial era. Railroad subsidies abounded during the age of building the transcontinentals, of course, and protective tariffs were almost as old as the Republic itself. In the early twentieth century government support of trade expansion abroad enlarged and gradually became a major thread of government policy. Resembling promotion but logically distinct in many respects is the fourth category of business-government interaction, the area of cooperative relationships. Few scholars, even those who believe ongoing conflict has chiefly characterized business-government relations, would deny that cooperation has occurred at certain points, as during American participation in the major wars of the twentieth century. But in recent years many writers who conceive of business-government relations as taking place within a "corporatist" framework have perceived the scope and continuity of cooperative tendencies as very broad.

These four categories describe the subjects or topics around which scholarly investigation of business-government relations has revolved. There is, however, another approach to analyzing the literature of this relationship, one in which we ask about a writer's interpretive perspective, the conceptualizations the writer brings to the subject. All historians and social scientists, including those who created the literature collected here, adopt an interpretive standpoint from which to view society and its workings. An interpretive standpoint is a way of understanding the structure of society and the way those structural elements relate and interact; in other words, it is a "model" of society. Several rival models have competed for acceptance among scholars in recent times. Readers will be better equipped for informed reading of the literature assembled in these volumes if they are knowledgeable about these interpretive standpoints and the aim here therefore is to define the most important of these and give them appropriate labels.

Until the 1950s the prevailing interpretation of business-government relations—indeed, of American history generally— was the progressive viewpoint. The term progressive refers in the first place to the reform ideology and activity of the early twentieth century, the period before World War I. The perspective of the progressive generation continued for many years to dominate historical writing, not only on the period itself but on the whole of American history. According to the progressive perspective, the rise of big business during the late nineteenth and early twentieth centuries created a radical shift in the balance of economic and political power in America in favor of concentrated wealth. The rise of the "trusts", the powerful firms that came to predominate in many industries in the years after 1880, and the creation of cartels and other arrangements for suppressing competition, threatened independent capitalists and consumers with raw economic exploitation. This concentration of economic power threatened to utterly suborn representative political institutions as well and reduce American democracy to a plutocracy. In the progressive view the predominating tone of business-government relations was therefore necessarily antagonistic and conflictual.

The progressive paradigm became deeply embedded in the American consciousness. Reformist politicians have often reverted to it in shaping their ideological and rhetorical appeals. Franklin D. Roosevelt's attack in the campaign of 1936 upon "economic royalists" and John Kennedy's denunciation in 1962 of Big Steel during the controversy over price guidelines as "utterly contemptuous of the public interest" are vivid examples. The progressive outlook is evidently a persistent element in the popular historical consciousness. The power of the progressive conception of American history is in fact readily confirmed by reference to the way twentieth-century history is periodized, in textbooks and popular histories, into epochs of reform (the Progressive, New Deal, Fair Deal and Great Society periods) and of reaction (the Twenties, the Eisenhower and Reagan eras).

But if the progressive interpretation of business government relations retains some force among some historians and in the consciousness of liberal opinion makers and the public, its hold on much of the academic mind has long since weakened. A reaction among historians and other academics against the progressive paradigm emerged soon after the end of the Second World War and gathered force during the 1950s. The reaction was especially sharp among historians writing business history. Writing at a time when a reinvigorated American economy appeared to have overcome the doldrums of the 1930s and to be demonstrating the superiority of capitalism over other systems, energetic business and economic historians completely revised the progressive interpretation of the founders of American big business. The revisionists interpreted the founders not as greedy robber barons but as heroes of the entrepreneurial spirit, the spirit of enterprise and productivity. This revisionist interpretation proved too one-dimensional and celebratory to be maintained without modification. Revisionism, however, did succeed in thoroughly discrediting the progressive point of view. This circumstance, together with the impact of interpretive concepts emanating from post-war social science, moved historians to replace the progressive paradigm with a new and more sophisticated framework for understanding American political economy, the pluralist framework.

Pluralism as the dominant interpretive mode replaced progressivism in the 1950s and 60s. Speaking broadly, the pluralist model understands public policy as the result of struggle between economic and social groups. A major by-product of industrialization is the sharpening of differences between groups playing distinctive economic roles and a heightened articulation of self-interested goals and purposes on the part of such groups. Thus, government-business relations, that is, the shape of government policies towards business, are the result of rivalries among the major interest groups, business, labor, consumers, and so on. But the nature of the struggle is complex because the major groups are themselves divided into more or less rivalrous sub-groups. Business itself is divided; both intra- and inter-industry rivalries exist, sometimes in acute forms. Government policy is not merely the result of nonbusiness groups seeking to shape that policy but also of some business interests seeking to impose their own wishes on others.

During the 1960s pluralist interpretation became more complex. One important source of this heightened complexity was what some commentators have called the "organizational" outlook. Again influenced by currents in American social science, this time sociology, practitioners employing the organizational perspective are struck by the ever-increasing importance of large bureaucratic organizations in American life since the onset of industrialization. Business has continuously evolved in terms of an ever larger role for the large corporation, but other spheres, including government and the professions, also are organized in terms of large hierarchical bureaucracies. Borrowing from Weberian sociological traditions, writers impressed by the organizational perspective have explored the thesis that large bureaucracies wherever situated have similar requirements and tend to develop in those who manage them similar values and expectations. Thus, this brand of pluralism stresses the extent to which group leaders, including the managers and technicians who run the large corporations, developed accommodative as well as merely self-seeking motives. Business leaders, many of them at least, came to share certain values, such as respect for stability in the overall economy, which leads them to seek harmonious and cooperative relationships between interest groups and between them and the government. Government is assigned the role, in this construct, of facilitating and stimulating cooperative modes of behavior and umpiring conflicts. In the literature on business and government, figures who have advocated this kind of polity are often dubbed "corporatists" or "corporate liberals." Broadly defined, corporatism is the practice of cooperation between government and the corporate world to resolve economic issues. The existence and the importance of corporatist relationships has been one of the major emphases of recent scholarship but there is much disagreement as to the intentions of its practitioners and its impact. Some scholars have interpreted corporatism in a more or less positive light, as an ideology and a practice entailing cooperation rather than conflict between government and business, as an alternative to an adversarial relationship, a way of obtaining desirable economic performance from business without resorting to governmental coercion.

But others, especially but not only those writing in the vein of the "New Left", have argued that members of the corporate elite have frequently pursued their own narrow interests under the cover of ostensibly cooperative endeavors. The New Leftists emerged in the 1960s, expounding a more radical criticism of business than the progressive-liberal historians had advanced. The New Leftists doubted or denied outright that the American system was pluralist at all in any meaningful sense. Control of public policy might appear as a contest between social groups, but in fact one group, or rather class, those who controlled big business, enjoyed such lopsided power that the contest was apparently not real. Behind the facade of political infighting over government policy toward business, the masters of the corporate world quietly steered events toward outcomes which cemented in place control of the economy by monopoly capital.

These four conceptualizations, the progressive, the pluralist, the corporatist, and the New Leftist, are essentially theories of the structure and process of American political economy. However, rarely are researchers slavishly devoted to a theoretical perspective. Thus, those who see, in the progressive vein, an ongoing conflictual relationship between the people and business sometimes argue against the reformers and in favor of the businessmen. Even more significant and widespread is the conclusion of many writers using the pluralist or corporatist modes of interpretation, that regulation has not fostered equity and economic progress but rather has hardened the economy's vital arteries. Pluralists initially assumed that policies arising from a political arena to which all organized interests have access will inevitably achieve benign results, that the policy outputs will construct a system of "countervailing power" among organized interest groups. The assumption of acceptable outcomes is still prevalent, but a skeptical version of the results of interest group rivalries became manifest in the late

1960s, holding that both in origin and ongoing impact, business regulation was too often subject to "capture." In this view, regulatory measures and agencies and other policies seeking to guide business behavior toward balanced and generally acceptable outcomes readily fall under the control of the very interests they were intended to regulate.

There has emerged in recent years still another approach to the origin and process of social-economic policy that has been applied to the business-government connection. In this interpretation of the connection, a few examples of which will be found in articles collected here, emphasis is placed on the relative autonomy of government administrators and regulators. Seen by the pluralists as merely the creatures of the organizational struggles that result in public policies, in this new view regulators are seen as possessing substantial room for independent action. Thus the state is not merely to be seen as a passive receptor and executor of outcomes that social forces determine but as having a partially autonomous role which the officers of the state presumably will use to extend their own interests rather than the interests articulated by social groups.

These categories, progressivism, pluralism, corporatism, Leftism and the "autonomous officialdom" viewpoint, represent the major schools of thought and interpretation that readers will discover in the literature reproduced in these volumes. Writers investigating specific historical incidents, trends or problems have, in most cases, written through the framework provided by one or another of these interpretive models. As an alert reader will discover, most writers do have certain assumptions about the structure and dynamics of social relationships, and these assumptions stem from one of the models that have been described.

Interpretation of the relationship between business and government in the age of industry has given rise to a literature that is large and complex. It presents a stimulating intellectual challenge and is certainly relevant for anyone seeking understanding of contemporary business-government relations and endeavoring to predict, or to shape, their future course.

INTRODUCTION

This period is traditionally known as the Progressive Era. Contemporaries, and historians after them, conceived of it as a period of seminal reform. These are the years of Presidents Theodore Roosevelt and Woodrow Wilson (1901–1909 and 1913–1921, respectively), each regarded as reformers of major stature.

One of the most important, probably the central issue of the era, was the "trusts", the giant combinations that in many cases dominated entire industries. The period 1897–1902, as the United States emerged from the depression of the 1890s, was one of intensive merger activity. In numerous industries, combinations through merger resulted in creation of one, or a few, dominant firms. The resulting industrial structure across a broad range of industries was one of near monopoly or of tight oligopoly, control by a few. During the 1890s, among Americans of all social strata, a broad and deep conviction developed that the corporate world was irresponsible, characterized by arrogance and disregard for the public good. An additional concern, exacerbated by the appearance around the turn of the century of so many powerful corporate giants, grew out of a long-standing dimension of American political ideology, the conviction that concentrated power, in whatever form, threatened democracy and liberty. A fear developed, in other words, as Richard McCormick shows in his essay in this volume, that the trusts would corrupt and dominate politics.

Roosevelt earned the sobriquet of "trust-buster" by successfully using the Sherman Antitrust Law in the 1902 *Northern Securities* case. For years, since the Supreme Court's 1895 decision in the *Knight* sugar trust case, legal opinion held that the Court would not sustain application of the Sherman Act to combinations produced by mergers. In numerous decisions the Court had agreed that cartels (agreements among independent firms) violated the Sherman's Act's prohibition against "restraint of trade." However, the Court's position in the *Knight* case, as well as lack of an aggressive determination on the part of the Justice Department, had persuaded promoters that "tight-knit" combinations produced by merger would escape unscathed. On the other hand, Roosevelt, convinced he had to respond to popular alarm, vigorously prosecuted Northern Securities, a combination of railroads in the American Northwest, under the Sherman Act and succeeded in breaking it up. Having demonstrated the government's potential capacity to dissolve big combinations, however, Roosevelt refrained until nearly the end of his presidency from further trust prosecutions. As Robert Wiebe and other authors represented here explain, Roosevelt preferred a policy of informal regulation to trust-busting. His successor, however, the Republican William Howard Taft, believed he was obligated by the law to move against the trusts and launched a remarkable number of prosecutions during his one-term presidency. Two cases proved especially important, *Standard Oil* and *American Tobacco*. Both were initiated late in Roosevelt's presidency. Taft's Attorney General, George Wickersham, fought the cases to a conclusion before the Supreme Court in 1911. The Court's ruling in these cases held immense importance for the future course of antitrust policy in the United States. While the Court accepted the Justice Department's demand for dismemberment of the two corporations, which at the time exerted quasi-monopoly control of their industries, it included in its decision a dictum that made future prosecutions of trusts difficult. Known as the "rule of reason," the Court's dictum held that big corporations were not liable to dissolution under the Sherman Act merely on account of their size. They would be held guilty of restraint of trade or monopolization only if they were found to have abused their relative economic power by using unfair or abusive tactics against rival firms.

Eventually, the result was governmental acceptance of a high degree of economic concentration in many industries. When the Democratic Party, after many years of Republican dominance, returned to power in 1912, gaining control of both the Presidency and Congress, it was unable, despite strong intentions to the contrary among important elements of the party, to reverse the policy the Supreme Court had fashioned in 1911. Some attempt was made to revive prosecution of trusts, but the main contribution of Wilson and his followers was to strengthen the government's capacity to prevent powerful corporations from using unfair tactics against competitors. In the Clayton and Federal Trade Commission Acts of 1914 the Democrats fashioned legal and administrative methods to foster a more vigorous competitive climate in which, they hoped, the relative size and monopolistic influence of the trusts would gradually be diminished.

The authors represented in this volume take up the points outlined in the foregoing paragraphs. As the reader will discover, some of these points are matters of controversy. What precisely the intentions and aims of the reformers were, and what the actual impact of their interventions was, are complex interpretive issues historians have long argued over and continue to debate.

From Peckham to White:
economic welfare and the rule of reason

BY JOHN R. CARTER*

I.

In his pronouncement of the rule of reason in the *Standard Oil* decision[1] Justice White maintained that there was no fundamental difference between his rule and the construction given to the Sherman Act more than a decade earlier by Justice Peckham. The rule of reason and Peckham's test of direct and indirect restraint were ultimately "one and the same thing."[2] Such a claim provoked a bitter dissent from Justice Harlan,[3] who found White's assertion to be as surprising as "a statement that black was white or white was black."[4] Harlan's interpretation of the Peckham rule was that every restraint of interstate trade was unlawful independent of its

---

* Assistant Professor of Economics, College of the Holy Cross, Worcester, Mass.

[1] Standard Oil Co. of New Jersey v. U.S., 221 U.S. 1 (1911).

[2] *Id.* at 66.

[3] Standard Oil Co. of New Jersey v. U.S., 221 U.S. 1 (1911) (Harlan, J., concurring and dissenting); U.S. v. American Tobacco Co., 221 U.S. 106 (1911) (Harlan, J., concurring and dissenting).

[4] U.S. v. American Tobacco Co., 221 U.S. 106, 191 (1911) (Harlan, J., concurring and dissenting).

reasonableness. White's pronouncement of the rule of reason, Harlan charged, was clearly a blatant act of judicial legislation.[5]

At least one antitrust scholar has found White's claim to be both sincere and convincing. Robert Bork argues that the inherent policy of the two constructions is the promotion of economic welfare, and that it is from this common policy that their fundamental identity is derived.[6] Bork builds his argument upon a critical reading of the Peckham and White opinions. The objective in this article is to supplement Bork's reading with a review of several lower court opinions written during the period between the Peckham and White decisions. It will be argued that Harlan's interpretation of the Peckham rule was exceedingly narrow, that there was evidenced in several lower courts a more flexible interpretation which constituted unmistakably a rule of reason, and that the policy implicit in this rule was the promotion of economic welfare.

II.

Justice Peckham's construction of the Sherman Act evolved in a sequence of five major opinions written between 1897 and 1899.[7] The first of these decisions was written by Peckham for the narrowest majority of five justices in *U.S. v. Trans-Missouri Freight Assoc.*[8] The case involved an association of 15 railroads formed with the express purpose of eliminating ruinous competition "by establishing and maintaining reasonable rates, rules, and regula-

---

[5] Standard Oil Co. of New Jersey v. U.S., 221 U.S. 1, 100 (1911) (Harlan, J., concurring and dissenting).

[6] Bork, "The Rule of Reason and the Per Se Concept: Price Fixing and Market Division," 74 *Yale Law Journal* 775, 801-05, 829-32 (1965). *See also* R. Bork, *The Antitrust Paradox* 33-41 (1978).

[7] U.S. v. Trans-Missouri Freight Assoc., 166 U.S. 290 (1897); U.S. v. Joint Traffic Assoc., 171 U.S. 505 (1898); Hopkins v. U.S., 171 U.S. 578 (1898); Anderson v. U.S., 171 U.S. 604 (1898); and Addyston Pipe and Steel Co. v. U.S., 175 U.S. 211 (1899).

[8] U.S. v. Trans-Missouri Freight Assoc., 166 U.S. 290 (1897).

tions on all freight traffic.'"[9] Apart from the question of the applicability of the Sherman Act to railroads, the paramount issue before the Court was whether the statute should be constructed to declare illegal only unreasonable restraints of trade, as was urged by the defense upon its reading of common law, or reasonable and unreasonable restraints alike.

The latter position was adopted by the Court. Peckham wrote:

> Under these circumstances we are, therefore, asked to hold that the act of Congress excepts contracts which are not in unreasonable restraint of trade, and which only keep rates up to a reasonable price, not withstanding the language of the act makes no exception. . . . This we cannot and ought not do.[10]

The *Trans-Missouri* decision declared that every restraint of trade was illegal under the Sherman Act, yet absent from the opinion was any explicit definition of what constituted such a restraint. After a brief review of the nature of the railroad association, Peckham concluded simply that "its direct, immediate and necessary effect is to put a restraint upon trade or commerce as described in the act." [11]

The *Trans-Missouri* decision provided the basis for Harlan's dissent to White's rule of reason. However, as Bork has noted,[12] and as the earlier excerpt from Peckham's opinion makes clear, the *Trans-Missouri* defense understood the reasonableness of the restraint to be synonymous with the reasonableness of the prices being maintained, and it is this standard of reasonableness that was rejected by Peckham. Moreover, it is dangerous and almost surely misleading to attempt to construct Peckham's interpretation of the statute on the basis of the *Trans-Missouri* opinion alone. As already suggested, Peckham's interpretation evolved over the course of several years and several decisions.

---

[9] *Id.* at 292.

[10] *Id.* at 340.

[11] *Id.* at 342.

[12] Bork, "The Rule of Reason," *supra* note 6, at 785-89.

The opportunity to clarify his Sherman Act construction was presented to Peckham in *U.S. v. Joint Traffic Assoc.*,[13] decided 19 months after *Trans-Missouri*. The facts were remarkably similar in the two cases, both involving railroad rate fixing associations. The defense was altered slightly in the second case. The earlier decision appeared to close the issue of reasonableness of prices while perhaps leaving open the meaning of trade restraint. The Joint Traffic defense was formulated accordingly. The industry was vulnerable to ruinous competition; such competition was destructive of trade; conversely, the agreed elimination of ruinous competition was promotive of trade; hence, the railroad association did not constitute a trade restraint.

Peckham and the Court's majority once again rejected the ruinous competition defense and held that the rate fixing association was in restraint of trade. In the course of the opinion the intended meaning of trade restraint was made clear. Having determined that the "natural, direct and necessary effect" of the association's articles was to eliminate competition among its members, Peckham pronounced:

> The natural, direct and immediate effect of competition is, however, to lower rates, and to thereby increase demand for commodities, the supplying of which increases commerce, and an agreement, whose first and direct effect is to prevent this play of competition, restrains instead of promoting trade and commerce.[14]

This pronouncement serves as an efficient summary statement of Peckham's test for unlawful restraint and is termed here the Peckham rule.

The Peckham rule enjoined only direct restrictions on competition as restraints of trade; indirect or incidental restrictions were deemed lawful. The rule therefore demanded in its application a standard of reason distinguishing between direct and indirect restrictions. From a reading of Peckham's remaining decisions it can be inferred that the distinction made by Peckham constituted a policy of promoting economic welfare.

---

[13] U.S. v. Joint Traffic Assoc., 171 U.S. 505 (1898).

[14] *Id.* at 577.

It is useful to review briefly the meaning of economic welfare in its conventional partial equilibrium sense. In the absence of externalities it is defined as the difference between consumer valuation and producer opportunity cost for a given rate of output. Thus, economic welfare may be viewed as the economic gains which arise from production and trade and which accrue to producers and consumers. These gains are increased by definition (1) if the valuation-cost differential is widened across rates of output and/or (2) if production and trade are extended toward that output for which price, and therefore marginal valuation, equals marginal cost. In the first instance there is said to occur an increase in productive efficiency; in the second instance there is said to exist an increase in allocative efficiency. Hence, promotion of economic welfare is synonymous with promotion of economic efficiency.

Profit seeking behavior of a firm normally acts on economic welfare by either inducing a gain in productive efficiency, a loss in allocative efficiency, or both.[15] An increase in productive efficiency will ordinarily be associated with an increase in both profits and output. A loss in allocative efficiency will be associated with an increase in profits but a decrease in output. A policy promoting economic welfare is then described as follows. Business conduct whose sole or primary effect is to restrict output and hence induce allocative inefficiency would be proscribed. Profit raising business conduct, whether enacted unilaterally or in combination, whose sole or primary effect is to induce productive efficiency would be sanctioned. Peckham's distinction between direct and indirect restrictions on competition constituted such a policy.

The five major opinions written by Peckham reveal clearly that he essentially defined unlawful trade restraint to be output restriction. As the rule quoted above reveals, Peckham appreciated that the natural effect of competitive rivalry was to lower prices and to extend trade. To directly eliminate competition permitted the enhancement of price and the diminution of output and thus restrained trade. An incidental restriction, however, which neither

---

[15] Exceptions would include some forms of price discrimination and cheating on a cartel agreement.

raised price nor reduced output, promoted trade and was therefore left outside of the Sherman Act. It is possible to document the validity of this interpretation of the Peckham rule with a critical reading of the Peckham decisions. This exercise has already been carried out by Bork and need not be repeated here.[16] However, several particularly lucid excerpts from the Peckham decisions are provided in the footnote below.[17]

---

[16]   Bork, "The Rule of Reason," *supra* note 6, at 785-96, 829-32.

[17]   Unlawful trade restraint is defined explicitly as output restriction in the following excerpt from *Addyston Pipe*, a case involving a bidding cartel of six pipe manufacturers:

"If iron pipe cost one hundred dollars a ton instead of the prices which the record shows were paid for it, no one, we think, would contend that the trade in it would amount to as much as if the lower prices prevailed. The higher price would operate as a direct restraint upon the trade, and therefore any contract or combination which enhanced the price might in some degree restrain the trade in the article. . . . And when by reason of the combination a particular contract may have been obtained for one of the parties thereto, but at a higher price than would otherwise have been paid, the charge that the combination was one in restraint of trade is not answered by the statement that the particular contract was in truth obtained and not prevented. The parties to such a combination might realize more profit by the higher prices they would secure than they could earn by doing more work at a much less price. The question is as to the effect of such combination upon the trade in the article, and if that effect be to destroy competition and thus advance the price, the combination is one in restraint of trade." Addyston Pipe and Steel Co. v. U.S., 175 U.S. 211, 245 (1899).

The sanction of indirect restrictions on competition which are promotive of trade is illustrated in *Anderson*, a case brought by the government against an open livestock traders' association, the by-laws of which stipulated a refusal to deal with nonmembers. Ruling in favor of the association (with Harlan dissenting), Peckham wrote:

"The [refusal to deal] rule has no direct tendency to diminish or in any way impede or restrain interstate commerce in the cattle dealt in by defendants. . . . [The agreement] has no tendency, so far as can be gathered from its object or from the language of its rules and regulations, to limit the number of cattle marketed or to limit or reduce their price or to place any impediment or obstacle in the course of the commercial stream which flows into the Kansas City cattle market." Anderson v. U.S., 171 U.S. 604, 617, 620 (1898).

III.

It has been maintained that over the course of several cases Justice Peckham fashioned a rule of reason supportive of economic welfare. Under that rule direct restrictions on competition whose main purpose or effect was to enhance price and diminish output were declared to be unlawful trade restraints. Restrictions whose primary object was to promote trade were termed indirect and incidental and were sanctioned under the rule. In the present section this interpretation of Peckham's rule will be supported with a review of five subsequent lower court decisions which cited the Peckham opinions for precedence and which were consistent with the maintained interpretation. Two cases pertaining to putatively exclusionary practices are outlined first, followed by three cases involving vertical and/or horizontal integration.

Judge Sanborn's opinion in *Whitwell v. Continental Tobacco Co.*[18] is indicative of the tone and rationale of the opinions to be reviewed in this section. The sole question decided was whether the practice of exclusive dealing constituted a conspiracy to restrain or an attempt to monopolize trade in violation of the Sherman Act. For a number of years Continental Tobacco, a dominant firm in the production of plug and chewing tobacco, had been in the practice of essentially selling for a much reduced price if the purchaser agreed to refrain from dealing in competitors' products for the 4-month duration of a contract. Whitwell, a tobacco jobber and an established customer of Continental, upon a renewal date of his contract refused to accept the restrictive condition of the purchase agreement. Continental in turn refused to supply Whitwell at the lower price. Electing not to buy at the higher price, Whitwell sued Continental for treble damages.[19] A demurrer to the complaint was

---

[18]   125 F. 454 (8th Cir. 1903).

[19]   The suit was brought against Continental and one of its sales agents. In his decision Sanborn conceded for argument but did not decide that there may exist a conspiracy to restrain trade between an employer and employee. *Id.* at 460.

sustained by the district court, and an appeal was heard before Judges Sanborn, Thayer, and VanDevanter in the Eighth Circuit. The judgment of the lower court was upheld.

Judge Sanborn's reading of the Peckham opinions was identical to the interpretation maintained in this article. Citing the Peckham decisions, Judge Sanborn enunciated the Peckham rule as follows:

> That purpose [of the Sherman Act] was to prevent the stifling or substantial restriction of competition, and the test of the legality of a combination under the act which was inspired by this purpose is its direct and necessary effect upon competition in commerce among the states. If its necessary effect is to stifle or to directly and substantially restrict free competition, it is a contract, combination, or conspiracy in restraint of trade, and it falls under the ban of the law. [Citations omitted.]

> If, on the other hand, it promotes or but incidentally or indirectly restricts competition, while its main purpose and chief effect are to foster the trade and to increase the business of those who make and operate it, then it is not a contract, combination, or conspiracy in restraint of trade, within the true interpretation of this act, and it is not subject to its denunciation. [Citations omitted.][20]

The reasoning employed by Sanborn was straightforward and concise. The practice of exclusive dealing was not a direct restriction on competition, and hence it did not constitute an unlawful restraint, because unlike the price fixing of *Trans-Missouri*, *Joint Traffic*, and *Addyston Pipe*, it involved no agreed elimination of competition among competitors. Sanborn wrote:

> But there was no restriction upon competition here, because this act left the rivals of the tobacco company free to compete for sales to the customers of the tobacco company by offering to them goods at lower prices or on better terms than they secured from that company.[21]

In essence, the exclusive dealing arrangement was part of, rather than a restraint on, the process of competition.

---

[20] *Id.* at 458-59.

[21] *Id.* at 461.

Identical reasoning was employed by Sanborn and the Eighth Circuit in *Phillips v. Iola Portland Cement Co.*,[22] issued simultaneously with *Whitwell*. In January of 1901 Parr and Company, a merchant in Texas, signed a contract with Iola for the purchase of a fixed quantity of cement at a specified price. Included in the contract was an agreement that Parr would not sell or ship the purchased cement outside of the State of Texas. During the term of the contract, Parr accepted and paid for approximately only one-half of the agreed allotment. Iola sued Parr for damages, and Phillips, a copartner of Parr, responded that the contract was void because its resale clause was in violation of the Sherman Act. The lower judgment in favor of Iola was sustained by the Eighth Circuit. Noting that the contract placed no restrictions upon the conduct of Iola's rivals, Sanborn added:

> If it had the effect to restrain Parr & Co. from using the product which they purchased to compete with other jobbers or manufacturers in the country beyond the limits of the state of Texas, this restriction was not the chief purpose or the main effect of the contract of sale, but a mere indirect and immaterial incident of it.[23]

Whitwell and *Phillips* illustrate Peckham's rule of reason and suggest its economic welfare policy objective. Particularly interesting and noteworthy is the conformity of Sanborn's reasoning to what may be termed today Director's analysis of exclusionary practices.[24] That analysis recognizes that restrictive clauses are not imposed freely by the seller but in essence must be purchased, typically by means of a price concession. This concession can augment market power if it imposes greater losses on rivals of the seller than are experienced by the seller. Since the conduct of rivals remains unrestrained, it is doubtful that this condition is satisfied. Dismissing induced market power as the rationale for the restrictive clause, efficiency or price discrimination is inferred as the objective. The

---

[22] 125 F. 593 (8th Cir. 1903).

[23] *Id*. at 595.

[24] For an early analysis, *see* Director and Levi, "Law and the Future: Trade Regulation," 51 *Northwestern University Law Review* 281 (1956). For more recent and complete statements, *see* R. Bork, *The Antitrust Paradox* (1978); R. Posner, *Antitrust Law* (1976).

concession might be made in order to encourage sales effort, to avoid free-rider effects, or to reduce transactions costs, presumptively thereby increasing economic welfare. Alternatively, the practice might serve as a means of increasing the returns from existent market power through price discrimination, in which case the effect on economic welfare is a priori indeterminate.

An interesting complement to *Whitwell* and *Phillips* was the case of *Wheeler-Stenzel Co. v. National Window Glass Jobbers Assoc.*,[25] decided upon appeal in 1907 by Judges Gray, Dallas, and Buffington. National Jobbers was a corporation engaged in the purchase of window glass for resale by its wholesaler stockholders, who allegedly accounted for better than 75 percent of the wholesale business. Wheeler-Stenzel, a Boston wholesaler suing for treble damages, charged that there existed since February of 1900 an unlawful combination among the defendant, its member wholesalers, and American Window Glass Company. The latter was the dominant manufacturer of window glass and a virtual monopoly in the better grades of such glass.

The combination was alleged to be elaborate.[26] National Jobbers agreed to purchase exclusively from American Window Glass provided that prices of rival manufacturers were no more than 5 percent below those of American. Furthermore, National Jobbers agreed to boycott any rival manufacturer who refused to close its plant or restrict its output upon instruction by American Window Glass. American Window Glass in turn allowed a 2½-5 percent discount on its glass sold to National Jobbers. The quantity of glass sold to each member wholesaler was fixed and limited jointly by National Jobbers and American Window Glass. Further horizontal restraints were alleged to exist between the member wholesalers. Wheeler-Stenzel declared that National Jobbers fixed "unreasonable and excessive prices" to retailers and also fixed the geographic resale territories of its members. Member wholesalers were permitted to sell to nonmember wholesalers only at the higher fixed retailer

---

[25]   152 F. 864 (3d Cir. 1907).

[26]   *Id.* at 869-70.

prices and were subject to pecuniary fine if discovered in violation of this rule.

Wheeler-Stenzel, finding its only alternatives were to buy quality glass either at a premium from American Glass or at the fixed retailer prices from National Jobbers, brought suit under the Sherman Act. A demurrer was entered and sustained by the lower court. The judgment was reversed upon appeal. In the appeal National Jobbers argued that the declared combination was lawful since it was merely an exclusive dealing agreement between a manufacturer and a group of wholesalers.[27] The defense was rejected by Judge Gray, who observed that there was "something more, however, set forth in the declaration affecting the character and operation of this contract."[28] Gray condemned the fixing of quantities, retailer prices, and geographic territories. Gray also found obnoxious the agreed boycott of manufacturers uncooperative with policy dictated by American Glass.[29]

It is possible to interpret the combination in its entirety as a (near) bilateral successive monopoly.[30] In the absence of combination, such a structure is expected to yield a final price which is higher and a quantity which is lower than the industry profit maximizing price and quantity. This divergence creates then the impetus for vertical integration either by ownership or by contract. The latter requires a price-quantity agreement between the monopolist seller and the monopsonist/monopolist resaler. If the agreement is complete, the quantity will be set as if the resaler is a price taker, and the joint profits will be divided according to the transfer price negotiated between the two parties. The vertical combination would permit a lower final price, a higher output, and hence an increase in economic welfare relative to the outcome without vertical combination.

---

[27] *Id.* at 870.

[28] *Id.* at 871.

[29] *Id.*

[30] For a lucid review of bilateral and successive monopoly, *see* F. Warren-Boulton, *Vertical Control of Markets* 51-64 (1978).

11

While this analysis explains the price-quantity agreement which existed between American Glass and National Jobbers, it does not vitiate Judge Gray's decision. In the bilateral monopoly model the existence of the monopsonist is granted as datum. However, in *Wheeler-Stenzel* the horizontal combination between the jobbers was itself charged unlawful. Unlike *Whitwell* and *Phillips*, the restriction on competition was direct. The horizontal combination could offer no welfare gain; indeed, a welfare loss followed to whatever extent the subsequent vertical price-quantity agreement was incomplete or costly to maintain. Furthermore, included in the vertical combination was an agreed group boycott organized to enforce collusive conduct at the manufacturing level.

In *Whitwell*, *Phillips*, and *Wheeler-Stenzel* a standard of reason was employed by judges which led to a distinction between horizontal and vertical combinations. This distinction was maintained in the joint venture case of *Arkansas Brokerage Co. v. Dunn & Powell.*[31] In 1906 five dominant jobbers doing business in Pine Bluff organized a brokerage company which was held exclusively by them but which was open to service other jobbers as well. As would be expected, the five jobbers removed their purchases from competing brokers unless prices were offered "sufficiently low to neutralize the advantages they would secure by making their purchases through their own agency."[32] One such competitor was Dunn & Powell, a regional broker with a branch office in Pine Bluff. Suffering loss of business to Arkansas Brokerage, Dunn & Powell withdrew from Pine Bluff and subsequently filed suit for treble damages, charging that the joint venture violated the Sherman Act. A judgment for the plaintiff was rendered in the trial court. The judgment was reversed in favor of Arkansas Brokerage upon appeal to the circuit court, where the case was heard by Judges Adams, Riner, and Amidon.

In its opinion the court emphasized the unrestrained openness of competition in the brokerage industry and discounted the import of Dunn & Powell's loss of business. Judge Adams wrote:

---

[31]   173 F. 899 (8th Cir. 1909).

[32]   *Id.* at 900.

The organization of the brokerage company as a competitor in business open to all had no natural tendency to directly or necessarily restrain commerce between the states, and the proof fails to show that it actually did restrain, lessen, or in any way stifle its free flow. The volume of that commerce, after as well as before the organization of the brokerage company, was determined by the fixed economic laws of demand and supply. . . . Any one who had been in the business before could remain in it, and any one who wished to enter it afterwards could freely do so; but they had necessarily to compete with others, including the brokerage company, with whatever advantages they possessed for conducting a prosperous business.[33]

Rather than as a restraint on competition, Adams viewed the joint venture by the jobbers as an expedient of competition with the object "to promote economy in the management of their existing business and to extend it into other fields of legitimate enterprise."[34] After citing Peckham's *Hopkins* and *Anderson* and Sanborn's *Whitwell* and *Phillips* decisions, Adams concluded his opinion with the following dictum:

Free competition is the life of trade and commerce, and it is quite as important to approve all lawful, fair, and reasonable expedients devised to promote individual success as it is to condemn vicious and unlawful practices which violate individual right and the public weal.[35]

In *Arkansas Brokerage*, as in the previous cases reviewed, the economic reasoning was concise and uncluttered. A few summary remarks are offered here in support of Judge Adams' decision. First, while the dominance of the five jobbers taken together in the Pine Bluff market was recognized, there was neither accusation nor evidence presented suggesting any horizontal collusion among the jobbers. Second, even if for the sake of argument monopoly power was imputed to the jobbers at the resale level, there would be no motive for backward integration other than increased economic efficiency. Finally, the vertical venture presented no threat of

---

[33] *Id.* at 901.

[34] *Id.* at 902-03.

[35] *Id.* at 903.

monopsonization inasmuch as Arkansas Brokerage purchased its wares from manufacturers selling in regional interstate markets if not national markets.[36]

The final decision to be reviewed in this section is *Bigelow v. Calumet & Hecla Mining Co.*[37] In 1907 Calumet acquired substantial stockholdings in a contiguous copper mine, Osceola Company, and in the solicitation of proxies explicitly vowed to vote a new board of directors pledged to the initiation of significant policy changes. Bigelow, president and stockholder of Osceola, sued for a permanent injunction restraining Calumet from voting its shares. It was charged by Bigelow that the purpose of the takeover was to suppress competition between the two mines and thereby obtain a monopoly. Calumet answered that the object was to secure a more economical management of the two firms by the common usage of mine shafts and machinery as well as the integration of smelting, refining, and distribution functions.[38] Judge Knappen initially

---

[36] Perhaps some elaboration on the first two comments is warranted. Conceivably one could argue that the vertical integration standardized costs between the jobbers and thereby facilitated horizontal resaler collusion. However, the argument would be highly speculative, and one would be pressed to explain why procurement cost differences in such a simple market would be anything other than ephemeral. On the second point, it is a well-known result that under the assumption of fixed proportions, vertical integration by a monopolist at one level of production into a second level which is competitive yields no increase in profits unless there is generated a cost reduction. It is true that under variable proportions vertical integration promises gains via the broadening of monopoly (albeit with ambiguous welfare effects); however, this result pertains only to forward integration. *See* McGee and Bassett, "Vertical Integration Revisited," 19 *Journal of Law & Economics* 17 (1976). The present case, of course, involves backward integration between successive stages of distribution for which the assumption of fixed proportions is probably adequate. Finally, entry barrier arguments relating to vertical integration are normally weak and would appear particularly ludicrous in the context of this case.

[37] Temporary injunction issued 155 F.869 (C.C.W.D. Mich.), *bill dismissed* 167 F. 704 (C.C.W.D. Mich.), *affirmed* 167 F. 721 (6th Cir. 1909).

[38] Calumet's testimony was summarized as follows:

granted a temporary injunction but upon final hearing dismissed the bill against Calumet. Knappen's decision was affirmed upon appeal.

Judge Knappen's decision for Calumet in the lower court is notable for its sophisticated application of the Peckham rule of reason. Knappen's articulation of that rule deserves quotation:

> It is settled that a combination does not violate the federal statute merely because it may indirectly, incidentally, or remotely restrain trade or tend toward monopoly. If its necessary effect is to stifle or to directly and substantially restrict interstate commerce, it falls under the ban of the law. On the other hand, if it only incidentally or indirectly restricts competition, while its main purpose and chief effect are to promote the business and increase the trade of the consumers, it is not denounced or voided by the law.[39]

As previously noted, in the four cases already reviewed the Peckham rule was used to distinguish explicitly or implicitly between horizontal and vertical combination. Restrictions essentially vertical in nature were believed to leave competition substantially unrestrained and thus were placed outside of the Sherman Act. The question arises whether under the Peckham rule an essentially horizontal combination would necessarily be enjoined by the statute. Knappen addressed this issue and answered as follows:

"The Kearsarge lode runs through the mines of the Calumet & Hecla, Osceola, Centennial, Allouez, La Salle, and Fratiot. The testimony tends to show that the Calumet & Hecla Company proposes by combining the Osceola with its other holdings to operate that company, the Calumet & Hecla, Centennial, Allouez, and possibly other mines, by sinking through Osceola lands shafts for other mines, shafts for the Osceola through the lands of other companies, and using for some or all of these mines on the lode drifts or openings from the lands of other mines, using machinery in common to some extent for two or more of such mines, including the Osceola, and having ores from all these mines stamped, smelted, refined and sold through Calumet & Hecla agencies." Bigelow v. Calumet & Hecla Mining Co., 155 F. 869, 872 (C.C.W.D. Mich. 1907).

[39] Bigelow v. Calumet & Hecla Mining Co., 167 F. 704, 712 (C.C.W.D. Mich. 1908).

15

The conclusion reached is that . . . the authorities do not go to the extent of holding that in the absence of intent, or of special features or conditions, every case of control by a manufacturing or a mining corporation over a competitor, through stock ownership and consequent direction of corporate management, creates per se, directly, immediately, and necessarily, a restraint upon trade; and I am not prepared to hold that such is its effect.[40]

The greater portion of Knappen's opinion involved then a review of evidence pertaining to the intent and expected effect of the takeover.

Four factors were significant in Knappen's decision for Calumet. First, testimony was cited which indicated that the productivity of the rock mined by Calumet was significantly diminished, and in the absence of expansion Calumet's reserves would be depleted within about 15 years.[41] Second, Knappen was convinced by the evidence that substantial technical economies were promised by the integration of the Calumet and Osceola mines.[42] Third, it was ob-

---

[40]   *Id.* at 716.

[41]   "The conglomerate rock mined by the Calumet & Hecla Company originally yielded 100 pounds of copper to the ton, but the percentage of copper has decreased with the depth at which the vein is mined, until now it yields but little more than 40 pounds. The testimony fairly indicates that the profitable life of the Calumet & Hecla Company, in mining upon the conglomerate lode, at the present rate of production, is about 15 years, and that when this lode is exhausted, unless considerably more territory is secured, the industrial life of the Calumet & Hecla Company will be greatly impaired, and several million dollars worth of equipment and plants rendered in large part valueless." *Id.* at 710.

[42]   "The Kearsarge lode can be most advantageously worked by the Calumet & Hecla Company, through friendly cooperation with the Osceola, Centennial, Allouez, and La Salle mines, not unusual between mining companies sustaining friendly relations toward each other. Certain abandoned shafts of the Osceola Company are thought by the Calumet & Hecla Company to be available for mining the Osceola amygdaloid lode as well as the conglomerate lode of the Calumet & Hecla Property, and certain shafts of the Osceola Company it is thought may ultimately be profitably extended into the Allouez and Centennial workings, and certain shafts upon other properties in which the Calumet & Hecla is interested it is believed can be advantageously used in the Osceola Company's territory. The relations between the Calumet & Hecla and the Osceola Companies were not such as to permit cooperation." *Id.* at 711.

16

served that Osceola and a number of associated mines sold their copper through a common sales agent, the United States Metals Selling Company. Any elimination of competition between Calumet and Osceola would be reciprocated with an increase in competition between Calumet and United States Metals.[43]

The fourth important factor considered by Knappen was the combined market position of Calumet and Osceola. The plaintiff Bigelow argued that copper mined in the territory around Lake Superior, for that reason called Lake copper, was distinguishable on the basis of chemical purity from copper mined elsewhere, designated Western or electrolytic copper. The respective market shares of Lake copper annual production for Calumet and Osceola were approximately 42 and 8 percent, while the corresponding shares with respect to all domestic copper, including both Lake and Western, were approximately 10 and 2 percent.[44] The combination of the two mines, charged Bigelow, would "directly and necessarily tend to substantially restrict competition and create a monopoly in Lake copper." [45]

Judge Knappen rejected Bigelow's charge, ruling in effect that Lake copper did not constitute the relevant economic market because recent and continuing technological advances in electrolytic refining had rendered Western copper highly substitutable and competitive with Lake copper.[46] "It would seem," wrote Knappen,

---

[43]   *Id.* at 716.

[44]   *Id.* at 717-18.

[45]   *Id.* at 716.

[46]   "The testimony shows that there is no inherent chemical or physical difference between equally pure furnace refined and electrolytically refined copper, provided the latter is subjected to the same final furnace process, as the testimony indicates it usually is for commercial sale. Electrolytic copper is capable of use for any purpose for which Best Lake is used. Lake copper and electrolytic are sold in direct competition with each other, both in this country and abroad, the Best Lake usually selling, on a normal market, at an average of about one-quarter cent per pound in excess of the best electrolytic. The preference of some purchasers, which results in this difference in price, is probably due, in large part at least, to

17

"that any attempt to artificially raise the price of Lake copper as against electrolytic would be offset by a larger use of electrolytic."[47] Knappen concluded that there was neither the intent nor the direct and necessary effect to restrain trade; hence, there was no violation of the Sherman Act.[48]

IV.

The cases presented in the preceding section are interesting for both their historical and analytical relevance. It is possible to read the Peckham decisions and conclude with Bork that Peckham, not White, should be honored in recorded history as the father of the rule of reason.[49] Whether in fact most courts subsequently understood the Peckham opinions to expound such a rule is a question which is perhaps unanswerable. In the vast majority of cases decided in the decade prior to *Standard Oil*, it was unnecessary to differentiate between opposing interpretations of the Peckham opinions. Many cases involved peripheral, legalistic issues such as the right to sue, the enforceability of contracts entered by unlawful combinations, and the relation between patent and antitrust law. Others involved naked, direct restraints which were equally unlawful under either a flexible or a narrow interpretation of the Peckham precedents.

---

the long existing reputation of the Best Lake for excellence, including uniformity of product, and to the fact that the present high state of electrolytic refining has but lately been reached. Lake copper is not locally consumed or sold. With the improvement in the electrolytic process, and by care in refining, the preference of some consumers for Lake copper is diminishing, and seems likely to disappear in the near future, except so far as it may be based upon the reputation of individual producers." *Id.* at 718.

[47]   *Id.* at 719.

[48]   *Id.* The circuit court of appeals concurred in full with Knappen's economic analysis of the takeover, supplementing his decision by reference to a lack of evidence that the combination would directly affect interstate trade. 167 F. 721 (6th Cir. 1909).

[49]   Bork, "The Rule of Reason," *supra* note 6, at 785.

The cases reviewed in this article are distinguished because the decisions rendered, with the exception of *Wheeler-Stenzel*, were crucially dependent upon the explicit adoption of a rule of reason discriminating between direct and indirect restraints. At a minimum, these decisions indicate that White's *Standard Oil* opinion hardly constituted the sharp break in antitrust policy which Harlan asserted it to be. Regarding the sincerity of White's contention that his rule and Peckham's rule were fundamentally the same, it is worth noting that in *Standard Oil* Justice White was affirming a lower court opinion written by Judge Sanborn.[50] It will be recalled that in his *Whitwell* and *Phillips* decisions Sanborn clearly articulated a rule of reason; this rule was repeated explicitly in his *Standard Oil* opinion, complete with its citations to the Peckham precedents.[51]

Apart from the issue of the historical origin of the rule of reason, the five decisions reviewed are interesting because taken together they outline a rational antitrust policy of promoting economic welfare. In the briefest of terms, the decisions served both to proscribe allocative inefficiency and to protect productive efficiency. Absent from the decisions was consideration of alternative antitrust objectives which are generally placed under the rubric of social purpose. In particular, protection of small business was given no weight, although the opportunity to do otherwise surely was presented. The practical objective stated in the cases was the promotion of open competition. However, the opinions reveal that competition was perceived by the judges as a process of action and rivalrous response rather than as a structural condition. This interpretation permitted a policy of competition wholly supportive of economic welfare.

Given their perception of competition, the judges distinguished two general classes of business conduct restricting rivalrous response. In one class, response was constrained by simple agreement among competitors. Such agreement constituted a direct lessening

---

[50]   U.S. v. Standard Oil Co. of New Jersey, 173 F. 177 (C.C.E.D. Mo. 1909).

[51]   *Id.* at 188.

of competition, permitting the enhancement of price and the reduction of output.[52] Since its expected effect was to lessen trade, conduct of this sort was judged under the Peckham rule to be an unlawful restraint. In the second class of conduct, rivalrous response was limited only by the superior efficiency of the initiating action. Such conduct was recognized to be an inherent part of competition, or in Judge Adams' words an expedient of competition, and was believed to be promotive of trade. Accordingly, it was placed outside of the Sherman Act.

This article is concluded with the following curious statement by Judge Sanborn. The statement first appeared in *Whitwell* and was repeated almost verbatim in his *Standard Oil* opinion. In the former Sanborn wrote:

> An attempt by each competitor to monopolize a part of interstate commerce is the very root of all competition therein. Eradicate it, and competition necessarily ceases—dies. Every person engaged in inter-

---

[52] Although in four out of the five cases an unlawful trade restraint was not found, it would be erroneous to infer that the judges did not recognize a positive role for the Sherman Act in proscribing direct agreements eliminating competition. For example, in *Whitwell* Judge Sanborn wrote:

"The right of each competitor to fix the prices of the commodities which he offers for sale, and to dictate the terms upon which he will dispose of them is indispensable to the very existence of competition. Strike down or stipulate away that right, and competition is not only restricted, but destroyed. Hence agreements of competing railroad companies to intrust their power to fix rates of transportation to the same man or body of men, and contracts of competitors in the production or sale of merchantable commodities to deprive each competitor of the right to fix the prices of his own goods, the terms of the sale, or the customers to whom he shall dispose of them, and either to fix these prices, terms, and customers by the agreement of the competitors, or to intrust the power to dictate them to the same man or body of men, necessarily have the effect either to stifle competition entirely, or to directly and substantially restrict it, because such contracts deprive the rivals in trade of their best means of instituting and maintaining competition between themselves." Whitwell v. Continental Tobacco Co., 125 F. 454, 459-60 (8th Cir. 1903) (citations omitted).

state commerce necessarily attempts to draw to himself, and to exclude others from, a part of that trade; and, if he may not do this, he may not compete with his rivals. . . .[53]

The terminology used by Sanborn is unusual, and perhaps for that reason the statement risks misinterpretation. But read in context, it is clear that Sanborn's reference was to exclusion by efficiency, that is, to exclusion derived wholly from a competitor's differential gain in productive efficiency. In the decisions reviewed in this article there was consistently evidenced a concern that the Sherman Act be interpreted to leave unrestrained the productive efficiency of vigorous and open competition. Indeed, the boldness with which this concern was given expression is refreshing when contrasted with the poor judgment and hostility displayed toward efficiency in more modern decisions such as *Alcoa*,[54] *Brown Shoe*,[55] and *Procter & Gamble*,[56] to list only a few. Perhaps recent decisions by the Burger Court signal a movement toward a sensible policy of antitrust grounded on an economic welfare objective.[57] As the opinions in this article reveal, Justice Peckham, in his rule of reason fashioned more than three-quarters of a century ago, provided the outline for precisely such a policy.

---

[53] *Id.* at 462. *See also* U.S. v. Standard Oil Co. of New Jersey, 173 F. 177, 191 (C.C.E.D. Mo. 1909).

[54] U.S. v. Aluminum Company of America, 148 F.2d 416 (2d Cir. 1945).

[55] Brown Shoe Co., Inc. v. U.S., 370 U.S. 294 (1962).

[56] FTC v. Procter & Gamble Co., 386 U.S. 598 (1967).

[57] *See, e.g.*, Continental TV v. GTE Sylvania, Inc., 433 U.S. 36 (1977).

The Taft Administration and the Sherman Antitrust Act

President Taft's conception and enforcement of the Sherman Antitrust Act was somewhat complicated by a rather naive attitude toward the Sherman Act and big business, by the influence of Attorney General George W. Wickersham, who was given great discretion in antitrust proceedings, by Taft's often emotional response to businessmen, and by the President's legalism—laws were to be "faithfully executed."

One fact is clear: The Sherman Act *was* enforced during Taft's administration. The Department of Justice initiated ninety suits, while during the period 1902–1908 Roosevelt's attorneys general had a total of forty-four suits. Roosevelt's record included eighteen civil and twenty-six criminal cases, resulting in twenty-two convictions and twenty-two acquittals. But Taft's four years showed fifty-four civil, thirty-six criminal suits. Taft's prosecutors secured fifty-five convictions, thirty-five acquittals.[1]

A glance at the list of cases also shows that Taft was not simply taking on easy targets. The corporations and industries that the Attorney General filed suit against or continued to prosecute were the then recognized giants of American business: United States Steel, Aluminum Company of America, Standard Oil, International Harvester, American Tobacco, United Shoe Machinery Company, National Cash Register, Westinghouse, General Electric and other members of the electric trust, Kodak, Dupont, Pacific Coast Plumbing Supply and American Standard Sanitary, Union Pacific, Southern Pacific, steamship combinations, American Coal Products and several coal producers and carriers, Associated Press, Central West Publishing, the beef trust (National Packing Company), the lumber trust (Eastern States Retail Lumber), the stone trust (Cleve-

---

[1] United States Library of Congress, Legislative Reference Service, *Congress and the Monopoly Problem*, Washington, 1956, 659. Included in the conviction category are cases concluded by consent decree. This Taft-Wickersham innovation involved negotiation between the business concerned and the Justice Department after a suit was filed. The difference between this and a Rooseveltian Gentlemen's Agreement was that the final agreement was issued by a federal court in the form of a decree, thus giving it the binding force of law. Homer Cummings and Carl McFarland, *Federal Justice*, New York, 1937, 342–3.

172

land Stone), a motion picture patent pool, an attempted cotton corner, a wine trust, a turpentine trust, a wall paper trust, a licorice trust, Corn Products Refining, American Thread, Keystone Watch and many others.

There is very little evidence to show that President Taft hesitated, for either personal or political reasons, to enforce the law. Despite pleas, for example, by political advisers the President refused to order Wickersham not to file criminal indictments against officers of the National Cash Register Company, in spite of the fact that this corporation was located in Taft's home state of Ohio and that several of the accused directors were personal friends. The President also would not follow suggestions that the antitrust prosecutions be halted, or at least slowed down in the months preceding the 1912 election.[2]

The President was unhappy when personal acquaintances were involved in actions taken under the Sherman Act. In one case, a friend of the President was a defendant in a criminal antitrust action, and Taft replied to a complaint from a mutual friend.

There seems to be a sort of feeling on the part of businessmen who violate the law that their prosecution for doing this calls for some explanation. I think the law is a good law and ought to be enforced, and I propose to enforce it. I greatly regret that in doing so I have to strain or break off relations with real friends. That is my misfortune. . . . I don't want to seem churlish or unkind in respect to Brooker, but what I have said above is the cold truth.[3]

It is easy to demonstrate that Taft enforced the Sherman Act on a broad, general scope, not on a restrictive or selective one. It is more difficult to explain just "why" he did this, to determine what his goals were. In his endeavor to "bust trusts," to "restore competition," Taft eliminated Roosevelt's distinction between "good" and "bad" trusts. Although the President used the standard rhetoric of progressivism, he did not really appear to have had a clear understanding of the antitrust crusade. On one level, from his actions, he could be described as being proto-Wilsonian in approach, but

---

[2] Senator T. E. Burton to Taft, Feb. 10, 1912, Taft Papers, Library of Congress, Series 6, casefile 2709. Hereafter cited as TP, Ser. 6. Wickersham to C. D. Hilles, Feb. 13, 1912, Department of Justice Files, National Archives, Record Group 60, file 60–51–0, sec. 1. Hereafter cited as DJ file. C. P. Taft to W. H. Taft, May 29, 1912, TP, Ser. 7, casefile 4, C. D. Hilles to Taft, Aug. 17, 1912, Wickersham to Taft, Aug. 23, 1912, Taft to Hilles, Aug. 26, 1912, TP, Ser. 7, casefile 227.

[3] Taft to Arthur Kimball, Nov. 21, 1911, TP, Ser. 8, Presidential Letterbook (hereafter PLB), XXXI, 42.

with much less intellectual underpinning. Although Taft was quite serious in his approach to monopoly, often he seemed to view the Sherman Act and business in general in terms of a very large and exciting game.

"Mr. Neff thinks he knows a trust that ought to be attended to . . . if there is any such trust that can be attacked, attack it," but "I fear however it is complicated with patents."[4] The President once commented to Wickersham that "generally . . . wherever we see a trust we hit it on the head, and that we have not had any favorites among the directors, but have treated all alike."[5] "If there is a case, go for them!"[6] Wickersham himself usually did not speak in this tone, but on occasion did evidence the same attitude, as when he described the electrical trust, in a rather mixed metaphor, saying "That 'octapus' [*sic*] seems to have extended its tentacles pretty far, and presents about as profitable a dragon as any St. George could desire!"[7]

One recent student of the antitrust campaign, William Baldwin, has noted that "it seems obvious that economic considerations had only a minor influence on antitrust policy in its formative years. Had every economist in the country supported the trust movement . . . there still would have been condemnatory legislation."[8] This can be extended a bit further to argue that there still would have been enforcement of the condemnatory legislation.

Taft was very much a product of this area of progressivism, and in terms of his naive view of the Sherman Act itself and his occasional emotional response to businessmen he was also a product of the intuitive branch of progressivism. Ignoring reality, he would say, "The trust act is clear enough under the decision of the court, . . ."[9] "I confess I don't see where the uncertainty arises in respect to future business. *The decisions of the Supreme Court are easily interpreted and anyone can follow them. . . .*"[10]

After one particularly intemperate letter of complaint from his banker friend Otto Bannard in New York, the President lost

---

4 Taft to Wickersham, Jun. 22, 1912, TP, Ser. 8, PLB, XXXVII, 463.
5 Taft to Wickersham, Jun. 6, 1912, TP, Ser. 8, PLB, XXXVII, 195.
6 Taft to Wickersham, Dec. 10, 1910, TP, Ser. 8, PLB, XX, 189.
7 Wickersham to Wade Ellis, Sept. 20, 1909, DJ file 60–90–0, sec. 2.
8 William L. Baldwin, *Antitrust and the Changing Corporation*, Durham, 1961, 38.
9 Taft to Horace Taft, Nov. 5, 1911, TP, Ser. 7, casefile 1194.
10 Taft to Henry L. Higginson, Sept. 8, 1911, TP, Ser. 8, PLB, IXXX, 264. (My italics.)

patience with his critics. The contradiction and simplistic view in this letter were typical of Taft's perception of the Sherman Act.

I can tell without the slightest difficulty whether a company is violating the law or not or intends to violate the law, and so can anybody else who wants to be genuine about it and look into the matter. The whole trouble with you, and with everybody else engaged in the matter, is that you are not willing to come up and face the music and agree that the methods of business ought not to include combination for the purpose of suppressing competition and driving other people out of business by methods akin to duress. . . . I am strongly in sympathy with the principals [*sic*] of the anti-trust law. . . . *Of course there must be some doubt as to the intent and purpose of particular combinations.* That is in the nature of things, and when the evidence seems to show that the intent and purpose is contrary to the statute, it is the business of the Government to come in and try to break up that which has been the result of original illegal purpose and illegal maintenance. . . . I believe in the gentle but continuous prosecution of all these combinations until they learn better . . . and if we can divide up the other trusts in some way, business people will finally learn that the law means something and that they have got to conform to it. But if they meet the matter in the spirit in which you speak of Wickersham and the administration policy, then we shall never accomplish anything.[11]

The President's impression of business and of businessmen was often colored by unthinking emotionalism. "The business men are fools, like some of the voters. For a time they don't see their real interests; they don't have the power of discrimination."[12] He would "just as lief punish them as much as possible," but unfortunately this was not always possible.[13] Taft often seemed to feel business was attempting to threaten him into abandoning prosecution.

They don't frighten me at all with the cry of panic in the stock market. There is no reason for a panic. . . . It has just percolated into the heads of some of these people that I mean what I say, and I don't have to reiterate my sentiments every five minutes to convince them that my messages are my decrees and that they are not written for political effect but to secure legislation.[14]

As you say, Wall Street, as an aggregation, is the biggest ass that I have run across.[15]

Ex-corporation lawyer Wickersham occasionally responded in the same way. "Sometimes I think that nothing more stupid and short-sighted and dishonest minded ever was than the average railroad

---

11 Taft to Otto Bannard, Jun. 29, 1912, TP, Ser. 8, PLB, XXXIX, 89. (My italics.)
12 Taft to C. P. Taft, Jun. 2, 1912, TP, Ser. 7, casefile 4.
13 Taft to Wickersham, Sept. 1, 1911, TP, Ser. 8, PLB, IXXX, 227.
14 Archie Butt, *Taft and Roosevelt*, 2 vols., Garden City, 1930, I, 265.
15 Taft to Henry Taft, Feb. 21, 1910, TP, Ser. 8, PLB, XII, 169.

man in his dealings with the public and in his shortsighted vision concerning the practical results of his dealings [*sic*]."[16]

There were three basic stages in the administration's antitrust campaign but like so much of the activity surrounding the Sherman Act in this period, these stages were really not truly separate or distinct. There was an apparent difference in feeling and emphasis. The evolution of the administration's policy can be seen during 1909–1910. This was basically an organizational period. Wickersham reviewed all suits initiated and prepared by Roosevelt's Department of Justice. He declined to prosecute many of these, feeling that the government's evidence would not prevail in court. This created adverse publicity as many "progressives" began to cry that Taft had "sold out to the interests." The Department continued the prosecution of Standard Oil and American Tobacco that had been initiated by Roosevelt. The administration, and the general public, believed that these cases would test the efficacy of the Sherman Act against large corporations. The desire to await the Supreme Court's decision accounts to a large degree for the hesitant attitude of the Justice Department. Only one civil suit under the Sherman Act was filed in 1909.

The Court ordered the dissolution of both the tobacco and oil companies, and in 1911–1912 there was a great flurry of antitrust activity. There was increased confidence on the part of the administration because the Supreme Court had ordered the breaking up of both of these corporations, and it seemed that the Sherman Act would be an effective weapon against corporate monopolies.

During 1912–1913 the level of prosecution continued as it did in the previous year, but the earlier sense of confidence was lacking, at least within the Department of Justice. The government had prevailed with American Tobacco and Standard Oil but now it seemed that the results were not as salutary or beneficial as originally thought. There were immense difficulties in arranging the practical details of dismemberment and the practice did not seem to be following the theory. So although prosecution continued, this was a period of relative confusion and uncertainty. In large part this is explained by the unsatisfactory reorganizations of the tobacco and oil industries.

When Taft entered office he believed without qualification that the Sherman Act should be used to eliminate "the supression of

---

16 Wickersham to Cornelius Wickersham, Mar. 1, 1911, George W. Wickersham Papers, Chocorua, New Hampshire.

competition, the controlling of prices and the monopoly ... [of] commerce ... [these] are not only unlawful, but contrary to the public good, and that they must be restrained and punished until ended."[17] These vaguely stated ideals were the goals. But since the Sherman Act had not previously been used in a concerted manner against monopoly, it was not known how effective the antitrust act could be.

The law prohibited contracts and combinations in restraint of trade, and also condemned any monopoly or attempt to monopolize business, trade or commerce. The statute did not attempt to define these terms. Prosecutions under the act could take place in both civil and criminal courts. Section six of the Sherman law stated that property owned by a business adjudged to be a party to restraint of trade or a monopoly could be forfeited to the United States under normal condemnation proceedings. Wickersham went further than most public officials when he asserted that "resort will have to be made to that section at some time,"[18] but no serious consideration was given to initiating condemnation proceedings under section six. Certainly the federal courts could, as the act stated, "prevent and restrain ... violations," but the most effective way to achieve this was yet to be determined.

The major test of the Sherman Act, in the mind of the administration, the public, and the business community, was to come in the important cases of American Tobacco and Standard Oil. These suits had been initiated by the Roosevelt administration and continued by Taft. Recognizing their significance, Attorney General Wickersham assumed responsibility for them and personally prepared the written briefs and presented the oral arguments before the Supreme Court. He asked that the high court order both corporations to disband and to dissolve into their constituent parts. The argument, basically, was that these two businesses were artificial creations, that they had not achieved their positions in the respective industries through the normal methods of business and commerce, and hence were guilty of violating the strictures of the Sherman Act. The government asserted that dismemberment would correct this inequity and would force and restore normal competition in both the tobacco and oil industries.

There was much satisfaction within the administration when the Court found for the government and ordered that both corporations

---

17 *The New York Times*, Jan. 7, 1910.
18 Wickersham to A. H. Walker, Feb. 24, 1911, quoted in Albert H. Walker, *President Taft and the Sherman Act*, New York, 1912, 27.

break down into their original parts. They thought the effectiveness of the antitrust law now could be tested; here was the opportunity, with two of the largest corporations in the nation, to—by edict—"restore competition." If this attempt were successful, then it could be used against all other major conglomerates that the government thought were violating the Sherman Act. Wickersham was ecstatic in a letter to his chief assistant. "Thank you for your congratulations. 'Us lets congratulate we'; there is glory enough for all. My only regret is that as the titular head of the Dept. I get really more credit than is my share."[19]

The confidence in the expected remedy of the antitrust law soon proved to be misplaced. The administration's experience with the Standard Oil and American Tobacco reorganization showed that use of the Sherman Act in this way was really not a viable solution to the problem of restoring competition and ending monopolistic conditions in the United States. Simply speaking, the Standard Oil decree ordered that within six months each of the subsidiary companies had to have an independent board of directors and executive officers; there was to be no common element between the companies. The original holding company had to distribute its stocks *pro rata* among the new thirty odd corporations to be created. After this, each corporation could go its own way and thus competition would be restored in the industry.[20]

Many citizens did not approve. Although they feared the power possessed by the original holding company, most consumers were more concerned with the price of oil. Under the control of Standard Oil the price of many oil products had been declining for twenty years. A number of people were afraid that this would now end. The Attorney General, defending administration policy, disagreed.

The newspaper clipping which you enclose assumes that oil and oil products will not be cheaper under the new condition of affairs than they were under the old. It is, on the contrary, the opinion of the best informed people, and the results of experience, that competition in a commodity results in reducing the price to the public, and that is the theory on which the

---

[19] Wickersham to Frank Kellogg, Jun. 1, 1911, DJ file 60–20, sec. 9.
[20] The responsibility for writing this decree rested with the Department of Justice. Gabriel Kolko's statement that "There is no indication that Wickersham participated in the formulation of the Standard dissolution plan...." (*The Triumph of Conservatism*, Chicago, 1967, 167), may be questioned. The Attorney General himself wrote the final decree which was issued by the Supreme Court. John Milburn to Wickersham, Jun. 13, 1911, Frank Kellogg to Wickersham, Jun. 19, 1911, Wickersham to Kellogg, Jun. 16, 1911, Wickersham to Milburn, Jun. 16, 1911, DJ file 60–57, sec. 3.

legislation of Congress was enacted. It will not do to begin, now that we are on the eve of restoring competitive conditions, to say that the result will not be accomplished. We must try it out and see.[21]

Because of the corporate organization of the original Standard Oil Company, it was not that difficult to effect dissolution. Since the many companies controlled by the holding corporation had retained their identities, breaking the organization down into its separate entities was not very complicated. But the theory was one thing, the actual results, another. Wickersham and Taft came to share consumer's concern about the price of oil. Wickersham replied to one correspondent:

I can quite understand your feeling that breaking up a trust is not such a beneficial thing as it promised to be. At the same time it is a little too early to determine just what the result will be. Competition is something that can't be established as a result of a pen stroke. It's a growth, just as combination was a growth.... At the moment, for some reason which I don't understand, the retail price of some fuel-oil has advanced; but I cannot believe that thirty different companies with separate managements, under the normal conditions of trade which will result, can either standardize or hold up the price in the face of competition which the universal experience of the past shows inevitably steps in unless there is an artificial control to keep it from working.[22]

This is based on the assumption that "competition" necessarily results in lower prices. Wickersham slowly began to realize that this result would not necessarily follow.

There has been some increase in the prices of some of the finished products, such as gasoline; on the other hand, there has been considerable increase in the price paid for raw crude oil. In addition to that, the disintegrated companies of both the oil and tobacco trusts are spending many times what was formerly spent by any one in advertising in the newspapers.... However, *we cannot guarantee the reductions of prices* on commodities dealt with by the trusts, but at all events we can guarantee the continued impartial enforcement of the law....[23]

The Attorney General began to recognize that there were some extremely complicated matters involved in trust busting. This became more apparent with his difficulties in writing the tobacco decree. His explanations of why the price of oil had not decreased are rather simplistic. Increased budgets for advertising was a valid argument why the theory that competition equals price decreases

---

[21] Wickersham to Philip G. Peabody, Aug. 4, 1911, DJ file 60–57, sec. 3.
[22] Wickersham to George Jonas, May 6, 1912, DJ file 60–57, sec. 4.
[23] Wickersham to Taft, Aug. 23, 1912, TP, Ser. 7, casefile 227. (My italics.)

did not work. This increased expense in part, at least, had been caused by government action. Increases in the cost of raw material also may have been caused by the loss of economy of distribution, again because of the action of the government. Recognition of these factors seems not to have existed to any large degree within the administration. Since conditions in the oil industry were not following theory, the Justice Department reacted instinctively in the only way it knew how: it investigated alleged violations of the court decree and alleged violations of the Sherman Act by the new Standard Oil companies. The Attorney General seemed slightly confused by the results—no violations could be found.[24]

But the dissolution of Standard Oil was a first, and it was not the fault of the administration if the result did not follow the theory. It was a general belief of the time that competition would result in price decreases. It was also understood, however, that combination could result in economy that could be passed on to the consumer. Yet it was clear that combination opened the way to possible abuse. The fear of abuse at this time outweighed the possible benefits of combination. There was the idea that combination, under control, could have beneficial results, but thinking along these lines had not yet really reached any state of practical action within the administration.

The dissolution of Standard Oil did help bring about more competition in the oil industry.[25] Competition may not necessarily have been the best solution for the problems within this industry, but it was what the Sherman Act and Wickersham and Taft were attempting to restore. The Attorney General and the President may not have understood everything that was happening, but they cannot be condemned for following both the letter and the spirit of the law. The results were not clear, but even more disillusionment was created by the parallel attempt to dissolve and re-create the American Tobacco Company.

American Tobacco was one of the most powerful of American industries. By virtually any definition of the word, there is little doubt that it was a monopoly. In 1910 its share of the tobacco industry was predominant. Its profits in 1908 were $30,000,000 and it was paying 46% earnings on common stock.[26]

---

24 Wickersham to Charles B. Morrison, Oct. 17, 1912, Wickersham to William F. Murray, Jan. 9, 1913, DJ file 60–57, sec. 5.

25 Simon N. Whitney, *Antitrust Policies: American Experience in Twenty Industries*, 2 vols., New York, 1958, II, 388.

26 Richard B. Tennant, *The American Cigarette Industry*, New Haven, 1950, 27–37.

The Supreme Court decided, as it did in the oil case, that the company was indeed guilty of violating the Sherman Act. The Court said this fact left it with two immediate alternatives: to prohibit it from doing any interstate business, or to appoint a receiver to sell its property. Instead of chosing either of these methods, the case was remanded to a circuit court with the requirement of issuing an acceptable decree ordering the dismemberment of American Tobacco within six months' time. If this could not be done, the circuit court was then instructed to turn the business into receivership.[27] The responsibility of writing an acceptable decree fell on the Department of Justice. Neither the Supreme Court nor the circuit court was willing to attempt to draw the guidelines for the dissolution of a $400 million corporation. Although the court would listen to challenges from the stockholders of American Tobacco, it was left to the Attorney General and his department to formulate the final decree.

The technique used in the Standard Oil reorganization did not apply in this case. American Tobacco was possessed of an extremely complex corporate organization since dissolutions and combinations of previous corporations in the tobacco industry, stock conveyances, mergers and consolidations had blended American Tobacco into an entirely new form. The difficulties in creating new corporate structures from a corporation as large as American Tobacco were compounded by the Supreme Court's insistence on a deadline of six months, with a possible extension of eight weeks.

It is not necessary to consider the specific details of the new arrangement. Suffice it to say that the decree proposed by the Justice Department and promulgated by the Court created many new companies, divided the tobacco business, the half billion dollars in assets, the plants and the brand names among many independent companies. American Tobacco itself was reduced to a fraction of its original size, and the rest of the tobacco business was divided among fifteen other corporations.[28]

---

27 *United States v. American Tobacco Co.*, 221 U.S. 106 (1911).

28 George Wickersham speech, "Recent Interpretation of the Sherman Act," Michigan State Bar Association, Jul. 6, 1911, 60–3, Wickersham Papers. Wickersham to James McReynolds, Jul. 12, 1911, DJ file 60–20, sec. 10, Wickersham to Taft, Aug. 30, 1911, TP, Ser. 6, casefile 2024, Taft to Wickersham, Sept. 1, 1911, TP, Ser. 8, PLB, IXXX, 227, Wickersham to T. W. Bickett, Sept. 15, 1911, DJ file 60–20, sec. 10, Wickersham to Henry C. Lodge, Oct. 2, 1911, DJ file 60–20, sec. 11, Wickersham to Cornelius Wickersham, Oct. 22, 1911, Wickersham Papers.

There was a dual purpose that had to be kept in mind while attempting to arrange the details of the reorganization. First and foremost was to restore competition in the industry; secondly, the Attorney General had to be careful to protect the interests of the original investors in American Tobacco. The Court had not confiscated the property of these investors.[29]

Wickersham, who had the responsibility to draw up a decree which had to protect the original investors, which had to restore competition, which had to end monopolistic conditions, and which had to meet the Supreme Court's six month deadline, began to realize that this method of using the Sherman Act to end monopoly and restore competition was extremely difficult, impractical, and perhaps impossible. He did believe that the final decree would restore competition, but he now understood fully—"the whole matter has impressed upon me the very unsatisfactory condition of law and procedure under which I have been acting"[30]—that simply citing the virtue of the Sherman law and mouthing cliches about restoring competition and destroying monopoly were not enough.

In an extremely long letter to the President, the Attorney General expressed his displeasure over the course he had to follow. He felt that the Department of Justice and the Attorney General should not have to assume the responsibility of drawing up reorganization decrees. "The questions involved are economic; they depend upon information which we cannot have in this department." Wickersham felt that there would be a number of similar cases in the future, but believed that the procedures following the preliminary court order had to be re-evaluated and modified. Some other administrative agency, perhaps the Department of Commerce and Labor, should draw up the reorganization plan. The problems in-

---

29 Wickersham to Henry C. Lodge, Oct. 2, 1911, DJ file 60–20, sec. 11.
30 Wickersham to Taft, Nov. 4, 1911, TP, Ser. 6, casefile 2024. There seems to be nothing to substantiate Gabriel Kolko's implication that Wickersham deceived the President, nor his assertion that the Attorney General tried to deceive the public (*Triumph of Conservatism*, 169). Kolko's statement that "Wickersham failed to formulate a detailed proposal, and rejected out of hand a receivership scheme advanced by one of his key attorneys, James C. McReynolds,..." is something of a distortion. It is true that Wickersham himself did not come up with a detailed proposal—it was probably impossible to do this. The final decree was the work of literally hundreds of men over a period of more than six months. And if McReynolds' plan was rejected "out of hand" it was only because Taft and Wickersham, for good reasons, did not want the combine to go into a receiver's sale. Kolko further implies that McReynolds' plan was dismissed because Wickersham wanted to accept the tobacco company's plan, which basically would make few major changes in the structure of the industry. This again is not correct, certainly not in terms of motivation.

volved, he claimed, were "economic and commercial questions and [should] not [be] guessed at by the law department."[31]

The thrust of his letter was to suggest that some other department or agency should take responsibility once the Justice Department had completed its job of proving violation of the Sherman law. The Attorney General felt that the methods used in both the Standard Oil and American Tobacco organizations were unsatisfactory for two basic reasons. First, the Department was really not qualified to deal with the economic and commercial problems involved in the re-structuring of a half billion dollar corporation. Secondly, the reorganization plan should be issued in some other way than by judicial decree. "If the disentanglement is embodied in the decree of a court, it becomes *res judicata;* and if found subsequently to be based on some mistake, the people must suffer." If the plan were issued administratively, it would not be binding for all time and the government would find it easier to correct mistakes which might have been made.[32]

The Sherman Act, said the Attorney General, should not be amended. It had been built upon by twenty years of case law, and Standard Oil and American Tobacco showed that it could be used against large corporations. He argued that it had to be supplemented by an administrative body. He was not certain what this body should be or what powers it should possess, but he was convinced that its creation was essential. "I do not believe that the whole commercial question can be settled by merely enforcing the Sherman Act."[33]

This then leads to the relatively old question of a federal incorporation law. Once again, Taft, although a nominal supporter of such a plan, showed no real understanding of the difficulties involved in enforcement of the Sherman Act under present procedures. A federal incorporation law was not novel to the Attorney General, Roosevelt had vaguely supported such a plan. The President did suggest enactment of an incorporation bill written by Wickersham in 1910, but he neither understood the idea behind it nor was he particularly interested in securing passage of it. "I am not greatly excited about it, so I have turned it over to George Wickersham.... But the first thing we have to do is to get the law passed, and I am not sitting up very late nights."[34] Taft continued

---

[31] Wickersham to Taft, Nov. 4, 1911, TP, Ser. 6, casefile 2024.
[32] *Ibid.*
[33] *Ibid.*
[34] Taft to C. H. Clark, Apr. 18, 1910, TP, Ser. 8, PLB, XIV, 363.

to quietly advocate such a bill, at least in part for partisan political reasons, but he did not make any meaningful effort to secure enactment. He showed small appreciation of the benefits that it might produce. In spite of his efforts, the Attorney General was unable to transmit to the President his difficulties and frustrations with the oil and tobacco reorganizations.[35]

There were many problems involved in drafting and securing agreement to a federal incorporation act: should it be voluntary or mandatory? If voluntary, what inducements could be offered to state chartered corporations to take out a federal charter? Could a corporation hold a dual charter with both state and national governments? What questions of national and state sovereignty were involved? What specific provisions should be enacted, for example, should a federal charter prohibit holding companies, as the Attorney General urged? Nevertheless, Wickersham, especially after American Tobacco, became more and more dissatisfied with using only the Sherman Act to try to restore competition and end monopoly. He began strongly to urge passage of an incorporation act, and with a rather radical addition.

The Attorney General recommended creation of a federal board, under the federal incorporation act, similar to the Interstate Commerce Commission. He felt that this proposed agency should have similar power and responsibility over commercial and industrial corporations as the I.C.C. had over transportation. Wickersham began to recognize that fair competition required combination to some degree, and therefore this should be allowed, but only under strict governmental control. He claimed that for many years prices in the United States in most major commodities had been set by agreement among the producers, and that the law of supply and demand was really not functioning in the nation. He said that although the country was accustomed to regulation of transportation rates, many citizens claimed that extension of that principle to commodities was both novel and radical. This, said Wickersham, was not true. Regulation of commodity prices was merely an extension of the principle of regulation of transportation rates. Going back to the principle enunciated in *Munn v. Illinois* in 1877, he noted that "when property is used in a manner to make it of public consequence

---

[35] Taft to Frank B. Kellogg, Oct. 12, 1910, TP, Ser. 8, PLB, IXX, 169, Taft to Eugene G. Hay, Dec. 11, 1910, TP, Ser. 8, PLB, XX, 208, Taft to Seth Low, Jan. 11, 1911, TP, Ser. 8, PLB, XXI, 445, Taft to William Lummis, Nov. 5, 1911, TP, Ser. 6, casefile 115.

and affect the community at large, it becomes clothed with a public use, and may be controlled by the public for the common good."[36] He felt that to require that prices of commodities sold in interstate commerce be reasonable was simply a new application of the old principle. "Indeed, unless prices be dealt with under such a law, it would fail to reach the essential evil; for 'unified tactics with regard to prices' has been authoritatively declared to be the essence of modern monopoly."[37]

Wickersham, originally a corporation lawyer, had modified his views about big business and the Sherman Act. His conception of the problems of monopoly had evolved as a result of his experience in attempting to enforce the antitrust statute. The President, on the other hand, had not budged from his original, almost intuitive view of the Sherman Act and big business. "I don't think there ought to be a right to fix prices in anybody. . . ."[38] Taft did not move toward a broader degree of regulation, and continued to attempt to use the Sherman Act to force competition in various industries and to use the threat of potential prosecution as a club to convince businessmen to behave themselves. In essence then, the President wanted to use the fear of prosecution to force businessmen to regulate themselves. The Attorney General did not disagree with this, but felt that the proceedings were quite unsatisfactory when business called the bluff and the government was forced to go to court. Wickersham favored continued prosecution but was also moving closer to the additional concept of government regulation.

In conclusion, in terms of basic administration policy the Sherman Act was viewed and used in essentially the same way in 1913 as it had been viewed and used in 1909. In spite of technical difficulties encountered in enforcing the Sherman Act, most clearly seen with American Tobacco, in spite of the fact that forced competition did not seem to accomplish a great deal, in spite of the suggestions of the executive officer most deeply involved in enforcement of the law, Taft's rather naive and simplistic view of the Sherman law did not change. It was essentially the same at the end of his administration as it had been at the beginning: monopoly had to be de-

---

36 George Wickersham speech, "What Further Regulation of Interstate Commerce is Necessary or Desirable," Minnesota State Bar Association, Duluth, Jul. 19, 1911, reprinted in George Wickersham, *The Changing Order*, New York, 1914, 158.
37 *Ibid.*
38 Taft to William Lummis, Nov. 5, 1911, TP, Ser. 6, casefile 115.

stroyed, competition had to be restored, the Sherman Act had to be enforced.

Enforcement continued unabated to the end of Taft's term. In fact, sixteen cases were instituted in the last two months of the administration. The President was unwilling, or unable, to view the problems of the American economy in terms other than those of the 1890 Sherman Antitrust Act. He appears to have gained no understanding of the larger questions involved in this very complex and complicated area. Essentially he did not recognize that the American economy and business structure, in a large sense, had qualitatively changed, and that the change demanded new solutions to what were basically new problems.

JAMES C. GERMAN, JR.

Temple University

*   *   *   *   *

By William Graebner

ASSISTANT PROFESSOR OF HISTORY
STATE UNIVERSITY COLLEGE
FREDONIA, N.Y.

Great Expectations: The Search for Order in Bituminous Coal, 1890-1917*

❦ *Arguing that the American bituminous coal industry suffered from "excessive competition," this study traces the industry's repeated failures to control output or prices, whether by various kinds of trade associations, mergers, or by attempts to secure government sanctions for cooperation. Although an over-zealous Department of Justice must bear some responsibility for the industry's "sick" condition, Professor Graebner concludes, the fundamental problem lay in the basic economic conditions in the industry.*

Between 1890 and 1917 the American bituminous coal industry experienced rapid growth, largely in response to exceptional demands for industrial and domestic steam coals and coking coals to service the iron and steel industry. Stagnant in the early years of the 1890s, bituminous production doubled between 1894 and 1901 and doubled again by 1912. In 1918 some 579,000,000 short tons were produced, a figure not reached again until 1942.[1] But in the midst of this expansion, conditions in the coal trade were widely regarded — by operators, miners and their unions, engineers, scientists, and government officials — as wasteful, inefficient, excessively competitive, and insufficiently profitable.[2] Operator attorney D. W. Kuhn said: "Among the Falstaff army of industries of this country, too poor to fight, too cowardly or too virtuous to steal, the coal mining industry presents itself as one of the most bedraggled members of these ragged recruits."[3] The military analogy also seemed

Business History Review, Vol. XLVIII, No. 1 (Spring, 1973). Copyright © The President and Fellows of Harvard College.

* The author wishes to thank the Research Foundation of the State University of New York for financial support in conducting the research for this study.

[1] U.S. Bureau of the Census, *Historical Statistics of the United States, Colonial Times to 1957* (Washington, D.C., 1960), 356.

[2] *United Mine Workers Journal*, May 12, 1910, 4, and May 20, 1910, 4; American Mining Congress, *Proceedings of the Thirteenth Annual Session*, XIII (1910), 225; clipping from *Nation's Business*, April 15, 1913, 12, found in United States Bureau of Mines, Records, Record Group 70, National Record Center, Suitland, Maryland, box 55; and H. M. Chance, "A New Method for Working Deep-Coal Beds," *Transactions* of the American Institute of Mining Engineers, XXX (February–September, 1900), 287.

[3] D. W. Kuhn, "Sherman Anti-Trust Law with Special Reference to the Coal Mining Industry," *AMC Proceedings*, XIV (1911), 264.

appropriate to Pennsylvania's Chief Mine Inspector, James Roderick. "The rapid growth of the industry," he said, "has prevented systematic development and today the operators constitute a great army of antagonistic elements and unorganized forces . . . they continue to indulge in a cut-throat war-fare." [4] As one public official commented, "the old idea of a coal baron is a myth." [5]

These subjective evaluations were based on fact. In most major coal markets east of the Mississippi, coals from several states were in competition. Pennsylvania, West Virginia, and Ohio coals moved by rail and lake steamer to the distribution and consumption centers of Chicago, Milwaukee, and Duluth-Superior, where they were competitively priced with lower-grade coals produced in Illinois and Indiana. Kentucky coals shipped north became significant market influences in every midwestern state from Ohio to Minnesota. The nation's two largest producers after 1910, Pennsylvania and West Virginia, effectively dominated the coal trade in the eastern tidewater, in select western markets like Cincinnati, and in one particular product market, coke. Seldom did Illinois and Indiana coals enter these or other eastern markets.[6] This interstate competition reflected the wide availability of coal and the labor to mine it, the relatively low capital requirements for its development, and the ease with which one coal (or an alternative energy source) could be substituted for another. The result was a low-profit industry with chronic and growing excess capacity and an extremely low level of concentration. The bituminous coal industry had its large firms, but none had significant market power beyond the local marketing area.[7]

From 1890 to 1917 coal operators, like businessmen in cotton textiles, agriculture, steel, and other industries, attempted to deal individually and cooperatively with the problems posed by excessive

[4] Commonwealth of Pennsylvania, *Report of the Department of Mines of Pennsylvania, Part II — Bituminous, 1910* (Harrisburg, 1911), 4.

[5] Herbert M. Wilson, "Safety Measures in the Bituminous Coal Mines of Western Pennsylvania," National Safety Council *Proceedings*, I (1912), 116. Wilson was with the U.S. Bureau of Mines.

[6] U.S. Department of the Interior, Geological Survey, *Mineral Resources of the United States, 1915, Part II — Nonmetals* (Washington, D.C., 1917), 487–492; *ibid.*, 1910, 32–33; E. L. Moran, "The Coal Traffic of the Great Lakes," *Journal of Geography*, XV (January, 1917), 150–159; *Coal Trade*, 1896, 58, and *ibid.*, 1911, 102; West Virginia, *Annual Report of the Department of Mines for the Year Ending June 30, 1910* (Charleston, 1911), 81–87; International Commerce, *Coal Trade of the U.S.*, 1900, 2853–2865.

[7] Walton H. Hamilton and Helen R. Wright, *The Case of Bituminous Coal* (New York, 1925), 56-57; U.S. Department of Commerce, Bureau of the Census, *Thirteenth Census of the United States*, Volume XI, *Mines and Quarries* (1909), *General Report and Analysis* (Washington, D.C., 1913), 204-231; *Twenty-Ninth Annual Coal Report of the Illinois Bureau of Labor Statistics, 1910* (Springfield, Ill., 1911), 1-2; and *Black Diamond*, XLVIII (January 6, 1912), 24. The lack of uniform accounting practices would make an accounting determination of profits virtually impossible before 1917 or 1918. This essay accepts the contemporary view that profits were low, a logical consequence of the industry's industrial and market structure.

competition; they tried to bring order to the chaos of competition that was the coal industry. Few of the cures had much effect; some made the patient worse, and none went to the source of the illness. Real progress became possible only after 1912, when the industry turned in earnest to the national government. Five years later it was clear that although the search had taken some new forms under the aegis of politics, operator expectations had not been fulfilled. For all its efforts, the industry of 1917 looked much the same as it had some thirty years earlier; only the mechanism for change — politics — was well established. Coal's search for order had been frustrating and essentially futile.[8]

The coal industry's most common response to disorder, logical for the firm but self-defeating on an industry-wide basis, was to attempt to cut costs of production and distribution or to prevent them from increasing. Concern with labor costs in part explains the rapid mechanization of the industry after 1900 and the operators' efforts to prevent unionization in the 1890s. Enthusiasm for cost-cutting also led to waste of natural and human resources and resistance to cost-increasing innovations such as state safety legislation.[9]

Just as ineffective as cost-cutting was the trade's effort to find foreign markets to absorb surplus output. The export movement, led by the American Consular Service and occasionally promoted by the journals of the coal trade, interested few operators. A 1908 trade association report suggesting that coal operators viewed the export market as a "safety valve . . . at a time when the demand in the home market may be slow," was wishful thinking or propaganda.[10] Aside from export surges in 1899–1900 and 1911–1913, shipments abroad, largely to Canada, Mexico, and Cuba, grew very slowly. Nor was a major proportion of total production exported during this period. In 1898 only 1.8 per cent of total bituminous production found its way abroad; by 1915 that had increased to a still unimpressive 4.2 per cent. It was not uncommon for European and South American consuls to report available but unexploited markets, and in 1911 *Coal and Coke Operator* speculated that the

[8] The title is, of course, from Robert H. Wiebe, *The Search for Order, 1877–1920* (New York, 1967). Wiebe's use of the term is much broader than its use here, but it includes industrial organization. For another discussion of the problem of order and organization, see Louis Galambos, "The Emerging Organizational Synthesis in Modern American History," *Business History Review*, XLIV (Autumn, 1970), 279–290.

[9] The word "waste" is not intended here to have a timeless economic meaning; it is conceivable that the use operators made of productive factors was economically viable, even in the long run. For an interesting statement of the problem, see Warren C. Scoville, "Did Colonial Farmers 'Waste' Our Land?" *Southern Economic Journal*, XX (October, 1953), 178–181.

[10] *A Report to the Bituminous Coal Trade Association on the Present and Future of the Bituminous Coal Trade, 1908* (n.p., 1908), 11.

foreign market could not serve as an outlet for surplus production because "we have no ships to carry it at a transportation rate that would enable us to meet the competition from European countries, Australia, and Japan." [11] While the coal industry could not help but participate in the national interest in foreign markets, there is no evidence that operators saw foreign markets as an industry panacea. They correctly perceived that the "Open Door" was largely irrelevant to an industry with chronic overcapacity and virtually unlimited productive potential.[12]

Cost-cutting and the search for markets placed coal operators within the traditional framework of competition. In these years, however, the operators began to move beyond this framework toward solutions which minimized competition. Of great appeal for many operators was the attempt to equalize costs of production and distribution over a competitive geographical area. When state legislation was a factor in increasing the cost of production, operators interested in cost equalization tried to insure that legislative increments to cost were roughly equivalent in competitive regions or states. The mechanism was uniform state legislation, pursued in matters of safety and accident compensation and a favorite project of Illinois operators who saw their marketing region invaded by eastern operators with lower production costs. Working with the National Civic Federation and other groups, the American Mining Congress achieved virtual uniformity in workmen's compensation legislation by about 1916; in that year, however, the movement for uniform state legislation was hopelessly stalled by the failure of Ohio and West Virginia representatives to participate in the Uniform Mining Laws Conference.[13]

A similar but more potent mechanism — national rather than uniform state legislation — was used to stabilize and equalize transportation costs. As Joseph Lambie has demonstrated, coal producers and the railroads serving them were both interested in

[11] XII (January 26, 1911), 62.
[12] Export statistics are computed from *Historical Statistics of the United States*, 356; *Coal Trade Bulletin*, XV (June 1, 1906), 35, and (August 1, 1906), 53; *Coal Trade Journal*, XXXV (September 16, 1896), 531, and XXXVIII (April 26, 1899), 217; *Black Diamond*, XXII (March 11, 1899), 267. On the Open Door idea, see William Appleman Williams, *The Tragedy of American Diplomacy* (New York, 1959); Martin J. Sklar, "Woodrow Wilson and the Political Economy of Modern United States Liberalism," *Studies on the Left*, I (Fall 1960), reprinted in James Weinstein and David W. Eakins, eds., *For a New America* (New York, 1970), 46–100; and Thomas J. McCormick, *China Market* (Chicago, 1967).
[13] *Report of the Uniform Mining Laws Conference*, Chicago, Illinois, November 13, 14, 15, 1916 (Springfield, Ill., n.d.); James Weinstein, "Big Business and the Origins of Workmen's Compensation," *Labor History*, VIII (Spring, 1967), 156–174; American Mining Congress, *Proceedings*, XIX (1916), 157–158. The U.S. Bureau of Mines was created in 1910 partly to provide a scientific underpinning for uniform legislation. See William Sievers Graebner, "Coal Mining Safety: National Solutions in the Progressive Period" (Ph.D. dissertation, University of Illinois at Urbana-Champaign, 1970), 67.

maintaining volume and prices. Price-cutting initiated through cutthroat rail competition was just as harmful to coal operators as self-initiated cutting, and before 1900 it was a regular feature of transportation into competitive markets like Cincinnati, Chicago, and the eastern tidewater.[14] The carriers' inability to maintain rates rendered futile attempts to fix prices and production such as that mounted in 1887 by the Seaboard Steam Coal Association for the tidewater trade. When the railroads moved beyond self-regulation to government regulation with the Elkins and Hepburn Acts, competition was not eliminated, only reduced through bureaucratization. Regional coal operators' associations continually sought redress from unfair competition at the offices of the Interstate Commerce Commission.[15] Most common were requests for rate adjustments from central Pennsylvania coal operators, who faced stiff Virginia and West Virginia competition in New England, and from Ohio producers who were fighting a losing battle to control the coal trade in their own state and to keep their share of the traffic on the Great Lakes. And, although the Interstate Commerce Commission denied having the authority or the intent to maintain inter-regional competition, that, rather than a diminution of the competition, appears to have been the overall impact of federal regulation.[16]

Cost equalization also played a minor though significant role in the epic struggle between operators and miners over unionization. Labor costs, some 75 per cent of production costs, were a critical element in a region's competitive ability; the disabilities of Illinois, Indiana, Ohio, and sections of Pennsylvania can in part be traced to the intimidating non-union competition of West Virginia, which survived the 1897 union drive untouched. Since one of its major goals was to raise wages and thus production costs, the union was, in one sense, the universal adversary. Non-union operators in West Virginia believed in the existence of a conspiracy of Illinois, Indiana, Pennsylvania, and Ohio operators to unionize the state; a 1912 governor-commissioned report found West Virginia operators "within their rights in declining to recognize a union which would place them in a helpless minority when joined to those of the four

[14] Joseph T. Lambie, *From Mine to Market: The History of Coal Transportation on the Norfolk and Western Railway* (New York, 1954), 59; U.S. House of Representatives, *Report on Discriminations and Monopolies in Coal and Oil*, Interstate Commerce Commission, H. Doc. 561, 50th Cong., 2d Sess., 1907.
[15] Lambie, 87ff., 180ff., 189–190; Gabriel Kolko, *Railroads and Regulation, 1877–1916* (New York, 1965), 94ff.
[16] *Coal Trade*, 1911, 22, 60, and *ibid.*, 1910, 33; *Mineral Resources, 1915, Part II*, 191–192 and 406; *Twenty-Fourth Annual Report of the Chief Inspector of Mines, To the Governor of the State of Ohio, for the Year 1898* (Columbus, Ohio, 1890), 9, 22–23, 303; *ibid.*, 1909, 5, and *ibid.*, 1912, 64.

competitive States."[17] In the regions participating in the Interstate Joint Conference, there were frequent complaints that mining rates were not uniformly drawn. Ohio operators threatened to walk out of the Joint Conference in 1910, a threat Illinois operators had carried out two years earlier.[18]

In another sense, however, the union was not an adversary but a mechanism for internal adjustment in the industry. Herman Justi, Commissioner of the Illinois Coal Operators' Association, said as much in his testimony to the U.S. Industrial Commission in 1901:[19]

> Severe as we find competition to-day in the bituminous coal field it has its limitations which it did not have before. The reason for this is plain. Relatively speaking, every operator in the bituminous field pays the same scale of wages and is governed by the same mining conditions. As the miner pays no rebates, each operator knows substantially what it costs his rival to produce coal, and hence the selling price is more nearly uniform.

When wages were not the subject of formal collective bargaining procedures, they were sometimes equalized locally through informal operator agreements. Wage fixing and price fixing were intimately related. In Iowa, for example, operators agreed on a wage scale at the same meeting at which they fixed prices. In Illinois in 1898, the union settlement led to an operator organization designed to fix selling prices. "This action," said the *Coal Trade Journal*, "has been forced upon the operators by the drift of circumstances. It is the natural sequence of the uniform mining scale."[20] The unionization of much of the bituminous industry in 1897 should be seen not only as the consequence of a victory of miners over operators, but as the result of a conscious decision on the part of farsighted operators to use the union to equalize an important cost of production. Even those operators who had strongly opposed the union could see that once their mines were unionized, they would remain at a disadvantage until competitive mines were also brought under union control. Although the primary union-operator relationship was and continued to be one of conflict, a secondary relationship found the two sides in rough agree-

---

[17] *Coal and Coke Operator*, XV (December 12, 1912), 369; *Coal and Coke Operator and The Fuel Magazine*, XXI (September 25, 1913), 486.

[18] *Coal and Coke Operator*, X (February 17, 1910), 107; letter A. J. Moorshead, Madison Coal Corporation, to T. L. Lewis, President, United Mine Workers of America (April 9, 1908), in Edward A. Wieck Papers, Archives of Labor History and Urban Affairs, Wayne State University, Detroit, Michigan, box 1, book 3. The Interstate Joint Conference was the bargaining forum for miners and operators.

[19] U.S. House of Representatives, Industrial Commission, *Report on the Relations and Conditions of Capital and Labor Employed in the Mining Industry*, XIII (Washington, 1901), 678.

[20] *Coal Trade Journal*, XXXVII (March 23, 1898), 157, and XXXV (September 2, 1896), 502.

ment on the economic problems of the coal industry. For a time this produced labor-management agreement on solutions as well, most notably a 1915 consensus that the Sherman Act was harmful insofar as it was interpreted to prevent trade agreements fixing the selling price of coal. In short, as early as 1897 labor was in a small way integrated into the coal industry's scheme of things and had adopted the major assumptions of the search for order.[21]

The culmination of this effort to bring order to the industry by stabilizing labor conditions came in 1912 with an abortive attempt to establish a national association of operators. No such organization would have been necessary had the joint conference functioned satisfactorily, but the efficiency of that body had been seriously impaired by the periodic absence of key groups of operators. Impetus for the new organization came from Illinois, the state which had earlier separated from the joint conference but which now found its competitive position eroding. Illinois, said Chicago's *Black Diamond*, "was pleading for some united action that would bring a harmonious result in the various states. She wanted to end the practice of the miners of dividing the operators into groups and whipping them piecemeal." [22]

Not long after negotiations began in 1909, it became clear that not all operators saw Illinois' suggestion of a national organization as benign. A. B. Fleming, former Governor of West Virginia and president of the mammoth Fairmont Coal Company, expressed the viewpoint of most West Virginia operators. "It seems to me," he said, "that it would be impossible for our West Virginia Association to become a member unless we intend to 'unionize' and recognize the United Mine Workers, as I suppose all will do who join the

[21] Letter John P. White, UMWA President, to Charles S. Keith, President, Central Coal and Coke Co., Kansas City, Mo. (September 20, 1915), in Federal Trade Commission, General Correspondence, 1914–1921, Record Group 122, National Archives, Washington, D.C., box 44, file 8149–13; letter T. L. Lewis to editor, *Pittsburgh Daily Headlight* (March 10, 1911), in Wieck Papers, box 16, book 3; Robert H. Harlan, "Is Uniform Mining Legislation Advisable?" AMC *Proceedings*, XIX (1916), 600–601; speech of William B. Wilson, in UMWA District 2 *Proceedings*, March 25, 1908 session (1908), 76–77; *United Mine Workers Journal*, October 28, 1915, 4, and November 4, 1915, 4; and U.S. House of Representatives, *Hearings Before the Committee on Mines and Mining, To Consider the Question of the Establishment of a Bureau of Mines*, 1908 (Washington, D.C., 1908), 32–33.

On the integration of labor into the corporate order, the place to begin is Ronald Radosh, "The Corporate Ideology of American Labor Leaders from Gompers to Hillman," *Studies on the Left*, VI (November–December, 1966), 66–88, and the comment on that piece by Philip S. Foner in the same issue, 89–96. David Brody briefly considers the problem in "Labor and the Great Depression: The Interpretative Prospects," *Labor History*, XIII (Spring, 1972), 231–244. Melvyn Dubofsky makes the argument in *When Workers Organize: New York City in the Progressive Era* (Amherst, Mass., 1968), 44. The above analysis is intended to supplement, not replace the more traditional views; it recognizes that the essence of labor-management relations (at least in this period) was conflict. Radosh goes considerably further, but then he was dealing with Samuel Gompers and the AF of L, not the United Mine Workers.

[22] *Black Diamond*, XLVIII (January 27, 1912), 35.

National Association." [23] Pittsburgh district operators, essential to the organization's success, also proved unwilling; they viewed the Illinois proposition as an attempt to impose costly western mining conditions on the eastern states. Like Ohio operators, they were incapable of assuming a leadership role or even of unified action. At a time when the coal trade needed a "Moses to lead it out of the wilderness of doubt and uncertainty to a land of steadiness and profit," Ohio operators required three associations to harbor their divisions, and Pittsburgh district producers could only "lag behind quarrel and fuss and fume, spit fire and hiss at each other like cats and dogs." [24] West Virginia, Ohio, and Pittsburgh remained out of the organizing meetings of the association, leaving Kentucky as the only participating state east of Indiana. These omissions were fatal. The American Federation of Coal Operators remained a regional, rather than a national association, and as such it was incapable of contributing much to the industry's search for stability.[25]

Cost equalization — whether through uniform state legislation, federal legislation, or unionization — was only one element in the coal industry's master plan for industrial reform. The heart of that plan was cooperation between coal operators, and its method (before 1899 at any rate) was the trade association. A great many of the associations serving the coal industry in the depression decade of the 1890s had no direct connection with trade conditions and were concerned with safety, education, or labor relations. The trade-oriented units were of two basic types. The more common type was the simple agreement to maintain prices among producers from a particular region or selling in a particular market. The price fixing agreement was generally considered inferior to the second type, the joint sales agency, under which producers agreed to sell their output through (or to) one sales agency at or above an established minimum price.

What was probably the first joint sales agency, the Coal Producers' Contract, was established in the Pocahontas region of West Virginia in 1886 to sell that area's output at tidewater. Oper-

[23] Letter Fleming to Neil Robinson (December 31, 1909), in Aretas Brooks Fleming Papers, West Virginia University Library, Morgantown, West Virginia, box August–December 1909; Coal and Coke Operator, XIII (December 14, 1911), 388.
[24] Coal and Coke Operator, XIII (August 10, 1911), 91; XIV (January 11, 1912), 24; XIV (January 18, 1912), 37; and XII (January 26, 1911), 60; Coal and Coke Operator and Fuel, XXI (May 15, 1913), 66; (May 8, 1913), 35.
[25] Coal and Coke Operator, XIII (December 14, 1911), 381; Arthur E. Suffern, The Coal Miners' Struggle for Industrial Status (New York, 1926), 168–170, and Suffern, Conciliation and Arbitration in the Coal Industry of America (Boston, 1915), 128–134. The stated objective of the association was to "promote the common interests of the coal operators of America by all lawful means; but the Federation shall not deal with matters relating to freight rates, prices or sale of coal."

ators received the average price of all the coal sold through the agency. After 1890 the sales agency was a common, though usually transient feature of other coal fields. By 1892 demoralized conditions had spawned talk of a huge company to buy and sell the entire ouput of the Hocking Valley, Ohio, coal mines. Like Ohio associations to follow, it fell apart when major operators, reluctant to submerge their identities and sensing benefits in railroad car distribution from remaining outside, refused to participate. When the object of the selling agreement was isolated to a particular market, the chances of success were better. Hocking operators apparently managed to coalesce for the purpose of marketing in the Chicago area. That city was also the target of the Northern Coal Association, selling out of Streator, Illinois, and the Brazil Coal Company, which sold most of the output of the Indiana Block district after 1896. Another highly competitive market, Cincinnati, was the focus of a West Virginia agency designed to eliminate price competition between producers in that state's Kanawha and New River regions. For varying periods, operators in the Indiana territory, the Jellico district of Tennessee, the Connellsville coke region of Pennsylvania, and the Mystic Block and Walnut Block areas of Iowa marketed all or much of their coal through one seller. Selling agencies appear to have been limited to producers in one state and usually to a region producing a single type of coal.[26]

Like the selling agencies, price fixing associations were widely used throughout the coal fields and were usually aimed at particular markets and distribution centers, notably Chicago, Cincinnati, the lake ports, and the eastern tidewater. Several were especially successful, including the American Coal Operators Association, which had some influence over coal prices in the Hocking Valley from 1892 to 1897. Perhaps because the commitment was a lesser one, interstate price agreements were more common than interstate selling agencies. One impressive interstate group was the Southern Coal Association, formed in 1895 of nearly all the leading operators in Tennessee, Alabama, and Kentucky and including nine coal producing districts and some eighty companies. Interstate arrangements were worked out among Virginia, West

[26] Lambie, 48; Coal Trade Journal, XXXI (December 7, 1892), 583; (December 14, 1892), 591; XXXII (January 4, 1893), 2; (January 11, 1893), 23; (February 15, 1893), 95; XXXIII (October 24, 1894), 780; XXXIV (September 25, 1895), 725; XXXVI (June 16, 1897), 309; Black Diamond, XXII (March 18, 1899), 300; Coal and Coke Operator, XI (November 24, 1910), 757; memorandum by U.S. Attorney on New River and Pocahontas Arrangement (January 31, 1917), in Department of Justice Central Files, Classified Subject Files, Correspondence, Record Group 60, National Archives, Washington, D.C., box 607, file 60–187–16 (these records are hereinafter referred to as DJ-CS); and letter C. P. McKenzie to James R. Garfield (January 25, 1907), in Bureau of Corporations Records, Record Group 122, National Archives, Washington, D.C., box 198, file 4439-9.

Virginia, and Pennsylvania operators serving Cincinnati in 1895 and in the Ohio-Pittsburgh district in 1896.[27]

Occasionally operators combined with dealers to fix prices in local markets. Usually, however, dealer associations were restricted to retailers, and when that was the case they did little to stabilize the trade on the production level. Indeed, these "local coal barons" sometimes engaged in buying-price agreements under which retailers and jobbers agreed to hold the selling price of coal at the mine as close as possible to the cost of production. As a result, said the *United Mine Workers Journal* in 1915, "many of our best friends among the operators are being forced to the wall." [28]

Price fixing associations and sales agencies multiplied rapidly during the 1893 depression and, in spite of ongoing declines in production and prices, there was some optimism among producers. Following the formation of several associations in the spring and summer of 1895, the *Coal Trade Journal* commented: "Observant men in the coal trade think they discern in these associations, proof of a drift toward conditions which might make it possible to bring soft coal under a control as concentrated as that dominating Anthracite." [29]

This sanguine view proved unfounded. From the beginning, coal trade associations were neither easy to form nor easy to keep together. The Southern Coal Association was troubled first by Tennessee operators who were in the association but insisted on competing with each other regardless of the fixed schedule of prices and grades, then by Alabama members who threatened to resign. The Indiana Block Coal Company, a sales agency, had to close its doors when important operators refused to join. Operators attempting to maintain association prices in the face of undercutting sustained heavy losses. Certain companies, the M. A. Hanna Coal Co. in the Pittsburgh district, for example, acquired reputations for price cutting, and a major operator in the central Pennsylvania region, Edward J. Berwind, reportedly "would never join any

[27] *Coal Trade Journal*, XXXII (February 15, 1893), 104; XXXIV (August 28, 1895), 627; (February 6, 1895), 101; (July 31, 1895), 564; (August 7, 1895), 573; (August 21, 1895), 615; XXXV (January 22, 1896), 46; (March 25, 1896), 178. For an account of the Seaboard Steam Coal Association, see Lambie, 87–110.

[28] October 7, 1915, 4; letter F. P. Carey, Clearfield, Iowa, to George B. Cortelyou (March 25, 1903), Bureau of Corporations Records, file 0–40–31; clipping from *San Francisco Chronicle* enclosed in letter F. A. Lacey to James R. Garfield (September 23, 1907), Bureau of Corporations Records, note 598, file 4439–14; *Coal Trade Journal*, XXXI (April 6, 1892), 185; *Coal and Coke Operator*, XIV (April 4, 1912), 224; *Coal and Coke*, IX (August 1, 1902), 18; and file 60–187–9 in DJ–CS, box 606. Retailers were also organized regionally and nationally, but beyond the local level their economic functions were increasingly restricted. KoKoal, the national retail organization, was largely a social institution.

[29] XXXIV (October 9, 1895), 758.

operators association, holding that they were all right for the ordinary operator but were beneath his dignity."[30] Such intra-regional differences produced situations such as that in the Pittsburgh district in 1898, when three different associations existed, "all having purposes in some instances radically different from the others."[31] If an association managed to survive internal strains, it might succumb to the interregional assaults of the Pittsburgh operators or non-union West Virginia.[32]

By 1900, moreover, the whole climate for price fixing and sales associations had noticeably soured. The return to normal trade conditions exacerbated centrifugal tendencies as operators found the associations less necessary. The near-lethal blow, however, was delivered by the national government with the prosecution and conviction in 1899 of the New River Consolidated Coal and Coke Company, organized to sell the output of the New River and Kanawha fields. The government case emphasized the destruction of competition through a minimum selling price, and the company was held to be a combination in restraint of trade under the Sherman Act. This decision was in line with the Supreme Court's new and profound hostility to any limitations on competition. Some associations continued to exist, but only because the Justice Department was remarkably inactive.[33]

By 1900 it was clear that price fixing and sales associations were no longer appropriate solutions to the problems of the coal industry. Legal liabilities aside, they had failed to bring significant structural change to the coal markets. Although operators continued to experiment with these organizational forms, the new century found the industry looking for a solution through a new mechanism, corporate consolidation. The first significant merger movement in the history of the bituminous coal industry began in 1898 or soon afterwards in most of the major coal producing regions and continued with some intensity until after 1910. Despite frequent claims that efficiency was the great motivator, consolidations were designed, like the associations before them, to achieve price stability and

[30] W. P. Tams, Jr., *The Smokeless Coal Fields of West Virginia* (Morgantown, 1963), 78; *Coal Trade Journal*, XXXV (January 22, 1896), 46; (June 10, 1896), 339; XXXVI (February 17, 1897), 87; (June 16, 1897), 309.
[31] *Coal Trade Journal*, XXXVII (February 16, 1898), 92; and U.S. Industrial Commission, *Report*, XIII, 119.
[32] *Coal Trade Journal*, XXXVIII (January 11, 1899), 19; *Coal and Coke Operator*, XIV (April 11, 1912), 233. The few attempts to limit output failed.
[33] DJ-CS, box 617, file 60–187–94; *Black Diamond*, XXII (May 13, 1899), 520; James D. Norris, "The Missouri and Kansas Zinc Miners' Association, 1899–1905," *Business History Review*, XL (Autumn, 1966), 334; Henry R. Seager and Charles A. Gulick, Jr., *Trust and Corporation Problems* (New York, 1929), 94–95 and 383–384; William Letwin, *Law and Economic Policy in America: The Evolution of the Sherman Antitrust Act* (New York, 1964), chapters 4 and 5.

restrict competition.[34] By 1901, operators in the Pittsburgh district had merged into two great operating companies. The Pittsburgh Coal Co. controlled, through purchase, more than 100 mines (including the M. A. Hanna property) which shipped their product by rail. To the south and east, the Monongahela River Consolidated Coal and Coke Co. acquired all those properties shipping down the Monongahela River through the city of Pittsburgh. Coke making was relatively concentrated as early as 1895, when the H. C. Frick Co. owned two-thirds of the ovens in the world famous Connellsville region. Although the Frick company continued to add to its oven holdings, the percentage of ownership changed little. Merger of merchant coke companies, producing for a market rather than captive producers for the steel industry like Frick, began in 1910.[35] Consolidation in West Virginia began in 1901, when coal properties in the state's northern counties were brought together under the Fairmont Coal Co. Two years later controlling shares in the Fairmont company and the Clarksburg Fuel Co., itself a major combination, were purchased by Consolidation Coal Co., an operating firm organized in 1860. By 1909, Consolidation mined coal in Maryland, West Virginia, and Pennsylvania and was producing almost 2 per cent of the total national production of bituminous coal. Major consolidation also took place in the state's Pocahontas field in 1900, in the New River district in 1905, and in the Cabin Creek district in 1907.[36]

To the west, operators also participated in the merger movement, but with less enthusiasm and fewer results. Consolidation in Illinois began early in the 1890s and culminated in the formation of a number of medium-sized corporations in 1905. Bridging the interstate barrier was the Dering Co., with interests in two Illinois and three Indiana counties. Ohio's equivalent was the 1905 merger of the Continental Coal Co. and the Sunday Creek Coal Co., with the product an interstate company with interests in West Virginia as

[34] This conclusion discounts the role of economies of scale (minimal in bituminous coal production) and is in general agreement with the findings of Alfred S. Eichner in *The Emergence of Oligopoly: Sugar Refining as a Case Study* (Baltimore, 1969). Unlike sugar refining, however, the problems of the coal industry were precipitated in part by the transportation-stimulated emergence of a national market. See Eichner, *Emergence*, 94, and Joe S. Bain, "Industrial Concentration and Anti-Trust Policy," in Harold F. Williamson, ed., *The Growth of the American Economy* (New York, 1951), 616–630.

[35] *Coal and Coke Operator*, X (June 9, 1910), 369; XI (November 24, 1910), 757; (December 22, 1910), 840; XVI (April 3, 1913), 252; U.S. Industrial Commission, *Final Report* (1902), 229–230; and *ibid.*, XIII (1901), 100–102; *Coal Trade Journal*, XXXII (June 28, 1893), 400; XXXVIII (May 17, 1899), 255; (August 23, 1899), 438; *Mineral Resources, 1900*, 274; 1905, p. 746; and 1915, 549; *Coal Trade*, 1896, 8; *Coal and Coke Operator*, X (June 9, 1910), 369.

[36] *Coal Trade*, 1901, 39; memorandum, October 11, 1911, in Fleming Papers, box September 1911–February 1912; Phil Conley, *History of the West Virginia Coal Industry* (Charleston, W. Va., 1960), 98, 168, 221, 235; *Moody's Manual of Railroads and Corporation Securities, 1910* (New York, 1910).

well as the Buckeye State. Between 1909 and 1911 there was talk in the Midwest of a scheme to consolidate the region's coal mining properties into a series of district companies, operated by a parent company. U. S. Steel and Standard Oil were conceived as models, and, according to *Coal and Coke Operator*, J. P. Morgan was asked to undertake the task of reorganization. Morgan's field agents, however, brought back reports of the excessive prices operators wanted for their properties. Although Morgan's 1911 European trip may have included a personal look at the German coal syndicates, the trade lost interest in this grand scheme after 1912. The Supreme Court's 1911 decision in the Standard Oil Case was no doubt the critical element in the change of opinion.[37]

Consolidation did not produce stability. Even in the coke markets, with a relatively homogeneous product and a natural price leader in the Connellsville product, price maintenance proved impossible. In the Pittsburgh district, where concentration was carried the furthest, independents continued to be a factor and the two giants, rather than cooperating, invaded each other's markets. Pessimism in midwestern trade circles was aptly expressed by *Black Diamond*: "It is apparently impossible for any consolidation of bituminous coal mines which falls short of a monopoly, to effect any radical increase in the price of fuel to the consumer." [38]

Behind this failure lay the same economic realities — widely available resources, easily developed — which had rendered powerless the price fixing and sales associations of the previous decade. Those realities were now abetted by an uncertain political atmosphere. Although no coal merger was prosecuted under Theodore Roosevelt or William Taft, neither President was receptive when operators presented their economic analyses of the industry. Whatever its role in other areas of the economy, the Bureau of Corporations functioned as a funnel for an undercurrent of public opposition to concentration in the coal industry, referring complainants to the dynamic center of federal opposition to consolidation, the Department of Justice. More than once coal operators found Justice officials uncooperative. In 1910, lawyer D. W. Kuhn of the Pittsburgh-

[37] *Coal Trade Journal*, XXXVII (March 23, 1898), 157; Harry Mitchell Dixon, "The Illinois Coal Mining Industry" (Ph.D. dissertation, University of Illinois, 1951), 74, 96; *Mineral Resources, 1905*, 505–506; *Coal Trade Bulletin*, September 1, 1906, 45, and October 1, 1906, 27; *Ohio Mine Inspectors' Report, 1909*, 5–6; *Coal and Coke Operator*, XII (February 23, 1911), 128–129; (March 2, 1911), 142–143; XIII (September 21, 1911), 186. A plan similar to the midwestern one was mentioned for the Appalachian region. See *Coal and Coke Operator*, XI (October 6, 1910), 642. For statistics on bituminous mergers, see Ralph L. Nelson, *Merger Movements in American Industry, 1895–1956* (Princeton, 1959), 46, 62, and Appendices B and C.
[38] *Black Diamond*, XL (February 22, 1908), 17; *Coal and Coke Operator*, XV (July 11, 1912), 27; *Coal and Coke*, IX (January 1, 1902), 12–13, and (April 1, 1902), 8–9.

Westmoreland Coal Co. thought the antitrust climate sufficiently threatening to warrant a letter to the Department of Justice. Kuhn explained and justified a proposed consolidation of seven or eight coal companies and requested assurance that Justice would not prosecute the combination. The Department refused. The same process took place in 1912 when the Pittsburgh Coal Co. sought a merger with the Monongahela River Consolidated Coal and Coke Co. Justice officials again would offer no advice and, upon receipt of newspaper notice of the merger, sent agents into the Pittsburgh district to conduct an inquiry. Little wonder that numerous operators saw the Sherman Act as the enemy of consolidation.[39]

The second post-1900 institution designed to confine competition within reasonable bounds was the statistical trade association. Also called open price associations, these organizations were based on the assumption that operators who were fully knowledgeable about prices, contracts, inventories, shipments, selling and production costs, and other terms of the trade would be less likely to sell below cost and more likely to maintain prices individually or by informal agreement.[40] The idea was introduced into the coal industry in 1897, but before 1911 there was only one statistical association of any importance. Established in February 1903, the Bituminous Coal Trade Association served operators shipping east from eight regions in Pennsylvania, West Virginia, Virginia, and Maryland. "The Association," explained its chairman, L. N. Lovell, "cannot take up individual questions of competition. . . . nor can there be any agreements on prices. The latter is a matter prohibited by law and, quite apart from that, always made inoperative by the exigencies of business. But the members can meet, confer on the various matters of mutual interests, and there is no law, statute or moral, to prevent [it]." [41]

[39] *Black Diamond*, XLVIII (April 13, 1912), 18; letter John Mitchell to Joseph A. Holmes (November 27, 1909), in John Mitchell Papers, Mullen Library, Catholic University, Washington, D.C., box A3–15, file 63; *The Independent*, LX (April 26, 1906), 991–992; letter U.S. Attorney, Topeka, Kansas, to Attorney General (April 10, 1912), in DJ–CS, box 607, file 60–187–21; letter D. W. Kuhn to W. S. Kenyon, Assistant Attorney General (April 28, 1910), *ibid.*, box 606, file 60–187–3; letter Cyrus E. Woods to George W. Wickersham (February 3, 1912), *ibid.*, and Wickersham to Woods (February 8, 1912), *ibid.*; letter J. F. Shotts to James R. Garfield (October 25, 1906), in Bureau of Corporations Records, box 598, file 4439–8; letter W. P. Atkins to Theodore Roosevelt (September 11, 1907), *ibid.*, file 4439–11; letter A. L. Brandenburg (January 20, 1909), *ibid.*, file 4439–18; *Coal and Coke Operator*, XV (July 11, 1912), 27; X (March 3, 1910), 137; Glenn W. Traer, "Conservation in the Coal Industry, Protection of Life and Prevention of Waste," AMC *Proceedings*, XI (1908), part 2, 161–163; and Letwin, *Law and Economic Policy*, 240–266.

[40] Milton Nels Nelson, "Open Price Associations," *University of Illinois Studies in the Social Sciences*, X (June, 1922), 9–10, 14–15; Seager and Gulick, 305, 318–319; and Louis Galambos, *Competition and Cooperation: The Emergence of a National Trade Association* (Baltimore, 1966), 78–83.

[41] From the Report of the Annual Meeting of February 11, 1904, 4–5, copy in Bureau of Corporations Records, file 5091–6; *Coal Trade Journal*, XXXVI (January 20, 1897), 29.

The coal industry participated in the national infatuation with such associations which began in 1911 and reached a peak about 1916. In coal, as elsewhere, the major reasons are clear. Most important, the industry's previous solutions to the problem of competition — sales agencies, price fixing associations, mergers — were now suspect. The case against mergers was simple; they completely failed to stabilize the industry. Sales agencies and price fixing associations, used extensively before 1900, had been on shaky legal ground since 1897 and particularly after Taft assumed the presidency. In November 1909, a committee of coal operators met with the President and asked for his cooperation in modifying the Sherman Act so that producers could " 'get together' and arrange for a price on bituminous coal at the mine." Taft, according to their report, "could see no escape from a continuance of the present system of vigorous competition." [42] All doubt concerning the administration position was dispelled the next spring, when Attorney General George W. Wickersham threatened a suit against a combination of New River and Pocahontas operators for price maintenance. With the U. S. Steel indictment in 1911, the administration placed the open price system itself under suspicion, and the election year found Justice Department agents investigating Pennsylvania merchant coke producers for uniform pricing based on uniform accounting systems. These actions insured Taft's alienation from the coal operators. One in particular, a prominent producer from the new Winding Gulf region of West Virginia, termed the President "unquestionably a stiff, with the judicial mind, who would sit still and let the country go to the devil while prosecuting every man and every concern in the country that had made good." [43]

The decreasing usefulness of mergers and price fixing made little difference between 1899 and 1909, years of growth in the coal industry. But when stagnation began in 1910, the statistical association took on increasing appeal as a new device for securing stability. Cautious because of the steel indictment and the new President, coal operators waited until May 1915. Then, with the industry in the depths of depression and reasonably sure that statistical associations would not be prosecuted, midwestern opera-

[42] Letter Holmes to Mitchell (no date), in Mitchell Papers, box A3–15, file 63.
[43] Letter Justus Collins to Isaac T. Mann (February 29, 1912), in Justus Collins Papers, West Virginia University Library, Morgantown, W. Va., series I, box 10, folder 67; *Coal and Coke Operator*, X (May 19, 1910), 314; (April 14, 1910), 236–237; XIII (September 28, 1911), 201; XV (July 11, 1912), 27; Robert H. Wiebe, *Businessmen and Reform: A Study of the Progressive Movement* (Chicago, 1968), 82–84; James Weinstein, *The Corporate Ideal in the Liberal State, 1900–1918* (Boston, 1968), 83–84 and 149–150; and James C. German, Jr., "The Taft Administration and the Sherman Antitrust Act," *Mid-America*, LIV (July 1972), 172–186.

tors took action, forming district statistical associations that eastern-ers "first met with scorn, then disbelief." [44] Within eighteen months, nearly every major producing district had its own association, "co-operating with the sanction of the Federal Trade Commission in the exchange of information." [45] The associations emphasized their informational functions and denied any intent to fix the price of coal. Since the numbers collected and dispensed by the asso-ciations were meaningless unless they represented comparable units, the open price movement implied and encouraged uniform sizing of coal and uniform cost accounting. [46]

The tone and performance of the Taft administration did a good deal more than motivate coal operators to consider the statistical association. In conjunction with the industry's ubiquitous economic problems, it convinced the operators of the need to redefine the government-industry relationship and make it predictable. Restive even under Theodore Roosevelt, in 1908 coal producers joined with the National Civic Federation and past and present Commissioners of the Bureau of Corporations in ill-fated support of amendments to the Sherman Act, predictably conceived to be restrictive, re-pressive, and partly responsible for the maintenance of destructive competition. [47] Their efforts centered on the Hepburn bill, which provided for the registration of corporations and associations with the Commissioner of Corporations and gave him, with the concur-rence of the Secretary of Commerce and Labor, the power to judge whether contracts or combinations filed with the Bureau of Cor-porations were "reasonable." [48]

Between 1911 and 1914 the operators again sought to make the federal government a full partner in the search for order and ap-pealed once more for a legislative solution to the problem of exces-

[44] *Coal Trade*, 1916, 70; *Fuel Magazine*, XX (February 5, 1913), 7–8.
[45] Edward W. Parker, "Cooperation, Conservation and Competition in Coal," AMC *Proceedings*, XIX (1916), 242; *Black Diamond*, LVI (January 1, 1916), 1; (June 17, 1916), 498.
[46] *Black Diamond*, LIV (March 13, 1915), 210–211; LVII (December 30, 1916), 578; letter Bulkley, Hauxhurst, Inglis, and Saeger, Attorneys, to Department of Justice (May 24, 1916), in DJ–CS, box 607, file 60–187–13; typescript of address by Robert E. Belt, FTC, delivered March 23, 1916, in FTC General Records, 1914–21, box 42, file 8140–2–8; American Mining Congress, *Proceedings*, XIX (1916) 78–83 and 186–192.
[47] *Report of the Pennsylvania Department of Mines*, 1909, iii; D. W. Kuhn, "Sherman Anti-Trust Law with Special Reference to the Coal Mining Industry," AMC *Proceedings*, XIV (1911), 259; *Coal and Coke Operator and Fuel*, XXI (October 23, 1913), 562; *Black Diamond*, LII (April 18, 1914), 312; *Coal Age*, I (November 11, 1911), 143; and *Outlook*, December 11, 1909, 797–798.
[48] Letter James R. Garfield to Henry Knox Smith (May 7, 1908), in James R. Garfield Papers, Manuscript Division, U.S. Library of Congress, Washington, D.C., Office Files, box 128; *Black Diamond*, XL (May 2, 1908), 17; *Coal and Coke Operator*, XI (October 6, 1910), 642; Gabriel Kolko, *The Triumph of Conservatism: A Reinterpretation of American History, 1900–1916* (Chicago, 1967), 133–138; Wiebe, *Businessmen and Reform*, 80–81; Weinstein, *The Corporate Ideal in the Liberal State*, 77–82; and George Cullom Davis, Jr., "The Federal Trade Commission: Promise and Practice in Regulating Business, 1900–1929" (Ph.D. dissertation, University of Illinois, 1969), 16–17.

sive competition. They were united on one specific proposition – the need to transfer regulatory functions from the Department of Justice, which had "caused so much uncertainty [and] disturbance to orderly pursuit of business," to a commission.[49] One suggestion, which appealed to the more radical operators, was for a National Mining Commission with "universal and complete jurisdiction over the mining business."[50] Advocates of such a commission viewed trade agreements as essential but inadequate solutions to destructive competition. Illinois operator A. J. Moorshead, for example, envisioned a commission which would restrict the opening of new mines and equalize supply and demand. Nonetheless, the vast majority of operators, represented in the American Mining Congress, again found common ground with the National Civic Federation in advocating a general commission which would investigate contracts, trade agreements, and combinations, and determine their legal status under the Sherman Act, amended if possible. The commission proposed by the AMC and the NCF would have the crucial power of prior approval – power to determine conclusively the legality of industrial arrangements submitted by corporations. If the commissioners found an agreement to be an unreasonable restraint of trade, they could request the participants to discontinue their illegal activities. Only if they failed to do so within a reasonable period would prosecution result.[51]

Operators were in general agreement not only on the means to be used in achieving industrial recovery, but on ends as well. Basic to their vision was the district confederation, a natural response to American conditions and one which reflected the widely admired German syndicate structure.[52] Under trade agreements sanctioned by a commission, operators within one production district (e.g., Indiana-Illinois, Pittsburgh, eastern Kentucky-western West Virginia) might limit production or restrict the opening of new mines; "group" output in order to eliminate seasonal overproduction; or employ a central sales agency to raise the price of coal or to achieve distributive economies. Differences between operators arose largely

---

[49] Coal and Coke Operator, XVI (February 27, 1913); and Weinstein, Corporate Ideal, 82.

[50] AMC Proceedings, XIV (1911), 39–41; Coal Age, I (January 6, 1912), 433; Coal and Coke Operator, XIV (April 11, 1912), 235; and Black Diamond, XLVIII (April 13, 1912), 18.

[51] A. J. Moorshead, "Condition of the Bituminous Coal Industry," AMC Proceedings, XIV (1911), 251; AMC Proceedings, XIV (1911), 42 and 279; Black Diamond, XLVIII (June 1, 1912), 20; LII (April 18, 1914), 312; Coal and Coke Operator, XIV (May 2, 1912), 278–279; and Coal and Coke Operator and Fuel, XXII (December 25, 1913), 137–138.

[52] Coal and Coke Operator, XIII (September 28, 1911), 196; (November 2, 1911), 281; and Coal Age, I (May 18, 1912), 1049–1050.

over the question of pricing. Speaking before the Senate Interstate Commerce Committee for the operators of Indiana, Walter S. Bogle emphasized production and selling agreements and admitted they would be of little value unless the result was some control over price. He was willing to see the federal government decide what constituted a reasonable price. Illinois operator Glenn Traer spoke in favor of restraint of trade but claimed to draw the line at output limitations or "arbitrary" control of prices. Admitting to the committee that he was "considerably at variance" with Bogle, Traer suggested that district operators agree to operate only enough mines to supply the trade. S. A. Taylor, representing the Pittsburgh Coal Operators' Association but also president of the American Mining Congress, did his best to emphasize possible economies of scale in sales and marketing; still, it was clear that his conception included control of supply, fixing of minimum selling prices, and the possibility of government regulation of prices. Industry spokesmen were aware of the need for a radical restructuring of the industry into a highly concentrated trade agreement oligopoly.[53]

Of the vocal members of the Senate Committee on Interstate Commerce, only West Virginia's Clarence Watson, a coal operator, showed much sympathy with the operators' recommendations or an understanding of industry economics. Chairman Moses Clapp of Minnesota traced industry difficulties to "poor business policy [in] opening these mines in excess of the real demand for their product."[54] Albert Cummins of Iowa and Frank Brandegee of Connecticut apparently could discern no difference between the coal industry and any other industry. Failing to recognize the problem (excessive competition), the Senators could hardly countenance the solution (the trade agreement). Nor could the committee conceive of an industrial structure between perfect competition and monopoly. American Mining Congress lobbyist James Callbreath told of a revealing exchange with Clapp. Clapp said: "When you will show me how it is possible to lock the stable door and still have it closed, or, having it closed, may at the same time have it open, I will understand how what you want can be accomplished." Callbreath replied: "Between the stable and the garden is a plot of grass going to waste and needing to be cropped. In the stable is a horse suffering for want of this grass. I am going to put a halter on that horse, give you the end of the halter-strap and allow you to supervise the

[53] U.S. Senate, Committee on Interstate Commerce, *Hearings Pursuant to Senate Resolution 98*, Vol. II, 62nd Cong., 1912, 2320-2332, 2354-2368, 2371, 2381-2393, 2400; *Coal and Coke Operator*, XV (August 29, 1912), 138; X (March 3, 1910), 137.
[54] Senate Committee on Interstate Commerce, *Hearings Pursuant to SR 98*, 2363.

grazing, and whenever the horse attempts to go into the garden you can pull him back, and, if he persists, you can put him back in the stable."[55]

It should come as no surprise that the Federal Trade Commission Act as signed into law on September 26, 1914, was not what the coal operators had requested. Prior approval was not mentioned. The hoped-for article on trade agreements was replaced with Section 5, declaring "unfair methods of competition" unlawful and empowering the commission to issue cease and desist orders in case such "unfair methods" were employed. Moreover, in spite of repeated requests, the coal industry did not succeed in placing the informed and politically adept Callbreath on the commission.[56] Nonetheless, the initial reaction to the trade commission was surprisingly favorable. *Coal Age* appreciated the commission's investigatory powers and predicted the body would make a careful study of the industry which "will lead to the tacit or open sanctioning of suitable working agreements."[57] A lengthy meeting between Indiana and Illinois operators and Interior Secretary Franklin K. Lane in December 1914 led to speculation that the commission would not only give advance advice on trade agreements but would declare most of them permissible. *Black Diamond* forecast "the co-operative era in American business" and looked forward to statistical associations and cooperative production, storage, and marketing.[58]

From the last days of 1914, however, the industry was profoundly ambivalent toward the FTC. Amid positive statements there was uncertainty and even hostility. Aware that the act itself offered little, *Black Diamond* wondered if Wilsonian cooperation might be limited to cost-reducing distribution schemes and sidestep the real need — cooperation to curtail production. A new and powerful spokesman for the industry, Charles S. Keith of Kansas City, Missouri, claimed the public was misinformed. The trade commission, he said, was not an administrative body to supervise restraint of trade, but an investigative body which reported to the Department of Justice: "It is consequently a repressive rather than a constructive measure. . . . under the new act, with the court ruling on facts as pre-determined by the Commission and by this same cause prejudiced against the defendant, we can expect more convictions,

[55] *Coal and Coke Operator*, XVI (February 20, 1913), 147; Senate Committee on Interstate Commerce, *Hearings Pursuant to SR 98*, 2324, 2331, 2334–2335, 2359, 2362, 2366, 2368, 2390, 2393, 2397, 2404; U.S. House of Representatives, Committee on Interstate and Foreign Commerce, *Hearings, Interstate Trade Commission, 1914*, 1914, 460–461.
[56] U.S. *Statutes at Large*, XXXVIII, 717ff.; *Black Diamond*, LIII (July 18, 1914), 50; (August 1, 1914), 90–91; (August 15, 1914), 131.
[57] *Coal Age*, VI (November 21, 1914), 844.
[58] LIII (December 19, 1914), 29, and (December 29, 1914), 525.

greater fears, less investment, and less initiative on the part of business." [59] By late 1915, it was clear to many operators, including Keith, that the FTC Act had failed to correct even the uncertainty which had prevailed under Taft and Roosevelt. They expressed their disappointment in a December 1915 appeal to the U. S. Chamber of Commerce for help in obtaining new legislation: "In the present state of the law business is prevented from indulging in co-operation due to the uncertain state of the law touching our Federal Trust statutes. . . . Doubt, itself, is equivalent to prohibition." [60]

These operators were responding to an FTC-Justice Department policy of cooperating with business that was extremely narrow in scope and hostile to all but the most primitive of trade agreements. Neither government agency exercised prior approval over any trade agreement, and their passive encouragement was limited to strictly statistical associations. Operators could take some solace in the views of FTC Vice-Chairman Edward Hurley, who publicly advocated cooperation through joint selling agencies. But Hurley's insistence that such cooperation "necessarily presupposes strict Federal regulation of the cooperating concerns" apparently involved too much federal interference for most operators.[61] Moreover, Hurley's legacy to the operators was not his broad vision but rather uniform accounting, a pet project which he promoted in coal, lumber, and other atomistic industries. Hurley's purpose, and the Commission's, was not to encourage price maintenance but to eliminate "unintelligent" competition based on faulty estimates of production cost. The end was notably conservative.[62]

The statistical associations, moreover, were carefully watched. An April 1915 memorandum prepared by an FTC agent asserted that a typical open price association in Franklin County, Illinois, "might be of considerable influence in preventing active price competition;" by early 1915, according to one report, "members of the Trade Commission [were] becoming increasingly suspicious of the operation of many of these trade asociations; they are not limiting

[59] *Black Diamond*, LIV (May 15, 1915), 414; and LIII (December 26, 1914), 525.
[60] December 2, 1915, in FTC General Correspondence, 1914–1921, box 44, file 8149–13. See also Davis, *The Federal Trade Commission*, 131; Nathan B. Williams, "The Federal Trade Commission Law," *Annals*, LXIII (January, 1916), 20–21; and AMC *Proceedings*, XIX (1916), 242.
[61] Edward N. Hurley, *Awakening of Business* (n.p., 1916), 202.
[62] Typescript of Belt Address, FTC Records; typescript of "Informal Conference with Illinois and Indiana Coal Operators," May 15, 1916, in FTC General Records, 1914–1921, box 201, file 8508–572-2–1, 7–8, 90; letter L. C. Boyle to Joseph Davies (March 30, 1916), FTC General Records, box 44, file 8149–13; FTC General Records, box 38, file 8116–2; and letter W. C. Saeger to Department of Justice (May 24, 1916), DJ–CS, box 607, file 60–187–13; Hurley, *Awakening of Business*, 197–200.

themselves to their legitimate functions, but are getting into the price-fixing, territory-dividing field." [63]

Justice Department officials remained largely uninvolved in the question of statistical associations until early 1917, when complaints of high coal prices led the attorney general to consider possible violations of the antitrust laws. Although the ensuing investigation emphasized dealer combinations, operator open price associations were examined to determine if they had been used "as a cover for price fixing purposes." [64] The Justice Department discovered that the Indiana Trade Bureau, ostensibly a straightforward statistical association, had been issuing circular selling instructions to its members in an effort to maintain prices. George Anderson, special assistant to the attorney general, wrote of "the desirability of wiping out of existence all these associations" because they engaged in illegal practices such as price fixing and division of territories. The FTC, he suggested, could do all the statistical work done by the associations. Nonetheless, as of 1918 Justice had entered no indictments against associations which limited their functions to collecting and disseminating statistics. Three West Virginia associations which transgressed department guidelines were indicted for price fixing through joint sales agencies; no convictions were obtained.[65]

The rest of the operator program for industry stabilization, including district confederations, sales agencies, and production restrictions, received no assistance from any branch of the federal government. A test case developed early in 1915 when a group of Indiana operators, led by Bogle and Callbreath, asked FTC approval for a sales corporation which would market some 80 per cent of the state's output and restrict production through a pooling of mine operating time. Their presentation emphasized anticipated economies in production and sales and the natural limits on price increases imposed by interstate competition. An FTC investigation revealed little empathy. It questioned whether the coal industry really suffered from excessive competition and low profits, criticized

[63] Letter George W. Anderson, Special Assistant to the Attorney General, to Attorney General (January 6, 1917), Department of Justice Central Files, Straight Numerical Files, box 1874, file 181092 (1–99) (these files are hereinafter referred to as DJ–SN); memorandum signed D. A. Morrow, "Preliminary Memoranda in Regard to Proposed Agreement of Indiana Coal Operators and Conditions in the Coal Mining Industry of Illinois," in FTC General Correspondence, box 196, file 8508–10–2–1; and *Declaration of Purposes, Articles of Association and By-Laws of the Franklin County, Illinois, Coal Operators' Association* (n.p., 1904), copy in FTC General Records, *ibid.*, file 8508–10–1–1.
[64] Letter Attorney General Thomas Gregory to William Howard, House of Representatives (July 25, 1917), DJ–SN, box 1874, file 181092 (310).
[65] Letter Anderson to Gregory (January 6, 1917), DJ–SN, box 1874, file 181092 (1–99); letter Anderson to Gregory (January 10, 1917), *ibid.* (100–179); Assistant to Attorney General to Charles F. Kingsley (June 15, 1917), *ibid.* (250–309); and DJ–CS, box 607, file 60–187–16.

the output and sales provisions of the agreement, and conjured the spectre of district sales agencies eventually combining to effect a monopoly.[66] Following meetings with trade commission and Justice officials in April 1915, there were reports of an agreement between the Justice Department and the Indiana operators. G. Carroll Todd, who handled these meetings for Justice, was upset by the suggestion of a deal and privately communicated his feeling that the coal operators were working "not quite fairly to create an atmosphere of having committed the Department to an approval of their plans."[67] It seems likely that the Federal Trade Commission and the Justice Department refrained from encouraging the Indiana operators in this critical test. Deprived of government aid, the Indiana association never became a major factor in the coal trade; prosecution was unnecessary.

The post-1914 "co-operative era" was punctuated with frustration and disappointment. While a few operators continued to see the FTC as the coal industry's benefactor, most were dissatisfied with an organization which tolerated only the most limited form of cooperation and was oblivious to the very real need — often articulated by industry spokesmen — for production restrictions.[68] Dissatisfied operators joined the United Mine Workers and the U. S. Chamber of Commerce in an attempt to secure amendments to the antitrust laws. "If the Commission as it is now construed," wrote one operator, "has not the power to advise with industries along broad and constructive lines, then, indeed, this power should be conferred upon it."[69] This group planned to secure amendments to Section 5 of the FTC Act, so as "to empower the Commission to permit reasonable cooperation in business and industry."[70] If the FTC was the captive of politically oriented big businessmen, coal operators were not among the captors.[71]

[66] Letter W. S. Bogle, et al., to Joseph E. Davies (March 25, 1915), FTC General Records, box 196, file 8508-10-1-1; D. A. Morrow, "Preliminary Memoranda."

[67] Letter Anderson to Gregory (January 10, 1917), DJ-SN, box 1874, file 181092 (100-179). Anderson's recollections were based on personal notes taken at the April 21, 1915 meeting between Todd and the Indiana operators (letter L. L. Bracken [February 23, 1917], in FTC General Records, box 190, file 8502-297).

[68] This is particularly obvious in the May 15, 1916 FTC-Illinois-Indiana Conference, report in FTC General Records, 12, 14, 83; also Black Diamond, LVI (May 27, 1916), 444-445. In 1962, G. Cullom Davis made the point that until 1925, the commission tried "to execute a strict regulatory policy in accordance with the progressive ideals of economic reform." But Davis dismissed the years before 1918 and offered little proof for his thesis before that date. See "The Transformation of the Federal Trade Commission, 1914–1929," Mississippi Valley Historical Review, XLIX (December, 1962), 437-455.

[69] Letter Boyle to Davies (January 22, 1916), FTC General Records, box 44, file 8149-13; Wiebe, Businessmen and Reform, 84.

[70] Letter Charles S. Keith and W. R. Fairley to Samuel Gompers and John Fahey (January 19, 1916), FTC General Records, box 44, file 8149-13; Black Diamond, LV (October 23, 1915), 325; and Coal and Coke Operator, XXI (February 1917), 15.

[71] Recent critiques of Progressivism from the New Left have overemphasized harmony and underemphasized conflict in business-government relationships. See Sklar, 78-79,

Contrary to what operators hoped, the FTC had not replaced Justice as the arbiter of trade agreements. And the attorney general had responded to an increasing flow of anti-coal operator mail with his own industry-wide investigation of coal trade associations and ultimately with indictments. "In regulating the coal business," commented *Black Diamond* in April 1917, "the government and the Department of Justice have tampered with the roots. They began to bear down on coal before any organization at all was effected. Therefore they began to hack at it before anything which makes for efficiency had become a part of the coal routine." [72]

On the eve of American entry into World War I, the coal industry remained undisciplined, wasteful of natural and human resources. Three decades of remedies for a sick industry had produced minor victories (a slight increase in concentration, some statistical associations, and a degree of uniformity in wages and other costs) and major defeats (price fixing associations, joint selling agencies, the merger movement, and the limited nature of FTC cooperation). An over-zealous Department of Justice, particularly under Presidents McKinley and Taft, must bear some of the responsibility for the industry's continued predicament, but fundamentally the problem lay not in politics but in the basic economic conditions in a natural resource industry with regional and national markets. These conditions did not change after 1917. Wartime surges in demand and price fixing brought relief in the form of higher profits, but it was only temporary and was accompanied by considerable friction between coal operators and federal officials. [73] After 1920 an increasingly divided industry, troubled by an anti-union southern wing, resisted the associational approach of Herbert Hoover and the Com-

---

Weinstein, *Corporate Ideal*, 89, 91, and Kolko, *Triumph of Conservatism*, 268–270. "The business community," states Kolko, "knew what it wanted from the commission, and what it wanted was almost precisely what the commission sought to do." (*Ibid.*, 278.) Only further research will indicate conclusively whether the coal industry's relationship to the federal government was typical or uniquely frustrating, the exception that proves the rule. There are indications that other groups, presumably without the divisions and disabilities of the coal industry, were also unable to obtain precisely what they wanted. The National Civic Federation, for example, was no more successful than the coal industry in getting Congress to act on its trust program. See Senate Committee on Interstate Commerce, *Hearings Pursuant to SR 98*, 515–516, 519, 521, 527, 529. There is reason to doubt Weinstein's claim that "the ideas embodied in the Federal Trade Commission Act represented a triumph of the agitation and education done by the NCF over the previous seven years" (*Corporate Ideal*, 89).

[72] *Black Diamond*, LVIII (April 28, 1917), 355; and JD–SN, box 1874, file 181092 (100–179).

[73] Daniel R. Beaver, *Newton D. Baker and the American War Effort, 1917–1919* (Lincoln, Nebraska, 1966), 64–66; Letter Anderson to Gregory (June 30, 1917), JD–SN, box 1874, file 181092 (250–309); letter Judge Isaac R. Oeland to Gregory (July 13, 1917), DJ–CS, box 607, file 60–187–16; memorandum, undated and unsigned, on formation of the National Coal Association, JD–SN, box 1874, file 181092 (250–309); *Black Diamond*, LVIII (June 30, 1917), 552; (July 28, 1917), 61; (August 4, 1917), 87; and (September 29, 1917), 249.

merce Department. Even the regulatory legislation of the New Deal reflected the industry's divisions and centrifugal tendencies, and not until late 1940 did the minimum price provisions of the Guffey-Vinson Act go into effect.[74] The great expectations of the 1890s were just beginning to be fulfilled.

[74] Ellis W. Hawley, "Secretary Hoover and the Bituminous Coal Problem, 1921–1928," *Business History Review*, XLII (Autumn, 1968), 247–270; James P. Johnson, "Drafting the NRA Code of Fair Competition for the Bituminous Coal Industry," *Journal of American History*, LIII (December, 1966), 521–541; and Ellis W. Hawley, *The New Deal and the Problem of Monopoly: A Study in Economic Ambivalence* (Princeton, 1966), 205–212.

Herbert Croly, Progressive Ideology, and the FTC Act

DOUGLAS WALTER JAENICKE

The proper interpretation of the national government's early twentieth-century intervention in the economy, especially in the form of regulatory agencies, is the subject of a continuing debate between two schools of thought. The first school, exemplified in the writing of Arthur Schlesinger, Jr., views government economic intervention as a democratic and progressive response to the threatening power of big business. His description of President Woodrow Wilson (1913–1920) captures the essence of Schlesinger's interpretation of early twentieth-century government economic intervention.

> As the election of 1916 approached, Wilson completed his acceptance of the main lines of the Progressive program of 1912. He now stood clearly for strong government, for administrative regulation, for some intervention on behalf of the farmer and the worker—in short, for affirmative federal action aimed to produce equality of opportunity. In a basic respect, Roosevelt seemed to have been right: the people's government had to be stronger than business if popular rule were to be effective.[1]

Schlesinger interprets the national government's intervention in the economy as being impelled by and embodying concern for the little man who sought an equal opportunity to succeed.

Recent scholarship by revisionist historians, most notably Gabriel Kolko, has challenged this democratic interpretation of early government intervention in the economy.[2] Instead, Kolko has argued that from 1900 to 1916 big business

[1] Arthur M. Schlesinger, Jr., *The Crisis of the Old Order* (Boston, 1957), pp. 34–35.
[2] Both Kolko and James Weinstein self-consciously pit their interpretations against the Schlesinger-type of argument. See Gabriel Kolko, *The Triumph of Conservatism* (Chicago, 1963),

DOUGLAS WALTER JAENICKE is an instructor in political science at Dickinson College. He is currently completing a study which develops the competing theories of political party in Jacksonian America.

pushed for and obtained a policy of government economic intervention in order to protect the large firms from the competitive threat of smaller ones. After studying the origins, intents, and consequences of federal regulatory legislation from 1900 to 1916, Kolko concluded that the economic regulatory legislation Schlesigner had praised as being democratic not only had been supported by but also had benefited big business. According to Kolko, ostensibly progressive and democratic legislation neither restored equal opportunity and business competition nor protected farmers and workers but, rather, intentionally aided and abetted the economic self-interest of big business; consequently, the era of 1900-1916 was nothing more than *The Triumph of Conservatism.*

Kolko argued that big business sought escape from the uncertainty and risk of economic competition. To attain this, big business first attempted to stabilize the relations among firms through voluntary agreements. However, these agreements failed since an individual firm would benefit from violating an agreement if the others complied.[3] Business then turned to mergers, but these also failed to stabilize industry since the resulting large corporations were inefficient and hence vulnerable to economic competition. Consequently, big business turned to the coercive power of the government to order the economy; big business needed and pushed for economic intervention by the national government—this government intervention would be dominated by big business—in order to stabilize economic relations and thereby institutionalize the dominant position of the large corporations.[4]

In accordance with their respective general interpretations, Kolko and Schlesinger offer mutually exclusive explanations of the original Federal Trade Commission (FTC) Act of 1914. Where Schlesinger sees a democratic creation, Kolko perceives a victory for big business. While agreeing with Kolko that Schlesinger's explanation of the original act as a "democratic victory" is incorrect, this article contends that the basis of *conscious*[5] support for the act cannot be understood purely in terms of big business's self-interest.

While avoiding Schlesinger's mistake, this article offers an alternative interpretation of the FTC Act which challenges, but does not exclude, Kolko's. Kolko's account of the origins and intentions behind the 1914 FTC Act neglects to confront that stream of progressive thought, exemplified in Herbert Croly's *The Promise of American Life* (1909), which sought both government encouragement and government control of economic consolidation for reasons of "individual excellence" and "national purpose."[6] This omission on Kolko's part

---

pp. 7-8, and *Railroads and Regulation, 1877-1916* (New York, 1965), p. 2, and James Weinstein, *The Corporate Ideal in the Liberal State: 1900-1918* (Boston, 1968), pp. xi-xii.

[3] For a formal explanation of this phenomenon, see Mancur Olson, *The Logic of Collective Action: Public Goods and the Theory of Groups* (Cambridge, Mass., 1971).

[4] Kolko, *Triumph*, esp. "Introduction" and chaps. 1, 2.

[5] Wanting to argue that people who fully understood the implications of the act could still support it for idealistic (disinterested) reasons, I emphasize "conscious."

[6] It is neither the purpose nor the need of this discussion to defend and explain *fully* what Croly meant by "public excellence" and "national purpose." The terms are solely to show that Croly

is due to his linking all conscious support for large economic units to support for the economic self-interest of big business. However, Croly defended the existence and regulation of large corporations, monopolies, and trusts from a perspective entirely distinct from economic interest; for Croly the national government's economic intervention was intended neither to further equal opportunity nor to serve big business's self-interest, but rather to provide and protect positions of concentrated power and responsibility for a few excellent individuals.

In 1914 Herbert Croly publicly endorsed the FTC Act.[7] This article will show how and why Croly could consciously support the act, not in terms of equal opportunity (business competition) or big business's self-interest, but rather for idealistic, disinterested reasons,[8] first by briefly sketching Croly's thought and then by demonstrating the harmony between the 1914 act and Croly's ideas.

CROLY'S PROGRESSIVE VISION:
EXCELLENCE AND THE LARGE CORPORATION

A number of factors justify using Croly as a representative of a distinctive stream of progressive thought. Students of the progressive era see Croly as exemplifying one style of progressivism.[9] Furthermore, many contemporaneous intellectuals recognized the distinctiveness of Croly's thought and agreed with him on fundamental points.[10] In addition, Croly's influence and recognition extended beyond intellectual circles to a broader audience. Theodore Roosevelt called Croly's *Promise* the "most powerful and illuminating study of our national condition which has appeared for many years." Croly had cited Roosevelt as the model reformer and his policy as the model progressive program.[11] Finally, Croly along with Walter Lippmann and Walter Weyl edited the *New Republic,* which along with its audience constituted indirect evidence of a wider reception for Croly's thinking. Thus, Croly's was not a lone voice.

Perceiving a positive role for the large corporations in the modern world, Croly arrived at a progressive vision that tried to avoid both the Scylla of big business's self-interest and the Charybdis of equal opportunity. His driving vi-

---

valued the large corporations for reasons other than big business's self-interest. Due to space constraints this article sketches what Croly meant by "excellence" but not "national purpose."

[7] Herbert Croly, "Restraint of Trade," *New Republic,* I (November 21, 1914), 9-10.

[8] "Idealistic" is used to emphasize that Croly's *ideas* would lead him to endorse the act.

[9] See Richard Hofstadter, *The Age of Reform* (New York, 1955), and Charles Forcey, *The Crossroads of Liberalism* (New York, 1961).

[10] See Walter Lippmann, *Drift and Mastery* (Englewood Cliffs, N.J., 1961, first published 1914). *Drift and Mastery* proposed the substitution of national purpose and individual excellence (taken together he termed them "mastery") made possible by economic concentration for the traditional American values of equal liberties, equal opportunity, business competition, and the profit motive.

[11] Quoted in Arthur M. Schlesinger, Jr., "Introduction," Herbert Croly, *The Promise of American Life* (Cambridge, Mass., 1965), p. xxiii. For Croly's praise of Theodore Roosevelt, see chap. 6, sec. 6, 7.

sion was the achievement of an economic and political structure that would enable excellent individuals to distinguish themselves. According to Croly, excellent individuals disciplined themselves by accepting the authority of their work, not the requirements of the market. Economic competition vitiated any such vocationalism since under conditions of competition individuals could not dedicate themselves exclusively to the excellence of their work but rather pursued economic gain. Furthermore, economic competition only allowed for quantitative differences among individuals—more or less economic success; but, Croly contended: "A genuine individual must at least possess some special *quality* which distinguishes him from other people . . ." (italics added).[12] Accordingly, he favored economic consolidation which promised to liberate all individuals from the economic scramble so that they could dedicate themselves to the demands and nature of their work.

Economic consolidation also provided the extraordinary individual with the decision-making responsibility and power congruent with exceptional ability. Public excellence required the concentration and institutionalization of power and decision-making responsibility through extensive subordination and hierarchy. Consequently, Croly embraced the large corporations and trusts which institutionalized positions of great power. Severely circumscribing the ambit of economic market competition, the large corporations could provide pinnacles of power and responsibility where exceptional individuals could effectively govern the economy. This concentration, institutionalization, and wielding of power would lift the excellent individual high above the mass and make him visible far and wide.[13]

In the 1890s the American economy witnessed the emergence and growth of truly national economic *institutions*—trusts, monopolies, and large corporations—which in effect constituted new structures of economic governance, since they concentrated economic decision making. Preempting the decision making of individual factories, these new national economic institutions extended the power of a few corporate positions first to individual factories, and later to the economy. Corporate headquarters now assumed the task of governing the corporation's factories which were dispersed across the country, thereby abrogating the previous practice of each factory deciding economic matters autonomously.[14]

---

[12] Croly, *Promise* (New York, 1965), p. 410. Hereafter, page references are to this edition of Croly's *Promise*. Expressing this same disdain for quantitative differences, Roosevelt designated the Jacksonian era the "millennium of minnows." Quoted in Marvin Meyers, *The Jacksonian Persuasion* (Stanford, Calif., 1957), n. 1, pp. 16–17.

[13] For Croly's discussion of the need for concentrated decision-making responsibility, see his *Promise*, pp. 200–201, 325, 330, 332, 336, 338. For examples of his discussion of economic concentration providing positions for exceptional individuals, see ibid., pp. 368, 432. For Croly's discussion of individual excellence and distinction, see ibid., chaps. 1, 3, 7, 13 and chap. 4, sec 3, 'Lincoln as More Than an American."

[14] The day-to-day operations—the efficient running of the factory—were still left to the factory managers, but corporate directors and trustees assumed responsibility for decisions concerning ex-

Transcending governance of the large corporation's own factories and the trust's own corporations, directors of the large corporations and trusts could also conrol other firms through a variety of techniques. Oligopolistic price leadership testified to the ability of a large corporation (or group of corporations) to govern other firms in the same sector. In a similar manner dominant corporations could coerce their competitors to accept a fixed percentage of the sector's total business volume.[15] Finally, vertical integration allowed a corporation that controlled the supply of raw materials and hence their price to govern its competitors.[16]

In addition to valuing the large corporations because they established positions of extraordinary power and responsibility, Croly also favored these new institutions because they were amenable to an ongoing government regulatory role.[17] To Croly, regulation of these governing corporations meant the creation of additional positions of visibility and authority; government regulation promised mastery rather than drift, excellence rather than mediocrity. Unlike the owner of a family firm who constituted the backbone of the National Association of Manufacturers (NAM) and on moral grounds defended the integrity of his business from government encroachment, the corporate director was liberated from such a moral imperative. Keeping this fact always before Croly, the National Civic Federation (NCF)—the national organization of the large corporations and finance capital—from 1900 to 1920 urged government intervention in the economy in order to secure and protect the governing role of its members, a role which was being attacked by equal opportunity advocates, especially NAM.[18]

Croly further argued that the existence of these dominant economic institutions was an irrevocable fact which paradoxically was the natural outcome of economic competition. Croly's analysis hinges on a psychological insight:

---

pansion, sources of raw materials, markets, prices, etc. At that time, a typical example of this phenomenon was the Standard Oil Trust whose nine trustees successfully governed the more than thirty participating corporations. See Ida M. Tarbell, *The History of the Standard Oil Company*, Vol. II (Gloucester, Mass., 1963; first published 1904).

[15] Standard Oil resorted to this tactic when the practice of driving its competitors into bankruptcy became too costly. Ibid., pp. 11-23.

[16] Controlling the supply of iron ore, United States Steel pursued this course. Croly, *Promise*, p. 114.

[17] It is important to distinguish regulation which accepts economic concentration (here labeled "ongoing") from regulation which sought to destroy and level large economic units. Obviously, Croly favored the former type of regulation.

[18] Kolko fails to differentiate the NCF and NAM. The NCF, which was the organization of the large corporations and finance capital, sought government regulation of the monopolies, trusts, and large corporations while NAM favored government intervention to destroy them. The NCF had developed a new ideology of social responsibility whereas NAM still adhered to business competition and equal opportunity. See James Weinstein, *Corporate Ideal*, and Gordon M. Jenson, "The National Civic Federation: American Business in an Age of Social Change and Social Reform," Ph.D. diss., Princeton University, 1956, pp. 54-65. Kolko's lumping together NCF and NAM leads him to make mistakes. See footnote 26.

Those businessmen engaged in competition, especially those who head corporations, seek to protect and consolidate their precarious advantages.[19] Any attempt to outlaw practices that result in economic consolidation would prove futile as well as pernicious since the real businessmen—who arose with the corporation—would be compelled either to develop new practices which had not yet been declared illegal or to break the law.

The demise of economic competition was due not only to the psychological desire explicated above but also to the coinciding of the economic interests of the large corporations. This coincidence of private interests encouraged cooperation among the large economic units which then furthered economic consolidation.[20]

Valuing the large corporations and also perceiving them as inevitable, Croly urged government discrimination in their behalf. The government's charting an antilargeness course would endanger Croly's vision as well as contravene historical necessity; therefore, Croly urged that government policy accept and encourage the large units while also controlling them.

Government control was exigent since economic consolidation could easily become mired in economic self-interest, bereft of excellence and national purpose; government control was needed in order to make consolidation serve public ends. For example, since consolidation abolished the natural selection of the meritorious through the market structure (that is, equal opportunity could not survive within a hierarchical society structured by large corporations), economic consolidation meant that individuals could rest upon and be content with their past laurels while still occupying the positions of power and that unworthy individuals could inherit governing positions. Consequently, Croly demanded artificial selection implemented by government to replace the moribund natural selection of the market.

However, this artificial selection did not seek to restore equal opportunity; though it was to select the best. Basically accepting the social Darwinist dictum that the best usually produce the best, Croly's solution made no pretense of ensuring equal starts and fair races. Neither accepting nor favoring a restoration of equal opportunity, Croly recognized its deleterious consequences. After crossing the many hurdles and passing through the many gates, the successful com-

---

[19] Croly, Promise, p. 111. Acknowledging this psychological motivation, Woodrow Wilson wrote that the "naturalness" of the trusts and monopolies lay in the natural desire of businessmen to escape the ambiguity and risk of competition. Wilson, The New Freedom (Englewood Cliffs, N.J., 1961, first published 1913), p. 102. Wilson, however, did not agree with Croly's conclusion that the psychological impetus precluded legislating against economic consolidation. Similarly, in History of the Standard Oil Company, Tarbell recounted Rockefeller's desire for business security; this desire to protect his success compelled him to utilize every means to establish a monopoly which was the only possible safeguard for his success.

[20] Croly cited the Northern Railroad's sale of its iron ore holdings to U. S. Steel, but not to small producers, as an example of this. Croly, Promise, p. 114. Such cooperation permeated other economic sectors; Rockefeller had utilized cooperation with the railroads to aggrandize Standard Oil. See Tarbell, History of the Standard Oil Company.

petitor was so exhausted and enervated that he could not fully exploit and enjoy the position of power and responsibility which he had eventually won.[21] Purposeful government discrimination was to affect the direction and character of the entire nation both by ensuring that the meritorious secured positions of honor and power congruent with their talents and by favoring those institutions that provided such positions.[22]

PROGRESSIVE ASPECTS OF THE ACT: A POLICY ANALYSIS

D.H. Lawrence warned: "Art-speech is the only truth. An artist is a damned liar, but his art, if it be art, will tell you the truth of his day. . . . Never trust the artist. Trust the tale."[23] Concerning politics, we are wise to obey an analogous dictum, for politics deals with the world of appearance as well as the underlying reality. The intellectual debate surrounding the FTC Act confronts us with three conflicting interpretations. If we continue to focus on the political process, we will be unable to resolve the issue since each author can point to political activity which supports his conclusion. For example, the legislative debate amply supports Schlesinger's thesis that the advocates of equal opportunity fought for enactment; however, Kolko has marshaled evidence that big business was also actively engaged in writing and supporting the act but for self-interested reasons. Consequently, a resolution of the debate demands that we get outside the political process perspective and analyze the actual policy. Only the final act can reveal which group's vision—that of Schlesinger's advocates of equal opportunity, of Kolko's big business, or of Croly—was more nearly embodied in the final law. The very recognition that a plurality of groups pursuing different ends sought a trade commission act compels a policy analysis.

Five major points about the 1914 FTC Act will help explain Croly's idealistic endorsement of it: (1) the "strange wording" of the public interest clause; (2) the provision of cease and desist orders; (3) the provision of consent decree power as related to cease and desist orders though in a different statute; (4) the particular and peculiar stress on information and the degree of punishment for misinformation; and (5) the FTC as a new official governing institution. Each of these points will be argued in turn as a case of Croly's outlook so that each will become a datum tending to confirm Croly's idealistic support for the act. The first three points demonstrate that the legislation would encourage economic consolidation and also provide for control of this process. Developing this latter argument, the fourth and fifth points contend that the FTC Act was written in such a manner that the FTC could be a governing agency. From this entire analysis will emerge a portrait of the FTC which challenges Gabriel Kolko's conclusion that conscious support for the FTC was simply the product of big business's self-interest.

[21] Croly, *Promise*, pp. 409–421.
[22] For the preceding paragraphs' discussion of discrimination, see ibid., chap. 7, sec. 2, 3.
[23] D. H. Lawrence, *Studies in Classic American Literature* (New York, 1961), p. 2.

From the perspective of early twentieth-century political economy, the FTC Act (1914) was not originally conceived as consumer protection legislation. (The transformation of the FTC into an ostensible consumer protection agency only occurred in the 1930s with the adoption of the Wheeler-Lea Act which outlawed deceptive advertising.) Declaring unfair methods of competition illegal, the original FTC Act was viewed as dealing with incipient monopolies, for the political economy of that day argued that unfair methods provided one means by which corporations developed into either monopolies or dominant corporations.[24] In addition, the creation of an agency that would proceed against incipient monopolies responded to the then widespread criticism that the Sherman Antitrust Act empowered the government to act only *after* the monopoly actually existed; the pernicious deficiency of the Sherman Act was that the government could only react to a fait accompli. Given this understanding of unfair competition as producing monopoly and the criticism of extant antitrust legislation, one understands the original FTC Act as enabling the government to proceed against incipient monopolies.

STRANGE WORDING

Taken at face value, the original FTC Act enacted an absolute standard, which represented an apparent victory for equal opportunity: "Unfair methods of competition in [interstate] commerce are hereby declared illegal" (Sec. 5).[25] However, the act moved immediately to withdraw the absolute by giving the FTC discretion to apply the standard according to the public interest. The statute actually recognized that some outright cases of unfair competition would be permissible by the strange provision that:

> Whenever the commission shall have reason to believe that any such person, partnership, or corporation has been or is using any unfair method of competition in [interstate] commerce, *and if it shall appear to the commission that a proceeding by it in respect thereof would be to the interest of the public*, it shall issue and serve . . . a complaint. (Sec. 5, italics added.)

At the very least the FTC would not proceed against an unfair practice when that practice benefited the public interest, that is, the FTC was to be guided by the bane of equal opportunity—the rule of reason.[26] In the case of the FTC Act,

---

[24] At that time the best-known example of this phenomenon was the Standard Oil Trust which Rockefeller had built into a near monopoly using rebates, drawbacks, other forms of railroad subsidization of Standard Oil, price cutting to kill competition, and similar unfair practices. See Tarbell, *History of the Standard Oil Company.*

[25] 38 Stat. 719. All references to the FTC statute are from 38 Stat. 717–724; therefore I will no longer footnote quotations from this act.

[26] In 1911, the Supreme Court had enunciated its rule of reason decision—a decision warmly applauded by Croly. Arguing that the antitrust laws did not outlaw monopolies and restraints of trade per se, this decision ruled that only unreasonable restraints of trade, i.e., those that injured the public interest, were illegal whereas reasonable restraints were legal. 221 U.S. 1; 31 S.Ct. 502; 54 L.

rather than distinguishing between reasonable and unreasonable restraints of trade, the FTC was to take the public interest as its standard and to evaluate unfair practices and its own proceedings accordingly. To state, as did Herbert Croly,[27] that the italicized phrase parallels the reasonable/unreasonable distinction is only partially correct. The statement is correct in that unfair competition per se will not necessarily be prosecuted since a standard of public interest will be employed. However, if the intent were merely to parallel the reasonable/unreasonable distinction, a different phrase would and could have been used: "and if such unfair method of competition injures the public interest. . . ."

Unlike the final version, the substitute language (above) would compel the FTC to prosecute any unfair practice that injured the public interest. But, according to the statute's strange wording, the FTC is directed to proceed only if the *proceeding* is judged to be in the public interest; a proceeding is not justified by the simple fact that the unfair practice injured the public interest. Consequently, the statutory phrase grants the FTC greater discretion in selecting cases with which to become involved than does the substitute wording. Beyond the obvious meaning that the FTC can refuse to prosecute when it judges that an unfair practice benefits the public interest, the strange wording also allows the FTC to refrain from prosecuting a *harmful* unfair practice on the reasoning that (1) the FTC should concern itself with serious violations and not squander its resources on petty violations or (2) though the unfair practice injures the public interest, to correct the abuse would damage that interest even more (for example, the stock market might fall and cause a panic).

This interpretation of the strange wording of the implementation phrase enables the FTC to narrow its jurisdiction—just such a narrowing had been fought for and sought by Senator Newlands. Originally planning to limit the FTC's jurisdiction to large corporations whose capital assets exceeded $5 million, Newlands later abandoned this threshold when he recognized that large corporations often used smaller corporations as weapons against competitors. Consequently, Newlands argued that the FTC's jurisdiction should encompass all corporations.[28] Upon the adoption of Cummins's amendment which extended the FTC's jurisdiction to individuals and partnerships as well as to corporations, Newlands immediately encouraged and supported the Pomerene amendment which sought to return the FTC to a jurisdiction including only corpora-

---

Ed. 619. *Standard Oil of New Jersey* v. *U.S.* (1911). NAM's opposition to the 1908 Hepburn bill which proposed statutory recognition for the reasonable-unreasonable distinction evidenced equal opportunity's opposition to this distinction; for the equal opportunity votary, this distinction is spurious because *all* trusts make a mockery of equal opportunity. Weinstein, *Corporate Ideal*, pp. 78–80. Kolko missed this reason for NAM's opposition and instead attributed it solely to the bill's recognition of labor unions. This is an instance where Kolko's lumping all business together causes him to err. Kolko, *Triumph*, p. 135.

[27] Croly, "Restraint of Trade," pp. 9–10.

[28] *Congressional Record*, Sixty-third Congress (1914), p. 11,602.

tions.[29] Although Newlands's two attempts to restrict the FTC's jurisdiction to corporations failed, the strange wording of the statute grants the FTC general discretionary power so that the FTC could avoid entanglement in petty violations—which was Newlands's intent.

Interpreting the strange wording in much the same manner as point 1 above, the Supreme Court in *FTC* v. *Klesner* (1929)[30] decided that the public interest was not served by the FTC's prosecution of Klesner even though Klesner had engaged in unfair competition, since Klesner's violation was minor. The court ruled that the FTC was to issue a cease and desist order only if the injury to the public interest was "specific and substantial." In addition,

> this requirement ["if it shall appear to the commission that a proceeding by it in respect thereof would be to the interest of the public"] is not satisfied by proof that there has been misapprehension and confusion on the part of the purchaser, or even that they have been deceived.

In spite of the Klesner ruling, the FTC has allowed itself to be entrapped by petty violations to the detriment of both the public interest and the FTC's governing role.

The discretion granted the FTC concerning its jurisdiction was increased by the fact that the strange wording liberated the agency from being bound by prior precedents. The wording of Section 5 is purely situational and particularistic since a proceeding against an unfair method might be in the public interest at one point in time but not at another. The difference between an FTC that possesses discretion in deciding when to proceed and one that is guided and bound by precedents is analogous to the difference between equity decisions that are and are not rule-bound.[31]

This liberation of the FTC from precedents coincided with Croly's avowed antipathy to lawyers. Croly argued that lawyers were unfit to govern for two reasons: (1) Their self-interest in litigation precluded them from being advocates of reform and change. (Note the contemporary opposition of lawyers to no-fault insurance.) (2) More importantly, even if they could transcend their self-interest, their "mental outlook" and "prejudices" disqualified them.[32] By this Croly meant that lawyers placed too great a faith in precedents and failed to grasp that precedents often need to be rejected. Applied to the FTC, Croly's point is that if the FTC became bound by precedents it would to that extent become less of a governing institution since the FTC commissioners would become the administrators of previous decisions rather than the creators and enforcers of policy that responded to changing circumstances; consequently, Cro-

---

[29] A brief discussion of this legislative history is given in the text in the section "Jurisdiction and Implementation," and in footnote 40.

[30] 280 U.S. 19; 50 S.Ct. 1; 74 L. Ed. 1929.

[31] For the transformation of equity law, see F. W. Maitland, *The Constitutional History of England*, H. A. L. Fisher, ed. (Cambridge, England, 1965), pp. 221–226, 466–471; and Walter Wheeler Cook, "Equity," *Encyclopedia of the Social Sciences*, Vol. 5 (New York, 1932), pp. 582–588.

[32] Croly, *Promise*, pp. 131–137.

ly favored granting wide discretion to the FTC to prevent it from becoming simply an administrative body.

The analysis of the strange wording of the public interest clause has revealed two Crolyesque aspects: (1) a statutory parallel to the reasonable/unreasonable distinction, and (2) the provision of the FTC with the discretion that is necessary for governing. Other reformers, such as La Follette, who sought the abolition of all unfair practices, were to that extent distinguishable from Croly. Croly opposed government action against all unfair competition on the grounds that such an indiscriminate policy would impede necessary economic consolidation.

However, the strange use of "public interest" is a necessary, but not sufficient, condition for realizing the role envisioned for the FTC by Croly. Note must also be taken of the type of sanction provided by the act—the cease and desist order.

CEASE AND DESIST ORDERS

Croly advocated experimentation as an essential feature of his reform program since no one could anticipate the consequences of various trade practices.[33] Precisely this uncertainty concerning consequences commended to Croly the choice of the cease and desist order enforced through the courts as the appropriate sanction for trade regulation. An absolute prohibition on unfair competition coupled with severe penalties such as heavy fines and imprisonment would almost certainly provide a powerful disincentive to experimentation. In contrast, the court-enforced cease and desist order, coupled with the public interest provision, would be ideally suited for a positive FTC role in the economy—positive in Croly's view. Cease and desist orders possess a unique ability to provide effective enforcement while removing most of the risk from a firm engaging in practices that might later be defined as illegal unfair competition. Under a cease and desist order, the offending corporation bears the minimal cost (consistent with effective enforcement) of giving up an unfair practice and returning to the status quo ante, but does not have to assume the *additional* costs of fines and imprisonment. More importantly, although the firm must return to the status quo ante, the public interest clause (the hope of having the FTC decide that a new unfair practice is in the public interest) and the relatively small costs imposed by the cease and desist order usually would not dissuade the firm from experimenting with *other* unfair methods.[34]

However, if the corporation refuses to obey the order, the FTC may appeal to the courts for enforcement. If the corporation continues to refuse obedience

[33] Ibid., pp. 315–332.

[34] In the congressional debates, critics of cease and desist orders argued that these orders were too weak and hence would be ineffective; instead they proposed legislating fines and imprisonment. The response to these critics was that the ambiguity of "unfair methods of competition" prevented legislating a stiffer sanction. They did not want to imprison a person who had unknowingly and unintentionally engaged in an unfair competitive practice. *Congressional Record*, Sixty-third Congress (1914), pp. 11,533, 11,539.

after the courts have upheld the order, the corporation is then subjected to contempt of court penalties. The real threat of contempt of court serves as a strong inducement for the corporation to comply with the initial court decision.

Of course, there are sanctions that impose smaller costs on a corporation than does a cease and desist order, but these sanctions would not guarantee the effective enforcement needed by the FTC as a governing institution. For example, fines can impose smaller costs than a cease and desist order since a corporation might willingly assume the costs of even a large fine (thereby treating it as a licensing fee) in order to continue a lucrative unfair practice.[35] However, a court-enforced cease and desist order allows for an orchestration of sanctions to ensure eventual compliance. It begins with the order to return to the status quo ante and can proceed to appropriate levels of punishment imposed by the courts if the offense persists. Courts are jealous of their authority and tend to impose stiff penalties whenever their authority has gone unheeded.

Under the guise of antitrust legislation the FTC Act embodied Croly's vision within the constraints imposed by democratic public opinion. The use of cease and desist orders, enforced through the courts, sought to occupy a narrow space between two extremes: (1) a government policy that destroys and/or prevents the emergence of large corporations, and (2) a government policy that only favors large corporations without controlling them. Though public opinion proscribed the outright statutory legalization of some monopolies and government regulation of them,[36] the FTC statute could still encourage the growth of large corporations while maintaining government supervision of their behavior. Through selective use of its power, the FTC could permit as well as prevent economic consolidation (which stopped short of becoming monopolistic) without risking a direct confrontation with the hostile advocates of equal opportunity. As the next section shows, Croly even witnessed an attempt to escape the limits imposed by the public antipathy to *all* monopolies.

CONSENT DECREES

Not fortuitously, three weeks after the passage of the FTC Act, a device similar to the cease and desist order was incorporated into the antitrust laws. The Clayton Act, an amendment to the Sherman Act, provided for government-business consent decrees which encourage experimentation with restraints of trade. To understand the significance of the consent decree provision, one must first comprehend the historical background. Croly praised the 1911 rule of reason (see note 26) which provided the opportunity for the existence of legally

[35] Large fines can be ineffective in preventing some business practices. Arguing that large corporations can simply treat fines as the licensing fee for an illegal practice, the Justice Department recently announced that it will request that courts impose eighteen-month prison sentences for convicted price fixers. "Justice Department Seeks Prison for Price Fixers" (AP news story), *The Ithaca Journal*, February 25, 1977.

[36] Croly recognized only too well the hostility of equal opportunity to his vision. For example, see Croly, *Promise*, pp. 6, 25, 175.

recognized monopolies other than municipal utilities. Yet Croly's joy was short-lived, for the triple damages provision of the Sherman Antitrust Act discouraged corporations from experimenting with various restraints of trade. Although the "rule of reason" had made some restraints legal, a corporation could not predict with certainty the legality of its particular restraint of trade and therefore its liability to civil suits seeking triple damages. In fact, the government possessed no statutory means of abolishing a monopolistic practice other than criminal prosecution,[37] and this meant exposing the convicted violator to later civil triple damage suits.[38]

The consent decree arms the government with a formal means of abolishing an unreasonable restraint of trade without exposing the violating corporation to the rigors of triple damages. Unlike conviction in a criminal case, the consent decree neither constitutes an estoppel to pleading innocent nor can be submitted as evidence in a civil case; nevertheless it carries the force of law with respect to future actions. As long as the triple damages provision of the antitrust laws hovered threateningly over their heads, corporations were leery of the opportunity created by the reasonable/unreasonable ruling. Yet once the consent decree removed that threat, they were free to act. The consent decree effectively removed the danger from experimenting with restraints of trade imposed by triple damages, and thereby encouraged further economic consolidation.[39] However, a consent decree can also induce corporations to accept the stipulations of the government in order to avoid being subject to criminal prosecution and the possibility of easily won triple damages. Thus consent decrees can serve both as an incentive to experimentation as well as an inducement to compliance with the dictates of the government.

INFORMATION AND PUNISHMENT FOR MISINFORMATION

As argued previously, Croly did not expect encouragement of corporate bigness to render government subservient to big business. Rather, he sought an independent government role unhampered by either the lack of information or false in-

---

[37] The *failure* of government-business gentlemen's agreements, which had no statutory foundation, to regulate restraints of trade during Theodore Roosevelt's administration is documented in Kolko, *Triumph*, chaps. 3–5.

[38] Under the antitrust acts, firms which have been injured by a monopolistic practice can sue for triple damages, which the plaintiff can win by proving (1) the defendant's violation of the law and (2) injury to itself as a result of the monopolistic practice. After a successfully prosecuted government case, the plaintiff can submit the court's decision as prima facie evidence of the defendant's violation of the law, thereby fulfilling the former condition and needing only to prove injury to itself. Conviction in the government case constitutes an estoppel forbidding the convicted corporation to deny in a civil suit that it had violated the law. Without the decision in the criminal case, the injured firm must prove not only injury to itself but also the guilt of the defendant. Objectively, the latter requirement is nearly impossible to fulfill since the injured firm might have been driven bankrupt by the monopolistic practice, the litigation costs might be too great for it to bear, etc.

[39] For an analysis of the consent decree which agrees with my analysis, see William D. Rogers, "Is It Trust-Busting or Window-Dressing?" *The Reporter*, November 1, 1956, pp. 21–23.

formation. Making this independent government role possible, the FTC Act empowered the commission to gather the information necessary to make complex political-economic decisions. Thus although punishment was relatively modest for violations of the substantive provision of the act, punishment was in fact quite severe for refusal to provide the FTC with the information it needed in order to judge unfair competitive practices. Quite simply, without the requisite information the FTC cannot rationally decide when to prosecute an unfair practice; and with false information, the FTC could easily reach a wrong decision.

In regard to acquisition of information, the FTC Act significantly improved upon the Interstate Commerce Commission (ICC) Act and its 1893 amendment. The relevant section of the FTC statute reads:

> Sec. 10. That any person who shall neglect or refuse to attend and testify, or to answer any lawful inquiry, or to produce documentary evidence, if in his power to do so, in obedience to the subpoena or lawful requirement of the commission, shall be guilty of an offense and upon conviction thereof by a court of competent jurisdiction *shall be punished by a fine of not less than $1,000 nor more than $5,000, or by imprisonment for not more than one year, or by both such fine and imprisonment.* (Italics added.)

Furthermore, individuals who falsify, alter, or fail to keep business records or refuse to furnish them to the FTC

> shall be subject . . . to a *fine of not less than $1,000 nor more than $5,000, or to imprisonment for a term of not more than three years, or to both such fine and imprisonment.* (Sec. 10, italics added.)

These sanctions, especially the possibility of immediate imprisonment, contrast vividly with the use of a cease and desist order to stop unfair competitive practices.

THE FTC AS A GOVERNING AGENCY

The first three sections explained in detail the FTC Act's encouragement of economic consolidation. In addition, the discretion granted the FTC by the strange wording, the enforcement of cease and desist orders through the courts, and the severe penalties for misinformation indicate that the FTC could become a new governing agency which would control the process of consolidation. Not only did Croly's program entail the transformation of corporations into governing institutions within the economy through the encouragement of economic consolidation; it also sought new official government agencies which would possess the power, responsibility, independence, and discretion necessary for controlling the process of economic consolidation effected by unfair competitive practices. Table 1 schematizes the battles that were fought in order to strengthen or weaken the FTC as a new governing agency,[40] and the following explains the

---

[40] Acting as chairman of the Interstate Commerce Committee, Senator Newlands submitted and defended the original Senate bill which he offered as a substitute for the House bill. After some debate, Cummins's amendment of Section 5 was adopted by the Senate. In response to Cummins's

TABLE 1

Metamorphosis of the FTC Bill

	Original Senate Bill	Cummins's Amendment (adopted)	Pomerene's Amendment (defeated)	1914 FTC Act (conference committee bill)
Jurisdiction	Corporations	Individuals, partnerships, and corporations	Corporations	Individuals, partnerships, and corporations
Implementation	Automatic; no public interest clause; no discretion until commission appeals to courts for enforcement	Same	Same	Strange wording
Sanction	Restraining and prohibiting	Cease and desist	Restraining and prohibiting	Cease and desist
Role of courts	Procedural review	Review of questions of law and fact	Review of questions of law	Review of questions of law with limited review of questions of fact

75

significance of these battles with regard to the FTC as a governing agency.

Jurisdiction and Implementation.[41] Granting the commission the broadest jurisdiction—over individuals, partnerships, and corporations—Cummins's amendment paradoxically would have substantially weakened it as a governing agency since, as Alan Stone convincingly demonstrated,[42] such an extensive jurisdiction without effective statutory means of limiting it necessarily debilitates a regulatory agency. Without this knowledge, common sense would have argued that such extensive jurisdiction actually enhances the commission's capacity to govern. Although the statute contained this same broad jurisdiction, the strange wording of Section 5 also contained the potential to liberate the FTC from the insidious consequences inherent in this grant, that is, the agency's entrapment in petty affairs at the expense of its regulation of large corporations. Since Pomerene's amendment directly responded to Cummins's amendment, especially in regard to the FTC's jurisdiction, one can reasonably conclude that the strange wording was purposefully devised in order to liberate the FTC from the enervation inherent in the broad jurisdiction.

Allowing the FTC to exercise discretion regarding the initiation of proceedings against unfair practices, the final version is superior to both the original and Pomerene bills. Without this discretionary provision, according to which the FTC could refuse to proceed against an unfair practice when such proceeding was not in the public interest, the FTC could not have effectively regulated the economy because it would have been unable to concentrate upon serious cases. Furthermore, the statute's grant of such broad discretion to the FTC is quite reasonable since even today savants are unable to generalize about what consequences flow from measurable economic features.[43]

Sanctions. All four versions employed basically the same sanction although two versions utilized "restraining and prohibiting" while the other two authorized "cease and desist" orders. The former phrase has the same consequence as the latter since both sanctions impose the minimal punishment consistent with effective regulation. The contrast of cease and desist orders to fines and imprisonment is also true for orders that restrain and prohibit. Furthermore, either of these sanctions would have to and can only be enforced by an appeal to the courts which secure obedience through the threat of contempt of court sanc-

---

success, the Interstate Commerce Committee at the behest of Newlands and after consultation with the Judiciary Committee authorized Senator Pomerene to draft another amendment to Section 5 in order to challenge Cummins's amendment; despite Newlands's support for Pomerene's amendment, it was defeated on the floor. Since the Senate and House versions differed, the bills were sent to conference committee. Except for a few minor modifications, the conference committee's bill became the FTC Act.

[41] Keeping in mind the strange wording section is particularly helpful here.

[42] Alan Stone, "The FTC and Advertising Regulation," *Public Policy* XXI (Spring 1973), 203-234. The FTC is de facto, though not de jure, without a means of limiting this broad jurisdiction because the FTC does not assert its statutory prerogative to exercise discretion.

[43] For example, see the selections in Walter Adams, ed., *The Structure of American Industry*, 4th ed. (New York, 1971).

tions. Finally, the language of "cease and desist" allows the FTC to issue mandatory (corrective) orders, just as the phrase "restraining and prohibiting" permitted the courts to issue mandatory injunctions. Therefore, in terms of sanctions,[44] no significant difference exists between the four versions.

Role of the Courts. Arguing that judges lacked the expertise to decide the complex political-economic issues involved in unfair competition and restraints of trade, Croly had constantly criticized the courts as inadequate forums for deciding these issues. After the passage of the FTC Act, Croly hoped that the commissioners would be further empowered to determine the reasonableness or unreasonableness of particular restraints of trade in monopoly cases.[45] Thus Croly sought to transfer authority *away from the courts* to new governing institutions.

The independence of the FTC from the courts was a function of the extent of judicial review over the FTC's cease and desist orders. Restricting the courts to procedural review, such as determining whether constitutional rights had been violated, the original Senate bill had confined the courts to the narrowest review powers—Newlands correctly characterized it as allowing only that minimal review which the courts would assume of their own accord without statutory recognition[46]—and consequently conferred the greatest autonomy on the FTC.

In contrast to the original bill, Cummins's amendment provided: "Jurisdiction is hereby conferred, upon said court to hear and determine any such suit and enforce obedience thereto according to the law and rules applicable to suits in equity."[47] In effect, this amendment sanctioned judicial review of questions of

---

[44] Although the two phrases have somewhat different consequences, the following analysis demonstrates the differences to be relatively unimportant. "Restraining and prohibiting" is the language of injunctions. By 1914, the precedent had been firmly established that courts could issue mandatory, as well as prohibitory, injunctions. A prohibitory injunction orders a person to cease or not to begin an activity, whereas a mandatory injunction compels positive performance of an act. Mandatory injunctions originated when the courts would restrain and prohibit a person from allowing a condition to continue. For an excellent discussion of the differences between prohibitory and mandatory injunctions and of the development of mandatory injunctions from prohibitory language, see Zachariah Chafee, Jr., "Injunction," *Encyclopedia of the Social Sciences*, Vol. 8 (New York, 1932), pp. 53–57.

Mandatory orders can emerge from a parallel employment of cease and desist (prohibitory) orders. In regard to mandatory orders, the advantage in using "restraining and prohibiting" rather than "cease and desist" is that by 1914 the precedent had been established that the injunctive language encompassed mandatory as well as prohibitory injunctions, whereas no such precedent had been established for "cease and desist." Another difference is that the language of "restraining and prohibiting" can prevent injury before it occurs while "cease and desist" cannot. As revealed by an analysis of the language, a cease and desist order cannot logically be used to prevent an unexecuted but planned action. By the nature of the words, "cease and desist" can only forbid current, not future, activity. Since the FTC must appeal to the courts for enforcement of its orders (whether they be couched in the language of injunctions or cease and desist), future-seeing orders are of little, if any, value to it.

[45] Croly, "Restraint of Trade," pp. 9–10.

[46] *Congressional Record*, Sixty-third Congress (1914). See p. 13,060 for Newlands's comment and p. 10,377 for the original Senate bill.

[47] Ibid., p. 12,817.

law and fact as was the practice at that time for appellate courts when deciding equity suits.[48] Consequently, this amendment abolished the FTC's autonomy and jeopardized its governing role. The threat posed by Cummins's amendment and the failure of Pomerene's amendment (Table 1) compelled the conference committee to incorporate judicial review of questions of law and a restricted review of questions of fact in the final version. Restricting judicial review primarily to questions of law, the statute provides that the courts can broach questions of fact only upon submission of new evidence, but such submission can occur only if "there were reasonable grounds for the failure to adduce such evidence in the proceeding before the commission" (Sec. 5). Thus in regard to the FTC's independence from the judiciary, the statute represented ground between the original and Cummins's version, but lay closer to the Cummins version.

The language of the bills contradicts Newlands's assertion that Pomerene's amendment provided broader judicial review than did that of Cummins.[49] Newlands's disingenuous comment underscores the importance of reading the bills carefully.

Rule Making. Table 2 introduces the concluding evidence establishing the FTC as a governing institution. The House proposed only an advisory and information-gathering agency with *procedural* (not legislative) rule-making powers whereas the Senate version offered an agency that would prosecute violations of the law without the aid of any (either procedural or legislative) rule-making powers. Rule-making and enforcement powers only coincided in the statute, thereby enabling the FTC to assume a governing role not provided by either the Senate or House versions.

The original act vested the FTC with legislative as well as procedural rule-making power: ". . . The commission shall also have power . . . from time to time to classify corporations and to make rules and regulations for the purpose of carrying out the provisions of this act" (Sec. 6g). Using such legislative power, the FTC can declare certain methods of competition unfair and submit its declaration in a court proceeding as prima facie evidence of the unfairness of the practice. This legislative rule-making power enables the FTC simply to refer the courts to its declaration that a given practice is unfair rather than having to prove such in each case it prosecutes. Prior to 1972 when the FTC first asserted this power, it had to prove not only that the defendant had engaged in the practice but also that the practice was unfair. (See the conclusion for a discussion of

[48] Henry L. McClintock, *Handbook of Equity* (St. Paul, Minn., 1936), p. 23. It is not clear why Cummins proposed this amendment and why a majority of the Senate passed it. Croly favored narrow review powers for the courts; similarly, equal opportunity reformers also sought restricted judicial review since the courts had historically castrated antitrust and other legislation aimed at restoring equal opportunity. Furthermore, according to Kolko, "business" also favored narrow judicial review. See *Triumph*, p. 266. Perhaps Kolko's failure to distinguish the NCF from the NAM hides the group that sought the broad judicial review proposed by Cummins and accepted by the Senate. Or perhaps wanting to be cautious in their innovation, the politicians favored broad judicial review.

[49] *Congressional Record*, Sixty-third Congress (1914), p. 13,066.

TABLE 2

Rule-Making Powers Conferred by the Various Bills

	Original House Bill	All Senate Versions	Final (1914) Act (conference committee bill)
Commission possesses any rule-making authority	Yes (procedural)	No	Yes (legislative and procedural)
Commission enforces standards	No	Yes	Yes

the FTC's renunciation of this power.) In 1972 an appellate court upheld the FTC's legislative rule-making power. Oil refiners had challenged this power when the FTC declared that failure to post the octane ratings of gasoline was an unfair competitive practice. Confirmed in its legislative capacity by the court decision, the FTC had only to prove that refiners had failed to post octane ratings, not that the failure to post was as an unfair practice.[50]

Eliminating the case-by-case determination of unfair methods, the FTC's authority to make legislative rules enhances its capacity to govern since this authority facilitates and expedites the FTC's prosecution of violations. Yet this rule making does not narrowly constrict the activity of the commission since the strange wording still allows the commission to decline prosecution of instances of unfair competition. From Croly's perspective the legislative rule-making authority together with the strange wording gave the FTC the best of all possible worlds.

THE FTC ACT: TRIUMPH OF EXCELLENCE OR INTEREST?

A careful analysis has revealed that a thinker like Croly could support the FTC Act for idealistic reasons. (By establishing the existence of idealistic support for a trade commission which would further economic consolidation, this article calls for, but does not attempt, a *re*-evaluation of the prime movers behind the legislation. Especially, those legislative leaders and actors whom Kolko ties to big business need to be *re*-examined in light of this new perspective.) In appearance the act granted the advocates of equal opportunity what they desired—antitrust legislation directed at incipient monopolies. However, the act would actually encourage the development of large corporations while imposing government regulation. Even so, why has the preceding interpretation which demonstrated the congruence between Croly's idealism and the act rarely, if ever, revealed itself in the FTC's practice? If the literature on the FTC

[50] 482 Fed. 2d 672 (1972). *National Petroleum Refiners' Association* v. *FTC*.

agrees on one point, it is that the FTC has seldom governed and served a larger public interest.

From the standpoint of consumer protection (which was not Croly's standpoint), Alan Stone argues that the FTC's inefficacy can be traced to its statute. Concentrating on deceptive advertising, Stone accounts for the FTC's failure to protect consumers by pointing to (1) the FTC's broad jurisdiction over persons (individuals, partnerships, and corporations) and subject matter (all deceptive advertising) and (2) its cease and desist orders. This broad jurisdiction makes the agency dependent upon business for information concerning violations; therefore the FTC becomes primarily and perniciously involved with cases that possess importance for business, but not for consumers. Furthermore, as has been demonstrated above, cease and desist orders can (and do) not prevent deceptive advertising; when a firm is ordered to cease one deceptive practice, it simply initiates another.[51]

Convincing as it is, Stone's analysis cannot be applied to the original statute with its Crolyesque meaning. If the defining perspective is both the encouragement and regulation of governing corporations which attain economic leadership through unfair competition, the vices cited by Stone—the FTC's dependence upon business and the cease and desist sanction—are transformed into virtues. In this Crolyesque context, there is no better source of information than the injured businesses and no better sanction than the cease and desist order. More importantly, Stone's analysis cannot account for the FTC's *self-renunciation* of its three most powerful weapons: (1) the discretionary power conveyed by the strange wording of Section 5; (2) the legislative rule-making power granted by Section 6g; and (3) the power to issue corrective (mandatory) orders. It is doubtful that Stone could ever trace this self-denial to the original statute as no necessary causal link exists between the statute and this remarkable *self-restraint*. Yet it is a historic fact that for many years the FTC denied or refused to exercise these very powers which could transform it into a governing institution. Only recently has the FTC asserted its legislative rule-making power and its power to issue corrective orders. More importantly, as evidenced by the FTC's behavior and Stone's article (Stone himself is an ex-FTC lawyer), the FTC still *refuses* to invoke the strange wording in order to narrow its jurisdiction.

Accounting for the FTC's failure to assume the governing role envisioned for it by Croly, the FTC adopted interpretations of (1) the strange wording of Section 5, (2) Section 6g, and (3) "cease and desist" which are different from the ones offered here. Reasoning that a proceeding is in the public interest whenever an unfair practice injures the public interest, the FTC throughout its history interpreted Section 5 not as has been done here but as directing the FTC to proceed against any injurious unfair method of competition.[52] Acting on this interpretation, the FTC becomes embroiled in petty affairs which obstruct its regula-

---

[51] Stone, "Advertising Regulation."

[52] One need only read the *Federal Trade Commission Decisions* to see the FTC's interpretation of the public interest clause. For example, see 35 FTC 335; 49 FTC 1190; 31 FTC 1076; 32 FTC 20.

tion of the large corporations. The FTC fails to acknowledge that although an unfair practice causes some public injury, a FTC proceeding still may be detrimental to the larger public interest. Although this article's interpretation of the strange wording of Section 5 may be more convincing than that of the FTC, the act undoubtedly permits both.

Until the 1970s, the FTC denied its possession of legislative rule-making authority. Since Section 6g only states that the FTC could "make rules" without specifying what kind of rules, the agency in interpreting this section referred to both the House and Senate bills which did not delegate *legislative* rule-making power to the agency; consequently the FTC *chose* to interpret this section as conferring only *procedural* rule-making powers. But the first time (1972) the FTC decided to assert its legislative rule-making power, the courts upheld the FTC's action. Again, the original act permitted both interpretations.

Further underscoring the fact that a straight line has not linked the final act with the FTC's actual behavior, the agency issued its first corrective (mandatory) order in October 1975.[53] A corrective order compels positive performance of an act whereas a prohibitory order merely commands cessation of an activity.[54] Prior to 1975, the FTC had chosen to interpret Section 5 to mean that the FTC could only stop unfair practices, not issue corrective orders.[55] However, the agency has come to realize that Section 5 and "cease and desist" do not logically preclude corrective orders but actually permit them. The FTC's current suit against the six largest cigarette manufacturers asks that they be made not only to stop their illegal practice (that is, the firms will now have to display the standard caution) but also to pay for *corrective* advertising;[56] such corrective advertising will warn of the hazards of smoking, thereby compensating for the harmful consequences of their prior failure to display the standard caution (Warning: The Surgeon General Has Determined That Cigarette Smoking Is Dangerous to Your Health).[57] In effect, the FTC has ordered them not only to cease and desist from a practice but also to correct the harmful conditions created by their previous illegal activity. A corrective order compels a corporation to correct the injurious state of affairs created by its unfair practice; such a correction attempts to prevent the corporation from reaping the benefits

---

[53] "U.S. Files Six Suits on Cigarette Ads," *The New York Times*, October 18, 1975, pp. 1, 43.

[54] Footnote 44 discusses the difference between prohibitory and mandatory injunctions and the development of mandatory injunctions from prohibitory language.

[55] Hence there are at least two meanings of "return to the status quo ante": (1) the return to the status quo ante can simply mean the absence of the unfair competitive practice, or (2) it can mean that corrective orders seek to reestablish to some degree the economic relations that existed prior to the implementation of the unfair competitive practice.

[56] Corrective orders should not be confused with affirmative disclosure orders. Affirmative disclosure requires that an offending firm disclose the fact that its product is of foreign origin, that oil is *re*refined, etc., but does not require in addition that the firm inform the public of its previous deceptive practice. For the FTC's decisions regarding affirmative disclosure, see 263 Fed 2d 818; 265 Fed 2d 246; 262 Fed 2d 741.

[57] "U.S. Files Six Suits on Cigarette Ads," pp. 1, 43.

81

of a harmful state of affairs which persists after the cessation of the actual unfair practice.

The FTC Act actually delineates an *exclusive range* of possible consequences rather than just one consequence. Consequently, the malaise of the FTC's regulatory role cannot simply be attributed to its organic statute, and therefore our faith must not simply repose in good laws. The act drew a circle around the administrators' activity but within this circle they or their superiors were (and still are) free to choose. As demonstrated previously, a cease and desist order combined with the public interest clause will encourage experimentation with unfair competitive practices and hence cannot possibly inhibit economic consolidation. Democratic appearances notwithstanding, the FTC Act did not seek to protect business competition and restore equal opportunity. But whether the FTC would become an agency that would control economic consolidation or instead become the tool of the large corporations was *not determined* by the act in and of itself.[58] The FTC Act presented (and still presents) the commission with a range of alternatives: (1) to use the strange wording to narrow the commission's jurisdiction or to proceed against petty violations; (2) to issue corrective orders or to refrain from so doing; and (3) to make legislative rules or to deny itself this power. The alternatives that the FTC chose were contingent on factors external to the act—the FTC's personnel, internal organization, and political environment; but these external factors operate only within the limits imposed by the act.

Therefore, the most basic cause for the failure of the FTC to realize Croly's vision in American practice was the fact that Croly's ideal easily merged with the self-interest of the large corporations. Whereas equal opportunity and economic consolidation are polar opposites, it is a mere step from Croly's vision to the National Civic Federation's self-interest. The ground shared by Croly and the NCF (Kolko's "big business") was that both favored economic consolidation supported by the government. They differed only with regard to the extent of the government's power over the large corporations. When the crucial interpretations of the ambiguous sections were being made, Croly and like-minded

---

[58] The fact that two different consequences can easily flow from the use of consent decrees further underscores that a statute permits an exclusive range of consequences. (1) From Croly's perspective, consent decrees would serve a twofold purpose: to encourage experimentation with restraints of trade and also to retain government control of the resultant economic consolidation. (2) However, as they have been utilized, consent decrees mark the government as the handmaiden of the large corporations. This discrepancy is attributable to the fact that it is within the discretion of the administrators to determine the requirements of a consent decree and consequently the strength or weakness of a decree. Underscoring the existence and importance of this type of administrative discretion, complaints by competitors that a proposed decree was too weak have at times prodded the government to impose tougher conditions. Recently, the complaints of the competitors of Xerox compelled the FTC to demand a stronger consent decree than was first offered by Xerox. (John Omicinski, "FTC Okays Xerox Agreement," *Ithaca Journal*, July 31, 1975, Gannett News Service, p. 24.)

others possessed no political power since their vision never commanded widespread popular appeal; however, the large corporations knew which interpretations favored them and mobilized to secure their choice. The final and unanswered question, then, is the most fundamental: Was Croly's vision a true alternative or does its easy transformation into serving the interests of large corporations deny it that status?*

* The author wishes to thank Diane Brannon, Eldon Eisenach, Theodore Lowi, Stephen Skowronek, and Bill Tetreault for their generous, invaluable help in the preparation of this article.

Theodore Roosevelt and the Bureau of Corporations

By Arthur M. Johnson

By the time Theodore Roosevelt succeeded to the presidency in 1901 the question of government control of large interstate business corporations had become a matter of pressing concern to the American public. Some federal legislation, notably the Sherman Antitrust Act, had been enacted, but none of it had measurably changed the drift toward concentration of economic power. The policies toward business which the new President would follow were not clearly perceived, but his character and past record suggested that the acquiescent attitude of the McKinley administration was not likely to be continued. The fears of some big businessmen proved to be well grounded, for Roosevelt soon sponsored a series of measures directed toward federal regulation of business interests. If he did not prove to be a wide-ranging "trustbuster," he nevertheless worked strenuously toward curbing some individual industrial combinations while proposing to bring all interstate corporations into federal — and presidential — harness. His policies and proposals matured during the presidency, but they all reflected his own vigorous self-confidence. One of the earliest projects to which he gave his support was the establishment of an agency of publicity about corporate affairs; and Congress finally brought such an agency into being in 1903 as the Bureau of Corporations. A study of Roosevelt's role in the establishment and early work of the Bureau reflects his heady conception of the presidential office and provides insight into the evolution of federal regulation and supervision of interstate corporations.

Roosevelt had earlier reached the conclusion that industrial combination was an inevitable and generally a desirable development, a view to which he adhered throughout his political career. As governor of New York he stated these views in a message to the legislature in January, 1900. He made it clear that he believed combinations were not in themselves injurious to the public, and he pointed out that "much that is complained about is not really the abuse so much as the inevitable development of our modern industrial life." [1] Although he cited various abuses by corporation managements, such as secrecy or misrepresentation concerning corporate organization, overcapitalization, unfair methods of competition, and the manipulation of prices, he urged caution in dealing with these problems. His immediate recommendation was phrased in these words: "The first essential is knowledge of the facts, publicity. Much can be done at once by amendment of the corporation laws so as to provide for such publicity as will not work injustice as between business rivals." [2]

Unexpectedly catapulted into the presidency, Roosevelt's first recommendations on federal policy toward big business were grounded on the approach he had advocated as governor. The first essential was again publicity. His endorsement of wider publicity for the affairs of interstate corporations had the initial advantage of constituting positive action without committing him to any given course of action. Publicity could be used as a substitute for, or a prelude to, more stringent measures. Thus, in his first annual message to Congress he declared: "Publicity is the only sure remedy which we can now invoke." He added, however, that it might lay the groundwork for broader action in the future.[3]

As Roosevelt observed in his *Autobiography*, the first problem that he confronted in dealing with big business was whether the national government had the power to control it.[4] In the same message that urged publicity as an initial step in correcting corporate abuses, he pointed out that a constitutional amendment might be necessary to permit federal supervision of interstate corporations. The constitutional problem assumed less significance by the fall of 1902. Legal actions had been undertaken to test the extent of the federal government's power under existing law, and Roosevelt's attorney general maintained that under the interstate commerce clause Congress had sufficient power to enact any additional legislation that

---

[1] William Griffith (ed.), *The Roosevelt Policy* (2 vols., New York, 1919), I, 19-20.
[2] *Ibid.*, 23.
[3] *Ibid.*, 168-69.
[4] Theodore Roosevelt, *An Autobiography* (New York, 1913), 464-65.

might be needed to deal with big business. At the same time he, too, endorsed publicity on the affairs of corporations and "visitorial supervision" over them.[5]

The main outlines of the administration's program were now clear: publicity to reveal corporate abuses, prosecution of the worst offenders, and general legislation to insure federal "supervision" of the great industrial combinations. The way had been cleared for congressional action, and in his second annual message to Congress Roosevelt renewed his demand for additional legislation to curb the abuses of interstate corporations. He called for an agency of publicity and an appropriation for better enforcement of the anti-trust law. At the same time, to quiet the fears of businessmen, he emphasized that he did not propose to destroy combinations but rather intended to do away with "any evil in them." [6]

During the summer of 1902, in a series of speeches throughout the East, Roosevelt had stressed the importance of publicity as a weapon in his campaign against business "evils." Speaking in Providence, Rhode Island, for example, he declared: "Such publicity would by itself tend to cure the evils of which there is just complaint; it would show us if evils existed, and where the evils are imaginary, and it would show us what next ought to be done." [7] Publicity, then, could provide factual information about business behavior as an aid to the formulation of public policy, and at the same time it might serve as a deterrent to abuses of private economic power. Here was a typical Rooseveltian approach: faith in small means to accomplish big ends and definition of an economic problem in ethical terms.

Since 1901 a number of bills calling for enforced publicity of corporation accounts had been introduced in Congress, but little progress was made until the second session of the Fifty-seventh Congress. In January, 1903, the House began consideration of a resolution offered by Representative Charles E. Littlefield of Maine, which, in addition to banning discriminatory transportation rates and pricing practices, provided that corporations should file reports with the Interstate Commerce Commission.[8] Failure to comply

---

[5] See speech of Attorney General Philander C. Knox before the Pittsburgh Chamber of Commerce in October, 1902, printed in *Cong. Record*, 57 Cong., 2 Sess., 413-15 (December 17, 1902).

[6] Griffith (ed.), *Roosevelt Policy*, I, 180-81.

[7] *Ibid.*, 38.

[8] House Resolution 17, 57 Cong., 2 Sess. (1903). Originally introduced in the first

would result in the offender being barred from the use of the channels of interstate commerce. The Commission would annually publish a list and summary of these reports, which presumably would reveal stock watering and other abuses.

Littlefield believed that his measure would be acceptable to the administration, but developments soon showed that he was mistaken. Attorney General Philander C. Knox gave the first hint of the administration's disapproval in a letter to Senator George F. Hoar, chairman of the Senate Judiciary Committee, early in January, 1903. Knox stated that he believed that the majority of the American people wanted regulation of combinations of capital and not their destruction. After recommending legislation against discriminatory practices destructive of competition, he came to the matter of publicity. Advocating the establishment of a commission to investigate the operations and conduct of corporations engaged in interstate commerce, he proposed that such a commission should have compulsory powers to obtain information, and that it should report its findings to the President, who would presumably use them for legislative recommendations to Congress.[9]

Although the Knox proposal was phrased in general terms, the President clearly was to play a key role under this plan. Read between the lines, it suggested that the Chief Executive could withhold or publicize derogatory information about corporate activities, in effect giving him the power to draw the line for the public between "good" and "bad" combinations. The proposal was obviously more to Roosevelt's liking than the Littlefield measure, which would give him no such power and which he reportedly regarded as "unconstitutional" and "too drastic."[10] Opposition of Republican senators to the bill probably strengthened his decision to oppose it.[11] Instead of supporting the Littlefield proposal, Roosevelt put his influence behind the bill to establish a Department of Commerce and Labor, the Elkins Anti-Rebate bill, and a bill to expedite the

session of this Congress, the resolution had been revised for consideration in the second session. See Hans B. Thorelli, *The Federal Antitrust Policy* (Baltimore, 1955), 538-39.

[9] Knox to George F. Hoar, January 3, 1903, *Senate Exec. Docs.*, 57 Cong., 2 Sess., No. 73 (Serial 4422), 15-21.

[10] New York *World*, February 11, 1903. See also Thorelli, *Federal Antitrust Policy*, 548.

[11] In a letter to William H. Taft on March 19, 1903, Roosevelt expressed a preference for working with men like Senators Marcus A. Hanna and Nelson W. Aldrich rather than with "radical 'reformers'" like Littlefield. Elting E. Morison (ed.), *The Letters of Theodore Roosevelt* (8 vols., Cambridge, 1951-1954), III, 450.

handling of cases originating under the antitrust and interstate commerce laws.

The first of these measures had been received in the House in January, 1903, shortly before that body began consideration of Littlefield's bill. A proposal to create a Department of Commerce and Labor had been under discussion for some years, but a special feature of the new bill was a provision for a Bureau of Corporations. Although the powers of the proposed Bureau were of a restricted nature, it was this agency to which the President was ultimately to turn in utilizing publicity as an aid in bringing about executive control of the trusts. The responsibilities of the Bureau, as set forth in the bill, were to be limited mainly to gathering, compiling, publishing, and supplying "useful" information about interstate corporations and those engaged in foreign trade.[12] No powers to compel testimony or the production of records were conferred on the Bureau, and an effort by Representative William Sulzer of New York, a Democrat, to add them was defeated on January 17 by a strict party vote.[13] Obviously, the Bureau's functions as proposed in the House bill fell far short of what Roosevelt had envisioned.

At the suggestion of Senator Knute Nelson of Minnesota, Roosevelt asked Attorney General Knox to draft an amendment to the bill to bring its publicity provisions more in line with the administration's views.[14] The result emerged from the conference committee on February 9 as the the so-called Nelson amendment, which greatly strengthened the powers of the Bureau and gave the President control of the publicity accorded its findings. The purpose of the Bureau was now stated to be the procurement of information and data to enable the President "to make recommendations to Congress for legislation" for the regulation of interstate commerce. Publication of the results of the Bureau's work was to be at his discretion. Common carriers subject to the Interstate Commerce Commission were specifically exempted from the jurisdiction of the new agency, but the Commissioner of Corporations was given the power already conferred on the ICC to compel testimony and the production of documents.[15]

---

[12] *Cong. Record*, 57 Cong., 2 Sess., 2003 (February 10, 1903).

[13] New York *Times*, January 18, 1903.

[14] Roosevelt to Knute Nelson, July 21, 1906, Morison (ed.), *Letters of Theodore Roosevelt*, V, 334-35.

[15] A comparison of the House provision and the Nelson substitute is in *Cong. Record*, 57 Cong., 2 Sess., 2003 (February 10, 1903).

The extent of presidential discretion under the Nelson amendment was attacked in the House debate. Although the publicity provision had the apparent advantage of protecting legitimate business secrets by making their publication a matter for the President to decide, at the same time it made him the arbiter of what the public and Congress should know about the results of the Bureau's work. The Democrats quickly seized on this point. William Richardson of Alabama told the House: "He [the President] can suppress all data, every scintilla of information. He can hold it secret and stand pat and say and do nothing, and no law can move him. Is that publicity?" David H. Smith of Kentucky also felt that the amendment gave the President too much power: "It is not so important, as I view the matter, that the President should be enabled to make recommendations as that Congress should be enabled to enact some intelligent effective legislation." [16]

By his insistence on executive discretion in throwing the spotlight of publicity on the affairs of interstate corporations, Roosevelt had offered his political opponents a tempting target. Since the Nelson amendment provided no yardstick by which the President was to be guided in deciding whether or not to release information gathered by the Bureau of Corporations, he was seemingly in a position to wield the big stick of publicity against corporations that he decided were "bad" while shelving adverse information on those that he thought were "good." It was this point that Richardson stressed in his attack on the amendment. "We all know," he declared, "that the President has repeatedly said that there are 'good and bad trusts.' Who should be the judge on such a question? It should not be one man. It should be the law, under the rules and regulations prescribed for eliciting the truth." [17] Such charges did not disturb Roosevelt, who had serene confidence in his own sense of justice. On the other hand, this type of reaction to the proposed legislation made it necessary to take positive steps to insure its passage.

With his sure grasp of political and publicity techniques, Roosevelt had already paved the way for adoption of the Nelson amendment. A first task was to stop the Littlefield bill and the plan it offered for publicity of corporation affairs. When the House passed

[16] *Ibid.*, 2005, 2007 (February 10, 1903).
[17] *Ibid.*, 2005.

the bill, on February 7, without a dissenting vote, Roosevelt moved quickly. That same day he told the press that he intended to call a special session of Congress unless he obtained the legislation that he demanded. At the same time he indicated that John D. Rockefeller had sent to six senators telegrams opposing the administration's antitrust legislation. This news made front-page headlines and though the administration's antitrust legislation embraced a variety of measures it was believed that the President's reference to Rockefeller opposition applied specifically to the Nelson amendment. The New York *Times* declared: "It is this legislation particularly that the Standard Oil Company so vigorously objects to, and which it hoped might be headed off or emasculated, through the appeals made to Senators, before it reached the stage of actual passage." [18]

Though Roosevelt had twisted the truth a bit by attributing to the senior Rockefeller a telegram that he had not sent, Standard Oil had actually provided him with the opportunity. In attempting to protect its interests, another Rockefeller — John D. Jr. — had sent a telegram.[19] Representatives of Standard Oil also apparently did express to various men in Washington a dislike for the Nelson amendment because of the opportunity that it offered for attacking large corporations.[20] It was even reported that a Standard-inspired substitute for the amendment was presented to the conference committee by a member who was ignorant of its origin.[21] The company lacked finesse in countering unwelcome legislation, and Roosevelt had made the most of its ineptitude. His adroit exploitation of popular hostility to Standard Oil helped to carry the day for the Nelson amendment. The amended Department of Commerce and Labor bill passed the House on February 10 by a vote of 252 to 10, the negatives being cast by the disgruntled Littlefield and nine Democrats; and the Senate approved the bill the next day.[22] Roosevelt himself attributed the favorable result in large measure to the publication of the Rockefeller telegram.[23]

[18] New York *Times*, February 8, 1903.
[19] Allan Nevins, *John D. Rockefeller: The Heroic Age of American Enterprise* (2 vols., New York, 1940), II, 516.
[20] New York *Times*, February 8, 9, 1903.
[21] *Ibid.*, February 9, 10, 1903.
[22] Thorelli, *Federal Antitrust Policy*, 553-54, gives the vote and some additional details.
[23] Roosevelt testimony in "Campaign Contributions," *Testimony before a Sub-*

Big business was now faced with a new expression of government power, the federal Bureau of Corporations. How effective the Bureau would be depended on the extent to which the President would use the broad discretionary powers which its charter granted him. Roosevelt himself had high hopes for the measure. "The enactment of this law," he told an audience in Milwaukee in April, 1903, "is one of the most significant contributions which have been made in our time toward the proper solution of the problem of the relations to the people of the great corporations and corporate combinations." At the same time he expressed his confidence that administration of the law would be "in a spirit of absolute fairness and justice and of entire fearlessness." [24]

The Bureau was organized and staffed in accordance with the high hopes that the Chief Executive held for it. As the first Commissioner of Corporations, Roosevelt selected James R. Garfield, son of the former President and a lawyer who had served under him in the Civil Service Commission. Z. Lewis Dalby, the clerk to the Commissioner, and Warren Choate, chief clerk, were lawyers, the latter also having served under Roosevelt in the Civil Service Commission. They formed the nucleus around which a capable staff was built, employing a remarkably efficient administrative system. [25]

Roosevelt had deliberately sought to make the new agency a vehicle for executive leadership in dealing with big business, and the decision as to whether the Bureau would be used for punitive purposes was one which depended on him. The first substantial indication of his attitude came in the presidential election year 1904. One of the early actions of the administration had been to obtain an injunction against the major beef-packing companies, and an investigation of the packers' compliance with it soon involved the Bureau of Corporations. In March, 1904, the Bureau, in response to a House resolution, had reluctantly agreed to investigate the wide margin between beef-cattle prices and the price of fresh beef and the possibility that illegal business practice was responsible. Meanwhile, the Department of Justice had been investigating possible violations of the federal court injunction issued against the beef-

committee of the Committee on Privileges and Elections, United States Senate, Sixty-second Congress, Second Session, Pursuant to S. Res. 79 . . . (2 vols., Washington, 1912-1913), I, 187.

[24] Griffith (ed.), Roosevelt Policy, I, 113-14.

[25] See Meyer H. Fishbein, "Records Management in the Bureau of Corporations," American Archivist (Washington), XVIII (April, 1955), 161-67.

packers. The Bureau of Corporations and the Justice Department were obviously probing along parallel lines and inevitably the question arose whether the findings of the Bureau would become part of the government's case against the packers. In September, 1904, the United States district attorney of the northern district of Illinois requested all the information that the Bureau had collected on the so-called Beef Trust.[26] Only Roosevelt could decide whether the request should be honored. If he decided in the affirmative, he would explode the claim that the Bureau was "not a detective agency." If he decided in the negative, he might have to forego a victory over the Beef Trust.

With the election a little over a month away, Roosevelt decided to postpone his decision. Big business interests were substantial contributors to his campaign, and Democrats charged that the threat of adverse publicity by the Bureau of Corporations had stimulated their largesse. To protect himself, Roosevelt on October 26 ordered Republican National Committee Chairman George B. Cortelyou — who as the first Secretary of Commerce and Labor had recently been "boss" of the Bureau — to return contributions from Standard Oil.[27] Four days later he advised Garfield that he was not yet ready to say whether the Department of Justice could utilize the information which the Bureau had obtained from the packers. "The law creating the Bureau," he said, "explicitly set forth this publicity which was to be attained by you as the main object of its creation. At the same time I do not wish as yet to commit myself on one side or the other of the proposition that incidental to this main object you may be able to secure information which will be of value in securing the better execution of the law through the Department of Justice." [28]

[26] In August, 1904, at the request of the Attorney General, Garfield had supplied a list of names of persons from whom information might be obtained concerning violation of the injunction. United States v. Armour & Co. et al., 142 Federal Reports 808. In his annual report at the end of 1904 Commissioner Garfield apparently took pains to regain the confidence of businessmen by declaring that "the immediate object of its [the Bureau's] inquiries is the suggestion of legislation, not the institution of criminal prosecutions"; but he also pointed out that if violations of federal statutes were encountered they would be reported to the President for such action as he deemed "appropriate or necessary." See "Report of the Commissioner of Corporations, December, 1904," House Exec. Docs., 58 Cong., 3 Sess., No. 165 (Serial 4830), 35-36.

[27] Roosevelt to George B. Cortelyou, October 26, 1904, Morison (ed.), Letters of Theodore Roosevelt, IV, 995-96. Roosevelt later intimated that Cortelyou neglected to carry out this order. See Roosevelt to Henry Cabot Lodge, September 21, 1907, ibid., V, 804.

[28] Roosevelt to Garfield, September 30, 1904, Bureau of Corporations Records, File 3161 (National Archives).

This respite, which in the light of subsequent developments was clearly dictated by political expediency, was welcomed by Garfield. The following day he replied to the President's letter with the observation that use of the Bureau's power of investigation as an arm of the Justice Department "would be in contravention of the express provisions of law." [29] In the case of the packers, moreover, it seemingly would have been a violation of confidence, for Garfield had obtained his information through what he believed to be their voluntary co-operation.

Republican party pressures against use of the Bureau as a law enforcement agency were also strong. In December, 1904, the manager of the successful Republican campaign, Charles G. Dawes, who earlier had aided the Bureau in obtaining information from the beef-packers, reminded Garfield that the Bureau had emphasized the fact that it was not an agent of the Justice Department.[30] Cortelyou, too, talked to Garfield, and said he felt sure that the Commissioner would "try to do what is wise and conservative." [31] Under the law, however, the President had the power of final decision on how the findings of the Bureau should be used, and he soon made his position clear.

Flushed with a smashing victory at the polls, Roosevelt seemed determined to launch a vigorous antitrust drive. His enthusiasm for publicity alone as a remedy for abuses of economic power had diminished, and he soon showed a greater readiness to use the Bureau of Corporations as an auxiliary to the Justice Department. The shift in his position was indicated on January 18, 1905, when he directed Garfield to furnish the United States district attorney with all the information at his disposal on the Beef Trust that might be required in contempt proceedings.[32] Garfield complied, and the Bureau's report on the beef industry was also made available to

[29] Garfield to Roosevelt, October 1, 1904, *ibid.*

[30] Charles G. Dawes to Garfield, December 29, 1904, *ibid.*, File 2170. For Dawes's view of this affair, see Bascom N. Timmons, *Portrait of an American: Charles G. Dawes* (New York, 1953), 124-25.

[31] Cortelyou to Dawes, December 31, 1904, Bureau of Corporations Records, File 2170.

[32] Roosevelt to Garfield, January 18, 1905, James R. Garfield Papers (Manuscript Division, Library of Congress). On January 30, 1905, the Supreme Court affirmed the final injunction issued against the packers in 1903. Swift and Company *v.* United States, 196 U. S. 375. For a detailed account of Garfield's relations with the packers and the Justice Department, see United States *v.* Armour & Co. *et al.*, 142 Fed. 808.

the public in March, 1905, just before a federal grand jury was called to consider possible antitrust law violations by the packers.

The adverse public reaction to the report illustrated some of the shortcomings of publicity as a primary weapon of public policy. Interest in the Beef Trust was already widespread as a result of charges made by muckrakers, particularly through a series of magazine articles by Charles E. Russell on "The Greatest Trust in the World." [33] The Bureau's report was widely expected to verify Russell's sensational charges. When it failed to do so, the public reaction was hostile to the Bureau and the Commissioner. The New York *Press*, for example, declared that "Commissioner Garfield, who has convicted himself of incapacity, should not wait for Beef Trust officials to go to jail before he goes out of office. He should get out now." [34] *World's Work* asserted that the report "was a shock to every reader, the personal experience of every individual consumer throughout the United States having been of a nature which led him to judge the case in advance." [35]

In the fiasco of the beef report, Roosevelt was brought face to face with two of the conflicting demands of his program for dealing with big business. The use of the Bureau for the investigation of economic conditions and business behavior as a basis for legislation demanded objectivity and restraint. Effective publicity to create widespread popular support for such legislation demanded sensationalism. In his initial foray, Roosevelt had chosen the first course, stressing that the beef report was to be unassailably correct in its facts and figures. Certain information, moreover, was withheld from publication to avoid interference with the pending antitrust prosecution of the packers. [36]

Garfield took comfort in the limitations imposed by these requirements. In a letter written shortly after the report appeared, he remarked: "I was fully aware that the papers whose proprietors desire sensation rather than facts would not primarily accept the conclusions, but as yet I have not seen a criticism which indicates wherein

[33] See *Everybody's Magazine* (New York), XII, No. 2 (February, 1905), to XIII, No. 3 (September, 1905).

[34] New York *Press*, March 21, 1905.

[35] *World's Work* (New York), X (May, 1905), 6122.

[36] Herbert K. Smith memorandum, February 28, 1905, Bureau of Corporations Records, File 2734; *Annual Report of the Commissioner of Corporations to the Secretary of Commerce and Labor for the Fiscal Year Ended June 30, 1905* (Washington, 1905), 4.

the statistics are incorrect." [37]   But he missed the point. As the New York *Sun* observed: "The public is not interested in tedious and voluminous reports. It wants to know why its steaks and its roasts cost more than they did a short time ago." [38]   In fact, the Bureau's first effort at publicity, which Roosevelt had seen as its main function, was the target of criticism from all sides: from the cattlemen for a failure to understand their problems, from the public for seemingly protecting the beef-packers, and from the packers for violating their confidence.

This situation seemed to require intervention by Roosevelt himself. Angered by the New York *Press* description of the report as "very silly," "quite disgraceful," and "preposterous," he called in Herbert Knox Smith, Garfield's deputy, and discussed a counterattack. The President wanted a supplement to the beef report to be prepared before the next session of Congress. According to Smith, it was "to deal positively and affirmatively with the general line of criticism on the beef report, meeting the intelligible points in detail." [39]   Apparently nothing came of this directive. While additional material was turned over to the Justice Department in October, 1905, it was used for prosecution of the beef-packers rather than for publication. [40]

Roosevelt's decision to throw the Bureau into the legal attack on the packers also boomeranged. Indictments were obtained in July, 1905, against four meat-packing companies and certain of their officers who were charged with violating the Sherman Antitrust Act. District Judge J. Otis Humphrey, however, accepted the defendants' contention that the Justice Department had relied on information obtained by the Bureau under conditions that amounted to compulsion. Accordingly, in March, 1906, he ruled that under the Fifth Amendment and the provisions of the act establishing the Bureau the officials of the companies were immune, as individuals, from prosecution for offenses that they had explicitly or inferentially admitted to the Bureau. [41]   Roosevelt was furious. Writing to Knute Nelson in July, 1906, he angrily commented: "No one of us had the

[37] Garfield to Franklin W. Moulton, March 13, 1905, Bureau of Corporations Records, File 2694.

[38] New York *Sun*, April 29, 1905.

[39] William Loeb to Garfield, March 23, 1905, Bureau of Corporations Records, File 2694 ; Smith memorandum (n.d.), *ibid*.

[40] United States *v*. Armour & Co. *et al.*, 142 Fed. 808.

[41] *Ibid*.

slightest reason for supposing that under it [the Nelson amendment] such a decision as that of Judge Humphrey was possible. Attorney General Knox has told me, as he has told you, that he did not regard Judge Humphrey's decision as good law." [42] Meantime, to plug the gaping hole in the Bureau's armor, he had recommended, and Congress had passed, legislation extending immunity only to natural persons who were forced by formal legal means to testify against themselves.[43]

Despite the reverses of the Bureau, it provided Roosevelt with the necessary executive agency to distinguish between "good" and "bad" combinations when he took up more actively the campaign for federal control of interstate corporations. His annual message to Congress for 1905, while acknowledging the benefits of combination, had called for federal regulation and supervision to prevent restrictions on competition and other abuses of corporate power.[44] This was but the first of a series of messages during the remainder of his term of office in which he recommended such legislation. While he did not initially specify the means to be employed, by 1907 it was clear that he had in mind the Bureau of Corporations,[45] which by that time had come to play an increasingly important role. Its revelations about railroad rate practices with relation to Standard Oil shipments were useful in securing passage of the Hepburn amendment to the Interstate Commerce Act. This same report, made in response to a congressional request, was equally important in providing the President with a new opportunity to exploit popular hostility to Standard Oil as a means of promoting federal jurisdiction over big business in general.

The oil probe, growing out of conditions in the Kansas oil fields, was begun early in 1905, about the same time that the Bureau's re-

[42] Roosevelt to Nelson, July 21, 1906, Morison (ed.), *Letters of Theodore Roosevelt*, V, 334-35.

[43] In a message to Congress, April 18, 1906, Roosevelt reviewed the Humphrey decision and pointed out that this interpretation of the law regarding immunity came near to making it "a farce." Merely by answering questions of the Commissioner of Corporations, an officer of a corporation, not formally summoned as a witness, could gain immunity for offenses that he admitted. Roosevelt therefore asked Congress to declare its "real intention." Griffith (ed.), *Roosevelt Policy*, II, 362-66. Congress responded with legislation specifying that "immunity shall extend only to a natural person who, in obedience to a subpoena, gives testimony under oath or produces evidence, documentary or otherwise, under oath." *United States Statutes at Large*, XXXIV, Part 1 (1906), 798.

[44] Griffith (ed.), *Roosevelt Policy*, I, 324-26.

[45] *Ibid.*, II, 661.

port on the Beef Trust was stirring controversy. Roosevelt was credited with saying at the outset of the investigation that "his aim would be to secure fair treatment for small producers, for dealers and for consumers, without doing injustice to the great company." [46] Obviously it was no more possible to satisfy all these groups than it was to reconcile the conflicting interests in the Beef Trust investigation. From the start it was clear that Standard Oil would be the focal point of inquiry, and Bureau records show that its agents were especially alerted to look for Standard Oil material in their investigation.[47] Although Roosevelt did not initiate the probe, he probably put it in proper perspective many years later when he stated: "It [Standard Oil] antagonized me before my election, when I was getting through the Bureau of Corporations bill, and I then promptly threw down the gauntlet to it." [48]

Roosevelt's use of the Bureau's report on oil transportation provides a superb example of his technique for winning congressional support. Railroad discriminations and Standard Oil had been linked in the public mind for many years, and the President must have seen that the Bureau's findings would give him leverage to obtain more power for the Interstate Commerce Commission. The evidence certainly points in this direction. Every precaution was taken to make the impact of the Bureau's report as great as possible. On March 19, 1906, Roosevelt asked Chairman Martin A. Knapp of the ICC, which was probing discriminations in oil and coal transportation, to avoid interference with the Bureau's oil inquiry.[49] Ten days later Garfield asked the Census Bureau not to release its study of industrial combinations until his report was published.[50] Finally, Roosevelt himself provided a synopsis of the Bureau's report in a special message to Congress on May 4, 1906, at a crucial point in the Senate debate on the Hepburn amendment. The most telling argument of the message was the announcement

[46] *Independent* (New York), LVIII (March 2, 1905), 453.

[47] Meyer H. Fishbein, "Bureau of Corporations: An Agency of the Progressive Era" (M. A. thesis, American University, 1954), 85, citing Luther Conant memorandum, April 20, 1905, Bureau of Corporations Records, File 3367.

[48] "Campaign Contributions," *Testimony . . . Pursuant to S. Res. 79* (62 Cong., 2 Sess.), I, 192-93.

[49] Roosevelt to Martin A. Knapp, March 19, 1906, Theodore Roosevelt Papers (Manuscript Division, Library of Congress).

[50] Bureau of Corporations memorandum, March 29, 1906, Bureau of Corporations Records, File 4071.

that "The report shows that the Standard Oil Company has benefited enormously up almost to the present moment by secret rates, many of these secret rates being clearly unlawful." [51]

The public and congressional response to the President's message was almost entirely favorable. The Pittsburgh *Daily Dispatch* exemplified the popular reaction when it declared: "The President's moves, while sometimes questionable in judgment, have always the merit of hitting something. But he has produced none that hit the mark more notably nor at such an effective moment as this one." [52] The Hepburn amendment, its path so well cleared by the Chief Executive, became law with little difficulty. Unquestionably the Bureau of Corporations had scored a triumph. The value of publicity was further vindicated by the disclosure that many allegedly illegal rates uncovered in investigation by the Bureau had been discontinued voluntarily.

With Roosevelt's approval, the Bureau's work was followed by federal prosecution of Standard Oil. Writing to Attorney General William H. Moody in September, 1906, Roosevelt said: "I do not see how we can refrain from taking action about them [Standard Oil]. I wish the formal report to be ready at the earliest day practicable in October, as I should like to dispose of the matter as soon as possible after my return to Washington." [53] By mid-November several suits had been initiated against Indiana Standard and New York Standard for violation of the Elkins Act, and a bill in equity had been brought against Standard Oil (New Jersey) for violation of the Sherman Act. The importance of the Bureau's role in these prosecutions cannot be overstressed. [54] As Charles B. Morrison, one of the government prosecutors, later told Herbert Knox Smith, who succeeded Garfield as Commissioner in 1907: "The help you have been to us is so great that it can hardly be estimated." [55]

Through its involvement in legal proceedings against Standard Oil, the Bureau once again found itself in the center of the conflicting demands of Roosevelt's program for dealing with big busi-

[51] *Cong. Record*, 59 Cong., 1 Sess., 6358 (May 4, 1906).

[52] Pittsburgh *Daily Dispatch*, May 5, 1906.

[53] Roosevelt to William H. Moody, September 13, 1906, Morison (ed.), *Letters of Theodore Roosevelt*, V, 409.

[54] Ralph W. and Muriel E. Hidy, *Pioneering in Big Business, 1882–1911: History of the Standard Oil Company (New Jersey)* (New York, 1955), 684.

[55] Charles B. Morrison to Herbert K. Smith, April 10, 1908, Bureau of Corporations Records, File 4167-54.

ness. As Bureau officials noted in August, 1906, a reversal for the government in the courts, even on technicalities, would reflect adversely on the Bureau and on the administration.[56] On the other hand, the legal desirability of withholding from publication critical parts of the findings of the Bureau clashed with its publicity function. The government prosecutors opposed releasing the remainder of the Bureau's findings on the oil industry for fear of prejudicing their case. Bureau officials, however, were more anxious to further Roosevelt's broader legislative plans for federal regulation and supervision of corporations. Publication, they argued, "would be the most convincing argument for the Federal-license plan [advocated by Commissioner Garfield and endorsed by Roosevelt] that could be advanced."[57] But Attorney General Moody cautioned against immediate publication. "I think," he said, "this would be expected in private litigation, and I see no reason why we should not set a good example to litigants."[58] For the time being this view prevailed.

In May, 1907, a year after publication of the Bureau's report on oil transportation, the first installment of its report on the petroleum industry, subtitled "Position of the Standard Oil Company in the Petroleum Industry," was released to the public. Although Roosevelt had ordered some information withheld because it would "interfere with the proper prosecution" of the pending suit against Standard Oil,[59] the report made good newspaper copy. The summary, designed to save busy editors the trouble of combing the whole document, sharply criticized the oil combination as a monopoly that owed its position to railroad discriminations, improper use of its control of pipelines, and unfair marketing methods.

While these charges helped to insure a climate of public opinion favorable to the administration's prosecution of Standard Oil, they were subject to qualification. Commissioner Smith, for example, castigated Standard because pipelines which it controlled did not serve as common carriers; yet the report itself pointed out that there could be no legal compulsion to transport oil unless the oil was offered for transport, and admitted that most independent refiners

[56] Smith to Garfield, August 14, 1906, *ibid.*, File 4167-1.
[57] Smith to Garfield, August 31, 1906, *ibid.*, File 3366.
[58] Moody to Garfield, November 9, 1906, *ibid.*, File 3366.
[59] *Report of the Commissioner of Corporations on the Petroleum Industry* (2 vols., Washington, 1907), I, xv.

"have not for years sought to have oil transported through Standard's pipe lines, because of the universal belief that the request would be refused." [60] The fact that the Pure Oil pipeline combination followed practices similar to those of Standard received scant attention in the summary.[61] Again, in arriving at a verdict on the extent of Standard Oil's power, the Commissioner included the facilities of all companies, except Pure Oil, in which the Standard combination held even a minority interest.[62] In short, while he unquestionably made the main outlines of his indictment good, Smith presented it more like a prosecuting attorney than the head of an impartial investigatory body.

The dangers of this approach were more clearly evident in the next installment of the oil report, subtitled "Prices and Profits," which in timing and substance seemed to substantiate Standard Oil's charge that the Roosevelt administration was deliberately seeking to shape public opinion concerning that combination. This report was released two days after Judge Kenesaw M. Landis levied a $29,240,000 fine against Indiana Standard for violations of the Elkins Act, a decision which provoked significant criticism of both Landis and the Roosevelt administration. In the view of the Providence *Journal*, the timing of the Bureau's report by the administration was a calculated effort to offset such unfavorable reaction by the public.[63]

The Bureau's report on "Prices and Profits," however, contained fresh accusations against Standard Oil, and concluded explicitly that Standard's price policies were responsible for excessive costs to consumers. Given the Bureau's relation to the Chief Executive, there was unquestionably a temptation, if not a compulsion, for the Commissioner of Corporations to overemphasize findings which met popular expectations. Thus, Commissioner Smith made the flat assertion that "The Standard Oil Company is responsible for the

[60] *Ibid.*, 158.
[61] *Ibid.*, 29-30.
[62] Hidy and Hidy, *Pioneering in Big Business*, 688.
[63] Providence *Journal*, August 6, 1907. The timing may have been simply part of general strategy, fixed in advance of the decision, to drive home the evil of Standard Oil practices. See Allan Nevins, *Study in Power: John D. Rockefeller, Industrialist and Philanthropist* (2 vols., New York, 1953), II, 368. Standard Oil in its efforts to counteract the Bureau's publicity published a collection of critical newspaper comments. See *From the Directors of the Standard Oil Company to Its Employees and Stockholders* (August, 1907).

course of the prices of petroleum and its products during the last twenty-five years." [64] A competent economist pointed out, however, that the adequacy of the Bureau's methods of handling data and interpreting the results was open to question. According to him, the changes in the margins between the price of crude oil and certain refined products could have been adequately explained in terms of known conditions of supply and demand instead of Standard Oil's manipulation.[65] The New York *Times* also felt that the Commissioner's conclusions were not proved.[66] There had been some doubt, in fact, even in the Bureau, that the data on profits were sufficient to stand up in court.[67] Yet again, in the main outlines of its report, the evidence was adequate to support the Bureau's condemnation of Standard Oil practices; as Allan Nevins has observed, "the gravamen of the report was unquestionably justified." [68]

While the Roosevelt administration subjected the oil combination to prosecution and the glare of relentless and prejudicial publicity, it quietly quashed action against another combination on "moral" grounds. When the question of prosecuting the International Harvester Company for violation of the Sherman Act arose in the summer of 1907, Roosevelt referred the matter to Commissioner Smith. Since the company had co-operated with the Bureau in an investigation begun at the request of the Senate in December, 1906, Smith stated to Roosevelt that prosecution would work a "moral injustice." This consideration had not influenced the action taken against the beef-packers; and Standard Oil had early reached the conclusion that co-operation with the Bureau would be no safeguard against prosecution.[69] The situation with respect to International Harvester was different, however, in that the Morgan interests had been supporting Roosevelt's campaign for federal regulation and supervision of corporations. As the Commissioner reported to Roosevelt, "It is a very practical question whether it is well to throw away now the great influence of the so-called Morgan

[64] *Report of the Commissioner of Corporations on the Petroleum Industry*, II, xxix.

[65] *Economic Bulletin* (Baltimore), I (September, 1908), 205-12. This is a review, by Lewis H. Haney, of *Report of the Commissioner of Corporations on the Transportation of Petroleum* (Washington, 1906), and *Report of the Commissioner of Corporations on the Petroleum Industry* (2 vols., Washington, 1907).

[66] New York *Times*, August 5, 1907.

[67] E. Dana Durand, "Memorandum Regarding Publication of Remainder of Oil Report" (August, 1906), Bureau of Corporations Records, File 3366.

[68] Nevins, *Study in Power*, II, 372.

[69] See Hidy and Hidy, *Pioneering in Big Business*, 677.

interests, which up to this time have supported the advanced policy of the administration . . . and to place them generally in opposition." [70] Although the proposed prosecution was dropped, apparently on these grounds, a Bureau report on the company released in 1913 suggests that Smith could have made a case for prosecution if he had so desired. [71]

Assuming that the combinations investigated by the Bureau of Corporations during this period were treated as they deserved, it is still clear that there were serious shortcomings in Roosevelt's proposal for federal supervision and regulation of business by an executive body. In recommending regulatory legislation in his 1907 message to Congress, he declared: "Such a law to be really effective must of course be administered by an executive body, and not merely by means of lawsuits." [72] Judging from the Bureau's experience, however, an agency of its type was held down and influenced by the President's own desires and policies. The pressure, though indirect, to make a case in a given situation to fit the Chief Executive's requirements was inherent in the Bureau's relationship to him. The resulting invitation to make arbitrary distinctions between "good" and "bad" combinations was too patently inconsistent with sound public policy to be institutionalized. In a scathing report in January, 1909, issued shortly before Roosevelt left office, the Senate Judiciary Committee rejected the administration's major effort to obtain congressional approval of such a proposal. To accept it, the committee report said, "would be a most serious departure from the fundamental principles of our Government, and would do violence to what we conceive to be due process of law." [73]

The Bureau of Corporations was the nearest Roosevelt came to obtaining an agency through which he could exercise substantial executive control in the regulation of big business. [74] In publicizing corporate abuses and in helping to prosecute offenders, the Bureau

[70] Smith to Roosevelt, September 21, 1907, *Senate Exec. Docs.*, 62 Cong., 2 Sess., No. 604 (Serial 6177), 5, 7-8.

[71] See Bureau of Corporations, *The International Harvester Co.* (Washington, 1913), especially pp. xviii, xxiii, 1.

[72] Griffith (ed.), *Roosevelt Policy*, II, 661-62.

[73] *Senate Reports*, 60 Cong., 2 Sess., No. 848 (Serial 5380), 9.

[74] The Bureau continued to function through the Taft administration, and in 1914 was abolished by the act creating the Federal Trade Commission. *United States Statutes at Large*, XXXVIII, Part 1 (1914), 718.

proved very useful to the President in his role as "trustbuster." Its uneven performance, however, reflected his own difficulty in maintaining his balance under pressure from both sides of the anti-trust question. While it helped him to meet the needs of a transition period in the development of public policy toward big business, the Bureau's work demonstrated the dangers of Roosevelt's pro-gram for exercising executive and administrative discretion in dealing with new forms of economic power.

By *Benjamin J. Klebaner*

ASSOCIATE PROFESSOR OF ECONOMICS

THE CITY COLLEGE OF THE CITY UNIVERSITY OF NEW YORK

Potential Competition and the American Antitrust Legislation of 1914

❪ *The concepts of actual and potential competition as natural checks on trusts are examined through the literature which accompanied the framing and passage of the Clayton and Federal Trade Commission acts. The contributions of professional economists to these discussions are especially significant in the evolution of the public policies ultimately adopted.*

Public concern over the trust problem in the United States between 1890 and 1914 was mirrored in the considerable contemporary literature on the subject.[1] Of particular importance to these discussions was the participation of many professional economists. Their thinking directly and indirectly influenced the antitrust legislation of 1914 in a way that cannot be said of the Sherman Act of 1890.[2] A survey of the more important of these professional writings should improve our comprehension of the implications of the vague phraseology of the Clayton and Federal Trade Commission acts. Especially relevant is the discussion generated over the concepts of actual and potential competition as natural checks on large-scale enterprise, popularly called "trusts."

POTENTIAL COMPETITION: A NATURAL CHECK ON TRUSTS

Clear-cut refinement of market categories of the type Edward Chamberlin has made familiar in our own day, is not to be found in most pre-1914 analyses of competition and monopoly. A rigorous and systematic definition of perfect competition was first attempted by Francis Y. Edgeworth in 1881, but it was not until forty years later that Frank Knight presented a complete formulation.[3] In the

---

[1] Appleton P. C. Griffin, *List of Books (with references to periodicals) Relating to Trusts* (3rd ed., Washington, 1907); Library of Congress, *List of References on Trusts 1907–1913* (Washington, 1913).

[2] Hans B. Thorelli, *The Federal Antitrust Policy* (Baltimore, 1955), p. 567. Allyn A. Young, "The Sherman Act and the New Antitrust Legislation," *Journal of Political Economy*, vol. XXIII (May, 1915), p. 204.

[3] George J. Stigler, "Perfect Competition, Historically Contemplated," *Journal of*

meantime, successive editions of Alfred Marshall's *Principles* (1890–1920) defined free competition simply as a situation where "buyers generally compete with buyers and sellers compete freely with sellers." He stated explicitly that his analysis did not assume competition was perfect.[4] Marshall's most distinguished American contemporary, John Bates Clark, did not specify anything more definite for competition than "the healthful rivalry in serving the public." [5]

Trusts, however defined, could not oppress the public, it was often argued. "Potential competition," defined by Clark as "competition of the mill that is not yet built but will be built if the trust becomes too extortionate," acted as an effective natural restraint on the trusts.[6] In the absence of legal barriers "the active influence of the potential competitor" was ever present, according to George Gunton. This friend of Standard Oil stated in 1888 that the "economic effect is substantially the same as if the new competitor were already there." As the community accumulates "surplus capital," Gunton reasoned, the probability of new competition is heightened.[7] Two decades later William Howard Taft similarly pointed to the "enormous floating capital awaiting investment" in good times; rarely, he thought, would it take more than a year for potential competition to become effective. The Republican presidential candidate of 1908 drew the usual conclusion: "Existence of actual plant is not . . . . necessary to potential competition." [8]

Political Economy, vol. LXV (February, 1957), pp. 6, 11. On the relationship between Chamberlinian market categories, earlier economic theorizing, and antitrust, see: Shorey Peterson, "Antitrust and the Classic Model," *American Economic Review*, vol. XLVII (March, 1957), pp. 60–78.

[4] Alfred Marshall, *Principles of Economics* (8th ed., New York, 1946), p. 341. The first edition has identical wording. A similarly vague definition appears in his *Industry and Trade* (London, 1919), p. 653. P. W. S. Andrews remarks, in Thomas Wilson and P. W. S. Andrews (eds.), *Oxford Studies in the Price Mechanism* (Oxford, 1951), p. 142, that as long as entry is possible, Marshall considers the industry competitive. Beginning with the second (1891) edition, Marshall included the sentence about perfect competition. *Principles* (9th ed., 2 vols., New York, 1961), vol. II, p. 569.

[5] John Bates Clark, *Essentials of Economic Theory* (New York, 1907), p. 374. See also Benjamin J. Klebaner, "Trusts and Competition; John Bates Clark and John Maurice Clark," *Social Research*, vol. XXIX (Winter, 1962), pp. 475–80.

[6] John Bates Clark, "The Real Dangers of the Trusts," *Century Magazine*, vol. LXVIII (October, 1904), p. 955; Charles J. Bullock, "Trusts and Public Policy," *Atlantic Monthly*, vol. LXXXVII (June, 1901), p. 741; William M. Coleman, "Trusts from an Economic Standpoint," *Journal of Political Economy*, vol. VIII (December, 1899), pp. 29–30; George A. Rich, "Trusts Their Own Corrective," *Popular Science Monthly*, vol. XLIV (April, 1894), p. 741.

[7] George Gunton, "The Economic and Social Aspects of Trusts," *Political Science Quarterly*, vol. III (September, 1888), p. 403; H. Hayes Robbins, "Powers and Perils of the New Trusts," *Gunton's Magazine*, vol. XVI (June, 1899), pp. 198–99; similarly, Gunton, *Principles of Social Economics* (New York, 1891), pp. 404, 406, 407. See also: Charles F. Beach, Jr., "Facts About Trusts," *Forum*, vol. VIII (September, 1889), p. 69; Beach, Jr., *The Trust: An Economic Evolution* (Chicago, 1894), p. 12; George E. Roberts, "Why the Trusts Cannot Control Prices," *American Monthly Review of Reviews*, vol. XX (September, 1899), p. 307. Roberts was director of the Mint.

[8] William H. Taft, *Presidential Addresses and State Papers* (New York, 1910), p. 15; see also p. 526. In our day, Joseph A. Schumpeter felt "creative destruction" was important even when "merely an ever-present threat." *Capitalism, Socialism, and Democracy* (3rd ed., New York, 1950), p. 85.

Andrew Carnegie had emphasized in 1889 that only freedom to compete was needed to make exceptional profits temporary. By 1900 he could point to the "ghosts of numerous departed trusts which aimed at monopolies." The final report of the United States Industrial Commission affirmed in 1902 that under modern conditions "a monopoly cannot abuse its power to any great extent without rivals springing up to dispute its supremacy." Perhaps the most important facts brought out by the Commission, in the opinion of an Illinois economist, were those revealing "the development of new competition side by side with the great consolidations." [9]

Economists agreed that in the absence of legal or natural monopoly or control of a basic material, a trust could not permanently exact excessive profits, thanks to the operation of potential competition.[10] In much the same vein as Gunton and Taft, the argument of surplus capital appeared in writings of Professors Franklin H. Giddings (1887) and Charles J. Bullock (1898). There was "always a large amount of uninvested capital seeking profitable employment." This would curb the price-raising tendencies of businessmen, the American Philosophical Society was told in 1903.[11] Economists pointed out that not only newcomers, but also existing (albeit small) firms already in the industry threatened the would-be perfect monopolist.[12]

LIMITATIONS OF POTENTIAL COMPETITION

Unlike the spokesmen for the trusts, however, some economists called attention to the limitations of potential competition. Its working was stayed by the existence of excess capacity in an in-

[9] Andrew Carnegie, "The Bugaboo of Trusts," *North American Review*, vol. CXLVIII (February, 1889), p. 150; "Popular Illusions about Trusts," *Century Magazine*, vol. LX (May, 1900), p. 149. See also: Henry Wood, *Political Economy of Natural Law* (Boston, 1894), pp. 66, 71; William R. Peters, "Benefits of Trusts," John P. Peters (ed.), *Labor and Capital* (New York, 1902), p. 53; U. S. Industrial Commission, *Report* (19 vols., Washington, 1900–1902), vol. XIX, p. 614; Maurice H. Robinson, "The Report of the Industrial Commission: V – Trusts," *Yale Review*, vol. XI (November, 1902), pp. 293–94.

[10] Jeremiah W. Jenks, "Trusts in America," *Economic Journal*, vol. II (January, 1892), pp. 92–93, 99; Richard T. Ely, *Monopolies and Trusts* (New York, 1900), p. 252; Theodore Marburg, "Trusts in America," *Economic Review*, vol. XI (January, 1901), p. 67; Irving Fisher, *Elementary Principles of Economics* (3rd ed., New York, 1912), p. 330.

[11] Franklin H. Giddings, "The Persistence of Competition," *Political Science Quarterly*, vol. II (March, 1887), p. 67; Charles J. Bullock, *Introduction to the Study of Economics* (Boston, 1897), p. 325; also in 3rd ed. (New York, 1908), p. 339; Bullock, in A. B. Nettleton (ed.), *Trusts or Competition?* (Chicago, 1900), p. 121; C. Stuart Patterson, *The Problem of Trusts* (Philadelphia, 1903), p. 9. The idle capital argument was also used by the De Pauw University economist James R. Weaver, in *Chicago Conference on Trusts, Speeches* (Chicago, 1900), p. 297, and in Lyman Horace Weeks, *The Other Side* (New York, 1900), p. 74. Marshall referred to potential competition in an 1890 presidential address, "Some Aspects of Competition," without using the phrase. A. C. Pigou, *Memorials of Alfred Marshall* (London, 1925), p. 288.

[12] Frank W. Blackmar, *Economics* (Topeka, 1900), p. 437; same in (New York, 1907) edition, p. 457; Gilbert H. Montague, *Trusts of To-day* (New York, 1904), p. 78.

ANTITRUST LEGISLATION OF 1914   165

dustry.[13] The slow response of potential competitors was one explanation offered for very large profits earned year after year without attracting rivals.[14] Considerable, time might be required to gain a foothold in an industry, Harvard's Silas Macvane noted in 1890. To construct a large plant took time.[15] The sheer magnitude of the necessary outlay might deter entry.[16] President E. Benjamin Andrews of Brown University, one of the few economists who was very dubious of the effectiveness of potential competition, found no economic laws which could "prevent the permanent existence of monopolies" exacting excessive prices. Even if the minimum capital needed in many industries was forthcoming, he told the American Social Science Association in 1889, months or years might elapse before the new firm could produce.[17] There was always a chance that a new rival might join forces with an existing trust. An even stronger trust might arise "out of the ruins of the first," Edward W. Bemis warned. "Trusts have more frequently driven competition from the field, than has competition the trusts," John Bascom of Williams College insisted in 1895.[18]

Many supporters of the combination movement claimed that actual competition was hopeless. Bullock of Harvard pointed out that if this claim was indeed true, the remedial power of potential competition was put in doubt. Moreover, monopoly "fairly and honestly" achieved could undersell rivals, thereby deterring new

[13] Harry E. Montgomery, *Vital American Problems* (New York, 1908), pp. 10–11; Jeremiah W. Jenks, *The Trust Problem* (Rev. ed., New York, 1903), p. 69; William M. Collier, *The Trusts* (New York, 1900), pp. 126–27; O. M. W. Sprague, in "Governmental Price Regulation — Discussion," *American Economic Review*, suppl. III (March, 1913), p. 137.

[14] Henry C. Adams, "Trusts," American Economic Association, *Publications*, 3rd ser., vol. V (May, 1904), pp. 96–97; Jenks, *Trust Problem*, p. 70; Montgomery, *Vital American Problems*, p. 13; Charles Van Hise, *Concentration and Control* (New York, 1912), p. 84; Edwin R. A. Seligman, *Principles of Economics* (New York, 1914), p. 369; in the 1st ed. (New York, 1905), on p. 368.

[15] Silas Macvane, *Working Principles of Political Economy* (New York, 1890), p. 117; Collier, *Trusts*, p. 116; James E. Le Rossignol, *Monopolies Past and Present* (New York, 1901), p. 241; Editorial, "The Real Danger in Trusts," *Century Magazine*, vol. LX (May, 1900), p. 153; Montgomery, *Vital American Problems*, p. 10.

[16] Macvane, *Working Principles*, p. 117; Victor S. Yarros, "The Trust Problem Restudied," *American Journal of Sociology*, vol. VIII (July, 1902), p. 73; Charles W. Baker, *Monopolies and the People* (3rd ed., New York, 1899), p. 159; Nettleton (ed.), *Trusts*, p. 79; Jenks, in *Amendment of the Sherman Antitrust Law* (Hearings, Senate Judiciary Committee, Washington, 1908), p. 109; Eliot Jones, *The Trust Problem in the United States* (New York, 1921), p. 277.

[17] E. Benjamin Andrews, "The Economic Law of Monopoly," *Journal of Social Science*, vol. XXVI (February, 1890), pp. 6, 11, 12. In 1894 he saw "the competitive system . . . fast giving way to . . . combination. It could benefit society greatly if men improved morally." "The Combination of Capital," *International Journal of Ethics*, vol. IV (April, 1894), p. 334.

[18] Alsen F. Thomas, *The Slavery of Progress* (New York, 1910), pp. 21–22; Edward S. Meade, "The Limitations of Monopoly," *Forum*, vol. XXXI (April, 1901), p. 217; Edward W. Bemis, "The Trust Problem — Its Real Nature," *Forum*, vol. XXVIII (December, 1899), p. 420; Edward D. Durand, "The Trust Problem," *Quarterly Journal of Economics*, vol. XXVIII (May, 1914), pp. 398–99. Durand's Harvard lectures also appeared in book form (Cambridge, 1915); John Bascom, *Social Theory* (New York, 1895), p. 410. See also 56 Cong., 1 Sess., *House Reports*, No. 1501, p. 5.

firms from appearing in the industry despite high profits.[19] Economists thus cited a variety of practical reasons why potential competition could not always be counted on to eliminate monopolistic pricing.

UNFAIR COMPETITION OBSTRUCTS POTENTIAL COMPETITION

Destructive tactics employed by existing firms were widely held to be a major (when not the main) obstacle to entry into their markets.[20] Combinations seeking complete control, Taft explained in 1914, used various devices of an "unfair character. . . . in order to keep out or destroy new competition." Professor Thomas N. Carver pointed out that "the more effectively the organization can terrorize the trade, and the greater the artificial risks it can create, the less competition it will have and the larger profits it can make." This Harvard economist saw the danger of competition "lapsing into the brutal struggle for existence, where self-interest leads to uneconomic as well as to economic, to destructive as well as to productive activity." [21]

Unfair competition took a variety of forms. William H. S. Stevens, the leading authority (and subsequently assistant chief economist of the FTC) analyzed in detail no fewer than eleven methods: local price cutting, bogus independents, fighting ships [22] and brands, tie-ins, exclusive dealings, rebates and preferential contracts, acquisitions of exclusive or dominant control of machinery or goods used in manufacturing, "manipulation," [23] boycotts, espionage, and coercive threats and intimidation. These tactics prevented potential competitors from becoming actual rivals of existing firms.[24] Stevens therefore advocated the prohibition of "any method except produc-

[19] Bullock, "Trusts and Public Policy," pp. 741–42; Walter E. Clark, "Control of Industrial Monopoly," *Rollins Magazine*, vol. II (July, 1912), p. 7; Jenks, in *Amendment of the Sherman Antitrust Law*, p. 108.

[20] Nettleton (ed.), *Trusts*, p. 80; Baker, *Monopolies*, pp. 85, 253; Herbert J. Davenport, *Outlines of Economic Theory* (New York, 1896), p. 205; Davenport, *Economics of Enterprise* (New York, 1913), p. 485. On the other hand, Charles J. Bullock, "Trust Literature: A Survey and a Criticism," *Quarterly Journal of Economics*, vol. XV (February, 1901), p. 204, argued that capitalists would not be permanently intimidated by destructive competition.

[21] William H. Taft, *The Anti-Trust Act and the Supreme Court* (New York, 1914), pp. 128–29; Thomas N. Carver, *The Distribution of Wealth* (New York, 1904), p. 267; Carver, *Essays in Social Justice* (Cambridge, 1915), p. 108.

[22] A fighting ship is used by a shipping conference to prevent a new line from getting business by the former's quoting unprofitable rates.

[23] Stevens uses the term for "certain practices and methods which have occasionally appeared."

[24] William H. S. Stevens, "Unfair Competition: I," *Political Science Quarterly*, vol. XXIX (June, 1914), pp. 283; *ibid.*: II (September, 1914), 489; Stevens, *Unfair Competition* (Chicago, 1917), p. 221. Earlier Stevens had written . . . "if the Sherman Act can eliminate certain piratical and predatory methods of competition, a larger proportion of the 'natural' tendency toward combination would dissolve into the thin air." "A Group of Trusts and Combinations," *Quarterly Journal of Economics*, vol. XXVI (August, 1912), p. 642.

ANTITRUST LEGISLATION OF 1914   167

tion and selling efficiency which prevents potential competition from becoming actual competition." [25] Ban unfair competition, it was often said, and only deserving trusts would survive.[26]

As a major (if not the basic) means of dealing with the trust problem, leading economists — among them John Bates Clark, J. Laurence Laughlin (Chicago), Herbert J. Davenport (Cornell), Henry R. Seager (Columbia), Frank A. Fetter (Princeton) and Frank W. Taussig (Harvard) — came to favor legislation forbidding all forms of unfair competition.[27] Attorney General Philander C. Knox expressed the conviction (1903) that monopoly would be impossible in the United States "if competition were assured of a fair and open field and protected against unfair, artificial and discriminating practices." [28]

Among these forms of unfair competition, many observers especially singled out price discrimination as a deterrent to potential competition. Already in 1889 Charles W. Baker, associate editor of *Engineering News* and author of the first comprehensive American study of the monopoly problem, demanded a law providing for nondiscrimination.[29] William M. Collier, Special Assistant Attorney General to enforce the antitrust laws in 1903–1904, had urged in 1900 that corporations be compelled to sell to all on equal terms.[30] John Bates Clark's authoritative voice spoke out in favor of a policy of uniform f.o.b. mill prices with some exceptions. Such a policy, Theodore Marburg told the National Conference on Trusts and Combinations (Chicago, 1907), "would re-establish the industrial 'open door' through which the potential competitor may enter." [31] Economists of the standing of Taussig, Bullock, Fetter,

[25] Stevens, "Unfair Competition: I," p. 490.

[26] Bruce Wyman, "Constructive Trust Control," *World To-Day*, vol. XXI (January, 1912), p. 1585; Clark, "Control of Industrial Monopoly," p. 8; Henry R. Seager, *Introduction to Economics* (3rd ed., New York, 1905), p. 508.

[27] John Bates Clark, "How to Deal with the Trusts," *Independent*, vol. LIII (May 2, 1901), p. 1003; J. Laurence Laughlin, *The Elements of Political Economy* (Rev. ed., New York, 1896), p. 71; Laughlin, in *Changes in Interstate Commerce Laws* (Hearings, Senate Interstate Commerce Committee, Washington, 1911–1912), p. 1004; Davenport, *Outlines*, p. 314; Henry R. Seager, "Government Regulations of Big Business in the Future," *Annals of the American Academy of Political and Social Science: Industrial Competition and Combination*, vol. XLII (July, 1912), p. 244, hereafter cited as *Annals*, XLII; Seager, *Principles of Economics* (New York, 1913), p. 469; Frank A. Fetter, *Principles of Economics* (New York, 1904), p. 332 (original in italics); again in 1913 ed., p. 332; Frank W. Taussig, in "Governmental Price Regulation — Discussion," *American Economic Review*, suppl. III (March, 1913), p. 132.

[28] *Senate Documents*, 57 Cong., 2 Sess., No. 73, p. 16.

[29] Baker, *Monopolies*, pp. 247, 249, 253. Baker was prepared to legalize contracts in restraint of trade and permit the establishment of monopolies.

[30] Collier, *Trusts*, p. 310.

[31] John Bates Clark, *The Control of Trusts* (New York, 1901), pp. 64–66; John Bates and John Maurice Clark, *Control of Trusts* (New York, 1912), p. 192; Theodore Marburg, in National Civic Federation, *Proceedings of the National Conference on Trusts and Combinations* (New York, 1908), p. 105. See also Ernest G. Stevens, *Civilized Commercialism* (New York, 1917), p. 170.

and Laughlin, as well as President Charles Van Hise of the University of Wisconsin all wanted to forbid price discrimination.[32] In 1902, the conservative United States Industrial Commission came out for stringent legislation making price discrimination for the purpose of destroying competition a crime.[33]

Among prominent scholars, Jeremiah W. Jenks of Cornell was almost alone on the other side. He emphasized the usefulness of discrimination when rivals wished to make headway against a great combination. Similarly, Gilbert H. Montague, though opposed to fraud, disparagement, and coercion, felt that both law and ethics sanctioned "free competition by underselling." [34]

One particular form of price discrimination, railway rebates, was sometimes stressed. To Henry Carter Adams, then chief ICC statistician, the railway problem was "at the bottom of the trust problem." A few months later the Democratic platform described rebates and discriminations by transportation companies as "the most potent agency" promoting and strengthening unlawful trusts. Other economists, Clark, Bemis, Bullock, Laughlin, and Edwin R. A. Seligman among them, although not necessarily going this far, agreed as to the need for strong laws against favoritism to large shippers.[35]

As economists analyzed the actual operation of competition in the rough-and-tumble of the market place, they were generally led to assign to the state the function of "jealously safeguarding the privileges of the potential competitor," to use the words of Theodore Marburg, vice-president of the American Economic Association in 1901. John Bates Clark also warned that "potential competition will be weak if the government shall do nothing to strengthen it." A theorist who wrote more extensively on the trust problem than any other American economist, Clark called on government to preserve "the right of every potential competitor of a trust to enter a field of business and to call on the law for protection whenever he is in danger of being unfairly clubbed out of it." Professor Fetter like-

[32] Van Hise, *Concentration*, p. 226. Van Hise was a geologist by profession. In his address before the National Convention of the Progressive Party, Theodore Roosevelt pronounced Van Hise's main thesis "unquestionably right." *Progressive Principles* (New York, 1913), p. 144; Frank W. Taussig, *Principles of Economics* (2 vols., New York, 1911), vol. II, p. 429; Bullock, *Elements*, p. 195; Fetter, *Principles*, p. 332, found also in 3rd ed. (New York, 1913), p. 332.

[33] U.S. Industrial Commission, *Report*, vol. XIX, p. 650.

[34] Jenks, *Trust Problem*, presents a hypothetical example of how a small firm might be harmed (pp. 325–26); Gilbert H. Montague, "The Ethics of Trust Competition," *Atlantic Monthly*, vol. XCV (March, 1905), p. 421. Montague had recently left Harvard's Department of Economics to embark on a distinguished career as an antitrust lawyer.

[35] Adams, "Trusts," p. 105; see also Bemis, "The Trust Problem — Its Real Nature," p. 120; Kirk H. Porter (comp.), *National Party Platforms* (New York, 1924), p. 248; Bullock, *Elements*, p. 193; John Bates Clark in Chicago Conference on Trusts, *Speeches*, p. 408; J. Laurence Laughlin, *Industrial America* (New York, 1906), p. 136; Edwin R. A. Seligman in Frank Fayant (ed.), "What Is To Be Done with the Trusts?" *New York Times Magazine Section* (December 5, 1909), p. 2.

wise thought (1905) that the proper direction of trust control lay in "maintaining potential competition through fair and free conditions of industry." Even George Gunton would "stringently . . . prohibit all arbitrary barriers to the easy mobility and the safe concentration of capital and productive enterprise." Thomas N. Carver spoke for most American economists when he insisted that Adam Smith's "invisible hand" could produce beneficent results only in the presence of "proper government interference and control." Unchecked by appropriate legislation, a trust could enjoy "no small measure of monopolistic power," Clark declared.[36]

Some economists believed in the sufficiency of a policy of preventing unfair competition. They reasoned like Bruce Wyman of Harvard Law School that fair competition would always be possible if unfair competition were forbidden.[37] Other writers, however, stressed the need for measures going beyond a ban on unfair competition. Laughlin considered the abolition of tariffs on trust-made goods "the one powerful means" to secure effective competition.[38] At the same time he supported legislation to ban unfair competition.

On this last point, agreement among impartial students was well-nigh universal. After all, even a believer in the inevitability of monopoly or the economic advantages of large-scale production should be prepared to test his theory under proper (i.e., fair) conditions of competition. The Clarks pointed out that "survival in predatory competition is likely to mean something else than fitness for good and efficient production." As a 1910 editorial in the *Nation* urged: "Let monopolies arise where, in the ordinary course of things, and without resort to unfair means, competition dies away; but do not let competition be killed with a club." Only in this way could the "natural monopoly of superior efficiency" be distinguished from "artificial monopoly," to use Laughlin's description of good and bad trusts.[39]

[36] Marburg, in National Civic Association, *Proceedings*, p. 332 (original in italics); Clark, *Essentials*, pp. 384, 385; Fetter, *Principles*, p. 332 (original in italics found in 1st and 3rd eds.); George Gunton, "Trusts and How to Deal with Them," *Chautauquan*, vol. X (March, 1890), p. 703; Carver, *Essays*, p. 109; Clark, "The Real Dangers of the Trusts," p. 955. In the 4th ed. of his popular *Trust Problem*, Jenks for the first time stated: "in the fair field, kept deliberately open let the honest cost-cheapening monopoly be welcomed, if it come" (New York, 1917), p. 276.

[37] Bruce Wyman, "Unfair Competition by Monopolistic Corporations," *Annals*, XLII p. 73; a similar statement is in his *Control of the Market* (New York, 1911), pp. 264–65.

[38] Laughlin, *Industrial America*, p. 133. A more moderate recommendation was made by John Bates Clark, "Monopoly and Tariff Reduction," *Political Science Quarterly*, vol. XIX (September, 1904), p. 389. Cf. George H. Walker, "What Shall be Done about the Trusts?" Washington State Bar Association, *Proceedings Eleventh Annual Session* (Olympia, 1899), p. 97. A critique of the popular theory is Frank L. McVey, "Trusts and the Tariff," *Journal of Political Economy*, vol. VII (June, 1899), pp. 382–84. Baker (*Monopolies*, 1899 ed., p. 257) had little faith in potential competition but urged removing the tariff where a trust earned enormous profits.

[39] John D. Clark, *The Federal Trust Policy* (Baltimore, 1931), p. 104; Clark and Clark, *Control*, p. 200; Robert L. Raymond, "Industrial Combinations: Existing Law and Suggested

Combination as such — distinguished from the unfair tactics which merged firms might use — was no special concern to most students of the trust problem. Crusading Henry D. Lloyd wrote in 1896 that combination neither could nor should be prevented, but when it acquired the power to "crush competition and manipulate prices . . . something must be done!" As Professor William Folwell of Minnesota told the National Civic Federation in 1912, "Take from corporations the power to exploit, to overcapitalize and monopolize, and 'scale' may be left to the operation of economic forces." [40] By the 1890's economists generally viewed the combination movement as a normal evolution of the competitive system. Dissolution was "hopeless as a permanent policy. The fact of combination and of monopoly tendency must be faced," Taussig told the Chicago Conference on Trusts (1907). [41]

Protesting that trusts were not a "natural growth," Edward Meade of the University of Pennsylvania was in the minority when he forecast increased efficiency and lower costs of production following the break-up of the larger combinations. On the other side, Jenks criticized the Supreme Court's *Tobacco* and *Oil* decisions of 1911 for insufficiently appreciating the efficiency of the great combinations, even though they might be monopolies. [42]

Men with legal training shared Jenks' viewpoint. To William M. Coleman trusts were "absolutely indispensable to the attainment of the ideal state in which men of the highest possible development produce the greatest possible amount of the most advantageous commodities." Impressed with the inherent soundness of the combination principle, a legal scholar like Wyman argued for regulation rather than destruction of the trusts. "If it is true that not all competition is beneficent," stated the *Independent* in 1914, "it is no less true that not all combination is harmful." [43]

Legislation," *Journal of Political Economy*, vol. XX (April, 1912), pp. 313, 319; "Monopolies and the Law," *Nation*, vol. XC (January 6, 1910), p. 4; J. Laurence Laughlin, "Good and Bad Trusts," *World To-Day*, vol. XXI (January, 1912), p. 1588.

[40] Caroline A. Lloyd, *Henry Demarest Lloyd* (2 vols., New York, 1912), vol. I, pp. 289–90. Similarly, John Bascom wrote in 1895 that "Combination, an inevitable incident of progress, must be accepted and brought into submission to our common life." *Social Theory*, p. 413. Folwell, in National Civic Federation, *The Trust Problem* (New York, 1912), p. 369. *Cf.* the comments of Seager and Baker in *ibid.*, pp. 362, 391.

[41] Jeremiah W. Jenks, "Trusts in the United States," *Economic Journal*, vol. II (March, 1892), p. 71; Thorelli, *Federal Antitrust*, p. 376; Taussig, in National Civic Federation, *Proceedings*, p. 376.

[42] Edward S. Meade, "The Fallacy of 'Big Business,'" *Annals*, XLII, p. 88; contrast Donald Dewey, *Monopoly in Economics and Law* (Chicago, 1959), p. 8; Jeremiah W. Jenks, "Economic Aspect of the Recent Decisions of the United States Supreme Court on Trusts," *Journal of Political Economy*, vol. XX (April, 1912), p. 357. Jenks would protect "the public interest from direct harm" by legislation or court action, but would keep "the benefits of combination," *ibid.*

[43] Coleman, "Trusts from an Economic Standpoint," p. 33; Wyman, *Control of the*

Economists differed, however, on the significance of market share. Even an 85 per cent market share did not confer monopoly power on a firm in an industry where competitors were freely in existence and entry was not obstructed, according to Jenks, author of the *Trust Problem*, a standard work which went through more editions than any other in the field. Professor E. Dana Durand, on the other hand, reasoned that the mere combining of the greater part of an industry, quite apart from cut-throat practices, would give the firm "an appreciable degree of monopoly power." The Minnesota economist argued cogently that banning unfair competition could only serve as an adjunct to a policy forbidding combination. In the congressional debate on the 1890 legislation Senator John Sherman, quoting the New York Supreme Court, asked where was there room for another firm once an all- or nearly all-embracing combination had been formed. As William M. Collier pointed out, combining all the plants capable of supplying the entire market leads to at least a temporary monopoly; this restraint on competition justified laws against "such all-absorbing combination." Another lawyer, Charles P. Howland, saw monopoly deriving from the size of corporations. He wanted limits set on capitalization depending on the size of the national market; if no firm were allowed to grow so large as to fill the market, at least some competition would be restored.[44]

For a long time John Bates Clark was leader of the school which thought that banning unfair competition was all that was needed to make potential competition effective. By 1912, even he was prepared to place some restriction on the size of corporations. Clark, who had once described "the rigorous individualists" who advocated strict laws against consolidation as "bulls against the comets, one and all," now included in his list of remedies for the trust problem preventing combinations from growing to such a size that competition with them would be impossible. He favored breaking them up when they had grown that large. A firm controlling half the market might be required to prove that enough competition remained "to safeguard the interests of the public." Before a Senate

---

Market, pp. 263, 276; See also Robert L. Raymond, "The Federal Antitrust Act," *Harvard Law Review*, vol. XXIII (March, 1910), p. 378, and Ernest G. Stevens, "Civilized Commercialism," *American Law Review*, vol. XLVIII (May–June, 1914), pp. 433, 438; *Independent*, vol. LXXVII (1914), p. 80.

[44] Jeremiah W. Jenks, in Herbert Friedman, "The Trust Problem," *Yale Law Journal*, vol. XXIV (April, 1915), pp. 502–503; Hadley, however, thought that the larger the percentage controlled, "the larger the chance that a monopoly may in fact exist," *ibid.*, p. 502; Durand, "The Trust Problem," pp. 389, 401; Sherman, in *Congressional Record*, 51 Cong., 2 Sess., 2460 (March 21, 1890); Collier, *Trusts*, p. 130; Howland, "Monopolies: The Cause and the Remedy," *Columbia Law Review*, vol. X (February, 1910), pp. 102, 106; Robert R. Reed proposed a $200,000,000 capital limit, except by special act of Congress. "American Democracy and Corporate Reform," *Atlantic Monthly*, vol. CXIII (February, 1914), p. 267.

committee he conceded in 1914 that there were difficulties in setting a precise limit on size. The rule of reason might be applied by court or commission in this connection, based on whether or not the market was monopolistic. Dissolution prospects would, he hopefully maintained, strengthen "other measures for checking the development of further monopolies." [45]

Also in 1912, Van Hise, who was convinced that potential competition was not a sufficient regulator in more than 90 per cent of the cases, proposed that a firm with over half of any line be considered an unreasonable restraint of trade, i.e., one which did not permit free competition. Somewhat inconsistently he informed the House Committee on Interstate Trade in 1914 that whether one, two, or even five firms comprised an industry made little difference, because they could "cooperate perfectly to control the market;" hence the need for government regulation.[46]

An economist then at Van Hise's university, Thomas S. Adams, told the National Civic Federation that a firm controlling over 40 per cent of an industry should be regarded *ipso facto* as a combination in restraint of trade. In the event the firm had acquired this share without engaging in unfair competition he wanted a commission to regulate its prices.[47]

In practice, the closest Congress came to considering a limit on size was the recommendation of the Stanley Committee in 1912, found also in the La Follette bill of 1913, which would have established a rebuttable presumption of unreasonable restraint of trade when a firm had more than 30 per cent of the relevant market. One committee member, Representative John A. Sterling (Illinois), urged the dissolution of the great combinations. Even if monopolistic power had been achieved by natural growth, he advocated a limit on the amount of capital that a firm could have. Another committee member, Representative Augustus P. Gardner (Massachusetts), doubted that elimination of unfair competition would suffice to restore competition: "Mere bigness . . . may result in a more or less perfect monopoly." Representative Dick T. Morgan of Oklahoma saw the alternatives for the giant corporation as size limits or government supervision.[48]

[45] Clark, in *Annals*, XLII, p. 66; Clark, "The Real Dangers of the Trusts," p. 958; Clark and Clark, *Control*, pp. 194–95; John Bates Clark, in *Interstate Trade* (Hearings, Senate Interstate Commerce Committee, Washington, 1914), p. 364. A similar proposal is in Lewis H. Haney, *Business Organization and Combination* (Rev. ed., New York, 1914), p. 409.

[46] Van Hise, in *Interstate Trade*, p. 98; and in *Interstate Trade Commission* (Hearings, House Interstate and Foreign Commerce Committee, Washington, 1914), pp. 348–49; Van Hise, *Concentration*, pp. 227, 252.

[47] National Civic Federation, *Proceedings*, pp. 492–93.

[48] Stanley Bill, H.R. 26130 (1912), in U.S. Congress, *Bills and Debates in Congress*

In 1907, William Jennings Bryan reactivated the old proposal for federal licensing of interstate corporations, with maximum limits on the share which one firm could control, based on experience. The Democratic platform of 1908 proposed the licensing of interstate corporations before they could control 25 per cent of an industry, and prohibiting control of more than 50 per cent. As its share increased from 25 to 50 per cent, Bryan suggested (during the 1908 campaign), the licensed firm should stop expanding.[49]

Theodore Roosevelt considered the Bryan proposal even "more foolish" than the antitrust law. In his seventh annual presidential message (December, 1907) he had specifically opposed corporations whose formation or operations involved monopoly. Roosevelt wanted a giant whose position had been attained "by sheer baseness and wrong doing" to be broken up. However, there was no point in dissolving firms whose sole offense was their size, he explained in the *Outlook* (1912). Large size he identified with efficiency. Since his early days as President he had argued publicly for federal regulation and supervision of big business. He did not visualize that it would be any more difficult to regulate Standard Oil or United States Steel than to regulate a large railroad.[50]

In his attitude toward bigness President William H. Taft was in essential agreement with his predecessor. His inaugural address (two years before the Supreme Court announced the Rule of Reason) proposed an amendment to the antitrust law which included the right to combine for the sake of efficiency, while distinguishing combination "formed with the intent of creating monopolies." In this context, combinations which continued to grow beyond the point of economy of management characteristic of

Relating to Trusts (3 vols., Washington, 1914), vol. III, p. 2542; La Follette Bill, S. 2552 (1913), *ibid.*, vol. III, pp. 3118–19. Cummins' bill would have had the trade commission judge whether the capital of a firm was so extensive as to "destroy or prevent substantially competitive conditions in the general field of industry in which such corporation is engaged," *ibid.*, vol. III, pp. 2430–31; elsewhere he argued for a 25 per cent limit, *Congressional Record*, 63 Cong., 1 Sess., 4283 (August 29, 1913). See also: Sterling, in *House Reports*, 62 Cong., 2 Sess., No. 1127, p. 345, and *Congressional Record*, 62 Cong., 2 Sess., 10529–30 (August 8, 1912); Gardner, in *ibid.*, 10627 (August 9, 1912); Morgan, in *Interstate Trade Commission*, p. 170.

[49] William J. Bryan, "Dissolution and Prevention," *The Reader*, vol. IX (May, 1907), p. 578; Porter (comp.), *Platforms*, p. 277; Bryan, *Speeches* (2 vols., New York, 1913), vol. II, pp. 136–37.

[50] Elting E. Morison, *et al.* (eds.), *Letters of Theodore Roosevelt* (8 vols., Cambridge, 1951–1954), vol. VI, p. 1314; *Compilation of the Messages and Papers of the Presidents* (20 vols., New York, n. d.), vol. XV, p. 7078 (Seventh Annual Message); Theodore Roosevelt, "The Trusts, the People, and the Square Deal," *Outlook*, vol. XCIX (November 18, 1911), p. 655; "The Taft-Wilson Trust Programme," *Outlook*, vol. CII (September 21, 1912), p. 105; *Messages and Papers of the Presidents*, vol. XIV, p. 6648; George E. Mowry, *The Era of Theodore Roosevelt, 1900–1912* (New York, 1958), pp. 132–33. In a 1903 speech before Milwaukee businessmen, Roosevelt described big corporations as "the result of an inevitable process of economic evolution," quoted in Walter F. Meier, "What Attitude Should Government Assume toward Trusts?" *American Journal of Sociology*, vol. IX (September, 1903), p. 213.

efficient, large-scale firms demonstrated monopolistic intent. The law was violated only where the purpose or necessary effect of the combination was to stifle actual and potential competition and establish a monopoly.[51]

Woodrow Wilson too was not opposed to size *per se.* "I am for big business and I am against the trusts," he flatly stated during the campaign of 1912. His party's platform, though less explicitly than in 1908, wanted to forbid by law "the control by any one corporation of so large a proportion of any industry as to make it a menace to competitive conditions." [52] This idea was forgotten in the anti-trust legislation of 1914.

PUBLICITY AS A REMEDY

Publicity was often proposed to help make potential competition effective. The theory here was that knowledge of high profits would lure competitors into the field, while public opinion would moderate the trust's exactions. Henry C. Adams considered publicity "the first step" in the solution of the trust problem. Jenks saw publicity as the "most effective means" to force the passing on to the public of the savings of combination. Many businessmen shared Waddill Catchings' faith that little if any further trust legislation would be needed beyond a publicity statute.[53]

In 1900 and again in 1902 the United States Industrial Commission recommended that large corporations be required to submit "properly audited" annual reports. The Bureau of Corporations (1903–1914) operated on the theory of publicity which, in the words of Commissioner Luther Conant, Jr., had the "broader motive of maintaining an open field for fair competition." [54] Publicity, then,

[51] *Messages and Papers of the Presidents,* vol. XVI, p. 7369. See also vol. XVII, pp. 7651, 7655, and Taft, *Presidential Addresses,* p. 527.

[52] Woodrow Wilson, *The New Freedom* (New York, 1913), pp. 180, 191; Ray Stannard Baker, *Woodrow Wilson* (6 vols., Garden City, 1927–1007), vol. IV, p. 337. Porter (comp.), *Platforms,* p. 322.

[53] Frank N. Judson, *The Rightful Relation of the State to Private Business Associations* (St. Louis, 1890), p. 16; Baker, *Monopolies* (1889 ed.), pp. 254–55; *ibid.* (1899 ed.), p. 357; Gunton, "Trusts and How to Deal with Them," p. 703; Robert L. Raymond, "A Statement of the Trust Problem," *Harvard Law Review,* vol. XVI (December, 1902), p. 90; Seligman, *Principles* (1914 ed.), p. 640; Taussig, *Principles,* vol. II, p. 433; Seager, in *Annals,* XLII, p. 244; Henry C. Adams, "What is Publicity?" *North American Review,* vol. CLXXV (December, 1902), p. 904; Jeremiah W. Jenks, in *Amendments to Sherman Antitrust Law* (Hearings, Senate Judiciary Committee, Washington, 1914), p. 307; Jenks, *Trust Problem* (1900 and 1914 eds.), pp. 223–24; Jenks, in *Amendment of the Sherman Antitrust Law,* p. 109; Catchings, head of Central Foundry Co., in *Interstate Trade Commission,* pp. 54–55.

[54] U.S. Industrial Commission, *Report,* vol. I, p. 6; U.S. Commissioner of Corporations, *Annual Report,* 1912 (Washington, 1913), p. 3. By 1902 it was said that the inadequacy of publicity as a remedy had been "widely recognized." Yarros, "The Trust Problem Restudied," p. 68.

shared with a ban on unfair competition the distinction of being the least controversial and most widely proposed trust remedies.

CONGRESS AND POTENTIAL COMPETITION: THE 1890's

In the debate on the antitrust measure of 1890, congressmen had expressed concern for what was soon to become widely known as "potential competition." Senator Sherman explained that one of the purposes of his original bill was "to prevent and control combinations made with a view to prevent competition." Trusts, he thought, had "a uniform design to prevent competition." One of the six unlawful purposes of a trust enumerated in Senator John H. Reagan's bill of 1890 was "to prevent competition." The section in the law of 1890 making unlawful every contract in restraint of trade was held to render superfluous a proposed amendment denouncing every agreement "for the purpose of preventing competition." [55] By passing the Sherman Act, Congress aimed to outlaw "artificial obstacles to entry;" private restrictions on competition were to be eliminated and prevented. As Myron Watkins later pointed out, "we were committed to the principle of offering full protection to . . . potential producers." [56]

Senator George Hoar, one of the sponsors of the bill which eventually became the Sherman Act, explained that the 1890 measure was intended to protect "fair competition" in interstate commerce. After the Supreme Court in 1895 defeated the government's efforts to break up the Sugar Trust, many friends of an antitrust policy proposed a constitutional amendment. If such action were taken, Congress would have "power to maintain an open field for honest competition," according to the House Judiciary Committee. Chairman George W. Ray specifically saw the need for laws which would maintain "fair and open opportunity to enter and engage in every honest pursuit." [57] With the Northern Securities (1904) and subsequent decisions, it became clear that constitutional amendment was not necessary in order to deal with the trust problem.

[55] Sherman, in *Congressional Record*, 51 Cong., 1 Sess., 2457, 2459, 2569 (March 21, 24, 1890); Reagan, in *ibid.*, 51 Cong., 1 Sess., 2469 (March 21, 1890); Culberson, in *ibid.*, 51 Cong., 1 Sess., 5951 (June 11, 1890); Young, "The Sherman Act and the New Antitrust Legislation," p. 213. Justice Holmes went so far as to argue that "there is no combination in restraint of trade, until something is done with the intent to exclude strangers to the combination from competing with it in some part of the business which it carries on." *Northern Securities Co. v. U.S.*, 193 U.S. 197, p. 409 (1905) (dissent).

[56] John M. Lishan, "The Sherman Act" (Ph.D. Dissertation, Harvard University, 1958), p. 38. Thorelli, *Federal Antitrust*, p. 571. See also John Perry Miller, *Unfair Competition* (Cambridge, 1941), p. 25. Myron W. Watkins, "The Sherman Act: Its Design and Its Effects," *Quarterly Journal of Economics*, vol. XLIII (November, 1928), p. 42.

[57] Hoar, in *Congressional Record*, 51 Cong., 1 Sess., 3152 (April 8, 1890); *House Reports*, 56 Cong., 1 Sess., No. 1501, p. 33; Ray, in *Congressional Record*, 56 Cong., 1 Sess., 6306 (May 31, 1900).

Certain quarters were dissatisfied with Supreme Court decisions from 1897 on, which appeared to forbid all contracts restraining trade. Montague estimated that two-thirds of the country's business was thereby being conducted "in defiance of law." Strict enforcement of the Sherman Act would prohibit "the normal growth of large commercial enterprise," he complained. The law appeared not to confine itself to forbidding unreasonable restraints of trade.[58]

The "rule of reason," enunciated in May, 1911 in the historic Standard Oil and Tobacco decisions, was hailed by economist Seager: the Supreme Court's interpretation condemning only unreasonable restraints had turned the law into "a constructive and regulative measure of reform." Law-Professor Wyman saw reasonableness as the common law standard by which "good" trusts would be separated from the "bad." New York corporation lawyer Felix Levy took issue with the 1912 Democratic platform allegation that the rule weakened the Sherman Act.[59]

While some denounced the rule of reason for weakening the Sherman Act, others thought the rule did not go far enough in that direction. Professor Laughlin claimed business was slowing up because the antitrust law was uncertain in its meaning. The Sherman Act was attacked before the American Mining Congress in October, 1911, as "a wet blanket upon industry." The law of 1890 was "an anachronism," according to James M. Beck, and "little more than a delusion:" men could not be compelled to compete if they did not want to. The law was "destructive in purpose and application," according to Arthur Eddy, the lawyer who wrote a famous plea for open price associations in 1912.[60]

[58] Gilbert H. Montague, "Defects of the Sherman Antitrust Law," *Yale Law Journal*, vol. XIX (December, 1909), pp. 88, 107, 109, reprinted almost verbatim as "Trust Regulation Today," *Atlantic Monthly*, vol. CV (January, 1910), pp. 1–8. The President of the National Association of Clothiers, Marcus M. Marks, also urged that reasonable agreements be made lawful in "Effects of Anti-Trust Legislation on Business," *Annals of the American Academy of Political and Social Science*, vol. XXXII (July–December, 1908), p. 48.

[59] Henry R. Seager, "The Recent Trust Decisions," *Political Science Quarterly*, vol. XXVI (December, 1911), pp. 610–11; Wyman, *Control of the Market*, p. 234; Levy, in *Trust Legislation* (Hearings, House Judiciary Committee, Washington, 1914), pp. 241, 247–48.

[60] Laughlin, "Good and Bad Trusts," p. 1586; D. W. Kuhn, *Sherman Anti-Trust Law* (Address before American Mining Congress, October, 1911), p. 5; James M. Beck, "The Supreme Court Decisions: The Quandary," *North American Review*, vol. CXCIV (July, 1911), p. 70. Beck was U.S. Solicitor-General, 1921–1925; he favored a government tribunal to hear complaints, *Annals*, XLII, p. 300. Arthur J. Eddy, *The New Competition* (New York, 1912), p. 333. The President of the Virginia Bar Association urged the repeal of the Sherman Act on the grounds that competition should not be the life of trade, and the "absolutely uncertain and vague" law did not distinguish between good and bad trusts. J. F. Bullitt, "The Present Status of the Trust Question," Virginia State Bar Association, *Report of the Twenty-fourth Annual Meeting* (n.p., 1912), pp. 170, 182.

ANTITRUST LEGISLATION OF 1914   177

In the 1890's it had been urged that industries be given the right to combine "under proper supervision" and to agree on reasonable prices and avoidance of competitive excesses. In the years just preceding the enactment of the antitrust legislation of 1914, Van Hise was perhaps the outstanding non-business proponent of an amendment to the Sherman Act which would permit combinations in restraint of trade involving division of territories and agreements on output and even prices provided they were not detrimental to the public welfare.[61]

Other critics argued the Sherman Act had failed to solve the monopoly problem, or to prevent the maturation of monopoly. Indeed, according to Jenks, it had "tended to breed monopoly" by forbidding certain other restraints.[62]

Despite such attacks, there was widespread support for the Sherman Act as a measure to ensure fair competition and to prevent exclusion.[63] Almost unanimous support for the principle of the Sherman Act, and a determination that big business should be regulated appeared in the replies to a questionnaire sent to 16,000 representative Americans by the National Civic Federation. Advocates of repeal or liberalizing amendments were people who had been violating the law, attorney Samuel Untermyer pointedly observed. Among popular authors, support for the Sherman Act policy was even more common than among scholars.[64]

Certainly the Taft administration made vigorous use of the 1890 law. More prosecutions of business combinations were instituted from 1909 to 1913 than during Theodore Roosevelt's two terms. Taft considered the law "the expression of the effort of a freedom-loving people to preserve equality of opportunity." He told Congress in December, 1912 that the trust question was "gradually solving itself" by enforcement of the Sherman Act.[65]

[61] Aldace F. Walker, "Unregulated Competition Self-Destructive," *Forum*, vol. XII (December, 1891), p. 515; Walker, "Anti-Trust Legislation," *Forum*, vol. XXVII (May, 1899), p. 262. Walker was a member of the original ICC, 1887–1889; from 1889–1892 he was connected with the Trunk Line and Central Traffic Associations; after 1894 he headed the Santa Fe. Van Hise, in *Interstate Trade*, pp. 95, 96; Van Hise, in *Trust Legislation*, p. 557; see also F. P. Fish (Boston attorney) in *ibid.*, p. 1511 and L. C. Boyle (Kansas City attorney for the Yellow Pine Manufacturers Association), *Interstate Trade Commission*, p. 442.

[62] Rep. Dick Morgan, in *Trust Legislation*, p. 4; Dean William D. Lewis, University of Pennsylvania Law School, in *ibid.*, p. 399; J. Newton Baker (D.C. attorney), "Regulation of Corporations," *Yale Law Journal*, vol. XXII (February, 1913), p. 329; Jenks, in *Amendments to Sherman Antitrust Law*, p. 302.

[63] Bennett, attorney for manufacturers of printing presses, in *Trust Legislation*, p. 301; Dushkind, attorney for Independent Tobacconists Association of N.Y.C., in *ibid.*, p. 702; Charles A. Boston, "The Spirit behind the Sherman Anti-Trust Law," *Yale Law Journal*, vol. XXI (March, 1912), pp. 358, 371.

[64] National Civic Federation, *Proceedings*, p. 8; Samuel Untermyer, "The Supreme Court Decisions: The Remedy," *North American Review*, vol. CXCIV (July, 1911), p. 77; Thorelli, *Federal Antitrust*, p. 576.

[65] *Messages and Papers of the Presidents*, vol. XVII, p. 7655 (1911 Annual Message);

During the presidential campaign of 1912 Woodrow Wilson spoke of his desire to create a situation "where every man knows that the business community is open for him to enter and that he will be welcome." The New Freedom was concerned with "men who are on the make rather than the men who are already made." Wilson therefore wanted to "check those who use big business to crush little business, who use power to prevent anybody coming into competition with their power by a power and intelligence of his own." His first annual message proposed that the 1890 law be left unaltered, but urged supplementary legislation to "clarify it." The aim — much sought after by businessmen and endorsed by the three major party platforms in 1912 — was to "practically eliminate uncertainty." [66]

Maintenance of competition remained the dominant philosophy and, though seldom mentioned explicitly in congressional discussions of the antitrust measures of 1914, potential competition was probably in the mind of legislators.[67] The Senate Committee on Interstate Commerce, reporting on its 1913 hearings, stressed the importance of creating and preserving competitive conditions so that actual competition would be most likely to take place. In the unusual case where there was no actual competition, there would at least be "a potential competition tending to prevent undue prices and unfair practices." The aim of the 1914 laws, Senator Thomas J. Walsh succinctly stated, was "to preserve competition where it exists, to restore it where it is destroyed, and to permit it to spring up in new fields." Senator William E. Chilton stressed the purpose "to create competition, to fix it so that there is an incentive for the little man to come in and take the field or a part of the field which is now occupied absolutely by these gigantic corporations," not to destroy or stop big business. President Wilson similarly described the 1914 legislation as aiming to make "men in a small way of

---

Congressional Record, 62 Cong., 3 Sess., 897 (December 19, 1912). See also Attorney-General George W. Wickersham, *The Administration's Anti-Trust Record* (Washington, 1912), p. 26.

[66] Woodrow Wilson, *Public Papers* (ed. by R. S. Baker and W. E. Dodd, 6 vols., Garden City, 1925–1927), vol. I., p. 29; Wilson, *New Freedom*, pp. 17, 191, 221; John W. Davidson (ed.), *A Crossroads of Freedom* (New Haven, 1956), p. 516; see also *ibid.*, pp. 78, 269, 464. For a similar stress on a free field see W. R. Hammond (Atlanta Judge), "Evil and Cure of Monopolistic Business Tendency," Georgia Bar Association, *Report of the Twenty-ninth Annual Session* (Macon, 1912), pp. 129, 131; Albert Shaw (ed.), *Messages and Papers of Woodrow Wilson* (2 vols., New York, 1924), vol. I, p. 42 (1913 Annual Message); *ibid.*, vol. I, p. 52 (1914 Special Message on Trusts).

[67] E. Dana Durand, "The Trust Legislation of 1914," *Quarterly Journal of Economics*, vol. XXIX (November, 1914), p. 73. *Cf.* Jones, *Trust Problem*, p. 335; Clark, *Federal Trust Policy*, p. 168.

ANTITRUST LEGISLATION OF 1914   179

business as free to succeed as men in a big way and to kill monopoly in the seed." [68]

CLAYTON ACT APPROACH

Compared to the aspirations of some antitrust advocates, the Clayton Act was "so weak that you cannot tell it from water," as Wilson wrote to Colonel Edward House. Senator James A. Reed (Missouri) exaggerated, however, when he described the measure as proclaiming "Peace on earth, good will toward the trusts." After all, the 1914 measure left the Sherman Act intact. The intention of Congress was to supplement the 1890 act, making certain practices — such as tying clauses and price discrimination — illegal which in themselves were not covered by the earlier law, and thus "to arrest the creation of trusts, conspiracies, and monopolies in their incipiency and before consummation." Some of these practices, such as price discrimination, had been singled out for condemnation prior to 1914. Tying clauses involving a patented product, however, had been upheld by the courts.

Prevention of monopoly rather than prosecution of trusts after they had been in operation was at the heart of the Clayton Act's approach. Congress forbade certain tactics "where the effect . . . *may* be to substantially lessen competition or tend to create a monopoly" and not merely where competition had already been damaged or eliminated. This was in harmony with the theory that it was preferable to keep "the field open for the beneficent effect of competition rather than wait until those channels of competition have been blocked up and then try to open them with a knife," as Henry L. Stimson phrased it in 1911.[69]

FTC AND POTENTIAL COMPETITION

A similar philosophy motivated the Federal Trade Commission Act. Senator Francis G. Newlands, the author, argued that making unfair competition unlawful would "protect the pygmies against the giants of the business and open the lines of competition." Senator Henry F. Hollis envisioned the FTC as "policing competition, so

[68] Senate Reports, 62 Cong., 3 Sess., No. 1326, pp. 3–4; Walsh, in Congressional Record, 63 Cong., 2 Sess., 16145 (October 5, 1914); Chilton, in ibid., 14326 (August 27, 1914); Wilson, Public Papers, vol. I, p. 189; see also, ibid., vol. II, p. 318.

[69] Arthur S. Link, Woodrow Wilson and the Progressive Era, 1910–1917 (New York, 1954), p. 73; Reed, "The New Way with the Trusts," quoted in Literary Digest, vol. XLIX (October 24, 1914), p. 778; Senate Reports, 63 Cong., 2 Sess., No. 698, p. 1; Henry L. Stimson(Secretary of War in Taft's Cabinet), Address at the Republican Club New York City on December 15, 1911, p. 6.

as to protect small businessmen, keep an open field for new enterprise, and prevent the development of trusts." The last, of course was related to the widespread view that unfair competition was (in the words of a House group endorsing the bill) the one effective means of "establishing and maintaining a monopoly" in the absence of control of raw materials or transportation discrimination. To prevent unfair competition was therefore "the most certain way to stop monopoly at the threshold." As Representative Rufus Hardy told the House in 1911, "By . . . ruinous competition combination builds itself into monopoly." [70]

The idea of a trade commission was in the air in the first decade of the twentieth century. Americans felt that regulation had to accompany combination. President Roosevelt envisioned it in 1907 as functioning to ratify "reasonable agreements between, or combinations of corporations." Wyman had suggested using the Sherman Act to dissolve combinations restraining trade, while a commission regulated firms with "substantial control over their market." Senator Newlands, the staunchest congressional advocate of the trade commission idea, explained in 1911 that the proposed agency would preserve "the good arising from commercial combination," while "curing the pernicious practices connected therewith." [71]

Commissioner of Corporations Herbert K. Smith argued for administrative regulation because application of the Sherman Act through the courts was haphazard. The Republican platform of 1912 viewed the commission as an agency for the prompt administration of the law. The Senate report on the FTC bill agreed that a commission would help to enforce the 1890 law. Moreover, the experts could aid the courts in fashioning effective dissolution decrees. [72] Advocates also envisioned the commission in the role of adviser to businessmen on the legality of their plans. [73]

[70] Newlands in *Congressional Record,* 63 Cong., 2 Sess., 12939 (July 29, 1914); Hollis, in *ibid.,* 12146 (July 15, 1914); 63 Cong., 2 Sess., *House Reports,* No. 1142, pp. 18–19; George Rublee, "The Original Plan and Early History of the Federal Trade Commission," *Academy of Political Science Proceedings,* vol. XI (January, 1926), pp. 117–18; Hardy, in *Congressional Record,* 62 Cong., 1 Sess., 1232 (May 16, 1911). The notion that monopoly was built on unfair practices was challenged by Progressive Donald Richberg in *Trust Legislation,* p. 419.

[71] Talcott Williams, "No Combination Without Regulation," *Annals of the American Academy of Political and Social Science,* vol. XXXII (July–December, 1908), p. 258; *Messages and Papers of the Presidents,* vol. XIV, p. 7079; Bruce Wyman, in *Annals,* XLII, p. 71; *Congressional Record,* 62 Cong., 1 Sess., 1212 (May 15, 1911).

[72] Herbert K. Smith, in *Amendments to Sherman Antitrust Law,* p. 333; see also, William Draper Lewis, in *Trust Legislation,* p. 398; Porter (comp.), *Platforms,* pp. 341, 354; *Senate Reports,* 63 Cong., 2 Sess., No. 597, pp. 9, 10, 12.

[73] James R. Garfield (ex-Secretary of the Interior), *Annals,* XLII, pp. 144–45; Henry R. Towne (of Yale and Towne), in *Trust Legislation,* p. 524.

Two groups, otherwise at odds, supported the commission idea. One — which included the Progressives — wanted to regulate what appeared to be inevitable monopolies. The other, which embraced the congressional sponsors of the 1914 measures, wanted to destroy monopoly and employ the commission as an instrument to preserve competition. Senator Newlands cleverly argued (1911) that a commission would not commit the country permanently to either school's approach.[74] Some opponents of the mild measure which became law in 1914 feared that it was the first step to the adoption of the policy of regulating rather than destroying private monopoly. To allay such misgivings, the House report on the bill pointed out that the commission had no power "to make terms with monopoly or in any way to assume control of business."[75]

By mid-1914 Wilson, originally critical of the Progressives' proposal for a strong trade commission came to advocate the Brandeis-Rublee plan for an effective regulatory agency for business. In the process he scrapped his original concept of an antitrust statute which would define trade restraints in precise terms.[76] The Commission, hailed by Professor Durand as "a great forward step," turned out to be "the most important feature of the new trust legislation," as he remarked shortly after the event.[77]

By the time Wilson submitted his special message on trusts and monopolies (January 20, 1914), Congress had already enacted two major measures which were intended in part to have an impact on this problem: tariff reduction and creation of a central banking system. For decades elimination of protectionism had been the main antitrust proposal of the Democratic Party. The Underwood Tariff of 1913 made a start in this direction. Creation of the Federal Reserve System followed a warning by the Pujo Committee that the "inner group" of leading banks had been "more destructive of competition than anything accomplished by the trusts, for they strike at the very vitals of potential competition in every industry that is under their protection."[78] The Federal Reserve System was established on a decentralized basis so as to make it impossible for

[74] Senate Reports, 63 Cong., 2 Sess., No. 597, p. 10; Gerard C. Henderson, The Federal Trade Commission (New Haven, 1925), pp. 21, 22; Henry R. Seager and Charles A. Gulick, Jr., Trust and Corporation Problems (New York, 1929), p. 415; Newlands, in Senate Reports, 63 Cong., 2 Sess., No. 597, p. 27.

[75] Dushkind, in Trust Legislation, pp. 711–712; House Reports, 63 Cong., 2 Sess., No. 533, p. 7.

[76] Link, Wilson and the Progressive Era, pp. 72–73. In his Special Message on Trusts, January 20, 1914 (loc. cit., note 66), pp. 85–86, Wilson advocated a trade commission. Durand, "The Trust Legislation of 1914," pp. 78, 90, 97; Porter (comp.), Platforms, p. 341 (Progressive plank).

[77] Wilson, Special Message on Trusts, January 20, 1914, pp. 81–88 (loc. cit., note 66).

[78] House Banking and Currency Committee, Report of the Committee . . . to Investigate the Concentration of Control of Money and Credit (Washington, 1913), p. 161.

the New York financial leaders to control the central bank. Yet another weapon intended to deal with banker control was forged in Section 8 of the Clayton Act.

HOLDING COMPANIES AND CORPORATE REFORM

In his January, 1914 statement Wilson observed that agreement was general that the holding company should be prohibited. Four years earlier Taft had made a similar recommendation for inclusion in a proposed federal incorporation law, reasoning that the device "has been such an effective agency in the creation of the great trusts and monopolies." The holding company facilitated the elimination of competition because a controlling interest in a firm could be purchased at small cost, Senator Theodore E. Burton pointed out.[79] Another important count against the holding company was that it was used to exploit minority shareholders.[80] The House Judiciary Committee considered a corporation whose primary purpose was to hold the stock of other companies "an abomination;" Section 7 of the Clayton Act was to eliminate the evil as far as possible.[81] Contrary to Wilson's original (impractical) notion, not all holding companies would be banned under this provision.

Effective antitrust action was linked, in the opinion of many, with restrictions on corporate powers and conduct, to be achieved (as a rule) by federal incorporation.[82] Some went so far as to claim that monopoly would be destroyed if corporate privileges — illustrated by the right of firms to hold the stock of other companies — were confined.[83] It remained for Chester Wright of the University of Chicago to point out that reform of corporation law would help only in a small way to solve the monopoly problem — insofar as

[79] Wilson, Special Message on Trusts, January 20, 1914, p. 87 (loc. cit., note 66); Taft, Special Message, January 7, 1910, Messages and Papers of the Presidents, vol. XVII, p. 7455; Theodore E. Burton, Corporations and the State (New York, 1911), p. 122. For a lawyer's arguments against holding companies see J. Newton Baker, "Regulation of Corporations," p. 330. For a lawyer's favorable attitude see Albert H. Walker, in Trust Legislation, p. 1396.

[80] Clark and Clark, Control, p. 191; Untermyer, in Trust Legislation, p. 858.

[81] House Reports, 63 Cong., 2 Sess., No. 627, p. 17. John Bates Clark also used the term "abomination" in "After the Trusts, What?" World To-day, vol. XXI (November, 1911), p. 1296. E. Dana Durand commented that Section 7 of the Clayton Act added "nothing of real value to the Sherman Act." "The Trust Legislation of 1914," p. 83. For the legislative history of Section 7, see David D. Martin, Mergers and the Clayton Act (Berkeley, 1959), chap. 2.

[82] Burton, Corporations, p. 174; Frederick H. Allen (corporation attorney), in Trust Legislation, p. 1168; R. M. Benjamin, "The Evolution and Prevention of Trusts and Monopolies," Albany Law Journal, vol. LXVIII (August, 1906), p. 246. A comprehensive discussion of remedies for corporate abuses is found in Haney, Business Organization, pp. 383–402.

[83] Robert R. Reed, "American Democracy and Corporate Reform," Atlantic Monthly, vol. CXIII (February, 1914), p. 259; Reed, in Interstate Trade Commission, pp. 332–33, 344; Reed, in Trust Legislation, pp. 591, 625.

ANTITRUST LEGISLATION OF 1914   183

promoters' profits stimulated the formation of trusts. He correctly observed: [84]

> . . . totally abolish all the evils of the corporation, stock-watering, manipulation, defrauding creditors, injuring minority stockholders, excessive promoters' profits, and all the rest, and you will still have the problem of trusts on your hands. Conversely, if you were so successful as to abolish all the trusts in creation, you would still have to face these evils which are due to our lax corporation laws.

Thoroughgoing corporate reform, however, was not on the program of action for the New Freedom.

THE LEGACY OF 1914

Spokesmen for laissez-faire — among them the eminent corporation lawyer John Dos Passos — looked to "the natural laws of trade" to "prevent or break up most commercial monopolies." [85] Between 1890–1914 the view became widespread that markets could function satisfactorily only if potential competition were an ever-present threat. Economists (and some others) pointed out that unregulated cut-throat competition often destroyed the possibilities of potential competition. They insisted that government assume the responsibility of forbidding activities which impeded the working of potential competition.

Price discrimination, exclusive dealing, holding-company acquisitions — business devices enumerated in the original Clayton Act as unlawful when they might "substantially lessen competition or tend to create a monopoly" — all menace potential competition. The "unfair methods of competition" declared unlawful in the FTC Act of 1914 can also reasonably be interpreted to include the variety of devices endangering potential competition.

The half-century which has elapsed since the passage of the two measures cannot be said to have seen the realization of the aspirations of some of the more enthusiastic supporters of the idea that a specialized independent agency aided by statutes forbidding various forms of unfair business conduct were adequate to preserve competition in the American economy.[86] Moreover, uncertainty was not eliminated in the 1914 laws, which left intact the rule of reason

---

[84] Chester W. Wright, "The Trust Problem: Prevention versus Alleviation," *Journal of Political Economy*, vol. XX (June, 1912), p. 582.

[85] John R. Dos Passos, *Commercial Trusts* (New York, 1901), p. 63.

[86] John Perry Miller, "Woodrow Wilson's Contribution to Antitrust Policy," in Earl Latham (ed.), *The Philosophy and Policies of Woodrow Wilson* (Chicago, 1958), pp. 134, 143.

interpretation of the Sherman Act. Indeed, the courts extended the principle to the Clayton Act as well.

Nevertheless, the antitrust heritage of 1914 remains of value even in today's world. Pure and perfect competition were repudiated as "direct goals of antitrust policy" by the eminent lawyers and economists who reported on the antitrust laws in 1955 to the Attorney General; but these men emphasized the fundamental importance of "relative freedom of opportunity for entry of new rivals . . . for effective competition in the long run." In effect, they restated the main point of the message of serious students of the trust problem between 1890 and 1914. A recent study of big business concludes that "the threat of competitive innovation and entry is continuous and omnipresent." [87] To the extent that this is true, the 1914 laws have contributed to the result. Antitrust decisions which focus on potential competition [88] are in the spirit of the thinking which lay behind the 1914 Clayton and Federal Trade Commission acts.

[87] Attorney-General's National Committee to Study the Antitrust Laws, *Report* (Washington, 1955), pp. 326, 334; A. D. H. Kaplan and Alfred Kahn, "Big Business in a Competitive Society," *Fortune*, vol. XLVII (February, 1953), sec. 2, p. 4.

[88] American Bar Association Section on Antitrust Law, *Proceedings*, vol. XII (Chicago, 1958), pp. 105–202, esp. pp. 177, 186, 202.

The Discovery that Business Corrupts Politics:
A Reappraisal of the Origins of Progressivism

RICHARD L. McCORMICK

ALMOST ANY HISTORY TEXTBOOK that covers the Progressive era and was written at least twenty years ago tells how early-twentieth-century Americans discovered how big business interests were corrupting politics in quest of special privileges and how an outraged people acted to reform the perceived evils. Commonly, the narrative offers ample anecdotal evidence to support this tale of scandal and reform. The autobiographies of leading progressives—including Theodore Roosevelt, Robert M. La Follette, William Allen White, Frederic C. Howe, and Lincoln Steffens, among others—are frequently cited, because all of them recounted the purported awakening of their authors to the corrupt politico-business alliance.[1] Muckraking journalism, not only by Steffens but also by David Graham Phillips, Charles E. Russell, Ray Stannard Baker, and numerous others, is often drawn upon too, along with evidence that the magazines for which they wrote achieved unprecedented circulation. Political speeches, party platforms, and newspaper editorials by the hundreds are also offered to buttress the contention that Americans of the early 1900s discovered the prevalence of illicit business influence in politics and demanded its removal. But all of this evidence would probably fail to persuade historians today that the old textbook scenario for progressivism is correct.

And for good reason. Every prominent interpretation of the Progressive movement now encourages us not to take the outcry against politico-business corruption too seriously. Some historians have seen progressivism as dichotomous: alongside the individualist, antibusiness strain of reform stood an equally

An earlier version of this paper was read at the Seventy-Second Annual Meeting of the Organization of American Historians, held in New Orleans, April 1979. Arthur S. Link, Peyton McCrary, and David P. Thelen provided exceptionally helpful comments and suggestions on that occasion, and, in addition, I am grateful to several of my colleagues at Rutgers University for reading and commenting upon one or more drafts of the paper: Rudolph M. Bell, Paul G. E. Clemens, William L. O'Neill, Herbert H. Rowen, and Barbara M. Tucker.

[1] Although it is a common autobiographical convention to recount one's growth from ignorance to knowledge, it is nonetheless striking that so many progressive autobiographies should identify the same point of ignorance and trace a similar path to knowledge. See Roosevelt, *An Autobiography* (New York, 1913), 85–86, 186, 297–300, 306, 321–23; La Follette, *La Follette's Autobiography: A Personal Narrative of Political Experiences* (Madison, Wisc., 1960), 3–97; White, *The Autobiography of William Allen White* (New York, 1946), 149–50, 160–61, 177–79, 192–93, 215–16, 232–34, 325–26, 345, 351, 364, 428–29, 439–40, 465; Howe, *The Confessions of a Reformer* (New York, 1925), 70–72, 100–12; and Steffens, *The Autobiography of Lincoln Steffens* (New York, 1931), 357–627.

vocal, and ultimately more successful, school that accepted industrial growth and sought even closer cooperation between business and government.[2] Other recent interpreters have described progressivism as a pluralistic movement of diverse groups, including businessmen, who came together when their interests coincided and worked separately when they did not.[3] Still other historians have seen businessmen themselves as the key progressives, whose methods and techniques were copied by other reformers.[4] Whichever view of the movement they have favored, historians have increasingly recognized the Progressive era as the age when Americans accommodated, rather than tried to escape, large-scale business organizations and their methods.[5] More often than not, the achievement of what used to be called reform now appears to have benefited big business interests. If our aim is to grasp the results and meaning of progressivism, the evidence in the typical textbook seems to lead in the wrong direction.

The currently dominant "organizational" interpretation of the Progressive movement has particularly little room for such evidence. Led by Samuel P. Hays and Robert H. Wiebe, a number of scholars have located the progressive impulse in the drive of newly formed business and professional groups to achieve their goals through organization and expertise. In a related study, Louis Galambos has described the progressive outcry against the trusts as merely a phase in the nation's growing acceptance of large corporations, and, with Hays and Wiebe, he has suggested that the rhetorical attack on business came to very little. The distinctive achievement of this interpretation lies in its account of how in the early twentieth century the United States became an organized, bureaucratic society whose model institution was the large corporation. Where reformers of the 1880s and 1890s had sought to resist the forces of industrialism, or at least to prevent their penetration of the local community, the progressives of the early 1900s accepted an industrial society and concentrated their efforts on controlling, ordering, and improving it. No interpretation of the era based on ideological evidence of a battle between the "people" and the "interests" can capture the enormous complexity of the adjustments to industrialism worked out by different social groups. Hays and Wiebe have succeeded better than any previous historians in describing and characterizing those adjustments and placing them in the context of large social and economic changes. In this light the

[2] Richard Hofstadter, *The Age of Reform: From Bryan to F.D.R.* (New York, 1955), 133; George E. Mowry, *The Era of Theodore Roosevelt, 1900–1912* (New York, 1958), 55–58; John Braeman, "Seven Progressives," *Business History Review*, 35 (1961): 581–92; and Sheldon Hackney, *Populism to Progressivism in Alabama* (Princeton, 1969), xii–xiii, 329–30.

[3] John D. Buenker, "The Progressive Era: A Search for a Synthesis," *Mid-America*, 51 (1969): 175–93; David P. Thelen, "Social Tensions and the Origins of Progressivism," *Journal of American History* [hereafter, *JAH*], 56 (1969): 323–41; and Peter G. Filene, "An Obituary for 'The Progressive Movement,'" *American Quarterly*, 22 (1970): 20–34.

[4] Robert H. Wiebe, *Businessmen and Reform: A Study of the Progressive Movement* (Cambridge, Mass., 1962); Gabriel Kolko, *The Triumph of Conservatism: A Reinterpretation of American History, 1900–1916* (New York, 1963); and Samuel P. Hays, "The Politics of Reform in Municipal Government in the Progressive Era," *Pacific Northwest Quarterly*, 55 (1964): 157–69.

[5] Samuel P. Hays, *The Response to Industrialism, 1885–1914* (Chicago, 1957); Robert H. Wiebe, *The Search for Order, 1877–1920* (New York, 1967); Louis Galambos, *The Public Image of Big Business in America, 1880–1940: A Quantitative Study in Social Change* (Baltimore, 1975); William L. O'Neill, *The Progressive Years: America Comes of Age* (New York, 1975); and David P. Thelen, *Robert M. La Follette and the Insurgent Spirit* (Boston, 1976).

progressives' claims to have discovered and opposed the corruption of politics by business seem to become a curiosity of the era, not a clue to its meaning, a diversion to the serious historian exploring the organizational achievements that constituted true progressivism, a suitable subject for old textbooks.[6]

Despite its great strengths, however, the organizational model neglects too much.[7] Missing is the progressives' moral intensity. Missing, too, are their surprise and animation upon discovering political and social evils. Also absent are their own explanations of what they felt and what they were doing. And absent, above all, is a description, much less an analysis, of the particular political circumstances from which progressivism emerged in the first years of the twentieth century. In place of these vivid actualities, the organizational historians offer a vague account of what motivated the reformers who advocated bureaucratic solutions and an exaggerated estimation of their capacity to predict and control events. Actually, progressive reform was not characterized by remarkable rationality or foresight; nor were the "organizers" always at the forefront of the movement. Often the results the progressives achieved were unexpected and ironical; and, along the way, crucial roles were sometimes played by men and ideas that, in the end, met defeat.

The perception that privileged businesses corrupted politics was one such ultimately unsuccessful idea of particular short-run instrumentality. Especially in the cities and states, around the middle of the first decade of the twentieth century, the discovery of such corruption precipitated crises that led to the most significant political changes of the time. When the crises had passed, the results for political participation and public policy were roughly those that the organizational interpretation predicts, but the way these changes came about is far from adequately described by that thesis. The pages that follow here sketch an account of political change in the early twentieth century and show how the discovery of politico-business corruption played this central, transforming role—though not with quite the same results that the old textbooks describe.

---

[6] Louis Galambos provided a sympathetic introduction to the work of the "organizational" school; see his "The Emerging Organizational Synthesis in Modern American History," *Business History Review*, 44 (1970): 279–90. For another effort to place the work of these historians in perspective, see Robert H. Wiebe, "The Progressive Years, 1900–1917," in William H. Cartwright and Richard L. Watson, Jr., eds., *The Reinterpretation of American History and Culture* (Washington, 1973), 425–42. In addition to the works by Wiebe, Hays, and Galambos, already cited, several other studies by Hays also rank among the most important products of the organizational school: Samuel P. Hays, *Conservation and the Gospel of Efficiency: The Progressive Conservation Movement, 1890–1920* (Cambridge, Mass., 1959), "Political Parties and the Community-Society Continuum," in William Nisbet Chambers and Walter Dean Burnham, eds., *The American Party Systems: Stages of Political Development* (New York, 1967), 152–81, and "The New Organizational Society," in Jerry Israel, ed., *Building the Organizational Society: Essays on Associational Activities in Modern America* (New York, 1972), 1–15. Although Wiebe and Hays share the same broad interpretation of the period, their works make quite distinctive contributions, and there are certain matters on which they have disagreed. Some of Wiebe's most important insights concern the complex relationships between business and reform, while Hays has demonstrated particular originality on the subjects of urban politics and political parties. Concerning the middle classes, they have differing views: Wiebe has included the middle classes among the "organizers," while Hays has emphasized their persistent individualism. Compare Wiebe, *The Search for Order, 1877–1920*, chap. 5, and Hays, *The Response to Industrialism, 1885–1914*, chap. 4.

[7] For related comments on the organizational model's shortcomings, see William G. Anderson, "Progressivism: An Historiographical Essay," *History Teacher*, 6 (1973): 427–52; David M. Kennedy, "Overview: The Progressive Era," *Historian*, 37 (1975): 453–68; O'Neill, *The Progressive Years*, x, 45; and Morton Keller, *Affairs of State: Public Life in Late-Nineteenth-Century America* (Cambridge, Mass., 1977), 285–87.

Admittedly, to interpret progressivism on the basis of its political and governmental side is a more risky endeavor than it once was. Indeed, a major thrust of contemporary scholarship has been to subordinate the Progressive era's political achievements to the larger social and economic changes associated with what Wiebe has called "the process of America's modernization."[8] From such a perspective, "developments in politics" become, as John C. Burnham has observed, "mere epiphenomena of more basic forces and changes."[9] But what if political behavior fails to fit trends that the rest of society seems to be experiencing? What conclusions are to be drawn, for instance, from the observation that American political rhetoric was preoccupied with attacking corporations at precisely the moment in the early twentieth century when such businesses were becoming ascendant in economic and social life? One approach simply ignores the anomalous behavior or, at most, considers it spurious or deceptive. Another answer lies in the notions that American politics is fundamentally discontinuous with the rest of national life and that, as several political scientists have suggested, it has always retained a "premodern" character.[10] A better solution, however, rests upon a close study of the ways in which apparently anachronistic political events and the ideas they inspired became essential catalysts for "modernizing" developments. Studied in this manner, politics has more to tell us about progressivism than contemporary wisdom generally admits.

SHORTLY AFTER 1900, American politics and government experienced a decisive and rather rapid transformation that affected both the patterns of popular political involvement and the nature and functions of government itself. To be sure, the changes were not revolutionary, but, considering how relatively undevelopmental the political system of the United States has been, they are of considerable historical importance. The basic features of this political transformation can be easily described, but its causes and significance are somewhat more difficult to grasp.

One important category of change involved the manner and methods of popular participation in politics. For most of the nineteenth century, high rates of partisan voting—based on complex sectional, cultural, and communal influences—formed the American people's main means of political expression and involvement. Only in exceptional circumstances did most individuals or groups rely on nonelectoral methods of influencing the government. Indeed, almost no such means existed within the normal bounds of politics. After 1900, this structure of political participation changed. Voter turnout fell, and, even among those electors who remained active, pure and simple partisanship became less

---

[8] Wiebe, "The Progressive Years, 1900–1917," 429.

[9] John D. Buenker, John C. Burnham, and Robert M. Crunden, *Progressivism* (Cambridge, Mass., 1977), 4. For some disagreements among these three authors about how central politics was to progressivism, see *ibid.*, 107–29.

[10] Samuel P. Huntington, *Political Order in Changing Societies* (New Haven, 1968), 93–139; Walter Dean Burnham, *Critical Elections and the Mainsprings of American Politics* (New York, 1970), 175–93; and J. G. A. Pocock, *The Machiavellian Moment: Florentine Political Thought and the Atlantic Republican Tradition* (Princeton, 1975), 549.

pervasive. At approximately the same time, interest-group organizations of all sorts successfully forged permanent, nonelectoral means of influencing the government and its agencies. Only recently have historians begun to explore with care what caused these changes in the patterns of political participation and to delineate the redistribution of power that they entailed.[11]

American governance, too, went through a fundamental transition in the early 1900s. Wiebe has accurately described it as the emergence of "a government broadly and continuously involved in society's operations."[12] Both the institutions of government and the content of policy reflected the change. Where the legislature had been the dominant branch of government at every level, lawmakers now saw their power curtailed by an enlarged executive and, even more, by the creation of an essentially new branch of government composed of administrative boards and agencies. Where nineteenth-century policy had generally focused on distinct groups and locales (most characteristically through the distribution of resources and privileges to enterprising individuals and corporations), the government now began to take explicit account of clashing interests and to assume the responsibility for mitigating their conflicts through regulation, administration, and planning. In 1900, government did very little in the way of recognizing and adjusting group differences. Fifteen years later, innumerable policies committed officials to that formal purpose and provided the bureaucratic structures for achieving it.[13]

Most political historians consider these changes to be the products of long-term social and economic developments. Accordingly, they have devoted much of their attention to tracing the interconnecting paths leading from industrialization, urbanization, and immigration to the political and governmental responses. Some of the general trends have been firmly documented in scholarship: the organization of functional groups whose needs the established political parties could not meet; the creation of new demands for government policies to make life bearable in crowded cities, where huge industries were located; and the determination of certain cultural and economic groups to curtail the political power of people they considered threatening. All of these developments, along with others, occurred over a period of decades—now speeded, now slowed by depression, migration, prosperity, fortune, and the talents of individual men and women.

---

[11] I have elsewhere cited many of the sources on which these generalizations are based; see my "The Party Period and Public Policy: An Exploratory Hypothesis," *JAH*, 66 (1979): 279–98. On the decline in turnout and the increase in ticket-splitting, see Walter Dean Burnham, "The Changing Shape of the American Political Universe," *American Political Science Review* [hereafter, *APSR*], 59 (1965): 7–28. On the rise of interest-group organizations, see Hays, "Political Parties and the Community-Society Continuum." For two studies that make significant contributions to an understanding of how the political changes of the early twentieth century altered the power relationships among groups, see J. Morgan Kousser, *The Shaping of Southern Politics: Suffrage Restriction and the Establishment of the One-Party South, 1880–1910* (New Haven, 1974); and Carl V. Harris, *Political Power in Birmingham, 1871–1921* (Knoxville, 1977).

[12] Wiebe, *The Search for Order, 1877–1920*, 160.

[13] McCormick, "The Party Period and Public Policy"; Robert A. Lively, "The American System: A Review Article," *Business History Review*, 29 (1955): 81–96; James Willard Hurst, *Law and the Conditions of Freedom in the Nineteenth-Century United States* (Madison, Wisc., 1956); Theodore J. Lowi, "American Business, Public Policy, Case-Studies, and Political Theory," *World Politics*, 16 (1964): 677–715; and Wiebe, *The Search for Order, 1877–1920*, 159–95.

Yet, given the long-term forces involved, it is notable how suddenly the main elements of the new political order went into place. The first fifteen years of the twentieth century witnessed most of the changes; more precisely, the brief period from 1904 to 1908 saw a remarkably compressed political transformation. During these years the regulatory revolution peaked; new and powerful agencies of government came into being everywhere.[14] At the same time, voter turnout declined, ticket-splitting increased, and organized social, economic, and reform-minded groups began to exercise power more systematically than ever before.[15] An understanding of how the new polity crystalized so rapidly can be obtained by exploring, first, the latent threat to the old system represented by fears of "corruption"; then, the pressures for political change that had built up by about 1904; and, finally, the way in which the old fears abruptly took on new meaning and inspired a resolution of the crisis.

LONG BEFORE 1900—indeed, since before the Revolution—Americans had been aware that governmental promotion of private interests, which became the dominant form of nineteenth-century economic policy, carried with it risks of corruption. From the English opposition of Walpole's day, colonists in America had absorbed the theory that commercial development threatened republican government in two ways: (1) by spreading greed, extravagance, and luxury among the people; and (2) by encouraging a designing ministry to conspire with monied interests for the purpose of overwhelming the independence of the legislature. Neither theme ever entirely disappeared from American politics, although each was significantly revised as time passed. For Jeffersonians in the 1790s, as Lance Banning has demonstrated, both understandings remained substantially intact. In their belief, Alexander Hamilton's program of public aid to commercial enterprises would inevitably make an agrarian people less virtuous and would also create a phalanx of privileged interests—including bank directors, speculators, and stock-jobbers—pledged to support the administration faction that had nurtured them. Even after classical republican thought waned and the structure of government-business relations changed, these eighteenth-century fears that corruption inevitably flowed from government-assisted commercial development continued to echo in American politics.[16]

[14] James Willard Hurst, *Law and Social Order in the United States* (Ithaca, 1977), 33, 36, and *Law and the Conditions of Freedom*, 71–108; and Grover G. Huebner, "Five Years of Railroad Regulation by the States," *Annals of the American Academy of Political and Social Science*, 32 (1908): 138–56. For a further account of these governmental changes, see pages 267–69, 271–74, below.
    [15] Burnham, "The Changing Shape of the American Political Universe," and *Critical Elections and the Mainsprings of American Politics*, 71–90, 115; and Jerrold G. Rusk, "The Effect of the Australian Ballot Reform on Split-Ticket Voting, 1876–1908," *APSR*, 64 (1970): 1220–38. For a contemporary effort to estimate and assess split-ticket voting, see Philip Loring Allen, "Ballot Laws and Their Workings," *Political Science Quarterly*, 21 (1906): 38–58.
    [16] Banning, *The Jeffersonian Persuasion: Evolution of a Party Ideology* (Ithaca, 1978); J. G. A. Pocock, "Virtue and Commerce in the Eighteenth Century," *Journal of Interdisciplinary History*, 3 (1972): 119–34, and *The Machiavellian Moment*, 506–52; Gordon S. Wood, *The Creation of the American Republic, 1776–1787* (Chapel Hill, 1969), 32–33, 52, 64–65, 107–14, 400–03, 416–21; Morton Keller, "Corruption in America: Continuity and Change," in Abraham S. Eisenstadt *et al.*, eds., *Before Watergate: Problems of Corruption in American Society* (New York, 1979), 7–19; and Edwin G. Burrows, "Albert Gallatin and the Problem of Corruption in the Federalist Era," *ibid.*, 51–67.

For much of the nineteenth century, as Fred Somkin has shown, thoughtful citizens remained ambivalent about economic abundance, because they feared its potential to corrupt them and their government. "Over and over again," Somkin stated, "Americans called attention to the danger which prosperity posed for the safety of free institutions and for the maintenance of republicanism."[17] In the 1830s the Democratic Party's official ideology began to give voice to these fears. Using language similar to that of Walpole's and Hamilton's critics, Andrew Jackson decried "special privileges" from government as dangerous to liberty and demanded their abolition. Much of his wrath was directed against the Second Bank of the United States. That "monster," he said, was "a vast electioneering engine"; it has "already attempted to subject the government to its will." The Bank clearly raised the question of "whether the people of the United States are to govern . . . or whether the power and money of a great corporation are to be secretly exerted to influence their judgment and control their decisions." In a different context Jackson made the point with simple clarity: "Money," he said, "is power." Yet Jackson's anti-Bank rhetoric also carried a new understanding of politico-business corruption, different from that of the eighteenth century. For the danger that Jackson apprehended came not from a corrupt ministry, whose tool the monied interests were, but from privileged monsters, acting independently from public authorities and presenting a danger not only to the government but also to the welfare of other social and economic groups ("the farmers, mechanics, and laborers") whose interests conflicted with theirs. Jackson's remedy was to scale down governmental undertakings, on the grounds that public privileges led to both corruption and inequality.[18]

Despite the prestige that Jackson lent to the attack on privilege, it was not a predominant fear for Americans in the nineteenth century. So many forms of thought and avarice disguised the dangers Jackson saw. First of all, Americans were far from agreed that governmental assistance for some groups hurt the rest, as he proclaimed. Both the "commonwealth" notion of a harmonious community and its successor, the Whig-Republican concept of interlocking producer interests, suggested that economic benefits from government would be shared throughout society. Even when differences emerged over who should get what, an abundance of land and resources disguised the conflicts, while the inherent divisibility of public benefits encouraged their widespread distribution. Especially at the state and local levels, Democrats, as well as Whigs and Republicans, freely succumbed to the nearly universal desire for government aid. Not to have done so would have been as remarkable as to have withheld patronage

---

[17] Somkin, *Unquiet Eagle: Memory and Desire in the Idea of American Freedom, 1815–1860* (Ithaca, 1967), 24.

[18] [Jackson] *Annual Messages, Veto Messages, Protests, &c. of Andrew Jackson, President of the United States* (Baltimore, 1835), 162, 165, 179, 197, 244. Numerous studies document the Democratic Party's use of the accusation that privileged business was corrupting politics: Lee Benson, *The Concept of Jacksonian Democracy: New York as a Test Case* (Princeton, 1961), 52–56, 96–97, 236; William G. Shade, *Banks or No Banks: The Money Issue in Western Politics, 1832–1865* (Detroit, 1972), 56–59; Marvin Meyers, *The Jacksonian Persuasion: Politics and Belief* (Stanford, 1957), 23–24, 30, 157–58, 196, 198; and Edward K. Spann, *Ideals and Politics: New York Intellectuals and Liberal Democracy, 1820–1880* (Albany, N.Y., 1972), 60, 68–78, 105–06. President Martin Van Buren's special message to Congress proposing the subtreasury system in 1837 contained accusations against the Bank similar to those Jackson had made, except that Van Buren expressed them more in "pure," eighteenth-century republican language; James D. Richardson, ed., *A Compilation of the Messages and Papers of the Presidents, 1789–1897*, 10 vols. (Washington, 1896–99), 3: 324–46.

from deserving partisans.[19] Nor, in the second place, was it evident to most nineteenth-century Americans that private interests represented a threat to the commonweal. While their eighteenth-century republican heritage warned them of the danger to free government from a designing ministry that manipulated monied interests, classical economics denied that there was a comparable danger to the public from private enterprises that were independent of the government. Indeed, the public-private distinction tended to be blurred for nineteenth-century Americans, and not until it came into focus did new threats of politico-business corruption seem as real as the old ones had in the 1700s.[20]

As time passed, Jackson's Democratic Party proved to be a weak vehicle for the insight that privileged businesses corrupted politics and government. The party's platforms, which in the 1840s had declared a national bank "dangerous to our republican institutions," afterwards dropped such rhetoric. The party of Stephen A. Douglas, Samuel J. Tilden, and Glover Cleveland all but abandoned serious criticism of politico-business corruption. Cleveland's annual message of 1887, which he devoted wholly to the tariff issue, stands as the Gilded Age's equivalent to Jackson's Bank veto. But, unlike Jackson, Cleveland made his case entirely on economic grounds and did not suggest that the protected interests corrupted government. Nor did William Jennings Bryan pay much attention to the theme in 1896. Unlike his Populist supporters who charged that public officials had "basely surrendered . . . to corporate monopolies," the Democrat Bryan made only fleeting mention of the political influence of big corporations or the danger to liberty from privileged businesses.[21]

From outside the political mainstream, the danger was more visible. Workingmen's parties, Mugwumps, Greenbackers, Prohibitionists, and Populists all voiced their own versions of the accusation that business corrupted politics and government. The Greenbackers charged that the major parties were tools of the monopolies; the Prohibitionists believed that the liquor corporations endangered free institutions; and the Populists powerfully indicted both the Democrats and Republicans for truckling to the interests "to secure corruption funds from the millionaires." In *Progress and Poverty* (1879), Henry George asked, "Is there not growing up among us a class who have all the power . . . ? We have

[19] McCormick, "The Party Period and Public Policy," 286–88. On the "commonwealth" ideal, see Oscar Handlin and Mary Flug Handlin, *Commonwealth—A Study of the Role of Government in the American Economy: Massachusetts, 1774–1861* (New York, 1947); and Louis Hartz, *Economic Policy and Democratic Thought: Pennsylvania, 1776–1860* (Cambridge, Mass., 1948). For a classic expression of the Whig concept of interlocking producer interests, see Calvin Colton, ed., *The Works of Henry Clay, Comprising His Life, Correspondence, and Speeches*, 5 (New York, 1897): 437–86; and, for a later Republican expression of the same point of view, see Benjamin Harrison, *Speeches of Benjamin Harrison, Twenty-Third President of the United States* (New York, 1892), 62, 72, 157, 167, 181, 197. For a discussion of the Republican ideology and economic policy, see Eric Foner, *Free Soil, Free Labor, Free Men: The Ideology of the Republican Party before the Civil War* (New York, 1970), 18–23.

[20] Lively, "The American System," 94; Carter Goodrich, "The Revulsion against Internal Improvements," *Journal of Economic History*, 10 (1950): 169; and Hays, *The Response to Industrialism, 1885–1914*, 39–40. On the reluctance of state legislatures to prohibit their members from mixing public and private business, see Ari Hoogenboom, "Did Gilded Age Scandals Bring Reform?" in Eisenstadt *et al., Before Watergate*, 127–31.

[21] Compare the Democratic platforms of 1840–52 with those for the rest of the century; see Donald Bruce Johnson and Kirk H. Porter, eds., *National Party Platforms, 1840–1972* (Urbana, 1973); for the People's Party platform of 1896, see *ibid.*, 104. For Cleveland's message of 1887, see Richardson, *Messages and Papers of the Presidents, 1789–1897*, 8: 580–91; and, for a compilation of Bryan's speeches of 1896, see his *The First Battle: A Story of the Campaign of 1896* (Chicago, 1896).

simple citizens who control thousands of miles of railroad, millions of acres of land, the means of livelihood of great numbers of men; who name the governors of sovereign states as they name their clerks, choose senators as they choose attorneys, and whose will is as supreme with legislatures as that of a French king sitting in a bed of justice."[22] But these were the voices of dissenters and frail minorities. Their accusations of corruption posed a latent challenge to an economic policy based on distributing privileges to private interests, but for most of the nineteenth century their warnings were not widely accepted or even listened to by the political majority.

The late 1860s and early and mid-1870s, however, offer an apparent exception. These were the years when the Crédit Mobilier and other scandals—local and national—aroused a furor against politico-business corruption. "Perhaps the offense most discredited by the exposures," according to C. Vann Woodward, "was the corrupting of politicians to secure government subsidies and grants to big corporations—particularly railroads." For several years, in consequence, there was a widespread revulsion against a policy of bestowing public privileges and benefits on private companies. Editorializing in 1873 on the Crédit Mobilier scandal, E. L. Godkin of the *Nation* declared, "The remedy is simple. The Government must get out of the 'protective' business and the 'subsidy' business and the 'improvement' and the 'development' business. It must let trade, and commerce, and manufactures, and steamboats, and railroads, and telegraphs alone. It cannot touch them without breeding corruption." Yet even in the mid-1870s, by Woodward's own account, it was possible for railroad and other promoters, especially in the South and Midwest, to organize local meetings that rekindled the fervor for subsidies in town after town. The fear of corruption that Godkin voiced simply was not compelling enough to override the demand for policies of unchecked promotion.[23]

Even the nineteenth century's most brilliant and sustained analysis of business and politics—that provided by the Adams brothers, Charles Francis, Jr. and Henry, in their *Chapters of Erie* (1871)—failed to portray the danger convincingly. Recounting the classic Gilded Age roguery of Jay Gould and Jim Fisk, including their corruption of courts and legislatures and their influence on the president himself, the Adamses warned that, as Henry put it, "the day is at hand when corporations . . . —having created a system of quiet but irresistible corruption—will ultimately succeed in directing government itself." But the Adams brothers presented Gould and Fisk as so fantastic that readers could not believe that ordinary businessmen could accomplish such feats. Rather than de-

[22] Johnson and Porter, *National Party Platforms, 1840–1972*, 90; and George, *Progress and Poverty—An Inquiry into the Cause of Industrial Depressions and of Increase of Want with Increase of Wealth: The Remedy* (New York, 1880), 481. For examples of other late-nineteenth-century dissenters who recognized the corruption of politics and government by business interests, see H. R. Chamberlain, *The Farmers' Alliance: What It Aims to Accomplish* (New York, 1891), 12, 37–38; and Henry Demarest Lloyd, *Wealth against Commonwealth* (New York, 1894), 369–404.

[23] Woodward, *Reunion and Reaction: The Compromise of 1877 and the End of Reconstruction* (Boston, 1951), 65; and Godkin, "The Moral of the Crédit Mobilier Scandal," *Nation*, 16 (1873): 68. Also see Allan Nevins, *The Emergence of Modern America, 1865–1878* (New York, 1927), 178–202; and John G. Sproat, *"The Best Men": Liberal Reformers in the Gilded Age* (New York, 1968), 72–73. For the ebb and flow of public aid to private enterprise in this era, see Keller, *Affairs of State*, 162–96. For other expressions of Godkin's opinion, see the *Nation*, 16 (1873): 328–29, and 24 (1877): 82–83.

scribing a process of politico-business corruption, the Adamses gave only the dramatic particulars of it. Words like "astounding," "unique," and "extraordinary" marked their account. Writing of the effort by Gould and Fisk to corner the market on gold in 1869, Henry said, "Even the most dramatic of modern authors, even Balzac himself, . . . or Alexandre Dumas, with all his extravagance of imagination, never have reached a conception bolder or more melodramatic than this, nor have they ever ventured to conceive a plot so enormous, or a catastrophe so original." Far from supporting the Adamses' thesis, such descriptions must have undermined it by raising doubts that what Gould and Fisk did could be widely or systematically repeated.[24]

Expressed by third parties and by elite spokesmen like Godkin and the Adamses, the fear that business corrupted politics exerted only minor influence in the late nineteenth century. When they recognized corruption, ordinary people seem to have blamed "bad" politicians, like James G. Blaine, and to have considered the businessmen guiltless. Even when Americans saw that corruption involved the use of money, they showed more interest in how the money was spent—for example, to bribe voters—than in where it came from. Wanting governmental assistance for their enterprises, but only sporadically scrutinizing its political implications, most people probably failed to perceive what the Adamses saw.[25] Nor did they, until social and industrial developments created deep dissatisfaction with the existing policy process. Then, the discovery that privileged businesses corrupted politics played a vital, if short-lived, role in facilitating the momentous transition from the nineteenth-century polity to the one Americans fashioned at the beginning of the twentieth century.

BY THE 1890s, LARGE-SCALE INDUSTRIALIZATION was creating the felt need for new government policies in two distinct but related ways. The first process, which Hays and Wiebe have described so well, was the increasing organization of diverse producer groups, conscious of their own identities and special needs. Each demanded specific public protections for its own endeavors and questioned the allocation of benefits to others. The second development was less tangible: the unorganized public's dawning sense of vulnerability, unease, and anger in the face of economic changes wrought by big corporations. Sometimes, the people's inchoate feelings focused on the ill-understood "trusts"; at other times, their negative emotions found more specific, local targets in street-railway or electric-power companies. Older interpretations of progressivism gave too much weight to the second of these developments; recently, only a few historians have sufficiently recognized it.[26]

---

[24] Adams and Adams, *Chapters of Erie* (reprint ed., Ithaca, 1956), 136, 107. Originally published as articles during the late 1860s and early 1870s, these essays were first issued in book form in 1871 under the title *Chapters of Erie and Other Essays* (Boston).

[25] For the vivid expression of a similar point, see Wiebe, *The Search for Order, 1877–1920*, 28.

[26] Hays, *The Response to Industrialism, 1885–1914*; and Wiebe, *The Search for Order, 1877–1920*. On the fear and anger of the unorganized, see Hofstadter, *The Age of Reform*, 213–69; Irwin Unger and Debi Unger, *The Vulnerable Years: The United States, 1896–1917* (Hinsdale, Ill., 1977), 102–08; and David P. Thelen, *The New Citizenship: Origins of Progressivism in Wisconsin, 1885–1900* (Columbia, Mo., 1972).

Together, these processes created a political crisis by making people conscious of uncomfortable truths that earlier nineteenth-century conditions had obscured: that society's diverse producer groups did not exist in harmony or share equally in government benefits, and that private interests posed a danger to the public's interests. The crisis brought on by the recognition of these two problems extended approximately from the onset of depression in 1893 until 1908 and passed through three distinct phases: (1) the years of realignment, 1893–96; (2) the years of experimentation and uncertainty, 1897–1904; and (3) the years of discovery and resolution, 1905–08. When the crisis was over, the American political system was different in important respects from what it had been before.

During the first phase, the depression and the alleged radicalism of the Populists preoccupied politics and led to a decisive change in the national balance of party power. Willingly or unwillingly, many former voters now ceased to participate in politics, while others from almost every social group in the North and Midwest shifted their allegiance to the Republicans. As a result, that party established a national majority that endured until the 1930s. Yet, given how decisive the realignment of the 1890s was, it is striking how quickly the particular issues of 1896—tariff protection and free silver—faded and how little of long-standing importance the realignment resolved.[27] To be sure, the defeat of Bryan and the destruction of Populism established who would not have control of the process of accommodating the nation to industrial realities, but the election of 1896 did much less in determining who would be in charge or what the solutions would be.

In the aftermath of realignment, a subtler form of crisis took hold—although several happy circumstances partially hid it, both from people then and from historians since. The war with Spain boosted national pride and self-confidence; economic prosperity returned after the depression; and the Republican Party with its new majority gave the appearance of having doctrines that were relevant to industrial problems. Soon, President Theodore Roosevelt's activism and appeal helped foster an impression of political command over the economy. However disguised, the crisis nonetheless was real, and, in the years after 1896, many voices quietly questioned whether traditional politics and government could resolve interest-group conflicts or allay the sense of vulnerability that ordinary people felt.

Central to the issue were the dual problems of how powerful government should be and whether it ought to acknowledge and adjust group differences. Industrialism and its consequences seemed to demand strong public policies based on a recognition of social conflict. At the very least, privileged corporations had to be restrained, weaker elements in the community protected, and

---

[27] The three most important studies of the electoral realignment of the 1890s are Paul Kleppner, *The Cross of Culture: A Social Analysis of Midwestern Politics, 1850–1900* (New York, 1970); Richard Jensen, *The Winning of the Midwest: Social and Political Conflict, 1888–1896* (Chicago, 1971); and Samuel T. McSeveney, *The Politics of Depression: Political Behavior in the Northeast, 1893–1896* (New York, 1972). A number of studies associate the realignment with subsequent changes in government policy: Walter Dean Burnham *et al.*, "Partisan Realignment: A Systemic Perspective," in Joel H. Silbey *et al.*, eds., *The History of American Electoral Behavior* (Princeton, 1978), 45–77; and David W. Brady, "Critical Elections, Congressional Parties, and Clusters of Policy Changes," *British Journal of Political Science*, 8 (1978): 79–99.

regular means established for newer interest groups to participate in government. But the will, the energy, and the imagination to bring about these
changes seemed missing. Deeply felt ideological beliefs help explain this paralysis. The historic American commitment, on the one hand, to weak government,
local autonomy, and the preservation of individual liberties—reflected in the
doctrines of the Democratic Party—presented a strong barrier to any significant
expansion of governmental authority. The ingrained resistance, on the other
hand, to having the government acknowledge that the country's producing interests were not harmonious—voiced in the doctrines of the Republican Party—
presented an equally strong obstacle to the recognition and adjustment of group
differences.[28]

Weighted down by their doctrines as well as by an unwillingness to alienate
elements of their heterogeneous coalitions, both parties floundered in attempting to deal with these problems. The Democrats were merely more conspicuous
in failing than were the Republicans. Blatantly divided into two wings, neither
of which succeeded in coming to grips with the new issues, the Democrats bla-
zoned their perplexity by nominating Bryan for president for a second time in
1900, abandoning him for the conservative Alton B. Parker in 1904, and then
returning to the Great Commoner (who was having trouble deciding whether to
stand for nationalizing the railroads) in 1908. The Republicans, for their part,
were only a little less contradictory in moving from McKinley to Roosevelt to
Taft. Roosevelt, moreover, for all of the excitement he brought to the presidency
in 1901, veered wildly in his approach to the problems of big business during his
first term—from "publicity" to trust-busting to jawboning to conspiring with
the House of Morgan.[29]

While the national leaders wavered and confidence in the parties waned, a
good deal of experimenting went on in the cities and states—much of it haphazard and unsuccessful. Every large city found it difficult to obtain cheap and efficient utilities, equitable taxes, and the variety of public services required by an
expanding, hetereogeneous population. A few, notably Detroit and later Cleveland and New York, made adjustments during the last years of the nineteenth
and the first years of the twentieth centuries that other cities later copied: the
adoption of restrictions on utility and transportation franchises, the imposition
of new taxes on intangible personalty, and the inauguration of innovative municipal services. But most cities were less successful in aligning governance with
industrialism. Utility regulation was a particularly difficult problem. Franchise
"grabs" agreed to by city councilmen came under increasing attack, but the

[28] For a discussion of the major parties' ideological beliefs, see Robert Kelley, "Ideology and Political Culture from Jefferson to Nixon," *AHR*, 82 (1977): 531–62. And, for a brilliant account of the resistance to
change, see Keller, *Affairs of State.*

[29] On the Democratic Party's doctrinal floundering in these years, see J. Rogers Hollingsworth, *The Whirli-
gig of Politics: The Democracy of Cleveland and Bryan* (New York, 1963). For the Republican side of the story, see
Nathaniel W. Stephenson, *Nelson W. Aldrich: A Leader in American Politics* (New York, 1930); and John M.
Blum, *The Republican Roosevelt* (Cambridge, Mass., 1954). Roosevelt's doctrinal uncertainties can be traced in
his annual messages as president; see Hermann Hagedorn, ed., *The Works of Theodore Roosevelt*, memorial edition, 17 (New York, 1925): 93–641. For a recent treatment of these matters, see Lewis L. Gould, *Reform and
Regulation: American Politics, 1900–1916* (New York, 1978).

chaotic competition between divergent theories of regulation (home rule versus state supervision versus municipal ownership) caused the continuance of poor public policy.[30] In the states, too, the late 1890s and early 1900s were years of experimentation with various methods of regulation and administration. What Gerald D. Nash has found for California seems to have been true elsewhere as well: the state's railroad commission "floundered" in the late nineteenth century due to ignorance, inexperience, and a lack of both manpower and money. These were, Nash says, times of "trial and error." Antitrust policy also illuminates the uncertainty that was characteristic of the period before about 1905. By the turn of the century, two-thirds of the states had already passed antitrust laws, but in the great majority the provisions for enforcement were negligible. Some states simply preferred encouraging business to restraining it; others felt that the laxity of neighboring states and of the federal government made antitrust action futile; still others saw their enforcement policies frustrated by court decisions and administrative weaknesses. The result was unsuccessful policy—and a consequent failure to relieve the crisis that large-scale industrialization presented to nineteenth-century politics and government.[31]

In September 1899, that failure was searchingly probed at a conference on trusts held under the auspices of the Chicago Civic Federation. Attended by a broad spectrum of the country's political figures and economic thinkers, the meeting's four days of debates and speeches amply expressed the agitation, the uncertainty, and the discouragement engendered by the nation's search for solutions to the problems caused by large business combinations. In exploring whether and to what extent the government should regulate corporations and how to adjust social-group differences, the speakers addressed basic questions about the nineteenth-century American polity.[32] Following the conference, the search for answers continued unabated, for there was little consensus and considerable resistance to change. In the years immediately following, pressure to do *something* mounted. And roughly by the middle of the next decade, many of the elements were in place for a blaze of political innovation. The spark that finally served to ignite them was a series of disclosures reawakening and refashioning the old fear that privileged business corrupted politics and government.

THE EVIDENCE CONCERNING THESE DISCLOSURES is familiar to students of progressivism, but its meaning has not been fully explored. The period 1904–08 com-

---

[30] Melvin G. Holli, *Reform in Detroit: Hazen S. Pingree and Urban Politics* (New York, 1969); Martin J. Schiesl, *The Politics of Efficiency: Municipal Administration and Reform in America, 1880–1920* (Berkeley and Los Angeles, 1977); Mowry, *The Era of Theodore Roosevelt, 1900–1912*, 59–67; Thelen, *The New Citizenship*, 130–201; and David Nord, "The Experts versus the Experts: Conflicting Philosophies of Municipal Utility Regulation in the Progressive Era," *Wisconsin Magazine of History*, 58 (1975): 219–36.

[31] Nash, "The California Railroad Commission, 1876–1911," *Southern California Quarterly*, 44 (1962): 293, 303; Harry L. Purdy *et al.*, *Corporate Concentration and Public Policy* (2d ed., New York, 1950), 317–22; Hans B. Thorelli, *The Federal Antitrust Policy: Origination of an American Tradition* (Baltimore, 1955), 155–56, 265, 352–55, 607; and William Letwin, *Law and Economic Policy in America: The Evolution of the Sherman Antitrust Act* (New York, 1965), 182–247.

[32] Civic Federation of Chicago, *Chicago Conference on Trusts* (Chicago, 1900).

prised the muckraking years, not only in national magazines but also in local newspapers and legislative halls across the country. During 1905 and 1906 in particular, a remarkable number of cities and states experienced wrenching moments of discovery that led directly to significant political changes. Usually, a scandal, an investigation, an intraparty battle, or a particularly divisive election campaign exposed an illicit alliance of politics and business and made corruption apparent to the community, affecting party rhetoric, popular expectations, electoral behavior, and government policies.[33]

Just before it exploded in city and state affairs, business corruption of politics had already emerged as a leading theme of the new magazine journalism created by the muckrakers. Their primary contribution was to give a national audience the first systematic accounts of how modern American society operated. In so doing, journalists like Steffens, Baker, Russell, and Phillips created insights and pioneered ways of describing social and political relationships that crucially affected how people saw things in their home towns and states. Since so many of the muckrakers' articles identified the widespread tendency for privilege-seeking businessmen to bribe legislators, conspire with party leaders, and control nominations, an awareness of such corruption soon entered local politics. Indeed, many of the muckraking articles concerned particular locales—including Steffens's early series on the cities (1902–03); his subsequent exposures of Missouri, Illinois, Wisconsin, Rhode Island, New Jersey, and Ohio (1904–05); Rudolph Blankenburg's articles on Pennsylvania (1905); and C. P. Connolly's treatment of Montana (1906). All of these accounts featured descriptions of politico-business corruption, as did many of the contemporaneous exposures of individual industries, such as oil, railroads, and meat-packing. Almost immediately after this literature began to flourish, citizens across the country discovered local examples of the same corrupt behavior that Steffens and the others had described elsewhere.[34]

In New York, the occasion was the 1905 legislative investigation of the life insurance industry. One by one, insurance executives and Republican politicians took the witness stand and were compelled to bare the details of their corrupt relations. The companies received legislative protection, and the Republicans got bribes and campaign funds. In California, the graft trials of San Francisco city officials, beginning in 1906, threw light on the illicit cooperation between

---

[33] For other analyses that indicate the importance of the year 1906 in state politics around the country, see Richard M. Abrams, *Conservatism in a Progressive Era: Massachusetts Politics, 1900–1912* (Cambridge, Mass., 1964), 131; and Dewey W. Grantham, Jr., "The Progressive Era and the Reform Tradition," *Mid-America*, 46 (1964): 233–35.

[34] The fullest treatment of the muckrakers is still Louis Filler's *The Muckrakers*, a new and enlarged edition of his *Crusaders for American Liberalism* (University Park, Pa., 1976). Filler's chronology provides a convenient list of the major muckraking articles; *ibid.*, 417–24. Steffens's initial series on the cities was published as *The Shame of the Cities* (New York, 1904). His subsequent articles on the states appeared in *McClure's Magazine* between April 1904 and July 1905; these essays were later published as *The Struggle for Self-Government* (New York, 1906). Blankenburg's articles on Pennsylvania appeared in *The Arena* between January and June 1905; Connolly's "The Story of Montana" was published in *McClure's Magazine* between August and December 1906. Other major magazine articles probing politico-business corruption include "The Confessions of a Commercial Senator," *World's Work*, April–May 1905; Charles Edward Russell, "The Greatest Trust in the World" [the meat-packing industry], *Everybody's Magazine*, 1905; and David Graham Phillips, "The Treason of the Senate," *Cosmopolitan Magazine*, 1906.

businessmen and public officials. Boss Abraham Ruef had delivered special privileges to public utility corporations in return for fees, of which he kept some and used the rest to bribe members of the city's Board of Supervisors. San Francisco's awakening revitalized reform elsewhere in California, and the next year insurgent Republicans formally organized to combat their party's alliance with the Southern Pacific Railroad. In Vermont, the railroad commissioners charged the 1906 legislature with yielding "supinely to the unfortunate influence of railroad representatives." Then the legislature investigated and found that the commissioners themselves were corrupt![35]

Other states, in all parts of the country, experienced their own versions of these events during 1905 and 1906. In South Dakota, as in a number of Midwestern states, hostility to railroad influence in politics—by means of free passes and a statewide network of paid henchmen—was the issue around which insurgent Republicans coalesced against the regular machine. Some of those who joined the opposition did so purely from expediency; but their charges of corruption excited the popular imagination, and they captured the state in 1906 with pledges of electoral reform and business regulation. Farther west Denver's major utilities, including the Denver Tramway Company and the Denver Gas and Electric Company, applied for new franchises in 1906, and these applications went before the voters at the spring elections. When the franchises all narrowly carried, opponents of the companies produced evidence that the Democratic and Republican Parties had obtained fraudulent votes for the utilities. The case made its way through the courts during the next several months, and, although they ultimately lost, Colorado's nascent progressives derived an immense boost from the well-publicized judicial battle. As a result, the focus of reform shifted to the state. Dissidents in the Republican Party organized to demand direct primary nominations and a judiciary untainted by corporate influence. These questions dominated Colorado's three-way gubernatorial election that fall.[36]

To the south, in Alabama, Georgia, and Mississippi, similar accusations of politico-business corruption were heard that same year, only in a different regional accent. In Alabama, Braxton Bragg Comer rode the issue from his position on the state's railroad commission to the governorship. His "main theme," according to Sheldon Hackney, "was that the railroads had for years deprived the people of Alabama of their right to rule their own state and that the time had come to free the people from alien and arbitrary rule." Mississippi voters heard similar rhetoric from Governor James K. Vardaman in his unsuccessful campaign against John Sharp Williams for a seat in the U. S. Senate. Georgia's

[35] Robert F. Wesser, *Charles Evans Hughes: Politics and Reform in New York, 1905–1910* (Ithaca, 1967), 18–69; Richard L. McCormick, *From Realignment to Reform: Political Change in New York State, 1893–1910* (Ithaca, 1981), chap. 7; George E. Mowry, *The California Progressives* (Berkeley and Los Angeles, 1951), 23–85; Spencer C. Olin, Jr., *California's Prodigal Sons: Hiram Johnson and the Progressives, 1911–1917* (Berkeley and Los Angeles, 1968), 1–19 ; Winston Allen Flint, *The Progressive Movement in Vermont* (Washington, 1941), 42–51; and the *Tenth Biennial Report of the Board of Railroad Commissioners of the State of Vermont* (Bradford, Vt., 1906), 25.

[36] Herbert S. Schell, *History of South Dakota* (Lincoln, Neb., 1961), 258–61; Fred Greenbaum, "The Colorado Progressives in 1906," *Arizona and the West*, 7 (1965):21–32; and Carl Abbott, *Colorado: A History of the Centennial State* (Boulder, 1976), 203–06.

Tom Watson conjured up some inane but effective imagery to illustrate how Vardaman's opponent would serve the business interests: "If the Hon. John Sharp Williams should win out in the fight with Governor Vardaman, the corporations would have just one more doodle-bug in the United States Senate. Every time that a Railroad lobbyist stopped over the hole and called 'Doodle, Doodle, Doodle'—soft and slow—the sand at the little end of the funnel would be seen to stir, and then the little head of J. Sharp would pop up." In Watson's own state, Hoke Smith trumpeted the issue, too, in 1905 and 1906.[37]

New Hampshire, Rhode Island, New Jersey, Pennsylvania, Ohio, Indiana, North Dakota, Nebraska, Texas, and Montana, among other states, also had their muckraking moments during these same years. Although the details varied from place to place, there were three basic routes by which the issue of politico-business corruption entered state politics. In some states, including New York, Colorado, and California, a legislative investigation or judicial proceeding captured attention by uncovering a fresh scandal or by unexpectedly focusing public attention on a recognized political sore. Elsewhere, as in New Hampshire, South Dakota, and Kansas, a factional battle in the dominant Republican Party inspired dissidents to drag their opponents' misdeeds into public view; in several Southern states, the Democrats divided in similar fashion, and each side told tales of the other's corruption by business interests. Finally, city politics often became a vehicle for spreading the issue of a politico-business alliance to the state. Philadelphia, Jersey City, Cincinnati, Denver, and San Francisco all played the role of inspiring state reform movements based on this issue. Some states took more than one of these three routes; and the politicians and reformers in a few states simply echoed what their counterparts elsewhere were saying without having any outstanding local stimulus for doing so. This pattern is, of course, not perfect. In Wisconsin and Oregon, the discovery of politico-business corruption came earlier than 1905–06; in Virginia its arrival engendered almost no popular excitement, while it scarcely got to Massachusetts at all.[38]

An anonymous Kansan, whose state became aware of business domination of

---

[37] Hackney, *Populism to Progressivism in Alabama*, 257; Watson's *Weekly Jeffersonian*, July 25, 1907, as quoted in William F. Holmes, *The White Chief: James Kimble Vardaman* (Baton Rouge, 1970), 184; Dewey W. Grantham, Jr., *Hoke Smith and the Politics of the New South* (Baton Rouge, 1958), 131–46; and C. Vann Woodward, *Origins of the New South, 1877–1913* (Baton Rouge, 1951), 369–95.

[38] Geoffrey Blodgett, "Winston Churchill: The Novelist as Reformer," *New England Quarterly*, 47 (1974): 495–517; Thomas Agan, "The New Hampshire Progressives: Who and What Were They?" *Historical New Hampshire*, 34 (1979): 32–53; Charles Carroll, *Rhode Island: Three Centuries of Democracy*, 2 (New York, 1932): 676–78; Erwin L. Levine, *Theodore Francis Green: The Rhode Island Years, 1906–36* (Providence, 1963), 1–19; Arthur S. Link, *Wilson: The Road to the White House* (Princeton, 1947), 133–40; Ransom E. Noble, Jr., *New Jersey Progressivism before Wilson* (Princeton, 1946), 24–81; Eugene M. Tobin, "The Progressive as Politician: Jersey City, 1896–1907," *New Jersey History*, 91 (1973): 5–23; Lloyd M. Abernethy, "Insurgency in Philadelphia, 1905," *Pennsylvania Magazine of History and Biography*, 87 (1963): 3–20; Hoyt Landon Warner, *Progressivism in Ohio, 1897–1917* (Columbus, 1964), 143–210; Clifton J. Phillips, *Indiana in Transition: The Emergence of an Industrial Commonwealth, 1880–1920* (Indianapolis, 1968), 93–100; Charles N. Glaab, "The Failure of North Dakota Progressivism," *Mid-America*, 39 (1957): 195–209; James C. Olson, *History of Nebraska* (Lincoln, Neb., 1955), 250–53; Alwyn Barr, *Reconstruction to Reform: Texas Politics, 1876–1906* (Austin, 1971), 229–42; Michael P. Malone and Richard B. Roeder, *Montana: A History of Two Centuries* (Seattle, 1976), 229–42; Robert S. Maxwell, *La Follette and the Rise of the Progressives in Wisconsin* (Madison, Wisc., 1956); Herbert F. Margulies, *The Decline of the Progressive Movement in Wisconsin, 1890–1920* (Madison, Wisc., 1968); Raymond H. Pulley, *Old Virginia Restored: An Interpretation of the Progressive Impulse, 1870–1930* (Charlottesville, 1968); and Abrams, *Conservatism in a Progressive Era*.

its politics and government in 1905 and 1906, later gave a description of the discovery that also illuminates what happened elsewhere. When he first entered politics in the 1890s, the Kansan recalled, "three great railroad systems governed" the state. "This was a matter of common knowledge, but nobody objected or was in any way outraged by it." Then "an awakening began" during Roosevelt's first term as president, due to his "hammering on the square deal" and to a growing resentement of discriminatory railroad rates. Finally, after the railroads succeeded in using their political influence to block rate reform, "it began to dawn upon me," the Kansan reported, "that the railway contributions to campaign funds were part of the general game. . . . I saw they were in politics so that they could run things as they pleased." He and his fellow citizens had "really been converted," he declared. "We have got our eyes open now. . . . We have seen that the old sort of politics was used to promote all sorts of private ends, and we have got the idea now that the new politics can be used to promote the general welfare."[39]

State party platforms provide further evidence of the awakening to politico-business corruption. In Iowa, to take a Midwestern state, charges of corporation influence in politics were almost entirely confined to the minor parties during the years from 1900 to 1904. Prohibitionists believed that the liquor industry brought political corruption, while socialists felt that the powers of government belonged to the capitalists. For their part, the Democrats and Republicans saw little of this—until 1906, when both major parties gushed in opposition to what the Republicans now called "the domination of corporate influences in public affairs." The Democrats agreed: "We favor the complete elimination of railway and other public service corporations from the politics of the state." In Missouri, a different but parallel pattern emerges from the platforms. There, what had been a subordinate theme of the Democratic Party (and minor parties) in 1900 and 1902 became of central importance to both parties in 1904 and 1906. The Democrats now called "the eradication of bribery" the "paramount issue" in the state and declared opposition to campaign contributions "by great corporations and by those interested in special industries enjoying special privileges under the law." In New Hampshire, where nothing had been said of politico-business corruption in 1900 and 1904, both major parties wrote platforms in 1906 that attacked the issuance of free transportation passes and the prevalence of corrupt legislative lobbies. Party platforms in other states also suggest how suddenly major-party politicians discovered that business corrupted politics.[40]

[39] "How I Was Converted—Politically: By a Kansas Progressive Republican," *Outlook*, 96 (1910): 857–59. Also see Robert Sherman La Forte, *Leaders of Reform: Progressive Republicans in Kansas, 1900–1916* (Lawrence, Kansas, 1974), 13–88.

[40] *The Iowa Official Register for the Years 1907–1908* (Des Moines, 1907), 389, 393; *Official Manual of the State of Missouri for the Years 1905–1906* (Jefferson City, Mo., 1905), 254; and *Official Manual of the State of Missouri for the Years 1907–1908* (Jefferson City, Mo., 1907), 365. Also see State of New Hampshire, *Manual for the General Court, 1907* (Concord, N.H., 1907), 61–63. State party platforms for the early 1900s are surprisingly hard to locate. For some states, particularly in the Northeast and Midwest, the platforms were printed in the annual legislative manuals and blue books, but otherwise they must be found in newspapers. Of the ten states—Iowa, Missouri, New Hampshire, New York, New Jersey, Indiana, Pennsylvania, Illinois, Wisconsin, and South Dakota—for which I was able to survey the party platforms of 1900–10 fairly completely (using the manuals,

The annual messages of the state governors from 1902 to 1908 point to the same pattern. In the first three years, the chief executives almost never mentioned the influence of business in politics. Albert Cummins of Iowa was exceptional; as early as 1902 he declared, "Corporations have, and ought to have, many privileges, but among them is not the privilege to sit in political conventions or occupy seats in legislative chambers." Then in 1905, governors across the Midwest suddenly let loose denunciations of corporate bribery, lobbying, campaign contributions, and free passes. Nebraska's John H. Mickey was typical in attacking "the onslaught of private and corporation lobbyists who seek to accomplish pernicious ends by the exercise of undue influence." Missouri's Joseph W. Folk advised that "all franchises, rights and privileges secured by bribery should be declared null and void." By 1906, 1907, and 1908, such observations and recommendations were common to the governors of every region. In 1907 alone, no less than nineteen state executives called for the regulation of lobbying, while a similar number advised the abolition of free passes.[41]

WHAT IS THE MEANING OF THIS AWAKENING to something that Americans had, in a sense, known about all along? Should we accept the originality of the "discovery" that monied interests endangered free government or lay stress instead on the familiar elements the charge contained? It had, after all, been a part of American political thought since the eighteenth century and had been powerfully repeated, in one form or another, by major and minor figures throughout the nineteenth century. According to Richard Hofstadter, "there was nothing new in the awareness of these things."[42] In fact, however, there was much that was new. First, many of the details of politico-business corruption had never been publicly revealed before. No one had ever probed the subject as thoroughly as journalists and legislative investigators were now doing, and, moreover, some of the practices they uncovered had only recently come into being. Large-scale corporation campaign contributions, for instance, were a product of the 1880s and 1890s. Highly organized legislative lobbying operations by competing interest groups represented an even more recent development. In his systematic study of American legislative practices, published in 1907, Paul S. Reinsch devoted a lengthy chapter to describing how business interests had developed a new and "far more efficient system of dealing with legislatures than [the old methods of] haphazard corruption."[43]

---

supplemented when necessary by newspapers), only two fail to support the generalization given here: Wisconsin, where an awareness of politico-business corruption was demonstrated in the platforms of 1900 and 1902 as well as those of later years; and New Jersey, where the Democrats used the issue sparingly in 1901 and 1904, while the Republicans almost completely ignored it throughout the decade.

[41] New York State Library, *Digest of Governors' Messages* (Albany, N. Y., 1903–09). This annual document, published for the years 1902–08, classifies the contents of the governors' messages by subject and permits easy comparison among them. For Mickey's and Folk's denunciations, see New York State Library, *Digest of Governors' Messages, 1905*, classifications 99 (legislative lobbying), 96 (legislative bribery).

[42] Hofstadter, *The Age of Reform*, 185.

[43] Reinsch, *American Legislatures and Legislative Methods* (New York, 1907), 231. On the history of party campaign funds, see James K. Pollock, Jr., *Party Campaign Funds* (New York, 1926); Earl R. Sikes, *State and Federal Corrupt-Practices Legislation* (Durham, N.C., 1928); and Louise Overacker, *Money in Elections* (New York, 1932).

Even more startling than the new practices themselves was the fresh meaning they acquired from the nationwide character of the patterns that were now disclosed. The point is not simply that more people than ever before became aware of politico-business corruption but that the perception of such a national pattern itself created new political understandings. Lincoln Steffens's autobiography is brilliant on this point. As Steffens acknowledged, much of the corruption he observed in his series on the "shame" of the cities had already come to light locally before he reported it to a national audience. What he did was take the facts in city after city, apply imagination to their transcription, and form a new truth by showing the same process at work everywhere. Here was a solution to the problem the Adams brothers had encountered in writing *Chapters of Erie*: how to report shocking corruption without making it seem too astounding to be representative. The solution was breadth of coverage. Instead of looking at only two businessmen, study dozens; explore city after city and state after state and report the facts to a people who were vaguely aware of corruption in their own home towns but had never before seen that a single process was at work across the country.[44] This concept of a "process" of corruption was central to the new understanding. Uncovered through systematic journalistic research and probing legislative investigations, corruption was now seen to be the result of concrete historical developments. It could not just be dismissed as the product of misbehavior by "bad" men (although that kind of rhetoric continued too) but had to be regarded as an outcome of identifiable economic and political forces. In particular, corruption resulted from an outmoded policy of indiscriminate distribution, which could not safely withstand an onslaught of demands from private corporations that were larger than the government itself.[45]

Thus in its systematic character, as well as in its particular details, the corruption that Americans discovered in 1905 and 1906 was different from the kind their eighteenth- and nineteenth-century forebears had known. Compared to the eighteenth-century republican understanding, the progressive concept of corruption regarded the monied interests not as tools of a designing administration but as independent agents. If any branch of government was in alliance with them, it was probably the legislature. In a curious way, however, the old republican view that commerce inherently threatened the people's virtue still persisted, now informed by a new understanding of the actual process at work. Compared to Andrew Jackson, the progressives saw big corporations not as monsters but as products of social and industrial development. And their activist remedies differed entirely from his negativistic ones. But, like Jackson, those

---

[44] Steffens later commented insightfully on his own (and, by implication, the country's) process of "discovery" during these years; see his *Autobiography*, 357–627. Also see his *Shame of the Cities*, 3–26; and Filler, *The Muckrakers*, 257–59.

[45] Around 1905 a social-science literature emerged that attempted to explain the process of corruption and to suggest suitable remedies. In addition to Reinsch's *American Legislatures and Legislative Methods*, see Frederic C. Howe, *The City: The Hope of Democracy* (New York, 1905), and *Privilege and Democracy in America* (New York, 1910); and Robert C. Brooks, *Corruption in American Politics and Life* (New York, 1910). Several less scholarly works also analyze the cause of politico-business corruption; see, for example, George W. Berge, *The Free Pass Bribery System* (Lincoln, Neb., 1905); Philip Loring Allen, *America's Awakening: The Triumph of Righteousness in High Places* (New York, 1906); and William Allen White, *The Old Order Changeth: A View of American Democracy* (New York, 1910).

TABLE 1

Selected Categories of State Legislation, 1903–08

Type of Legislation	1903–04	1905–06	1907–08	1903–08
Regulation of Lobbying	0	2	10	12
Prohibition of Corporate Campaign Contributions	0	3	19	22
Regulation or Prohibition of Free Railroad Passes for Public Officials	4	6	14	24
Mandatory Direct Primary	4	9	18	31
Regulation of Railroad Corporations by Commission	5	8	28	41
TOTALS	13	28	89	130

NOTE: Figures represent the number of states that passed legislation in the given category during the specified years.

SOURCE: New York State Library, *Index of Legislation* (Albany, N.Y., 1904–09).

who now discovered corruption grasped that private interests could conflict with the public interest and that government benefits for some groups often hurt others. The recognition of these two things—both painfully at odds with the nineteenth century's conventional wisdom—had been at the root of the floundering over principles of political economy in the 1890s and early 1900s. Now, rather suddenly, the discovery that business corrupts politics suggested concrete answers to a people who were ready for new policies but had been uncertain how to get them or what exactly they should be.

Enacted in a burst of legislative activity immediately following the awakening of 1905 and 1906, the new policies brought to an end the paralysis that had gripped the polity and constituted a decisive break with nineteenth-century patterns of governance. Many states passed laws explicitly designed to curtail illicit business influence in politics. These included measures regulating legislative lobbying, prohibiting corporate campaign contributions, and outlawing the acceptance of free transportation passes by public officials. In 1903 and 1904, there had been almost no legislation on these three subjects; during 1905 and 1906, several states acted on each question; and, by 1907 and 1908, ten states passed lobbying laws, nineteen took steps to prevent corporate contributions, and fourteen acted on the question of passes (see Table 1). If these laws failed to wipe out corporation influence in politics, they at least curtailed important means through which businesses had exercised political power in the late nineteenth and early twentieth centuries. To be sure, other means were soon found, but the flood of state lawmaking on these subjects, together with the corresponding attention they received from the federal government in these same years, shows how prevalent was the determination to abolish existing forms of politico-business corruption.[46]

Closely associated with these three measures were two more important categories of legislation, often considered to represent the essence of progressivism in the states: mandatory direct primary laws and measures establishing or strengthening the regulation of utility and transportation corporations by commission. These types of legislation, too, reached a peak in the years just after 1905–06, when so many states had experienced a crisis disclosing the extent of politico-business corruption. Like the laws concerning lobbying, contributions, and passes, primary and regulatory measures were brought forth amidst intense public concern with business influence in politics and were presented by their advocates as remedies for that problem. Both types of laws had been talked about for years, but the disclosures of 1905–06 provided the catalyst for their enactment.

Even before 1905, the direct primary had already been adopted in some states. In Wisconsin, where it was approved in 1904, Robert M. La Follette had campaigned for direct nominations since the late 1890s on the grounds that they would "emancipate the legislature from all subserviency to the corporations." In his well-known speech, "The Menace of the Machine" (1897), La Follette explicitly offered the direct primary as "the remedy" for corporate control of politics. Now, after the awakening of 1905–06, that same argument inspired many states that had failed to act before to adopt mandatory direct primary laws (see Table 1). In New York, Charles Evans Hughes, who was elected governor in 1906 because of his role as chief counsel in the previous year's life insurance investigation, argued that the direct primary would curtail the power of the special interests. "Those interests," he declared, "are ever at work stealthily and persistently endeavoring to pervert the government to the service of their own ends. All that is worst in our public life finds its readiest means of access to power through the control of the nominating machinery of parties." In other states, too, in the years after 1905–06, the direct primary was urged and approved for the same reasons that La Follette and Hughes advanced it.[47]

---

[46] The figures in this paragraph (and in the accompanying table) are based on an analysis of the yearly summaries of state legislation reported in New York State Library, *Index of Legislation* (Albany, N.Y., 1904–09). The laws included here are drawn from among those classified in categories 99 (lobbying), 154 (corporate campaign contributions), 1237 (free passes), 160 (direct nominations), and 1267, 1286 (transportation regulation). The legislative years are paired because so many state legislatures met only biennially, usually in the odd-numbered years; no state is counted more than once in any one category in any pair of years. The *Index of Legislation* should be used in conjunction with the accompanying annual *Review of Legislation* (Albany, N. Y., 1904–09).

[47] Ellen Torelle, comp., *The Political Philosophy of Robert M. La Follette* (Madison, Wisc., 1920), 28; and Hughes, *Public Papers of Charles E. Hughes, Governor, 1909* (Albany, 1910), 37. Also see Maxwell, *La Follette and the Rise of the Progressives*, 13, 27–35, 48–50, 53–54, 74; Allen Fraser Lovejoy, *La Follette and the Establishment of the Direct Primary in Wisconsin, 1890–1904* (New Haven, 1941); Wesser, *Charles Evans Hughes*, 250–301; Direct Primaries Association of the State of New York, *Direct Primary Nominations: Why Voters Demand Them. Why Bosses Oppose Them* (New York, 1909); Ralph Simpson Boots, *The Direct Primary in New Jersey* (New York, 1917), 59–70; Grantham, *Hoke Smith and the Politics of the New South*, 158, 162, 172–73, 178, 193; Schell, *History of South Dakota*, 260; Olin, *California's Prodigal Sons*, 13; and Charles Edward Merriam and Louise Overacker, *Primary Elections* (Chicago, 1928), 4–7, 60–66.

The creation of effective regulatory boards—progressivism's most distinctive governmental achievement—also followed upon the discovery of politico-business corruption. From 1905 to 1907 alone, fifteen new state railroad commissions were established, and at least as many existing boards were strengthened. Most of the new commissions were "strong" ones, having rate-setting powers and a wide range of administrative authority to supervise service, safety, and finance. In the years to come, many of them extended their jurisdiction to other public utilities, including gas, electricity, telephones, and telegraphs. Direct legislative supervision of business corporations was also significantly expanded in these years. Life insurance companies—whose corruption of the New York State government Hughes had dramatically disclosed—provide one example. "In 1907," as a result of Hughes's investigation and several others conducted in imitation of it, Morton Keller has reported, "forty-two state legislatures met; thirty considered life insurance legislation; twenty-nine passed laws.... By 1908 ... [the basic] lines of twentieth century life insurance supervision were set, and thereafter only minor adjustments occurred." The federal regulatory machinery, too, was greatly strengthened at this time, most notably by the railroad, meat inspection, and food and drug acts of 1906.[48]

The adoption of these measures marked the moment of transition from a structure of economic policy based largely on the allocation of resources and benefits to one in which regulation and administration played permanent and significant roles. Not confined for long to the transportation, utility, and insurance companies that formed its most immediate objects, regulatory policies soon were extended to other industries as well. Sometimes the legislative branch took responsibility for the ongoing tasks of supervision and administration, but more commonly they became the duty of independent boards and commissions, staffed by experts and entrusted with significant powers of oversight and enforcement. Certainly, regulation was not previously unknown, nor did promoting commerce and industry now cease to be a governmental purpose. But the middle years of the first decade of the twentieth century unmistakably mark a turning point—that point when the direction shifted, when the weight of opinion changed, when the forces of localism and opposition to governmental authority that had sustained the distribution of privileges but opposed regulation and administration now lost the upper hand to the forces of centralization, bureaucratization, and government actions to recognize and adjust group differences. Besides economic regulation, other governmental policy areas, including health, education, taxation, correction, and the control of natural resources, increasingly came under the jurisdiction of independent boards and commissions. The establishment of these agencies and the expansion of their duties meant

---

[48] Huebner, "Five Years of Railroad Regulation by the States"; Robert Emmett Ireton, "The Legislatures and the Railroads," *Review of Reviews*, 36 (1907): 217–20; and Keller, *The Life Insurance Enterprise, 1885–1910: A Study in the Limits of Corporate Power* (Cambridge, Mass., 1963), 257, 259. The manner in which the states copied each other's legislation in this period is a subject deserving of study; for a suggestive approach, see Jack L. Walker, "The Diffusion of Innovations among the American States," *APSR*, 63 (1969): 880–99.

that American governance in the twentieth century was significantly different from what it had been in the nineteenth.[49]

The developments of 1905–08 also changed the nature of political participation in the United States. Parties emerged from the years of turmoil altered and, on balance, less important vehicles of popular expression than they had been. The disclosures of politico-business wrongdoing disgraced the regular party organizations, and many voters showed their loss of faith by staying at home on election day or by casting split tickets. These trends had been in progress before 1905–06—encouraged by new election laws as well as by the crisis of confidence in traditional politics and government—but in several ways the discovery of corruption strengthened them. Some reigning party organizations were toppled by the disclosures, and the insurgents who came to power lacked the old bosses' experience and inclination when it came to rallying the electorate. And the legal prohibition of corporate campaign contributions now meant, moreover, that less money was available for pre-election entertainment, transportation to the polls, and bribes.[50]

While the party organizations were thus weakened, they were also more firmly embedded in the legal machinery of elections than ever before. In many states the direct primary completed a series of new election laws (beginning with the Australian ballot in the late 1880s and early 1890s) that gave the parties official status as nominating bodies, regulated their practices, and converted them into durable, official bureaucracies. Less popular now but also more respectable, the party organizations surrendered to state regulation and relinquished much of their ability to express community opinion in return for legal guarantees that they alone would be permanently certified to place nominees on the official ballot.[51]

Interest organizations took over much of the parties' old job of articulating

---

[49] Among the best accounts of this transformation in policy are Herbert Croly, *Marcus Alonzo Hanna: His Life and Work* (New York, 1912), 465–79; Hurst, *Law and the Conditions of Freedom*, 71–108; and Wiebe, *The Search for Order, 1877–1920*, 164–95.

[50] The causes of the decline in party voting have been the subject of considerable debate and disagreement among political scientists and historians in recent years. Walter Dean Burnham began the controversy when he first described the early-twentieth-century changes in voting behavior and explained them by suggesting that an antipartisan industrial elite had captured the political system after the realignment of the 1890s; "Changing Shape of the American Political Universe." Jerrold G. Rusk and Philip E. Converse responded by contending that legal-institutional factors could better account for the behavioral changes that Burnham had observed; Rusk, "The Effect of the Australian Ballot Reform on Split Ticket Voting"; and Converse, "Change in the American Electorate," in Angus Campbell and Philip E. Converse, eds., *The Human Meaning of Social Change* (New York, 1972), 263–337. All three political scientists carried the debate forward—and all withdrew a bit from their original positions—in the September 1974 issue of the *American Political Science Review*. At present, the weight of developing evidence seems to indicate that, while new election laws alone cannot explain the voters' changed behavior, Burnham's notion of an elite takeover after 1896 is also inadequate to account for what happened; McCormick, *From Realignment to Reform*, chap. 9. What I am suggesting here is that the shock given to party politics by the awakening of 1905–06 played an important part in solidifying the new tendencies toward lower rates of voter participation and higher levels of ticket splitting. On the relative scarcity of campaign funds in the election of 1908, see Pollock, *Party Campaign Funds*, 37, 66–67; Overacker, *Money in Elections*, 234–38; and Brooks, *Corruption in American Politics and Life*, 234–35.

[51] Peter H. Argersinger, "'A Place on the Ballot': Fusion Politics and Antifusion Laws," *AHR*, 85 (1980): 287–306; Merriam and Overacker, *Primary Elections*; and William Mills Ivins, *On the Electoral System of the State of New York* (Albany, 1906).

popular demands and pressing them upon the government. More exclusive and single-minded than parties, the new organizations became regular elements of the polity. Their right to represent their members before the government's new boards and agencies received implicit recognition, and, indeed, the commissions in some cases became captives of the groups they were supposed to regulate. The result was a fairly drastic transformation of the rules of political participation: who could compete, the kinds of resources required, and the rewards of participation all changed. These developments were not brand new in the first years of the twentieth century, but, like the contemporaneous changes in government policy, they derived impressive, decisive confirmation from the political upheaval that occurred between 1905 and 1908.

POLITICAL AND GOVERNMENTAL CHANGES thus followed upon the discovery that business corrupts politics. And Americans of the day explicitly linked the two developments: the reforms adopted in 1907–08 were to remedy the ills uncovered in 1905–06. But these chronological and rhetorical connections between discovery and reform do not fully explain the relationship between them. Why, having paid relatively little heed to similar charges before, did people now take such strong actions in response to the disclosures? Why, moreover, did the perception of wrongdoing precipitate the particular pattern of responses that it did—namely, the triumph of bureaucracy and organization? Of most importance, what distinctive effects did the discovery of corruption have upon the final outcome of the crisis?

By 1905 a political explosion of some sort was likely, due to the accumulated frustrations people felt about the government's failure to deal with the problems of industrialization. So combustible were the elements present that another spark besides the discovery of politico-business corruption might well have ignited them. But the recognition of such corruption was an especially effective torch. Upon close analysis, its ignition of the volatile political mass is unsurprising. The accusations made in 1905–06 were serious, widespread, and full of damaging information; they explained the actual corrupt process behind a danger that Americans had historically worried about, if not always responded to with vigor; they linked in dark scandal the two main villains—party bosses and big businessmen—already on the American scene; they inherently discredited the existing structure of economic policy based on the distribution of privileges; and they dramatically suggested the necessity for new kinds of politics and government. That businessmen systematically corrupted politics was incendiary knowledge; given the circumstances of 1905, it could hardly have failed to set off an explosion.

The organizational results that followed, however, seem less inevitable. There were, after all, several other known ways of curtailing corruption besides expert regulation and administration. For one, there was the continued reliance on direct legislative action against the corruption of politics by businessmen. The lobbying, anti–free pass, and campaign-contribution measures of 1907–08 exemplified this approach. So did the extension of legislative controls over the offending corporations. Such measures were familiar, but obviously they were considered inadequate to the crisis at hand. A second approach, favored by Edward Alsworth Ross and later by Woodrow Wilson, was to hold business leaders personally responsible for their "sins" and to punish them accordingly. There were a few attempts to bring individuals to justice, but, because of the inadequacy of the criminal statutes, the skill of high-priced lawyers, and the public's lack of appetite for personal vendettas, few sinners were jailed. Finally, there were proposals for large structural solutions changing the political and economic environment so that the old corrupt practices became impossible. Some men, like Frederic C. Howe, still advocated the single tax and the abolition of all privileges granted by government.[52] Many more believed in the municipal ownership of public utilities. Hundreds of thousands (to judge from election returns) favored socialist solutions, but most Americans did not. In their response to politico-business corruption, they went beyond existing legislative remedies and avoided the temptation to personalize all the blame, but they fell short of wanting socialism, short even of accepting the single tax.

Regulation and administration represented a fourth available approach. Well before the discoveries of 1905–06, groups who stood to benefit from governmental control of utility and transportation corporations had placed strong regulatory proposals on the political agendas of the states and the nation. In other policy areas, the proponents of an administrative approach had not advanced that far prior to 1905–06, but theirs was a large and growing movement, supported—as recent historians have shown—by many different groups for varied, often contradictory, reasons.[53] The popular awakening to corruption increased the opportunity of these groups to obtain enactment of their measures. Where their proposals met the particular political needs of 1905–08, they succeeded most quickly. Regulation by commissions seemed to be an effective way to halt corruption by transferring the responsibility for business-government relations from party bosses and legislators to impartial experts. That approach also possessed the additional political advantages of appearing sane and moderate, of meeting consumer demands for government protection, and, above all, of being sufficiently malleable that a diversity of groups could be induced to anticipate favorable results from the new policies.[54]

In consequence, the passions of 1905–06 added support to an existing movement toward regulation and administration, enormously speeded it up, shaped

[52] Ross, *Sin and Society: An Analysis of Latter-Day Iniquity* (Boston, 1907); John M. Blum, *Woodrow Wilson and the Politics of Morality* (Boston, 1956); John B. Roberts, "The Real Cause of Municipal Corruption," in Clinton Rogers Woodruff, ed., *Proceedings of the New York Conference for Good City Government*, National Municipal League publication (Philadelphia, 1905), 148–53; and Howe, *Privilege and Democracy in America*.

[53] For an astute analysis of which groups favored and which groups opposed federal railroad legislation, see Richard H. K. Vietor, "Businessmen and the Political Economy: The Railroad Rate Controversy of 1905," *JAH*, 64 (1977): 47–66; and, for an excellent survey of the literature on regulation, see Thomas K. McCraw, "Regulation in America: A Review Article," *Business History Review*, 49 (1975): 159–83. The best account of the emergence of administrative ideas is, of course, Wiebe, *The Search for Order, 1877–1920*, 133–95.

[54] On the adaptability of administrative government, see Otis L. Graham, Jr., *The Great Campaigns: Reform and War in America, 1900–1928* (Englewood Cliffs, N.J., 1971), 50–51; and Wiebe, *The Search for Order, 1877–1920*, 222–23, 302.

the timing and form of its victory, and probably made the organizational revolution more complete—certainly more sudden—than it otherwise would have
been. These accomplishments alone must make the discovery of corruption piv-
otal in any adequate interpretation of progressivism. But the awakening did
more than hurry along a movement that already possessed formidable political
strength and would probably have triumphed eventually even without the
events of 1905–06. By pushing the political process toward so quick a resolution
of the long-standing crisis over industrialism, the passions of those years caused
the outcome to be more conservative than it otherwise might have been. This is
the ultimate irony of the discovery that business corrupts politics.

Muckraking accounts of politico-business evils suggest one reason for the discovery's conservative impact. Full of facts and revelations, these writings were
also dangerously devoid of effective solutions. Charles E. Russell's *Lawless Wealth*
(1908)—the title itself epitomizes the perceptions of 1905–06—illustrates the
flaw. Published originally in *Everybody's Magazine* under the accusatory title,
"Where Did You Get It, Gentlemen?," the book recounts numerous instances of
riches obtained through the corruption of politics but, in its closing pages,
merely suggests that citizens recognize the evils and be determined to stop them.
This reliance on trying to change how people felt (to "shame" them, in Steffens's phrase) was characteristic of muckraking and of the exposures of 1905–06.
One can admire the muckrakers' reporting, can even accept David P. Thelen's
judgment that their writing "contained at least as deep a moral revulsion toward capitalism and profit as did more orthodox forms of Marxism," yet can
still feel that their proposed remedy was superficial. Because the perception of
politico-business corruption carried no far-reaching solutions of its own or genuine economic grievances, but only a desire to clean up politics and government,
the passions of 1905–06 were easily diverted to the support of other people's
remedies, especially administrative answers. Had the muckrakers and their local
imitators penetrated more deeply into the way that business operated and its
real relationship to government, popular emotions might not have been so readily mobilized in support of regulatory and administrative agencies that business
interests could often dominate. At the very least, there might have been a more
determined effort to prevent the supervised corporations themselves from shaping the details of regulatory legislation. Thus, for all of their radical implications, the passions of 1905–06 dulled the capacity of ordinary people to get reforms in their own interest.[55]

The circumstances in which the discovery of corruption became a political
force also assist in explaining its conservatism. The passions of 1905–06 were primarily expressed in state, rather than local or national, politics. Indeed, those
passions often served to shift the focus of reform from the cities to the state capitals. There—in Albany, or Madison, or Sacramento—the remedies were worked
out in relative isolation from the local, insurgent forces that had in many cases

[55] Russell, *Lawless Wealth: The Origin of Some Great American Fortunes* (New York, 1908), 30–35, 52–55, 274–79;
and Thelen, "Lincoln Steffens and the Muckrakers: A Review Essay," *Wisconsin Magazine of History*, 58 (1975):
316.

originally called attention to the evils. Usually the policy consequences were more favorable to large business interests than local solutions would have been. State utility boards, for example, which had always been considered more conservative in their policies than comparable local commissions, now took the regulatory power away from cities and foreclosed experimentation with such alternatives as municipal ownership or popularly chosen regulatory boards. In gaining a statewide hearing for reform, the accusations of politico-business corruption actually increased the likelihood that conservative solutions would be adopted.[56]

Considering the intensity of the feelings aroused in 1905 and 1906 ("the wrath of thousands of private citizens . . . is at white heat over the disclosures," declared a Rochester newspaper) and the catalytic political role they played, the awakened opposition to corruption was surprisingly short-lived. As early as 1907 and 1908, the years of the most significant state legislative responses to the discovery, the messages of the governors began to exhibit a more stylized, less passionate way of describing politico-business wrongdoing. Now the governors emphasized remedies rather than abuses, and most seemed confident that the remedies would work. Criticism of business influence in government continued to be a staple of political rhetoric throughout the Progressive era, but it ceased to have the intensity it did in 1905–06. In place of the burning attack on corruption, politicans offered advanced progressive programs, including further regulation and election-law reforms.[57] The deep concern with business corruption of politics and government thus waned. It had stirred people to consciousness of wrongdoing, crystalized their discontent with existing policies, and pointed toward concrete solutions for the ills of industrialism. But it had not sustained the more radical, antibusiness possibilities suggested by the discoveries of 1905–06.

Indeed, the passions of those years probably weakened the insurgent, democratic qualities of the ensuing political transformation and strengthened its bureaucratic aspects. This result was ironical, but its causes were not conspiratorial. They lay instead in the tendency—shared by the muckrakers and their audience—to accept remedies unequal to the problems at hand and in political circumstances that isolated insurgents from decision making. Once the changes in policy were under way after 1906, those organized groups whose interests were most directly affected entered the fray, jockeyed for position, and heavily shaped the outcomes. We do not yet know enough about how this happened, but studies such as Stanley P. Caine's examination of railroad regulation in Wisconsin suggest how difficult it was to translate popular concern on an "issue" into the details of a law.[58] It is hardly surprising that, as regulation and adminis-

---

[56] Nord, "The Experts versus the Experts"; and Thelen, *Robert M. La Follette and the Insurgent Spirit*, 50–51.

[57] Rochester *Democrat and Chronicle*, October 18, 1905; and New York State Library, *Digest of Governors' Messages, 1907, 1908*. In a number of states where politico-business corruption had been an issue in the party platforms around 1906, the platforms were silent on the subject by 1910.

[58] Caine, *The Myth of a Progressive Reform: Railroad Regulation in Wisconsin, 1903–1910* (Madison, Wisc., 1970), 70. Also see Mansel G. Blackford, *The Politics of Business in California, 1890–1920* (Columbus, Ohio, 1977); Bruce W. Dearstyne, "Regulation in the Progressive Era: The New York Public Service Commission," *New York History*, 58 (1977): 331–47; and McCraw, "Regulation in America." These and other studies cast considerable doubt on the applicability at the state level of Gabriel Kolko's interpretation of regulatory legislation;

tration became accepted public functions, the affected interests exerted much more influence on policy than did those who cared most passionately about restoring clean government.

But the failue to pursue antibusiness policies does not mean the outcry against corruption was either insincere or irrelevant. Quite the contrary. It was sufficiently genuine and widespread to dominate the nation's public life in 1905 and 1906 and to play a decisive part in bringing about the transformation of American politics and government. Political changes do not, of course, embrace everything that is meant by progressivism. Nor was the discovery that business corrupts politics the only catalytic agent at work; certainly the rise of consumer discontent with utility and transportation corporations and the vigorous impetus toward new policies given by Theodore Roosevelt during his second term as president played complementary roles. But the awakening to corruption—as it was newly understood—provided an essential dynamic, pushing the states and the nation toward what many of its leading men and women considered progressive reform.

The organizational thesis sheds much light on the values and methods of those who succeeded in dominating the new types of politics and government but very little on the political circumstances in which they came forward. Robert H. Wiebe, in particular, has downplayed key aspects of the political context, including the outcry against corruption. Local uprisings against the alliance of bosses and businessmen, Wiebe has stated, "lay outside the mainstream of progressivism"; measures instituting the direct primary and curtailing the political influence of business were "old-fashioned reform."[59] Yet those local crusades, by spreading the dynamic perception that business corrupts politics, created a popular demand for the regulatory and administrative measures that Wiebe has claimed are characteristic of true progressivism; and those "old-fashioned" laws were enacted amidst the same political furor that produced the stunningly rapid bureaucratic triumph whose significance for twentieth-century America Wiebe has explained so convincingly. What the organizational thesis mainly lacks is the sense that political action is open-ended and unpredictable. Consequences are often unexpected, outcomes surprising when matched against origins. While it is misleading, as Samuel P. Hays has said, to interpret progressivism solely on the basis of its antibusiness ideology, it is equally misleading to fail to appreciate that reform gained decisive initial strength from ideas and feelings that were not able to sustain the movement in the end.[60] The farsighted organizers from business and the professions thus gained the opportunity to complete a political transformation that had been begun by people who were momentarily shocked into action but who stopped far short of pursuing the full implications of their discovery.

---

for that position, see his *The Triumph of Conservatism*. Commonly, the affected interests opposed state regulation until its passage became inevitable, at which point they entered the contest in order to influence the details of the law. Businessmen often had considerable, but not complete, success in helping shape such legislation, and they frequently found it beneficial in practice.

[59] Wiebe, *The Search for Order, 1877–1920*, 172, 180.
[60] Hays, "The Politics of Reform in Municipal Government."

Losing to Win: U.S. Steel's Pricing, Investment Decisions, and Market Share, 1901–1938

THOMAS K. MCCRAW AND FOREST REINHARDT

U.S. Steel held two-thirds of the American market in 1901, but by the 1930s its share had dropped to one-third. Such a decline is consistent with the economic theory of oligopoly pricing and capacity expansion, but the available data offer limited opportunities for formal testing of hypotheses. A close examination of U.S. Steel's early history leads us to argue that Chairman Elbert Gary's desire for price stability, his fear of antitrust litigation, and shortcomings in the firm's organizational capability constrained it from the unbridled pursuit of discounted profits that the economic theory assumes.

An examination of the United States Steel Corporation's declining market share over its first four decades permits a useful exploration of several themes: the underlying nature of oligopolistic competition; the interrelationships among pricing policy, capacity utilization, and investment decisions; and the effects of public antitrust policy on private decision making in dominant firms. Standard historical accounts of U.S. Steel's decline, following the lines pursued by the Justice Department in its antitrust litigation against the firm from 1911 to 1920, have focused on pricing policies and the umbrella U.S. Steel held over the industry. Yet the company's pricing behavior by no means tells the whole story, even when re-examined in the light of modern economic theory. U.S. Steel's decisions on capacity expansion were equally important. Here again, modern oligopoly theory cannot fully account for the firm's secular decline. A more complete explanation must consider not only U.S. Steel's pricing and investment decisions but also the constraints imposed by the threat of antitrust prosecution, together with other objectives pursued by the firm.

The 1901 merger that created U.S. Steel was capitalized at $1.4 billion, a sum that included a fair amount for anticipated earnings (later estimates placed the "overcapitalization" of the company at about 40 percent). The most important company going into the merger was Carnegie Steel, for which the financial syndicate headed by J. P. Morgan paid $480 million. In 1901 Gross National Product was $20.7 billion, so

The Journal of Economic History, Vol. XLIX, No. 3 (Sept. 1989). © The Economic History Association. All rights reserved. ISSN 0022-0507.

Thomas K. McCraw is Straus Professor of Business History, Harvard University, Boston, MA 02163. Forest Reinhardt is a Ph.D. candidate in Business Economics, Harvard University, Cambridge, MA 02138.

the capitalization of U.S. Steel was equivalent to about 6.8 percent of GNP. A commensurate transaction today, with GNP at about $5 trillion, would be $340 billion. Andrew Carnegie and his colleagues would receive nearly $117 billion.

Carnegie's company represented by far the most efficient competitor in the industry. Much of its success was derived from a combination of management techniques that have since become standard in efficient big businesses: recruitment of topflight executives, construction and acquisition of modern plants, systematic vertical integration, and continuous rationalization of process technology. What made the Carnegie enterprise distinctive, however, were two additional policies: hard driving and scrap and build. Hard driving meant pushing blast furnaces beyond their rated capacities, through hotter blast, greater volume, and constant pressure to get additional output. It was much like what a twentieth-century test pilot does in "pushing the envelope" with a jet airplane: see how fast and high it might be made to fly regardless of what its designers had predicted.

Under the related policy of scrap and build, whenever any superior production method appeared, Carnegie Steel rapidly adopted it, with apparent disregard of the short-term cost. Andrew Carnegie did not pioneer new technology so much as he rapidly commercialized it, and he went to extraordinary lengths to discover less expensive ways of producing steel. Once when his young assistant Charles Schwab reported the development of a superior design for a rolling mill, Carnegie ordered him to raze and reconstruct an existing three-month-old mill. Carnegie Steel thoroughly deserved its international reputation as the most relentless, ruthless competitor in the steel industry.[1]

As for the newly merged entity: "It is difficult to convey any adequate idea of the magnitude of the Steel Corporation," journalist Ray Stannard Baker wrote in *McClure's* in 1901.

> A mere list of the properties owned or controlled would fill an entire number of this magazine. It receives and expends more money every year than any but the very greatest of the world's national governments; its debt is larger than that of many of the lesser nations of Europe. It absolutely controls the destinies of a population nearly as large as that of Maryland or Nebraska. . . . It owns or controls 115 fine steamships on the great lakes, and six important railroad lines and several smaller ones. In Pennsylvania, its coal possessions cover over 75,000 acres of land worth $1200 an acre, besides 30,000 acres of other land and quarries, and 98,000 acres of leased natural-gas lands. It owns no fewer than 18,309

[1] Harold C. Livesay, *Andrew Carnegie and the Rise of Big Business* (Boston, 1975), pp. 116–17, 150. On Carnegie Steel, see also Joseph Frazier Wall, *Andrew Carnegie* (New York, 1970); and James Howard Bridge, *The Inside History of the Carnegie Steel Company* (New York, 1903). For Charles Schwab's favorable predictions of the results of the merger, see Charles Schwab, "What May Be Expected in the Iron and Steel Industry," *North American Review*, 172 (May 1901), pp. 655–64.

coke-ovens. . . . Of blast furnaces it owns eighty, producing 9,000,000 tons of pig iron yearly, and of steel plants its owns about 150.[2]

The response of the American public to the formation of this new trust to end all trusts was mostly negative.[3] Perhaps more important, the reaction of the capital markets was overwhelmingly favorable. Despite press complaints about the watering of U.S. Steel's stock, all securities sold expeditiously. Investors were apparently reassured by the earning potential of the new giant and by Morgan's underwriting. In time they were proven right.[4]

Once the ink was dry on the new securities, Morgan installed Schwab as head of the company. Many observers expected Schwab to proceed with a rationalization along the lines of Carnegie Steel. Instead, Schwab made a series of social and political blunders and resigned after only two years at the helm. Morgan's fateful choice of a replacement was Elbert Gary, a lawyer who had chaired U.S. Steel's executive committee. This shift in 1903 from the production-oriented Schwab to the lawyer-financier Gary provided an appropriate symbol for the future corporate strategy of U.S. Steel. Gary remained chairman for almost 25 years, until his death in 1927. Under his leadership the company followed a series of policies that differed radically from the hard-driving, low-dividend, scrap-and-build regime epitomized by Andrew Carnegie.

Unlike most successful mergers, U.S. Steel under Gary did little to rationalize production facilities, innovate product lines, or consolidate management structure. Through U.S. Steel's Pittsburgh-plus system, the firm facilitated price coordination with smaller competitors, but saddled itself with a locational inertia that minimized its ability to

---

[2] Ray Stannard Baker, "What the U.S. Steel Corporation Really Is, and How It Works," *McClure's*, 18 (Nov. 1901), p. 6. Many other accounts of U.S. Steel take the same awestruck tone. The U.S. District Court's opinion in the antitrust case of 1915 begins as follows: "The subject-matter of the litigation is of such magnitude and complexity, and the record is of such size, that the effort to set bounds to this discussion has not been easy." See *United States v. United States Steel Corporation et al.*, District Court, New Jersey, 223 Federal Reporter (1915), p. 58. On the first page of a three-part 1936 *Fortune* series, one reads: "It is extremely difficult, if not impossible, to visualize the workings of the Steel Corporation as a whole." See "The [United States Steel] Corporation," *Fortune*, 13 (Mar. 1936), p. 59.

[3] Much was made in the American popular press about the size, overcapitalization, and antitrust implications of the merger. Nor was the reaction confined to the United States alone. Britain's *Iron and Coal Trades Review*, for example, was quoted in *The Iron Age*, 67 (Mar. 14, 1901), pp. 2–3, to the effect that U.S. Steel would be too "vast . . . cumbersome . . . unnatural and . . . subversive of public and vested interest" to survive.

[4] See George J. Stigler, "The Dominant Firm and the Inverted Umbrella," *Journal of Law and Economics*, 8 (Oct. 1965), pp. 167–72. For elaborations and some differing views, see Donald D. Parsons and Edward John Ray, "The United States Steel Consolidation: The Creation of Market Control," *Journal of Law and Economics*, 18 (Apr. 1975), pp. 181–219; and Michael E. Burton, "The 1901 Establishment of the U.S. Steel Corporation: For Monopoly and/or Efficiency?" (Ph.D. diss., University of California at Los Angeles, 1985).

exploit new opportunities in growing geographical markets.[5] Organizationally it persisted in the form of a loose holding company, long keeping intact about 200 subsidiaries—including such giants as Carnegie Steel, Illinois Steel, American Sheet and Tin Plate, and American Steel and Wire. Many of these subsidiaries had overlapping markets and duplicate sales forces.[6] Overall, between 1901 and the 1930s, U.S. Steel's share of the American market dropped from about two-thirds to one-third. Gary, as chairman and chief strategist, therefore seems guilty of a profligate dissipation of the market power and organizational capabilities he had inherited.

Yet Gary's strategy also yielded strong profits for shareholders and brought stability to an industry long plagued with price wars and producer distress. In addition, U.S. Steel, unlike several other famous trusts, escaped dissolution under the Sherman Act. Viewed in this light, Gary's policies seem remarkably successful.

During his long tenure, the company endured constant public scrutiny by the press. It underwent two detailed investigations by the Bureau of Corporations and the Stanley Committee of the House of Representatives. It defended itself in a prolonged antitrust suit (1911–1920), several smaller investigations during World War I, and still another thorough investigation by the Federal Trade Commission (1921–1924). The records of these proceedings provide an abundance of primary evidence on the company's behavior.[7]

The performance of U.S. Steel and its competitors over its first decades is detailed in the following tables and figures. Table 1 shows, in brief, what happened in different segments of the market during Gary's chairmanship. U.S. Steel's share of the broadest product category,

[5] Under the Pittsburgh-plus system, prices of steel products of different locales were standardized through the device of adding phantom freight charges from the "basing point" of Pittsburgh, regardless of where the products had actually originated. Later a few other basing points were added.

[6] U.S. Steel represented a combination of combinations, climaxing a series of mergers of about 180 iron and steel companies existing in the late 1880s into nine very large firms in the late 1890s, and finally into one giant holding company in 1901. The U.S. Steel merger was part of a great wave of combinations in many industries, a movement that began in 1895, peaked in 1899, and finally ended in 1904. During this period, more than 1,800 manufacturing firms merged into 157 consolidated corporations. Many of these, such as General Electric, National Biscuit, and International Harvester, dominated their industries for generations to come and, like U.S. Steel, became household words in American society. The standard work is Naomi R. Lamoreaux, *The Great Merger Movement in American Business, 1895–1904* (New York, 1985).

[7] The best original documentary sources are U.S. Department of Commerce and Labor, *Report of the Commissioner of Corporations on the Steel Industry*, 3 parts (Washington, DC, 1911 to 1913); U.S. House of Representatives, *Hearings before the Committee on Investigation of the United States Steel Corporation*, 8 vols., 62nd Cong., 2nd sess. (Washington, DC, 1911), the Stanley Committee hearings; U.S. House of Representatives, *Report on the Investigation of the United States Steel Corporation*, 3 parts, 62nd Cong., 2nd sess. (Washington, DC, 1911), the Stanley Committee report; and the voluminous records of the antitrust case cited in fn. 2. The availability of this copious primary data goes far to offset the disadvantage that U.S. Steel's corporate archives remain closed to independent scholars.

TABLE 1
PERCENTAGE OF TOTAL OUTPUT PRODUCED BY UNITED STATES STEEL

Category of Product	1901	1911	1913	1919	1927
Iron Ore	45.1%	45.8%	46.4%	42.1%	41.4%
Blast-furnace Products	43.2	45.4	45.5	44.0	37.7
Steel Ingots and Castings	65.7	53.9	53.2	49.6	41.1
Steel Rails	59.8	56.1	55.5	62.0	53.3
Heavy Structural Shapes	62.2	47.0	54.0	43.8	38.8
Plates and Sheets	64.6	45.7	49.1	44.3	36.5
Wire Rods	77.6	64.7	58.4	55.4	47.4
Wire Nails	65.8	51.4	44.6	51.9	42.0
Tin and Terne Plate	73.0	60.7	58.6	48.4	40.5
Total Finished Products	50.1	45.7	47.8	44.6	37.7
Unweighted Average	61.9	52.3	51.7	49.1	42.1
Standard Deviation	10.8	6.7	5.1	6.2	4.9

Notes: Average and standard deviations exclude "total finished products."
Source: N.S.B. Gras and Henrietta M. Larson, Case Book in American Business History (New York, 1939), p. 612.

ingots and castings, fell from 66 percent in 1901 to 41 percent in 1927, and continued downward to 33 percent in 1934. Thus, the corporation lost half of its overall share during its first three decades. Another clue to the company's passive strategy may be inferred from its market share decline in the most dynamic growth sectors of the industry: structural shapes (essential to bridge and building construction) and light flat rolled products (notably sheet and tin plate for the powerful new automobile and consumer goods industries). In Table 1 we see structural shapes declining from about 62 percent share to about 39 percent, plates and sheets from 65 to 37 percent, and plate from 73 to 40 percent. The table also shows that the company standardized its shares in all product lines, as Gary had said he intended to do.

Other important aspects of U.S. Steel's business may be observed from the numbers in Table 2. The first is the immense magnitude of the undertaking: for many years, U.S. Steel remained the largest manufacturing enterprise in the country by any measure. Yet the numbers also reveal a striking cyclicality of the firm's business. In 1916, U.S. Steel increased its employment by 62,000 workers. Five years later, it laid off 76,000. The sales figures tell a similar story. In 12 of the 35 years between 1903 and 1938, the company's sales rose by 20 percent or more over the figure for the previous year. In seven other years, sales fell by more than 20 percent. Fully half of all years, therefore, were characterized by either explosive sales growth or severe contraction. Similarly, annual profits ranged from almost a half billion dollars during World War I to large losses during the Great Depression.

In general, U.S. Steel's profits were respectable even when one ignores the huge spike caused by World War I. Profitability fell

TABLE 2
SELECTED DATA ON UNITED STATES STEEL, 1901 to 1938

Year	Workers (thousands)	Sales ($ million)	Percentage Change in Sales on Previous Year	Profits ($ million)	Profits as Percentage of Sales	Ingot Capacity (million gross tons)	Percentage Market Share of Ingot Production
1901						9.4	66%
1902	168	$ 561		$140	25%	10.0	65
1903	168	537	−4%	116	22	11.2	63
1904	147	444	−17	80	18	11.5	61
1905	180	585	32	126	22	12.9	60
1906	202	697	19	163	23	13.4	58
1907	210	737	6	167	23	14.8	56
1908	165	482	−35	67	14	15.6	56
1909	196	646	34	101	16	17.2	56
1910	218	704	9	125	18	17.8	54
1911	197	615	−13	93	15	18.1	54
1912	221	746	21	88	12	18.8	54
1913	229	797	7	117	15	18.5	53
1914	179	558	−30	58	10	19.0	50
1915	191	727	30	110	15	19.2	51
1916	253	1,231	69	313	25	20.8	49
1917	268	1,706	39	487	29	22.0	45
1918	269	1,749	3	441	25	22.2	44
1919	252	1,445	−17	159	11	22.3	50
1920	268	1,757	22	176	10	22.4	46
1921	192	997	−43	72	7	22.7	55
1922	215	1,101	10	72	7	22.7	45
1923	261	1,577	43	155	10	22.8	45
1924	247	1,271	−19	126	10	22.8	43
1925	250	1,412	11	133	9	23.1	42
1926	253	1,515	7	160	11	22.7	42
1927	232	1,318	−13	126	10	23.2	41
1928	222	1,382	5	147	11	23.8	39
1929	254	1,502	9	220	15	24.2	39
1930	253	1,175	−22	113	10	25.2	41
1931	216	725	−38	−1	0	26.1	39
1932	164	355	−51	−5	−2	27.8	36
1933	173	521	47	−30	−6	27.3	35
1934	190	589	13	−12	−2	27.3	33
1935	195	776	32	12	2	27.3	33
1936	222	1,100	42	67	7	26.7	35
1937	261	1,396	27	130	9	25.8	37
1938	202	767	−45	3	0	25.8	33

Sources: U.S. Steel Corporation, *T.N.E.C. Papers* (New York, 1940) [Exhibits prepared for the Temporary National Economic Committee], vol. 2, pp. 138, 142 (capacity and market share); and Gertrude D. Schroeder, *The Growth of Major Steel Companies, 1900–1950* (Baltimore, 1955), appendix, table 1, p. 216 (other data).

gradually over time, and U.S. Steel, like its competitors, lost money during part of the Great Depression. Overall, the firm's profit margins do not suggest any obvious superiority or inferiority of management. Table 3 shows average annual profit figures for the top seven firms

TABLE 3
PERCENTAGE PROFITABILITY, 1901 TO 1930: ANNUAL AVERAGES

Company	Profitability
U.S. Steel	12.6%
Bethlehem	10.3
Republic	10.1
Jones & Laughlin	8.2
Youngstown	16.3
Inland	16.9
Armco	13.7

Source: Gertrude D. Schroeder, *The Growth of Major Steel Companies, 1900–1950* (Baltimore, 1955), p. 175.

during the period 1901 to 1930, expressed as a percentage of gross fixed assets. Clearly, the American steel industry enjoyed healthy profits— under policies worked out primarily by U.S. Steel.

"COMPETITION" UNDER CARNEGIE AND GARY

Buried in the volumes of testimony taken by the antitrust prosecutors and the investigators from the Bureau of Corporations and the Stanley Committee is a vast array of comments on competition by lawyers, economists, and steel executives. Throughout the antitrust proceedings, the word competition and its cognates occur thousands of times. The meaning of the words varies widely, yet, as a whole, these comments provide a detailed picture of what was happening in the industry after 1901.

Gary himself was called to the stand during the trial. He had this to say about pricing policies: "The Steel Corporation has endeavored to prevent sudden and violent fluctuations downward by its advice, but more particularly by its own action in fixing its prices, and has endeavored to prevent the unreasonable increase in prices at times when the demand was greater than the supply and there was a general disposition in the trade to take advantage of these conditions and unduly increase prices."[8]

However self-serving, Gary's testimony was corroborated by U.S. Steel's customers. An agricultural implement manufacturer who purchased bars and plates from U.S. Steel's Carnegie subsidiary described the firm's practices: "Our experience has been that, on advancing markets, the Carnegie Company were [sic] as low and frequently lower than competitors, while on declining markets they were generally a little higher." The president of Pacific Coast Steel, a competitor of Gary's, said: "I have always found the competition of the United States Steel

[8] *United States v. United States Steel Corporation* (1915), p. 90.

163

Company and its subsidiaries fair; its existence has been beneficial to the steel and iron trade of the country."[9]

The policies of the old (pre-1901 merger) system were attacked sharply in the testimony by witness after witness, including Gary himself:

> There was a competition that was bitter, fierce, destructive. If it did not absolutely drive competitors out of business, it so harassed and injured them as to prevent them from extending their business, or from taking advantage of their location, and at times compelled them to close their mills, discharge their employes [sic], and disrupt their organization, and in fact, was a competition that, in the opinion of those in charge of the United States Steel Corporation, I might say the opinion of those in control of the industry generally in this country at the present time, was calculated to destroy, to injure instead of build up, to prevent extensions of the trade, to limit the capacity or the opportunity of many who were engaged in the trade.[10]

Exonerating U.S. Steel in the antitrust case, the court summarized as follows: "[A] single large concern, by lowering the price of any substantial steel product it sells, can depress the obtainable price." On the other hand, "[N]o single large concern, by raising or even maintaining the price of any substantial steel product, can raise the obtainable price." As important as the policies of U.S. Steel were, in the end the forces of supply and demand remained decisive. All prices depended "on whether the consumption of steel was such that the mills were crowded with orders from buyers, or whether buyers were crowded with offers from mills. . . . [T]he prices at which steel products have been bought from the Steel Company and its competitors have been fixed by business conditions—over demand or over supply."[11]

Ultimately, the court pronounced the old competition bad, and the new better: "[N]o testimony has been produced on this record that a return to the old trade war system of ruinous competition would, as a matter of fact, benefit the public interests. On the contrary, the proof is that present business methods and ethics are more to be desired."[12] A concurring opinion put the issue in even broader compass, holding that the 1901 merger had been for horizontal not vertical reasons and that a monopoly had been intended but not achieved. Yet, despite their more skeptical view of U.S. Steel, the concurring judges concluded as follows:

> The testimony abundantly shows that the power of the [U.S. Steel] corporation to control prices was efficient only when in cooperation with its competitors. It has

[9] Ibid., pp. 78, 90–91.
[10] Ibid., p. 95.
[11] Ibid., pp. 88–89.
[12] Ibid., p. 95. Although the court drew a distinction between the old competition and the new, its remarks on prices, on pp. 88–89, downplay the market power U.S. Steel possessed. The concurring opinion partly alleviated this apparent contradiction.

never raised and maintained prices by its own action. It has done it only by joint actions, and when joint action was either refused or withdrawn, the corporation's prices were controlled by competition. . . . There is no evidence that it attempted to crush its competitors or drive them out of the market, and in its competition it seemed to make no distinction between large and small competitors. In fact, its conduct towards its competitors, as shown by the testimony, has been conspicuously free from that business brutality, meanness, and unfairness which characterized the conduct of certain large corporations found guilty of violating the Anti-Trust Law.[13]

When the Supreme Court upheld the lower court ruling, it followed the lead of this concurring opinion.

All opinions at both levels exhibit consistent ambiguity toward the idea of competition. For the judges it implied price competition, for which the critical data obviously pertained to U.S. Steel's pricing behavior. Yet is also encompassed vaguer notions of fairness that were difficult to measure and for which the ultimate evidence was not intent or behavior but results: in particular, the decline in the company's market share, which had as much to do with investment decisions (notably the expansion of capacity) as with pricing. Let us take up these two topics sequentially.

PRICING

In their attempts to understand U.S. Steel's behavior during the early period of its existence, contemporary observers paid a great deal of attention to its pricing policies. For these observers, as for modern economic historians, monopoly power was, almost axiomatically, the power to set monopoly prices. Today, in "strategy" courses taught at leading business schools, market power is defined as a firm's ability to raise prices without provoking an adverse competitive response. The ability to set monopoly prices is simultaneously the most visible symptom of market power and the source of allocative inefficiency and social inequity.

Did U.S. Steel possess this kind of power in the early years after its formation? Scholars have long known, in a general way, that prices stabilized after 1902 under the leadership of U.S. Steel. The trends evident in the following figures show a little more precisely what happened in important product markets. In Figure 1 we see that between 1895 and 1900, prices for wire and nails first doubled, then fell back to their original level, then almost tripled, and finally fell by about 30 percent. After the U.S. Steel merger in 1901, prices stabilized and showed little fluctuation even during the Panic of 1907. Similar patterns hold for other important products, as shown in Figure 2. The same

[13] Ibid., pp. 165–66, 172. The reference in the last sentence of this quotation is to the 1911 cases against Standard Oil and American Tobacco.

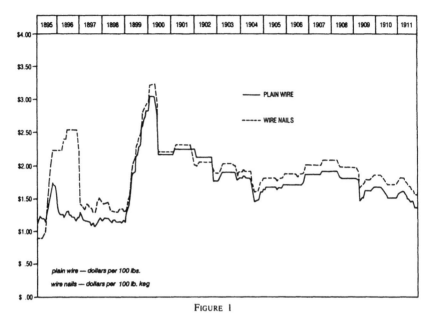

FIGURE 1

AVERAGE MONTHLY PRICE OF PLAIN WIRE AND WIRE NAILS AT PITTSBURGH,
1895–1911

Source: United States vs. United States Steel Corporation et al., District Court, New Jersey,
Government Exhibits 218 and 219, Nov. 19, 1912.

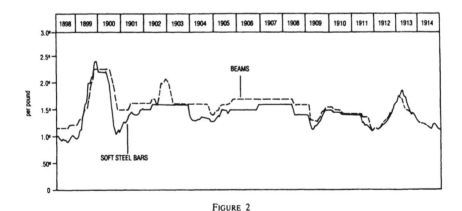

FIGURE 2

PRICES OF BEAMS AND BARS, 1898–1914

Source: Adapted from *The Iron Age*, 95 (Jan. 7, 1915), pp. 16ff.

166

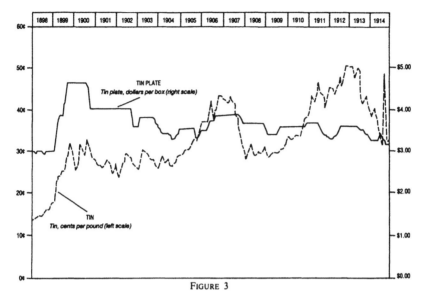

FIGURE 3

TIN AND TIN PLATE PRICES, 1898–1914

Source: See Fig. 2.

pattern appears again in Figure 3, which contrasts the rapid movement in the price of tin, which steel companies had to purchase in a more or less open market, with the more stable price of tin plate, which they manufactured.[14]

According to Gary's testimony in the antitrust case, the company decided at the end of each year what its prices were going to be during the coming year, and then actually kept them at that level.[15] This policy did bring an unprecedented measure of price stability to the industry, as the figures suggest; but it also gave U.S. Steel's competitors an opportunity to undercut the leader's prices and thus increase their market share. The competitors did so, and Gary's own managers often grumbled that his pricing policies were misguided.[16]

Gary, however, together with the company's admirers, was extremely pleased with U.S. Steel's record of bringing price stability to a wildly cyclical industry. While the famous system of Gary dinners involving executives from many companies lasted only a short while, the company's policy of publishing its prices for the upcoming year

[14] Roughly speaking, the metallurgical content of tinplate is about one percent tin, which accounts for about 15 percent of the final product's price.
[15] *United States v. United States Steel Corporation et al.*, District Court, New Jersey (1912–1915), Transcript of Trial Testimony, pp. 4882–83.
[16] Robert Hessen, *Steel Titan: The Life of Charles M. Schwab* (New York, 1975), pp. 186–87.

remained a lasting force for stabilization.[17] Thus, U.S. Steel's policies gave rise to a chorus of accolades of the sort quoted earlier from testimony in the antitrust case, and, ironically considering some of the presumed aims of antitrust policy, they contributed mightily to the company's victory in that case.

Additional evidence suggests that Morgan and Gary regarded their activities in steel as a means to stabilize not only the industry, but the macroeconomy. Gary, in fact, sometimes advocated governmental pricing of steel in the pattern of the Interstate Commerce Commission's supervision of railroad rates. He seems to have conceived of the steel industry as a type of industrial utility.[18] Then, too, the purchase by Gary and Morgan in 1907 of the Tennessee Coal, Iron, and Railroad Company (TC & I), the antitrust implications of which were later scrutinized by the Justice Department, appears to have been motivated primarily by a desire to avert financial panic rather than to obtain assets at bargain prices. Gary secured the personal approval of President Theodore Roosevelt and Secretary of State Elihu Root before purchasing TC & I, and they at least regarded the macroeconomic considerations as important. Gary's testimony in the antitrust case and in many other proceedings shows him unmistakably to have been preoccupied with the pursuit of stability, both for his own industry and for the national economy. As for Morgan, his activities both in steel and in finance (as during the national liquidity crises of 1894 and 1907, when he performed the role of central banker) also demonstrate an overriding concern with stability.

As Gary and other witnesses testified, U.S. Steel's practice was to cut prices last in recessions, thereby losing market share to more aggressive competitors but maintaining higher profit percentages for as long as possible. In upturns, U.S. Steel raised prices last, thereby recapturing some market share at the expense of short-term profit percentage. This policy, along with the three other possible pricing strategies for market leaders at different stages of the business cycle, can be summarized in Table 4.

At about the same time U.S. Steel was following the first of these policies, companies such as Standard Oil and Du Pont were pursuing different courses. Their objectives seem to have been to keep their manufacturing plants running full and steady regardless of business conditions. Although the patterns by no means were always the same, in general they often cut prices ahead of their rivals in recessions,

---

[17] For a discussion of the Gary dinners and their aftermath, see Maurice H. Robinson, "The Gary Dinner System: An Experiment in Cooperative Price Stabilization," *The Southwestern Political and Social Science Quarterly*, 7 (Sept. 1926), pp. 137–61.

[18] See, for example, *The Iron Age*, 87 (June 8, 1911), pp. 1404–7, for a summary of Gary's testimony before the Stanley Committee; and *The Iron Age*, 89 (Feb. 29, 1912), pp. 540–41. Gary's proposals along this line did not often sit well with other steel executives. See editorial in *The Iron Age*, 87 (June 15, 1911), p. 1446.

TABLE 4
ACTUAL AND POTENTIAL PRICING POLICIES

	In Recessions	In Upturns
U.S. Steel's actual policy	Cut prices last: lose market share, maintain high margins	Raise prices last: gain market share, forgo high margins
What the reverse policy would have been	Cut prices first: gain market share, sacrifice profit margins	Raise prices first: lose market share, increase profit margins
How best to maximize short-term profitability	Cut prices last: lose market share, maintain profit margins	Raise prices first: lose market share, increase profit margins
How best to maximize market share and (perhaps) long-term profitability	Cut prices first: gain market share, sacrifice profit margins	Raise prices last: gain market share, forgo high margins

sacrificing some profitability in order to maintain scale economies and take a larger share of a shrinking market. In upturns, they often gave back this market share and enhanced their profitability. As demand recovered, they sometimes undertook new construction programs and sometimes did not; and, as we will suggest below, this kind of investment decision was as important as pricing policy. Overall, unlike U.S. Steel, they tried to pass on to their rivals most of the capacity utilization effects of cyclicality. Standard Oil specifically priced at levels that would discourage competitors from investing in new plant, a policy deliberately eschewed by U.S. Steel.[19]

A dominant firm could also cut prices last in recessions but lead price increases in expansions. This could result in loss of market share both in good times and bad, but it might also allow maximum absolute profits over the entire business cycle. In the steel industry, as we have seen, neither Gary nor Carnegie followed any such pattern. Carnegie, in fact, pursued the only remaining policy mentioned in Table 4: he cut prices first in recessions and raised them last in upturns, maximizing capacity utilization and long-term market share at the expense of short-run profitability.

Whatever the motivation for U.S. Steel's pricing policies, many modern business strategists would argue that the company deserved its competitors' praise since it was essentially giving them its markets. Certainly the policy of announced prices made it easy for the smaller firms to undercut U.S. Steel's prices and thereby increase their sales. As Schwab's biographer notes: "Gary's blueprint for stability within the industry often worked against the dominant position of his own

[19] Ralph W. Hidy and Muriel E. Hidy, *Pioneering in Big Business, 1882–1911* (New York, 1955), pp. 28, 117–18, 194.

corporation." U.S. Steel's fixed prices "served as a magnet to draw aggressive smaller firms into price and product competition with the giant steel corporation."[20]

In modern economics, dynamic limit pricing theory implies that, in order to maximize the present value of future profits, market leaders ordinarily should lose share gradually over time. That is, a monopolist should set the price of its product somewhere on a spectrum between the price that maximizes short-run profits and the highest price that maximizes long-term market share. If the price is set to maximize short-run profits, these excess profits will induce other firms to enter the business, resulting in a rapid erosion of market share. On the other hand, the dominant firm may be able to set prices low enough that no rival will think it worthwhile to enter.[21]

The appropriate strategy under dynamic limit pricing ordinarily lies between these extremes and depends on subjective appraisals by the market leader of the likelihood of entry under different conditions. The entry-deterring price depends on the elasticity of demand for the product, on potential entrants' costs, and on potential rivals' perceptions of possible profits after they enter the market. All of these factors are difficult for the dominant firm to estimate. Further, each factor changes over time, so the entry-deterring price and the optimal price will change over time as well.

It is hard for a dominant firm to estimate these parameters contemporaneously, and even harder for historians to reconstruct such subjective estimates long after the fact. Because of the dynamic nature of the model, no single pattern of market share decline uniquely confirms the theory. Probably for this reason, attempts to apply dynamic limit pricing theory directly to historical market share and profit data for U.S. Steel or any other industry leader have been few. U.S. Steel's pattern of market share decline is consistent with the theory on a qualitative level, and one could reconstruct determinations that would lead to the kind of market share decline the firm in fact experienced. Yet this would be an exercise in speculation, and corroborating evidence from corporate archives would be necessary to clinch the argument. For now, the available data on market share and profits neither directly confirm nor refute the model.

Dynamic limit pricing theory is especially hard to apply to the case of

---

[20] Hessen, *Steel Titan*, p. 187.

[21] Darius W. Gaskins, Jr., "Dynamic Limit Pricing: Optimal Pricing Under Threat of Entry," *Journal of Economic Theory*, 3 (Sept. 1971), pp. 306–22; Morton Kamien and Nancy Schwartz, "Limit Pricing and Uncertain Entry," *Econometrica*, 39 (May 1971), pp. 441–54; and Morton Kamien and Nancy Schwartz, *Dynamic Optimization: The Calculus of Variations and Optimal Control in Economics and Management* (New York, 1981), pp. 206–11. See also Hideki Yamawaki, "Dominant Firm Pricing and Fringe Expansion: The Case of the U.S. Iron and Steel Industry," *Review of Economics and Statistics*, 67 (Aug. 1985), pp. 429–37.

U.S. Steel because of the high probability that the company's top management had other objectives besides maximizing long-term discounted profits. The theory does not readily accommodate the possibility that decision makers might be interested in stability for its own sake, let alone constrained by fears of antitrust litigation—as was clearly the case with U.S. Steel.

At a more general level, any theory that emphasizes pricing policies necessarily downplays decisions about capacity expansion, even though these obviously can have a decisive effect on long-term market share. In U.S. Steel's case, the available data on capacity expansion and utilization strongly suggest that price is not the whole picture and perhaps not even the most important single factor.

CAPACITY

If U.S. Steel's pricing policies were encouraging entry, it should follow that other firms' capacity expansions and utilizations consistently exceeded U.S. Steel's. Yet historically this was not the case, as Table 5 shows. From 1902 until the Great Depression, U.S. Steel maintained a higher level of capacity utilization than its competitors, and often much higher. These numbers (the fourth and fifth columns in Table 5) appear to refute any proposition that U.S. Steel, by adhering to rigid pricing policies, ordinarily allowed its rivals' mills to run more steadily than its own. The peculiar patterns of capacity expansion for U.S. Steel and for the industry as a whole are shown in columns 8 through 11 of Table 5. In four of its first six years, U.S. Steel added more ingot capacity than the rest of the industry combined; in four of its first eight years, it increased capacity by 10 percent or more. Given the huge base figures, these additions represented large jumps. Such behavior seems uncharacteristic of the passive giant portrayed in most historical accounts of U.S. Steel.

On the other hand, after 1907 U.S. Steel expanded capacity much less rapidly than did other companies. As Table 5 shows, in only six of the next 30 years did it add more or retire less capacity than did the rest of the industry. In Figure 4 we have condensed the information in Table 5 to permit a more vivid presentation of trends in production, capacity growth, and capacity utilization on the part of U.S. Steel and its competitors.

This sustained policy of not matching, much less preempting, competitors' capacity expansions is crucial to any understanding of the decline of U.S. Steel's market share. It contrasts sharply with the behavior of other "trusts"—Standard Oil in the nineteenth century, Alcoa in the twentieth—and also with the investment patterns modern business strategists would recommend. Without U.S. Steel's record of sluggish capacity expansion during the 30 years after 1907, its decline in

TABLE 5
STEEL INGOT CAPACITY, PRODUCTION, AND EXPANSION, 1901–1938

Year	Total Capac- ity[a]	Total Produc- tion[a]	Capacity Utilization		U.S. Steel share of:		Capacity Expansion[b]		Change in Capacity on previous year	
			U.S. Steel	Others	Capac- ity	Produc- tion	U.S. Steel	Others	U.S. Steel	Others
1901	21.5	13.5	94%	38%	44%	66%				
1902	22.7	14.9	97	41	44	65	602	635	6.4%	5.3%
1903	23.9	14.5	82	42	47	63	1,178	22	11.7	0.2
1904	25.2	13.9	73	40	46	61	337	953	3.0	7.5
1905	26.3	20.1	94	60	49	60	1,334	−224	11.6	−1.6
1906	27.4	23.4	101	71	49	58	563	537	4.4	4.0
1907	28.5	23.4	89	75	52	56	1,332	−232	9.9	−1.7
1908	30.3	14.0	50	42	51	56	813	987	5.5	7.2
1909	34.0	24.0	78	63	50	56	1,567	2,133	10.1	14.5
1910	35.2	26.1	79	69	51	54	688	512	4.0	3.0
1911	36.0	23.7	71	61	50	54	238	562	1.3	3.2
1912	38.0	31.3	90	75	50	54	739	1,261	4.1	7.0
1913	39.0	31.3	90	71	47	53	−326	1,326	−1.7	6.9
1914	39.7	23.5	62	56	48	50	502	187	2.7	0.9
1915	41.3	32.2	85	71	47	51	230	1,375	1.2	6.6
1916	45.8	42.8	100	88	46	49	1,613	2,881	8.4	13.1
1917	49.6	45.1	92	90	44	45	1,205	2,621	5.8	10.5
1918	52.5	44.5	88	82	42	44	161	2,766	0.7	10.0
1919	54.5	34.7	77	54	41	50	133	1,809	0.6	6.0
1920	55.6	42.1	86	69	40	46	13	1,141	0.1	3.5
1921	57.4	19.8	48	25	40	55	341	1,399	1.5	4.2
1922	58.4	35.6	71	55	39	45	0	1,040	0.0	3.0
1923	58.6	44.9	89	69	39	45	108	120	0.5	0.3
1924	59.4	37.9	72	59	38	43	14	773	0.1	2.2
1925	61.1	45.4	82	70	38	42	309	1,396	1.4	3.8
1926	57.8	48.3	89	80	39	42	−376	−2,948	−1.6	−7.8
1927	60.0	44.9	80	72	39	41	428	1,791	1.9	5.1
1928	61.5	51.5	85	83	39	39	585	848	2.5	2.3
1929	63.8	56.4	90	87	38	39	440	1,879	1.9	5.0
1930	65.2	40.7	66	60	39	41	961	421	4.0	1.1
1931	69.0	25.9	39	37	38	39	912	2,902	3.6	7.3
1932	70.3	13.7	18	21	40	36	1,766	−406	6.8	−0.9
1933	70.2	23.2	29	35	39	35	−499	350	−1.8	0.8
1934	69.8	26.0	32	41	39	33	0	−436	0.0	−1.0
1935	70.0	34.1	41	54	39	33	0	291	0.0	0.7
1936	69.8	47.8	63	72	38	35	−685	429	−2.5	1.0
1937	69.8	50.6	72	73	37	37	−885	870	−3.3	2.0
1938	71.6	28.4	36	41	36	33	18	1,801	0.1	4.1

[a] Total capacity and total production are listed in million tons.
[b] Capacity expansion is listed in thousand tons.
Source: U.S. Steel Corporation, *T.N.E.C. Papers* (New York, 1940) [Exhibits prepared for the Temporary National Economic Committee], vol. 2, pp. 138, 142.

market share could not have occurred (given industry pricing patterns), unless its utilization rate compared with that of other companies had fallen much faster than it did in fact. (Again, see Table 5 and Figure 4.)

Sometimes game theory is useful in analyzing investment decisions

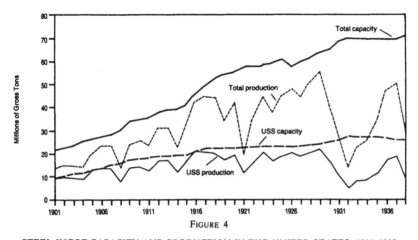

FIGURE 4

STEEL INGOT CAPACITY AND PRODUCTION IN THE UNITED STATES, 1901–1938

Source: Calculated from United States Steel Corporation, *T.N.E.C. Papers*, vol. 2, pp. 138–39, 142–43.

such as U.S. Steel's. For a well-specified set of technologies and costs, game-theoretic models can be employed to derive equilibrium investment strategies both for the leader and for potential entrants.[22] The application of these models to the historical data is difficult, however, and to our knowledge has not been attempted for U.S. Steel. The company's own perception of available technologies and costs can be estimated, but not with much precision throughout the long period of decline, which covered three decades. If U.S. Steel's archives were open to independent scholars, such a task would be more plausible. Even so, the possibility that the firm was constrained by other considerations such as antitrust tends to confound game-theoretic models. It is impossible to say, simply by examining the pattern of U.S. Steel's decline, whether the company was behaving in accordance with game-theoretic concepts developed some 60 years later. Further, even if U.S. Steel could be shown not to have behaved as game theory would predict, it would remain unclear whether this implied poor management on the part of the company, some weakness in the theory, or the presence of additional constraints.

We have seen that dynamic limit pricing provides a useful conceptual framework but is not amenable to direct empirical testing. Game-theoretic models of investment are also useful as behavioral paradigms, but are equally difficult to test against historical data.[23] Both sorts of

---

[22] Jean Tirole, *The Theory of Industrial Organization* (Cambridge, MA, 1988), contains numerous examples and comprehensive bibliographies.

[23] One implication of both dynamic limit pricing theory and of game-theoretic models of investment is that higher barriers to entry should lead to higher profits for the dominant firm, slower

models, furthermore, assume that the sole objective of the firm is the maximization of discounted profits and that the firm is unconstrained by either legal problems or other institutional factors. To provide a more satisfying explanation of U.S. Steel's decline, we need to relax these counterfactual assumptions. As we have seen, U.S. Steel was concerned with industry stability as well as with its own profits. The fear of antitrust litigation and the apparent inability of its managers to overcome inadequacies in organizational structure and performance also played important roles in its decline.

ANTITRUST CONSTRAINTS

Lurking in the background of U.S. Steel's management decisions in its first two decades is the long shadow of the Department of Justice. The avowed purpose of the firm's creation, as Gary expressed it, was "to form and complete an organization which would give us a self-contained, complete, rounded-out business proposition that would enable us to manufacture at the lowest cost all of the principal forms of

---

declines in its market share, or both. Steel is ordinarily regarded as having substantial barriers to entry. Comparative work on turn-of-the-century mergers, however, shows that barriers to entry in steel were not especially high and that U.S. Steel's loss of market share was not atypical of that of contemporary trusts.

Richard Caves, Michael Fortunato, and Pankaj Ghemawat have used the qualitative analytic framework provided by dynamic limit pricing to investigate the declining market share of major trusts of the early twentieth century. They have shown that a sample of 34 companies with a mean market share of 69 percent in 1905 had dropped by 1929 to a mean of 45 percent. They examined the effects of entry barriers, profit levels of the largest participant in each industry, and erosion of market share experienced by each dominant firm. As one might predict, they found that trusts protected by high entry barriers maintained higher profits, slower erosion of market share, or both. The table below shows some of their findings for U.S. Steel and the other 33 companies studied:

	U.S. Steel	Mean of All Trusts Studied
Profit Rate, 1901–1916 (Return on Invested Capital)	6.41%	7.16%
Profit Rate, 1917–1933	6.71%	7.36%
Percentage of market supplied by average plant of dominant firm	0.90%	5.08%

See Richard E. Caves, Michael Fortunato, and Pankaj Ghemawat, "The Decline of Dominant Firms, 1905–29," *Quarterly Journal of Economics*, 99 (Aug. 1984), pp. 523–46. The quoted data come not only from that article but also from the working papers behind it, which are available from its authors.

The last line of numbers listed is a measure of one kind of entry barrier. The authors also examined others, including degree of vertical integration, presence of patent protection, capital investment required for a plant of minimum efficient scale, and so on. For most of these categories, barriers in the steel industry were lower than average.

Less recent but still useful literature on the subject includes Dean A. Worcester, Jr., "Why 'Dominant Firms' Decline," *Journal of Political Economy*, 65 (Aug. 1957), pp. 338–46; Shaw Livermore, "The Success of Industrial Mergers," *Quarterly Journal of Economics*, 50 (Nov. 1935), pp. 68–96; and Eliot Jones, *The Trust Problem in the United States* (New York, 1921).

finished steel [to sell to] all parts of the world.''[24] Yet, even before the company was formed, Gary had considered the possibility that it could be successfully prosecuted under the Sherman Act. He is reported to have said to Morgan in 1901:

> If there should be a direct attack by the Attorney General against the new corporation at the beginning of its business career, the attack would probably be successful for the reason that so large a percentage of the iron and steel business is included in the new company; as the intentions of the organization have not been demonstrated, the Corporation is liable to be held a monopoly in opposition to the Sherman Law. But I also think that if the Corporation with its business is properly managed and it is allowed to continue in business until it has proven that the intentions of the managers are good, that there is no disposition to exercise a monopoly or to restrain legitimate trade, then in that case, if there is a contest, the company will be held to be legal.[25]

Gary was a first-rate lawyer, and in this case he was exactly right.

Until 1907–1908, as the numbers in Table 5 suggest, U.S. Steel did not behave as if it were seriously concerned with the danger of antitrust prosecution. Then it reversed course. Several events occurred during the period 1906 to 1908 that might have made the company adopt a more careful approach to its drive to expand capacity. In 1906 Gary publicly expressed his fear of "unreasonable political action," noting that "the atmosphere seems to be charged with distrust and suspicion," falling on "good and bad enterprises alike." Accordingly, he urged that "Every one in charge of great [business] responsibilities should be stimulated to use greater efforts to promote what is good, and to prevent what is bad."[26] And, indeed, in 1906 the Justice Department launched major antitrust suits against American Tobacco and Standard Oil, the second and third largest industrial corporations after U.S. Steel. Then, during the Panic of 1907, U.S. Steel purchased the Tennessee Coal, Iron, and Railroad Company. Gary's publicly proclaimed purpose in making this acquisition was to rescue a Wall Street brokerage firm from bankruptcy, and U.S. Steel portrayed its purchase as an act of industrial statesmanship. Even so, Gary was sufficiently sensitive to the antitrust implications to board a train for Washington and secure clearance for the merger from President Theodore Roosevelt.[27] Meanwhile, the Panic itself prompted a new wave of criticism of trusts, and the Bureau of

---

[24] Testimony of Elbert Gary, *United States v. United States Steel Corporation*, p. 4757.

[25] Quoted in Ida M. Tarbell, *The Life of Elbert H. Gary: The Story of Steel* (New York, 1925), pp. 123–24.

[26] Quoted in *The Iron Age*, 77 (Mar. 29, 1906), p. 1117.

[27] See Robert H. Wiebe, "The House of Morgan and the Executive, 1905–1913," *American Historical Review*, 65 (Oct. 1959), pp. 49–60; and Robert H. Wiebe, *Businessmen and Reform: A Study of the Progressive Movement* (Cambridge, MA, 1962), chap. 4. Gary's anxious state of mind in the 1906 to 1908 period is vividly recalled in a long retrospective interview he gave with Bureau of Corporations investigators on Oct. 6, 1911. See the interview transcript in the Bureau's records, Steel Investigation, File 1940-1, National Archives, Washington, DC.

Corporations began a long investigation into the affairs of U.S. Steel. In Congress, important bills were introduced foreshadowing the antitrust legislation eventually passed in 1914.[28] Also, in the presidential election of 1908, even the more conservative of the two candidates, William Howard Taft, urged vigorous antitrust prosecution. The Republican Taft, who won the election, was steeped in a kind of literal legalism and known to be committed to antitrust as a matter of principle. His Democratic opponent, William Jennings Bryan, was seen by many voters as an antibusiness radical.

Ida Tarbell, who interviewed Gary at length during the 1920s and prepared his biography, believed that he limited his company's market share so as to ensure victory in potential antitrust cases. Gary's strategy, wrote Tarbell,

> was not to allow in any branch [product line] over 50 per cent of the business, and oddly enough, it was William Jennings Bryan who set this per cent figure for him! Along in 1906 Bryan was advocating 50 per cent as a legal limit for the size of a business, and Judge Gary had seized the figure. 'If we confine ourselves voluntarily to a size approved by the most popular and trusted of radicals, we surely cannot be attacked for monopoly,' he told his associates. They had acquiesced and had succeeded fairly well in keeping the percentage down, even in the leading products.[29]

The idea that fear of antitrust litigation constrained U.S. Steel should not be overdrawn. Clearly, some of the firm's aggressive capacity expansions during its first six years—both through acquisition and new construction—could well have provoked antitrust prosecution. Even after capacity expansion slowed, U.S. Steel inaugurated the famous (if short-lived) Gary dinners, at which prices were openly discussed. Later, these dinners were held to be in violation of the Sherman Act, although the point was moot since they had ceased before the antitrust case was brought in 1911. Also, if antitrust fears had been *the* binding constraint of U.S. Steel's expansion, one might expect its relative decline to reverse or abate after the Supreme Court's decision of 1920 in the company's favor.

Yet antitrust considerations likely had a central role in explaining the capacity expansion figures presented in Table 5. In the final decision of 1920, the company escaped dismemberment by the narrowest possible margin. Four justices voted for the defendant U.S. Steel, three for the

---

[28] An editorial in *The Iron Age*, 81 (Feb. 13, 1908), p. 518, complained: "The scope and severity of laws to regulate business have vastly increased within a few years, and if the growth of legislation continues it will be a comparatively short time until every man who conducts an industry or business will be technically, at least, a law breaker." On the agitation within Congress, especially the powerful Hepburn Bill of 1908, see the middle chapters of Martin J. Sklar, *The Corporate Reconstruction of American Capitalism, 1890–1916: The Market, the Law, and Politics* (Cambridge, 1988).

[29] Quoted in Tarbell, *Life of Gary*, pp. 257–58. See also Bureau of Corporations Interview with Gary cited in fn. 27.

government. Two others, Louis Brandeis and James McReynolds, recused themselves. Brandeis had written muckraking articles against the company before coming on the Court in 1916; McReynolds, as President Woodrow Wilson's attorney general, had been indirectly involved in prosecuting the case. Had both of these men actually voted the verdict almost surely would have been five to four against the company.

The decision, in both the District Court and the Supreme Court, turned on the firm's behavior, just as Gary had foreseen in 1901. The opinions in the case refer repeatedly to U.S. Steel's loss of market share. Given the logic of the jurists' reasoning, it seems certain that had the company's share not dropped significantly from the 66 percent figure of 1901, it would have been dismembered.[30] The trade paper *Iron Age* summarized the outcome: "Here is the greatest corporation in the world, one whose coming many viewed with alarm, but where is one that has less power to turn to the right or to the left to carry out its own will, as against that of any related interest? It has had to be all things to all men—the servant of its competitors, its customers, its employees and the public."[31]

INSTITUTIONAL CONSTRAINTS

It is conceivable that U.S. Steel declined because it was constrained by limited access to capital or because its managers were overcautious in their appraisals of the likely growth of a market for steel. The first idea seems implausible after even a cursory look at the firm's board of directors, which included the greatest industrial capitalists and investment bankers of the period. U.S. Steel had access to whatever capital it wished to expend; indeed it built the world's largest integrated works at Gary's eponymous Chicago suburb. The second notion seems equally unlikely as an explanation for the sustained, systematic deterioration evident in Table 5.[32]

A more promising set of explanations for U.S. Steel's decline can be based on a close analysis of its organizational structure. The company did not adopt the kind of well-defined managerial hierarchy character-

[30] The contemporary press reporting of the District and Supreme Court decisions in 1915 and 1920, like the texts of those opinions, makes much of the decline of U.S. Steel's market share and the rise of competitors' share. See, for example, *Wall Street Journal*, June 4, 5, and 7, 1915; *Commercial and Financial Chronicle*, June 5, 1915, pp. 1860–61, 1873–75; *The Iron Age*, June 15, 1915, pp. 1299–1321; *Literary Digest*, June 12, 1915, p. 1386; *Literary Digest*, Mar. 13, 1920, pp. 17–18; *Wall Street Journal*, Mar. 2 and 3, 1920; and *New York Times*, Mar. 2, 3, and 4, 1920.

[31] *The Iron Age*, 95 (June 10, 1915), pp. 1302–4.

[32] A different focus altogether is evident in Parsons and Ray, "The Creation of Market Control." They are preoccupied with the company's control of ore, its building of market power, and foreign trade. We believe that control of ore was less important than they argue (partly because the company divested very substantial portions of its ore interests), and that the company did not possess as much market power as their argument implies.

istic of the most successful giant corporations. Leading firms in other industries (oil, chemicals, automobiles—even some in steel, such as Bethlehem) developed extraordinarily efficient structures that allowed them to track costs and allocate resources rationally across product divisions and functional activities. This accomplishment, in turn, enabled them to reap economies of scale, scope, and throughput, and to build sustainable cost advantages.[33] U.S. Steel, by contrast, operated as a loose federation topped by a holding company. Elbert Gary maintained his headquarters in New York, far from any important manufacturing complex or from U.S. Steel's traditional markets. (In fact, the company virtually ceded the East Coast market to Bethlehem and other rivals.) Gary's orientation and that of top management in general remained legal and financial as opposed to industrial. In 1941 the magazine *Fortune*, in a careful retrospective, contrasted the company unfavorably with Bethlehem Steel: "U.S. Steel is a combine, born of finance; Bethlehem was born of steel. The primary job of U.S. Steel's management has been administrative. The primary job of Bethlehem's management has been creative."[34]

The view that this kind of institutional orientation and capability is central to the history of managerial capitalism originated with Alfred D. Chandler, Jr., who has recently criticized U.S. Steel for failing to rationalize its operations. The senior managers, writes Chandler, "who were lawyers and financiers, failed to appreciate the value of operating full and steady." Although some rationalization did take place after 1901, especially in the area of plant specialization, U.S. Steel "made no attempt to create a single overall centralized, functionally departmentalized structure."[35]

Such arguments help to explain the questions about sluggish capacity expansion posed earlier. They also suggest reasons why the company's capacity utilization rates tended to fall. If the managers in New York cared little about field operations, then the company would be unlikely to pursue product and process innovations as aggressively as did such competitors as Bethlehem and Republic. Nor would it fully exploit available scale and scope economies. The only other managerial expla-

---

[33] Alfred D. Chandler, Jr., *Strategy and Structure: Chapters in the History of the American Industrial Enterprise* (Cambridge, MA, 1962); and Alfred D. Chandler, Jr., *The Visible Hand: The Managerial Revolution in American Business* (Cambridge, MA, 1977).

[34] "Bethlehem Steel," *Fortune*, 23 (Apr. 1941), p. 62. The same article contains the following comment about the reasons why U.S. Steel allowed Bethlehem to prosper through such deals as access to Minnesota iron ore: "The answer is that however much U.S. [Steel] disapproved of Bethlehem's upsurge, it was too big to become any bigger, for political and operating reasons. Judge Gary simply had to sit back in a forbearing, Christian manner and offer Bethlehem his blessing" (p. 144). For an insightful analysis of U.S. Steel's first three decades, see "The [United States Steel] Corporation" (cited in fn. 2).

[35] Alfred D. Chandler, Jr., *Scale and Scope: The Dynamics of Industrial Capitalism* (Cambridge, MA, forthcoming).

nation for the downward trend in capacity utilization is sheer incompetence. Yet this seems difficult to accept. It is true that Gary was a lawyer-financier and not an engineer or production man, but a review of his exhaustive testimony in the antitrust case and other proceedings reveals that he was solidly in control of his data and well versed in operational knowledge. Further—and again we believe this to be the most important point—U.S. Steel's utilization rates remained above the industry average for 25 years after the company's formation.

The most plausible managerial explanation of the phenomena exhibited in Table 5 and Figure 4 would run approximately as follows. First, in the early years after the company's formation, Gary, Morgan, and the executive team pursued a strategy of completing the rounded out, vertically integrated, full line of products company they had originally envisioned. They did this primarily by acquisition but also by constructing, over several years, the gigantic and efficient Gary mills in Indiana.

Second, beginning in the period 1906 to 1908, with the Gary mills under construction and their rounding out strategy more or less complete, U.S. Steel's managers now faced intensified antitrust sentiment. Accordingly, they tempered further construction and acquisition programs. Elbert Gary began to focus more on U.S. Steel's role as a stabilizing dominant firm, emphasizing intraindustry cooperation, especially with respect to prices. Meanwhile, little innovative product development and no huge new projects on the scale of the Gary mills were contemplated, despite an almost certain growth of demand.

Third, within the corporate organization, the holding company form persisted. Subsidiaries operated without much coordination except with respect to price. The best operating executives, notably Schwab and other members of the crack team assembled earlier by Carnegie, either retired or left for other steel companies where they would enjoy more entrepreneurial challenges than were possible under the Gary regime.[36]

Fourth, by the time U.S. Steel won its antitrust suit in 1915 and defeated the government's appeal in 1920, the company's organizational capabilities had long since atrophied. Now, U.S. Steel was poorly positioned as an organization to respond to the challenges of Bethlehem, Republic, and other aggressive firms which had been helped by the spurt in demand brought on by World War I.

Thus, a combination of forces, all in sequential reinforcement of each

[36] In 1911, Gary told Bureau of Corporations investigators "that he had been criticized sharply by his own presidents [of subsidiary companies], because they claimed that this plan [of price maintenance] was practically building up the Steel Corporation's competitors, inasmuch as the fair maintenance of prices by the Steel Corporation and the frequent failure to observe the schedule[d] prices by its competitors enabled such competitors to enlarge their proportion of the business (I have this sentence noted as 'confidential') [wrote the Bureau of Corporations investigator]; but Judge Gary said further that in his opinion the Steel Corporation from the start had too great a proportion in tubes, wire, and tin plate, and that it was his policy to let their proportion in those lines of the business be reduced." See interview citation in fn. 27.

other, ended by the 1920s with U.S. Steel still at the head of the industry—but, as an organization, one far different from the aggressive, intensely competitive company pioneered by Andrew Carnegie. Within a remarkably short time after U.S. Steel's formation in 1901, it had dissipated the legacy of managerial capability Carnegie had bequeathed it.[37]

AN OVERALL ASSESSMENT

For three decades, U.S. Steel followed patterns of pricing and investment that guaranteed an erosion of its market share. Instead of raising barriers to entry into the steel industry, it lowered them. It neither tried vigorously to retain its existing markets nor to take advantage of new growth opportunities in structural and rolled products. For possible explanations of this puzzling behavior, we must turn to the sum of evidence presented in this article. As Tibor Scitovsky once remarked: "Nothing is ever so simple that a single explanation will adequately explain it."[38] So with the case of U.S. Steel and its declining market share.

When the company was created in 1901, its founders had at least three objectives. They wanted to end cut-throat competition with its wild price fluctuations and instability that had characterized the steel business in the 1890s. To do so, they assembled the largest industrial enterprise the world had yet seen. They were not ignorant of the enormous underwriting profits that would accompany the formation of such a company. And they wanted to continue to operate the firm both to reap profits and maintain stability within the industry.

The company could hardly have been more explicit about its intentions. Its very first *Annual Report* highlighted an innovative "Policy as to Prices":

> The demand for the products of the several [operating] companies has been so great that prices could easily have been advanced. Indeed, higher prices have been voluntarily offered by consumers who were anxious for immediate execution

[37] Although cross-national comparisons are not central to our argument, we note that steel giants which merged more recently in other countries have lost share as well. In Britain, 14 companies combined in 1967 to form British Steel. The new firm had a total work force of 257,000 and a domestic market share of about 70 percent. By 1980, its share had dropped to only 48 percent. It recovered to 59 percent in 1983, by which time total employment had shrunk to about 80,000, less than one-third the original total. See Sara Coles, *The British Steel Corporation, 1967–1983* (n.p., Dec. 1983).

In Japan, the controversial merger during 1967 to 1970 of the two leading companies, Yawata and Fuji, to form Nippon Steel was also followed by loss of market share: in pig iron, from 45 percent in 1967 to 38 percent in 1984; in raw steel, from 36 to 28 percent; in hot rolled finished steel, from 37 to 31 percent. See Tsutomu Kawasaki, *Japan's Steel Industry* (Tokyo, 1985), p. 698. These figures pertain to total production, not to the domestic market alone as in the case of British Steel.

[38] Tibor Scitovsky, *Human Desire and Economic Satisfaction: Essays on the Frontiers of Economics* (New York, 1986).

of orders, but the companies have firmly maintained the position of not advancing prices, believing that the existing prices were sufficient to yield a fair return on capital and maintain the properties in satisfactory physical condition, and that the many collateral advantages to be gained in the long run by refusing to advance prices would be of substantial and lasting value, not only to the companies, but also to the general business interests of the country. The strong position thus taken by the companies for stability in prices both of raw material and finished products, has had a reassuring effect on the trade, and has contributed greatly toward restoring confidence in the general business situation and creating the present large demand for steel products, by dispelling any doubt as to prices in the future.[39]

In 1902, when this statement was issued, corporations were not required to publish annual reports at all, and U. S. Steel received widespread plaudits for its pioneering example of openness.[40]

If we take at face value the "Policy as to Prices" and combine it with other evidence, then it is hard to escape the conclusion that the founders of U.S. Steel succeeded brilliantly in their aims. The company returned respectable dividends to its shareholders, and prices stabilized to a degree that would have been inconceivable in the nineteenth century.[41] Whether management's aims were good for the company, the industry, or the macroeconomy remain other questions. Clearly, the cost of U.S. Steel's policy was an inexorable loss of market share: not only because of pricing but even more because of decisions not to innovate with new products and not to build new plants at a rate commensurate with the pattern of overall demand. Ultimately, Gary's pursuit of "stability" had drifted into an obsession with maintaining the status quo—an ominous development for any firm, however powerful.

In economic theory, as we have seen, it is far from axiomatic that a loss of market share, taken by itself, constitutes evidence of a company's failure. Relinquishment of share by the market leader over time is consistent with at least some prescriptions of optimal business

[39] United States Steel Corporation, *Annual Report 1901* (New York, 1902), p. 14.

[40] The company, while criticized for its "overcapitalization," was also praised for its adherence to the "Policy as to Prices" in the face of very high demand for steel in 1901 to 1902. See, for example, *The Nation*, Mar. 13, 1902, p. 205: "The Steel Corporation started with a heavy [financial] strain on its resources. It is very fortunate for the company that this year's market for its products should have developed demands far beyond what the most sanguine prophet could have foreseen. It is still more fortunate that this tidal wave of prosperity in the iron trade should have failed to sweep away the company's managers from their original position as to prices."

[41] In 1920 Gary was still evangelizing on the virtues of stability: "We think stability in business is of the highest importance and that every man, to the extent of his opportunity and ability, and even at some sacrifice, is obligated to assist in stabilizing and maintaining prices on a fair and sane level. The producer, consumer and workman will be benefited by this attitude"; *The Iron Age*, 106 (Nov. 25, 1920), p. 1428. The context was Gary's announcement that U.S. Steel would not increase prices despite increases in its costs. His obsession with stability almost never wavered, and can be followed in detail over a 20-year period in his many appearances before congressional committees and in his speeches, many of which were published in the *Proceedings* of the American Iron and Steel Institute, of which he was the perennial president. The Bureau of Corporations Records (National Archives) also has a broad collection of Gary's speeches to other groups.

behavior. Dynamic limit pricing, game-theoretic approaches to capacity expansion, and industrial organization analyses all describe circumstances in which the loss of share might benefit the leader.

On the other hand, any of these theoretical approaches to the U.S. Steel story would predict very substantial excess profits during the period of market share losses. What happened to these profits? In all likelihood, they failed to materialize fully for the same reasons that the company's market share declined so quickly: the pursuit of stability, the fear of antitrust litigation, and an institutional structure incapable of exploiting the rich legacies the company inherited from Carnegie Steel.

In the end, the overall meaning of the theoretical and empirical evidence is not a determinate matter but one of historical judgment. In our interpretation, the antitrust constraint and other political factors, together with the related deterioration of the company's managerial capabilities, loom large in explaining both the declining market share and the absence of extraordinary profits. In the first decades of the twentieth century, Gary and other top managers of U.S. Steel watched as American Tobacco, Standard Oil, Du Pont, and other giant firms lost antitrust suits and were forced to divest major portions of their companies. U.S. Steel, being much larger than any of these other firms, lived in an even more fragile glass house. Gary and his colleagues understood this and behaved accordingly.[42] They coddled their competitors, forbore to build a modern administrative structure for their own company, took special pains to issue informative annual reports, and often made their corporate records public—sometimes even including their own cost data. And when they did come before the bench in a major antitrust suit, they won, unlike their counterparts in other industries.

Consider as one final contrast the history of Alcoa, a primary metals firm like U.S. Steel. During the first four decades of the twentieth century, both Alcoa and U.S. Steel integrated vertically and horizontally. Yet Alcoa also adopted a centralized management structure, engaged in a zealous policy of preemptive capacity expansion, and took

---

[42] The evidence of U.S. Steel's attempts to stay out of trouble with the government is overwhelming. For example, an editorial titled "The Steel Corporation Helps Its Competitors," *The Iron Age*, 88 (Aug. 24, 1911), praised U.S. Steel for its actions during a strike in Britain that led to a shortage of tin in the United States: "If the United States Steel Corporation had chosen to use all its advantages for its own purposes and to ignore its competitors the opportunity here existed for reaping important benefits. This would have been ordinary commercial selfishness, and would by no means have been illegal restraint of trade. The Steel Corporation chose to do otherwise, however, and thus signally manifested its liberality and magnanimity."

Gary and others were in fact shocked when the antitrust case was actually brought against them. As the prominent banker Frank Vanderlip wrote privately in 1911, "The Steel people, however, have been hopeful up to the last that this would not happen and have tried to do everything possible to avoid it and to bring themselves in line with official opinions." Quoted in Sklar, *The Corporate Reconstruction*, p. 375, fn. 71. See also the Gary interview with Bureau of Corporations officials cited in fn. 27.

part in an international cartel. In the ultimate reckoning, Alcoa, like Standard Oil and American Tobacco, lost its big antitrust case, whereas U.S. Steel a quarter of a century earlier had won.

Seen in this light, the U.S. Steel story becomes not just an epic of administrative failure, or an example of oligopolistic inevitability, or, necessarily, a harbinger of American industrial decline. It may be all three; but fundamentally it is a story of political economy. It constitutes a vivid instance of the interrelated nature of public policy and business behavior—an exemplar of the proposition that "success" in twentieth-century American business has sometimes been defined not only in the marketplace but also in the court of public opinion. In an open democratic polity, if a firm is perceived as too large and powerful, then its management might behave too conservatively for the good of their own company; and this is what Gary and his colleagues did.

Kansas City Stockyards

Missouri and the Beef Trust:
Consumer Action and Investigation
1902

BY STEVEN L. PIOTT*

When William McKinley ran a successful campaign for reelection in 1900 on a slogan that promised the American worker a "full-dinner pail," he indeed appeared optimistic. Perhaps more people were working and the worst aspects of the depression had passed, but severe fluctuations in the cost of living and retail price indexes created a more dreary picture. From 1891 through 1897, real hourly earnings in all industries remained almost stationary and from 1898 through 1902 rose only slightly. But after falling 9 percent for 1891-1897, the cost of living index ominously pushed upward after 1898. By 1902 it had increased 9 percent above the 1898 level. Similar results appeared in the retail price index for food. For 1891-1897, food prices dropped 5.2 percent, but in 1898-1902, they

*Steven L. Piott is assistant professor of History at the University of Kansas, Lawrence. He has the B.A. and M.A. degrees in History from the University of Utah, Salt Lake City; and the Ph.D. in History from the University of Missouri-Columbia.

31

actually jumped 8.3 percent.[1] Prosperity had not come to rural and urban America, but to corporate America. Such changes created problems of serious consequence. The director of the Board of Charity of St. Joseph, Missouri, worried that monthly grants of money, usually not more than $5.00 per family, would soon be inadequate to meet rising food prices. The cheapest kind of beef had increased in cost from 5 cents a pound to 12½ cents a pound in just one year. Potatoes had more than doubled in price in a year from 40-50 cents to $1.05 a bushel. According to the director, an allotment which had once been good for the purchase of twenty pounds of soup meat and two bushels of potatoes would now have to be stretched to buy twelve pounds of meat and one bushel of potatoes.[2] Price increases had accentuated the age-old problem of making means and ends meet.

As price increases continued during the "trust era" which began in 1898, people, in their roles as consumers, increasingly pointed the finger of blame at the trusts. They sought their own means of meeting the problem through consumer boycotts and popular pressure for legal action. Consumers understood their declining purchasing power to be directly linked to corporate consolidation or, in the term most commonly used at the time, the trusts. Over 100 trusts were incorporated during 1899 alone, more than doubling the number in existence prior to that time. By 1903, the number had increased to over 300.[3]

People struggled to grasp the connection between rising prices and corporate consolidation. Occasionally, newspapers helped. The *St. Louis Post-Dispatch*, in August 1899, found prices higher on nearly every necessity of life. In fact, the cost of these necessities, on the average, proved 15 percent higher than they had been a year earlier. This trend occurred at a time of plentiful crops, when the supply of raw materials of all kinds had never been larger, and when the amount of manufactured products exceeded previous years. These facts called into question presumed "laws" of supply and demand. The *Post-Dispatch* concluded, that without unnatural manipulation, these conditions would cause a decrease in prices instead of an increase. But trusts had forced price increases upon

---

[1] U.S. Bureau of the Census, *Historical Statistics of the United States, 1789-1945* (Washington, D.C., 1949), 235-236; Paul H. Douglas, *Real Wages in the United States, 1890-1926* (Boston, 1930), 205.

[2] *St. Joseph Gazette*, April 28, 1902.

[3] Hans B. Thorelli, *The Federal Antitrust Policy* (Baltimore, 1955), 294-303; *St. Louis Post-Dispatch*, March 9, 1899.

the people to "make dividends for largely over-capitalized combinations."[4] In some instances, such as with the Beef Trust, the large slaughtering houses linked price increases to shortages in cattle. But butchers and consumers refused to accept these explanations. Price advances forced many butchers out of business, especially in the poorer urban sections of the city where demand declined. Butchers blamed the increase on price-fixing by the large packing concerns, and consumers easily accepted these assertions when they learned that the price of cattle had gone up 5 percent while consumer prices had advanced an average of 33 percent.[5] High beef prices in St. Louis in 1899 caused consumer pressures and butcher dissatisfaction with the trust. The situation provoked retail butchers in the city to follow preliminary plans drawn up by the National Retail Butchers' Cooperative Association, to erect cooperative slaughterhouses and sell to subscribers directly.[6]

Consumers and butchers appeared justified in their suspicions. By the turn of the century the Beef Trust possessed economic power over an industry exceeded only in extent by the Standard Oil Trust. Gustavas Swift had combined refrigerated railroad cars and refrigerated warehouses to create the first national meat packing company in the late 1880s. Other packinghouses quickly followed his example and soon formed a system based on a mutuality of interest. About 1885 these major meat packers, especially the

---

[4] *Ibid.*, August 20, 1899.
[5] *Ibid.*, July 25, 1899.
[6] *Ibid.*, August 23, 1899.

Armour Packing Company, Kansas City, About 1902

Armour, Swift and Morris concerns, combined their efforts. They formed a pool to dominate a large portion of the food industry by controlling and regulating shipments of dressed meats to the markets. By 1893, the packers had expanded their combination. For the next three years, representatives of cooperating companies met weekly on Tuesday to divide the country into territories and determine the volume of shipments each house could make for that week. The combine worked well and, by 1898, had expanded to include six leading companies. They shared statistical reports and proportioned shipments on that basis. Any company exceeding its percentage of shipments paid a 40-cent fine (later 75 cents) per hundred pounds of excess. Companies short of their quotas received this fee as compensation. A group of auditors kept a check on the system. To complete the arrangement, the pool adopted a uniform method of figuring the cost of fresh meat so that profit margins would remain identical. This pooling agreement continued in undisturbed form until the spring of 1902.[7]

Producers, not consumers, initiated the first protests against the meat packing industry. The Beef Trust maintained tight secrecy about its pooling agreements, but its activities aroused the suspicions of western cattlemen and butchers. In response to complaints from these groups, a special committee of U.S. senators from Missouri, Kansas, Illinois, Texas and Nebraska began hearings in St. Louis in November 1888, to investigate the industry. The senators selected St. Louis because the International Cattle Range Association and the Butchers' National Protective Association met there. After two years of investigation the committee issued the Vest Report in 1890. It confirmed the existence of a "Beef Trust" which included the Armour, Swift, Nelson Morris and Hammond companies. The committee found convincing proof of collusion in the price fixing of beef, the division of territory and business, including public contracts, and the compulsion of retailers to purchase from the major packers. Conditions revealed by the Vest Report helped facilitate the passage of the Sherman Antitrust Act on July 2, 1890. Livestock producers, alarmed over low stock prices, prompted a federal grand jury to hold hearings in 1895. However, it brought no indictments.[8]

---

[7] Federal Trade Commission, *Report on the Meat-Packing Industry* (Washington, D.C., 1919), Summary and Pt. I, 46-48, 237-256; *ibid.* (Washington, D.C., 1918), Pt. II, 11-17; Rudolf Alexander Clemen, *The American Livestock and Meat Industry* (New York, 1923), 745-767.

[8] Federal Trade Commission, *Report*, Pt. II, 13; *ibid.*, Summary and Pt. I, 46; Clemen, *American Livestock*, 748-750.

By the turn of the century, anger at the Beef Trust may have attracted readers to H. G. Wells's story, "When the Sleeper Wakes," which told of a universal food trust. When the people came under the food trust the slot machine lunch would be universal. On the walls above the machines, mottos would direct: "Help Yourself," "No Tips" and "Be Your Own Waiter." The trust's first economy would put all waiters out of work. Of necessity, consumers would take what the trust's slot machine offered or go hungry. This very well might be meatless sandwiches, chicory coffee, oleo butter and other articles, "that a trust may put before its customers so as to secure dividends for its stockholders." Consumers found it useless to smash the slot lunch machine, "as a man does not quarrel with his bread and oleo." After all, the trust might forget to refill the machines![9]

Fear of a food trust, control of meat products and rising consumer costs increased in November 1901. Reports surfaced that certain Chicago dealers had combined to corner the egg market. The large packinghouses entered the chicken killing business, bought eggs in enormous amounts and placed them in cold storage for speculative purposes. One would-be poet contemplated the results as he put his thoughts to rhyme:

Now the gentle egglet seeketh
For admission to the trust,
And it sayeth (loud it speaketh);
Lemme in there, or I'll bust;
I, too long have lingered lowly
At a dime or two a doz.;
Now I seek a higher goal, a
Taller price than used to wuz
At a dollar a doz., the waiter
Will no longer yell 'Ham and;'
I'll be brother to the tater,
As to price, and rule the land.[10]

A common rumor spread that greedy packing corporations busily worked hens overtime, feeding them red pepper and raw meat to stimulate their laying power. Reportedly in four and one-half months, Chicago's big cold storage houses of Armour and Swift gained control of 500,000 cases of eggs, enough to manipulate prices.[11] As long as prices increased moderately, or high levels did not continue for extended periods of time, consumers remained

---

[9] *St. Louis Post-Dispatch,* June 1, 1900.
[10] *Ibid.,* November 14, 1901.
[11] *Ibid.*

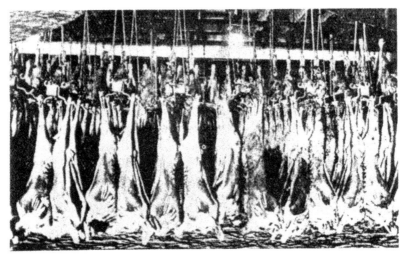

The *St. Joseph Journal of Commerce* depicted this sheep chill room at Nelson Morris & Co., in 1900.

cynical commentators and sporadic grumblers. As temporarily shown with beef in St. Louis in 1899, however, consumers and butchers could potentially unite to directly confront the trust.

News of exorbitant price increases for beef frequented newspapers during the first months of 1902, telling consumers what they already knew. According to the *St. Joseph Gazette*, people of moderate means severely felt the recent advance in nearly all food products. Along with the increased cost, few of them had experienced a corresponding increase in their annual incomes. Supposedly, the country experienced a period of "unexampled prosperity," but curiously, it seemed restricted to certain corporations and trusts. If the Beef Trust had advanced meat prices only a fraction of a cent, claims of shortages might have been accepted without challenge. Advances of from three to four cents a pound seemed to stretch credibility.[12] The *Lamar Leader* determined that, with the price of beef "soaring among the clouds" and the manufacturers of tinware forming a trust, the average workman would find the promised "full-dinner pail" to be "chimerical."[13] The editor of the *St. Joseph Daily News* noted that four straight years of price increases had forced the poor to quit using all but the cheaper grades of beef. Market butchers blamed the price elevation on a conspiracy of packers. They asserted that the rise in the price of

12 *St. Joseph Gazette*, April 10, 1902.
13 Cited in *Sedalia Democrat*, April 16, 1902.

dressed meat appeared well out of proportion to the increase in the price of cattle.[14]

Packers and consumers also differed in their explanations of rising beef costs and the affects of those costs upon people. The major beef packers claimed that conditions required the advance in meat prices. In their defense the packers pointed to a light corn crop, caused by drouth, which had raised the price of cattle feed. They also accused farmers of holding out for higher prices which, linked to the growing consumer demand, made the cost of beef dear to consumers.[15] Charles W. Armour, head of the Armour Packing Company, repeatedly denied knowledge of a Beef Trust. He maintained that "natural causes" led to expensive dressed meats and livestock. In fact, the workingman need not fear increased costs. Armour contended that: "The man who lives on prime rib roasts and porterhouse steaks pays for the advance in the prices of beef, while the price to the purchasers for cheaper cuts is kept down."[16] Such statements made no sense at all to the editors of the *St. Louis Labor Compendium*. They responded that "the most unpopular man these days is he who tries to prove there is no meat trust."[17] George Marr, an agent for Armour and Company in Houston, Texas, supported his employer when he spoke of the effects of high meat prices on the workingman. In Marr's opinion, workingmen ate too much:

> Their appetites don't suit their resources. The laborer of England is contented with the soup bone and porridge, and craves for nothing more, while the average negro and the poor white man . . . , with a wage of $2 or $3 a day, wants porterhouse, demands porterhouse and, in the past, has been able to get porterhouse because the market was easy and within reach of his purse.[18]

Working people held a different view. Alois Bilker, a St. Louis Street Department sweeper, earned $1.50 a day and voiced his own opinion of the meat situation:

> We have meat but once a day now at our house. It is too high to expect a poor man to serve it at every meal. As long as I have had a family I do not know when it was so high. Nowadays we buy round steak, cut as thin as paper almost, for twenty cents or perhaps fifteen cents,

---

14 *St. Joseph Daily News*, April 16, 1902.
15 St. Louis *Butchers and Packers' Gazette*, April 26, 1902.
16 *St. Louis Star*, April 29, 1902.
17 *St. Louis Labor Compendium*, May 4, 1902.
18 *St. Louis Post-Dispatch*, May 3, 1902.

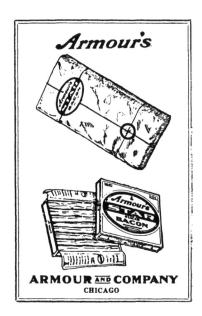

Armour's

ARMOUR AND COMPANY
CHICAGO

and we are lucky in getting it at that. Generally we have to buy shoulder and neck pieces, because we get more of that part of the cow for the money. We have to fall back on beans and cheap things to take the place of meat. There is much grumbling down in my neighborhood around Geyer Avenue. We all believe that a few rich men get together and make the prices. That story about higher beef and scarcity of corn and so on may do for some, but we do not believe that it is necessary to send up the price of meat the way they do.[19]

The assumed inability of workers to purchase select cuts of meat concealed a powerlessness to purchase a sufficient quantity of meat or any meat at all.

The federal government offered a strange kind of assistance. H. W. Wiley, head of the Bureau of Chemistry of the United States Agriculture Department, encouraged the adoption of cereal substitutes for high-priced beef products. Only half-jokingly, he predicted that vegetarianism might become a fad if beef prices continued to soar.[20] The editor of the *Baltimore American* joked along similar lines. Linking production and consumption, he put his suggestion to rhyme:

Mary had a little lamb,
    With mintsauce on the side;
When Mary saw the meat trust's bill,
    It shocked her so she cried.

Mary had a little veal—
    A cutlet, nicely broiled
Her papa, to pay for that veal,
    All morning sorely toiled.
Mary had a little steak—
    A porterhouse quite small,
And when the bill came in, she sighed;
    No dress for me next fall.

19 *St. Louis Republic,* April 27, 1902.
20 *St. Louis Post-Dispatch,* May 4, 1902.

> Mary had a little roast—
>   As juicy as could be—
> And Mary's papa simply went
>   Right into bankruptcy.
>
> Mary isn't eating meat;
>   She has a better plan;
> She vows it's ladylike to be
>   A vegetarian.[21]

A more graphic story involved a seventeen-year-old boy who attempted suicide with morphine. When asked the reason for this near fatal attempt, the boy replied:

> Since we came from the country two months ago I have supported mother and sister on my wages of $7 a week. I earned that sum setting type . . . , but last week I lost my job, and Wednesday I got work as a pantry boy at the Westmorland Hotel. But my earnings would not meet our expenses. Meat was so high and all the world seemed against me. So I decided to die.[22]

To consumers living on the margins of survival, the slighest increase in food prices could be catastrophic.

In mid-April 1902, the precipitous rise in meat prices and popular dissatisfaction prompted mild action from the attorney general's office. On April 14, U.S. Attorney General Philander C. Knox instructed William Warner, U.S. District Attorney in Kansas City, to take preliminary steps to investigate the so-called Beef Trust.[23] Traffic officials of eastern and western railroads added to the problems of the major packinghouses. They asserted that in Chicago plans to corner the beef market had been implemented. They based this belief on the fact that beef provisions destined for export had rapidly declined in the last month. The export figure appeared smaller than at any time in the past several years. The not-so-subtle hint by those officials revealed stockpiling by large packinghouses for speculative purposes.[24]

---

21 *St. Joseph Gazette*, April 26, 1902.
22 *St. Louis Post-Dispatch*, May 3, 1902.
23 *St. Joseph Gazette*, April 14, 1902. Antitrust investigations also were begun on the state level. Attorney General M. A. Breeden of Utah began proceedings against the alleged Beef Trust in Salt Lake City by requesting statistics of the state food and dairy commissioner relating to the recent advance in the price of meat. *St. Joseph Daily News*, April 26, 1902. In Denver, Colorado Attorney General C. C. Post began an attempt before the state board of equalization to prove that the Armour car lines were owned by the packing company, and, therefore, part of the Beef Trust. His avowed intention was to "assess the beef trust out of the state." *Kansas City Journal*, April 27, 1902.
24 *St. Louis Chronicle*, April 16, 1902.

**U.S. Attorney General
Philander C. Knox**

Missourians, like other citizens, raised many questions concerning the ethics of the meat packing industry. One Missouri stockman found no excuse for the "squeeze" in beef prices:

> The packers are the people who are making the money out of this upward flight of the price of meat, for while we are getting good prices for our cattle, feed is high, making the cost of feeding higher than formerly. The packers' raise is way out of proportion to the increase in the price of cattle. The big fat steers which can be bought for 6 cents a pound now have not been below 5 cents for the past five years. It is certainly hard on the common people.[25]

The *Springfield Leader and Democrat* also raised questions concerning the sale of beef in Missouri. Located in the heart of the drouth section, dealers in Springfield, Missouri, somehow could sell beef a good deal cheaper than dealers in Kansas City, the state's leading cattle market and slaughterhouse center. Some cuts

---

[25] *Kansas City Journal,* April 19, 1902.

sold in Kansas City at almost twice the price as in Springfield. What possible explanation could be given? Charges for delivery service, supply depots and wagons proved comparable, and Kansas City packers even had to pay railroad duties to ship to the southern part of the state. The *Leader-Democrat* concluded that the only explanation lay in the type of business conducted. Springfield packers had competition, and the Kansas City trust did not. Many local Springfield butchers continued to do their own killing. In most other places, the packers had forced the butchers to quit killing by establishing their own local meat market outlets. According to a Springfield newspaper: "That was never done here, and old-fashioned ways still prevail to an extent in the butchers' trade." The reading public slowly received a lesson in trust policy and pocketbook economics, in addition, they realized the threat to their nearly self-sufficient lifestyle and values of economic independence.[26]

Many people began to fear the formation of an even greater food trust from within the Beef Trust. The Retail Butchers and Meat Dealers' Protective Association also condemned the meat combine for the "almost prohibitive" prices of meat. Members alerted consumers that trust control might extend to foodstuffs in general. J. A. Hoffman, second vice president of the organization commented:

> The Beef Trust is taking advantage of the fact that there is a natural cause for the rise in beef and is using it as a lever to advance the price of meats beyond any real necessity. The Beef Trust is not content to run up the price of meat beyond reason, but it is also controlling, to a great extent, the vegetable market. The price of potatoes is today regulated by this same Beef Trust . . . . . Butter and eggs are not beyond the grasp of this same trust.[27]

In one week, Swift and Company reportedly rushed 100,000 cases of eggs into cold storage for speculative purposes. The *St. Louis Chronicle*, on April 23, 1902, reported that 50,000 cases of eggs had been stored by St. Louis speculators endeavoring to force up the price of eggs three cents in one week. A day later, the *Kansas City Star* reported that major packers were uniting to control the supply of eggs and poultry. It also claimed to possess information that major packers directly bought from the farmers, thereby

---

[26] *Springfield Leader-Democrat*, April 28, 1902; *Kansas City Star*, April 14, 1902.

[27] *St. Louis Republic*, April 26, 1902.

shutting out the concession men. Eggs, which sold at 10 cents a dozen in 1901, sold for at 18 cents a dozen in April 1902.[28]

Reporters for the *Kansas City Journal*, on April 19, 1902, had informed their readers of the Beef Trust's ultimate objective to corner all food products and form a colossal food combination. Readers, as consumers, feared the dream of H. G. Wells might be possible. Citizens of Philadelphia and other eastern cities realized the Beef Trust's power in the butter, egg and poultry line. The trust also aimed to corner the vegetable and fruit market. Reportedly for two years prior to 1902, the big packing firms had been anticipating the formation of one gigantic trust. As a result, the various concerns increased plant capacities which would enhance profits in the event of a trust agreement. Plant expansion had increased cold storage room beyond storage needs. With the surplus space, the packers could control the cold storage facilities of every great market and buy up provisions to hold until a corner could be effected.[29] Exorbitant price figures appeared on every kind of perishable food preserved in a refrigerator. Spring chickens which had been killed in 1901, wrapped up in "trust tissue paper" and laid away by carloads in cold storage plants, sold at a cost far greater than 1902 broilers. Apparently the Beef Trust held back all food supplies to create a "ficticious scarcity" that would assure higher prices. The *Mirror* reported: "The man who eats broilers and truffles and the man who pampers his family on pot-roast and cabbage, are at one in their grievance against the beef trust."[30] Consumers became a powerful potential force for resistance.

In many cities consumers began expressing attitudes of resistance to what they regarded as trust imposition. Although the advance in consumers' meat cost had not proven a conspiracy, "an impression of this kind could result in nothing else than general agitation and resentment . . . ."[31] In the smaller St. Louis meat shops, butchers found their customers "complaining lustily." In the city, the consumption of meat fell off 5 percent in two weeks. Fish became the staple for many as the demand trebled. Butchers and consumers began to unite to resist the "extortion" of the Beef Trust. In the words of one retail butcher: "Our interests are the same as those of the public." This same butcher noted that consumers had begun to advocate cooperative butcher shops, "like

---

[28] *Sedalia Democrat*, April 20. 1902: *St. Louis Chronicle*, April 23, 1902; *Kansas City Star*, April 24, 1902.
[29] *Kansas City Journal*, April 19, 1902.
[30] *Mirror*, XII (April 24, 1902), 2.
[31] *Kansas City Star*, April 29, 1902.

The *St. Joseph Journal of Commerce* depicted the beef killing department at Swift & Co., in 1900.

A hog cutting scene at Nelson Morris & Co., also appeared in the *Journal of Commerce.*

those started in New York by butchers to fight the trust."[32] In Indianapolis, Indiana, grocers who had conducted meat businesses for years, discontinued the sale of beef and beef products. They notified suppliers that they would not resume the trade until they witnessed a "substantial" reduction in prices. Several butcher shops, not connected with grocery stores, also closed or refused to buy from Chicago packers. In some instances the boycott caused butchers to contemplate cooperative resistance in which they would buy live cattle and do their own slaughtering.[33]

Workers yielded to their roles as consumers, using their producer-oriented forms of organization to boycott the trust. In Bloomington, Illinois, 2,000 employees of the Chicago and Alton Rail-

[32] *St. Louis Post-Dispatch,* April 24, 1902.
[33] *Kansas City Journal,* April 23, 1902.

road shops agreed that none of their members would eat meat for a thirty-day period. The workers hoped to encourage others to follow their example and force the Beef Trust to reduce the prices of meat. Dayton, Ohio, protestants started an endless chain letter crusade against the Beef Trust. Thousands of letters broadcasted the high price of meat and encouraged abstinence for one week. Four hundred workers in Bellefontaine, Ohio, signed an agreement refusing to eat any meat for thirty days. The Central Labor Union of Amsterdam, New York, composed of twenty-five subordinate unions and 5,000 members, began a thirty-day boycott to abstain from using any meat handled by the so-called "meat trust."[34]

Popular outcry against the Beef Trust and the notice of potential federal litigation provoked legal action in Missouri. On April 29, 1902, Missouri Attorney General Edward C. Crow filed a petition with Chief Justice Gavon D. Burgess of the state supreme court. He requested representatives of the major packinghouses in Missouri to testify concerning the alleged Beef Trust's control of meat prices. Crow based his petition on violations of the state's antitrust law which prohibited packers from conspiring to fix the wholesale and retail prices of all beef, pork and dressed meats. Judge Burgess complied with the order and asked representatives to appear before the court on May 6, 1902.[35] Crow noted that federal authorities had instituted suits against the Beef Trust but would not hear any evidence for some time. He remarked that his investigation would be the first in the country to reveal the real conditions among the packers. The attorney general had spent six weeks researching the causes for the current high meat prices before filing his petition. He noted that the investigation was "arousing interest throughout the country . . . ."[36]

On May 6, 1902, "Beef Trust" hearings began in Jefferson City before the Missouri Supreme Court. None of the representatives from the packing companies appeared. Their legal counsel had advised them to object to the hearings by questioning the constitutionality of the antitrust law.[37] The court also subpoenaed more

---

[34] *St. Louis Republic*, April 25, 1902; *St. Louis Chronicle*, April 30, 1902; *Kansas City Journal*, April 30, 1902; *Sedalia Democrat*, May 4, 1902.

[35] Among those summoned were Charles W. Armour (Armour Packing Co.), J. C. Dold (Jacob Dold Packing Co.), O. W. Waller (Swift and Co.), Gust Bischoff (St. Louis Dressed Beef Co.), and Walter Pfeiffer (St. Louis Butchers' Union). *St. Louis Star*, April 29, 1902.

[36] *St. Joseph Gazette*, May 2, 1902.

[37] They were represented by attorneys Frank Hagerman and Alexander New of Kansas City. *St. Louis Star*, May 6, 1902.

than forty retail butchers from St. Louis, Kansas City and St. Joseph. They did appear and told of trust methods in those cities. These butchers testified that representatives of Armour, Swift, Cudahy, Morris—the "Big Four"—fixed a uniform price for meat and fined their agents, salesmen or companies if they sold at a lower price.[38] Some butchers testified that they received rebates on purchases, some in cash and others in an extra supply of meat. Packinghouse salesmen had cautioned them to keep the dealings secret. They levied fines if others found out. This tightly controlled system, including a blacklist of delinquent creditors, forced butchers to buy from the Big Four packers or fear a boycott by the combine.[39]

The second day of the inquiry revealed further evidence of the combine's efforts to control prices. Testimony showed that

---

[38] One butcher stated that the prices in St. Joseph had been raised four or five times since January alone. An arbitrator represented the leading packing companies and it was his duty to supervise the accounts of retail dealers with the wholesale houses he represented. A retailer who failed to pay his bill on time, and whose indebtedness had been made known to the arbitrator, would be placed on a delinquent list and allowed future goods on a cash basis only.

[39] *St. Louis Post-Dispatch*, May 6, 1902; *St. Louis Chronicle*, May 6, 1902; *St. Louis Star*, May 6, 1902.

Wounded.

Farm Machinery in July 11, 1905, reprinted this *Indianapolis News* cartoon of the federal grand jury's indictments of the Beef Trust.

**Missouri Attorney General
Edward C. Crow**

salesmen of Swift, Armour, Nelson Morris and other large concerns undersold the smaller packing companies, with the intention of driving them out of business.[40] Retail butchers felt similar trust pressure. Maurice Prendiville, a St. Louis butcher, stated that Armour damaged the interests of some butchers by operating de- livery wagons and selling to customers direct and at a prohibitively lower price. Evidently designed as a lesson, the practice taught butchers to buy only "trust" beef and at a regular fixed price. Even shippers appeared at the mercy of the combine. If shippers did not sell all their goods to the trust, it would refuse to make any purchase, whatsoever. If a shipper refused their price and chose to reship his meat to Chicago, he faced similar results. The packers merely wired their offer to Chicago and the shipper would receive the same price there.[41]

---

[40] The Mound City Packing Company and the North St. Louis Packing Company were two firms that had gone under.
[41] *St. Louis Chronicle,* May 7, 1902; *St. Louis Star,* May 7, 1902; *St. Joseph Gazette,* May 7, 1902.

Testimony not only confirmed that the trust artificially increased meat prices, but it also forced consumers to purchase an inferior product. According to one St. Louis meat dealer, "the number of cattle sold and killed in East St. Louis this season has been unusually large." He quickly noted that most of that meat had been placed in cold storage and withheld from the market. When the public learned that the big packers had sold diseased meat to St. Louis consumers, the term "concession" beef entered the consumer's vocabulary. Under this practice wholesalers sold "ripe," "aged," "stale" or "beginning to spoil" meat to butchers at a reduced price, after the packing firms granted a price concession to the wholesaler. During the hearings Captain T. L. O'Sullivan, a St. Louis meat dealer, under oath revealed the sale of decayed meat in that city. It had been rubbed to remove "whiskers," painted to restore a wholesome color, and preserved with amonia. "Lumpy-jawed" cattle, condemned by government inspectors in East St. Louis, were smuggled over the bridge at night and sold in the St. Louis market at a discount as concession beef. These revelations prompted public attention on several fronts. The St. Louis House of Delegates considered measures to provide for the proper inspection of cattle. Mayor Rolla Wells and Health Commissioner Dr. Max C. Starkloff held a conference and decided to add three additional meat inspectors.[42]

Following these exposures the state's legal apparatus began to respond. The selling of life threatening adulturated meat provoked Circuit Attorney Joseph W. Folk to initiate his own investigation. Folk requested the St. Louis grand jury to proceed against the Beef Trust and stated: "This has become a subject for the criminal courts and the matter will be investigated as have been the bribery scandals, and I have no doubt but that men who have been selling diseased and decayed meat to St. Louisans will be landed behind the bars of the penitentiary."[43] The same feeling prompted Attorney General Crow to indicate that he meant not merely to break up the combine charging outrageous prices, but also to force the packers to furnish better meat. Confident that ample evidence had been obtained, on May 10, Crow asked for a writ of ouster against

---

[42] No general meat inspection had been made since August 1900, when three of the four St. Louis meat inspectors were discharged to economize. *Springfield Leader-Democrat,* May 7, 1902; *St. Louis Post-Dispatch,* May 8, 9, 1902; *St. Louis Chronicle,* May 8, 1902; *St. Louis Star,* May 9, 1902; *Chicago Tribune,* May 9, 1902.

[43] *St. Joseph Gazette,* May 9, 1902; *St. Louis Star,* May 12, 1902.

the major meat packing firms in the state. He alleged violations of the antitrust laws of Missouri. In the writ the attorney general charged that a combine of packing companies owned, controlled and supplied at fixed prices to the general public, 90 percent of all meats sold in Missouri. The Missouri investigation received national attention.[44] U.S. District Attorney William Warner of Kansas City, speaking for U.S. Attorney General Philander C. Knox, asked to procure a copy of the evidence obtained by Crow for use in the federal government investigation.[45]

The information revealed by the Missouri investigation, the anticipation of federal and state actions elsewhere, increased newspaper comment and the persistent high beef cost, all served to intensify popular reaction. At Lynn, Massachusetts, nearly 1,700 employees of the General Electric Company, representing at least 4,000 consumers, formed an antibeefeating league. Members pledged to abstain from beef consumption for thirty days, and promoters expected 5,000 company employees to join before the boycott ended. In Middletown, New York, 300 members of the Laborers' Union voted unanimously to abstain from western beef for one month. The Central Labor Union in Portland, Maine, unanimously adopted a resolution protesting the advance in meat prices and organized a similar thirty-day boycott. In Topeka, Kansas, 2,500 Sante Fe Railroad shop employees began a thirty-day beef boycott and caused an immediate 50 percent drop in meat sales in the workingclass neighborhoods. The continued high beef prices in St. Joseph, Missouri, and Omaha, Nebraska, caused consumers to switch to a fish diet. And in New York City 500 Jewish men and women met and formed the Ladies Anti-Beef Trust Association, threatening to start their own cooperative stores if the price of meat did not come down.[46]

---

44 See *New York Times,* May 7, 10, 1902; *Chicago Tribune,* May 7, 8, 9, 10, 1902; *Washington* [D.C.] *Post,* May 6, 7, 8, 1902. Events in Missouri seemed to have an accelerating and grassroots influence on investigations elsewhere. On May 11, District Attorney S. H. Bethea in Chicago asked for an injunction against the combination of beef packers and commented: "Owing to the communications from all over the country, volunteering evidence of the illegal practices of the trust, . . . the district attorneys throughout the country have been directed to examine into the testimony offered and to forward the same to the department." *St. Louis Star,* May 11, 1902. One week after the Missouri hearings the attorney general of New York began an investigation against the Beef Trust in his state. *Ibid.,* May 15, 1902; *Kansas City Journal,* May 16, 1902.
45 *St. Louis Post-Dispatch,* May 7, 9, 1902; *St. Louis Star,* May 10, 1902; *Jefferson City State Tribune,* May 8, 1902.
46 *St. Louis Chronicle,* May 7, 1902; *St. Joseph Gazette,* May 8, 13, 17, 19, 1902; *Washington Post,* May 8, 1902.

These consumer responses succeeded. As soon as beef reached prohibitive price levels, the consumption fell off. People simply stopped eating meat. Thousands of small meat shops closed and the public responded by substituting cereal foods for meat. In the words of one editor:

> The people stopped eating eggs when the egg dealers pushed the prices too high. The people likewise shut down on butter. They quit sugar and coffee the same way, under the same circumstances. They revolted and they stopped eating meat . . . when their common sense told them that the prices asked were asked only because the beef barons thought they had the supply so thoroughly cornered that they could charge anything they pleased.[47]

An indication that the packers felt consumer pressure appeared in mid-May 1902, when beef prices stabilized. In the opinion of local butchers this action resulted from popular agitation and legal prosecutions.[48]

In addition to the reactions to price fixing, trade restraints and corporate arrogance some individuals questioned corporate consolidation itself. The Beef Trust's ability to control the butcher and small farmer, and dictate costs to consumers, resulted from unchecked corporate consolidation. As one labor leader suggested: "It seems probable that a new era will distinguish the lives of farmers when the food trust gets the nation absolutely organized and systematized."[49] In earlier days a farmer living near a small town might have had a calf, hog or young steer for sale. He probably would have taken his animal to the local butcher. The butcher paid him a fair price, slaughtered the animal and sold the meat at reasonable prices to his customers. But things had changed. Agents of the Beef Trust watched the local butcher, and if they found him trading independently, they became concerned. They required the local butcher to buy all his meat from the trust. If he refused, the trust would cut off his regular supply of pork, mutton, veal or beef. The local farmer could only supply on occasion, but the butcher needed supplies daily. Conditions forced the butcher to curtail his trade with the farmer and buy from the

---

47 *Mirror*, XII (May 15, 1902) , 3.
48 On May 20, Judge P. S. Grosscup of the U.S. Circuit Court in Chicago granted a temporary injunction against the Beef Trust. The government charged the packers with controlling 60 percent of the fresh meat business in the United States and of conspiring to fix meat prices to dealers and consumers. *St. Louis Post-Dispatch*, May 21, 1902; *Mirror*, XII (May 15, 1902) , 3; *Kansas City Journal*, May 27, 1902; Omaha, Nebraska, *Morning World Herald*, May 6, 1902.
49 *St. Louis Labor Compendium*, May 4, 1902.

trust, while the farmer had to sell his stock to the trust or keep them himself. Even when the butcher dealt with the trust, other worries remained. The old-fashioned methods of many small retail butchers placed them at a distinct disadvantage. Butchers experienced difficulty competing with larger, modern concerns that operated more efficiently and utilized every part of the slaughtered animal. Thus, consumers confronted the final result, purchasing trust-made products at trust-made prices.[50]

The people did not regard this "modernizing" process as just, and they resisted its implications. Reverend George Lloyd, pastor of the Church of the Redeemer in St. Louis, expressed these feelings well in a sermon:

> Combination and centralization, they tell us, are the mark of the age; that we can not help ourselves; that in a big age big combinations may naturally be expected, and that all these great combinations of manufacturers and purveyors are facilitated by a marvelous development in rapid transit. Such reasoning is faulty, inasmuch as it takes for granted that what is naturally expected to be is right, without considering its character and its effect on people.[51]

[50] *Ibid.;* St. Louis *Butchers and Packers' Gazette,* May 10, 1902.
[51] *St. Louis Republic,* May 5, 1902.

Kemper Meat Market, Clinton, Early 1900s

Citizens, as consumers, taxpayers, workers and housewives, recognized the larger forces pressing down upon them. They understood the "us-and-them" relationship to "the interests," and reacted against those perceptions.

On June 28, 1902, the Missouri Supreme Court acted on Attorney General Crow's request for ouster proceedings against the Beef Trust in Missouri. The court appointed I. H. Kinley of Kansas City as a special commissioner to gather further testimony. Kinley finally filed his report on January 3, 1903. He confirmed the earlier findings of Attorney General Crow that certain companies had entered a combine in Missouri to regulate the prices of meats. A week later attorneys for the packers filed exceptions to the report of the commissioner, but to no avail.[52] Finally, on March 20, 1903, the Missouri Supreme Court awarded judgement to the state against the Armour, G. H. Hammond, Cudahy, Swift, and Schwarzschild and Sulzberger packing companies. Fined $5,000 plus court costs, each of the five Missouri packing companies was required to pay within thirty days or be ousted from the state. By April 12, 1903, all defendants had complied with the order. Drafts totaling $27,136 reached the supreme court.[53]

The struggle against the Beef Trust drew upon a tradition which stressed the need to preserve the economic independence of an individual in a democratic society. Farmers knew the reason for disappearing local butchers. Butchers also realized why they were being forced out of business, and consumers recognized who dictated the prices of their goods. Conscious of their situation, citizens ably formulated their own explanations. They sensed their sacrifice to a larger process of corporate modernization, and they resisted. Consumers altered their diet, stopped eating meat and participated in formal, organized boycotts. Their actions forced the judicial system to respond. Investigations at the state level, such

---

52 The packers charged that evidence they deemed important was not allowed to be submitted, while much that was submitted would have been inadmissable in a court of law. St. Louis *Butchers and Packers' Gazette,* January 10, 1903. The various companies, in their objections to the testimony, also raised the question that the agents of the companies, even if they did make agreements to fix prices, were not shown to have been authorized by their "principals" to enter into and make such agreements. Commissioner Kinley responded to their objection in his report and disagreed: "The local agents of the dressed beef companies did it [fixed prices] and all knew it and their knowledge is the knowledge of their companies and their acts are the acts of their companies." St. *Louis Post-Dispatch,* January 4, 1903.
53 St. *Louis Post-Dispatch,* June 28, 1902, January 4, March 20, 1903; *New York Times,* April 13, 1903.

as the one in Missouri, exposed corporate arrogance which, in turn, deepened consumer indignation. These investigations not only served as an example for national policymakers, they also showed the popular reaction to economic consolidation. This consumer-oriented response to the Beef Trust served as a model for state antitrust activity and for progressivism.

————————

The Petroleum Industry in Transition: Antitrust and the Decline of Monopoly Control in Oil

JOSEPH A. PRATT

The discovery of vast oil fields in Texas after 1901 encouraged competition in an industry previously dominated by Standard Oil of New Jersey. The manner in which the state of Texas enforced its antitrust and corporation laws hastened the growth of several major new oil companies, most notably Gulf Oil and The Texas Company, by constraining the activities of Standard in the new fields. In so doing, these Texas laws shaped the transition from near monopoly to near oligopoly in the oil industry. Such beneficial results of state laws were, however, largely accidental, since weaknesses in the government's capacity to monitor changes in the burgeoning industry undermined its ability to define and implement systematic regulatory policies. Problems of adjustment that accompanied government's early efforts to regulate market structure in oil have continued to hamper subsequent efforts to regulate other aspects of the industry's operations.

THE energy crisis of the 1970s has revived political interest in using antitrust to make the petroleum industry more competitive. Ongoing debates on this controversial issue have been notably lacking in historical perspective. Proponents of antitrust have largely ignored the historical record, which offers little encouragement for their crusade to restore "free" or even "freer" competition in the energy industries.[1] Defenders of the existing market structure in oil generally have treated oligopoly—that is, competition among numerous large firms—and vertical integration—that is, the organization in a single corporation of production, refining, transportation, and marketing—as natural, almost inevitable, products of the evolution of the petroleum industry. They argue that economics, not politics, have determined the structure of the industry, and that public policy aimed at changing existing arrangements would destroy a delicate balance that reflects fundamental economic realities underlying the operations of the industry.[2] When historians have entered the debate at all, they

Journal of Economic History, Vol. XL, No. 4 (Dec. 1980). © The Economic History Association. All rights reserved. ISSN 0022-0507.

The author is Assistant Professor, School of Business, University of California, Berkeley, CA 94720. He would like to acknowledge the assistance of Louis Galambos, Richard Abrams, John O. King, and Mary Yeager in the preparation of this paper. Funds for the research came from the School of Business and the Institute of Business and Economic Research at the University of California, Berkeley, the Lincoln Educational Foundation, and the Historians Office of the Department of Energy.

[1] For several strong proponents of antitrust, see John Blair, *The Control of Oil* (New York, 1976) and Norman Medvin, *The Energy Cartel* (Washington, D.C., 1976). For a history of antitrust in oil, including documents, see Burton Kaufman, *The Oil Cartel Case* (Westport, CT, 1978).

[2] For a collection of views on recent attempts at divestiture in the oil industry, see George Reigeluth and Douglas Thompson, eds., *Capitalism and Competition: Oil Industry Divestiture and the Public Interest* (Baltimore, 1976).

have generally supported this position, citing a well-developed body of historical literature that stresses the primacy of economic forces in defining the structure of the modern American petroleum industry. The events and processes described in this literature are, however, open to a different interpretation than that thus far offered by business historians. A reexamination of the emergence of oligopoly in oil places current debates about antitrust in the industry in a new historical perspective while suggesting the long-run impact of early efforts to enforce antitrusts laws on the history of government-business relations in the petroleum industry.

HISTORICAL INTERPRETATIONS OF THE DECLINE OF STANDARD OIL

The modern market structure in the petroleum industry emerged in the first two decades of the twentieth century, as new competitors rose to challenge the monopoly position exercised by Standard Oil in the late nineteenth century. The symbol for this change both in the popular mind and in the historical literature has been the U. S. Supreme Court's dissolution of Standard Oil in 1911. The intense passions that accompanied the antitrust cases against John D. Rockefeller and the "octopus" have remained to color historical accounts of this crusade, and much of the resulting literature reflects both the assumptions and the tone of the original dispute between the trustbusters and the defenders of Standard Oil.[3]

The reformers' view that the dissolution marked a turning point in the evolution of the modern oil industry market structure held sway until the 1950s before being challenged by the careful research of a new generation of "revisionist" business historians.[4] Foremost among their works were the excellent three-volume *History of Standard Oil Company (New Jersey),* which drew extensively on the internal records of that company, and the two-volume *American Petroleum Industry,* which presented a detailed account of the first century of petroleum history from 1859 to 1959.[5] Along with several other major works that appeared at approximately the same time,[6] these histories argued convincingly that for several decades before

[3] For a detailed account of both federal and state antitrust cases against Standard Oil at the turn of the century, see Bruce Bringhurst, *Antitrust and the Oil Monopoly: The Standard Oil Cases, 1890-1911* (Westport, CT, 1979).

[4] Works that reflect reform views are discussed briefly in Harold Williamson and Ralph Andreano, "Competitive Structure of the American Petroleum Industry, 1890-1911: A Reappraisal," Staff of *Business History Review,* eds., *Oil's First Century* (Boston, 1960), pp. 71-84.

[5] The three volumes of the *History of Standard Oil Company (New Jersey)* are: Ralph Hidy and Muriel Hidy, *Pioneering in Big Business, 1882-1911* (New York, 1955); George Gibb and Evelyn Knowlton, *The Resurgent Years, 1911-1927* (New York, 1956); and Henrietta Larson, Evelyn Knowlton, and Charles Popple, *New Horizons, 1927-1950* (New York, 1971). See also Henrietta Larson and Kenneth Porter, *The History of Humble Oil and Refining Company* (New York, 1959). The citation for the two-volume history of the American petroleum industry is as follows: Harold Williamson and Arnold Daum, *The Age of Illumination, 1859-1899* (Evanston, IL, 1959) and Harold Williamson, Ralph Andreano, Arnold Daum, and Gilbert Klose, *The Age of Energy, 1899-1959* (Evanston, IL, 1963).

[6] In particular, see John McLean and Robert Haigh, *The Growth of Integrated Oil Companies* (Boston, 1954); Staff of the *Business History Review,* eds., *Oil's First Century;* and Arthur Johnson, "The Early Texas Oil Industry—Pipelines and the Birth of an Integrated Oil Industry, 1901-1911," *Journal of Southern History,* 32 (Nov. 1966), 516-28.

1911 "autonomous market forces" had begun to undermine Standard's dominance in oil. Contrary to the "progressive" interpretation, political intervention did not abruptly make the existing market structure more competitive. Rather, the Supreme Court's decision merely accelerated ongoing economic processes set in motion earlier by "the size, quality, and location of crude discoveries and the limited success in restricting market space in the new fields on the part of the Standard Oil Company."[7]

Among the flush fields that hastened such changes, Spindletop—the first major oil deposit found in Texas—is accorded special importance. The discovery of oil at Spindletop in 1901 probably had a greater impact on the petroleum industry's market structure than did the development of any other American oil field in the twentieth century. Gulf Oil and Texaco were born at Spindletop. It was there that Shell Trading and Transport Company first entered oil transporting in the United States on a large scale; its transportation investments later led it into other aspects of the industry. Sun Oil grew much stronger at Spindletop. The Magnolia Oil Company, absorbed by Standard of New York (now Mobil) in the 1920s, sprang from the new field. The men who later organized Humble Oil and Refining (now part of Exxon) got their start at Spindletop. The major new firms that grew out of the Gulf coast fields brought the first substantial alterations in the old order of near monopoly control by Standard Oil, and their subsequent growth, along with the expansion of several of the companies created by the dissolution of Standard in 1911, formed the core of the oligopolistic order that has since characterized the petroleum industry.[8]

The leading historians of the petroleum industry offer several slightly different explanations for Standard's inability to control the early Texas oil fields. Henrietta Larson, who directed the research and writing of the Standard Oil history, cites a form of administrative fatigue, arguing that Standard lacked both sufficient managerial resources and adequate market outlets for Texas crude.[9] The authors of *The Age of Energy*, the second volume of *The American Petroleum Industry*, add that Standard "was much less active in the Gulf development than in other areas" because of "a hostile legal climate and more attractive opportunities elsewhere."[10] In *Pioneering in Big Business*, the first volume in the *History of Standard Oil Company (New Jersey)*, Ralph and Muriel Hidy also mention the "un-

---

[7] Ralph Andreano, "The Emergence of New Competition in the American Petroleum Industry" (Ph.D. diss., Northwestern Univ., 1960). See also Harold Williamson, et al., *The Age of Energy*, p. 5.

[8] The size of the field, its location near the Gulf coast, and Texas laws prohibiting Standard's open entry into Texas are cited as reasons for Spindletop's importance. See Joseph Pratt, *The Growth of a Refining Region* (Greenwich, CT, 1980), pp. 33–60. See also Henrietta Larson and Kenneth Porter, *History of Humble Oil*, p. 13; Harold Williamson, et al., *The Age of Energy*, pp. 16 and 97. For a general account of the development of the Spindletop field, see James Clark and Michel Halbouty, *Spindletop* (New York, 1952).

[9] Henrietta Larson, "The Rise of Big Business in the Oil Industry," in *Oil's First Century*, pp. 38–40.

[10] Harold Williamson, et al., *The Age of Energy*, p. 76.

friendly" political environment before asserting that "more important than any other factor explaining Standard Oil's relatively slight interest in Texas was the overwhelmingly greater attractiveness of activity in Mid-Continental petroleum."[11] When discussing the Gulf coast fields, these accounts thus acknowledge that political constraints limited Standard's participation, but they emphasize economic considerations in explaining the rise of new competition. More important, when they leave the subject of the Gulf coast fields and begin to generalize about the causes for the transformation of the national petroleum industry market structure, these influential works stress market forces to the near exclusion of public policy considerations.

Their overriding conclusion that antitrust laws essentially ratified changes previously initiated by economic forces has gained general acceptance. Its broad implications for historians of the American economy are most evident in the synthesis of the history of the modern corporation contained in the works of Alfred D. Chandler, Jr., who attributes a distinctly secondary role to antitrust in explaining the transition from monopoly to oligopoly.[12] Chandler argues that "markets and technology and not antitrust laws have determined why the automobile, rubber and oil industries have always been concentrated and that the furniture, apparel, and leather industries have almost never been. . . . Clearly the passing of laws will not readjust the fundamental structure of a modern industrial economy."[13] This lesson from the past is supported by the best historical accounts of the development of the modern petroleum industry.

A reexamination of events in the industry in the first decades of the twentieth century suggests, however, that existing research generally underestimates the impact of legal and political factors in explaining the rise of oligopoly in oil. One reason for the relative neglect of antitrust is simply a matter of focus. The earliest and most far-reaching impact of antitrust was felt at the state, not the national, level. The dissolution of Standard in 1911 did indeed ratify an ongoing economic process that had previously generated new competition, but this process had been shaped in crucial ways by the enforcement of state antitrust laws before 1911. Events in Texas were of special importance in these years, and the manner in which that state enforced its corporation laws encouraged the transition from near monopoly in oil in 1900 to near oligopoly by 1911. The

[11] Ralph and Muriel Hidy, *Pioneering in Big Business*, p. 394. At this point, it is essential to acknowledge the debt that any student of the history of the oil industry owes to the last generation of petroleum scholars. Their excellent research prepared the way for subsequent work by scholars with different perspectives.

[12] For Chandler's treatment of antitrust, see Alfred D. Chandler, Jr., *Strategy and Structure* (Cambridge, MA, 1962), pp. 383–86. Also, Alfred D. Chandler, Jr., *The Visible Hand: The Managerial Revolution in American Business* (Cambridge, MA, 1977), pp. 350–53, 373–76.

[13] Reigeluth and Thompson, eds., *Capitalism and Competition*, pp. 8–9. Chandler's quotation is from a paper delivered as a historical introduction to a symposium on the feasibility of antitrust as a public policy toward the oil industry in the late 1970s.

"autonomous" market forces at work in the industry before the Supreme Court's decision had been unleashed, or at the very least channeled into numerous new firms, by the efforts of Texas and other states to challenge the monopoly power of Standard Oil.

The relative importance of economic versus political forces in determining the modern market structure in oil is less interesting and less useful in understanding the past or the present than is the question of how the two interacted. Antitrust was the focal point of the initial confrontation between the state and national governments and the young Gulf coast companies that emerged as new competitors to Standard Oil. A closer look at the early efforts to enforce antitrust laws supplements the existing histories of the oil industry while directing attention to political variables that have become increasingly important over the course of the twentieth century.

POLITICAL CONSTRAINTS FACING STANDARD IN TEXAS

A very hostile political environment blocked Standard's open and aggressive entry into the newly discovered Texas oil fields. Legal obstacles to its operations and strong public suspicion of its motives and methods made Standard the focus of much political attention. Such constraints did not completely prevent Standard from entering the field, but they did limit the extent to which "the Trust" could attempt to control this major new source of oil.

Under the antitrust law in effect in Texas at the time of the Spindletop discovery, Standard could not operate legally in that state. Passed in 1889, one year before the Congress of the United States passed the Sherman Antitrust Act, this strict law prohibited combinations in restraint of trade and blocked one company from owning stock in another. Its passage had been pressed by farmers and ranchers who sought to regulate the companies that controlled the price of cotton bagging, beef, and other similar products, but it applied equally to the oil industry.[14] The general corporation laws of the state reinforced this strong antitrust law by limiting each business chartered in the state to one particular corporate purpose. Strictly interpreted, these laws forbade vertically integrated operations within one oil company, and Standard had built its monopoly by coordi-

---

[14] For general background on the passage of the Texas antitrust law of 1889, see Alwyn Barr, *Reconstruction to Reform: Texas Politics, 1876-1906* (Austin, 1971), p. 108. For a description of efforts to enforce the antitrust law as it applied to the Texas oil industry, see Bringhurst, *Antitrust and the Oil Monopoly*, pp. 40–68. See also, John O. King, *Joseph S. Cullinan: A Study in Leadership in the Texas Petroleum Industry, 1897-1937* (Nashville, 1970), pp. 112–45; Jewel Lightfoot, *Anti-Trust Laws of Texas* (Austin, 1907); H.R. Seager and Charles Gulick, Jr., *Trust and Corporation Problems* (New York, 1929); Tom Finty, Jr., *Anti-Trust Legislation in Texas: An Historical and Analytical Review of the Enactment and Administration of the Various Laws Upon the Subject* (Dallas, 1916); and John Allison, "Survey of the Texas Antitrust Laws," *Antitrust Bulletin*, 20 (Summer 1975), 215–308.

nating production, refining, transportation, and marketing in a single organization.[15]

The actual enforcement of the law was more important than its wording, and enforcement was strict, if uneven, in the first decades after the law's passage. A special target of the state was the Waters-Pierce Oil Company, a Standard Oil marketing affiliate active in much of the Southwest. Waters-Pierce first came under attack in Texas in 1899, when the state revoked its charter because of its ties to Standard Oil. In the next decade the Waters-Pierce case remained at the center of a heated controversy that dominated Texas politics as charges and countercharges of wrongdoing in the original case flew back and forth between Senator Joseph Bailey and his political opponents.[16] The Bailey controversy kept the issue of antitrust violations attributed to Standard Oil and its affiliates in the press and on the campaign stump throughout the early history of the Texas oil industry. By couching much of the debate over antitrust in the oil industry in highly personal terms, the Bailey controversy encouraged public officials to make choices on antitrust policy based on personalities, not on changing economic circumstances in the industry.

In the twenty years after Spindletop, Standard remained the object of public scrutiny and the focus of the antitrust activities of the Texas attorney general. Standard's vertically integrated operations meant that it was, by definition, in restraint of trade, and any Texas company with close ties to it faced suspicion and legal harassment from the state. After an even stricter antitrust law in 1907 replaced the 1889 law, for example, Waters-Pierce and other Standard affiliates were prosecuted for the second time in a decade. Such legal actions in Texas were strengthened by similar court cases in neighboring states and by a national investigation by the Bureau of Corporations in 1905 and 1906 of Standard's involvement in all aspects of the industry.[17]

The legal and political objections to Standard arose in Texas at least as much from the company's national image as from its actual behavior in the state. Before 1901, Standard's business in Texas was almost entirely in marketing. Even after the Spindletop discovery it did not openly and ag-

---

[15] On the eve of the Spindletop discovery, Standard Oil dominated all phases of the oil industry in the United States. In 1899 Standard still controlled about 85 percent of crude supplies, 80 percent of refining capacity, 85 percent of the market for kerosene—the most important refined product of that time—and most of the pipeline and tanker capacity in the nation. See Harold Williamson, et al., *The Age of Energy*, p. 7.

[16] For contemporary accounts of the controversy, see William A. Cocke, *The Bailey Controversy in Texas*, 2 vols. (San Antonio, 1908) and W.L. Crawford, *Crawford on Baileyism* (Dallas, 1907). For historical accounts, see Sam Acheson, *Joe Bailey, The Last Democrat* (New York, 1932); Bob Holcomb, "Senator Joe Bailey, Two Decades of Controversy" (Ph.D. diss., Texas Technological College, 1968); and Bringhurst, *Antitrust and the Oil Monopoly*, pp. 40–68.

[17] A summary of this investigation was published as U.S. Bureau of Corporations, *Report of the Commissioner of Corporations on the Petroleum Industry*, 2 vols. (Washington, D.C., 1907). The records of the investigation are in Record Group 122, Records of the Bureau of Corporations, National Archives, Washington, D.C.

gressively enter Texas and attempt to drive out competition. If Standard's actions were restrained, however, its image was more than potent enough to attract political attention. Populist sentiment had run high in Texas, and a major concern was the power of the trust, especially that of Standard Oil, one of the oldest, most powerful, and most visible of the industrial combinations. Its large size and widespread reputation for secretiveness and ruthlessness made Standard a popular symbol of the evils of concentration. Therefore, it was not surprising that after the discovery of the vast new supplies of oil in Texas many citizens—taking a cue from politicians and newspapers—became obsessed with protecting the newfound wealth of Texas from the Trust.

The rhetoric used by the attorney general of Texas in explaining the 1907 antitrust law reflected the passion of the opposition to Standard. In describing "the most drastic antitrust law enacted by any state," he vowed to use it to "drive every trust and unlawful combination out of Texas," since their "well known purpose was to appropriate the territory of Texas for their greed and exploitation."[18] Such harsh words reflected both the conviction of the speaker and the political benefits to be gained from attacking Standard Oil.

Area newspapers reinforced this passionate opposition to Standard by printing exaggerated accounts of its involvement in the booming Gulf coast fields. Many articles were little more than unsubstantiated rumors, but repetition gave them at least the appearance of fact. Perhaps the depths of such sensationalism came in 1903 when a Fort Worth paper printed a story that was subsequently reprinted in eastern newspapers. In what the *Oil Investors' Journal* referred to with admirable candor as a "jack-assey story," these papers printed as fact an incredible account of an alleged Standard Oil project to build, under cover of darkness, a pipeline from the Gulf of Mexico to the Spindletop field. The reported purpose of this secret project was to pump salt water from the Gulf of Mexico into the field, thereby stopping production by Standard's competitors.[19] Similar though less extreme reports of devious maneuvers by Standard appeared almost daily, as local papers vied with each other to uncover its secret efforts to "take over the field."[20] At one time or another, a printed report linked every major company active in the field to the Trust, and executives of these companies felt sufficiently threatened by popular sentiment to make repeated public avowals of their independence.[21] Under-

[18] Lightfoot, *Anti-Trust Laws of Texas*, p. 51.

[19] *Oil Investors' Journal* (September 15, 1903), 4. See also undated newspaper clipping, file marked "1902-The Texas Co. (Ancient History, Clippings, etc.)," Box 14, Papers of James Lockhart Autry, Rice University, Houston, Texas.

[20] See, for example, *Oil Investors' Journal* (December 15, 1902), 10; ibid. (November 1, 1904), 6; ibid. (May 18, 1905) 6–8; *Port Arthur Herald* (May 4, 1901), 1; and *Beaumont Enterprise* (January 17, 1901), 1.

[21] *Oil Investors' Journal* (January 15, 1903), 3. For Texaco's statement and a response, see Arnold Schlaet to Joseph Cullinan, letter dated March 6, 1903, vol. 2, *Texas Company Archives*, in the Texas Company Archives, White Plains, New York.

mining the effectiveness of the companies' rejoinders was the publicity given to Ida Tarbell's series of articles in *McClure's,* which outlined Standard's past ruthlessness, and to the widely publicized report of the Bureau of Corporation's damning investigation of Standard in 1906.[22]

Such condemnations of the Trust were, however, at least partially offset by the recognition that Standard's participation could hasten the rapid development of the Texas oil industry. Often side by side with accusations of wrongdoing by the company ran stories that pointed out important economic benefits to be gained from its involvement in the field. The *Oil Investors' Journal,* which was perhaps less biased against Standard than any other local paper, captured this sentiment while discussing Standard's financial backing of the largest refinery in Beaumont, Texas, the town nearest Spindletop. After noting that the plant was "an immense undertaking and is ample evidence of Standard's presence in the Southern fields," the *Journal* concluded that "it does not, however, cause any jealousy in the public mind; on the contrary, it lends an element of permanency and stability to the situation which is not unpleasant."[23] Earlier, a group of small producers had even sent a telegram to Standard asking if it planned to serve as a common carrier for all the production of the field.[24] In response, a delegation of "Standard visitors" came to Beaumont to inspect the field. On their departure, they proclaimed that their company "would willingly enter" the field except that the Texas antitrust laws were "in the way."[25] One local paper that carried regular attacks on Standard aptly expressed the existing ambivalence toward the Trust by answering that Beaumont was "the one place on earth where Standard is to be devoutedly wished."[26] Recognizing and even fearing the company's power, many of those involved in the development of the Gulf coast fields nonetheless saw the advantages to be gained from the entry of the highly organized, much experienced company, with its access to markets, transportation, and technical expertise.

STANDARD'S ROLE IN THE EARLY TEXAS OIL INDUSTRY

As a result of such ambivalence, Standard's arrival in Texas was accepted in the way an older, nonbelieving child greets the arrival of Santa Claus: winking at Standard's disguise, many in the region gladly accepted the economic gifts that it brought. Despite strict antitrust laws and strong political rhetoric, Standard was allowed to operate in all phases of the industry. Its involvement was a well-known secret, and, within the limits set

---

[22] For the comments of local papers on Ida Tarbell's articles see, for example, *Oil Investors' Journal* (December 15, 1902), 5.

[23] *Oil Investors' Journal* (January 1, 1903), 3. This journal is the forerunner of the *Oil and Gas Journal,* and it established a widespread reputation for accuracy from its earliest issues.

[24] *Beaumont Daily Enterprise* (April 4, 1901), 1.

[25] *Beaumont Daily Enterprise* (April 12, 1901), 2; (April 13, 1901), 1.

[26] *Port Arthur Herald* (May 4, 1901), 1.

for it by the threat of antitrust, the company played a major role in the development of the youthful Texas oil industry.[27]

Standard entered the field as aggressively as the potentially hazardous political environment allowed. This meant widespread participation in production, transportation, and refining. To make its activities less conspicuous and therefore less open to political attack, it made use of thinly disguised subsidiaries and of other, less formal arrangements with independent companies.

Both the importance of Standard's early role and the constraints imposed by the political environment were evident in its operation of a large refinery during the first decade of the development of Gulf coast oil fields. In 1902 a mysterious stranger, one George Burt, got off a train in Beaumont, bought a large tract of land near Spindletop, constructed a high fence around the land, and built one of the largest and best equipped refineries in the state. Burt's plant, later acquired by the Security Oil Company, was paid for by people connected with Standard Oil, operated by former Standard employees, and sold its products almost exclusively to Standard. Security owned no producing wells. It simply bought oil from others, processed it, and shipped it by railroad tank car and tanker to Standard and its subsidiaries. For all practical purposes, Security was itself a Standard subsidiary. Most of those involved in the region's oil business understood and tolerated this arrangement. Standard was one of the few organizations with access to the capital, the expertise, and the markets needed to build and operate a refinery large enough to purchase substantial quantities of oil from the expanding area fields. As a result, those concerned with the rapid development of these fields and of the city of Beaumont ignored Security's ties to the "octopus." Recognizing that the company "was a potent force in the prosperity of South East Texas,"[28] they were not eager to cut off the tentacle that was feeding them.

Although Security did not own producing properties, it developed a series of very close ties with a number of large producers. Strong evidence suggests that Standard gained control over the Higgins Oil Company (a large producer in the early years after Spindletop) and perhaps also secretly directed the activities of several other regional producing companies.[29] Actual ownership of a majority of stock in a company was not, however, required for Standard to exercise great influence over its development. As the largest available market for crude, Standard's decisions

---

[27] Throughout the early years after Spindletop, it appears that almost everyone connected with the Texas oil industry knew of Standard's role. In fact, most seemed to assume that Standard's involvement went beyond control of Security to include a measure of control over other major companies active in Texas.

[28] *Oil Investors' Journal* (November 19, 1907), 12.

[29] Support for this conclusion comes from *Oil Investors' Journal* (December 15, 1902), 10; (May 15, 1903), 12. For interviews with the managers of many of the small companies at Spindletop, see Bureau of Corporation's Petroleum Investigation, Record Group 122, National Archives, Washington, D.C.

determine the fate of many producers in the first years after Spindletop. A Bureau of Corporation's study in 1906 showed that in the five years after the opening of the coastal fields, Standard was the major purchaser of Gulf coast crude. Almost half of all tanker shipments from the new fields in the period between January 1904 and June 1905 went to Standard. Excluding the shipments of Gulf Oil, which by then had begun to develop its own tanker system and marketing network, Standard bought more than two thirds of the oil shipped by tanker from the rest of the companies on the Gulf coast.[30] This was not the action of a company that lacked markets for Texas crude. Indeed, as the primary East coast purchaser of Gulf coast crude, Standard exercised a large measure of control over the pace of the development of the early Texas oil industry.

Despite antitrust laws that banned its open entry, Standard thus had a substantial interest in all phases of the early Texas oil industry. The company's widespread involvement in the Gulf coast fields suggests that it recognized the potential importance of that area as a producing and refining center. State laws, which posed a constant threat to Standard, were at least as important as the "overwhelmingly greater attractiveness" of other fields in limiting the company's participation in the Texas fields. Indeed, without such politically imposed constraints on its economic decisions, the company would have played an even greater—and probably controlling—role.

Such a strong statement is supported by an examination of the impact of political forces on the growth of the Security Oil Company. Although this Standard affiliate had been allowed to operate in the early years after Spindletop, its sustained growth finally brought a response from the Texas attorney general's office. In 1906 Security planned to expand its refinery and to build a costly pipeline from the Mid-Continent fields in Oklahoma to Beaumont, but antitrust action against the company blocked its proposed expansion. In response to the increasingly hostile political environment in Texas, Standard transferred many of its key employees and all of its projected investment dollars to the more favorable political climate of Louisiana, selecting Baton Rouge as the site for a new refinery that subsequently grew into one of the largest refineries in the world.[31]

After finding Security Oil Company in violation of the antitrust law in 1909, the state of Texas forced the sale of its properties. The history of the Beaumont plant in the next two decades reveals much about the working of the political system, and further suggests its impact on the growth of this important regional company. Before John Sealey, a Galveston capitalist, purchased Security's refinery out of receivorship, he disclosed to the

---

[30] File 3386, "Texas Shipments of Domestic Petroleum by Vessels," Bureau of Corporation's Petroleum Investigation, Record Group 122, National Archives, Washington, D.C.

[31] *Oil Investors' Journal* (February 6, 1909), 59; (April 20, 1909), 1 and 24. See also, Mobil Oil Company Publications Staff, "History of the Refining Department of the Magnolia Petroleum Company" (Beaumont, TX, n.d.). A copy is filed in the library of the Mobil refinery at Beaumont.

attorney general that most of his financial backing came from the same Standard of New York interests that had originally built the plant. Despite this, the sale was approved and the company, now renamed the Magnolia Petroleum Company, reopened. Several years later, however, a different attorney general discovered the arrangement and brought another suit that resulted in the loss of the ability of the Standard investors to vote their stock. In response, Magnolia asked for an opinion by the Federal Trade Commission on the legality of an outright sale of the plant to Standard of New York. Even in 1917, six years after the dissolution of Standard, the FTC replied unfavorably to such a proposal. Finally, in 1925 the formal, legal purchase of Magnolia by Standard of New York took place. Thus, for twenty-four years the growth of this "secret" Standard affiliate was shaped by the political system's periodical assaults on its Standard connections.[32] In the process of harassing the various owners of this company, state officials groped down a path that ultimately increased competition in the oil industry by encouraging both Standard Oil of New Jersey (Exxon) and Standard Oil of New York (Mobil) to build large Gulf coast refineries that supplied many of the same markets.

Prevented by law from taking control of the Texas oil industry through the aggressive expansion of a directly owned subsidiary, Standard sought indirect control over its development. In light of existing political constraints, its strategy was logical and fairly successful. While profiting from the handling of large quantities of Gulf coast crude, Standard attempted to check the growth there of any company capable of breaking out of the regional market and posing a challenge to its near monopoly position in the national oil industry.

The first president of Texaco, Joseph S. Cullinan, correctly summarized this strategy:

... while 26 [Standard] wants the goods, they are running a kind of incubator, fostering local competition, which will in turn assure their getting the supplies wanted at a very nominal margin as between cost of production and delivery to them, and this is a feature that we should aim to correct, if we undertake to expand and handle the business on broader lines.[33]

When Gulf Oil sought to expand to "broader lines" by entering into competition with Standard for eastern markets, Standard demonstrated the accuracy of Cullinan's appraisal by providing information to Texaco that allowed it to undercut Gulf in bidding for regional business.[34] Such a

[32] Information on these events comes from several sources. See, for example, *Oil Investors' Journal* (November 19, 1907), 12. For a somewhat confused account of Magnolia's problems with the Texas antitrust laws in this period, see Charles Wallace, *Nine Lives: The Story of the Magnolia Companies and the Anti-Trust Laws* (Dallas, 1953). See also, File 1-1434-3, Federal Trade Commission's Oklahoma Oil Investigation, Record Group 122, National Archives, Washington, D.C.

[33] Joseph Cullinan to Arnold Schlaet, letter dated May 5, 1904, vol. 30, *Texas Company Archives*, Texas Company Archives, White Plains, NY.

[34] Arnold Schlaet to Joseph Cullinan, letter dated September 26, 1904, vol. 34, *Texas Company Archives*, Texas Company Archives, White Plains, NY.

strategy encouraged the growth of numerous competing companies, all incapable of challenging Standard's dominance in the national petroleum industry. A reasonable assessment of political realities, not "administrative fatigue," underlay this choice of strategy. Recognizing that its traditional market position would inevitably be eroded, Standard nevertheless attempted to adjust by shaping a new market structure in which it would occupy the position of a giant among pygmies.

As indicated by the Cullinan statement, the pygmies were by no means content with their status. In trying to grow large enough to assert their independence from Standard, Gulf Oil and Texaco each saw the necessity of building a vertically integrated company patterned after Standard. To operate outside of the incubator, these companies had to become "mini-trusts" with sufficient production, transportation, refining, and marketing capacities to withstand the economic retaliation that would inevitably accompany a direct challenge to Standard. In the transitional decade after Spindletop, the symbol of the old order in petroleum thus provided an organizational model—vertical integration—for those companies that were building the new order. Standard's potential ability to crush its much smaller competitors also provided powerful incentives for the new companies to adopt this structure as rapidly as possible.[35]

In addition to furnishing a model for organization, Standard also furnished many of the people who filled these organizations. Texaco was especially fortunate in acquiring talented executives and technical experts who had gained experience while working for Standard subsidiaries in the eastern oil fields. Joseph Cullinan, perhaps the single most able and influential oil man in the formative years of the Texas industry, had learned the business while working in various Standard affiliates, as had Texaco's first chemist, its early marketing expert in New York, and the heads of its pipeline and refinery. Gulf's first manager and the head of its first refinery shared this background. Security, the "secret" subsidiary, was of course staffed with employees from other Standard operations.[36] Not all men with the skills needed to be good managers, drillers, or refiners had acquired their knowledge as employees of the Trust. What was important was practical experience, and in the last thirty years of the nineteenth century, most of those who had worked in the oil industry had worked for Standard. Such men were sometimes looked upon with suspicion as

[35] For an excellent account of this process, see McLean and Haigh, *The Growth of Integrated Oil Companies.* For a slightly different interpretation of the move toward vertical integration in oil, see Melvin G. de Chazeau and Alfred Kahn, *Integration and Competition in the Petroleum Industry* (New Haven, CT, 1959), pp. 75–118.

[36] The best source of biographical information on Texaco employees is a bound volume of biographical sketches filed in the Texas Company Archives in White Plains, New York. For Gulf Oil, see W.L. Mellon, *Judge Mellon's Sons* (Pittsburgh, 1948), pp. 161 and 275. For a thorough account of Cullinan's role, see King, *Joseph S. Cullinan.* For information on Security's early employees, see Mobil Oil Publications Staff, "History of the Refining Department of the Magnolia Petroleum Company."

agents of their former employer with secret missions to deliver the field to Standard. Despite such generally understandable but unfounded worries, these men were still eagerly sought after in a booming field with scarce managerial and technical skills. As the training school for those who developed the southwestern oil fields, Standard provided a service essential for orderly growth.

The much-maligned Trust thus filled several practical and essential roles in the emerging Texas oil industry. In addition, it filled a symbolic role that was perhaps even more important to the survival and growth of Gulf Oil and Texaco. As the focus of public and political attention, Standard protected the growing Gulf coast companies from political forces that might have blocked their expansion. From their inception, these new oil companies were larger than most corporations previously chartered in Texas, but because they were perceived as smaller, "Texas" alternatives to the giant "foreign" Standard Oil Trust, they enjoyed a great deal of political leeway in their operations. In particular, they quickly became in fact, if not in strict legal terms, vertically integrated oil companies, despite Texas laws that forbade this form of organization.[37] These growing companies therefore had the best of both worlds. They could grow into vertically integrated minitrusts in an oil-rich area from which their prime competitor—and their model of organization—was legally banned from open entry. Yet they could also benefit from the limited participation of Standard in the field since the legal strictures against its activities were only loosely enforced.

THE EVOLUTION OF COMPETING FIRMS

By expanding the economic space available to the growing Gulf coast oil companies, political constraints on Standard shaped the rise of important new competitors to the former monopolist. This is not to say that public officials in Texas consciously or systematically implemented this policy for economically and politically sound reasons. Rather, they reacted to popular opinion by attempting to use existing antitrust laws to banish the evil octopus from the state. Because they lacked sufficient authority, information, or popular support to root out all violations of the law, however, these officials only partially banished Standard, leaving several other vertically integrated companies largely untouched. So, as much by accident as by design, Texas officials allowed Standard to encourage the growth of its emerging competition but prevented it from absorbing these new companies. In so doing, the state political system defined the boundaries within which market forces shaped the rise of new competition.

[37] Texaco and Gulf Oil avoided potential legal problems by never formally absorbing the producing companies that supplied their crude oil. Instead, individual stockholders in the two large companies bought substantial blocks of stock in these smaller "independent" producing concerns.

Gulf Oil was the earliest major competitor to Standard to emerge from the Spindletop field. It entered the field with larger resources than any other firm, and the continued financial backing of its Mellon interests put it in the best position of all Gulf coast companies to challenge Standard. It was plagued, however, by administrative problems. When the Mellons had previously faced such a situation in the eastern oil field in 1895, they had elected to sell out. In Texas, as earlier in the East, Standard was the only logical buyer for the substantial properties of Gulf Oil. But whereas only seven years before Standard had eagerly absorbed the smaller, Mellon-run oil company, it refused to consider the offer to buy Gulf Oil in 1902. The proposed purchase would have altered greatly the development of the early Texas oil industry, since Gulf was by far the largest and most rapidly growing company there. Indeed, Standard's acquisition of Gulf Oil would have gone a long way toward giving it effective control of the field. Standard's reason for refusing such an attractive opportunity to strengthen its dominance in oil was simple: it did not want to risk more money in the hostile political environment of Texas.[38]

To protect its substantial investment, Gulf Oil then turned to a policy of aggressive expansion, filling out a vertically integrated structure as rapidly and thoroughly as possible. Once spurned by Standard, Gulf recognized the necessity of competing independently with its much larger rival. The most obvious answer, a merger with Texaco, was seriously considered. The combination of Gulf's resources and Texaco's superior managerial talent would have created a major new force in the regional and national oil industry. After extensive negotiations, the companies seemed very close to merger in 1905, but several difficult problems could not be resolved. The first was the exact exchange value of each company; equally bothersome were the legal implications of a merger. The two companies spent considerable time and effort in lobbying the Texas legislature for a new law to make such a combination possible. They were unsuccessful, in part because their efforts were perceived by some opponents as a Standard Oil-backed ploy to take control of the field.[39] Without such a legal change, both companies recognized that the state government was unlikely to allow their merger. Officials previously had looked the other way as these two growing companies operated in ways that were, strictly speaking, against the law; after all, the growth of such Texas companies would weaken Standard's dominance in oil. The possibility of a merger of these two potential giants raised considerable political opposition, however, especially in light of a widely held fear that one or both were secretly controlled by Standard.

Aside from blocking its proposed merger with Gulf Oil, suspicions of

---

[38] Mellon, *Judge Mellon's Sons*, pp. 269–70.

[39] For material on this proposed merger, see John O. King, *Joseph S. Cullinan*, pp. 159–83. See also, Joseph Cullinan to J. W. Gates, letter dated March 8, 1905, Drawer 1–A, Papers of Joseph Stephen Cullinan, Metropolitan Research Center, Houston Public Library, Houston, Texas.

Texaco's links to Standard did not prove particularly harmful to its growth. Perhaps more than any other company, Texaco benefited from the political constraints on Standard. In its formative years, Texaco did not possess the financial resources to expand as aggressively and quickly as did Gulf Oil. To develop more gradually into a major, vertically integrated oil company, Texaco remained in the incubator provided by Standard longer than had Gulf.

One price of this period of heavy dependence on Standard was considerable political harassment. Several Texas attorneys general as well as the investigator for the Bureau of Corporations speculated that Texaco was controlled by Standard. On another occasion, Texaco was forced to defend itself publicly against similar accusations leveled by the perennially embattled Senator Joseph Bailey. Local newspapers, of course, printed these "revelations" and others, fueling the belief that Texaco was a secret subsidiary of Standard Oil.[40]

In retrospect, it is clear that Texaco was not an affiliate of Standard. An examination of the close cooperation between Texaco and Standard in this period, however, helps to explain why the younger company faced such frequent accusations of domination by Standard. Texaco's first president, Joseph S. Cullinan, had only recently left the employment of a Standard affiliate, and most of his closest officers and technical help had similar backgrounds. These men also sold much of the oil they produced to their former employer. Indeed, Texaco's contract to sell Standard more than $1 million worth of oil (1.225 million barrels) over a seven-month period in 1903 provided a substantial portion of the large, secure market required for growth during its earliest years.[41] In refining, as in production, Standard furnished much of the market necessary for Texaco's early expansion. While planning its first major refinery, Texaco sought the advice of Standard and promised to offer the finished products to Standard before looking for other markets. After its Port Arthur works began operations, Texaco sent samples of its first refined products to Standard, which voiced its disappointment over the quality of the samples. In response, Texaco's marketing agent in New York—who had become "chummy" with his counterpart at Standard through his "frequent visits"—asked for a written criticism of the product.[42] Although Texaco remained in independent hands, it directed many of its activities toward filling a portion of the needs of Standard. Due to that company's continued domination in transportation and marketing, almost all of Texaco's early water shipments went from the Gulf coast to the East coast in Standard-owned tank-

---

[40] King, *Joseph S. Cullinan*, pp. 124–25.

[41] Fisher to Joseph Cullinan, letter dated April 18, 1903, Drawer A-2, Cullinan Papers.

[42] Arnold Schlaet to Joseph Cullinan, letter dated January 20, 1904, vol. 23, *Texas Company Archives*; Schlaet to Cullinan, letter dated September 29, 1903, vol. 19, *Texas Company Archives*; Schlaet to Cullinan, letter dated December 24, 1903, vol. 21, *Texas Company Archives*; Schlaet to Cullinan, letter dated September 26, 1904, vol. 35, *Texas Company Archives*. All of the above volumes are located in the Texas Company Archives, White Plains, NY.

ers. When Texaco decided to obtain its own tankers, it purchased part of the original fleet from Standard. Texaco thus drew very heavily on the expertise, the transportation network, and the established markets of its much larger competitor, and its access to the facilities and talents of a company that was, in theory, excluded from Texas shaped its early development.

Partly because of these close ties, Texaco recognized the necessity of creating a more favorable legal environment. In 1903 Texaco withstood strong local sentiment by "Texas" companies in support of a law establishing stricter controls on Standard's activities in the state. Texaco's spokesman argued that the proposed law was "an extremely dangerous precedent" and represented "a very low order of legislative sentiment" that should be "frowned upon." He added that:

If, at this time, legislation can be influenced and controlled upon a popular prejudice against the Standard Oil Company . . . would it not be true that at the next and succeeding legislatures it would be expected that bills would be introduced with reference to their application to other corporations individually singled out where popular prejudice can be aroused?[43]

In the first decade of existence, Texaco devoted considerable effort to opposing such sentiment and to lobbying for new laws to legalize vertically integrated operations within a single company.

Texaco did not prove immediately successful in its efforts to alter a hostile and potentially dangerous political environment. Several "Texaco bills" aimed at easing existing legal restraints against vertical integration failed in the Texas legislature, at least partially as a result of the success of small producers in using the fear of Standard to mobilize political support for their opposition to such changes. So strong was this sentiment that Texaco did not succeed in getting a new law passed that enabled oil companies to incorporate along broader lines until 1917.[44]

One other major participant on the Gulf coast, Shell Transport and Trading Company, was not initially in violation of the pre-1917 law that prevented one company from operating in all branches of the oil industry. At the turn of the century, Shell was primarily a transport company. It played a substantial role at Spindletop by providing tanker transport outside of Standard's control. Gulf Oil and Shell had especially close ties, and Gulf's access to European markets supplied by Shell accelerated its early development. There is evidence, however, that the political sentiment against Standard affected even Shell's early growth. In 1901, Shell's primary owner, Marcus Samuel, reportedly gave serious consideration to an attractive offer to sell out to Standard. The major stumbling block to the deal was Standard's fear of the political repercussions in the United

[43] Memo dated March 2, 1903, Drawer A-1, Cullinan Papers.

[44] Newspaper clippings, vol. 49, *Texas Company Archives*, p. 82. See, also, King, *Joseph S. Cullinan*, p. 123.

States from the proposed acquisition. To avoid a possible public outcry, Standard insisted that the transfer of ownership remain secret so that Shell could retain the appearance of independence. Samuel felt uncomfortable with such an arrangement, and for this and other reasons, the purchase fell through. In this case, as with Standard's dealings with Texaco and Gulf Oil, political considerations limited economic choices.[45]

The historian ventures onto uncertain ground when he begins to focus on what might have been, not on what actually occurred. A bit of speculation is useful, however, in understanding the far-reaching implications of some of the decisions affected by political constraints during this formative period for the oil industry's modern market structure. Had Shell agreed to Standard's offer, it is highly unlikely that it would later have merged with the Royal Dutch Company. Also, it would not have grown into a major vertically integrated company capable of competing with Standard. Similarly, the acquisition of Gulf Oil by Standard in 1902 could well have forestalled the emergence of any strong Gulf coast competitors to Standard. Finally, the merger of Gulf Oil and Texaco would have hastened the rise of such competition while limiting it to one, not two, new companies. Each of the above alternatives was considered; each was made impossible by the political environment.

As is often the case with antitrust, the threat of prosecution, not actual court cases, dictated these choices. As an often obscure part of the general decision-making calculus that persuaded individual corporate managers to avoid specific acquisitions, the impact of antitrust laws on the market structure that finally emerged in the oil industry has been slighted by historians.[46] Events in the early Texas oil industry, however, strongly suggest that antitrust and the fear of antitrust had a pervasive and far-reaching effect on the rise of oligopoly in oil. Without these laws, Standard Oil would have faced fewer and weaker competitors in the twentieth century. Such results obviously were more modest than had been hoped for by those who saw antitrust as a tool for returning "perfect competition" to the industry. Yet they were also more significant than a generation of business historians has since argued. State laws in Texas and elsewhere released new competitive pressures in the oil industry in the first decade of the twentieth century. In 1911 the United States Supreme Court climaxed this process by dissolving Standard Oil into numerous smaller companies, thus improving the competitive position of the companies that had begun to grow before 1911 while setting the stage for the gradual emergence of

---

[45] Interview with C.H. Ruhl dated June 2, 1905, Drawer 396, folder 3203, part 1, Bureau of Corporations Petroleum Investigation, Record Group 122, National Archives, Washington, D.C. See also, Kendall Beaton, *Enterprise in Oil: A History of Shell in the United States* (New York, 1957), p. 48.

[46] Antitrust is an issue that looks dramatically different from different vantage points. To reformers on the lookout for corporate abuses, the history of antitrust all too often appears to be a history of missed opportunities. To oil executives, however, the same events are viewed as evidence of an ongoing antitrust tradition that has been all too effective while remaining a constant threat to their operations.

competition among the companies that had formerly made up Standard Oil. Whether or not such changes represented fundamental readjustments in the industry's structure remains open to debate. What seems beyond dispute, however, is that antitrust laws at both the state and national levels redefined the boundary within which market forces were allowed free rein. In the oil industry, these laws channeled such forces into a market structure with more companies capable of competing with Standard Oil on relatively equal terms.

PUBLIC POLICY AMID PUBLIC CONFUSION

Measuring the impact of antitrust with any great accuracy is complicated by several characteristics of the public agencies that sought to administer the law in this transitional period. Rhetorical denunciations of monopoly by public officials far outstripped forceful, unambiguous policy aimed at reversing the trend toward economic concentration. Even when policy was clearly defined, the government quite often lacked the capacity to implement it. The state and national governments were ill equipped to deal effectively with the dynamic young oil companies that sprang up in the Gulf coast fields. Public institutions inherited from the less demanding days of the late-nineteenth century proved inadequate to understand, much less to react to, the rapid changes in the petroleum industry in the first decades of the twentieth century. In its initial efforts to regulate the modern petroleum industry, the public sector's capacity to govern effectively fell far short of its strong rhetorical commitment to tame the trusts. The result was a confusing lack of direction and coherence in public policy toward the major oil companies active in Texas.

A great deal of this confusion reflected the government's lack of reliable information about the petroleum industry. John D. Rockefeller had made secretiveness a trademark of Standard Oil, and most of the new oil companies on the Gulf coast followed suit. Standard's traditional use of "blind tigers"—that is, ostensibly independent companies secretly affiliated with Standard—caused a great deal of uncertainty.[47] Public officials not only lacked knowledge about the operations of individual companies, they could not even be sure of one most basic fact, the ownership of "independent" companies. Each dramatic disclosure of secret ties between Standard and a blind tiger cast suspicion on all independent concerns. The largest such companies, Gulf Oil and Texaco, also developed secret ties with numerous producing companies in order to avoid possible violations of the Texas antitrust laws. In confidential testimony to the Bureau of Corporations in 1906, Texaco's president, Joseph Cullinan, summarized his company's control of numerous producers while acknowledging

[47] A. W. Clem (General Manager, Clem Oil Company) to R.V. Davidson (Attorney General of Texas), letter dated November 17, 1906, "December 1905-July 1907-Anti-Trust letters" file, Box 4-8/386, Attorney General's Correspondence, Record Group 302, Texas State Archives, Austin, Texas.

that he was making a "fuller statement than we would have been willing to make ... to the local Texas authorities." Cullinan justified Texaco's lack of candor with state authorities by reminding the bureau that "sometimes these antitrust laws have been invoked in a very unfair way by local officers and have been made the means of oppression." Although Cullinan asserted his company's innocence, "both of purpose and of act," he acknowledged that "candidly we are not inviting inspection and criticism of our positions by the officers referred to."[48] Cullinan and other oil executives thus sought to minimize what they considered the meddling of unreasonable government officials by limiting the access of these officials to information about the operations of their companies.

To fill the resulting void in information, the government turned to several alternative sources for "facts" about the oil industry. One particularly unreliable source was newspapers. Much misinformation resulted from sensationalism designed to sell papers. Many half-truths appeared as facts when reporters from local newspapers attempted to report on complex events from limited and biased sources. Such journalistic accounts were matched in tone by the more thorough reporting of Ida Tarbell, whose damning account of the early history of Standard Oil was appearing in national magazines during the early years of oil development in Texas.

When government agencies sought to augment such unreliable sources by investigating conditions in the oil industry, they generally had extremely limited resources with which to attempt to unravel a complex and rapidly changing situation. The attorney general's office in Texas had to rely on a variety of questionable sources in its efforts to discover antitrust violations. Small competitors of Texaco and Gulf Oil were only too happy to describe the secret ties of these companies to Standard Oil.[49] An anonymous letter submitted to the attorney general by a "wise witness" in 1909 exemplified the quality of much of the information available to public officials. The letter correctly outlined many of the connections between Texaco and Standard Oil before asserting that the author could prove that Texaco, Gulf Oil, and four other large Gulf coast companies were controlled by Standard.[50] In the politically charged atmosphere of the time, such claims were generally treated without the skepticism they deserved. The national investigation of the Bureau of Corporations also relied heavily on hearsay testimony taken in personal interviews throughout the nation with those involved in the oil industry. The bureau's investigators seemed particularly interested in recording the charges of every aggrieved competitor of Standard Oil, and the general approach to the investigation

[48] Joseph Cullinan to James R. Garfield, letter dated June 20, 1905, Bureau of Corporations Numerical File 3208, Record Group 122, National Archives, Washington, D.C.

[49] Arthur Johnson, "Public Policy and Concentration in the Petroleum Industry, 1870–1911," in *Oil's First Century*, pp. 57–70.

[50] W.J. Weaver to P.P. Vanulett, letter dated June 7, 1909, "June 1907–November 1909, K-V, Anti-Trust Letters" file, Box 4-8/396, Attorney General's Correspondence, Record Group 302, Texas State Archives, Austin.

was somewhat short of objective.[51] The bureau appears to have set out to prove that Standard Oil controlled the entire oil industry, not to determine conditions in the industry. Thus, even after a thorough investigation that included personal interviews with all major oil executives in the Texas fields, the bureau's investigators concluded that "the unusual secretiveness of the Texas Company and other suspicious circumstances gave ground for the belief that it is connected with the Standard Oil Company."[52] This deceptively inconclusive statement contained enough qualifiers to remove the burden of proof from the bureau, but it nonetheless tarnished Texaco's standing with the public and with public officials. Despite its outraged denials of this "charge," Texaco remained less than comfortable defending its position, for it was, of course, closely "connected" to Standard in ways that stopped just short of illegality. In the chaotic formative years of the modern oil industry, such distinctions were usually lost amid the half-truths and rumors that hovered around the largest companies like gasoline fumes in search of a match.

The government was not alone in its inability to monitor, much less to control, changes in the oil industry. Even the major companies active in Texas were uncertain about the relationship of their competitors with Standard and with each other. Sun Oil's leading representative in Texas wrote frequent reports to his superiors asserting that "there is no doubt, of course, that Security Company is the Standard Oil Company and ... I think it is probable the Texas Company is very close to them." He earlier had advised that "I have no doubt that the Guffey Company (Gulf Oil), at least their refining end, is in the hands of the Standard, as I have previously suggested to you."[53] Texaco's executives were never quite certain of the affiliations of Security or of Gulf Oil, and those in charge at Waters-Pierce, a Standard affiliate, testified that they did not know if Gulf Oil and Texaco were controlled by Standard.[54] On occasion such ignorance was self-serving, as oil men justified their inability to obtain contracts or to defeat a competitor in selling oil by calling forth the invisible empire of Standard Oil. It is certainly not surprising that public officials did not know more about the industry than those involved in its everyday operations; nor is it surprising that politicians, like their counterparts in the industry, should at times seek to hide behind the image of an all-powerful concern to excuse their own shortcomings. It is worth point-

[51] For an overview of the Bureau of Corporation's investigations, see Arthur Johnson, "Theodore Roosevelt and the Bureau of Corporations," *Mississippi Valley Historical Review*, 45 (March 1959), 571–90.

[52] John Porter Hollis to Commissioner of Corporations, Report No. 2, July 29, 1906, Bureau of Corporations Numerical File 3208, Record Group 122, National Archives, Washington, D.C.

[53] J. Edgar Pew to J. Howard Pew, letter dated February 17, 1904, "J.E. Pew, January–May 1904" folder, Series 21-A, Administrative Files, Sun Oil Collection, Eleutherian Mills Historical Library, Wilmington, Delaware.

[54] Testimony of Clay Arthur Pierce, "The State of Texas versus Waters-Pierce Oil Company—Stenographer's Report," "Attorney General, 1906—General Files," Box 2-10/603, Attorney General's Correspondence, Record Group 302, Texas State Archives, Austin.

ing out, however, that oil men demanded more of government officials than they themselves could deliver.

The powerful, overriding image of Standard Oil brought a certain order to the confusion and uncertainty created by the absence of reliable information. If something went wrong, or even if something could not be easily explained, surely Standard Oil was to blame. Politicians were both victims and beneficiaries of such attitudes. Like the general public, they faced a bewildering lack of hard facts on which to base policy. Unfortunately, they often masked their own confusion by appealing to the lowest, most commonly shared political sentiment; they couched oil policy in language that attacked Standard Oil.

Such symbolic politics certainly characterized much of the enforcement of Texas's antitrust laws, but even the symbol at which these laws were directed was outdated. Before the discovery of oil in Texas, antitrust sought to control the activities of the "foreign" Standard Oil Company in Texas. Amid the changed economic realities brought by the early Texas oil boom, however, such laws and attitudes proved very difficult to adjust. If strictly enforced, they would have hampered the rise of strong, independent firms in Texas by preventing such companies as Texaco and Gulf Oil from copying the vertically integrated organizational structure that Standard employed throughout the nation. Indeed, Texaco's first attorney recognized the potential impact of these "very far-reaching" laws and sought "so far as possible, to remain on the safe side of the line of doubt."[55] While attempting to move the "line of doubt" by lobbying in Texas legislature for a broader incorporation law, Texaco remained "on the safe side" by obtaining much of its crude oil from nominally independent subsidiary companies that were in fact directly tied to it. As it became clear that the state would not challenge the use of such subsidiaries, Texaco became more open in their use. This, of course, presented a dilemma to public officials, since such arrangements were, strictly speaking, against the law. Their solution was expedient, if not wholly consistent; strong antitrust laws remained on the books but were enforced only sporadically and only against Standard.

More than expediency explains this policy of partial enforcement. The state attorney general's office suffered from the general absence of trustworthy information, and it also lacked sufficient resources to seek out and prosecute all offenders. The state's indignation in the face of "the abuse of corporate privileges" far outran its capacity to find and correct such abuses. As of 1901, the Texas attorney general's office had an annual budget of less than $18,000, and the staff consisted of the attorney general, three assistants, one stenographer, and one clerk.[56] By way of contrast,

---

[55] James Autry to Joseph Cullinan, letter dated May 12, 1904, "1904" folder, Box 27, Papers of James Lockhart Autry, Rice University, Houston, Texas.

[56] *Annual Report of the Comptroller of Public Accounts of the State of Texas for the Year Ending August 31, 1900* (Austin, 1900), p. 123.

Gulf Oil's original charter authorized a capitalization of $15 million. Such companies quickly outgrew state boundaries and became national and international concerns. Texas officials responded by seeking to share information about the oil industry with other states such as Missouri, which was also seeking to prosecute Standard Oil, but such ad hoc and temporary cooperative arrangements could not alter the central fact that the individual states lacked the clear legal authority or the resources to pursue nationally active concerns across state lines.[57] To defend themselves on intrastate matters, these companies generally had excellent legal staffs and a strong interest in assuring that the antitrust laws were not enforced against them. As if the companies' advantages in manpower and legal resources over the attorney general's office were not enough, biennial elections gave the public agency a much shorter time horizon than the private companies, making continuity of investigation, much less prosecution, most difficult. Faced with such problems, public officials generally focused their rhetoric and their attempts at enforcement of the existing antitrust laws on the largest and most vulnerable targets.

Strong public backing for strict enforcement of the antitrust laws might perhaps have forced the state government to surmount its own weaknesses. The polity was not, however, strongly or even unambiguously committed to antitrust. At times many Texans seemed almost obsessed with antitrust as a useful weapon with which to fight monopoly in the petroleum industry, but most were also committed to rapid development of the newfound regional wealth. When forced to choose between these two commitments, the public, through its political system, usually chose rapid growth at the expense of vigorous antitrust enforcement. At times both were possible. Attacks on the octopus allowed politicians to stand up against the most potent of all symbols of monopoly without impeding the growth of other large, dynamic firms that became the primary generators of regional prosperity.[58]

Such distinctions often were lost on executives in these other companies, who tended to listen to what public officials said instead of watching more carefully what they did. These executives interpreted the lack of coherent public policy as evidence of the opportunism or incompetence of politicians, not as the consequence of the weaknesses and confusion of a public sector trying to make very difficult adjustments to dramatically altered conditions:

[57] A.W. Whitfield, Jr. to Jewel Lightfoot, letter dated June 21, 1909, "June 1907-November 1909, K-V, Anti-Trust Letters" file, Box 4-8/396, Attorney General's Correspondence, Record Group 302, Texas State Archives, Austin. See also, Bringhurst, *Antitrust and the Oil Monopoly*, pp. 89–107.

[58] In this way, politicians avoided—at least temporarily—the conflicting views toward antitrust that Ellis Hawley has discussed in detail in analyzing the confusion of purpose in the enforcement of antitrust laws in the 1930s. See Ellis Hawley, *The New Deal and the Problem of Monopoly* (Princeton, 1966).

The oil business is young in Texas. Its operations are to a degree spectacular and attractive to public attention. Its profits are supposed to be large. It is the kind of shining mark which attracts the attention of the average politician.[59]

As products of the late-nineteenth century, these oil executives were predisposed to assume that the government could not intervene effectively and intelligently in economic affairs. The sporadic enforcement of the Texas antitrust laws and the exaggerated rhetoric that accompanied the ebb and flow of antitrust provided them with little evidence to the contrary. Indeed, many no doubt came to share the disdain of Texaco's first attorney for "the cheap *newspapers* and the cheaper *politicians*, and the still cheaper unions and ignorant *public sentiment* upon which both the former feed and which both encourage."[60] One logical response from the point of view of the individual firm was that of Texaco, which vigorously entered the political arena in an effort to control political uncertainty.

Business-government relations in this formative era in the evolution of the modern petroleum industry thus left a highly uncertain legacy. Despite an underlying confusion of purpose, antitrust policy ultimately encouraged the growth of new competitors to Standard. A strong antitrust law that the government was unable or unwilling to enforce systematically allowed Standard Oil to take a limited role in developing the new Texas field, yet blocked the former monopolist from crushing its youthful competitors. The subsequent growth of these new competitors was central to the emergence of oligopoly in oil.

Such largely accidental results should not, however, obscure the problems of adjustment that confronted both state and federal governments in their initial attempts to implement antitrust policies for an industry undergoing rapid, fundamental changes. This early confrontation between oil and state revealed a clear lag between the organizational capacities of the modern corporations that emerged from the Texas oil fields and those of the inexperienced and sparsely staffed and funded government agencies that sought to regulate the oil industry. Working within public institutions originally designed to deal with a much simpler political economy, officials in both Austin and Washington groped toward ill-defined—if forcefully proclaimed—regulatory goals. Their strained interaction with the young and growing Gulf coast oil companies shaped the transition from monopoly to oligopoly in oil while foreshadowing many of the difficulties that continue to accompany a broader transition at the heart of the subsequent evolution of the petroleum industry, the transition from monopoly control over oil policy by private corporations to shared control between private and public institutions.

[59] James Autry to Joseph Cullinan, letter dated May 12, 1904, "1904" folder, Box 27, Papers of James Lockhart Autry, Rice University, Houston, Texas.

[60] James Autry to John Porter Hollis, letter dated June 3, 1905, Bureau of Corporations Numerical File 3208, Record Group 122, National Archives, Washington, D.C.

THE POLITICS OF BUREAUCRATIZATION AND THE U. S. BUREAU OF CORPORATIONS*

WILLIAM G. ROY

University of California, Los Angeles

Journal of Political and Military Sociology 1982, Vol. 10 (Fall):183-199

The U.S. Bureau of Corporations, which existed from 1903 to 1914, is examined in the context of the transition from an electoral to a bureaucratic mode of politics. The rise of the Bureau is explained, in part, by conflict within the capitalist class over the relationship between the state and economy, resulting in a proto-bureaucratic organization incapable of solving the problem it was mandated to address. It lacked the anti-trust power desired by small businessmen but failed to rationalize the economy as desired by corporate capitalists. Its incomplete bureaucratization was both a result of this conflict and sustained the level of conflict. By the second decade of the century, the early supporters of the Bureau had abandoned it in favor of creating the Federal Trade Commission, which was vested with more formal authority than the Bureau but, because of its more bureaucratic structure was endowed with greater autonomy from instrumental political influence. The result was to depoliticize the anti-trust impulse. The paper's conclusion discusses the relationship between class conflict and the historical construction of state autonomy.

The U. S. Bureau of Corporations was an agency created in 1903 to deal with corporate evils as part of the new Department of Commerce and Labor. It operated until it was replaced in 1914 by the Federal Trade Commission, an agency independent of any cabinet department. The Bureau served as the symbolic centerpiece of Theodore Roosevelt's anti-trust policy, and was thus a critical component of the relation between the federal government and the economy during an era in which that relation was being dramatically redefined. Both those associated with the rise of the corporation and those who opposed it turned to the Bureau as a means of achieving their goals. The anti-trust movement wanted a more systematic, sustained, and effective means of busting the trusts than the cumbersome litigation required to enforce the Sherman Anti-Trust Law. Corporation leaders, especially financiers like J. P. Morgan, wanted to rationalize the economy in order to prevent the ruinous cycle of competition, speculation, and collapse that had been escalating since the Civil War. But its promise to contain corporate power or to rationalize the economy was never fulfilled. Its early demise, an unusual event for typically immortal

---

* A previous draft of this paper was presented at the 1981 Annual Meeting of the American Sociological Association at Toronto, Ontario. The research was supported by the Academic Senate of the University of California. Research assistance has been performed by Ann B. Beardsley and Amy Beckman. The paper has benefitted from the helpful comments of Nancy DiTomaso, W. Lawrence Neuman, Erik O. Wright, and three anonymous reviewers of this journal. William Regensburger has greatly assisted in all phases of the endeavor.

231

government agencies, suggests that it failed not only by its inability to fulfill its legislative mandate — a forgivable political sin — but by a more deeply rooted inability to resolve or deflect problems that underlay its formation. By 1914 the stage was set for replacing the highly politicized Bureau of Corporations (BoC) with an "independent" Federal Trade Commission. The FTC was a more autonomous and more bureaucratic agency that more successfully depoliticized the issues, even if it did not resolve them.

The most influential political-economic analysis of the Progressive era has been the corporate liberal perspective (Kolko 1963,1965; Weinstein 1969; Williams 1966; Eakins 1966), in which the rise of American governmental bureaucracy during the Progressive Era is treated as a resounding victory for far-sighted corporate elites. The corporate liberal perspective has impressively demystified the conventional liberal perspective, which interpreted Progressive reforms as the result of popular agitation in counterbalance to the "excesses" of the robber barons (Key 1958; Hartz 1955). However this perspective has been criticized for overemphasizing the power of the corporate elite, for neglecting the historic contribution of the working class, and for treating the state as a passive object of corporate liberal manipulation (Wrigley 1980; Block 1977; Lehman 1975).

While corporate liberal theorists have made a valuable contribution to our understanding of the Progressive era, this paper will attempt to go beyond them by emphasizing how conflict within the capitalist class (in the context of conflict between classes) underlay the transformation from an electoral mode of politics to a bureaucratic mode. The electoral mode of politics designates structures and processes by which political parties and legislative bodies mediate between class interests and the state. Interests are vested by placing friendly individuals in powerful positions. In the bureaucratic mode of politics, interests vested during the original formation of procedures and policies become embedded in administrative tasks that are carried out relatively independently of personal characteristics of administrative functionaries. A group's interests can be reliably served without sustained mobilization to instrumentally influence the agency, at least until the agency's activity becomes repoliticized (Roy, 1981).

Autonomy refers to the relative state independence from the instrumental power of contending groups (in the sense of an actor's ability to assert his will over another actor despite resistance). The state is autonomous to the extent that it proactively initiates action rather than reacts to initiatives of others. To the extent that the state is autonomous, one cannot adequately explain why the state pursues particular courses of action by reference to the constellation of power among external groups but must integrate the articulation of internal and external power.

THE HISTORICAL CONTEXT: ENTREPRENEURIAL AND CORPORATE CAPITAL

The politics of the early twentieth century pitted corporate capitalists, who had only recently emerged as a defined group but who had not yet institutionalized their political role, against an entrepreneurial segment that was well organized and institutionalized on the local level but was reluctant to use the full power of the national state when their interests were threatened.

Corporate capital was based on a fusion of financial and industrial capital,[1] institutionalized through the corporate form with capital mobilized by investment banks, brokerage houses, and the stock market. Its emergence represented a fundamental restructuring of the capitalist class, a bifurcation of the class into two industrial segments which shared many interests but which were often in conflict over issues concerning the role of the state, the structure of finance, and working class organization.[2]

The railroad industry pioneered the basic corporate forms and mobilized the wealth that capitalized the corporate revolution. Initially corporate capital was appropriated less through direct profit on production than through tax subsidies to the railroads, monopolistic freight charges, and high interest payments on railroad securities. This indirect expropriation pitted the corporate segment against the other capitalist interests as well as against workers and farmers. The conflict erupted into open struggle in the form of populism (Goodwin 1978; Rochester 1943), the anti-trust movement (Hofstadter 1955; Dudden 1957; Weinstein 1969), and working class militancy (Foner 1955; Lens 1974).

Capital mobilized by railroads and and investment banks was potentially available for investment in productive industry, except that the locally entrepreneurial mode of ownership was not conducive to large scale financial investment or financial control (Navin and Sears 1955; Myers 1951; Mead 1912; Davis 1965, 1971). In the course of capital concentration, local capitals were (often forcibly) combined into national (and international) capital, while partnerships were incorporated, sooner or later offering securities on the open market. In the process the typical entrepreneur became a corporate manager, rentier capitalist, or excapitalist. A few became corporate capitalists. Entrepreneurial capital was directly controlled by one or a few capitalists, and capital flows were administered through commercial banking. This was the stronghold of the traditional bourgeoisie, deeply embedded in American civilization, highly organized on a local basis through political, religious, and civic organizations. The emergence of corporate capital caught them in a political bind. On one hand they favored economic coordination among competitors, and when competition became "ruinous," they welcomed government support. On the other hand they were mistrustful of any threat to property rights or any sustained government regualtion. They wanted such acts as predatory pricing or labor strikes outlawed, but they did not want proactive intervention on a regular basis. Their ideal was a reactive state, ready to intervene when necessary but otherwise absent, allowing them dominance within civil society. The segment was well organized on a local basis and was often successful in winning battles against monopolies at the state level.

The conflict between these two segments structured the formation and operation of the Bureau of Corporations, although labor militancy and farmer

---

1. In Marxian terms, segments of the capitalist class are in competition with each other over the distribution of the surplus value expropriated from the working class. In discussing the relationship of finance to industry, Marx claimed that "both interest and profit express relations of capital. As a particular form, interest-bearing capital stands opposite, not labour, but rather opposite profit-bearing capital. . . . The mode of production does therefore not yet undergo essential change" (1973a, p. 853).

2. The distinction between entrepreneurial and corporate segments of the capitalist class is based not on size of firm but on the form of property relations. Within the corporate segment the property relation is socialized, so that each firm has many owners and each owner holds property in many firms. In contrast, entrepreneurial owners and workers are related through direct property relations, one owner to one firm.

electoral contention were also critical factors. Labor militancy forced class-wide interests to prevail over any tendency toward rupture within the capitalist class, and labor militancy precluded electoral cooptation as a capitalist strategy. Rather than meeting populist insurgency by exchanging concessions for electoral support, the strategy was to neutralize the working class electoral strength by discouraging them from voting at all (Foner, 1955). The lesson of the contentious 1896 election was the vulnerability of electoral politics. The populist challenge was defeated but the price of victory was high in terms of material costs and the challenge to legitimacy.

The labor threat and the populist threat together underscored the advantages of a more "rational" political process that operated according to "business principles" and administrative efficiency. But translating capitalist intentions for a more rational politics into practice was not automatic nor in the long run entirely successful. Not only was there conflict between and within the classes, there was the structure and operation of the state itself. A state that operated through the electoral mode was hardly the structure to displace that mode with a bureaucratic state. The congress and major party leaders were unenthusiastic about creating new agencies. The Southern-dominated Democratic Party stubbornly resisted any national agencies that would weaken states' rights. Thus the contentious state of class conflict and legislatively constituted state itself meant that the movement toward a bureaucratic state unfolded in fits and starts.

Although the relationship was far from perfect, entrepreneurial capitalists tended to be associated with the Democratic Party while corporate capitalists tended to be Republicans. Intra-capitalist divisions also corresponded to divisions within the structure of the state. The base of entrepreneurial power was the state legislature, where most of the successful attempts to restrain the growth of monopolies had taken place and where local boards of trade, chambers of commerce, protective associations, and employers' associations were most highly mobilized. Nationally organized corporations did not have the resources to fight on so many fronts at once. Even at the national level, entrepreneurial legislative power probably outweighed corporate influence. In the House, entrepreneurs and farmers grossly outnumbered corporate-oriented Congressmen. In the Senate, corporate capital was growing stronger as leadership positions were assumed by men like coal and traction magnate Marcus Hanna, Rockefeller son-in-law Nelson Aldrich, and former N.Y. Central Railroad president Chauncy M. Depew. However, despite popular alarm over Senate plutocracy, it was hardly a reliable protector of corporate interests. What direct political influence corporate capital possessed was in the executive. Each of the Presidents from Grover Cleveland (a former railroad lawyer) was closely associated with corporate capital, while cabinet officials tended to be disproportionately recruited from the corporate ranks (Mintz 1975).

Even though many of the new agencies created around the turn of the century effectively centralized power in the executive branch and contributed to the decline of legislative power, the legislators did not seem to realize that this would happen. Most legislators perceived government operation through the prevailing model of the period — formal constitutional law. Congressional powers were clearly distinguished and new laws were explicitly framed in terms of formal legislative or executive powers. New agencies, even when they were placed within the executive branch, were not seen as expanding executive powers because they did not explicitly create new powers. For example, in the initial presentation of the legislation creating the Department of Commerce and Labor in 1902, it was stated that the new department did not create any new presidential powers even though there would be a new cabinet member. Original cabinet members like the Secretary of State that exercised presidential power were distinguished from those like the Secretary of Agriculture who merely executed legislative initiatives. The new Department of Commerce and Labor was to be clearly of the latter type. Congressmen could not envision that the administrative power they were creating would extend beyond the ability of Congress to monitor.[3] In this way the electoral mode was a vessel that contributed to its own transcendence.

THE BUREAU OF CORPORATIONS AS A STANDOFF IN CLASS CONFLICT

First suggested during hearings of the U.S. Industrial Commission in 1901-1902 (called by Congress to investigate relations between capital and labor), the BoC was created as an investigative body to uncover corporate abuses and contribute to drawing corporate legislation. Roosevelt appointed James Garfield, son of the late President, as the first Commissioner of Corporations. During the decade of its existence, the BoC investigated several of the most notorious trusts and produced reports that remain among the best sources of information about them. They also compiled and codified state laws on a number of topics such as corporate taxation and corporate regulation. However, the bureau neither curtailed the trusts nor rationalized the economy. More importantly, many of the issues with which it was associated remained topics of controversy, as did the bureau itself.[4]

The Bureau of Corporations was the creation of no particular class or segment but was the manifestation of contradictory pressures primarily from entrepreneurial capital (in alliance with agrarian interests) and corporate capital. Many corporate capitalists felt that reckless speculation had been a major cause of the depression of the 1890's and that competition had undermined profits in major industries. The legal basis of their new form of property was still insecure, which not only created ambiguity and opportunities for privateering but also perpetuated the frequent charge that corporations were illegal combinations of capital. As leaders of the segment, like Morgan and Roosevelt, developed a conception of a corporate liberal society with rationalized economy and negotiated class conflict, the reality they faced defied their hopes. Anti-trust sentiment flourished among small businessmen, farmers

---

3. This distinction was also made in the BoC's first annual report, which described the bureau as "arm of the legislative branch. . . placed under the executive branch of the goverment for the purpose of administration and continuity of action" (U.S. Bureau of Corporations, 1904).

4. Some of the important issues were resolved, such as the legitimacy of the corporate form itself. The issue changed from the evil of the corporation itself to corporate evils. From the perspective of corporate capitalists, the BoC was successful in this regard.

and middle-class professionals. Working class mobilization partially subsided with the end of the depression and the Spanish-American War, but then revitalized after the turn of the century (Peters, 1902).

To anti-monopoly entrepreneurs, the Bureau of Corporations represented a means to strengthen enforcement of anti-trust laws. But their political vision, in the context of a state whose powers were based on policing powers, made an ironic contribution to the eventual rise of bureaucratic politics and limited their ability to resist the political ascendence of corporate capital. In the first place, the most highly mobilized anti-monopolists were bound within the framework of private property, severely restricting the measures they could propose without challenging the social relations upon which they themselves depended. Secondly, the most successful anti-trust initiatives pushed the economic concentration toward a set of pre-existing institutional economic arrangements (the stock market and investment banking) that was well established for transportation and communication but had formerly been considered inappropriate for industrial organization. Even though anti-monopolists attacked Wall Street, criticism was framed in terms of anti-trust, anti-combination, and pro-competition ideology rather than in anti-corporate terms. Their nostalgia for a free competitive economy blinded them to the unfolding transformation of property and restructuring of class relationships in which they were participating. In contrast, many corporate leaders favored, as an alternative to state level incorporation or federal licensing, either of which would require an extensive bureaucratic agency. It was also felt that stock market privateering could be reduced through collection and dissemination of stategic information on the corporate sector. But the corporate leaders lacked the legislative influence to achieve these goals.

Thus both entrepreneurial and corporate capitalists favored the creation of a Bureau of Corporations, but for very different reasons. The political process of reconciling these conflicting expectations resulted in a proto-bureaucratic agency lacking both the authority and the organization to achieve the goals sought by corporate officials while vested with only minimal powers to combat the trusts. The goal of entrepreneurial capitalists to combat trusts was reduced to publicly exposing corporate evils without any power to prosecute. The corporate capitalist hope for federal incorporation or licensing was never realized.

PUBLICITY AS AN ANTI-TRUST WEAPON

The Bureau's major task was studying and publicizing the operation of certain corporations and certain industries, one area in which the anti-trust and corporate leaders could find some common ground. To the anti-trust movement, publicity could expose corporate evils, galvanizing public opinion to force corporate reform. The rationale for the power of publicity was twofold: faith in the power of Truth, and the belief that the government's timidity against trusts stemmed partly from lack of evidence. As Rep. Sulzer (D- NY) argued in the House of Representatives, if the Bureau of Corporations effectively publicized corporate practices, "no trust in this country, no corporation, no monopoly, would or could violate the law" (*Congressional Record*, 1903:918).

The corporations themselves, while they did not invite publicity, would tolerate it as the least threatening of the anti-trust weapons. As early as 1886, *The Commercial and Financial Chronicle* stated: "We most decidedly favor publicity in corporate management, believing it to be the best cure for very many of the abuses which now to a greater or less extent prevail. Yet of course no part of the purpose of the Government officer in his regulation to attain that end can be either punitive or annoying (March 20, 1886, p. 350)." Pro-corporate political figures framed the publicity of corporate evils in terms of the distinction between good and bad trusts. Theodore Roosevelt, the most visible spokesman for this point of view, eloquently denounced and publicly prosecuted a few "bad" trusts, earning himself a reputation as a trust buster. But he was equally adamant, although less flamboyant, in his insistence that the "good" trusts were good. Roosevelt threw his support behind the creation of the Bureau of Corporations as the centerpiece of his anti-trust policy (Leinwald, 1962) because the bureau, he felt, would expose the abuses of the bad trusts and correct the public misconceptions of the good trusts.

Publicity was acceptable to both groups, but satisfied neither the entrepreneurs' goal to legally constrain the corporations nor the corporate capitalists' hope for governmental sanction of their existence and practice. As the later history of the Bureau demonstrates, both groups continued to seek more substantive functions, and in the end both groups retreated from their commitment to publicity.

Organizational Structure and Agency Failure

The internal organization of the Bureau also reflected the standoff in class power between the two major segments of the capitalist class. The Bureau was staffed by rationalizers whose organizational model was inspired by newly instituted corporate models of bureaucratic organizations. Over the period that the agency existed, each commissioner attempted to rationalize and bureaucratize it by regularizing record-keeping, routinizing the studies conducted, and changing staff procedures to conform with civil service practices (Fishbein 1955).

But the agency's incomplete bureaucratization contributed to its long-term failure and replacement by the more bureaucratic Federal Trade Commission. It could neither depoliticize the contentious issues that it faced nor insulate itself from continued partisan pressure. Groups that might have been demobilized by depoliticizing the issues continued to vigorously press for their goals through the bureau.

Rather than following well established administrative procedures, each investigation, after being commissioned by Congress, was assigned to staff members on an *ad hoc* basis, and conducted as a self-contained project. Many staff members were hired for a particular investigation, either because of special expertise or as lower level clerical help. Permanent investigators worked on only one project at a time. The Commissioners attempted to routinize the tasks by placing the staff under civil service regulations, adopting regular reporting procedures, and other measures, but each investigation nonetheless was a unique task, tailored by a Congressional Act to study a particular corporation or particular industry. Thus each revealed new information on well known and often infamous "trusts," including the meat packers, International Harvester,

Standard Oil, and U.S. Steel. Each was released with fanfare and critical review. Most of the investigations were intended as anti-trust salvos by the initiating Congressmen, and most were interpreted in that light, repoliticizing the trust question.

The lack of any enforcement powers also mandated sustained politicization. The corporate liberals who ran the Bureau were deeply dedicated to a rationalized social order of cooperative relationships among the classes, led by a responsible business elite. They were offended by apparent corporate excesses, but would have preferred to negotiate redemption gentleman to gentleman. But since they lacked authority and since corporate officials were not always gentlemen, publicity offered the best means at their disposal to rationalize their chaotic society.

The failure to insulate the Bureau is indicated in the accountability structure within which it was situated, which conformed closely to the electoral mode of politics: interests between social actors and the government were mediated by political parties and other plebescitarian structures. Instead of creating an independent agency like the Interstate Commerce Commission, Congress created the Bureau as an agency of the Department of Commerce and Labor, with the Commissioner of Corporations accountable directly to the Secretary of Commerce and Labor and indirectly to the President. Each investigation was initiated by Congress and, when complete, was sent directly to the President, who was empowered to release or withhold the report.[5] Continued operation and new initiatives were dependent on explicitly political structures. Such an accountability structure offered an influence route for all groups whose interests were affected by bureau actions and thus hindered autonomy.

THE FAILURE TO ESTABLISH FEDERAL INCORPORATION

The primary positive achievement that corporate capitalists hoped the Bureau would lead to was a system of federal incorporation, or at least federal licensing, as a possible solution to recurrent state level defeats. The most far-reaching form would have been to authorize the federal government to incorporate firms conducting interstate business.[6] However, state level political leaders, including Congressmen, opposed this notion too intensely to make it a practical proposition. So the alternative of federal licensing was proposed. Federal licensing would be a (presumably voluntary) legal status granted to businesses conducting interstate commerce. Firms would still be incorporated by individual states but would be granted a federal license contingent on a number of requirements including public release of financial data and responsible behavior. Licensing would also have provided an opportunity to legally sanction corporate practices before they were instituted. Instead of adopting new practices that might be prosecuted, licensed corporations would be able to preemptively check their legality with the bureau. Once sanctioned,

---

5. All the reports produced by the Bureau were released, but some were delayed for political reasons. Moreover, the number of copies of each released report was limited by the organic act to dampen the impact of the more sensational reports (U.S. National Archives).

6. There was some legal precedent for federal incorporation. Certain businesses that had no single state locus, such as navigation along rivers dividing states or companies headquartered in the District of Columbia, had been incorporated by special acts of Congress (U.S. National Archives).

the practice would be immune from prosecution.

These two plans were first proposed by corporate liberal economists like J.W. Jenks around the turn of the century (Thorelli, 1964), but the most vocal advocate during the next decade was the Bureau of Corporations. Every Annual Report thoroughly discussed the merits and demerits of the plans.[7] The Bureau's close ally, Senator Newlands of Nevada, invited them to produce model legislation which he frequently brought before Congress. The Morgan interests, especially George Perkins, supported the idea. At one point Perkins wrote Commissioner Smith concerning the effort for federal incorporation:

> If the opponents to Governmental supervision could only know how intelligently and how fairly you have worked for the very highest and best interests of American corporations, I am sure they would abandon their present attitude and join in trying to help you work out some of the knotty problems that are bothering you so much (April 18, 1908. U.S. National Archives. File 5589).

The movement for federal incorporation or federal licensing failed. Opponents accurately labelled it as an attempt to remove corporations to a more congenial jurisdiction than the unpredictable and decentralized individual states. Once it became obvious that neither plan would succeed, corporate support for the Bureau substantially eroded.

THE RISING TIDE OF DISENCHANTMENT

The two major segments that had contributed to forming the Bureau of Corporations became more and more unhappy with its performance. By the end of its first decade disenchantment had risen high enough to sweep the Bureau away and replace it with an entirely new agency, the Federal Trade Commission. Many of the problems built into the Bureau were resolved in the FTC, but it in turn embodied a number of contradictions inherent in the BoC.

Several factors contributed to the changing stance of the entrepreneurial capitalists. The most important in relations to the Bureau was that their faith in the power of publicity was severely strained. The Bureau's reports were obviously not breaking up the corporations. The only report contributing to a successful anti-trust prosecution was the Standard Oil report, which provided much of the evidence for Standard's dissolution in 1911. The authority to prosecute remained in the Justice Department and the courts, where the small businessmen lacked influence. So it was hoped that the creation of an agency free from dependence upon the Justice Department and courts would be more effective. Secondly, the merger wave that had engulfed the country during the first years of the century has subsided after 1904. The recession of 1907 shifted attention away from monopolistic, predatory anti-competitive practices toward particular practices of Wall Street financing. Public debate was increasingly framed in terms of corporate evils rather than the evil of the corporation itself. Finally, as the Socialist Party scored impressive electoral showings and the working class remobilized the labor movement, entrepreneurial businessmen became more willing to accept the existence of the corporate form. Class-wide interests were looming larger than they had in 1903.[8]

---

7. Typically annual reports of government agencies are dry, straight-forward reviews of the year's work, emphasizing budgeting and personnel matters, with modest proposals for enhancing the agency's domain. Such a sustained and intense advocacy of a radical change in the relationship between business and government was highly unusual.

8. Montgomery (1979), for example, describes (contra Weinstein) how the National Civic Federation and the National Association of Manufacturers moved closer together over the first decade of the century, at least on the labor issue, as more businessmen became intolerant of even moderate unionism.

It is clear from the agency's records that the small businessmen of America initially saw it as more than an agency of publicity. There were literally thousands of letters from the victims of anti-competitive practices and other abuses. They clearly assumed the agency to be a policeman ready to punish the corporate bullies. The Commissioner politely answered each letter explaining that they lacked authority to prosecute. If the petitioner could contribute information to an ongoing study, he was given an investigator's name. Otherwise, he was advised that authority to prosecute lay entirely within the Justice Department and corresponding state agencies (U.S. National Archives).

The common misunderstanding of the Bureau by these small businessmen stemmed partly from the extensive publicity given the Bureau's formation. Many newspapers carried lengthy articles and political cartoons portraying the Bureau in such metaphors as David's sling about to slay the monopoly Goliath. The image was further fuelled by the news stories of the investigations as they proceeded. Congressional initiators hailed each investigation as the answer to the problem of whatever trust was being investigated. Speculation about spectacular revelations continued until completion, at which time wide coverage tacitly implied that something was being done about the evils exposed, a presumption the Bureau did little to change. As the various studies were completed without remedial action, and as the Bureau's lack of real enforcement authority became more widely known, entrepreneurial support for the agency eroded.

Corporate support also waned. In the first place, they were stung by the Bureau's critical reports which contributed to their legitimacy problems. The first report (U.S. Bureau of Corporations, 1905), on the meat packing industry, was relatively harmless. It thoroughly documented the organizational aspects of the meat packers, presented evidence on past anti-competitive practices, and revealed financial data on pricing, cost of materials, and profits. It concluded that while the packers had formerly employed anti-competitive practices, there was no evidence of continued abuses, and that, in fact, the corporations were free of watered stock and gained only modest profits. The nation's press greeted the report with the charge of "whitewash," questioning the Roosevelt Administration's true commitment to anti-trust. The negative reaction troubled the Bureau's top officials and substantially altered the conduct of the later investigations (U.S. National Archives). The Standard Oil reports (U.S. Bureau of Corporations, 1906; 1907) documented evidence of widespread railroad rebates, predatory pricing practices, and exorbitant profits on invested capital. The Bureau's data then served as the basis of evidence in U.S. vs. Standard Oil, which disturbed many corporate officials. It was especially distressing because the first commissioner, James R. Garfield, eschewing Congressionally granted subpoena powers, had gained cooperation by assuring investigatees that no information would be used to prosecute them. Many felt that Garfield had betrayed the business world.

Garfield's (involuntary) betrayal precipitated a revaluation of the personalistic relationship formed between the Bureau and major corporate officials. The history of the ICC had shown that if friendly officials were appointed, the public would be satisfied with a visible symbol while concrete corporate interests would be little threatened. This personalistic stance toward regulatory agencies continued with the formation of the BoC. The commissioner thoroughly dominated the internal structure of the Bureau, as was characteristic of contemporary government agencies. Few hierarchical levels separated the commissioner from the staff. He alone mediated all communication with the outside, signing all communication, even to investigators in the field, and his personal style shaped the investigations. The general orientation toward political appointees and the commissioner's central organizational role coincided to intensify the political consequences of his actions. When corporate officials lost faith in the personalistic relationship with the commissioner, they lost faith in the agency itself. The events after Theodore Roosevelt left the White House followed such a pattern.

In the early days of the Bureau, the Roosevelt administration forged a "detente" with several corporate leaders, especially the Morgan interests (Wiebe, 1959; Kolko, 1963), by which corporate officials agreed to cooperate with the investigations in exchange for informal immunity from prosecution. This helps explain why the Meat Packing report was so benign. Although the Rockefeller interests enjoyed no such detente (since Standard Oil was Roosevelt's archtypal "bad trust"), Garfield personalistically negotiated the next investigation with them. Although Garfield abnegated his subpoena power, he threatened to publically expose their non-cooperation. Standard relinquished enough information so that, when it was added to their competitor's generous offerings, the resulting studies were devastating. The revelations rekindled the fires that had subsided as Lloyd's *Wealth Against Commonwealth* and Tarbell's *The History of Standard Oil* faded in the public memory. The corporate world was put on notice that the Bureau would not neccessarily produce what they considered responsible reports. However, the Morgan interests remained confident that the Bureau would honor their gentleman's agreement. As long as Roosevelt was in office, they were given reason to sustain their confidence. Congress had initiated studies on two Morgan corporations, U.S. Steel and International Harvester, but the Bureau stretched out the investigations over a number of years. The Steel report was then withheld pending the outcome of other Federal investigations, because Garfield adamantly refused to renege on his pledge to his friends in USS. The Harvester investigation also dragged out pending anti-trust litigation. However, when the celebrated "trust-buster" Roosevelt was succeeded by the "pro-business" Taft, the situation ironically changed. Taft had not agreed to the detente and vigorously prodded the Bureau to complete the two reports. Moreover, he felt no compunction against using the Bureau information as evidence in anti-trust litigation. In 1907 Garfield had been promoted to Secretary of the Interior, yielding leadership to his former assistant, Herbert Knox Smith. Although Smith was hardly anti-corporate, and in fact was personally close to Morgan's lieutenant, George Perkins, he was a highly principled man committed to public service. He thus conscientiously completed the reports despite knowing that they would probably be used for prosecution (U.S. National Archives). Although neither U.S. Steel nor International Harveste1 were successfully prosecuted, the conclusions drawn within the corporate world emphasized the uncertainty of the type of personal and informal agreement between Morgan and Roosevelt. Corporate leaders increasingly supported the creation of a new agency that would be less dependent on personal relationships with the incumbent officials. Instead they proposed an independent agency less accountable to Congress, operating according to more "neutral" administrative business principles, similar to municipal agencies being created by progressive reformers (Schiesl, 1981). Most importantly, they favored an agency that would not single out particular industries and corporations for public exposure.

THE FORMATION OF THE FEDERAL TRADE COMMISSION

By 1914, entrepreneurial and corporate support for the bureau of Corporations had all but disappeared. Entrepreneurial capitalists wanted an agency with anti-trust teeth but were disappointed. Corporate capitalists hoped in vain for federal incorporation or federal licensing. Both were then receptive to the proposal generated within the BoC to create an agency modelled after the British trade commission. When the BoC disappointed its original supporters, replacing it with a new bureau was more feasible than entirely dismantling it. The FTC was created in direct reference to, and in explicit contrast with the BoC. A higher level of bureaucratization in the FTC was attractive because of the low level of bureaucratization in the BoC.

It is beyond the scope of this paper to provide a full treatment of the formation and functioning of the Federal Trade Commission, but a brief outline will contrast the FTC to the BoC and describe how the former solved some of the contradictions faced by the BoC while embodying some of its own.

The particular structure of the FTC reflected the balance of power between capitalist class segments in the context of the pre-existing state structure. Entrepreneurial capitalists successfully strengthened anti-trust authority by empowering the FTC to prohibit "unfair methods of competition." Corporate capitalists successfully rationalized government coordination of the economy and depoliticized government regulation by insulating the agency from Congressional and Presidential interference. The relationship between the agency and the business world was mediated by interest groups rather than electoral parties. The FTC continued to collect and distribute information on the conduct of business, not by investigating particular industries or corporations and publicizing their conduct by name, but by conducting surveys and releasing only the aggregate results. The studies were initiated from within the agency itself and conducted by full time professional staff members rather than ad hoc investigators. Full time staff members had a built-in incentive to maintain ongoing cordial relationships with their subjects, with whom they would be repeatedly interacting. The resulting reports were typically written in administrative language cluttered with statistics, revealing little that could be sensationally interpreted. The reports were thus depoliticized.

The nature of the agency's leadership also discouraged politicizing issues. In place of a single politically appointed and accountable commissioner, the FTC was directed by five commissioners appointed for fixed overlapping terms. Not only were they less accountable to politicians, but each held limited authority. Had any of them been motivated to steer the agency toward anti-corporate activism, he would have probably been blocked by the others.[9]

The FTC's insulation from electoral political structures and the absence of a strong head protected it from the control of political parties and elected officials. The most direct route to influence the agency was via its clients and professional staff. This structure benefitted corporate capitalists by depoliticizing government regulation within a bureaucratic mode of operation, thus displacing conflict to the administrative arena, where they could more effectively mobilize than could small businessmen. Political activity could take the form of interorganizational relationships, bureaucracy to bureaucracy.

Thus like the Bureau of Corporations, the Federal Trade Commission neither effectively restrained the power of the corporations as sought by small businessmen, nor rationalized or thoroughly legitimized corporate actions as sought by the corporations. While the BoC could effectively politicize corporate issues and was organized to mobilize in a coordinated fashion if led by a motivated commissioner, it lacked any authority to materially affect the conduct of economic actors. On the other hand, the FTC was granted broader and potentially more effective authority, but its bureaucratic structure insulated it from the groups that would have had the strongest reason to mobilize it on their behalf. The structure was also too unwieldy to perform any decisive action.

CONCLUSION

The process illustrated here is this: conflict between the two major segments of the capitalist class, set in the context of the overall class structure and the structure of the state, contributed to the transformation of the American state from an electoral to a bureaucratic mode. The consequence was movement toward the historical construction of state relative autonomy. The organization of classes and class segments determined their relative capacity for instrumental mobilization. The structure of the state dictated the effectiveness of instrumental mobilization and the relativity of state autonomy. Conflict between capitalist class segments in the context of conflict between classes incapacitated any effective instrumental mobilization, even against a rather non-autonomous state. More specifically, the previously dominant entrepreneurial segment was threatened by the emerging corporate class segment. But its reliance on state policing powers, its commitment to property rights, and conflict with farmers and workers limited its ability to use the state to restrain the new segment. Although the state structure was dominated by electorally oriented bodies, several elements combined to facilitate centralization of power within the executive and expand bureaucratic power. First, legislators were willing to deflect the intense inter- and intra- class conflict from themselves to new agencies. Secondly, the legislators' formal constitutional orientation obscured their sensitivity to the centralization of power to which they were contributing.

A related issue is the tension between instrumental mobilization and state

9. The decentralized structure of having many commissioners was partly overcome in the formative stages by E.L. Davies, the last Commissioner of Corporations, who played a dominating role in the agency's early years.

autonomy, and how the interaction of mobilized political contenders and the state itself facilitated greater autonomy. Neither class segment enthusiastically pursued greater autonomy. The entrepreneurial segment, because of its power base in the legislature and its reliance on the policing powers of the state, had no interest in autonomy. Although corporate leaders could imagine a more active state, they initially treated bureaucratization as an instrumental device, serving their interests only when administered by friendly officials, and useful more as a means of coopting and depoliticizing mobilized contenders than as a positive goal. The initiative for creating both the BoC and FTC came from within the government itself, motivated by a desire to rationalize conflict between segments of the capitalist class and to develop a uniform and fair procedure for dealing with corporate affairs, especially corporate abuses.

Increased autonomy did not occur automatically or inevitably. The BoC's retarded bureaucratization stimulated instrumental mobilization by repoliticizing anti-trust issues. The non-routine nature of each investigation facilitated its continued politicization, spurring interested parties to mobilize and undermining the BoC's independence in conducting its investigations. Had the entrepreneurial segment been stronger, they might have won a servant agency, like the farmers had won the Department of Agriculture. Had the corporate segment been stronger they might have won government sponsorship of syndicates and cartels, as found in France or Germany. Since both class segments were disappointed in the BoC, they became more amenable to a bureaucratic solution and both helped shape the new commission. It was thus through this complex process that state autonomy was historically constructed.

Out of this case study several theoretical implications emerge which suggest lines for further research. It appears that the need for instrumental influence varies according to the structure of the state and the degree of conflict. The more bureaucratized the state, the more the state itself reproduces the pattern of vested interests and the less the need for instrumental mobilization to maintain the status quo. But bureaucracies are formed and altered partly by instrumental mobilization, often in the context of political conflict. Political conflict affects bureaucratization in at least two ways. Increased conflict heightens contenders' sensitivity to how well their interests are being served and thus politicizes the activities of those agencies that contenders interpret as insufficiently serving their intersts, thereby thwarting bureaucratic functioning. Secondly, executive officials typically resist attempts to politicize administrative activities, often self-consciously using depoliticization as a tool to restore order and reduce conflict. Thus social conflict often motivates state officials to act autonomously while it escalates contenders' attempts to instrumentally control the state. One of the factors that affects the outcome is the preexisting level of state bureaucratization. Highly bureaucratized states with large administrative agencies can more effectively resist influence attempts by administratively resolving conflict. Whose interests are thereby served depends on such factors as the relative ability of contenders to instrumentally influence the state, the structure of the state's own interests (such as how taxes are raised relative to expanding and contracting economic sectors), and the state's political imperatives and goals (such as the basis of its legitimacy or place in the international state system).

The experience of the BoC highlights the historical contingency of state autonomy, raising the issue of what types of factors affect the degree of autonomy in a given situation. Three necessary conditions for autonomy are suggested here. First, the state must possess power proportionate to its penetration into society, the deeper the penetration, the more power needed. A state that claims jurisdiction over social relations without the power to exercise that jurisdiction typically sacrifices autonomy to maintain the appearance of authority. For example, the Bureau of Corporations was granted subpeona powers for its investigations into corporate affairs, but it lacked the litigational apparatus to enforce those powers. To compensate, it emphasized a cooperative stance toward the corporations, relying on voluntary compliance to requests for information, putting the corporations in a strong negotiating position to demand (and win) concessions about the scope and nature of the investigations. Secondly, autonomy from instrumental control requires that the state have power appropriate to the intensity of class conflict. If the state lacks the power to maintain order in the face of social conflict, it may have to seek a coalition with a major contender. Thus the chaotic relationships between and within major classes partly accounts for the government's tendency to sanction and at times cooperate with Morgan's attempts to "stabilize" the tumultuous and rancorous economy. Thirdly, state autonomy requires that state authority be proportionate to the level of mobilization of various political contenders: the higher the level of mobilization, the greater the need for state authority. The American government did not have the authority to effectively counteract the increasing mobilization of the entrepreneurial and corporate segments against the Bureau of Corporations which eventually contributed to the bureau's demise.

State autonomy thereby can be treated not as an immanent systemic attribute, but as the result of real historical actors, acting in the context of structural constraints. In other words, autonomy is historically constructed, not structurally determined. The relative autonomy of the state is a historical variable that changes over time; it is neither a constant nor does it vary only as a function of impersonal structural forces. There are situations in which one class is so nearly hegemonic that the state takes on the attributes of an instrument of class rule. But there are other situations in which the struggle between the classes (or between class segments) is more evenly matched, in which classes (or class segments) turn to the state as a resource in the struggle.

The bureaucratic state is not an inevitable outgrowth of modern corporate capitalism. It is a historically specific mode of politics, stemming from and expressing contingent class relationships. Recent events have highlighted how vulnerable state bureaucracies are to repoliticization as well as how conditionally corporate leaders embrace government regulation. There is nothing inherent in bureaucratization or government regulation that predisposes corporate capitalists to favor them. When they interpret government bureaucracy and regulation as hurting them, they mobilize for deregulation. When they perceive it as beneficial, they support regulation. Whether they are successful or not depends on the structure of class power and the actions of the state itself. The critical theoretical and historical question is not so much whether bureaucracy favors one class or another, but the circumstances under which one class or another is favored and the circumstances under which class conflict in the context of the historically specific state creates and dismantles bureaucratic agencies.

REFERENCES

Block, Fred
    1977   "Beyond Corporate Liberalism." Social Problems 24: 352-361.
Commercial and Financial Chronicle
    1886   New York: William B. Dana and Co.
Davis, Lance E.
    1965   "The investment market, 1870-1914: The evolution of a national market." Journal
                of Economic History 25:355-399.
    1971   "Capital mobility and American growth. Pp. 285-300, in Robert W. Fogel and
                Stanley L. Engerman (ed). The Reinterpretation of American History. New York:
                Harper and Row.
Dudden, Arthur P.
    1957   "Men against monopoly: The prelude to trust-busting." Journal of the History of
                Ideas 18:587-593.
Eakins, David
    1966   The Development of Corporate Liberal Policy Research in the United States,
                1885-1965. Unpublished Ph.D. dissertation. University of Wisconsin.
Fishbein, Meyer H.
    1955   "Records Management in the Bureau of Corporations." The American Archivist
                18:161-167.
Foner, Philip S.
    1955   History of the Labor Movement of the United States. Vol. II. New York:
                International Publishers.
Goodwin, Lawrence
    1978   The Populist Moment: A Short History of the Agrarian Revolt in America. Oxford:
                Oxford University Press.
Hartz, Louis
    1955   The Liberal Tradition in America. New York: Harcourt, Brace & World.
Hilferding, Rudolf
    1979   "The capitalist monopolies and the banks." in Tom Bottomore and Patrick Goode
                (eds.) Austro-Marxism. Oxford: Clarendon Press.
Hofstadter, Richard
    1955   The Age of Reform. New York: Vintage.
Key, V.O., Jr.
    1958   Politics, Parties, and Pressure Groups. New York: Thomas Y. Crowell Co.
Kolko, Gabriel
    1963   The Triumph of Conservatism: A Reinterpretation of American History, 1900-
                1916. Chicago: Quadrangle Books.
    1965   Railroads and Regulation, 1877-1916. New York: W.W. Norton.
Lehman, Ingrid
    1975   "Corporate capitalism and the liberal state: The Kolko-Weinstein thesis."
                Kapitalistate 3:159-166.
Leinwald, Gerald
    1962   A History of the United States Federal Bureau of Corporations. Unpublished
                Ph.D. dissertation. New York University.
Lens, Sidney,
    1974   The Labor Wars. Garden City, N.Y.: Anchor.
Marx, Karl
    1974   "The Eighteenth Brumaire of Louis Bonaparte" in Political Writings: Vol II:
                Surveys From Exile. New York: Vintage.
    1973   Grundrisse. New York: Vintage.
Mead, Edward S.
    1912   Corporation Finance. New York: D. Appleton & Co.

Mintz, Beth
  1975   "The President's Cabinet, 1897-1972." Insurgent Sociologist 5(3):131-148.
Montgomery, David
  1979   Workers' Control in America: Studies in the History of Work, Technology, and
            Labor Struggles. New York: Cambridge University Press.
Myers, Margaret
  1951   "The investment market after the civil war." Pp. 571-584 in Harold F. Williamson
            (ed). The Growth of the American Economy. Englewood Cliffs, N.J.: Prentice-
            Hall.
Navin, T.B. and M.V. Sears
  1955   "The rise of a market for industrial securities, 1877-1902." Business History
            Review 29:105-138.
Peters, John P. (ed.)
  1902   Labor and Capital. New York: G.P. Putnam's Sons.
Rochester, Anna
  1943   The Populist Movement in the United States. New York: International Publishers.
Roy, William G.
  1981   "From electoral to bureaucratic politics: Class conflict and the financial-industrial
            class segment." Pp. 173-202 in Maurice Zeitlin (ed.) Political Power and Social
            Theory. Vol. II. Greenwich, Conn.: JAI Press.
Schiesl, Martin
  1981   The Politics of Efficiency. Berkeley: University of California Press.
Thorelli, Hans B.
  1964   Federal Anti-Trust Policy. Baltimore: Johns Hopkins University Press.
U.S. Bureau of Corporations
  1904   Annual Report of the Commissioner and Corporations. Washington: General
            Printing Office.
  1905   Report of the Commissioner of Corporations on the Beef Industry. Washington:
            Government Printing Office.
  1906   Report of the Commissioner of Corporations on the Transportation of Petroleum.
            Washington: General Printing Office.
  1907   Report of the Commissioner of Corporations on the Petroleum Industry.
            Washington: General Printing Office.
U.S. House of Representatives, Committee on Banking and Currency.
  1913   Report of the Committee Appointed Pursuant to House Resolution 429 and 504 to
            Investigate the Concentration and Control of Capital. Report No. 1593. 52nd
            Congress. 3rd Session. Washington: Government Printing Office.
U.S. Industrial Commission
  1900-1902 Reports. 19 Vols. Washington: Government Printing Office.
U.S. National Archives
            Records of the Bureau of Corporations. Record Group 122. Washington.
United States Congress.
  1903   Congressional Record. Washington: Government Printing Office.
Weinstein, James
  1969   The Corporate Ideal and the Liberal State. Boston: Beacon Press.
Wiebe, Robert
  1959   "The House of Morgan and the Executive, 1905-1913." American Historical
            Review 65:49-60
Williams, William A.
  1966   The Contours of American History. Chicago: Quadrangle
Wrigley, Julia
  1980   "Class politics and school reform in Chicago." Pp. 153-171 in Maurice Zeitlin (ed.)
            Class, Class Conflict, and the State. Cambridge: Winthrop.

WOODROW WILSON AS "CORPORATE-LIBERAL": TOWARD A RECONSIDERATION OF LEFT REVISIONIST HISTORIOGRAPHY

ALAN L. SELTZER

University of Maryland Baltimore County

SCHOLARS who view the American polity as governed by a "ruling class" or "power elite" hold that major U.S. political party leaders, especially the modern Presidents, have all tried to provide for the well-being of the giant corporate-industrial order and to perpetuate its underlying class structure. Since at least the turn of the century, according to this view, the senior officials of the executive branch — as partners of corporate executives — have shaped public policy to preserve corporate capitalism's hegemony. For instance, in a provocative textbook along these lines, Ira Katznelson and Mark Kesselman argue that federal government policies assured corporate capitalism's "initial success" during its "critical period," the several years following the turn of the century which are commonly known as the Progressive Era.[1] Katznelson and Kesselman have accepted as valid the findings and interpretations of left revisionist historical studies of that period,[2] apparently without independently reconsidering the evidence. Their textbook exemplifies a growing tendency among political scientists to utilize such studies in support of radical critiques of the American polity. This tendency makes it timely and appropriate for political scientists to participate more actively in discussions of the adequacy of that historiography.

This study will take issue with Martin J. Sklar's influential left revisionist argument about Woodrow Wilson's contribution as President to the success of large corporate-industrial capitalism.[3] According to his associates, Sklar's essay was "seminal" to radical scholars in their "development of a new view" of Wilson's liberalism.[4] For present purposes, Sklar's essay has been singled out because, unlike Gabriel Kolko,[5] Sklar focused in part on Wilson's thought, which he regarded as "the immediate parental source" of the "present-day fundamentals" of "twentieth century United States liberalism, which may be accurately referred to as corporate-liberalism...."[6]

The term "corporate-liberalism" — applied by New Left activists during the

NOTE: I should like to thank Morton S. Baratz, Philip Brenner, Robert D. Cavey, Lewis Anthony Dexter, J. David Greenstone, Ellis W. Hawley, Thomas D. Hyde, Theodore J. Lowi, Grant McConnell, and three anonymous readers, for their perceptive comments on an earlier draft. I also should like to acknowledge the assistance of the staffs of the Manuscript Division, Library of Congress, and the Manuscript and Archives Division, Sterling Library, Yale University. Part of the research was supported by a faculty research grant awarded by the Graduate Council, University of Maryland Baltimore County.

[1] *The Politics of Power: A Critical Introduction to American Government* (New York: Harcourt, 1975), p. 121.

[2] See ibid., pp. 112–22 *passim*. Among such studies, the two most well known are Gabriel Kolko, *The Triumph of Conservatism: A Reinterpretation of American History, 1900–1916* (New York: Free Press, 1963), and James Weinstein, *The Corporate Ideal in the Liberal State, 1900–1918* (Boston: Beacon, 1968).

[3] "Woodrow Wilson and the Political Economy of Modern United States Liberalism," *Studies on the Left*, Fall 1960 [Indianapolis: Bobbs-Merrill Reprint H-468; (hereafter Sklar)]. Cited by Katznelson and Kesselman, *Politics of Power*, p. 120n., from *For a New America: Essays in History and Politics from Studies on the Left, 1959–1967*, ed. James Weinstein and David W. Eakins (New York: Random House, 1970), pp. 46–100.

[4] Weinstein and Eakins, *New America*, p. 46.

[5] *Triumph*, pp. 204–12, 217–78.

[6] Sklar, pp. 41, 43.

early sixties to the contemporary American political economy and its ethos,[7] and later by James Weinstein to the outlook of leading participants in the National Civic Federation during the Progressive Era[8] — was first used in print some years earlier in Sklar's essay on Wilson. As will become clear in what follows, the term had there a theoretically interesting and precise meaning; for that reason, it merits careful examination. But the alternative interpretation to be presented here should also make necessary the reconsideration of other left revisionist studies; in particular, several themes of Kolko's chapters on Wilson. This point deserves emphasis because radical political scientists are today more likely to rely on Kolko's work than Sklar's. If this study in some measure succeeds in supporting an argument against the latter, that accomplishment will not lack significance for those who rely on the former. For instance, in another current textbook, Michael Parenti quotes Kolko's observation that none of the Progressive Era Presidents, neither Theodore Roosevelt nor Taft nor Wilson, "had a distinct consciousness of any fundamental conflict between their political goals and those of business."[9] Confining ourselves here mainly to Wilson, we shall see that this assertion is demonstrably false.

Focusing, then, on Sklar's essay, it differed sharply with standard interpretations of Wilson. The latter hold that Wilson's domestic program aimed at restraining private power and maintaining or restoring competition.[10] Indeed, nonsocialist adversaries of corporate power still seek inspiration from Wilson's economic views.[11] Moreover, both defenders and critics of Wilson's foreign policy have traditionally understood him to have argued "that the moral duties between nations were the same as those within a nation, ..."[12] Sklar, on the other hand, argued that Wilson's "world view" had as its central themes "large-scale corporate capitalism at home and economic expansion abroad," and that he thereby shared the outlook of most leading political, intellectual, and big business figures of his

---

[7] Students for a Democratic Society, "America and the New Era" (1963), reprinted in two parts in *New Left Notes* (Chicago), December 9 and 16, 1966 [Wooster, Ohio: Micro Photo Div. of Bell & Howell, Underground Newspaper Collection, Reel 1, n.d.], excerpts in Massimo Teodori, ed., *The New Left: A Documentary History* (Indianapolis: Bobbs-Merrill, 1969), pp. 172–82; Carl Oglesby, "Trapped in a System," speech delivered at Washington, D.C., march against Vietnam war, November 27, 1965 [original title, "Liberalism and the Corporate State"], ibid., pp. 186–87.

[8] *Corporate Ideal, passim.* Peter G. Filene, for instance, attributed the term to Weinstein in his important article, "An Obituary for the Progressive Movement," *American Quarterly* 22 (Spring 1970): 26.

[9] *Democracy for the Few*, 2nd ed. (New York: St. Martin's, 1977), p. 67, quoting Kolko, *Triumph*, p. 281. See also Kenneth Prewitt and Alan Stone, *The Ruling Elites: Elite Theory, Power and American Democracy* (New York: Harper & Row, 1973), pp. 35–44 and especially p. 51 n. 15; Kenneth Prewitt and Sidney Verba, *An Introduction to American Government*, rev. 2nd ed. (New York: Harper & Row, 1977), p. 22.

[10] Arthur S. Link, *Wilson* (Princeton: Princeton University Press, 1947–65), 1: 488–93.

[11] See especially Joel F. Henning, "Corporate Social Responsibility: Shell Game for the Seventies?" in *Corporate Power in America*, ed. Ralph Nader and Mark J. Green (New York: Grossman, 1973), quoting *A Crossroads of Freedom: The 1912 Campaign Speeches of Woodrow Wilson*, ed. John Wells Davidson (New Haven: Yale, 1956), pp. 111, 493–94 (hereafter *Crossroads*); Simon Lazarus, "Halfway Up from Liberalism: Regulation and Corporate Power," in Nader and Green, *Corporate Power*, pp. 219–20, quoting *The New Freedom* (Englewood Cliffs: Prentice-Hall, 1961), pp. 121–22 (hereafter *NF*); J. Philip Sipser, "Looking into Corporate Power," Op. Ed. column, *New York Times*, August 22, 1975, p. 31.

[12] Harley Notter, *The Origins of the Foreign Policy of Woodrow Wilson* (Baltimore: Johns Hopkins, 1937), p. 228; Robert E. Osgood, *Ideals and Self-Interest in America's Foreign Relations: The Great Transformation of the Twentieth Century* (Chicago: University of Chicago Press, 1953), chs. 9–12 and *passim*; Hans J. Morgenthau, *In Defense of the National Interest: A Critical Examination of American Foreign Policy* (New York: Knopf, 1951), pp. 13, 23–31; George F. Kennan, *American Diplomacy, 1900–1950* (Chicago: University of Chicago Press, 1951), ch. 4; Daniel P. Moynihan, "Was Woodrow Wilson Right?" *Commentary*, May 1974, pp. 25–31; cf. Sklar, p. 26 n. 35, quoting Charles A. Beard, *The Idea of National Interest* (New York: Quadrangle, 1966; 1934), pp. 121–22.

day. Differing with that view, I shall argue here that there were, during the Progressive Era, substantial differences among major political leaders over the industrial order, and that Wilson in particular did not, on balance, sympathize with or reflect the views and purposes of large corporate interests. Instead, I shall suggest, Wilson's moral understanding prompted him to argue rather consistently that independent small businessmen and small and medium size corporations should retain or be restored to central significance as America strove to shape its industrial order. I shall show that Wilson and his associates, in formulating their policies toward big business, followed a pattern quite in harmony with Wilson's argument. More specifically, I shall show that the Wilson Administration's most significant antitrust prosecutions are best understood as comprising a vigorous but unsuccessful effort to restructure the economy along lines opposed by the then dominant corporate interests. I shall give lesser attention to Wilson's foreign trade policies than Sklar did; I shall suggest, however, that Wilson himself was more concerned with small than with big business in formulating those policies. Finally, I shall argue that revisionists who, like Sklar, take public rhetoric seriously must reconsider the proposition that Wilson's public statements on the moral problems associated with economic penetration of other countries by U.S. corporations show him attentive to conflicts between morality and economic self-interest rather than believing that capitalist interests, even at their best, are simply in harmony with proper moral principles.

According to Sklar, the "unifying conception" of "corporate-liberalism" is the view that the giant corporation is "an organic growth."[13] Applying Karl Mann-heim's distinction between outlooks that support or countenance the deliberate framing of governments and those that advocate "allowing things to grow"[14] to justifications of the rise of giant corporations in America, Sklar contended that the legitimacy of a basic social institution depends, for modern liberals, on its not having resulted from deliberate planning. In his view, Edmund Burke's political philosophy decisively influenced Wilson, disposing him to hold that deliberate political reform must be limited to "facilitating natural evolution" of existing social institutions by promoting "rational adjustments ... to irrational processes,"[15] more specifically, adjustment of government institutions and law to the giant corporation's emergence as America's predominant economic institution. Taking note of Wilson's 1912 campaign argument that large corporations had developed naturally and inevitably, whereas "trusts" had been artificially and deliberately contrived by "financiers ... for monopolistic advantage," Sklar declared that this same distinction was "decisive" when Theodore Roosevelt and his associates or even leading corporate spokesmen grappled with "the trust question," as it was then called.[16]

Contrary to an economic determinist viewpoint, the central theme of left revisionist interpretations of early twentieth-century U.S. government-business

---

[13] Sklar, p. 41, quoting Adolph A. Berle, Jr., Foreword to *The Corporation in Modern Society,* ed. Edward S. Mason (New York: Atheneum, 1973; c. 1959), p. ix.

[14] Sklar, p. 40, quoting *Ideology and Utopia: An Introduction to the Sociology of Knowledge,* trans. Louis Wirth and Edward Shils (New York: Harcourt, n.d. [1955]), pp. 120–21; cf. Burke, *Works,* 6th ed. (Boston: Little, Brown, 1880), 3: 272; ibid., 5: 373; Leo Strauss, *Natural Right and History* (Chicago: University of Chicago Press, 1953), pp. 312–16; Morton J. Frisch, "Rational Planning versus Unplanned Becoming," *Classical Journal* 47 (April 1952): 288–90; Kurt H. Wolff, ed., *From Karl Mannheim* (New York: Oxford, 1971), pp. 120, 145–48, 169, 184–85 n. 3, 194, 206 and n. 1, 207.

[15] Sklar, pp. 41, 21–22; see also p. 19.

[16] Sklar, pp. 22, 40, 42, citing *NF* [pp. 101–3] and *The Public Papers of Woodrow Wilson,* ed. Ray Stannard Baker and William E. Dodd (New York: Harper, 1925–27), 2: 29 (here-after *PPWW*: the 3 vols. are in 6 pts., not consecutively numbered or paged; references shall be to pt. nos. as follows: pts. 1 and 2 of vol. 1 [1875–1913] are here cited as vols. 1 and 2 respectively; pts. 1 and 2 of vol. 2 [1913–1917] are here cited as vols. 3 and 4 respectively; pts. 1 and 2 of vol. 3 [1917–1924] are here cited as vols. 5 and 6 respectively).

relations is that most liberals and progressives mistakenly considered the giant corporation economically and technologically inevitable, whereas in actual fact policies formulated by the Presidents or within the federal executive branch in collaboration with spokesmen for corporate interests established and legitimated big business, while other possible alternatives were ignored or consciously rejected.[17] Sklar himself held that giant corporations were economically superior to smaller ones, particularly in their ability to compete in world markets. Nevertheless, he contended that big business developed through the determined perseverance of Progressive Era reformers, especially Wilson. The key figures, he argued, were large corporate spokesmen and their political and intellectual allies; they "fought hard and consciously" with ideas as well as economic, political, and legal schemes, "to establish the large corporation, in a historically short period of time, as the dominant mode of business enterprise, and to attain popular acceptance of that development." According to Sklar, Wilson provided this movement with "ideological and political leadership" (though he was not responsible for initiating it) because he broadly agreed with its aims, as articulated by other reformers as well as prominent businessmen. Thus, Sklar argued, the Wilson Administration shared "a community of agreement" with large corporate interests, and united with representatives of such interests to pursue commonly held goals.[18]

Going further than mainstream consensus historians, Sklar recommended that scholars "discard" the distinction between Theodore Roosevelt's New Nationalism and Wilson's New Freedom.[19] More precisely, he argued that Wilson synthesized Roosevelt's position on the trust question with that of William Howard Taft. According to Sklar, Wilson sought to legitimate judicially defined reasonable restraints of trade and encourage trade association cooperation with government for both domestic and foreign purposes, insisting only on "reasonable *intercorporate* competition," that is, on preventing unfair competition and prohibiting *unreasonable* restraints of trade.[20]

In addition, emphasizing the Wilson Administration's promotion of foreign trade and investment, Sklar viewed its domestic and foreign economic policies as essentially interlinked. He argued that the Administration, together with large corporate spokesmen, shaped tariff and banking reforms and sponsored a merchant fleet, for instance, to provide for the requirements of an expanding foreign trade. He also stressed how certain provisions of New Freedom antitrust law reforms paved the way for the Webb-Pomerene Act's exemption of export associations from antitrust prohibitions.[21]

Insisting that Wilson's policies served and were intended to serve the interests of big business, Sklar nevertheless acknowledged Wilson's well-known concern with "the little man," the independent small businessman, but suggested that it had as its basis Wilson's determination to counteract the influence of radical movements. For socialism in particular was bound to have increasing appeal to Americans if opportunities for upward mobility through capitalist economic activity dwindled. By achieving his domestic reforms and extending foreign trade, then, Wilson would make it possible for large and small business concerns to coexist.[22]

---

[17] Cf. Kolko, *Triumph,* especially pp. 11–56; Walter Adams and Horace M. Gray, *Monopoly in America: The Government as Promoter* (New York: Macmillan, 1955), ch. 1.

[18] Sklar, pp. 25–26, 29, 33, 34, 35, 39–41.

[19] Ibid., pp. 40, 47; see below, pp. 192–93 & n. 60; cf. Richard Hofstadter, *The American Political Tradition* (New York: Vintage, 1948), chs. 9 and 10, *passim;* cf. also *Crossroads,* pp. 480, 511.

[20] Sklar, pp. 25, 29; emphasis in quotation in original. On the antitrust positions of Roosevelt, Taft, and Wilson, see pts. III and IV below.

[21] Sklar, pp. 44, 36–39, 27, 29.

[22] Ibid., p. 43 and n. 84, quoting *PPWW,* 2: 446, 449–51.

In thus reinterpreting both the thought and actions of Wilson and his associates, Sklar took Wilson's public rhetoric seriously.[23] His approach was consistent with the orientation of his teacher, William Appleman Williams, who has since declared that policy-makers, fallible though they may be, use their minds to determine policies, and scholars should consider not whether such men thought, "but how and what they thought."[24]

This orientation somewhat resembles that of the present author.[25] The safest procedure in studying political leaders' deeds is to take seriously their own explanations of what they were doing or intended to do, linking such explanations — when possible — with their more comprehensive visions of the political and human good. Wilson's public rhetoric in particular provides an important indication of his intentions. According to his authorized biographer, if Wilson's confidential conversations had been transcribed, their disclosure would not have affected our knowledge of him in any essential way.[26] In addition, a President's words are in a sense more like acts. More specifically, presidential leadership apparently was a major determinant of public attitudes toward big business during the Progressive Era in particular,[27] and Wilson's supporters were apparently more committed to his principles than to the man himself.[28] Assuming, then, that Wilson's rhetoric had a profound impact on public opinion,[29] that rhetoric can be shown to have retarded, instead of hastening, the broad acceptance of giant corporations as permanent and legitimate features of American life. Moreover, the Wilson Administration's acts (in the more conventional sense), particularly its vigorous efforts to enforce the Sherman Antitrust Law, were remarkably consistent with the vision propounded in Wilson's speeches and writings.

I

Since this essay will contend that Wilson consciously sought fundamental economic reform, it is appropriate to consider first the problematical character of the view that Wilson, influenced by Burke's thought, was a proponent of "the 'allowing-things-to-grow' doctrine. . . ."[30] Sklar's interpretation appears to gain support from certain characteristically Wilsonian observations. For example, "In politics nothing radically novel may safely be attempted. No result of value can ever be reached . . . except through slow and gradual development, the careful adaptations and nice modifications of growth." Or (like Burke), "democracy in America had, almost from the first, a truly organic growth," a growth "by slow circumstance and . . . habit," which made it more solidly grounded than democracies which come into being out of discontent and revolution. Nevertheless, since American habits and customs, also from the first, were hospitable to the written framing and recasting of forms of government, Wilson transcended the dichotomy

---

[23] Consider especially Sklar, p. 17, the headnote [quoting *PPWW*, 2: 430].

[24] "A Profile of the Corporate Elite," in Ronald Radosh and Murray N. Rothbard, eds., *A New History of Leviathan: Essays on the Rise of the American Corporate State* (New York: Dutton, 1972), p. 1; cf. Kolko, *Triumph*, p. 210. Although Williams was discussing the Pentagon Papers, the context indicated that the point should be applied to public rhetoric as well.

[25] Cf., however, Sklar, p. 18 n. 1, citing Mannheim, *Ideology and Utopia*, pp. 59–70; Williams, "Confessions of an Intransigent Revisionist," *Socialist Revolution*, September-October 1973, pp. 94–95.

[26] Ray Stannard Baker, "Wilson as President: An Appraisal," in *Woodrow Wilson: A Profile*, ed. Arthur S. Link (New York: Hill & Wang, 1968), pp. 118–19.

[27] Louis Galambos, *The Public Image of Big Business in America, 1880–1940: A Quantitative Study in Social Change* (Baltimore: Johns Hopkins, 1975), pp. 120–33, 154, 156, 166–75, 185–86, 259.

[28] Charles E. Merriam, *Four American Party Leaders* (New York: Macmillan, 1926), p. 94.

[29] Cf. Link, *Wilson*, 2: 149–52.

[30] Sklar, p. 41.

Sklar took from Mannheim and suggested that the deliberate approach was consistent with the American experience, and therefore with his "rule of historical continuity."[31] There is, indeed, abundant evidence to support the standard interpretation that Wilson advocated deliberate constitutional reform, and found ways during his public life of bringing about fundamental governmental reforms even within the framework of existing written constitutions. From an early age, he repeatedly became absorbed in writing or revising constitutions,[32] a character trait not readily explainable in Burkean terms. Indeed, Wilson criticized Burke for not seeing that "progress" sometimes required "changes which seem to go even to the substance." As early as 1889, he indicated his weariness with the metaphor of growth as applied to government and his distress over the too literal interpretation of Walter Bagehot's writings. As President of Princeton, he once likened the life of the academic student of politics to that of an architect, suggesting that the scholar's leisure and insulation provided opportunities to construct proposed improvements through "fixed calculation."[33] His own well-known proposals for imitating the British model of responsible party and cabinet government and transforming public administration expressed his specific concern over the dominance of corporate interests, not just in Congress alone but in the whole of modern society.[34] In his 1910 New Jersey gubernatorial campaign and again in his 1912 presidential campaign Wilson went so far as to call for "reconstruction" of America's entire economic and political order.[35] He apparently spoke with determination; for consistent with his announced intentions, Wilson tried dramatically to transform both his gubernatorial and presidential offices, seeking to be a kind of prime minister by combining constitutional powers, popular mandate, and influence on public opinion, to try to achieve dominance over legislative bodies. Indeed, after a conversation with Wilson in September 1914, Colonel House observed that the President thought "our form of government can be changed by personal leadership, . . ."[36]

---

[31] *The State: Elements of Historical and Practical Politics,* rev. ed. (Boston: Heath, 1898), pp. 639, 455; "Character of Democracy in the United States," in *An Old Master and other Political Essays* (New York: Harper, 1893), pp. 115, 120; *Boston Herald,* November 12, 1889, p. 2; see also *The Papers of Woodrow Wilson,* ed Arthur S. Link et al. (Princeton: Princeton University Press, 1966–), 5: 67–69; ibid., 6: 228–30 (hereafter *Papers*); *PPWW,* 1: 177; Ray Stannard Baker, *Woodrow Wilson: Life and Letters* (Garden City: Doubleday, Page, 1927–39), 1: 310, 312–13 (hereafter Baker); *Constitutional Government in the United States* (New York: Columbia, 1908), pp. 52–53, 57; cf. Kent A. Kirwan, "Historicism and Statesmanship in the Reform Argument of Woodrow Wilson," paper presented at Annual Meeting of American Political Science Association, Chicago, September 1976, pp. 3–7.

[32] Baker, 1: 45, 94, 123–24, 198–99, 302–3; Link, *Wilson,* 1: 5, 7, 10, 12; Alexander L. and Juliette L. George, *Woodrow Wilson and Colonel House: A Personality Study* (New York: Dover, 1964), pp. 17, 18, 22, 26–27, 198; Alexander L. George, "Some Uses of Dynamic Psychology in Political Biography: Case Materials on Woodrow Wilson," in *A Source Book for the Study of Personality and Politics,* ed. Fred I. Greenstein and Michael Lerner (Chicago: Markham, 1971), pp. 86–89.

[33] "The Interpreter of English Liberty," in *Mere Literature and other Essays* (Boston: Houghton Mifflin, 1896), p. 153; *Papers,* 6: 335; ibid., 17: 515.

[34] *PPWW,* 1: 28, 133–34; *Congressional Government* (Cleveland: Meridian, 1956), pp. 54, 72; cf; cf. *NF,* pp. 65, 81–82; Kirwan, "Historicism and Statesmanship," pp. 5–6; R. Jeffrey Lustig, "Corporate Liberalism or Liberal Corporatism? The Origins of Modern American Political Thought" (Ph.D. Dissertation, University of California, Berkeley, 1975), p. 384.

[35] *Papers,* 21:119, 94; ibid., 18: 330; *Crossroads,* pp. 449–50; *NF,* pp. 31–32, 25, 43–44; *Princeton Alumni Weekly* 13 (November 6, 1912): 131–32; see also Address at Mass Meeting of Princeton Students, October 12, 1911, news report in Wilson Papers (hereafter Mss.), Series 7-A, reel 476, Library of Congress (hereafter LC).

[36] "The Cooperation of the States," Address to National Governors' Conference, Frankfort, Ky., November 29, 1910, copy in ibid.; Governors' Conference, *Proceedings* 4 (September 1911): 49–50; *PPWW,* 1: 342; ibid., 3: 23–24, 40; Baker, 4: 125, 415; Link, *Wilson,* 1: 527; *The Diary of Edward M. House,* September 28, 1914, House Papers (hereafter EMH), Sterling Library, Yale University (hereafter SL, Yale). For Wilson's mature understanding of the Presidency, see *Constitutional Government,* ch. 3; cf. *The*

Regarding the economy, although Wilson was not entirely consistent in making the distinction between the natural and the artificial which Sklar stressed, it generally was central to his view of the rise of big business. When we consider how Wilson applied it, however, we discover that he scarcely shared "a community of agreement" with either Theodore Roosevelt and his associates or large corporate spokesmen. As for consistency, Wilson did remark that big business had arisen as a result of "natural history" and "irresistible forces,"[37] but he also repeatedly disagreed with social contract theorists, and opposed the naturalness of both political and family life to the artificial, merely legal character of corporations.[38] Roosevelt and corporate spokesmen did believe, as Wilson never tired of pointing out, that giant business on the scale of U.S. Steel, for instance, was economically and technologically inevitable.[39] Wilson, on the other hand, distinguished between the growth of firms through internal expansion and their artificial combination through mergers. He differentiated himself from the Colonel in 1912 by repeatedly describing the steel corporation as an artifact of the House of Morgan, formed by merging "units of every kind, good plants with bad plants, efficient business with inefficient business," principally to eliminate competition and achieve a lavish "bonus" for the promoters. Such mergers should be broken up, Wilson argued, dissected into their "individual elements, . . ."[40] Far from undertaking to establish the hegemony of giant corporate combinations by political means, Wilson advocated structural reform of the industrial economy as a deliberate aim of public policy. If there is a criticism which can be made of Wilson at this point which remains within his frame of reference by making use of *his* distinction between natural growth and artificial combination, it is that he failed to grasp that highly concentrated or oligopolistic market structures can arise just as easily through internal expansion

---

State, pp. 546, 571. On his legislative and party leadership as Governor and President, see Link, *Wilson,* 1: 220, 228, 236, 246–50, 282; ibid., 2: 145–76; David Lawrence, *The True Story of Woodrow Wilson* (New York: Doran, 1924), pp. 310–12, 327–28; Merriam, *Party Leaders,* pp. 53, 60; William F. Willoughby, *Principles of Legislative Organization and Administration* (Washington: Brookings, 1934), pp. 71–72, 559–61, 566–69, 576; George and George, *Wilson and House,* pp. 133–54, 321–22; Edward S. Corwin, *The President: Office and Powers,* 4th rev. ed. (New York: NYU, 1957), pp. 267–70, 467–69; Wilfred E. Binkley, *President and Congress* (New York: Vintage, 1962), ch. 11; Randall B. Ripley, *Majority Party Leadership in Congress* (Boston: Little, Brown, 1969), pp. 52–69.

[37] *PPWW,* 2: 377, quoted by Sklar, p. 19.

[38] *Papers,* 5: 68–69, 77–78; ibid., 6: 309; ibid., 17: 336; "The Law and the Facts," *American Political Science Review* 5 (February 1911): 9, 11; *NF,* p. 85; cf. *The State,* pp. 637–38. On the question of consistency, see also *Papers,* 21: 191; Lawrence, *True Story,* p. 94; *PPWW,* 2: 377, 428; ibid., 3: 190; *St. Paul* (Minn.) *Pioneer Press,* May 25, 1911, news report in Mss., Series 7-A, reel 476; *Crossroads,* pp. 252, 262–63, 464–65; *NF,* pp. 77–78, 97, 103; cf. *Constitutional Government,* p. 210.

[39] *Crossroads,* pp. 162, 168, 182, 277, 291, 293–94, 357, 409, 495; *NF,* pp. 101–2, 117–18, 120–21, 126; cf. Roosevelt, Annual Messages of December 2, 1902, and December 3, 1907, in *Compilation of the Messages and Papers of the Presidents, 1789–1924,* ed. James D. Richardson (New York: Bureau of National Literature, 1897–1924), 14: 6711, 7075; U.S. Department of Commerce and Labor, *Reports,* 1908 (Washington: Government Printing Office, 1909), p. 306; *Letters of Louis D. Brandeis,* ed. Melvin I. Urofsky and David W. Levy (Albany: SUNY, 1971–75), 2: 688.

[40] *Crossroads,* pp. 281–82, 169, 183, 208, 163, 359; *NF,* pp. 102, 109, 119, 113–14. The formation of U.S. Steel has been widely discussed in government documents and secondary literature. See especially U.S. Bureau of Corporations, *Report of the Commissioner of Corporations on the Steel Industry,* July 1, 1911, Pt. 1 ch. 1; U.S. Congress, House, Committee on Investigation of United States Steel Corporation, *Report,* H. Rept. 1127 (62d Cong., 2d sess., 1912), pp. 3–51 and sources cited therein; *United States v. United States Steel Corp.,* 223 F. 55 (D. N.J., 1915): 114–43; Ida M. Tarbell, *The Life of Elbert H. Gary: The Story of Steel* (New York: Appleton, 1925), pp. 107–25; George Harvey, *Henry Clay Frick — The Man* (New York: Scribner's, 1928), ch. 19; Burton J. Hendrick, *The Life of Andrew Carnegie* (New York: Harper & Row, 1969; c. 1932), 2: 114–46; Frederick Lewis Allen, *The Great Pierpont Morgan* (New York: Harper, 1949), ch. 9.

as through mergers. If Wilson was correct about the economic[41] — and, as we shall presently see, the moral and political — effects of combination, his analysis (as he seems not to have clearly appreciated) would have similar force, as applied to industries that had become concentrated without combination.[42]

II

Wilson sought to reconstruct the industrial economy because he was alarmed over the possible and even probable decline of independent small businessmen as dominant social models in America. His thought is not adequately understood if it is believed that he accepted, either eagerly or grudgingly, the increasing economic predominance of giant corporations and merely sought to provide more room for "the little man." This is because his central emphasis on the individual as "moral agent" was the foundation of his economic arguments.[43]

According to Sklar, Wilson shared with other U.S. "corporate and political policy-makers" a cohesive, all-encompassing outlook which held that capitalism embraced "the highest morality," with the result that "the strength and spread of morality" appeared to such policy-makers to be "the function of the strength and spread of capitalism." Sklar argued that classical economics, Burke's political philosophy, and Puritanism — all three customarily regarded as major influences on Wilson's thought — contributed to his moral justification of large-scale corporate capitalism. Adam Smith and the Manchester liberals provided both "indefeasible economic principles" and "secular moral sanction for the bourgeois-democratic political economy. . . ." Not that Sklar regarded Wilson as a defender of laissez faire; quite the contrary. He argued that Burke's thought influenced Wilson to affirm the "prescriptively ordained" inevitability and moral indisputability of the evolved social system, and therefore the inevitable "demise of the freely competing entrepreneur at the hands of the large corporation."[44] In Sklar's view, the teaching of Burke's famous statement opposing government interference with farm prices during hard times in eighteenth-century England — that "the laws of commerce . . . are the laws of nature, and consequently the laws of God"[45] — could be applied by Wilson, with appropriate modifications, to the twentieth-century corporate economy. Further, Sklar argued that Puritanism, instead of distinguishing between economic activity and morality, "sanctioned, indeed posited, capitalist social and economic relations," so much so that to Wilson "religious conviction and 'market-place materialism' " were both "practical" and functionally related; that is, "mutually interdependent and interwoven like the white and purple threads of the single holy cloth."[46]

In contrast with this interpretation, it seems more accurate to understand Wilson to have advocated fundamental economic reform because he recognized and was troubled by *the moral costs* of capitalism's material and political benefits. Far from offering a moral justification of corporate capitalism, he understood — as some radical left critics of capitalism do not — that capitalism's most serious, penetrating, and perspicacious advocates never considered it to embrace "the highest morality."

---

[41] Contrast, for example, Harold Demsetz, *The Market Concentration Doctrine*, AEI-Hoover Policy Study 7 (Washington, D.C.: American Enterprise Institute for Public Policy Research, 1973).

[42] Albert M. Kales, "Good and Bad Trusts," *Harvard Law Review* 30 (June 1917): 852; cf. p. 203, below.

[43] Cf. William Diamond, *The Economic Thought of Woodrow Wilson* (Baltimore: Johns Hopkins, 1943), p. 125; John Morton Blum, *Woodrow Wilson and the Politics of Morality* (Boston: Little, Brown, 1956), pp. 197–98.

[44] Sklar, pp. 47, 18–19, 23–24, 42.

[45] "Thoughts and Details on Scarcity," *Works*, 5: 157, quoted by Sklar, p. 19.

[46] Sklar, pp. 22, 18.

Wilson was aware of Adam Smith's sharp distinction between capitalistic self-interest and the requirements of precise morality, defined in terms of concern for others or benevolence.[47] He wrote that Smith's moral philosophy proper, as presented in *The Theory of Moral Sentiments,* had "reckoned with the altruistic motives"; on the other hand, in *Wealth of Nations* Smith concentrated exclusively on self-interest and expediency, so as not to force altruistic motives into economics, where selfishness unquestionably predominated.[48] Self-interest, Wilson implied, although not fully grounded in morality, is a more dependable economic motive than benevolence. This also was Edmund Burke's view,[49] though on the question of the morality of capitalism Wilson was more strongly influenced by his Puritan religious beliefs than by either Smith's or Burke's teaching.

Wilson's religious convictions, decisive for understanding his character and thought,[50] constituted the foundation of his reformative cast of mind, and led him to emphasize the need "to bring business and Christianity together," as he once put it.[51] His Puritanism had little or nothing in common with the attitudes discussed by Weber and Tawney in their classic works on the Protestant ethic, for Wilson upbraided those who believed that mere material success was the path to heaven.[52] Instead, he stressed subordinating the interested pursuit of gain to Christian moral standards, and frequently urged businessmen to focus attention on their conduct and qualities of character.[53] He declared himself "the enemy" of those who said "I am not in business for my health," suggesting that the use of that old saw evinced indifference to moral health. And when businessmen repeated the motto, "Business is business," Wilson observed frequently, they were implicitly contending that business had nothing in common with Christianity or morality, thereby exposing their "grasping failure to see and appreciate" anything beyond self-interest. Thus, Wilson's religious principles, instead of reinforcing in his mind the economic teachings of Smith and Burke, caused him to believe that America was paying too high a price to enjoy capitalism's benefits. He urged that the country's "spiritual processes" should be elevated above her "material processes"; he observed that business served material but not spiritual needs; he insisted that business "solvency and expediency" must be subordinated to "the rule of right and justice, ..." For as he indicated in his first presidential inaugural, the Government, without "sentimentalizing" American life, could try to prevent a crude heartlessness from accompanying a hasty quest for success. (While President-elect, Wilson once even remarked extemporaneously that the nation's aggregate wealth was "less important" than its equitable distribution, though this probably was not his settled judgment.)[54]

---

[47] See Joseph Cropsey, *Polity and Economy: An Interpretation of the Principles of Adam Smith* (The Hague: Nijhoff, 1957); idem, "Adam Smith," in *History of Political Philosophy,* ed. Leo Strauss and Joseph Cropsey, 2nd ed. (Chicago: Rand McNally, 1972), pp. 607–30.

[48] *Old Master,* pp. 17–18; cf. *The State,* p. 632; Henry Wilkinson Bragdon, *Woodrow Wilson: The Academic Years* (Cambridge: Harvard, 1967), p. 443 n. 54; Sklar, p. 21 n. 15.

[49] *Annual Register* 2 (1759): 485; Thomas W. Copeland, gen. ed., *The Correspondence of Edmund Burke* (Chicago: University of Chicago Press, 1958–70), 1: 129–30; ibid., 3: 153.

[50] Cf. Baker, 1: 49.

[51] *Boston Herald,* November 12, 1889, p. 2; cf. *Papers,* 16: 319.

[52] Sklar, p. 20, referred explicitly to the works of both Weber and Tawney; see also Melvin I. Urofsky, *A Mind of One Piece: Brandeis and American Reform* (New York: Scribner's, 1971), p. 80; cf. *PPWW,* 1: 485–86; ibid., 2: 297–99; Arthur S. Link, "Presbyterian in Government," in *Calvinism and the Political Order,* ed. George L. Hunt (Philadelphia: Westminster, 1965), pp. 168–70.

[53] Cf. Kurt Samuelsson, *Religion and Economic Action: A Critique of Max Weber,* ed. D. C. Coleman (New York: Harper, 1964), pp. 28, 40–41.

[54] *New York Times,* April 25, 1911, p. 3; ibid., December 18, 1912, p. 3; *Boston Herald,* November 12, 1889, p. 2; *Crossroads,* p. 227; Bragdon, *Academic Years,* p. 168; *Papers,* 18: 648; *PPWW,* 2: 401–2; ibid., 3: 3; "Law and Facts." p. 8.

It would be easy to reply that the ideas just sketched are consistent with aiming to elevate the moral tone of large corporate capitalism. After all, revisionist arguments sometimes even insist that enlightened businessmen urged their associates to live up to the standards of *noblesse oblige* and concerned themselves with the heartlessness that accompanied unbounded selfishness. While Wilson too occasionally explained the benefits of enlightened self-interest,[55] he departed from the corporate argument because his Calvinist emphasis on the individual as "moral agent" was the basis of his belief that government had to foster individual liberty and opportunity for economic independence. The richness of opportunities "for individual initiative and action" would largely determine the country's "moral soundness," he argued, because individual moral responsibility was impossible without "freedom of individual choice, . . ." For there was "no such thing as corporate liberty or . . . morality"; only individuals could be "free or moral."[56]

Wilson foresaw sharply diminished opportunities for individual moral choice and therefore an inescapable moral decline if future generations of citizens had to become, almost necessarily, corporate employees. Although he exhorted corporate employees to maintain high moral standards and heed individual conscience, he believed that "perpetual subordination" would erect virtually insurmountable barriers to their continuing to do so. In a large organization, Wilson believed, there would be no practical significance to an employee's determination that an order was morally wrong or otherwise objectionable. By disobeying or ignoring objectionable orders, employees would be endangering their "connection with modern affairs." Their counsel unsought, their protests unheard, they would become "mere cogs in a machine which has men for its parts."[57]

Setting himself against such a vision of the future during the 1912 presidential campaign, Wilson — although he could not deny large firms out of existence — expressed reservations on moral grounds about the then prevailing structure of corporate industry, and even about the modern corporation as such, precisely because of the danger that independent small businessmen might become peripheral and, as he put it, were already "swimming against the stream. . . ."[58] To be sure, he did not want "the little man" to despair of opportunities for success and therefore turn to socialism, but he was less fearful of a radicalized proletariat — certainly during the prewar years — than of a precarious and visionary attempt at benevolent paternalism through regulation of industry or if over-regulation brought about state ownership. Indeed, he usually dismissed electoral support for socialists as merely a protest vote.[59]

Wilson instead emphasized "the little man" because he believed that his way of life was intrinsically desirable: superior to both socialism and a society dominated by giant corporations. Convinced that such a way of life would be hard to maintain without a determined effort through public policy, Wilson rejected the

---

[55] "The New States' Rights," Address before Commercial Club, Lincoln, Neb., May 26, 1911, copy in Mss., Series 7-A, reel 476; *Papers*, 18: 648–49; *New York Times*, April 14, 1911, p. 3.

[56] *Papers*, 18: 329, 331, 327; ibid., 20: 328; ibid., 17: 336; *PPWW*, 2: 292, 145, 196; *Constitutional Government*, pp. 16, 18.

[57] *Crossroads*, pp. 334. 284, 269, 456; *NF*, pp. 20, 23, 157, 166–67; *Papers*, 18: 325–26, 328–29, 332; ibid., 19: 642–43; *PPWW*, 2: 179–82, 253; cf. Kermit Vandivier, "Why Should My Conscience Bother Me?" in Robert L. Heilbroner et al., *In the Name of Profit: Profiles in Corporate Irresponsibility* (Garden City: Doubleday, 1972), pp. 3–31; Ralph L. Stavins, "Losers Weepers," Op. Ed. column, *New York Times*, October 11, 1976, p. 29.

[58] *PPWW*, 2: 388; *NF*, pp. 26, 59–60.

[59] *The State*, pp. 629–33; *Papers*, 17: 256; Address at Columbia, S.C., June 2, 1911, pp. 6–7, in Mss., Series 7-A, reel 476; Baker, 3: 225; *PPWW*, 2: 449, quoted by Sklar, p. 43 n. 84; *Crossroads*, p. 335; *NF*, p. 30; cf. *PPWW*, 6: 537–38; Link, "Presbyterian in Government," pp. 170–71; Baker, 4: 380.

contention that the gulf between him and the Bull Moose Progressives was a matter of tweedle-dum versus tweedle-dee. The 1912 presidential election, he said, involved a "fundamental" choice, which he called "the parting of the ways," not as a mere flourish of campaign oratory but because, as he went on to explain, he believed himself to be unique among the three candidates in his deep concern as to whether some semblance of the American dream could be sustained. America, he said, must remain "a place . . . where a man may choose his own career," not only for the moral reasons previously set forth but also because opportunities for independence were essential to the country's collective energy. Every society was renewed "from the bottom," he argued, from "the genius which springs up from the ranks of unknown men. . . ."[60]

It is a mistake for scholars to concede to Roosevelt the validity of the belief that independent entrepreneurs had already become "irrelevant" to the manufacturing sector of the industrial economy,[61] or to view Wilson's rhetoric as involving an impossible romantic longing "to return to an idyllic (and perhaps semimythical) past. . . ."[62] For Wilson himself stressed that "independent enterprises still unabsorbed by the great economic combinations" predominated in the small Midwestern towns where he had been campaigning in 1912. Addressing a Kokomo, Indiana, audience, for instance, he claimed that about 85 percent of the industries there were "locally owned and . . . controlled." He spoke of trying to maintain this pattern, even of enabling such towns to multiply, by preventing "the concentration of industry . . . in such a shape and on such a scale that towns that own themselves will be impossible."[63]

III

Wilson's 1912 presidential campaign was largely directed against Theodore Roosevelt, the Bull Moose candidate, whose position on the trust question he repeatedly attacked. President Taft's regular Republican candidacy was virtually ignored.[64] Far from sharing "a community of agreement" with Roosevelt and large corporate spokesmen, Wilson criticized T.R. for his close ties to E. H. Gary, U.S. Steel's chief executive, and to George W. Perkins, the Colonel's 1912 campaign manager, who had organized International Harvester for J. P. Morgan, Sr., and was also Morgan's principal representative on the boards of the Steel and Harvester corporations, among other large firms.[65]

"It is one of history's small ironies," George E. Mowry has written, "that Roosevelt never once in his public life argued that trust busting would cure the

---

[60] *Crossroads*, pp. 325, 360, 420, 496, 50–51; *NF*, pp. 24–27, 59, 114, 121, 165; *PPWW*, 2: 388; *Papers*, 19: 641. On tweedle-dum vs. tweedle-dee, cf. William Allen White, *Woodrow Wilson* (Boston: Houghton Mifflin, 1924), p. 264, with *PPWW*, 2: 383, 416, 453; *Crossroads*, p. 322; *NF*, p. 136; Daniel Aaron, *Men of Good Hope: A Story of American Progressives* (New York: Oxford, 1951), pp. 281–82; Sidney Fine, *Laissez Faire and the General Welfare State: A Study of Conflict in American Thought, 1865–1901* (Ann Arbor: University of Michigan Press, 1956), pp. 386–87 *et seq.*; Filene, "Obituary," pp. 21–22.

[61] Sklar, p. 43.

[62] Urofsky, *Mind of One Piece*, p. 84; cf. ibid., pp. 79–80.

[63] *Crossroads*, pp. 348, 330, 333.

[64] Baker, 3: 390; Link, *Wilson*, 1: 475, 511; cf. ibid., p. 517; Louis D. Brandeis, "Labor and the New Party Trust Program," *LaFollette's Weekly Magazine*, October 12, 1912, p. 6. The outcome of the election showed that the Wilson forces had correctly gauged voter sentiment. Wilson received 41.8% of the popular vote; Roosevelt, 27.4%; Taft, 23.2%; Debs, 6.0%, while the electoral vote tally was Wilson, 435; Roosevelt, 88; Taft, 8; Debs, 0; *Presidential Elections Since 1789*, ed. Robert A. Diamond (Washington, D.C.: Congressional Quarterly, 1975), pp. 27, 84.

[65] *Crossroads*, pp. 382–84; *NF*, p. 117; John A. Garraty, *Right-Hand Man: The Life of George W. Perkins* (New York: Harper, 1960), pp. 126–46. Although severing his formal association with the House of Morgan on December 31, 1910, Perkins remained a director of both the Steel Corporation and International Harvester; ibid., pp. 238–50.

industrial problem."[66]   Instead, he sought to regulate giant corporations through an executive agency empowered to distinguish between "combinations which do good and those . . . which do evil,"[67] that is, between reasonable and unreasonable restraints of trade. (These two distinctions, as applied by Roosevelt and his associates, were synonymous.) Roosevelt's position departed sharply from the approach traditionally taken by courts in applying the common law "rule of reason." As Taft had explained in a classic opinion while a federal judge (1898), restraints of trade traditionally were declared reasonable if "merely ancillary to the main purpose of a lawful contract, . . ." For example, a seller of a business, so as not to diminish its value, might agree within specified limits not to compete with a buyer. On the other hand, if the main purpose was to restrict competition, judges were not empowered to say this was "in the public interest, . . ."[68] In addition, a line of cases at common law dealt with ordinary fraud as "unfair competition"; for instance, appropriating a competitor's trade name. No later than 1900, however, many people were applying the term "unreasonable restraint of trade" to refer to a powerful corporation that used predatory or so-called cutthroat practices — for instance, local price wars — to drive competitors out of business. Quite typically, the practices themselves were said to be unfair.[69] When Roosevelt illustrated what he meant by a bad trust, he usually spoke of Standard Oil, notorious for its predatory practices, contrasting it with U.S. Steel and International Harvester. Despite the questionable circumstances surrounding formation of the steel corporation in particular,[70] these were among companies that both cooperated with the investigations of Roosevelt's Bureau of Corporations and adopted a "live and let live" policy toward their rivals.[71] Roosevelt therefore considered them combinations which did good, or reasonable restraints of trade. Toward the end of his second presidential term, he unsuccessfully sponsored the Hepburn bill of 1908, to empower the Bureau of Corporations to decide which giant combinations restrained trade unreasonably; that is, did evil. However, he opposed bills intended to give express power to the federal courts to make this determination in the first instance in the course of deciding Government lawsuits. Antitrust prosecutions, except as a last resort, were unwarranted, Roosevelt believed; they interfered with the ordinary course of business without providing the everyday supervision and scrutiny which regulation could offer.[72]

The Supreme Court did seem to assume such power in May 1911 when Chief Justice White, in his majority opinions against Standard Oil and American Tobac-

---

[66] *The Era of Theodore Roosevelt* (New York: Harper, 1958), p. 132.

[67] Annual Message of December 3, 1906, in *Messages and Papers*, 14: 7041.

[68] *United States* v. *Addyston Pipe and Steel Company*, 85 F. 271 (6th Cir. 1898): 281–84; Henry F. Pringle, *The Life and Times of William Howard Taft* (Hamden, Conn.: Archon, 1964; c. 1939), 1: 143–47; ibid., 2: 654.

[69] William H. S. Stevens, *Unfair Competition* (Chicago: University of Chicago Press, 1917), pp. 2–9.

[70] See references cited in n. 40, above.

[71] Robert H. Wiebe, "The House of Morgan and the Executive, 1905–1913," *American Historical Review* 65 (October 1959): 49–57; testimony of Perkins in U.S. Congress, House Committee on Investigation of United States Steel Corp., *Hearings* (62d Cong., 1st and 2d sess., 1911–12), 2: 1534.

[72] U.S. Congress, House Committee on the Judiciary, *An Act to Regulate Commerce, etc., Hearings on House Bill 19745* (60th Cong., 1st sess., 1908); National Conference on Trusts and Combinations, Chicago, October 22–25, 1907, *Proceedings* (New York, 1908); Roosevelt, Annual Message of December 3, 1907 and Special Message of March 25, 1908, in *Messages and Papers*, 14: 7071–80; ibid., 15: 7343; Elting E. Morison, ed., *The Letters of Theodore Roosevelt* (Cambridge: Harvard, 1951–54), 6: 987, 1374, 1379; Arthur M. Johnson, "Theodore Roosevelt and the Bureau of Corporations," *Mississippi Valley Historical Review* 45 (March 1959): 589; idem, "Antitrust Policy in Transition, 1908: Ideal and Reality," ibid. 48 (December 1961): 423–24, 426–31, 433; Robert H. Wiebe, *Businessmen and Reform: A Study of the Progressive Movement* (Cambridge: Harvard, 1962), pp. 79–81.

co, deviated from the traditional "rule of reason" and intimated that thereafter the Court would only hold "undue" restraints illegal.[73] But it was by no means a foregone conclusion that White's enigmatic opinions — "expressed in sentences sometimes nearly impenetrable"[74] — had legitimated so-called good trusts; that is, businesses possessing market power but which avoided cutthroat practices. While Justice Harlan in dissent was of that opinion,[75] some observers thought White had broadened the Sherman Act's reach, as if reason in the form of common sense had made the justices realize that certain obviously anti-competitive practices ought to be stopped by enforcing the Act before the prohibited result appeared imminent.[76] Since the Court's 1911 decisions were against so-called bad trusts, an unequivocal statement that good trusts were not "undue" restraints would have been dictum. White did not take the opportunity to offer it, and outsiders could not know how the eight justices in the majority would divide on that issue.[77]

President Taft believed that White's opinions were entirely consistent with his own earlier interpretation of the Sherman Act while on the bench. As a result, in October 1911 he ordered antitrust proceedings initiated against U.S. Steel, implicating Roosevelt for permitting it to purchase the Tennessee Coal and Iron Company (ostensibly to avert a Wall Street crisis during the Panic of 1907). In addition, the following April, Taft approved similar proceedings against International Harvester, immediately after releasing Roosevelt Administration correspondence about that firm which showed how T.R. preferred covert negotiation to prosecution. These two Government lawsuits had great importance (as contemporary news accounts stressed) because the two combinations or holding companies attacked were the most significant examples of so-called good trusts.[78] These were test cases in the most literal sense, raising the entire question of the legitimacy of corporate power or oligopoly.[79]

---

[73] *Standard Oil Co.* v. *United States,* 221 U.S. 1 (1911); *United States* v. *American Tobacco Co.,* 221 U.S. 106 (1911).

[74] William Letwin, *Law and Economic Policy in America: The Evolution of the Sherman Antitrust Law* (New York: Random House, 1965), p. 265.

[75] 221 U.S. 1 (1911): 82–105; 221 U.S. 106 (1911): 189–93.

[76] *New York Times,* June 1, 1911, p. 3; cf. A. D. Neale, *The Antitrust Laws of the United States of America: A Study of Competition Enforced by Law,* 2nd ed. (Cambridge, Eng.: Cambridge University Press, 1970), p. 25; Alfred S. Eichner, *The Emergence of Oligopoly: Sugar Refining as a Case Study* (Baltimore: Johns Hopkins, 1969), p. 306 n. 47, and references cited therein.

[77] Of those eight, five were still on the Court to hear and decide the U.S. Steel case. Two of those became dissenters; that is, they would have upheld the Government's contentions and dissolved the steel corporation into smaller, competing units; see *United States* v. *United States Steel Corp.,* 251 U.S. 417 (1920): 436, 457, 466; Leon Friedman and Fred L. Israel, eds., *The Justices of the Supreme Court, 1789–1969: Their Lives and Major Opinions* (New York: Chelsea House/Bowker, 1969), 4: 3208–11.

[78] *New York Times,* September 19, 1911, p. 5; ibid., October 27, 1911, p. 1; ibid., April 25, 1912, p. 6, 1; ibid., April 29, 1912, p. 1; ibid., May 1, 1912, p. 5; ibid., November 3, 1913, p. 3; Taft, Annual Message — Part I, December 5, 1911, in *Messages and Papers,* 15: 7645–46; U.S. Congress, Senate, *Prosecution of the Harvester Trust,* S. Doc. 604 (62d Cong., 2d sess., 1912); *Congressional Record* 48 (62d Cong., 2d sess., 1912): 5258–59, 5317–29; Mowry, *Era of Roosevelt,* pp. 218–19, 286–91; idem, *Theodore Roosevelt and the Progressive Movement* (New York: Hill & Wang, 1960; c. 1946), pp. 188–91; Henry F. Pringle, *Theodore Roosevelt: A Biography* (New York: Harcourt, 1931), pp. 441–45; idem, *Taft,* 2: 666, 671–76; Garraty, *Right-Hand Man,* pp. 210–14, 251–53, 257–58; Johnson, "Bureau of Corporations," p. 588; Wiebe, "House of Morgan," pp. 53–60; James C. German, Jr., "Taft, Roosevelt, and United States Steel," *Historian* 34 (August 1972): 598–613; cf. *Crossroads,* pp. 293–94; Stevens, *Unfair Competition,* pp. 223–27.

[79] Nearly a year before Taft's Justice Department filed suit against U.S. Steel, it launched an important case against a business with a quite spotty record, the American Sugar Refining Co. With the passage of time, this case was viewed as similar in character to those against the other "good trusts," because of the sugar company's successful efforts to portray itself as a good trust, which previously — say, prior to around 1907 — had been a bad one; Eichner, *Emergence,* pp. 304, 307–9, 316, 318.

Partly on economic grounds and consistent with the 1912 Democratic platform, Wilson and his associates rejected Roosevelt's distinction between reasonable and unreasonable restraints, or good and bad trusts.[80] On a crude political level, Wilson could not afford to alienate William Jennings Bryan's huge populist following. After sounding out the Great Commoner in April 1911 to test the presidential waters, Wilson was even touring Bryan country when the decisions of the Court were announced.[81] Bryan's antipathy to what appeared to be the new interpretation of "the rule of reason" was shared by Louis D. Brandeis, Senator Robert M. LaFollette's advisor. Brandeis supported Harlan's profound reservations about White's opinions, and before lending aid to Wilson's cause in late August 1912 had collaborated with LaFollette in proposing legislation that conceded the "unreasonable restraint" concept as legal precedent, but tried to shift the burden of proving reasonableness to business by specifying that certain predatory practices were per se unreasonable, and more importantly by stipulating that a 40 percent market share or more gave rise to a rebuttable presumption of unreasonableness.[82] As for Wilson, he did say that corporations were "indispensable to modern business enterprise" and did acknowledge the inevitability of "big business in the modern world. . . ."[83] But, as previously discussed, he argued that the great merger movement of the turn of the century had artificially combined competing businesses without regard to efficiency, resulting in giant firms which — although able to dominate their industries without resorting to cutthroat practices — were too huge and clumsy to be efficient. Along with Brandeis, he argued that the results of the merger movement should, to a significant extent, be undone. As Brandeis put it, "In attempting to dismember existing illegal trusts, we are . . . not interfering with a natural growth; we are endeavoring to restore health by removing a cancer: *for if the phrase be used in its proper economic and social sense, there is no such thing as a 'good trust.'*"[84]

---

[80] *Crossroads*, pp. 293, 409; see also ibid., pp. 128, 156; *NF*, p. 118; cf. Sklar, p. 25; Donald Bruce Johnson and Kirk H. Porter, eds., *National Party Platforms, 1840–1972*, 5th ed. (Urbana: University of Illinois Press, 1973), p. 169.

[81] For Byran's view, see Bryan to Wilson [ca. August 15, 1911], facsimile copy in James Kerney, *The Political Education of Woodrow Wilson* (New York: Century, 1926), facing p. 164. On Wilson's pre-presidential campaign activities during this period, see Link, *Wilson*, 1: 316–28.

[82] Cf. Sklar, p. 25 and n. 31, with *New York Times*, August 22, 1911, p. 6; Belle C. and Fola LaFollette, *Robert M. LaFollette, June 14, 1855—June 18, 1925* (New York: Macmillan, 1953), 1: 336–37, 345–46, 380–81; Brandeis, *Letters*, 2: 435–36, 438–39, 442–43, 510–12, 527, 561, 660–61, 686–94; Testimony of Brandeis in U.S. Congress, Senate Committee on Interstate Commerce, *Control of Corporations, Persons, and Firms Engaged in Interstate Commerce . . . Hearings* (62d Cong., 1st and 2d sess., 1911–12), 1: 1146–1291, and in U.S. Congress, House Committee on the Judiciary, *Trust Legislation, Hearings*, Serial No. 1 (62d Cong., 2d sess, 1912), pp. 13–54, 106–7, 129–30; Brandeis, *The Curse of Bigness* (Port Washington, N.Y.: Kennikat, 1965; c. 1934); idem, *Business: A Profession* (New York: Kelley, 1971; c. 1914); [idem], "The Method," *Collier's*, October 19, 1912, p. 8; Link, *Wilson*, 1: 491–93; Brandeis to Amos Pinchot, July 18, 1913, Amos Pinchot Papers, box 15, LC. LaFollett strongly opposed Roosevelt's position on antitrust and quietly supported Wilson in 1912; *La Follette's Autobiography* (Madison: University of Wisconsin Press, 1960), pp. 207–8, 248, 262–63, 270–71, 287, 290–99; Link, *Wilson*, 1: 468 and n. 6, 518; Brandeis, *Letters*, 2: 710n.

[83] *PPWW*, 2: 254, quoted by Sklar, p. 22; *Crossroads*, pp. 281, 291.

[84] *Papers*, 21: 206–7; *PPWW*, 2: 362, 337–38, 463; *Crossroads*, pp. 291–92; *NF*, pp. 103–4; 108–9, 154; [Brandeis], "Monopoly," *Collier's*, September 7, 1912, p. 8, emphasis in original; cf. Sklar, p. 23 and n. 22. In a letter to the author, February 20, 1976, Ellis W. Hawley has observed that Wilson's position at this time essentially resembled John Bates Clark's; see Clark, "The Parties and the Supreme Issue," *Independent* 73 (October 17, 1912): 893–94; John B. and John M. Clark, *The Control of Trusts*, rev. ed. (New York: Kelley, 1971; c. 1912), pp. 132, 194–97; B.M. Anderson, Jr., to Wilson, October 15, 1912, Mss., Series 2, reel 31. Clark sent *Control of Trusts* to Wilson during the 1912 campaign saying it would disclose the "grave . . . error" of the Bull Moose program of monopolistic price regulation; whether Wilson was directly influenced by it or even read it may be impossible to demonstrate; Joseph Dorfman, "John Bates Clark and

To be sure, Roosevelt was well aware that corporate power might be used for selfish purposes, but he believed that bigness brought relative freedom from competitive pressures, making it likely that large rather than small business could blend moral considerations into its operations and give serious attention to what are now called (too often for mere reasons of public relations) "corporate social responsibilities." In the Colonel's view, however, giant size was acceptable only if accompanied by watchful regulation. The propriety of T.R.'s regulatory proposals depended heavily on the assumption that the regulated interests would not be able to capture their regulators, but the broad discretion he proposed for the bureaucracy enabled Wilson to charge both that Roosevelt sought excessive government interference with business and that he would permit too close a relationship to develop between the regulators and the regulated. This issue had grown in salience after Roosevelt left the Presidency in March 1909, as the various details of his Administration's relationship with Morgan-dominated businesses gradually became known. Perkins' designation to head the third party's 1912 campaign created a campaign issue on which Wilson seized, public apprehension about the Colonel's ties to big business having already made his audiences receptive.[85]

Denying that he was impugning the character or motives of the businessmen close to Roosevelt and expressing indifference about how the Colonel's campaign was being financed, Wilson continually returned to a criticism of the thought of Perkins and Gary.[86] He knew Perkins had advocated "a national business court," to consist of enlightened businessmen who were supposed to be industrial statesmen; he also knew that Gary had proposed giving such a body price-fixing authority over highly concentrated industries.[87] The choice, Wilson therefore remarked, lay between "a government such as the United States Steel Corporation, . . . think the United States ought to have" and "a government such as we used to have before these gentlemen succeeded in setting up private monopoly." If Roosevelt were returned to the White House, he warned, a "partnership" between public officials and corporate executives would very likely become established,[88] not as a result of the Colonel's personal, political, or financial relationships with big businessmen, but because discretionary regulation would confront corporate executives with an overwhelming temptation to capture whatever regulatory agency was established.[89] The Colonel's program, Wilson argued, would also "perpetuate and license the concentration of control," legitimating the so-called good trusts as "the instruments" of U.S. industrial development, and recognizing them "as a permanent part of our economic order." According to Wilson, spokesmen for this position argued in effect that America could no longer liberate herself from the "mastery" of her industrial leaders, but could make her masters "pitiful and kind," "patriotic," "benevolent," and "philanthropic." Wilson even suggested a cartoon, which someone immediately drew, depicting Roosevelt trying to lead the country's

---

John Maurice Clark on Monopoly and Competition," in *Control of Trusts*, pp. 8–9 [separately paged], quoting Clark to Wilson, September 20, 1912, J. B. Clark Papers, Columbia University.

[85] Mowry, *Progressive Movement*, p. 270; Garraty, *Right-Hand Man*, pp. 271, 277–79; *Crossroads*, pp. 171, 361, 382, 384.

[86] Ibid., pp. 336, 360–61, 376, 164, 299, 382, 389, 405; *NF*, p. 124.

[87] Testimony of Perkins and Gary in Senate Committee on Interstate Commerce, *Control of Corporations*, 1: 1089–1145, 721, 726, 731; Testimony of Gary in *Steel Hearings*, 1: 79; Perkins, "Corporations in Modern Business," *North American Review* 187 (March 1908): 388–98; idem, "Business: The Moral Question," *World's Work* 22 (June 1911): 14465–71; idem, "Strangulation or Regulation," *World Today* 21 (November 1911): 1298–98b; idem, "Wanted — A National Business Court," *Independent* 71 (November 23, 1911), 1173–77; Garraty, *Right-Hand Man*, pp. 215–18, 247–51; cf. *Crossroads*, pp. 80n., 166, 175–76, 239; Brandeis, *Letters*, 2: 525, 666, 670.

[88] *Crossroads*, pp. 361, 96–97, 156, 207, 211, 238, 371; cf. *Papers*, 20: 300–301.

[89] *Crossroads*, pp. 77, 97.

"biggest monopolies" in the Hallelujah Chorus.[90] Brandeis, while less sarcastic, was at once more candid and more bitter; "the Roosevelt position on the trust question," he confided to *Collier's* editor Norman Hapgood, was "that of a pervert. . . ."[91]

Wilson himself was not very resolute, it must be said, about making sure his own Administration avoided public-private partnerships. Thus, Sklar was at his best in showing that the national Chamber of Commerce was heavily involved in drafting the section of the Federal Trade Commission (FTC) Act that led to the Webb-Pomerene Act authorizing export combinations. (It should be added in passing, however, that Brandeis's associate, George Rublee, who had joined forces with the Chamber, was a very independent-minded lawyer who was quite capable of engaging in reverse lobbying.) In addition, Sklar showed that some of Wilson's key appointees had played prominent roles in important business organizations; that one such appointee — Secretary of Commerce William C. Redfield — apparently was expected to remain heavily involved in such bodies after joining the Administration; and that under Redfield's auspices the Administration virtually sponsored the first National Foreign Trade Convention, at which the line between public and private was very blurred indeed.[92] Even Redfield, however, largely accepted Wilson's argument against giant corporate combinations. His first annual report in December 1913 questioned the relationship between bigness and efficiency, and his subordinate, Corporations Commissioner Joseph E. Davies, called for legislation placing the burden of proving reasonableness on the party claiming it.[93]

IV

Although Redfield's activities as business promoter did involve the nation's largest corporations, including those being prosecuted under the Sherman Act, the prosecutions themselves are more indicative of the Administration's position as to the legitimacy of giant business and of its longer run aims regarding industrial structure. Antitrust enforcement throughout Wilson's two presidential terms shows much greater consistency with his 1912 arguments than either radical or mainstream scholars have discerned. Wilson did have a specific antitrust program,[94] which was more than a legislative program. His Justice Department continued proceedings begun by the Taft Administration against so-called "good trusts," and initiated its own major cases against similar businesses, all on the basis of views Wilson had sharply differentiated from Roosevelt's during the presidential campaign. However, Wilson's antitrust policy has been seriously misunderstood because scholarly discussion has centered upon legislative history almost exclusively,[95] with emphasis on the rationale of the FTC Act, and with some additional though lesser attention given to the Clayton Act, mainly to its labor "Magna Carta." But even confining ourselves momentarily to the New Freedom legislative reforms, the scholarly interpretations seem somewhat problematical.

---

[90] Ibid., pp. 111, 358, 361, 373–74, 97, 129, 356–57, 281, 384, 182, 211, 371, 493–94, 238, 277, 360, 362–63; cf. pp. 191, 193, above; Adam Smith, *Wealth of Nations* (New York: Modern Library, 1937), pp. 14, 423; August Heckscher, "Woodrow Wilson: An Appraisal and Recapitulation," in *The Philosophy and Policies of Woodrow Wilson*, ed. Earl Latham (Chicago: University of Chicago Press, 1956), pp. 257–58.

[91] *Letters*, 2: 683.

[92] Sklar, pp. 26, 28–31, 36, and p. 28 n. 39; see further pp. 41–42, below. For the strong appeal to Wilson of Rublee's "independence of mind," see Baker, 6: 115 n. 3.

[93] U.S. Department of Commerce, *Reports*, 1913 (Washington: Government Printing Office, 1914), pp. 16–17, 71.

[94] Cf. Sklar, p. 39; Urofsky, *Mind of One Piece*, pp. 73, 78, 85–87; idem, *Big Steel and the Wilson Administration: A Study in Business-Government Relations* (Columbus: Ohio State University Press, 1969), pp. 52–53.

[95] Sklar's essay omitted consideration of Wilson's Justice Department, while Link devoted about a page to its prosecutions of so-called good trusts, specifically mentioning only the U.S. Steel case; *Wilson*, 2: 419–20; cf. Urofsky, *Big Steel*, pp. 24–27, 42–45, 78–83, 181–82, 340–43.

In planning his legislative program, the President adopted the approach Brandeis too had taken earlier as LaFollette's spokesman. The proposed statutory presumption of unreasonableness above a 40 percent market share was dropped, though section seven of the final version of the Clayton Act would restrict anticompetitive mergers.[96] Although neither the FTC nor the Justice Department presented significant court tests of the latter provision until the twenties, the Department did decide to ask the courts to adopt a percentage criterion in its Sherman Act prosecutions. (The Clayton Act, after all, could not be applied ex post facto to pre-1914 mergers.)

In calling for supplementary legislation, Wilson first advocated prohibiting certain specific unfair practices and enlarging the old Bureau of Corporations, transforming it into a trade commission with essentially ministerial functions. As Sklar indicated, Wilson's advisors (including Brandeis) persuaded him to drop this approach in favor of prohibiting unfair competition in general terms; they based their new position on the catch-all provisions which courts typically added to final decrees when enjoining specific unfair practices. In addition, the President accepted their proposal that the commission be empowered to order particular firms to cease such practices, subject to judicial review.[97]

Scholars have too readily interpreted Wilson's endorsement of a strong trade commission as signifying his agreement with or conversion to the Bull Moose program. To be sure, the general prohibition of unfair practices was being urged upon Congress by Bull Moosers. Moreover, George Rublee, who had come to Washington as Brandeis's associate to help draft the New Freedom legislative reforms and to lobby in their behalf, had also been close to Roosevelt, and in urging a strong FTC had advised Wilson that "without the use of unfair methods no corporation can grow beyond the limits imposed" by efficiency. However, the commission had not been empowered to determine whether restraints of trade were reasonable (the key power Roosevelt had sought for the Bureau of Corporations in 1908). It "will have no power," Rublee had told Wilson, "to authorize the use of a method of competition, or to give immunity from the Sherman Act." As Rublee saw its purposes, it would "protect small business men, keep an open field for new enterprise, and prevent the development of trusts." However, since most of Wilson's first appointees were poor choices, the agency was weak and unimpressive at the outset. It thereby served big business interests through inadvertence, though G. Cullom Davis has concluded that for a few years beginning around 1918 it did work hard to fulfill the original intentions of its creators.[98]

[96] *Stat.* 38 (1914): 731–32 (Public Law 212, 63d Cong., 2d sess., 1914); *U.S. Code* (1970), 15: 18.

[97] *PPWW*, 3: 75–76, 85–86; *New York Times*, January 23, 1914, p. 3; ibid., January 27, 1914, p. 7; ibid., June 13, 1914, p. 13; Sklar, p. 25; *The Reminiscences of George L. Rublee* (1951), pp. 105, 107, 110–15, in The Oral History Collection of Columbia University (hereafter Rublee, *OHC*); Rublee, "Memorandum Concerning Section 5 of the Bill to Create a Federal Trade Commission," enclosed with Franklin K. Lane to Wilson, July 10, 1914, Mss., Series 2, reel 60, pp. 7–14, 17–20 (hereafter Rublee, "Memo"); Rublee, "The Original Plan and Early History of the Federal Trade Commission," *Proceedings of the Academy of Political Science* 11 (January 1926): 667–69; *Everybody's Magazine* 32 (May 1915): 655; Link, *Wilson*, 2: 425–26, 435–41.

[98] Ibid., p. 433; idem, *Woodrow Wilson and the Progressive Era* (New York: Harper, 1954), pp. 70, 74–75; Testimony of Donald R. Richberg in U.S. Congress, House Committee on Interstate and Foreign Commerce, *Interstate Trade; Hearings* (63d Cong., 2d sess., 1914), p. 263; Testimony of William Draper Lewis in U.S. Congress, House Committee on the Judiciary, *Trust Legislation: Hearings* (63d Cong., 2d sess., 1914), p. 403; Testimony of Richberg in ibid., p. 420; Rublee, *OHC*, pp. 116–19; Rublee, "Memo," pp. 3, 21; Rublee, "Original Plan," p. 671; Brandeis, *Letters*, 3: 393–94; 581, 600–601; Alpheus T. Mason, *Brandeis: A Free Man's Life* (New York: Viking, 1956), pp. 406–7; Davis, "The Transformation of the Federal Trade Commission, 1914–1929," *Mississippi Valley Historical Review* 49 (December 1962): 440–41. For the FTC Act, see *Stat.* 38 (1914): 717–24 (Public Law 203, 63d Cong., 2d sess., 1914); *U.S. Code* (1970), 15: 41–51.

In urging a strong trade commission, Rublee sought to relieve the Justice Department "of a load of burdensome work" it was ill-equipped to perform, so it could focus attention on antitrust dissolution suits, which he believed the Sherman Act adequately covered. Thus, his view about the link between unfair methods and inefficient bigness did not prevent him from supporting the actions that had begun to take place in Wilson's Justice Department. Its officials agreed with their predecessors that the ambiguity of the Supreme Court's 1911 opinions left open the possibility that the Sherman Act could be used as a weapon against giant business combinations. Wilson's appointment of James C. McReynolds as Attorney General signified the intention to pursue an even more stringent antitrust policy than Taft's. McReynolds, to be sure, later showed himself to be a reactionary and bigoted Supreme Court justice, but he gained his early fame as a Justice Department trust buster who had a detailed grasp of the Sherman Act. Having sought a dissolution decree against American Tobacco that would have prohibited major stockholders from receiving shares in more than one of the new units established, he had resigned in protest when this was overruled by Attorney General George W. Wickersham, with Taft's approval. (There is conflicting evidence on whether this dispute had much to do with McReynolds' selection as Attorney General.) As his assistant in charge of antitrust, McReynolds chose his law partner, G. Carroll Todd, an adroit man esteemed by his colleagues, who had extensive experience in the field going back to his work for Roosevelt on the Northern Securities case (1902–4). Rep. John W. Davis (D., W. Va.), who had earlier expressed views on trusts similar to Bryan's, was appointed Solicitor General, a major step in the development of his distinguished legal career.[99]

Wilson's antitrust program involved a two-pronged attack. Harmful practices would be stopped, he said, and an intolerable "economic control . . . broken up." In attempting enforcement of the Sherman Act through the courts, the Justice Department moved vigorously against combinations not intended to be reached by the New Freedom reforms, the so-called good trusts becoming and remaining its principal targets. McReynolds considered the Sherman Act "amply sufficient," believing its energetic enforcement was the only acceptable solution of the trust question. Although Wilson, in 1910 and 1911, had opposed dissolving giant corporations, the Department routinely sought that remedy. White's 1911 opinions could not be ignored, but the Department's efforts to circumscribe and define the term "undue restriction of competition" resembled Brandeis's 1911 legislative proposals for LaFollette. The test of an undue restriction, Davis told the Supreme Court in 1916, depended "primarily on the extent of the restriction," and though it was impossible "to draw the exact line, the restriction is certainly undue where the combination embraces units which together occupy a preponderant position in a given industry." The "preponderant position" criterion, in turn, had to be defined, Davis said, on an industry-by-industry basis, mainly considering the extent of control over production on the one hand, and over raw materials, transporta-

---

[99] Rublee, "Memo," pp. 5–6; Burton J. Hendrick, "James C. McReynolds," *World's Work* 27 (November 1913): 26; *New York Times Magazine*, March 9, 1913, p. 4; Brandeis, *Letters*, 3: 35–36, 41; see also ibid., p. 256; *New York Times*, July 26, 1913, p. 2; William H. Harbaugh, *Lawyer's Lawyer: The Life of John W. Davis* (New York: Oxford, 1973), pp. 56–57, 86–88. On McReynolds' appointment, cf. *New York Times*, June 7, 1913, p. 2; ibid., August 19, 1914, p. 9; Ray Stannard Baker, "Memorandum of Conversations with Thomas W. Gregory at Houston, Texas, March 14 and 15, 1927," p. 6 (hereafter "Gregory Memo"), in R. S. Baker Papers (hereafter RSB), Series 1, box 35, LC, with *House Diary*, February 15, 16, and 20, 1913; Charles Seymour, "Memorandum of Conversation with Edward M. House," March 31, 1922, Seymour Papers, SL, Yale. On Todd, see John W. Davis to John Lord O'Brian, December 12, 1947, box 47, John W. Davis Papers (hereafter JWD), SL, Yale; Robert D. Cuff, "Business, the State, and World War I: The American Experience," in *War and Society in North America*, ed. R. D. Cuff and J. L. Granatstein (Toronto: Nelson, 1971), pp. 15–16.

tion, and distribution on the other hand. His rule of thumb was control of around 50 percent (or more) of any of these factors in a given industry. Not an attempt at restoring the pre-1900 industrial structure, this policy aimed at what economists would now call workably or effectively competitive markets. By asking courts to order that so-called good trusts be partitioned into several competing units, the Department pursued a deliberate, albeit ultimately futile, policy of industrial deconcentration.[100]

Developments occurred swiftly after Wilson's inauguration. Henry C. Frick, without informing his colleagues, sought out Colonel House to propose an out-of-court settlement of the Steel case. He suggested that the giant holding company could be transformed into "a single unobjectionable corporation," as if this superficial organizational change would suffice to bring it into compliance with Wilson's rhetorical distinction between large corporations and trusts. With House keeping the President and McReynolds fully informed of such contacts, they all reached the decision that while Frick's scheme was unacceptable the Attorney General would begin negotiations with U.S. Steel's attorneys. They all agreed, however, that no consent decree would be approved unless Secretary of State Bryan concurred. In the event, the Commoner did not have to be consulted, possibly because Gary was uncompromising and rejected terms stiff enough to satisfy the equally intransigent Wilson and McReynolds. Preliminary hearings had, in the meantime, continued in both the Steel and Harvester cases. In the latter, the new Administration — unlike Taft's, which had given explicit assurances to the contrary — threatened to charge Perkins with criminal violations of the Sherman Act! Around the same time (June 1913), the Government filed suit in Chicago against the Quaker Oats Company, another so-called good trust, asking the district court to order the firm enjoined from interstate commerce until the case was settled! Its officers too were warned shortly thereafter that criminal charges might be brought.[101] While the Government did not get its injunction, its threats of criminal prosecutions were not empty. Until John H. Patterson of the National Cash Register Company successfully appealed his conviction on such charges in March 1915 and the Supreme Court denied *certiorari* (in a case that involved blatantly unfair competitive practices) the Justice Department seemed quite prepared to carry out such threats.[102] As the Harvester case proceeded to trial, McReynolds himself wrote the Government's lower court brief, proposing the same remedy he had earlier sought in the tobacco decree; he journeyed personally to St. Paul to participate in oral argument in early November 1913. On his return, he ordered that charges be filed in Baltimore against the American Can Company (which then controlled just under half of U.S. can production) and the *Baltimore Sun* viewed the case as equal in importance to the landmark oil and tobacco prosecutions.[103] In yet another case, in which the issue of good conduct was more debatable, a special

---

[100] *PPWW*, 3: 242; ibid., 2: 254, quoted by Sklar, p. 23; *New York Times*, September 8, 1913, p. 6; ibid., September 4, 1915, p. 5; *House Diary*, April 12, 1914; Hendrick, "McReynolds," pp. 30–31; *San Francisco Chronicle*, May 17, 1911, news report in Mss., series 7-A, reel 476; Davis, "The Argument" (summary of the Government's Supreme Court brief in the Harvester case, October term, 1916), copy in JWD, box 67; cf. Kolko, *Triumph*, pp. 256–57; Urofsky, *Big Steel*, pp. 82–83; William F. Swindler, *Court and Constitution in the Twentieth Century, The Old Legality: 1889–1932* (Indianapolis: Bobbs-Merrill, 1969), p. 181.

[101] *House Diary*, March 22, 24, 25, 29, 1913; April 1, 2, 3, 10, 13, 14, 1913; May 11, 1913; September 30, 1913; Tarbell, *Gary*, p. 235; Urofsky, *Big Steel*, p. 26; *New York Times*, June 20, 1913, p. 1; ibid., June 12, 1913, p. 6; ibid., November 14, 1913, p. 2.

[102] *United States* v. *Patterson*, *cert. denied*, 238 U.S. 635 (1915); *New York Times*, March 14, 1915, sec. 3, p. 10; ibid., April 1, 1915, p. 20; ibid., May 19, 1915, p. 14; ibid., June 15, 1915, p. 14; ibid., June 22, 1915, p. 24.

[103] Ibid., November 3, 1913, p. 3; ibid., November 30, 1913, sec. 2, p. 6; ibid., sec. 8, p. 6; *Baltimore Sun*, November 30, 1913, p. 5; ibid., June 23, 1914, p. 14.

prosecutor recommended — with McReynolds' support — what a student of industrial organization would later call the "radical restructuring" of the sugar industry, to establish "the maximum degree of competition compatible with technical economies of scale."[104] Roosevelt, who clearly perceived the Department's aims, insisted that "harm would result" if the various companies were ordered divided into smaller units. Reacting to the lower court decision in the Government's favor in the Harvester case, the Colonel defended the firm as a good trust, telling an off-year campaign audience in upstate New York that there was a fundamental difference between his program of supervision and control and the Democratic program "of disintegration" exemplified by the Harvester prosecution. The *New York Times,* principal editorial defender of so-called good trusts, consistently attacked the Department throughout Wilson's two Presidential terms for pursuing precisely the latter objective. "The light of reason . . . has ceased to burn," the *Times* charged; "the issue," it said, "is whether there can be any good trust, or whether 'every' combination in restraint of trade is bad." This was indeed the issue. When the Harvester case ultimately reached the Supreme Court, the Government brief proclaimed that there was no such thing as a good or benevolent trust.[105]

The President fully approved of this policy. Colonel House assumed that Wilson himself would eventually decide whether the Steel case was to proceed to trial, though the matter of an out of court settlement would first be referred to McReynolds. Although the President acquired the reputation of giving his Cabinet officers, as House put it, "a very free hand" in running their departments, House confided to his diary that he and the President thoroughly went over nearly every policy of any significance. This was to some extent true even with McReynolds, who often brooded about not getting enough of Wilson's time. In September 1913, about to give up hope of settling the Steel case out of court, the Attorney General spoke of his own and Wilson's determination to establish "real competition. . . ." After a federal district court ruled against the Government in the case in June 1915, the President personally endorsed an appeal to the Supreme Court. Privately, he told a friend who advised against that course that the company itself would benefit by having the high Court authoritatively affirm the opinion below; this even Perkins considered somewhat desirable. But Attorney General Thomas Watt Gregory, who had taken office the previous September after his predecessor was named to the Court, announced the decision to appeal by expressing "complete accord" with the Taft Administration's view of the law. Considering the importance of the matter and the close ties that had begun to develop between Gregory and the President, the Attorney General very likely was speaking for Wilson. Perkins, at any rate, thought so. He furiously denounced Gregory's statement, and identified the Administration's policies with those of Bryan and his 1908 Democratic platform, which called for "dissolution of our large industrial corporations."[106]

Wilson frequently decided on appointees on the basis of antitrust considerations. Just after the lower court announced its decision in the Steel case, Bryan re-

---

[104] Eichner, *Emergence,* p. 315; see also n. 79 above.

[105] Roosevelt, *Works,* ed. Hermann Hagedorn, Memorial ed. (New York: Scribner's, 1923–26), 19: 547; *United States* v. *International Harvester Co.* 214 F. 987 (D. Minn., 1914); *Rochester* (N.Y.) *Union and Advertiser,* October 16, 1914, p. 3; *New York Times,* October 16, 1914, p. 18; ibid., November 5, 1913, p. 12; ibid., February 18, 1917, sec. 1, p. 14.

[106] *House Diary,* March 24, 1913, March 29, 1914, April 12, 1914, September 30, 1913; Urofsky, *Big Steel,* p. 44 and n. 19; *New York Times,* June 5, 1915, p. 1; ibid., June 6, 1915, sec. 2, p. 3; Frank P. Glass, editor of *Birmingham* (Ala.) *News,* to Wilson, June 3, 1915, enclosing his editorial of that date, and Wilson to Glass, June 8, 1915, Mss., Series 4, reel 272, case file 428; Glass to Wilson, June 14, 1915, and Wilson to Glass, June 17, 1915, ibid., Series 2, reel 71; Wilson to George W. Anderson, June 19, 1916, ibid., Series 4, reel 199, case file 76A; Wilson to House, July 23, 1916, EMH, box 121, folder 4266; House to Wilson, July 25, 1916, ibid. For citation of lower court decision in Steel case, see n. 40, above.

signed in protest against Wilson's response to German submarine warfare, and Robert Lansing, Counselor of the State Department, was named the new Secretary. Needing a replacement in his old job, Lansing sought Solicitor General Davis just after he had argued the Harvester case in the Supreme Court. The Court had ordered reargument the following term, presumably to decide it with its full complement of nine justices, and Davis was at the same time preparing the appeal of the Steel case. According to Davis's biographer, his personal commitment to the Government's position in these cases was deeper than to any others he argued during his tenure as Solicitor General and he had invested himself totally in preparing them. "He is the best Solicitor General of the last twenty years," said the President in vetoing the transfer, "and the docket . . . is crowded with cases of the first moment to the Government which he has studied thoroughly."[107] With McReynolds on the Court and obliged to disqualify himself from hearing these cases, an important consideration in passing over both Gregory and Davis for the 1916 vacancies was that they too would certainly be ineligible to participate. In addition, when Wilson was considering Judge John H. Clarke of Ohio for the vacancy created when Justice Hughes resigned to become the 1916 Republican presidential candidate, doubts arose about Clarke's position on antitrust; the newly appointed Secretary of War, Newton D. Baker (a former mayor of Cleveland who was his old friend), was dispatched to find out. Only after receiving Baker's favorable report did the President send Clarke's name to the Senate.[108]

The Justice Department's arguments against the "good trusts" reminded of Wilson's 1912 campaign rhetoric. Quite characteristically, it argued that the the Sherman Act did not limit the size of a business if attained "by internal expansion — by growth from within," because such growth would, in its view, be limited by the requirements of economic efficiency and not endanger "the competitive system. . . ."[109] As previously suggested, this seems a questionable economic argument, but the Department's lawyers were undoubtedly more concerned with the legal argument, and knew they could not attack internal expansion on Sherman Act grounds.[110] As in the political campaigns, the briefs and oral arguments stressed the artificial character of the combinations being prosecuted. McReynolds, in his 1913 Harvester brief in the lower court, for instance, had argued that the Company's "formation . . . was not a normal and natural development of the commerce in harvesting machinery. It was the child of one not . . . interested in the business, George W. Perkins, a banker and insurance man, who stepped in at an opportune time to bring the rival manufacturers together; . . ."[111] This kind of argument, just as characteristically, was rejected by the other side. Counsel for U.S. Steel argued, for instance, that its organization "was but a natural and normal development from existing trade and manufacturing conditions, and was only notable because of the largeness of the conception which underlay it, and the courage exhibited in undertaking to carry it out, . . ."[112] Again we see that while Sklar's concept of "corporate-liberalism" correctly stated that the Administration distinguished between internal expansion and mergers, the distinction

---

[107] *New York Times,* April 9, 1915, p. 15; ibid., June 22, 1915, p. 24; Harbaugh, *Lawyer's Lawyer,* p. 113; Wilson to House, July 12, 1915, copy in RSB, container 7; cf. Gregory to House, July 14, 1915, EMH, box 51, folder 1628.

[108] John W. Davis to John J. Davis, January 6, 1916, and to Anna K. Davis, July 5, 1916, JWD, box 2; Harbaugh, *Lawyer's Lawyer,* p. 121; Jacob M. Dickinson [special prosecutor in U.S. Steel case] to Wilson, January 6, 1916, and reply, January 10, 1916, Mss., Series 4, reel 199, case file 76A; N. D. Baker to Wilson, July 10, 1916, ibid., Series 2, reel 81; cf. R. S. Baker, "Gregory Memo," p. 12.

[109] *Baltimore Sun,* September 4, 1915, p. 8.

[110] See pp. 189–90, above.

[111] *New York Times,* November 3, 1913, p. 3.

[112] Ibid., October 21, 1914, p. 5.

was applied in the course of advocating the drastic restructuring of major industries. Instead of being the source of "a community of agreement" with Roosevelt and corporate spokesmen, it led to deep disagreement with them.

The Justice Department, consistent with Wilson's earlier rhetoric and Brandeis's testimony and writings against bigness, laid great stress on the power of these combinations. In the International Harvester case, it argued that Congress's "objections to substituting a despotic organization of industry for the competitive system were quite as much social and political as economic."[113] This accurately summarized views expressed by Senator John Sherman in 1890 during floor debate on the Act which bears his name. As he then put it,

> If we will not endure a king as a political power we should not endure
> a king over the production, transportation, and sale of any of the necessaries of life. If we would not submit to an emperor we should not submit to an autocrat of trade, with power to prevent competition and to fix
> the price of any commodity.[114]

Presumably familiar with these remarks, Davis told the Supreme Court that the Sherman Act was passed because kings were ruling interstate commerce. The Congress that framed the statute would not have been satisfied, he contended, to know "that the power which they feared was . . . being exercised benevolently." For benevolence could never justify "absolutism," no more so in industrial organization than in governmental organization. "Forced to admit" — as Davis confided to his father — the fundamental contention of the so-called good trusts, to the effect that they had not demonstrably abused their power, and admitting more specifically the Harvester Company's "consistent good conduct," Davis nevertheless attacked his adversaries' position on the ground that it lost sight entirely "of the broader purpose and basis of the act," by failing to recognize that Congress had intended to strike "at undue concentration of economic power" before its evils had occurred or become imminent. Possession of potential power, rather than either mere bigness or improper exercise of power in the past, was the decisive issue according to the Government's theory, because such combinations could, if they chose, exercise their power and drive all their competitors out of business. If they exercised forbearance, it was only to avoid prosecution. Moreover, the Government charged, such power could be and had been used to exact "non-competitive prices from the general public" as in the steel industry, where other iron and steel firms became "co-conspirators" with U.S. Steel "in the artificial maintenance of prices. . . ."[115]

The Court did not resolve the controversy until 1920. Brandeis, although disqualifying himself from its consideration of the Steel case, did participate in the Harvester case,[116] thereby deadlocking the latter. Both were ordered reargued, presumably to avoid the disturbing predicament of different results in two major cases presenting virtually the same issues. (In a tied case, the Court might ordinarily affirm the judgment below. But the lower court had decided the Harvester case in the Government's favor, while the Supreme Court was leaning four to three against it in the Steel case. Moreover, Davis appears to have had the foresight to intertwine the Government's briefs in the two cases, incorporating 68

---

[113] Ibid., February 18, 1917, sec. 1, p. 14.

[114] *Congressional Record* 21 (51st Cong., 1st sess., 1890): 2457. To be sure, Sherman — unlike Davis — might have been thinking of *monopoly*, strictly speaking (which of course shares a common stem with *monarchy*).

[115] *New York Times*, April 9, 1915, p. 15; ibid., February 18, 1917, sec. 1, p. 14; ibid., October 30, 1914, p. 13; ibid., March 14, 1917, p. 13; ibid., November 5, 1913, p. 12; ibid., October 22, 1914, p. 14; John W. Davis to John J. Davis, April 11, 1915, JWD, box 2.

[116] Brandeis, *Letters*, 4: 274–75 and n. 1; *New York Times*, March 8, 1917, p. 13; ibid., March 10, 1917, p. 10.

pages of the Harvester brief into the Steel brief by reference.)[117] As it turned out, the war prompted the Administration to accept a compromise settlement with International Harvester in August 1918,[118] clearing the decks for the relatively unambiguous plurality decision in U.S. Steel's favor in March 1920.[119]

It must be emphasized that there was no true "community of agreement" between the Administration and big business representatives, even during the war. There may be some force to the argument that by depending on large corporations during the war, and indeed on the very businesses it was fighting in court, the Government conferred a kind of legitimacy upon them and promoted the integration of the industrial economy.[120] Counsel for U.S. Steel assuredly reminded the Court of the wartime experience when the case was reargued.[121] Moreover, the Sherman Act was generally held in abeyance during the war, and the Department's one major effort to invoke it was easily repelled by the War Industries Board's (WIB) forceful objections.[122] On grounds such as these, many historians have suggested that the war fulfilled businessmen's hopes for permanent economic integration and new relationships with the Government. But after an exhaustive study, Robert D. Cuff has recently concluded that "the keynotes of business-government relations during the war" were "complexity, hesitancy, and ambiguity," indicating that "the kind of trends implied by 'industrial-military complex, 'political capitalism,' and 'corporate-liberalism' were comparatively weak."[123] Indeed, Wilson and Gregory were particularly cautious and stressed that the coordination which the war agencies had effected was justified only because of the extraordinary emergency.[124]

The steps leading to postponement until after the war of the major antitrust cases set down for argument or reargument during the Supreme Court's October 1917 term nicely illustrate how the Administration remained ambivalent despite wartime exigencies. Gregory at first opposed postponements, and the President — contrary to a widely perpetuated error — explicitly approved his position![125] Years later, with all his official papers left behind, Gregory vaguely recalled that the cases were postponed to avoid disrupting the firms being prosecuted, since so much of their output was supporting the war effort.[126] Contemporary evidence indicates, however, that Gregory may have been remembering only a second postponement, in October 1918. Wilson and Gregory decided to seek a January postponement, on the other hand, when the Treasury Department besought them to consider the widespread borrowing that would be triggered by the high Court, in competition with the Government's own wartime financial needs, if the companies were

---

[117] Davis, "The Argument."

[118] *International Harvester Co. v. United States, appeal dismissed*, 248 U.S. 587; U.S. Department of Justice, *Annual Report of the Attorney General*, 1918 (Washington, D.C.: Government Printing Office, 1918), pp. 61–62.

[119] For citation, see n. 77, above.

[120] William E. Leuchtenberg, *The Perils of Prosperity, 1914–32* (Chicago: University of Chicago Press, 1958), p. 42; see also Baker, 4: 380, 385.

[121] *New York Times*, September 28, 1919, p. 14.

[122] Cuff, "Business, the State," pp. 12–17.

[123] Idem, *The War Industries Board: Business-Government Relations during World War I* (Baltimore: Johns Hopkins, 1973), p. 7.

[124] Idem, "Business, the State," p. 12; *Ann'l Rep't of the Att'y Gen'l*, 1918, pp. 60–61.

[125] Gregory to Wilson, October 5, 1917, quoted by Homer Cummings and Carl McFarland, *Federal Justice* (New York: Macmillan, 1937), pp. 346–47; Wilson to Gregory, October 10, 1917, Mss., Series 3, reel 152. Just after Wilson's death, Gregory — providing some material for former Navy Secretary Josephus Daniels' memoir of the Wilson era — failed to recall "a single instance" when the President refused to support his "policies and views"; Gregory to Daniels, February 19, 1924, p. 3, in Thomas Watt Gregory Papers, box 2, LC.

[126] R. S. Baker, "Gregory Memo," pp. 6–7; Gregory to R. S. Baker, August 29, 1931, RSB, Series 1, box 35; Cuff, "Business, the State," p. 12; Urofsky, *Big Steel*, p. 182.

ordered dissolved.[127] This truce in the legal battle was even accepted under protest by U.S. Steel, since its officers had been hoping for a prompt decision in its favor.[128]

During the postwar reconversion period, particular agencies and officials within the Administration supported temporary or even permanent modification of previous antitrust policy, but official Justice Department policy resumed its prewar course, Wilson having opposed businessmen's demands for further relaxation of antitrust and continued government supervision of industry. Bernard Baruch, chairman of the WIB, refused to support such proposals either publicly or privately because he feared that his and his agency's wartime reputation would be damaged by bad publicity or adverse litigation. He also refused to participate in a move to have the WIB petition Congress for permanent antitrust revisions. As Robert F. Himmelberg has reported, an associate of Baruch expressed "his fear of 'the cry which . . . would be made that Mr. Baruch's last act, before he went back to business, was to try to have the antitrust laws, . . . suspended.' " As Himmelburg also concluded, Baruch himself was not yet willing to concede "that the antitrust tradition had become obsolete." Again, in 1919, when the Industrial Board of the Department of Commerce initiated postwar industry-wide price agreements modeled on wartime arrangements — ostensibly to pevent a depression but actually as a step toward permanent revision of antitrust law — Attorney General A. Mitchell Palmer, who had by then succeeded Gregory, ruled them illegal despite the argument that the Government itself was a party.[129] And despite Gary's major role in wartime mobilization of the steel industry, the Administration continued to press ahead to see the Steel case through to a judicial outcome.[130] It sufficed as the test case whereby the Court would hold that oligopoly was legal. As George W. Stocking has suggested, then, the judiciary "validated the new industrial structure,"[131] and not the executive branch under Wilson, for the Wilson Administration's antitrust suits show that it opposed that course. The difference is important; although many complain about the Court's pro-business judicial doctrines during this period, the Court as an institution insulates the justices from the day-to-day contacts with business that the revisionists have argued characterize policy formation in the executive branch. Moreover, a distinguished Solicitor General, preeminent perhaps over all who have held that office, used all the persuasive power he could command to try to convince the Court to adopt the Government's position.

The most that can be said, since the cases against the "good trusts" called for statutory rather than constitutional construction, is that Congress's inaction signified a more general acceptance of big business. We must remember, however, that the Clayton Act's anti-merger provision could not, after all, be applied expost facto. To be sure, almost nothing was done to try to overturn the Steel decision legislatively, though defenders of the antitrust tradition must have been convinced that the Clayton Act would suffice for post-1914 anti-competitive mergers.[132] In addition, the White House of course undertook no legislative initiatives, but with the

[127] Gregory to George W. Murray, December 29, 1917, copy in JWD, box 67; Harbaugh, *Lawyer's Lawyer*, p. 115; *New York Times*, October 8, 1918, p. 10; ibid., January 3, 1918, p. 15; *Commercial and Financial Chronicle* 106 (January 5, 1918): 33.

[128] *New York Times*, May 23, 1917, p. 14; ibid., January 3, 1918, p. 15.

[129] Robert F. Himmelberg, "The War Industries Board and the Antitrust Question in November 1918," *Journal of American History* 52 (June 1965): 59–74; idem, "Business, Antitrust Policy, and the Industrial Board of the Department of Commerce, 1919," *Business History Review* 42 (Spring 1968): 1–23; Cuff, "Business, the State," pp. 17–18; *Opinions of the Attorney General* 31 (1919): 411–19; *New York Times*, May 11, 1919, sec. 1, p. 12; cf. ibid., January 4, 1918, p. 10.

[130] *New York Times*, July 24, 1919, p. 20.

[131] *Workable Competition and Antitrust Policy* (Nashville: Vanderbilt, 1961), p. 139; cf. Eichorn, *Emergence*, pp. 330–31.

[132] Cf. ibid., p. 330.

"one track mind"[133] of an infirm President preoccupied by the fight over the League, it would go too far to say that he accepted the decision. And it would be sheer speculation to suggest that Congress would have reacted differently if the Court had upheld the Government's position.

But what of the Wilson Administration's promotion of the domestic trade association movement? There is no denying that Wilson was willing to support the cost accounting and standardization activities of such associations after Federal Trade Commissioner Edward N. Hurley drafted an appropriate letter for his signature.[134] Moreover, industrial mobilization during the war fostered their growth, with some of their unobjectionable activities — conservation programs, for instance — transferred to Commerce Department sponsorship at war's end.[135] Nevertheless, after the Supreme Court's Steel decision, the Justice Department dropped the other cases against the so-called good trusts, though Palmer was at first unconvinced the Court had mandated such a course, and began to negotiate settlement of the Sugar Trust case.[136] It was, however, in a good position to try to salvage the Sherman Act because during the high cost of living controversy of 1919 it had begun investigating price control by what economists refer to as loose combinations, giving specific attention to trade associations which provided for exchange of price information through the kind of "open competition plan" that Arthur J. Eddy had initiated. Proceedings had been filed in February 1920 to enjoin the hardwood lumber manufacturers from participating in such a plan; when the lower court responded favorably just sixteen days after the steel decision, a delighted Palmer announced that the Department would proceed against all such groups. Cases against thirty open price associations were considered, and an important one against the so-called linseed oil trust was launched by late June. Moreover, the Department repeatedly explained that the filing of information about such price stabilization schemes with the FTC, the Commerce Department, or other government agencies, provided no immunity.[137]

V

On the whole, then, consideration of the Wilson Administration's antitrust policies suggests that Wilson should not be understood to have been a supporter of or spokesman for large corporate interests. On the other hand, as Sklar did show, Wilson's positions on expansion of foreign trade were to a considerable extent consistent with the interests of large corporations. But here too, the well-being of small

---

[133] *House Diary*, July 10, 1915, June 23, 1916, May 19, 1917; James Hart, "Classical Statesmanship," *Sewanee Review* 33 (October 1925): 403; David F. Houston, *Eight Years with Wilson's Cabinet* (Garden City: Doubleday, Page, 1926), 2: 169; Baker, 4: 218; George and George, *Wilson and House*, pp. 115, 158, 183; cf. A[lfred] M. Low, *Woodrow Wilson: An Interpretation* (Boston: Little, Brown, 1918), pp. 282–83.

[134] Wilson to Hurley, May 12, 1916, in Hurley, *The Awakening of Business* (Garden City: Doubleday, Page, 1917), frontispiece; cf. Kolko, *Triumph*, p. 275.

[135] Himmelberg, "War Industries Board," pp. 70–71; idem, "Industrial Board," pp. 4–5.

[136] *United States v. American Can Co.*, 230 F. 859 (D. Md., 1916), *appeal dismissed on motion of gov't*, 256 U.S. 706 (1921); *United States v. Quaker Oats Co.*, 232 F. 499 (N.D. Ill., 1916), *appeal dismissed on motion of gov't*, 253 U.S. 490 (1920); Commerce Clearing House, *The Federal Antitrust Laws* (New York: CCH, 1949), p. 84; *New York Times*, June 2, 1920, p. 9; ibid., March 12, 1920, p. 12; *Baltimore Sun*, June 7, 1921, p. 3; U.S. Department of Justice, *Annual Report of the Attorney General*, 1921 (Washington: Government Printing Office, 1921), p. 19; Eichner, *Emergence*, pp. 324–25.

[137] *United States v. American Column and Lumber Co.*, 263 F. 147 (W.D. Tenn., 1920), aff'd, 257 U.S. 377 (1921); *United States v. American Linseed Oil Co.*, 275 F. 939 (N.D. Ill., 1921), *rev'd*, 262 U.S. 371 (1923); *New York Times*, February 15, 1920, sec. 1, p. 8; ibid., March 17, 1920, p. 10; ibid., March 18, 1920, p. 15; ibid., July 1, 1920, p. 23; cf. ibid., February 28, 1917, p. 7; Milton Nels Nelson, "Open Price Associations," *University of Illinois Studies in the Social Sciences* 10 (June 1922): 190–92, 297; on Eddy, see his *The New Competition*, 4th ed. (Chicago: McClurg, 1915).

businessmen was a more central concern than Sklar indicated. During Wilson's first term, as Sklar readily demonstrated, he successfully pressed Congress to lower tariff barriers, reform international banking operations through the Federal Reserve Act, and develop a merchant marine. These measures did serve large corporate interests, although the Administration did not expect the largest firms necessarily to get the greatest benefits. Giant firms did not necessarily possess technological, financial, or marketing advantages in foreign trade over those of more moderate size. The Underwood tariff reform of 1913 aimed at improving industrial efficiency, Sklar argued, "by inviting world-wide competition . . . in the capital and durable goods industries, . . ."[138] But both Wilson and Brandeis had argued that giant size did not necessarily bring with it greater technological and economic efficiency. In the iron and steel industry, U.S. Steel had indeed built up a substantial export trade,[139] but newer and smaller firms were more innovative and less encumbered by outmoded plant and equipment.[140] Moreover, decentralized banking and investment freed moderate size exporters from dependence on large internal reserves, or — as Sklar himself suggested — close Wall Street connections.[141]

Further, although big business representatives spearheaded a movement to exempt export combinations from the Sherman Act, eventually succeeding when Congress passed the Webb-Pomerene Act in 1918, they enjoyed the President's support because small businessmen also favored the proposal and because he expected it to diminish the foreign trade advantages of giant corporations. Large firms favored such legislation because it would enable them to combine more effectively against foreign combinations of producers and purchasers, sell their exports at better prices, undertake concerted sales promotion activities, and reduce marketing and distribution costs.[142] But in pressing for such legislation, large and small businessmen formed a broad coalition and argued convincingly that the proposal would benefit small business.

As Sklar reported, such legislation was supported by Secretary Redfield — who had been prominently associated with large corporate interests — and by the National Foreign Trade Council, a body headed by James A. Farrell, president of U.S. Steel, that had been formed through Redfield's efforts and that largely represented such interests.[143] But both the larger manufacturers and the FTC emphasized the advantages of export combinations to small business and on that ground gained the President's support. As Redfield told Wilson, "a small man who may need the foreign market and of whom it is of national importance to give a full chance to get it, is largely now excluded because he cannot alone afford the expenses of either travelers or agencies." The FTC argued along similar lines. Agreeing, Wilson told the U.S. Chamber of Commerce in 1915 that the decisive issue related to the problems of "the smaller merchants, . . . the younger and

[138] Sklar, p. 38.

[139] Burton I. Kaufman, *Efficiency and Expansion: Foreign Trade Organization in the Wilson Administration, 1913–1921* (Westport, Conn.: Greenwood, 1974), p. 52; National Foreign Trade Convention (hereafter NFTC), *Official Report* 2 (Washington, D.C., 1915): 64–65.

[140] Grant McConnell, *Private Power and American Democracy* (New York: Knopf, 1966), p. 55; idem, *Steel and the Presidency, 1962* (New York: Norton, 1963), pp. 28–30; Walter Adams, *The Structure of American Industry*, 3rd ed. (New York: Macmillan, 1961), pp. 151–52.

[141] Sklar, p. 42; cf. ibid., p. 35; Urofsky, *Mind of One Piece*, pp. 81–84; Kolko, *Triumph*, ch. 9, especially pp. 252–54.

[142] U.S. Federal Trade Commission, *Report on Cooperation in American Export Trade* (Washington, D.C.: Government Printing Office, 1916), 1: 4–9, 372–75.

[143] Sklar, pp. 28–30; NFTC, *Official Report* 1 (Washington, D.C., 1914): 203–4; Kaufman, *Efficiency and Expansion*, pp. 82–84.

weaker corporations" that sought a share of the export trade.[144] In addition, while a special committee of the national Chamber did play a major role in drafting this legislation, with the board chairmen of Westinghouse and Ingersoll-Rand serving as committee members,[145] the Chamber itself was not, on the whole, dominated by "large corporate spokesmen," nor established, as Sklar suggested,[146] largely through their efforts. It had been created in 1912 largely through the efforts of the Boston Chamber of Commerce and the Chicago Association of Commerce, working in conjunction with the Taft Administration at a time when big business disaffection with Taft was at its peak. Harry A. Wheeler, the Chicago banker who became the Chamber's first president, reportedly observed that "big business was out of sympathy with the new undertaking, . . ." Some large corporations postponed affiliating with the new organization, and E. H. Gary reportedly believed that it wouldn't amount to anything.[147] And in pressing for the Webb-Pomerene Act, the national Chamber too stressed the difficulties facing smaller manufacturers when they attempted to engage in export trade, being joined in this effort by such influential groups as the Merchants Association of New York, a body that earlier had actively lobbied against efforts to write into law Roosevelt's distinction between good and evil trusts.[148]

VI

Although space does not permit thorough consideration of left revisionist explanations of Wilson's foreign policy, it is important to show here how the moral understanding previously set forth characterized the rhetoric of Wilson and his associates when they spoke about the expansion of foreign trade. Because Sklar indicated that Wilson's rhetoric should be taken seriously, we must be attentive to Wilson's own way of stating the relative priority of economic and moral considerations when he articulated the foreign trade policy of his Administration.

Since there had already been penetration of the "less developed countries"[149] through European initiatives, Wilson, as William Diamond has shown, early raised the question of the terms on which the U.S. should participate, emphasizing not economic but moral considerations. The "peculiar duty" of both the United States and England, he argued in 1901, was "to moderate the process in the interests of liberty. . . ."[150] Moreover, in discussing American contacts with such countries, Wilson distinguished between morality, liberty, and economic opportunity on the

---

[144] NFTC, *Official Report*, 1: 168; ibid., 2: 64, 241–47, 251–52; Burton I. Kaufman, "The Organizational Dimension of United States Economic Foreign Policy, 1900–1920," *Business History Review* 46 (Spring 1972): 37, quoting Redfield to Wilson, February 3, 1915; see also Redfield to Wilson, September 18, 1914, Mss., Series 4, reel 307, case file 1105; NFTC, *Official Report* 3 (Washington, D.C.: 1916), 457; *New York Times*, July 19, 1916, p. 15; FTC, *Export Trade*, 1: 6–7; *PPWW*, 3: 275; cf. Carl P. Parrini, *Heir to Empire: United States Economic Diplomacy, 1916–1923* (Pittsburgh: University of Pittsburgh Press, 1969), pp. 28–31; Kolko, *Triumph*, p. 275.

[145] Sklar, pp. 26, 28 n. 39, 36; Chamber of Commerce of the U.S.A., *American Export Trade: Legislation Permitting Combinations* (Washington, 1916; hereafter Chamber, *Legislation*); U.S. Congress, Senate Committee on Interstate Commerce, *Promotion of Export Trade, Hearings . . . on H.R. 17350* (64th Cong., 2d sess., 1917), pp. 138–43 (hereafter *Trade Hearings*).

[146] Sklar, pp. 27, 29.

[147] Harwood L. Childs, *Labor and Capital in National Politics* (Columbus: Ohio State University Press, 1930), pp. 13, 25 and nn. 13, 45; Wiebe, *Businessmen and Reform*, pp. 35–40, 154; *New York Times*, April 23, 1912, p. 16; cf. ibid., April 25, 1912, p. 1; cf. also A. H. Baldwin to Charles Nagel, April 16, 1912, Department of Commerce Records, RG 40, File 70503, National Archives.

[148] Chamber, *Legislation*, p. 6; Senate Committee on Interstate Commerce, *Trade Hearings*, pp. 30–31, 139, 141; House Committee on the Judiciary, *Act to Regulate Commerce*, pp. 152–65, 241 ff.

[149] *PPWW*, 4: 232.

[150] Ibid., 1: 412; W. Diamond, *Economic Thought*, p. 137.

one hand, and commercialism on the other hand. As Bryan also put it while Secretary of State, there was "more hope in the heart" of the average American "than anywhere else on earth," and the U.S., by cultivating even higher moral standards, could "assist" other peoples in improving theirs.[161] The nation was morally committed to world-wide economic prosperity, he implied, because of her moral commitment to the well-being of ordinary people everywhere. A moral commitment to elevating even further the "hope in the heart" of the average American required, in Bryan's view, a moral commitment to foreign trade and investment as a means of improving living standards at home. But so too, he expected economic contact with America to improve living standards abroad, thereby transforming into hope the terrible burden of despair felt by ordinary people in most parts of the world. Wilson insisted that American businessmen must not impose upon and exploit "the mass of the people" in the countries where they traded. "I am willing to get anything for an American that money and enterprise can obtain," he declared, "except the suppression of the rights of other men."[162]

Sklar understood Wilson to argue that economic expansion abroad would be "in no way morally invidious" since it would be "a civilizing force," carrying with it "principles of democracy and Christianity as well as bonds of international understanding and peace." He stressed as *"the important point,"* however, that Wilson, key members of his Administration, and business leaders "held in common the assumption that expansion of markets and investment abroad was indispensable to the stability and growth of the political economy."[163] But this formulation begs the question because Wilson recognized the possibility of conflicts between what Sklar called "the imperatives of modern capitalism" and the demands of a "transcendent" morality.[164] Wilson insisted that in foreign affairs particularly capitalist interests must be considered subordinate to moral considerations. This country and its citizens, he warned, must not dare turn "from the principle that morality and not expediency is the thing that must guide us and that we will never condone iniquity because it is most convenient to do so." Consider also Wilson's way of handling the question of national interest:

> It is a very perilous thing to determine the foreign policy of a nation in the terms of material interest. It not only is unfair to those with whom you are dealing, but it is degrading as regards your own actions.... and there is a reason and a compulsion lying behind all this which is dearer than anything else to the thoughtful men of America. I mean the development of constitutional liberty in the world. Human rights, national integrity, and opportunity *as against material interests* — that,... is the issue which we now have to face.... the United States ... must regard it as one of the duties of friendship to see that from no quarter are material interests made superior to human liberty and national opportunity.... We have seen material interests threaten constitutional freedom in the United States. Therefore we will known how to sympathize with those in the rest of America who have to contend with such powers, not only within their borders but from outside their borders also.[155]

Such a statement need not be understood to repudiate the concept of national interest, for it may instead be viewed as involving a reinterpretation of that concept to include express concern with the well-being, liberties, and opportunities of peoples everywhere. Without being able to discuss here whether, or to what extent,

---

[151] *Journal of the American Asiatic Association* 14 (February 1914) : 13; cf. Sklar's quotations, pp. 30, 33.
[152] *PPWW*, 3: 143.
[153] Sklar, pp. 26–27, 34, emphasis supplied.
[154] Ibid., p. 47.
[155] *PPWW*, 3: 66–69, paragraphs omitted, emphasis supplied.

the policies and actions of the Wilson Administration deviated from this principled understanding of the nation's interest, we may simply observe again that according to Wilson capitalism's expansionist interests did not necessarily harmonize with proper moral principles. What the revisionists should try to do is to demonstrate how, in cases of real conflict between the two, moral considerations gave way for Wilson to economic considerations. But this would require the revisionists to recognize that in Wilson's view capitalist imperatives did not represent "the highest morality."

CONCLUSION

We turned to Sklar's essay as a first step toward the critical reexamination of the radical left historical studies on which a growing number of political scientists rely when sketching the development of the twentieth-century American polity and economy. There, we found the term "corporate-liberalism" applied to the "world view" which Wilson was said to have shared with prominent contemporaries in the political, intellectual, and big business communities. This outlook was said to have been influenced by Burke, and therefore to have considered the large corporation "an organic growth," a natural development, which required a political response in the service of large corporate interests. The alternative interpretation presented here has shown that if we try to see how Sklar's distinction between natural growth and artificial or deliberate contrivance applies to Wilson's thought and policies, we discover in it Wilson's justification for trying to apply the Sherman Act to break up giant corporate combinations. In this respect, surely, the last thing Wilson and his associates shared with giant corporate spokesmen when they applied that distinction was "a community of agreement." This study has in no way attempted to take issue with radical scholars' analyses of present-day American political and economic life. Its purpose has only been to show that the general applicability of "ruling class" or "power elite" models to the polity and economy of the Progressive Era is questionable, and particularly unsatisfying as applied to Wilson and his Administration. Radical left historians seem to have adopted a revised version of consensus historiography. Their writings argue that with the exception of a few neo-populists, perhaps LaFollette, Industrial Relations Commissioner Frank P. Walsh, or Amos Pinchot,[156] those in the political mainstream during the early twentieth century unhesitatingly and out of conscious conviction fostered the emergence of large-scale corporate capitalism and the enhancement of corporate power. If this view were sound, the attempts of many present-day liberal reformers to draw upon a genuine American mainstream tradition of distrust for unchecked power would be exposed as mythical or fraudulent, and their efforts to preserve or restore an effectively competitive economy would come to be viewed not only as mere romanticism today but also as involving a position that no mainstream American political leader of past decades seriously sought to implement. Thus, radical left interpretations of the Progressive Era would contribute to radical left movements for a socialist America.[157]

In explaining in what manner the term "radical" means "pertaining to the root," Joseph Cropsey has observed that "if there were a perfect radicalism, it would consist of a perfect understanding of its object and therewith of that object's root; and of an undistractable animus to destroy that object as its root." Should a "radicalism" possess only the understanding without the animus to destroy, he continued, it "would be a wisdom," a perfect "scrutiny of the regime," and while "there are grave questions as to the manner in which the regime should be subjected

---

[156] Weinstein, *Corporate Ideal,* pp. 142–52, 185–213.

[157] Cf. Weinstein and Eakins, *New America,* p. 6.

to scrutiny, there is no question as to the importance of scrutinizing it."[158] The present reconsideration of Wilson suggests that at least one radical left understanding of the development of the present-day American polity, and perhaps others as well, should be understood to have scrutinized the regime imperfectly, especially by those political scientists most predisposed to accept it. If radical scholars desire to provide us with a defensible radical criticism of the development of the present day American polity and economy, they will have to offer a more accurate explanation of how Wilson's thought and deeds were related to that development.

---

[158] "Radicalism and Its Roots," *Public Policy* 18 (Spring 1970) : 301–2.

Woodrow Wilson and the Political Economy of Modern United States Liberalism

Martin J. Sklar

The author is a candidate for the master's degree in the Department of History of the University of Wisconsin. He wishes to acknowledge the aid of the Fund for Social Analysis whose recent research grant has facilitated his study of the institutional and ideological roots and development of United States imperialism, of which this paper forms a small part. A condensed version of this paper was read before the Graduate History Symposium of the Wisconsin Historical Society, May 11, 1960.

" . . . Most persons are so thoroughly uninformed as to my opinions that I have concluded that the only things they have not read are my speeches."

—Woodrow Wilson, 1912.

PERHAPS THE GREATEST source of historical misconception about Woodrow Wilson is the methodological compartmentalization of his mentality into two distinct components, the "moralistic" and the "realistic" or "commercialistic," as if they were discrete and mutually exclusive. From this point of departure, if one thinks or acts "moralistically," he can not be considered capable at the same time of thinking and acting "realistically," at least not consistently: if one is a "moralist," his political behavior can be considered as deriving only secondarily, if at all, from an understanding of, or a serious concern for, the affairs of political economy.

According to this approach, wherever Wilson is perceived to have spoken or acted for the "little man," "democracy," "liberty," "individual opportunity," and the like, he was "liberal" and moralistic; wherever he is perceived to have spoken or acted for corporate interests, economic expansion abroad, and the like, he was "conservative," "commercialistic," "expedient," or realistic. Where Wilson supported measures promoting large corporate interests at home or abroad, he is considered to have forsaken his moralism, to have been driven by political expediency, personal egoism, or implacable social and economic forces, or to have gathered the unintended consequences of a misdirected moralism. In this view, Wilson the moralist is generally considered the true type, and Wilson the realist, the deviant.

Aside from objections that may be raised against the naiveté and

17

theoretical deficiencies of such an approach to social thought and ideology in general,[1] certain specific objections may be raised against such an approach to Wilson, particularly should the main ideological components generally attributed to Wilson's mentality be granted at the outset, and their implications accorded a modicum of examination.

First, the "Puritan ethic," to which students of Wilson have attached fundamental importance as basic to his mentality, made no such mutually exclusive distinction between a transcendent morality and the world of political economy. Puritanism embraced a morality applicable not merely to the world beyond, but as well to the living individual and existing society; it sanctioned, indeed posited, capitalist social and economic relations. The affirmation of capitalist society was therefore implicit in Wilson's Protestant morality. From the straightest-laced New England Puritan of the seventeenth century to Poor Richard's Benjamin Franklin, to Gospel-of-Wealth Andrew Carnegie, to New Freedom Woodrow Wilson, religious conviction and "market-place materialism" were each practical, each the uplifting agent of civilization and Providence, each the necessary condition for personal salvation and general human improvement, each a function of the other, mutually interdependent and interwoven like the white and purple threads of the single holy cloth. To the extent, then, that Puritanism entered significantly into Wilson's world-view, the affirmation of the capitalist system in the United States (and throughout the world) was a function of his morality, not merely an auxiliary prepossession.

Second, Wilson's moral affirmation of capitalism sanctioned by Puritan conceptions found powerful confirmation in the economic writings of Adam Smith (himself a professor of moral philosophy), John Bright, and Richard Cobden; as student and professor he had become firmly grounded in their theories of political economy which he admired and enthusiastically espoused, and it is not difficult to perceive that such writings would strongly appeal to one reared on Puritanism. In Smith, Bright, and Cobden, Wilson found secular moral sanction for the bourgeois-democratic political economy as well as indefeasible economic principles. Private, competitive enterprise manifested natural law in the realm of political economy, and went hand in hand with republican institutions, comprising together the essential conditions of democracy, individual liberty, and increasing prosperity. To Wilson, much of whose economic thinking was based upon the assumption of the growing superiority of United States industry, the arguments of Smith, Cobden, and Bright were compelling: they, in their day, spoke for an industrially supreme Great Britain, and recognizing Britain's position, argued that the optimum condition for the nation's economic growth and expansion rested upon the "natural" flow of trade, a "natural" international division of labor, uninhibited by "artificial" hindrances.

Taken together, Puritanism and Smithian-Manchestrian economics instilled Wilson with the compulsion to serve the strengthening and extending of the politico-economic system he knew in the United States as a positively moralistic commitment, since that would strengthen and extend the sphere of liberty, democracy, prosperity, and Providence, and accorded with natu-

---

1 See Karl Mannheim, *Ideology and Utopia* (Harvest Book edition), 59-70. Mannheim here distinguishes between the "particular conception of ideology" and the "total conception of ideology"; it is in terms of the latter that Wilson's world view is comprehended in this essay.

18

ral law. As William Diamond observes, such assumptions were to become "basic" to Wilson's "thought on foreign policy."[2]

Third and finally, the organismic view of society that Wilson derived from Edmund Burke and Walter Bagehot provided him with the concept that whatever social phenomena or social system evolved "naturally" from the traditions and customs of the past, from the working of natural law through "irresistible" social forces, were not only inevitable as prescriptively ordained but morally indisputable. They represented both the evolution of the genius of human custom and institutions and the assertion of God's will in human affairs. To Burke, whom Wilson revered and assiduously studied, the market economy manifested the working of natural law, which in turn manifested divine law. In Burke, Wilson could find a reverence for the market economy akin to religious awe: "the laws of commerce . . . are the laws of nature, and consequently the laws of God," Burke had said.[3] American Puritan doctrine, as developed by Johnathan Edwards, had itself become firmly anchored in the natural law of Newton and Locke; it required the intensive study of society's concrete development and condition, in order to comprehend God's work in the universe. In this respect, Puritanism and Burke stood on common ground. Here both religious and secular morality converged upon the affirmation of things as they were and as they appeared to be evolving. That which was "natural" was moral. The part of wisdom, morality, and statesmanship was to comprehend, affirm, and work for the necessary institutional adjustments to, "natural" evolution and "the well-known laws of value and exchange."[4] This evolutionary-positivist or conservative-historicist[5] approach to society served to modify whatever predilections Wilson may have had for atomized economic relations; it provided him with philosophical ground for rejecting the doctrine of unrestricted competition, as did the institutional economists he encountered at Johns Hopkins in the 1880's, and for affirming, as an inevitable result of the laws of commerce and natural social evolution, the demise of the freely competing entrepreneur at the hands of the large corporation. As Wilson once remarked, explaining his approval of large-scale industrial corporations, " . . . No man indicts natural history. No man undertakes to say that the things that have happened by operation of irresistible forces are immoral things. . . . "[6]

2 William Diamond, The Economic Thought of Woodrow Wilson (Balt., 1943), 29. As revealed by his life, speeches, and writings, Wilson's concern was to protect the private enterprise system, as beneficent in itself and in its effects, from those dishonest, unscrupulous men who threatened to misuse and pervert it (and from socialists who threatened to abolish it). It was in keeping with his intense commitment to his moral principles that Wilson, early and late in his life, viewed an activist political career as his "heart's first—primary—ambition and purpose," as opposed to pure academic pursuits. Wilson to Ellen Axson, Feb. 1885, cited in Arthur S. Link, Wilson: The Road to the White House (Princeton, 1947), 19 (hereafter cited as Link, Wilson, I). Emphasis in original. Cf. ibid., 20, 23, 97, 123, 130; and Ray S. Baker, Woodrow Wilson, Life and Letters (8 vols., N.Y., various dates), I, 229, II, 98. It was therefore only natural that in the 1880's and 1890's and thereafter, far from being a head-in-the-clouds "idealist," Wilson made himself intimately conversant with the concrete political and economic issues of the day.

3 Burke, Thoughts and Details on Scarcity (World Classics edition), VI, 22, also 6, 9, 10.

4 See, e.g., Wilson's "The Making of the Nation," Atlantic Monthly, LXXX (July 1897), in Ray S. Baker and William E. Dodd (ed.), The Public Papers of Woodrow Wilson (4 vols., N.Y., 1925, 1926), I, 328 (hereafter cited as P P W W); and "Democracy and Efficiency," Atlantic Monthly, LXXXVII (March 1901), Ibid., 400.

5 The term conservative-historicist is used in the technical sense defined by Mannheim, op. cit., 120, 121, and is not meant here to denote "conservatism" as against "liberalism" as those terms are conventionally used.

6 "Richmond Address," delivered before the General Assembly of Virginia and the City Council of Richmond, Feb. 1, 1912, P P W W, II, 377.

19

To the extent that the characterization of Wilson's mentality as "moralistic" connotes Sunday school platitudes or pollyanna ingenuousness, therefore, it is not only irrelevant, but fundamentally misleading. Since Wilson's writings, speeches, policy decisions, and actions simply do not correspond with such "moralism" the tendency of those who view his mentality in this manner is to judge both Wilson's utterances and actions, and the great events with which he was concerned, either in terms of a Faustian personality torn between the forces of high idealism and gross materialism, or less charitably, in terms of a sophisticated hypocrisy: " . . . Beneath the layer of Christian moralism is the shrewdness of the Puritan merchant. . . ."[7]

But Wilson's moralism was not simply a veneer "beneath" which lurked supposedly amoral "commercialism." It was a genuine and basic component of his ideological framework, though, it is submitted, no more so than in that of William Howard Taft, Philander C. Knox, Theodore Roosevelt, or Huntington Wilson. Woodrow Wilson's "wrung heart and wet hanky," we may be sure, were "real enough."[8] His thought in matters of political economy embraced a body of moralistic concepts, just as his moralism presumed certain principles of political economy and corresponding social relations. Whether or not in human thought and ideology the two have often failed to be inextricably interrelated, in Wilson they certainly were. A view of ideology that cast morality and ethics into one realm and political economy into another, that sees history as a struggle between the "ethical" men and the "materialistic" men, between the lofty and the commercialistic, suffers from an inverted economic determinism that overlooks the possibility that commitment to an economic way of life may go hand in hand with the most intense and highly systematized morality; with respect to Wilson, it forgets that just as classical political economy, "despite its worldly and wantion appearance—is a true moral science, the most moral of the sciences;"[9] so Puritanism, as the works of R. H. Tawney and Max Weber suggest, despite its heavenly concern, is a truly worldly doctrine.

For Wilson, like Burke, ideals and principles, to the extent that they validly applied to society, arose from and satisfied, not rationally deduced abstract precepts, but practical experience with the concrete conditions of society drawn in the light of "the inviolable understandings of precedent."[10] "Will you never learn this fact," he lectured Boston real estate men in January, 1912, "that you do not make governments by theories? You accommodate theories to the circumstances. Theories are generalizations from the facts. The facts do not spring out of theories . . . but the facts break in and ignore theories . . . and as our life is, as our thought is, so will our Government be."[11] Accordingly, Wilson insisted upon the necessity of adjusting legal institutions to the changed circumstances of economics and politics: " . . . if you do not adjust your laws to the facts, so much the worse

---

7 Richard W. Van Alstyne, "American Nationalism and Its Mythology," Queen's Quarterly, LXV, 3 (Autumn 1958), 436.

8 For this reference to Wilson by D. H. Lawrence, see his Studies in Classic American Literature, 1922 (Anchor edition: N.Y., 1951), 32-33, which contains a valuable insight into the morality showed by Wilson in the chapters on Benjamin Franklin and Hector St. John de Crevecoeur, pp. 19-43.

9 Karl Marx, Economic and Philosophic Manuscripts of 1844 (Foreign Languages Publishing House, Moscow, n.d.), 119.

10 "The Ideals of America," Atlantic Monthly, XC (Dec. 1902), P P W W, I, 422; Baker, Wilson, Life and Letters, II, 104.

11 "Efficiency" (Jan. 27, 1912), P P W W, II, 361.

20

for the laws, not for the facts, because law trails after the facts. . . . we must [adjust the laws to the facts]; there is no choice . . . because the law, unless I have studied amiss, is the expression of the facts in legal relationships. Laws have never altered the facts; laws have always necessarily expressed the facts; adjusted interests as they have arisen and have changed toward one another."[12] It was the necessity, the "facts," which Wilson recognized that determined his world view.

Time and again Wilson emphasized that the facts of modern life to which adjustment was most urgent were economic in character. Indeed, Wilson viewed economic relations as basic to all other social relations. He analyzed conditions in the United States, its troubles and opportunities, as essentially the result of rapid industrialization aggravated by the passing of the continental frontier. He conceived the major issues of his time as "questions of economic policy chiefly," and defined in this manner not only the tariff, coinage and currency, trust, and immigration questions, but also, significantly, "foreign policy" and "our duty to our neighbors."[13] The life of the nation, he declared in 1911, was not what it was twenty, even ten, years before: economic conditions had changed "from top to bottom," and with them "the organization of our life."[14] As New Jersey governor-elect Wilson noted, "the world of business [has changed], and therefore the world of society and the world of politics. . . . A new economic society has sprung up, and we must effect a new set of adjustments. . . ." And as candidate for the Democratic presidential nomination in 1912, he declared, " . . . business underlies every part of our lives; the foundation of our lives, of our spiritiual lives included, is economic." Business, he emphasized, "is the foundation of every other relationship, particularly of the political relationship. . . ."[15]

Wilson's view of economic relations as basic to social, political, and spiritual life, fit altogether consistently into his conservative-historicist, natural law approach to society. Understood in these terms, Wilson's "idealism" arose, therefore, from his conception of practical experience, of "natural" social evolution, of the genius of evolved social institutions, custom, habit, and traditions, of "irresistible" social forces, and the laws of commerce. It was that mixture of classical nineteenth century liberalism with conservative-historicism that made Wilson the Progressive he was: rational adjustments, determined by enlightened men concerned with the general welfare, were

12 *The New Freedom* (N. Y., 1914), 33, 34, 35; "Richmond Address" (Feb. 1, 1912), *P P W W*, II, 376. For an interesting comparison worth noting here, see Karl Marx, *The Poverty of Philosophy* (1847): "Indeed, an utter ignorance of history is necessary in order not to know that at all times sovereign rulers have had to submit to economic conditions and have never been able to dictate laws to them. Both political and civil legislation do no more than recognize the will of economic conditions. . . . Law is nothing but the recognition of fact." Translation is that found in Franz Mehring, *Karl Marx, the Story of His Life* (London, 1951), 123. (*Cf. The Poverty of Philosophy* [For. Lang. Pub. House, Moscow, n.d.], 83). For a present-day view that regards law as subordinate to economic fact, specifically with respect to the rise of the corporation as the predominant form of business organization, *cf.* Edward S. Mason (ed.), *The Corporation in Modern Society* (Cambridge, Mass., 1959), 1, where Mason, in his Introduction, states: ". . . law in a major manifestation is simply a device for facilitating and registering the obvious and the inevitable. . . ."

13 "Leaderless Government," address before Virginia State Bar Association, Aug. 4, 1897, *P P W W*, I, 354.

14 "Issues of Freedom," address at banquet of Knife and Fork Club of Kansas City, Mo., May 5, 1911, *P P W W*, II, 285; *The New Freedom*, 3.

15 Inaugural Address as gov.-elect of New Jersey, Jan. 17, 1911, *P P W W*, II, 273; "Government in Relation to Business," address at Annual Banquet of the Economic Club, New York, May 23, 1912, *ibid.*, 431, 432. In 1898, Wilson had observed, "For whatever we say of other motives, we must never forget that in the main the ordinary conduct of man is determined by economic motives." Quoted in Diamond, *op. cit.*, 52 n.

21

made to irrational processes, that is, to processes not determined by men but evolving irresistibly in accordance with supra-human natural law or predetermination.

Wilson's position on the "trust" question cannot be accurately understood apart from his firm conviction that law must correspond with the facts of economic life, must accommodate the people, their habits and institutions to, *and facilitate,* natural economic development, and in the process achieve the general welfare or national interest.

He defined the general welfare or national interest not in terms of abstract reasoning or visionary dreams, or from "pure" moral principles, but historically in terms of the "facts" of the existing economic structure and business organization. To Wilson, the "facts" were that the large corporation and large-scale industry had replaced the individual entrepreneur and small producing unit as the central and dominant feature of modern capitalism. Accordingly, the adjustments to be made, in Wilson's mind, involved not an attempt to restore the entrepreneurial competition of by-gone days nor the dissolution of large corporations, but on the contrary, "the task of translating law and morals into terms of modern business . . . ."[16] More precisely, the problem to be defined was that " . . . Our laws are still meant for business done by *individuals;* they have not been satisfactorily adjusted to business done by great *combinations,* and we have got to adjust them. . . . there is no choice."[17] What was needed were "open efforts to accommodate law to the material development which has so strengthened the country in all that it has undertaken by supplying its extraordinary life with necessary physical foundations."[18]

Usually overlooked in discussions about the great "anti-trust" debates of the pre-World War I period is that the leading participants were concerned not so much with the abstract idea of "competition versus monopoly" as with the role of the corporation in the new industrial order and its relation to the state. This was as true of Wilson as it was of Roosevelt, Taft. George W. Perkins, Elbert H. Gary, and Herbert Croly. In his writings and speeches on the "trusts," Wilson placed particular emphasis upon "the extraordinary development of corporate organization and administration,"[19] as the dominant mode of modern capitalist enterprise, upon the corresponding decline of unrestricted competition and the growth of "cooperation," and furthermore, of particular importance, consistent with his over-all view, upon the legitimacy of the process, the need to affirm and adjust to it. Large corporations were "indispensable to modern business enterprise"; "the combinations necessarily effected for the transaction of modern business"; "society's present means of effective life in the field of industry" and its "new way of massing its resources and its power of enterprise"; "organizations of a perfectly intelligible sort which the law has licensed for the convenience of extensive business," neither "hobgoblins" nor "unholy inventions of rascally rich men."[20]

16 "Politics (1857-1907)," *Atlantic Monthly,* C (Nov. 1907), *P P W W,* II, 19.
17 "Richmond Address" (Feb. 1, 1912), *Ibid.,* 376.
18 *The New Freedom,* 117-118.
19 "The Lawyer and the Community," annual address delivered before the American Bar Association, Chattanooga, Aug. 31, 1910, *P P W W,* II, 253.
20 *Ibid.,* 254-257, 262; "Bankers and Statesmanship," address before the New Jersey Bankers' Association, Atlantic City, May 6, 1910, *ibid.,* 229; *The New Freedom,* 5; Inaugural Address as gov.-elect of New Jersey (Jan. 17, 1911), *P P W W,* II, 271.

22

As institutions that had developed "by operation of irresistible forces," large corporations could not be considered "immoral"; " . . . to suggest that the things that have happened to us must be reversed, and the scroll of time rolled back on itself," Wilson declared in 1912, " . . . would be futile and ridiculous. . . . "21 On more than one occasion during the campaign of 1912, as he had in the past, Wilson declared: "I am not one of those who think that competition can be established by law against the drift of a world-wide economic tendency; neither am I one of those who believe that business done upon a great scale by a single organization—call it corporation, or what you will—is necessarily dangerous to the liberties, even the economic liberties, of a great people like our own . . . I am not afraid of anything that is normal. I dare say we shall never return to the old order of individual competition, and that the organization of business upon a great scale of co-operation is, up to a certain point, itself normal and inevitable."22 Or, as he put it on another occasion, " . . . nobody can fail to see that modern business is going to be done by corporations . . . We will do business henceforth when we do it on a great and successful scale, by means of corporations. . . . "23

With respect to remedies in the matter of "trusts," the task according to Wilson was "not to disintegrate what we have been at such pains to piece together in the organization of modern industrial enterprise"; a program of dissolution of the large corporations would only calamitously derange the economy; it would "throw great undertakings out of gear"; it would "disorganize some important business altogether."24 Rather, the task was to prevent the misuse of corporations by individuals, make guilt and punishment individual rather than corporate, prescribe in law those practices corporations might and might not undertake, prohibit unfair and coercive methods of competition, require reasonable competition among the large corporations, and assure that corporations operate in the public interest.25

Historians have argued over when it was that Wilson first declared in favor of commission regulation of business, as if this were of fundamental importance to his over-all view of the trust question.26 To Wilson, however, the question of commission regulation did not involve that of *laissez-faire*

21 "Richmond Address," *ibid.*, 376-377.

22 Address accepting Democratic party presidential nomination, Aug. 7, 1912, *Official Report of the Proceedings of the Democratic National Convention*, 1912, 407. The "certain point" referred to by Wilson was the point of diminishing returns. The enterprise that made money in the market without recourse to coercive or "artificial" practices was normal, its size justified by its pecuniary success.

23 "The Tariff and the Trusts," address at Nashville, Tenn., Feb. 24, 1912, *P P W W*, II, 410-411. In this connection, more than a decade before Theodore Roosevelt denounced the "rural tories" as reactionaries whose passion for unrestricted competition and small business units would turn back the clock of progress, Wilson, in December, 1900, had applied the same criticism to Populists and Bryan-Democrats: ". . . Most of our reformers are retro-reformers. They want to hale us back to an old chrysalis which we have broken; they want us to resume a shape which we have outgrown. . . ." "The Puritan," speech before the New England Society of N.Y.C., Dec. 22, 1900, *ibid.*, I, 365.

24 "The Lawyer and the Community" (Aug. 31, 1910), *ibid.*, II, 254.

25 ". . . You cannot establish competition by law, but you can take away the obstacles by law that stand in the way of competition, and while we may despair of setting up competition among individual persons there is good ground for setting up competition between these great combinations, and after we have got them competing with one another they will come to their senses in so many respects that we can afterwards hold conference with them without losing our self-respect." Wilson, Jackson Day Dinner Address, Jan. 8, 1912, *ibid.*, 348.

26 See, *e. g.*, John W. Davidson (ed.), *A Crossroads of Freedom: The 1912 Campaign Speeches of Woodrow Wilson* (New Haven, 1956), 80.

23

versus "positive" government, or regulation of monopoly versus enforcement of competition. It involved instead, the question of whether the ground rules of the new corporate system were to be left to arbitrary decisions of executive officers, subject to change with each administration, and possibly productive of both interference with personal and property rights and irrational attacks upon corporations, or whether, as he advocated, they were to become institutionalized in law. As had the corporate leaders themselves who testified before congressional committees, what Wilson wanted was "the certainty of law." Within that context, he favored "as much power as you choose."[27]

Whether one examines Wilson's thought before or during his "New Freedom" years, it is evident that what is thought of as *laissez-faire* Jeffersonianism is not one of its characteristics. In 1908, for example, pointing to "the necessity for a firm and comprehensive regulation of business operations in the interest of fair dealing," Wilson stated, " . . . No one now advocates the old *laissez-faire* . . . "[28] As if to emphasize his conviction that the popular notion of Jeffersonianism bore little direct relevance to the problems of modern times, Wilson took the occasion of the Democratic party's Jefferson Day Banquet in 1912 to assert, " . . . We live in a new and strange age and reckon with new affairs alike in economics and politics of which Jefferson knew nothing."[29] With respect to the government's role in particular, as William Diamond summarizes the record, " . . . Throughout his political life . . . [Wilson] was willing to use the government as a positive instrument in the economic life of the nation. . . ."[30]

In two most basic areas of policy and thought, then, that of the extent of government intervention in the economy and that of the "trust" question, Wilson was no more a "Jeffersonian" than was Theodore Roosevelt, Edward D. White, Oliver Wendell Holmes, George W. Perkins, or Herbert Croly. If "Jeffersonian" is meant to connote a return to an agrarian yeoman republic, or to the regime of unrestricted competition among independent entrepreneurs or small business units, or a government policy of *laissez-faire*, then much as it obscures more than clarifies in applying the term to any leading twentieth century figure in United States history, it certainly fails even allegorically to characterize, or provide much insight into, Wilson's thought or policy positions.

Accordingly, Wilson's "New Freedom" years, 1912-1914, may be more accurately comprehended not as a break with his past, just as his decision to make commission regulation the core of his "trust" program may be better understood not as a break with his "New Freedom" views. Before, during, and after 1914, Wilson's views on the "trust" question, like those of large

27 "The Vision of the Democratic Party" (New Haven Address, Sept. 25, 1912), *ibid.*, 264-265. Davidson points out (see fn 26 above) that Wilson declared for commission regulation at his Buffalo speech of September 2, 1912, at least three weeks prior to the New Haven address, but the point Wilson made on these occasions was in no essential respect different from that which he made more than four years earlier, when insisting "everywhere upon definition, uniform, exact, enforceable," he stated (in criticism of the pending Hepburn amendments to the Sherman Act), ". . . If there must be commissions, let them be, not executive instrumentalities having indefinite powers capable of domineering as well as regulating, but tribunals of easy and uniform process acting under precise terms of power in the enforcement of precise terms of regulation." "Law or Personal Power," address delivered to the National Democratic Club, N. Y., April 13, 1908, *P P W W*, II, 28.
28 *Ibid.*, 25.
29 "What Jefferson Would Do," *ibid.*, 424.
30 Diamond, *Econ. Thought of Wilson*, 130.

24

corporate spokesmen within the Chicago Association of Commerce, Nation Civic Federation, and the United States Chamber of Commerce, and like those of Roosevelt and Bureau of Corporations chiefs James R. Garfield and Herbert K. Smith, embodied the common law-Rule of Reason doctrine ultimately handed down by the Supreme Court in its American Tobacco and Standard Oil decisions of 1911. Like the others, Wilson had opposed the Court's earlier decisions prohibiting both "reasonable" and "unreasonable" restraints of trade; like them his approach affirmed large-scale corporate organization, sought the institutional legitimization of reasonable restraints of trade and the prohibition of unreasonable restraints or "unfair" competition, as determined at common law and by judicial precedent, with the public interest as the central consideration.

Wilson's position on the "trust" question as of 1912-1914 may be looked upon as a synthesis of the positions of Taft and Roosevelt: on the one hand, acknowledgement of the demise of *individualistic, entrepreneurial* competition, but the affirmation of and insistence upon reasonable *intercorporate* competition; on the other hand, the prevention of "unfair competition" and affirmation of "reasonable" combination and intercorporate arrangements consistent with the "public interest" or "general welfare," under a government regulatory policy rooted in the settled precedents and practices of common and civil law jurisprudence, whether enforced by the courts or by an administrative commission or by a combination of both.

To cite the fact that Louis D. Brandeis exerted decisive influence in Wilson's acceptance of the trade commission bill as evidence of a basic alteration in Wilson's views on the trust question, is either to overlook Brandeis' public utterances at the time and the program he advocated, or to disregard Wilson's previous writings and statements. Brandeis' position avowedly embodied the Supreme Court's Rule of Reason decisions of 1911; he advocated "reasonable" restraints of trade (including limitations upon competition by trade associations) and the prohibition of "unfair practices."[31] The issue involved in Wilson's abandoning the Clayton bill was primarily the impracticality of specifying every unfair practice to be proscribed, and the severity with which, in its original form, it threatened to interfere with corporate practices. The Rule of Reason decision, on the other hand, provided the general term, "unfair competition," with a recognized meaning at common law as evolved over the past decades in court decisions. And after its establishment, when the Federal Trade Commission sought to define "unfair methods of competition," it began by cataloguing all practices that had been found by the courts to be unreasonable or unfair at common law.[32] The trade commission act, while not providing full certainty of law, as Wilson had wished, satisfied the basic elements of his position in removing regulatory powers from the arbitrary decisions of commissioners and grounding them in judicial precedent.

It should also be noted, within the context of the community of agree-

31 See, *e.g.*, Brandeis' testimony before House Comm. on the Jud., *Trust Legislation* (Ser. No. 2)—*Patent Legislation* (Ser. No. 1), *Hearings on H. R. 11380, H. R. 11381, H. R. 15926, and H. R. 19959*, Jan. 26, 27, and Feb. 19, 1912, 62d Cong., 2d Sess. (Wash., 1912), 13-54 (Brandeis testified on Jan. 26, 1912); and Brandeis, "The Solution of the Trust Problem," *Harper's Weekly*, LVIII (No. 2968), Nov. 8, 1913, 18-19.
32 *Memorandum on Unfair Competition at the Common Law* (printed for office use only by the Federal Trade Comm., 1915), cited and discussed in Thomas C. Blaisdell, Jr., *The Federal Trade Commission* (N.Y., 1932), 21-23.

25

ment on the "trust" question between Wilson and large corporate spokesmen, that the circumstances surrounding the writing of the bill bear no
anomaly. As Arthur S. Link shows, Brandeis and George L. Rublee worked
closely tógether and in consultation with Wilson in drafting the legislation;
Rublee actually wrote the bill.[33] Generally unknown, however, is that at
the time Rublee worked in Washington writing the measure, he was serving
as a member of a special committee on trade commission legislation of the
United States Chamber of Commerce. (Brandeis had been an initial member of the Chamber's committee, but retired in favor of Rublee under the
press of other affairs).[34]

But all this is not to imply that Wilson "sold out," that he was obliged
reluctantly to submit to "implacable" forces, or that his views or policies
had undegone any basic change. Rather, it is to suggest that, viewed
within the context of Wilson's over-all thought and programmatic approach,
the "New Freedom" years are not best understood as a distinctive period
in his intellectual or political life, nor as "anti-Big Business" in nature or
intent.

This view may be all the more forcefully substantiated if the inter-
relationship between the "New Freedom" legislation of 1913-1914 and promotion of United States economic expansion abroad is appreciated. Here
again, it may be seen that, consistent with Wilson's previous and subsequent
views, the "New Freedom" was not directed against large corporate developments at home or abroad.[35]

That prior to 1912-1914 Wilson had been a firm advocate of United
States economic expansion abroad is a matter of record upon which there
is general agreement by historians. His views in this respect have been
sufficiently observed and analyzed elsewhere.[36] The main elements of his
thought may be briefly summarized here. As an early adherent of Turner's
frontier thesis Wilson defined the nation's natural political-economic development and its prosperity as a function of westward expansion. With
the end of the continental frontier, expansion into world markets with the
nation's surplus manufactured goods and capital was, in his view, indispensable to the stability and prosperity of the economy. It was also no
more than a natural development in the life of any industrial nation, and,
to him, in no way morally invidious since in his view, the nation's economic
expansion was a civilizing force that carried with it principles of democracy

---

33 Link, *Wilson: The New Freedom* (Princeton, 1956), 436-438, 441 (hereafter cited as Link, *Wilson*, I). See also, George Rublee, "The Original Plan and Early History of the Federal Trade Commission," *Proceedings of the Academy of Political Science*, XI, 4 (Jan. 1926), 114-120.

34 Senate Comm. on Interstate Commerce, "Promotion of Export Trade," *Hearings on H. R. 17350*, 64th Cong., 2d Sess., Jan. 1917 (Wash., 1917), 10-12.

35 For a characteristic formulation of the conventional interpretation of the "New Freedom," particularly with respect to foreign relations, see Charles A. Beard, *The Idea of National Interest*
(N. Y., 1934), 121, 122, 464. In this valuable theoretical work designed to demonstrate that
United States foreign policy has historically been based not upon abstract ideals, but upon the
pursuit of national interest as defined by the realities of political economy, Beard felt obliged
to classify Wilson as an exception to the rule. According to Beard, Wilson "turned a cold shoulder"
to the great economic interests that had "on the whole, supported and benefited by dollar diplomacy." "From the turn of the century," Beard explains, "the practice of giving aggressive support
to the interests of American citizens abroad grew until it appeared to attain almost world-wide
range and received the authority of a positive official creed in the conception of dollar diplomacy.
. . . After a brief setback during the Wilson regime, the pattern was restored again with the return
to power of a Republican administration in 1921. . . ." But, "in the main, the policies of President
Wilson, both domestic and foreign, ran counter to corporate development and commercial expansion
under the impulse of dollar diplomacy, with their accompanying interpretations of national interest. . . ."

36 Diamond, *op. cit.*, 131-161..

26

and Christianity as well as bonds of international understanding and peace. Given the United States' superior industrial efficiency she would assume supremacy in the world's markets, provided artificial barriers to her economic expansion were eliminated. Accordingly, Wilson admired and championed Hay's open door policy and advocated vigorous government diplomacy and appropriate government measures to attain the ends in view.

Within this broad framework of thought, the application of the expanding-frontier image to economic expansion abroad, assumed a significance more fundamental than the invocation of a romantic metaphor: the West had been developed by the extension of railroads, the opening of mines, the development of agriculture—in short by the extension of the sphere of enterprise and investment that resulted in the widening of the internal market and fed the growth of large-scale industry. Markets for manufactured goods were in this way actively *developed, created,* in the West, by the metropolitan industrial and finance capitalists, and not without the significant aid of the federal government. Similarly with such markets abroad: foreign investments and industrial exports were seen by the corporate interests most heavily involved and by like-minded political leaders, such as Wilson, as going hand in hand, centered as their concern was on the needs of an industrial capitalist system in general and heavy industry in particular. Accordingly, the idea of "development" of agrarian areas in other parts of the world, and "release of energies," is prominent in Wilson's approach to economic expansion abroad.

Wilson's emphasis on exports of manufactures, his belief in their indispensability to the nation's prosperity, and his conception that the government should play a leading role in these matters, coincided in every essential respect with the views of the so-called Dollar Diplomatists, and of large corporate spokesmen within the U. S. Chamber of Commerce, the American Asiatic Association, the Pan-American Society, the American Manufacturers Export Association, and the National Foreign Trade Council. In like manner his advocacy of appropriate government measures to encourage an effective merchant marine and adequate international banking facilities flowed from this common concern for expanding the economic frontier; and his support of a low tariff was in large part informed by his belief that it was necessary to the nation's assumption of its proper role in world economic affairs.

But these were not merely the views of a supposedly "early" Wilson, later to be abandoned by the "New Freedom" Wilson; on the contrary, he carried them most emphatically, along with programmatic proposals, into his presidential campaign of 1912. Wilson's consistent theme, in this respect, during his bid for the presidency, is summarized in his address accepting the Democratic Party's presidential nomination: " . . . Our industries have expanded to such a point that they will burst their jackets if they cannot find a free outlet to the markets of the world . . . Our domestic markets no longer suffice. We need foreign markets. . . . " The alternative, as he had previously put it, was "a congestion that will operate calamitously upon the economic conditions of the country." The economic imperatives, therefore, required institutional adjustments on the governmental and private business levels to break an outmoded "chysalis," in

27

order to "relieve the plethora," and "use the energy of the [nation's] capital." They also pointed to "America's economic supremacy" (a phrase, which Wilson shared with Brooks Adams): " . . . if we are not going to stifle economically, we have got to find our way out into the great international exchanges of the world"; the nation's "irresistible energy . . . has got to be released for the commercial conquest of the world," for "making ourselves supreme in the world from an economic point of view." He stressed three major reforms to meet the new necessities of the time—the downward revision of the tariff, the development of a strong merchant marine ("The nation that wants foreign commerce must have the arms of commerce"), and laws permitting foreign branch banking tied to a commercial-acceptance system (" . . . this absolutely essential function of international trade . . . ").[37]

Wilson's concern for the promotion of foreign trade and investment found expression in some of his key appointments upon assuming the presidency. To China, for example, he sent Paul S. Reinsch, long a prominent spokesman for economic expansion abroad. He appointed his intimate friend, Walter H. Page, as ambassador to Great Britain; as editor of *World's Work*, Page had published series of articles on such topics as "the industrial conquest of the world," to which Reinsch contributed.[38] Wilson's appointments of Edward N. Hurley and George L. Rublee to the newly formed Federal Trade Commission proved decisive, in its first few years, in making it a leading agency of foreign trade promotion, an aspect of its activities that was not then widely anticipated nor since been sufficiently appreciated.[39]

Wilson appointed William C. Redfield to head the Department of Commerce, which, with its Bureau of Foreign and Domestic Commerce, shared with the State Department the central responsibility within the federal government for promoting foreign economic expansion. It is a mistake to dismiss Redfield, as Link does with the remark that "perhaps his chief claim to fame was the fact that he was the last man in American public life to wear side whiskers. . . . "[40] For Redfield was a prominent member of the corporate community, enjoying the respect and confidence of corporate leaders. As a New York manufacturer of iron and steel products he spent many years abroad developing markets and as a "business

37 See in particular his speeches, "Efficiency" (Jan. 27, 1912), *P W W*, II, 357-360, 372-375, 380; "The Tariff and the Trusts" (Feb. 24, 1912), *ibid.*, 407-409; and "Speech of Acceptance" (Aug. 7, 1912), *ibid.*, 471-472.

38 See, *e. g.*, Walter H. Page to Paul S. Reinsch, Aug. 13, Nov. 15, Dec. 10, Dec. 28, 1900, in *Paul S. Reinsch Papers, Correspondence, 1892-1908*. Collection owned by State Historical Society of Wisconsin (Madison).

39 As a member of the Chamber of Commerce's special committee on trade commission legislation, Rublee played a leading role in the Chamber's campaign to authorize the Commission to investigate world trade conditions and make appropriate recommendations to Congress. Hurley was a prominent Illinois industrialist who had introduced the pneumatic tool industry to the United States, had been an active member and president of the Illinois Manufacturers Association, and, as an articulate advocate of economic expansion abroad, had played a leading role in the organization of the National Foreign Trade Council. In 1913 he toured Latin America as an official trade commissioner for Wilson's Department of Commerce to investigate market and investment opportunities for United States industry and finance.

40 Link, *Wilson*, II, 139. It might also be noted that Link errs in stating (*Woodrow Wilson and the Progressive Era, 1910-1917*, N. Y., 1954, 74) that Rublee was prevented from serving on the Federal Trade Commission due to the Senate's refusal to confirm his nomination in deference to Senator Jacob H. Gallinger (Repub.—N.H.), who declared Rublee "personally obnoxious." Actually, Rublee served, under a recess appointment by Wilson, for about eighteen months, from March 16, 1915, to Sept. 8, 1916, before he was obliged to retire. See *Federal Trade Commission Decisions* (March 16, 1915, to June 30, 1919), Wash., 1920, I, p. 4; and Rublee, *op. cit.*, 120.

28

statesman" much of his time expounding the theme of expansion and downward revision of the tariff. Like Wilson he had been a gold-Democrat, and the views of the two men were strikingly similar in matters of trade expansion and the tariff. Indeed, Wilson, in January, 1912, acknowledged that "I primed myself on Mr. Redfield's [tariff] speeches."[41] Of greater significance, indicating Redfield's prominence in the corporate community and the degree to which he represented corporate opinion, Redfield had been president of the American Manufacturers Export Association (organized in 1910), which, to use Robert A. Brady's terminology, was a peak association of large corporate interests. As Secretary of Commerce, with Wilson's support and approval, he immediately undertook to reorganize the Bureau of Foreign and Domestic Commerce for more efficient service in promoting foreign trade, and submitted a bill to Congress for the creation of a system of commercial attachés and agents, and trade commissioners, which Congress passed in 1914. Between the two of them, Redfield and Hurley, again with Wilson's approval, instituted many of the mechanisms of business-government cooperation in domestic and foreign trade, including the encouragement of trade associations, that are usually regarded as initially introduced by Herbert Hoover while Secretary of Commerce during the 1920's. Finally, it is important to note that while Wilson permitted Secretary of State William Jennings Bryan to make many ambassadorial appointments on the basis of patronage obligations, he refused to permit Bryan to disturb the consular service.

Against this background, the attitude of corporation leaders toward the three major pieces of "New Freedom" legislation of 1913-1914 (Underwood Tariff, Federal Reserve, and Federal Trade Commission acts), as well as the extent to which that legislation affected foreign trade expansion and to which, in turn, the nature of the legislation was determined by considerations relating to such expansion, may be more clearly understood.

Between 1910 and 1914, corporate leaders, particularly those connected with the large corporations and banking houses, were unusually active in organizing themselves for the promotion of their interests and programmatic objectives in domestic and foreign affairs. In 1910 industrial corporations organized the American Manufacturers Export Association (AMEA); in 1912, these corporations, along with other business organizations, such as the American Asiatic Association (AAA), established the United States Chamber of Commerce; and in 1914 the AMEA, the AAA, and the Pan-American Society joined together to form the National Foreign Trade Council (NFTC). These were all what might be called "peak associations" of large corporate interests; but the NFTC may be legitimately considered a peak association of peak associations. The officers and memberships of these associations interlocked as intricately as did the directors of the huge industrial corporations and finance houses of the time.

Of the more significant manifestations of the Wilson administration's concern for the promotion of foreign trade and of the community of agreement between large corporate interests and that administration, therefore, one was its endorsement of the purposes of the first National Foreign Trade Convention, convened in Washington, D. C., May 27 and 28, 1914. The Convention, presided over by Alba B. Johnson, and the National Foreign

---

41 "The Tariff" (Jan. 3, 1912), *P P W W*, II, 330.

29

Trade Council subsequently established, with James A. Farrell as its president, were led and dominated by men representing the nation's greatest industrial, mercantile, and financial corporations.[42] As Johnson related, "This Convention had its inception at a meeting in New York some time ago" with Secretary of Commerce Redfield. He gave the idea for such a convention "his most cordial approval, and, therefore, it is fair to say" that he "is in a sense the Father of this Convention. . . ."[43] Edward N. Hurley, the first vice-chairman and later chairman of the Federal Trade Commission, also played a leading role in the organization of the Convention and in the Council's subsequent affairs.[44]

The Convention met in the afterglow of Secretary of State Bryan's appearance, in January, 1914, as guest of honor at the annual dinner of the American Asiatic Association, of which Willard Straight was then president.[45] At that time, the Underwood Tariff and Federal Reserve acts, measures most closely associated with the "New Freedom," had been passed by Congress. The Association's expressed purpose for inviting Bryan to the dinner, which was attended by leaders of the corporate community, was to exchange views with him on, and have him clarify, the administration's foreign policy. Emphasizing that the "era upon which we are entering is not only that of the Pacific Ocean, it must be one of Pacific development as well," Straight cited the new tariff as a stimulant for "carrying the war into the enemies' camp and competing abroad with those who will now invade our own market. . . ." And to the cheers of the diners, he observed that with the Panama Canal and the opportunity provided by the reserve act for the extension of foreign banking and investment, ". . . we are in a better position than at any time in our history aggressively to undertake the development of our export trade."[46] In response, Bryan pointed out that his duties as Secretary of State kept him "in touch with the expansion of American Commerce and the extension of American interests throughout the world," with which both he and the President were in "deep sympathy," and he assured the business men that the administration "will see that no industrial highwayman robs you. This government stands committed to the doctrine that these United States are entitled to the greatest possible industrial and commercial development." In this respect, like Straight, he singled out the tariff and reserve acts as decisive instrumentalities for giving the doctrine practical effect.[47]

42 *Official Report of the National Foreign Trade Convention* (1914), 15, 16, 457-458 (hereafter cited as NFTC, Proceedings). Johnson was himself president of the Baldwin Locomotive Works, and Farrell the president of the United States Steel Corporation.

43 *Ibid.*, 203-204.

44 *Ibid.*, 15, 17, 457.

45 Straight had served as agent of the American Banking Group in China during the days of the Six-Power Consortium, was associated with the House of Morgan, and was a leading participant in the organization of the NFTC.

46. The reserve act, as Straight noted, permitted "the establishment of branches of American banking institutions abroad," and with its provision for a commercial-acceptance system promised to "free vast sums for use in an international discount market and for the purchase of desirable foreign securities." *Journal of the American Asiatic Association*, XIV, 1 (Feb. 1914), 8 (hereafter cited as AAA *Jour.*).

47 The reserve act, according to Bryan, as a law the nation "long needed," would stimulate foreign trade "not only in the Orient but also throughout South America"; the new tariff meant "a larger commerce between our nation and the world, and in this increase the Orient will have her share," to the advantage not only of the public in general, but "especially" of "those merchants and manufacturers now turning their eyes to the Far East." McKinley's advocacy of tariff reduction "as a means of extending . . . our exports," was "a prophetic utterance": we "must buy if we would sell." *Ibid.*, 12-13.

30

The administration's endorsement of the National Foreign Trade Convention the following May assumed tangible forms. Secretary of Commerce Redfield delivered the opening address of the Convention on the morning of May 27 and he served as toastmaster at its banquet that night; Secretary of State Bryan delivered the main after-dinner speech at the banquet; and Wilson the next day received the delegates at the White House for a short interview.

As the Council later announced, the national importance of the Convention was "attested by the fact that its purpose [to promote foreign trade and a coordinated national foreign trade policy based upon the cooperation of government and business] was cordially indorsed by the President of the United States, who received the delegates at the White House; by the Secretary of State, who delivered, at the banquet, an outline of the administration's policy toward American business abroad; and by the Secretary of Commerce, who opened the convention. . . . "[48]

In his address to the delegates in the East Room of the White House, after having been introduced to them by Edward N. Hurley, Wilson declared his "wish to express . . . the feeling of encouragement that is given by the gathering of a body like this for such a purpose." For, he said, "There is nothing in which I am more interested than the fullest development of the trade of this country and its righteous conquest of foreign markets." Referring to Secretary Redfield's address of the previous day, Wilson confided: "I think that you will realize . . . that it is one of the things that we hold nearest to our heart that the government and you should cooperate in the most intimate manner in accomplishing our common object." He expressed the hope that this would be "only the first of a series of conferences of this sort with you gentlemen." In reply, Alba B. Johnson assured the President that as business men they realized "the deep interest which this government takes in promoting legitimate foreign trade. . . . "[49]

Bryan delivered two addresses at the banquet on the night of May 27, 1914, the first a short, prepared statement for release to the press, the second a lengthier extemporaneous speech. In the prepared speech Bryan declared the administration "earnestly desirous of increasing American foreign commerce and of widening the field of American enterprise. . . . " He reiterated its intention to cooperate with the business community to this end, and speaking for his own department he emphasized its "earnest purpose" to "obtain for Americans equality of opportunity in the development of the resources of foreign countries and in the markets of the world." Accordingly it was his "intention to employ every agency of the Department of State to extend and safeguard American commerce and legitimate American enterprises in foreign lands," consistent with the "sovereign rights of other governments."[50]

---

48 NFTC, *Proceedings* (1914), 8.
49 *Ibid.*, 392-393.
50 *Ibid.*, 206, 207. That this represented administration policy, not merely edifying rhetoric to win the favor of corporate interests, is corroborated, *inter alia*, by the exchange of notes during the summer of 1913 between Bryan and E. T. Williams (U. S. Chargé d' Affaires at Peking). Williams requested instructions "as to the attitude to be taken by this Legation towards financial transactions between American capitalists and the Chinese Government," in view of President Wilson's statement of March 18, 1913, repudiating the Six-Power Consortium and the Reorganization Loan. Referring to the passages in that statement that the American people "wish to participate . . . very generously, in the opening . . . [of] the almost untouched and perhaps unrivaled *(continued at bottom of next page)*

31

In his extemporaneous remarks, Bryan explained to the men of capital that his department's policy was Wilson's policy—what it "does in foreign affairs is but what the President desires." This meant, he said, "policies which will promote our industry abroad as well as home"; already, in the short time of the administration's existence, it had taken measures that would "tend directly and necessarily to promote commerce," such as the tariff and reserve acts. But "more than that," Bryan continued, the administration's efforts to win friends for the United States, safeguard the peace, and conclude commercial treaties constituted a broad contribution to the stabilization and extension of foreign economic expansion. "One sentence from President Wilson's Mobile speech has done a great deal to encourage commerce." When he there renounced territorial conquest as an object of United States policy in Latin America, " . . . he opened the doors of all the weaker countries to an invasion of American capital and American enterprise. (Applause.)"[51] As Bryan had put it at the Asiatic Association

resources of China," and that the U. S. government "is earnestly desirous of promoting the most extended and intimate trade relationship between this country and the Chinese Republic," Williams suggested as his understanding of the administration's policy that the State Department would support "industrial" loans and investments for the development of railways and mineral resources, secured upon the assets and earnings of such enterprises, but not "financial loans" to the Chinese provincial and central governments secured upon government revenues. Bryan replied that ". . . the Legation is right in assuming that the Department is extremely interested in promoting, in every proper way, the legitimate enterprises of American citizens in China and in developing to the fullest extent the commercial relations between the two countries." He continued, "It may be stated, in general, that this Government expects that American enterprise should have opportunity everywhere abroad to compete for contractual favors on the same footing as any foreign competitors, and this implies also equal opportunity to an American competitor to make good his ability to execute the contract. . . . [This Government] stands ready, if wrong be done toward an American citizen in his business relations with a foreign government, to use all proper effort toward securing just treatment for its citizens. *This rule applies as well to financial contracts as to industrial engagements.*" (Emphasis added). Dept. of State, *Papers Relating to the Foreign Relations of the United States*, 1913, 183-187, 170-171. It is essential to note that the conditions outlined by Bryan in this note and in one cited by him from Secretary of State Richard Olney to Minister Charles Denby in 1896 (*ibid.*, 1897, 56), delimiting the extent of government support for U. S. enterprise abroad (*i. e.*, refusing special support for one U.S. firm to the exclusion of others, refusing to guarantee the execution of contracts or the success of an enterprise, and renouncing any commitment to intercede forcibly in the internal affairs of foreign nations on behalf of U.S. capitalists), were all well established principles affirmed alike by the Dollar Diplomatists (such as Taft, Knox, Calhoun, Straight, Warren, Mark) in their public statements and diplomatic notes, and by their predecessors. These delimiting principles were in no way peculiar to the Wilson administration, and cannot be considered as distinguishing its policy from that of Taft and Knox.

51 NFTC, *Proceedings* (1914), 208-210. Along with the Mobile speech, the statement repudiating the Six-Power Consortium is most often cited to substantiate the view that Wilson repudiated Dollar Diplomacy. If this is meant as a repudiation of government support of corporate interests in expanding investments and exports abroad, then as already indicated in the immediately preceding text and in footnote 50, above, neither the Mobile speech nor the consortium statement is amenable to such interpretation. Wilson's consortium statement not only emphasized the government's intention to promote United States participation in the development of China and the closest of commercial relations between the two countries, but also specifically declared, ". . . The present administration will urge and support the legislative measures necessary to give American merchants, manufacturers, contractors, and engineers the banking and other financial facilities which they now lack and without which they are at a serious disadvantage as compared with their industrial and commercial rivals. This is its duty. This is the main material interest of its citizens in the development of China. . . ." *Foreign Relations*, 1913, 171. *Cf.* the versions of and references to the statement in George H. Blakeslee (ed.), *Recent Developments in China* (N. Y., 1913), 159-160; John V. A. MacMurray (ed.), *Treaties and Agreements with and concerning China, 1894-1919* (N. Y., 1921), II, 1025; Charles Vevier, *The United States and China, 1906-1913* (Rutgers Univ. Press, N. J., 1955), 210. All these versions include the reference to banking and other financial facilities needed for effective competition in Chinese markets. (These facilities were regarded as essential by corporate interests to foreign economic expansion and were provided in 1913 by sections 13, 14, and 25 of the Federal Reserve Act, which permitted branch banking abroad and the establishment of a domestic discount market for foreign trade commercial acceptances). Unfortunately, in the widely used *Documents of American History*, edited by Henry S. Commager, the consortium statement, there entitled "The Repudiation of 'Dollar Diplomacy'," is entirely reproduced, except for the passage referring to the banking and other financial facilities (5th ed., 1949, Doc. #390). For further evidence regarding the Wilson administration's intentions in repudiating the consortium, see Secretary of State Bryan's address before the Asiatic Association in January, 1914, where he explained, ". . . The new administration in withdrawing approval from the Chinese loan did not question the good faith or good intent of those who had seen in it a means of increasing our influence, prestige and commercial power in China. The

(continued at bottom of next page)

dinner, " . . . The doctrine of universal brotherhood is not sentimentalism—it is practical philosophy . . . The government could not create trade, but it was its "duty" to "create an environment in which it can develop."[52] He looked forward with "great expectations" to the extension of United States trade and investment abroad; the Convention itself provided "evidence that we are going forward," and the statistics showing the increase in exports of manufactured goods left "no doubt" that the United States could compete successfully with the European industrial nations "in the newer countries that are awaiting complete development," and that the United States would thus become "an increasing factor in the development" of such countries.[53]

Bryan's approach to economic expansion exemplifies a unified world view, embracing "moralism" and "commercialism" as interdependent and mutually consistent elements, that was so common to the expansionists of the time; the underlying assumptions of the "Good Neighbor" policy of later administrations were not basically different; and like the policy of Wilson or Straight it emphasized not merely trade but also "development" of agrarian countries, and the government's responsibility to foster those operations.

Promising the complete support of his Department for the extension of markets and investments abroad, and inviting the close co-operation between the business men and the State Department, Bryan told the corporate leaders, "I promise you that the State Department—every agency of it—will be back of every honest business man in pushing legitimate enterprise in all parts of the world. (Applause.)" To emphasize the community of purpose between the Department and the corporate interests, he continued by extending a colorful analogy: "In Spanish-speaking countries hospitality is expressed by a phrase, 'My house is your house.' . . . I can say, not merely in courtesy—but as a fact—my Department is your department; the ambassadors, the ministers and the consuls are all yours. It is their business to look after your interests and to guard your rights." If any of them failed to fulfill his responsibility, advised Bryan, "we shall be pleased to have you report them." For his part, the Department would "endeavor to open all doors to you. We shall endeavor to make all people friendly to you . . . "[54]

Given the general approach to expansion shared by men such as Wilson, Straight, Bryan, and corporate spokesmen, the question of "inner" motive is somewhat irrelevant. For example, what may be said of Straight's "inner" motive when he spoke of trade as the means to peace; or of the

President believed that a different policy was more consistent with the American position, and that it would in the long run be more advantageous to our commerce. . . ." See also Willard Straight's remark on the same occasion that though many business men ". . . have interpreted the announcement . . . to mean that the American Government would not extend to our bankers the support which those familiar with trade conditions in China consider necessary . . . I personally feel assured that this impression . . . is not justified. . . ." AAA *Jour.,* XIV, 1 (Feb. 1914), 12, 8-9; cf. editorial in *ibid.,* 2. The present author examines this question in greater detail in his master's thesis.

52 AAA *Jour,* XIV, 1 (Feb. 1914), 13. *Cf.* Straight's remark: "The true armies of world peace . . . are the merchants engaged in international trade. In this army, the Secretary of State is a Chief of Staff, and the Ambassador a Corps Commander. We of this [Asiatic] Association are the rank and file. . . ." *Ibid.,* 8. Also, that of M. A. Oudin, manager of the Foreign department of General Electric Co., that while the government could not create trade, it could "point the way to private enterprise." NFTC, *Proceedings* (1914), 366, 367, 379-380.

53 *Ibid., Proceedings* (1914), 207, 208.

54 *Ibid.,* 210-211.

33

Steel Corporation's president, James A. Farrell, when he told the Convention: " . . .there is no factor which is so much involved in . . . [the nation's] material prosperity as the export trade," and then proceeded to say that "due to its great significance with respect to the economic conditions of our financial relations with the markets of the world, the export trade is likewise a vital factor in international affairs . . . The contest today is for supremacy in the trade of the world's markets, because that country which is a commerical power is also a power in other respects."[55] The important point is that they held in common the assumption that expansion of markets and investment abroad was indispensable to the stability and growth of the political economy. As Redfield had put it at the banquet while introducing Bryan as the next speaker, the mission of his fellow diners was "to make this land of ours one of continual increasing prosperity." For he continued:

> . . . we have learned the lesson now, that our factories are so large that their output at full time is greater than America's market can continuously absorb. We know now that if we will run full time all the time, we must do it by reason of the orders we take from lands beyond the sea. To do less than that means homes in America in which the husbands are without work; to do that means factories that are shut down part of the time. And because the markets of the world are greater and steadier than the markets of any country can be, and because we are strong, we are going out, you and I, into the markets of the world to get our share. (Applause.)[56]

The record leaves no reason to doubt that the knowledgeable corporate leaders understood and accepted as genuine the administration's policy statements.[57] The difficulty in their view, lay not with the administration, but with the people. In this respect, upon closer examination, it is apparent that many of the pronouncements by business men in this period that have been interpreted as directed against the Wilson administration, were more often directed against an "unenlightened" public and/or hostile senators or congressmen. As one business man put it, the public must realize "that governmental assistance to American shipping and the American export trade is not only a business but a patriotic policy, pertaining to national defense as well as to our industrial welfare."[58] Or as Willard Straight phrased it, under current conditions of public opinion, "any administration may be attacked if it utilizes the power of the Government for the profit of private interests, no matter what indirect advantage might accrue to the country as a whole." The problem was to educate the people to accept government support of private foreign investments as action not on behalf of a special, but of the national, interest.[59]

In the context of Wilson's approach to both foreign trade and the "trust" question, and of the community of views between large corporate interests and his administration in these areas, the significance for foreign trade of the Federal Trade Commission Act, as the legislative embodiment of the Rule of Reason, may be better comprehended.

55 *Ibid.*, 35, 36.
56 *Ibid.*, 205. For similar expressions on the indispensability of exports to the nation's prosperity by business and political leaders, see *Ibid.*, 6, 7, 70, 74, 80, 86, 117, 140, 141, 214, 218, 230-231, 285.
57 See, *e. g.*, the remark of M. A. Oudin of General Electric, *Ibid.*, 366, 367, 379-380.
58 P. H. W. Ross, president of the National Marine League, *Ibid.*, 143.
59 *Ibid.*, 174-187.

34

It was generally recognized in business circles that the large industrial corporations were most suited to successful export trade, and that the rapid rise in exports of manfacurers from the late 1890's to 1914 had been due largely to the operations of these corporations. The large corporations enjoyed low unit costs necessary for competition in world markets, particularly in the capital and durable goods industries. Their superior reserves and intimate connections with the great financial institutions enabled them to carry the expense of foreign sales promotion, offer attractive foreign credit facilities, and reap the benefits of foreign loans and concessions, all indispensable to an expanding and stable export trade. It was these corporations that were most intimately involved in the "development" of agrarian nations. Since the export of manufactured goods was considered primary in maintaining the nation's international exchanges, in liquidating foreign debts, and in guaranteeing domestic prosperity, the success of any business or governmental policy looking to the promotion of export trade and the achievement of these related objectives appeared to stand or fall with the large corporation. A domestic policy, therefore, designed to atomize large corporations could only prove self-defeating.

These were the points emphasized by such prominent spokesmen for large corporate interests as John D. Ryan, president of the Amalgamated Copper Company, M. A. Oudin of General Electric, and Alba B. Johnson of the Baldwin Locomotive Works.[60] As Johnson put it, "To attack our business interests because by reason of intelligent management they have grown strong is to cripple them in the struggle for the world's trade."[61] But their views, in so far as they related to the maintenance of large business units, were in no essential respect different from those of Wilson, whose attitude, as already indicated, may be summed up by the declaration in his Acceptance Speech: " . . . I am not afraid of anything that is normal."[62]

It is important to note, therefore, that the criticisms of "antitrust" bills pending in Congress by speakers at the 1914 National Foreign Trade Convention were leveled not against Wilson and his administration, but against "radicals" in Congress and what was considered misguided and dangerous public opinion. They particularly applied to the policy of the previous Taft administration, which in its last year and a half had "mined the Sherman Act for all it was worth."[63] But Wilson's position on the "trust" question was clear to all who read or heard his speeches, at any rate by early 1914; indeed, in his special address on the "trusts" to Congress in January, 1914, he had specifically declared, " . . . no measures of sweeping or novel change are necessary. . . . our object is *not* to unsettle business or anywhere seriously to break its established courses athwart."[64] Programmatically his position centered upon the legislative proposals advanced since the Hepburn amendments of 1908-1909, by large corporate interests

---

60 See their remarks in *Ibid.*, 167, 168, 375-378, 327-328.

61 *Ibid.*, 327-328.

62 *P P W W*, II, 464; *ibid.*

63 Robert H. Wiebe, "The House of Morgan and the Executive, 1905-1913," *American Historical Review*, LXV, 1 (Oct. 1959), 58. *Cf. The Federal Antitrust Law with Amendments, List of Cases Instituted by the United States, and Citations of Cases Decided Thereunder or Relating Thereto,* Jan. 1, 1914, in Sen. Comm. on the Jud., *Hearings . . . together with Briefs and Memoranda . . . Compiled for Use in Consideration of H. R. 15657,* 63d Cong., 2d Sess. (Wash., 1914), 164-183.

64 *P P W W*, III, 82, 83. Emphasis in original.

35

through such organizations as the Chicago Association of Commerce, the National Civic Federation, and later the Chamber of Commerce. And by the end of 1914, large corporate interests found that they could look with satisfaction upon the status of the nation's "antitrust" laws.[65]

The "New Freedom" legislation on "trusts" bore upon matters of foreign trade expansion in a more overt way. In February, 1914, the Chamber of Commerce devoted its principal session, in which Secretary Redfield participated, to a discussion of the administration's trust program.[66] It was here that the Chamber appointed its special committee on trade commission legislation, of which William L. Saunders and Rublee were members. Other members included president of the Chamber R. G. Rhett, Professor Henry R. Seager of Columbia University, Charles R. Van Hise, president of the University of Wisconsin, and Guy E. Tripp, chairman of the board of directors of the Westinghouse Electric Manufacturing Company. One of the committee's recommendations, issued in the spring of 1914, urged that Congress "direct the Commission [when established] to investigate and report to Congress at the earliest practicable date on the advisability of amending the Sherman Act to allow a greater degree of cooperation" in the export trade. By a vote of 538 to 67 the Chamber's membership approved this specific recommendation (as did the National Foreign Trade Convention in May, 1914), along with the broader one supporting a trade commission act.[67] Accordingly, in the drafting of the act, which Rublee wrote, it was this Chamber committee that inserted word for word section 6(h), which authorized the trade commission to investigate world trade conditions and submit appropriate recommendations to Congress.[68] With Rublee and Hurley appointed by Wilson as two of the agency's five commissioners, the FTC undertook and completed in its first year of operation four investigations, three of which dealt with foreign trade conditions.[69] One of these resulted in the two volume *Report on Cooperation in American Export Trade,* which recommended that Congress pass what was to become the Export Trade (Webb-Pomerene) Act of 1918 permitting cartels in the export trade, a bill which Wilson strongly supported.

The requirements of foreign trade promotion also influenced, in a negative way, the nature of the Clayton Act. As Oudin reported to the Foreign Trade Convention of May, 1914, " . . . the Committee on the Judiciary of the House . . . has reported a bill containing strict prohibitions against

---

65 See, *e.g.,* the report of William L. Saunders to the second National Foreign Trade Convention in January, 1915. Chairman of the board of the Ingersoll-Rand Company, Saunders was also a charter member of the National Foreign Trade Council, and had served with Rublee on the Chamber of Commerce's special committee that played a leading part in drafting the trade commission act. Saunders observed that the Sherman law prohibited only those restraints of trade that were "unreasonable or contrary to the public welfare," and that there was "no likelihood" of its becoming "any more drastic." The Clayton Act "defines a monopoly and . . . announces certain moral principles to which we all agree;" while the trade commission act "prevents unfair methods of competition," and as such "is the most wholesome legislation . . . that has been passed recently" in the matter of trusts. Saunders criticized *opponents* of the trade commission act for not seeing that "cooperation among business men—cooperation and concentration—is wholesome business and a good economic condition." NFTC, *Proceedings* (1915), 54, 56.

66 See *La Follette's Weekly,* VI, 8 (Feb. 21, 1914), 1-2.

67 Sen. Comm. on Interstate Commerce, "Promotion of Export Trade," *Hearings,* 64th Cong., 2d Sess., 11.

68 *Ibid.,* 10-12.

69 *Annual Report of the Federal Trade Commission for the Year Ended June 30, 1916,* 18.

36

discriminations in prices for exclusive agencies, but providing that such prohibitions shall apply only in respect to commodities sold within the jurisdiction of the United States. This emphatic recognition of the distinction between domestic and export commerce reflects the growing disposition of the Government to render sympathetic assistance to American exporters. . . . "[70]

Just as the character of "New Freedom" legislation concerning the regulation of business related to the requirements of foreign trade promotion and reflected a community of views between the corporate community and the Wilson administration, the same was true, as already indicated, of the two most important "New Freedom" laws passed in 1913, the Underwood Tariff and the Federal Reserve Acts.

When Bryan, in his banquet address to the Foreign Trade Convention delegates, cited the tariff and reserve acts as measures taken by the administration for the promotion of foreign trade, he was not assuming the posture of protesting too much, nor was he merely waxing politically expedient to please his audience: the large corporate spokesmen among the delegates analyzed the two laws in precisely the same way. The two laws, it should be noted, were passed against the background of a trend among large industrial and financial interests, which had visibly emerged at least a decade before, toward tariff and banking structures oriented *(inter alia)* to their foreign trade and investment requirements. Bryan pointed to the elementary principle underlying the new tariff: "if we are to sell abroad, we must buy from people beyond our borders." The reserve act "will do more to promote trade in foreign lands than any other one thing that has been done in our history"; it had "set a nation free."[71] From no less a figure in large corporate circles than John E. Gardin, vice-president of the National City Bank of New York, came a similar view. Complaining of the nation's immaturity in matters of international finance, Gardin found encouragement in the tariff and reserve acts. " . . . The administration . . . certainly has given us two things of which we might be proud: one, the reduction of the tariff . . . opening up the markets of the world,—if we want to sell we have got to buy; and the other is the Federal Reserve Law, which relieves us from the bondage" of an outmoded banking law, providing "relief just as important as the emancipation of the slaves. . . ." In view of these laws, Gardin looked forward to the projected program of the NFTC, as working "for the benefit of all those who wish to partake . . . of the new freedom."[72]

Among those spokesmen of industrial and financial interests who

---

70 NFTC, *Proceedings* (1914), 379; *cf.* House Comm. on Jud., *Hearings on Trust Legislation* (2 vols.), 63d Cong., 2d Sess., Serial 7, 1914, II, 1960-1963.

71 NFTC, *Proceedings* (1914), 208-209.

72 *Ibid.*, 249, 250-251. See also the remarks of Fred Brown Whitney, chairman of the board of directors of the Lake Torpedo Boat Co., Alba B. Johnson, Clarence J. Owens, managing director of the Southern Commercial Congress (at whose convention in 1913 Wilson had delivered his Mobile address), Herbert S. P. Deans, manager of the foreign exchange department of the Merchants Loan and Trust Company Bank of Chicago, Edward N. Hurley, representing the Illinois Manufacturers Association. *Ibid.*, 251, 22-23, 90-91, 304, 291. Whitney: the reserve act represented the people's "mandate—eternal and omnipotent—that the United States shall become a World Power in international finance and trade. . . ." Johnson: the new tariff was "part of the preparation . . . for this great forward movement in the world's market;" the reserve act "is designed particularly to facilitate exchange transactions with other nations. . . ." Owens: along with the Panama Canal the reserve act "announced the beginning of a period of direct financial relations" with Latin American markets, "giving America the chance, for the first time, to compete in this regard with Great Britain and Germany."

37

praised the Underwood Tariff, representatives of smaller interests were conspicuously absent. It is a mistake to view the Underwood measure as part of a "New Freedom" crusade against large corporations. It *was* part of the "New Freedom" program; but the heathens were not necessarily the large corporations. It was part of an attack on "special privilege" conceived to be in conflict with the national interest understood in terms of the conditions of modern times; but it was the special privilege cherished by smaller and by non-industrial interests, no longer needed by the larger interests as export trade became increasingly more important to them.

Aside from its immediate intent to stimulate export trade, the tariff, consistent with Wilson's views, sought to enforce industrial efficiency by inviting world-wide competition, which would result in making United States industry and finance a more formidable competitor in world markets. The larger industrial interests could withstand, and expect to fatten on, such competition, but not the smaller. Those items placed on the free list by the tariff were, in the majority, articles of food, clothing, and raw materials, industries occupied by the "little man." Large corporations engaged in the capital and durable goods industries, and most heavily involved in the export trade so far as manufactures were concerned, could approve this provision, because should the tariff have the intended effect, it would operate to keep wage levels down, reduce costs of materials, and in the process enable more effective competition in world markets, aside from increasing the profit rate. The issue was analogous to the great Corn Law debates in England during the previous century, where the industrialists sought to abolish import duties at the expense of producers of food and raw stuffs. Wilson, after all, had learned well from Cobden and Bright, the apostles of what has been aptly termed the "imperialism of free trade."[73]

At the same time, those items of heavy industry placed upon the free list, such as steel rails and agricultural machinery and implements, were already produced by the larger United States corporations with an efficiency and at a cost of production sufficient to permit not only successful competition in world markets in general, but within the national markets of the European industrial nations as well, a point Wilson frequently made. Of further aid to such competition, moreover, the Underwood Tariff granted drawbacks on exported items comprised in part or in whole of imported materials subject to import duties.[74]

In effect, the Underwood tariff strengthened the position of the larger corporations as against the smaller, and as against producers of agricultural materials. In this case, legal reform served the interest of those seeking to buttress the socio-economic *status quo*, while adherence to established law and institutions rallied those whose interest lay in forestalling the onward rush of that *status quo*. Accordingly, the greatest danger to the Underwood bill's downward revisions while pending in Congress "came

---

73 See John Gallagher and Ronald Robinson, "The Imperialism of Free Trade," *The Economic History Review*, VI, 1, Second Series (Aug. 1953), 1-15. This is not meant to imply that the Underwood Tariff was a free trade tariff; it was, in Taussig's terms, a "competitive tariff." F. W. Taussig, *The Tariff History of the United States* (8th edition: N.Y., 1937), 418-422.

74 Federal Trade Commission, *Report on Cooperation in American Export Trade* (2 vols.), June 30, 1916, I, 162; Taussig, *op. cit.*, 425-449.

38

from a horde of lobbyists," among whom the "owners and managers of industries that produced the great bulk of American industrial products were unconcerned and took no part. . . . " As Link concludes, the Underwood duties assumed their greatest significance "in so far as they reflected a lessening of the pressure from the large industrial interests for a McKinley type of protection."[75] It is understandable, therefore, that among the Congressional critics of the Underwood tariff, as with the reserve law and the trade commission and Clayton acts, were "radical" and insurgent Democrats and Republicans claiming to represent the smaller and agrarian interests. In so far as the tariff, perhaps more dramatically than other issues, brought into unified focus the elements of efficiency, bigness in business, foreign trade, and an expanding sphere of enterprise—the last holding out the promise of more room for the "little man"—it may be accurately described as one of the high points of Wilsonian reform.

It is not meant to imply that the corporate community had no criticisms of the Underwood Tariff or Federal Reserve Act; but large corporate interests in particular viewed the new tariff either as a worthwhile experiment or more positively as sound policy, and business opinion overwhelmingly viewed the reserve law as basically sound, in need of perfecting amendments, rather than as a measure directed against their interests. The conflict over the reserve system bill during 1913 had not revolved so much around the provisions of the bill as around the question of how and by whom those provisions should be administered, except in so far as the "radical" and agrarian Republicans and Democrats insisted upon provisions that Wilson rejected. Otherwise, with respect to the manner of administering the system, the division lay not between Wilson and the "small" interests on the one side and "big business" on the other: the large corporate interests themselves were divided, particularly, the evidence indicates, along industrial and financial lines. As Link notes, the great mass of non-banking business opinion approved the bill, and in October, 1913, for example, both the Merchants Association of New York and the United States Chamber of Commerce (the latter by a vote of 306-17) endorsed it.[76]

The Federal Reserve Act may be interpreted, with respect to the issues raised here, in terms of a movement of large finance and industrial corporate interests, extending back to and before the National Monetary Commission, for branch banking, a commercial acceptance market for the facilitation of foreign trade and investment, and a reserve system that would protect the gold stock from foreign and domestic runs; a movement that, by expanding the credit structure, would reduce industrial corporations' dependence upon the money markets for investment capital, and insulate industrial operations from stock market fluctuations and speculators; a movement that Wilson approved and responded to favorably without himself being in any way responsible for its initiation, just as in the case of the movement for the Federal Trade Commission Act.

Indeed, upon his election, Wilson had no well-defined specific program; he had a general approach, and even his "specific" proposals were

---

75 Link, *Wilson*, II, 186, 196. The lobbyists included representatives of such interests as wool, sugar, textile manufacturers, citrus fruits.

76 Link, *Wilson and the Progressive Era*, 51.

couched in general terms. He had identified himself with, and then given ideological and political leadership to, those movements with which his general approach corresponded, and which therefore corresponded with the concept of national interest embraced by that general approach. These movements—what are known as the Progressive reform movements (and they were reforms)—were movements led by and consisting of large corporate interests and political and intellectual leaders affirming the large corporate industrial capitalist system, and convinced of the necessity of institutionalized reforms, legal and otherwise, to accommodate the nation's law and habits, and the people's thinking, to the new corporate business structure and its requirements, domestic and foreign. As Wilson had put it, laws "meant for business done by individuals" had to be "satisfactorily adjusted to business done by great combinations," requiring "open efforts to accommodate law to the material development which has so strengthened the country."

Wilson's careful and emphatic distinction between the large corporation and the "trust" may be cited as one of the more forceful illustrations substantiating this formulation. A corollary of his evolutionary historicism, this distinction, in terms of Wilson's programmatic proposals, was decisive to his approach to the "trust" question, just as it was to that of the Bureau of Corporations under Garfield and Smith, and to that of Roosevelt, Taft, Perkins, Gary, and Croly. The large corporation, in this view, and the restriction of competition by corresponding forms of "cooperation," were the inevitable product of natural economic development. The "trust," however, was an artificial contrivance of predatory design, deliberately created by unscrupulous business men for undue ends. Accordingly, Wilson believed that while " . . . the elaboration of business upon a great co-operative scale is characteristic of our time and has come about by the natural operation of western civilization," this was different from saying that the "trusts" were inevitable. " . . . Big business is no doubt to a large extent necessary and natural. The development of business upon a great scale, upon a great scale of cooperation, is inevitable, and, . . . is probably desirable. But that is a very different matter from the development of trusts, because the trusts have not grown. They have been artificially created; they have been put together not by natural processes, but by the will, the deliberate planning will, of men who . . . wished to make their power secure against competition." On the other hand, " . . . any large corporation built up by the legitimate processes of business, by economy, by efficiency, is natural; and I am not afraid of it, no matter how big it grows. . . ."[77]

Conservative-historicism, with Edmund Burke as one of its more prominent spokesmen, regards the politico-economic sphere of society "as a completely irrational one which cannot be fabricated by mechanical methods but which grows of its own accord. This outlook relates everything to the decisive dichotomy between 'construction according to calculated plan' and 'allowing things to grow.' . . . " " . . . A mode of thought is thus created which conceives of history as the reign of pre- and super-rational forces."[78]

77 *The New Freedom*, 163-165, 166.

78 Mannheim, *Ideology and Utopia*, 120, 121.

40

This mode of thought, transmitted to Wilson in particular from Burke, may be traced as a central thread winding not only through the early twentieth century liberalism (Progressivism) of Theodore Roosevelt, Croly, *et al.*, as well as Wilson, but also through the liberalism of such presently prominent bourgeois ideological leaders as Adolf A. Berle, Jr., who states: " . . . Unlike the socialist commissariat, the American corporation is not a product of doctrine and dogma; it is an organic growth. . . . "[79] With respect to the basic structure of society, modern liberalism regards as legitimate only those institutions that it conceives as emerging independently of and beyond the deliberate, conscious determination of men; the underlying principle is submission to natural law, as distinguished, for example, from Marxism, which demands the understanding of objective laws of social development operating independently of man's will precisely in order to subject social development to man's conscious will; and as distinguished also from French Enlightenment social thought, which assumed that man could determine his society in accordance with Reason.[80] Conscious determination by men assumes its legitimate and proper function, from the modern liberal standpoint, only in facilitating natural evolution (as manifested in the basic structure of society as it is), and devising appropriate adjustments to it through parliamentary means (reforms).

The sharp and protracted ideological and social conflicts of the late nineteenth and early twentieth century, revolving around the corporate reorganization of the economy and erupting in the great "anti-trust" debates of that period, suggest that the growth of the corporation was not so "organic" as modern United States liberals insist; that capitalists and like-minded political and intellectual leaders fought hard and consciously, with "doctrine and dogma" and with economic, political, and legal strategem, to establish the large corporation, in an historically short period of time, as the dominant mode of business enterprise, and to attain popular acceptance of that development. Nevertheless, the "allowing-things-to-grow" doctrine achieves a triumphant renaissance, as the unifying conception, in twentieth century United States liberalism, which may be accurately referred to as corporate-liberalism (though now Burke is left neglected backstage and Croly given the curtain calls). It is the fundamental element that makes modern United States liberalism the bourgeois Yankee cousin of modern European and English social-democracy.[81]

Within this essentially natural-law framework, while consistently hold-

---

79 In his Foreword to Mason (ed.), *The Corporation in Modern Society*, p. ix. In the same way, and characteristically, Wilson anticipated the downward revision of the tariff not "because men in this country have changed their theories," but because "the condus of America are going to bust through [the high tariff]. . . ." " Efficiency" (Jan. 27, 1912), *P P W W*, V, 360.

80 In this connection, Wilson's conservative-historicism was reinforced by his adaptation of Darwin's theory of biological organic evolution to social evolution, though not in the form of survival-of-the-fittest "Social Darwinism" associated with Spencer, Sumner, and Fiske. See *Constitutional Government in the United States* (N. Y., 1908), 56-57, 199-200, and *The New Freedom*, 46, 47-48, where Wilson describes his view of government and social life as organic, Darwinian, as distinguishd from the mechanistic, Newtonian conception of Montesquieu, the Enlightenment thinkers, and Jefferson. *Cf.* also, Diamond, *Econ. Thought of Wilson*, 39, 47, and Link, *Wilson*, I, 21-22.

81 Herbert Marcuse, *Reason and Revolution* (2nd edition: N.Y., 1954), 398-401. Since completing this essay the author's attention has been drawn to Arnold A. Rogow's "Edmund Burke and the American Liberal Tradition," *The Antioch Review* (Summer, 1957), 255-265, which analyzes the decisive relevance of Burke to Wilsonian liberalism in particular and modern U.S. liberalism in general.

41

ing that the large industrial corporations were natural and beneficent products of social evolution, Wilson attributed much of the evils with which they were popularly associated to financiers, *dei ex machina*, manipulating corporate securities and practices for speculative profit and creating artificial corporate structures for monopolistic advantage.[82] At the same time, by tying credit and currency mechanisms to the "natural laws" of commerce, that is, by basing the banking system upon commercial paper rather than upon government bonds, and building up a reserve system, measures long sought by large financial and industrial corporate interests, the federal reserve law corresponded with Wilson's view that trade and investment should be set "free" to pursue their "natural" course, unhindered by the arbitrary will of a few financiers; in theory, it would encourage greater competition (through greater opportunities for investment borrowing), and permit "little men" to obtain credit with which to start or maintain a business enterprise of their own, though no longer in the central areas of production, transportation, or communication. *Mutatis mutandis*, Wilson's position on the tariff flowed from similar considerations: the government's role was to provide business with the "environment" best suited to the assertion of its "natural" course.

Wilson held no dogmatic views on the question of the extent of government intervention in economic affairs—he had long believed that the state should intervene so far as "experience permits or the times demand"—and with respect to the reserve law, he had by June, 1913, firmly decided upon government control of the central reserve board, in the face of stiff banker opposition. The compromise that resulted constituted a concession to the large banking interests. After the bill's passage, and the announcement of Wilson's appointments to the central reserve board, the large banks' spokesmen, as well as spokesmen for large industrial corporations, expressed widespread satisfaction,[83] just as they had in the case of the Underwood Tariff and Federal Trade Commission acts.

In this way, Wilson emerged as a foremost ideological and political leader of a social movement affirming industrial corporate capitalism, and as the pre-eminent personality in the nation's public life acting as a bridge of communication between that movement and the public (or, the electorate to which the movement appealed), popularizing the movement's ideology and program, and making them understandable and acceptable to the people in terms of the nation's traditions, evolutionary development, and "destiny." The ideology embraced a neo-Comtean positivism that (in European

---

82 See, *e. g.*, "Law or Personal Power" (Apr. 13, 1908), *P P W W*, II, 29.

83 See annual address of American Bankers' Association president Arthur Reynolds at the 1914 convention, and his later remarks at the same convention. *Proceedings of the Fortieth Annual Convention of the American Bankers' Association*, Richmond, Va., Oct. 12-16, 1914, pp. 57-68, 312-315. See also letters expressing approval of the Federal Reserve Act from George M. Reynolds, president of Continental and Commercial National Bank of Chicago, A. Barton Hepburn, chairman of the board, Chase National Bank, and A. J. Hemphill, president of Guaranty Trust Company of N.Y., to F. H. Goff (president of Cleveland Trust Co.), president of Bankers' Association's Trust Company Section, dated Sept. 23, Oct. 9, Oct. 5, 1914, respectively, in *ibid.*, 305-308. *Cf. La Follette's Weekly*, VI, 4 (Jan. 24, 1914), 3, where Jacob H. Schiff of Kuhn, Loeb & Co., is quoted praising the reserve law as "legislation highly pleasing to me." La Follette, who opposed the measure, remarked, ". . . The published reports that Wall Street banking interests were fighting the Administration's currency bill tooth and nail now appear somewhat pale in the light of the enthusiastic approval Wall Street is bestowing upon this law." See also, Link, *Wilson*, II, 451-452, 454-455.

42

terms) Wilson, the conservative-historicist and modified Manchestrian liberal, was eminently qualified to serve. Wilson's position was not that of a representative of the "little man," or the "middle class," *against* "big business"; but that of one who, affirming the large corporate industrial capitalist system, was concerned with establishing the legal and institutional environment most conducive to the system's stability and growth, while at the same time preserving some place within the system for the "little man." His formula was fair competition and impartial access to credit at home, and expansion of the economic frontier abroad, upon the assumption that the wider the market and the more impersonal its conditions, the more room and opportunity for the "little man" to coexist side by side with the big. The very conditions of industrial production and of foreign economic expansion, however, made the "little man," as an independent entrepreneur, increasingly irrelevant to the national economy, except in peripheral spheres of services and distribution. Theodore Roosevelt sought to meet this disturbing reality by acknowledging it and insisting upon equal opportunity for every young man to rise within the established corporate structures. While similarly insisting upon such equality, Wilson refused to concede the irrelevance of the "little man"; but his refusal was not a matter of sentimentality: it stemmed from his fear that given a growing irrelevance of "little men" in the nation's economy, fewer and fewer people would retain a stake in the capitalist system, and more and more would lose hope for betterment under capitalism and turn toward socialism or other forms of radicalism.[84] As such, the Wilsonian and Rooseveltian variants of Progressivism signified, if not the birth, then the coming of age, of twentieth century United States liberalism, whose present-day fundamentals, converging upon large-scale corporate capitalism at home and economic expansion abroad, remain genetically true to the components of Wilson's worldview, their immediate parental source.

According to the generally accepted interpretation offered by Arthur S. Link, Wilsonian Progressivism, as applied and developed during Wilson's two terms as president from 1913 to 1921, can be divided into two periods:

84 As Wilson advised leading business men in his address at the Annual Banquet of the Economic Club in New York, May 23, 1912 (*P P W W*, II, 446, 449-451): ". . . How would it suit the prosperity of the United States, how would it suit the success of business, to have a people that went every day sadly or sullenly to their work? How would the future look to you if you felt that the aspiration has gone out of most men, the confidence of success, the hope that they might change their condition, if there was everywhere the feeling that there was somewhere covert dictation, private arrangement as to who should be in the inner circle of privilege and who should not, a more or less systematic and conscious attempt to dictate and dominate the economic life of the country? Do you not see that just as soon as the old self-confidence of America, . . . as her old boasted advantages of individual liberty and opportunity are taken away, all the energy of her people begins to subside, to slacken, to grow loose and pulpy, without fibre, and men simply cast around to see that the day does not end disastrously with them."

"What is the alternative, gentlemen? You have heard the rising tide of socialism. . . Socialism is not growing in influence in this country as a programme. It is merely that the ranks of protestants are being recruited. . . If it becomes a programme, then we shall have to be very careful how we propose a competing programme . . . the programme of socialism would not work; but there is no use saying what will not work unless you can say what will work.

". . . If you want to oust socialism you have got to propose something better. It is a case, if you will allow me to fall into the language of the vulgar, of 'put up or shut up.' . . . It is by constructive purpose that you are going to govern and save the United States. . . .

"Very well, then, let us get together and form a constructive programme, [that posterity will say that after America had passed through a simple age] . . ., when the forces of society had come into hot contact, . . . there were men of serene enough intelligence, . . . of will and purpose to stand up once again . . . [and who found out] how to translate power into freedom, how to make men glad that they were rich, how to take the envy out of men's hearts that others were rich and they for a little while poor, by opening the gates of opportunity to every man. . . ."

43

the first, the period of the "New Freedom," characterized by government attempts to regulate and stand in hostile posture apart from "big business," and directed at restoring some semblance of a *laissez-faire,* free-competition social order; the second, characterized by a government policy of cooperation with "big business" and active regulatory intervention in the economy. The divide, according to this view, lay somewhere around November, 1914 (though at points the divide is rolled back to early 1914, as a response to the continuing depression, leaving scarcely a year to the "New Freedom" phase). Thus, it is argued, the "New Freedom" was capable of serving the cause of Progressivism for only a short time; Progressivism gained new life after November, 1914, through the abandonment of the "New Freedom" and the move toward Herbert Croly's and Theodore Roosevelt's "New Nationalism."

If Wilson is properly understood in terms of the widely current evolutionary-positivistic world view that he shared alike with leading industrial and finance capitalists and with prominent politicians and intellectuals within the bi-partisan Progressive movement, and if the approaches taken by his administration to both foreign and domestic affairs are viewed as basically interrelated, rather than compartmentalized, as affecting each other, rather than operating in isolated spheres, then it is of greater analytical value to view the attitude assumed by Wilson and his administration toward "business" before and after November, 1914, as undergoing consistent development, rather than fundamental change. That attitude corresponded with a world view that affirmed large-scale corporate industrial captalism as the natural and inevitable product of social evolution, and that regarded foreign investments and exports, defined in terms of the needs of industrial and finance capital, as indispensable to the nation's prosperity and social well-being. Beneficence at home and abroad, in this view, was a function of necessity. Large corporate production appeared as the vehicle of domestic material progress; foreign economic expansion, considered a decisive condition of such production, promised to carry "civilization," bourgeois-liberal ideas and institutions, and a better way of life, to the agrarian areas of the world, particularly as "development" of natural resources in those areas was considered essential to such expansion.

It no more occurred to such liberals as Wilson than it did to the so-called Dollar Diplomatists before him, or than it does today to the "internationalist" liberals, that investment in, and ownership of, other nations' resources, railroads, and industry, by United States capitalists, constituted imperialism or exploitation. Imperialism to them meant British- and European-style colonialism or exclusive spheres of interest; exploitation meant unscrupulous gouging, exorbitantly profitable concessions gained by undue influence with corrupt government officials, and the like, in short, "unfair practices" analogous to those characteristics that distinguished the "trust" from the large corporation in domestic affairs. Open door expansion, on the other hand, appeared to them as simply the implementation of the natural international division of labor between the industrialized and agrarian nations; it meant mutually beneficial (and beneficent) business relationships and trade; it meant the assumption by the United States of its natural place in the world economy *vis-á-vis* the other industrial nations, by the elimination of "artificial" impediments to the operation of the laws of competitive commerce; it meant "free trade."[85]

In the Wilsonian manner, former president Truman recently remarked, "The Open Door policy is not imperialism; it is free trade." Unfortunately, the bourgeois-liberal mind seems unable to understand how any transaction that involves the exchange of equivilent for equivalent can carry with it any quality of injustice or exploitation. In the economic realm, morality and justice are defined as exchange at value, so long as it is devoid of any element of extra-pecuniary coercion; in more sophisticated ideological terms, morality and justice correspond with natural law. But it is precisely in the relationship defined by natural law, precisely in the exchange of equivalent for equivalent (assuming the free and competitive exchange of equivalents in the first place, though this is often not the case), that the exploitation, the injustice, the immorality, from the point of view of the agrarian peoples, resides. For, while the relationship is reified by the liberal mind as purely an exchange of goods, a confrontation of things, of private properties, what is really involved is a relationship between human beings. Concern for the nicely balanced exchange of things according to their market value—"a fair field and no favor"—blinds the liberal mind to the real relationship between people, of which the exchange of goods is but a consequence, and to the resulting conditions of life (the "human relations" and "individual dignity" with which the liberal is so articulately preoccupied.)[86] Hence, the innocent shock consistently evinced by liberals at anti-Americanism and resentment in the agrarian areas of the world regardless of whether United States foreign policy is of the "Dollar Diplomacy" or the "Good Neighbor" variety.

For, the essence of open door expansion involved an international system of economy identical to that established by England and the European industrial nations with their colonies and other agrarian areas. The latter were to become increasingly familiar with modern relations of capital and labor, but with capital appearing in the form of the foreigner and labor in the form of the indigenous population; they were assigned the role of suppliers of raw materials and markets for industrial goods and capital invest-

---

85 See, e. g., Wilson's "Be Worthy of the Men of 1776," July 4, 1914, P P W W, III, 142-143: "The Department of State . . . is constantly called upon to back up the commercial . . . and the industrial enterprises of the United States in foreign countries, and it at one time went so far in that direction that all its diplomacy came to be designated as 'dollar diplomacy.' . . . But there ought to be a limit to that. There is no man who is more interested than I am in carrying the enterprise of American business men to every quarter of the globe. I was interested in it long before I was suspected of being a politician. I have been preaching it year after year as the great thing that lay in the future for the United States, to show her wit and skill and enterprise and influence in every country in the world. . . . [But if] American enterprise in foreign countries, particularly in those . . . which are not strong enough to resist us, takes the shape of imposing upon and exploiting the mass of the people . . . it ought to be checked and not encouraged. I am willing to get anything for an American that money and enterprise can obtain except the suppression of the rights of other men. I will not help any man buy a power which he ought not to exercise over his fellow-beings."

86 ". . . we are told that free trade would create an international division of labor, and thereby give to each country the production which is most in harmony with its natural advantages. You believe perhaps, gentlemen, that the production of coffee and sugar is the natural destiny of the West Indies. Two centuries ago, nature, which does not trouble herself about commerce, had planted neither sugar-cane nor coffee trees there." "If the free-traders cannot understand how one nation can grow rich at the expense of another, we need not wonder, since these same gentlemen also refuse to understand how within one country one class can enrich itself at the expense of another." ". . . the protectionist system is nothing but a means of establishing large-scale industry in any given country, . . . of making it dependent upon the world market, and from . . . [that] moment . . ., there is already more or less dependence upon free trade. . . ." Marx, "On the Question of Free Trade," public speech delivered before the Democratic Association of Brussels, Jan. 9, 1848, in The Poverty of Philosophy, 22-223, 224.

45

ment; and, of particular importance, control over, and investment decisions affecting, decisive sectors of their economies were to be transferred from their determination to that of capitalists in the United States. Those sectors of their economies were to become "complementary" to, and integrated with, the United States corporate economy, each an *imperium in imperio* within its respective nation, with all the implications of economic dislocation, political instability, and restriction of national economic and political independence. To Wilson, such implications were no necessary part of open door expansion, but rather of imperialism and exploitation as he narrowly conceived them; as for the rest, it all appeared as only natural in relations between "capital surplus" and "capital deficient" nations, and as the mode of progress in international affairs.[87]

It was the part of statesmanship to make law the expression of the necessities and facts of the time: to institutionalize the ground rules of the corporate economy at home and the mechanisms of economic expansion abroad, so that day to day business, the laws of commerce, and the government's role with respect to them, might flow smoothly along settled paths, rather than by the fits and starts of fire-brigade policy or executive fiat. As Wilson had put it in 1907, " . . . an institution is merely an established practice, an habitual method of dealing with the circumstances of life or the business of government. . . . "[88] In Wilson's view, it was this, with respect to modern circumstances of the modern industrial order, that the legislation of 1913-1914 promised to do.

Historians who have studied Wilson appear to harbor guilt-feelings about capitalism: a policy based upon considerations of the economic imperatives of capitalism is sordid, immoral, or amoral; a policy based upon

---

87 See, *e. g.*, the report of Edward E. Pratt, chief of the Bureau of Foreign and Domestic Commerce under Wilson, for the fiscal year July 1, 1914, to June 30, 1915: ". . . we can never hope to realize the really big prizes in foreign trade until we are prepared to loan capital to foreign nations and to foreign enterprise. The big prizes . . . are the public and private developments of large proportions, . . . the building of railroads, the construction of public-service plants, the improvement of harbors and docks, . . . and many others which demand capital in large amounts. New countries are generally poor. They look to older and richer countries to supply them with the capital to make their improvements and to develop their resources. The country which furnishes the capital usually sells the materials and does the work . . . there is no doubt that the loans of one nation to another form the strongest kind of economic bond between the two. It is commonly said that trade follows the flag. It is much more truly said that trade follows the investment or the loan." ". . . A foreign commercial policy . . . is gradually taking shape under a wise and careful administration. American investments abroad are being encouraged. The fact that investment must precede trade and that investments abroad must be safeguarded is fully recognized." *Reports of the Department of Commerce*, Oct. 30, 1915 (Wash., 1916), 247, 249. *Cf.* the more recent statement of the prominent liberal spokesman, Dean Acheson: ". . . in the nineteenth century an international system of sorts not only kept the peace for a century but also provided highly successful economic working arrangements. It brought about the industrialization of Europe and of many other parts of the world—our own country, for one. It stimulated production of raw materials and led to a great, though unevenly distributed, rise in the standard of living. This was accomplished by the export of capital, primarily by Great Britain, but also by all of Western Europe." ". . . a system for the export of capital, much greater than our present . . . efforts, is necessary. The system has been destroyed which expanded the power of Western Europe. . . . One to replace it will be devised, managed, and largely (but not wholly) financed by the United States; otherwise, it is likely to be provided by the Soviet Union, under circumstances destructive of our own power. . . ." "Foreign investment can provide wider opportunity for use of national energies. This can well enhance pride in national achievement and relieve frustrations among members of the populace now denied opportunity to use their full capabilities and training. This should tend to lessen xenophobia, strengthen social fabric and political stability, and bring new meaning to national independence. . . . " Acheson, *Power and Diplomacy* (Cambridge, Mass., 1958), 18, 19-20, 22. The first chapter of the book includes a subsection entitled, "The Collapse of a World Order," referring to the disintegration of the imperial system of the 19th century, and argues the necessity of replacing it with one similar to it, in its economic aspects, led by the United States. Acheson prefaces the chapter with lines of verse from Alfred Noyes: "When his hundred years expire / Then he'll set hisself a-fire / And another from his ashes rise most beautiful to see!"

88 Wilson, *Constitutional Government*, 14.

46

non-economic principle is moralistic. The corporate and political policy-makers of the United States, Wilson included, have had no such guilt-feelings or compulsion to make such a division in their thinking. To them there was (and is) nothing immoral about capitalism; it embraces the highest morality. The strength and spread of morality appear as the function of the strength and spread of capitalism. Historians, however, disregarding the imperatives of modern capitalism, while assuming its existence all the same, seem to have created an ideal construct of what liberalism ought to be, arbitrarily imputing to it certain characteristics of a transcendent nature and withholding from it others, particularly those relating to the affairs of political economy. It is an academic, idealized liberalism, not the responsible political liberalism as it operates as a functional ideology outside the university walls; it is a liberalism from which historians have written history in the manner of advice, consent, and dissent, rather than history that analyzes the nature of liberal ideology as it operates and appears in the hurly-burly of political economy. Accordingly, historians have tended to appraise the nature of the Wilsonian liberal (or Progressive) movement by deduction from, and in comparison with, the supposed nature of its ideology, instead of basing their analyses on an empirical study of the movement and comprehending the ideology of its leaders as emerging from and interacting with that movement and its adversaries. Particularly is the latter approach essential to an analysis of Wilson, to whom the great issues of his day turned upon concrete economic interests and questions.

Finding that Wilson's thought and policies often deviated from the ideal model, many historians have concluded superficially that Wilson was a "hypocrite" or a conservative in liberal's clothing. The point raised here, however, is not a quarrel as to whether Wilson was in fact a liberal or Progressive; on the contrary, it is submitted that a successful, comprehensive effort at analyzing precisely what Wilsonian liberalism or Progressivism was (and modern United States liberalism in general) has yet to be made.

It would be conducive to a more impartial and comprehensive understanding of Wilson and Wilsonianism to discard as a tool of analysis both the "New Freedom"—"New Nationalism" formula and the "Moralism"-vs.-"commercialism" presumption. This approach sees behind the "New Freedom" the shadow of a misconstrued Brandeis, who is taken inaccurately to symbolize an anti-"big business" program for the restoration of some sort of *laissez-faire*, free-competition society; more accurately, it sees behind the "New Nationalism" the shadow of Croly as represented in his book, *The Promise of American Life*. At the outset, and only at the outset, it may be more pertinent and analytically suggestive to a re-evaluation of Wilson and Wilsonianism, to see instead the shadow of Croly-the-adolescent behind the earlier years of Wilson's presidency, Croly-the-strapping-young-man behind the later (and lingering into the 1920's), with Croly-the-nearly-mature biding his time until the advent of the New Deal. In view of the present "national purpose" campaign of corporate spokesmen, liberal political and intellectual leaders, the Luce publications and the New York *Times*, short of a basic reordering of United States society, Croly-the-mature may yet arrive, and then the nation will surely be in need of a new freedom.

47

*M*ID-*A*MERICA

An Historical Review

Louis D. Brandeis, the New Freedom and the State

Philippa Strum
City University of New York: Brooklyn College
and The Graduate Center

The New Freedom was born during Woodrow Wilson's 1912 campaign for the presidency of the United States. It represented a view of the state as the foe of unchallenged power in the sphere of business and industry as well as in that of politics; as the appropriate body to "correct" the direction of capitalism when it took a mistaken road; and as the champion of the individual's right to economic as well as political liberty. But the New Freedom would not have come into existence had Louis D. Brandeis not provided Wilson with his vision of it, and so any examination of the conception of the state implicit in Wilson's campaign must begin with an examination of the ideas that Brandeis brought to Wilson.[1]

Brandeis, ever scornful of theory rather than facts, never set down his conception of the state in a systematic way. It is apparent nonetheless in a number of sources: the speeches he made, both as a lawyer and a statesman, during his pre-judicial career; the articles and letters he wrote about various aspects of the

---

[1] Arthur S. Link, *Wilson: The Road to the White House* (Princeton: Princeton University Press, 1947), pp. 488-493 (hereafter Link: *Road*); Arthur S. Link: *Wilson: The New Freedom* (Princeton: Princeton University Press, 1956), p. 95 (hereafter Link: *Freedom*).

subject; the advice he gave to Wilson during the 1912 campaign; and the suggestions he made once Wilson was in the White House.[2]

One of his most specific statements appeared in yet another forum: his famous concurrence in *Whitney* v. *California*. There he wrote,

> Those who won our independence believed that the final end of the State was to make men free to develop their faculties; and that in its government the deliberative forces should prevail over the arbitrary. They valued liberty both as an end and as a means. They believed liberty to be the secret of happiness and courage to be the secret of liberty. They believed that freedom to think as you will and to speak as you think are means indispensable to the discovery and spread of political truth; that without free speech and assembly discussion would be futile; that with them, discussion affords ordinarily adequate protection against the dissemination of noxious doctrine; that the greatest menace to freedom is an inert people; that public discussion is a political duty; and that this should be a fundamental principle of the American government. They recognized the risks to which all human institutions are subject. But they knew that order cannot be secured merely through fear of punishment for its infraction; that it is hazardous to discourage thought, hope and imagination; that fear breeds repression; that repression breeds hate; that hate menaces stable government; that the path of safety lies in the opportunity to discuss freely supposed grievances and proposed remedies; and that the fitting remedy for evil counsels is good ones.[3]

Close examination of this eloquent testament to free speech yields Brandeis's basic ideas about the state. First, human beings are both "good" in their ability to act intelligently, and "bad" in their susceptibility to the pitfalls of power and illogic. Second, the State is properly created by human beings to achieve goals unattainable without a State, among them the liberty necessary to develop individual talents.

---

[2]See, e.g., speeches and articles collected in Brandeis, *Business — A Profession* (Boston: Small, Maynard, 1914); Brandeis and Josephine Goldmark, *Women in Industry* (New York: National Consumers' League, n.d.); Brandeis, *Other People's Money and How the Bankers Use It* (New York: Stokes, 1914); Osmond K. Fraenkel, ed., *The Curse of Bigness* (New York: Viking Press, 1934); articles listed in Philippa Strum: *Louis D. Brandeis: Justice for the People* (Cambridge: Harvard University Press, 1984), pp. 486-488; Melvin I. Urofsky and David Levy, *Letters of Louis D. Brandeis* (Albany: State University of New York Press, 1972-1978). Also see the advice he later gave to President Franklin D. Roosevelt, as well as his opinions while on the Court. Nelson L. Dawson, *Louis D. Brandeis, Felix Frankfurter and the New Deal* (Hamden, Conn.: Archon Books, 1980), passim; Strum, *Brandeis*, chs. 15-19; Alexander M. Bickel, ed., *The Unpublished Opinions of Mr. Justice Brandeis* (Cambridge: Harvard University Press, 1957); Alfred Lief, ed., *The Social and Economic Views of Mr. Justice Brandeis* (New York: Vanguard Press, 1930); Alpheus T. Mason, *Brandeis, Lawyer and Judge in the Modern State* (Princeton: Princeton University Press, 1933).

[3]*Whitney* v. *California*, 274 U.S. 357, 375 (1927)

Third, and following logically from the second, the State must be democratic; i.e., responsive to the expressed will of the people. Fourth, and again following logically from earlier premises, the State must not act arbitrarily or in an illegitimately repressive manner, and mechanisms must be incorporated into the State's structure to prevent such phenomena — such phenomena being, by definition, a threat to liberty. (If there was a single element in Brandeis's conception of the State that was central to it, it was this: that the criterion by which the legitimacy of any regime is measured is its success in creating conditions — political, economic, social — that aid citizens in their search for individual liberty.)

Fifth, no State is to be trusted, no matter who its administrators are, and must constantly be subjected to examination by the people. For that reason, one of the functions of the State is maintenance of the free flow of ideas. Sixth, stability of government is desirable, because instability may be harmful to liberty; but stability is of lesser value than the liberty for whose sake it is sought. Finally, the State inevitably is an imperfect instrument, not only because arbitrary forces will challenge deliberate forces, but because it is in the nature of humanity to generate and heed "evil counsels," at least temporarily.

The primary goal of the State, then, is to create the conditions necessary for liberty. And Brandeis, no philospher but a practicing attorney and man of business and political affairs, whose ideas were derived from his experience in practicing his profession, recognized that in the early twentieth century the challenge was to create a system which would give all individuals the possibility of achieving *economic* liberty in an industrialized state. Because the development of trusts and monopolies threatened both economic and political liberty, the government had to wrestle with the problem of the trusts; i.e., the state had a positive role to play vis-à-vis economic institutions.

Both to understand his proposed policy, which in part became Wilson's, and to counter charges that it was economically naïve, it is necessary to follow the chronological development of Brandeis's ideas. The son of a small businessman, he began his legal career as the representative of small businessmen in New England. Perhaps his best known experience in that capacity occurred in 1902 at the McElwain shoe factory in Bridgewater, Massachusetts. Confronted both with a business slump and his employees' refusal to accept a wage cut, McElwain called upon Brandeis for advice.

Brandeis visited the plant and quickly discovered that while the employees were as well paid as McElwain claimed, their work was seasonal, and there were many days when there was no work — or pay — to be had. Brandeis immediately developed a method for spreading out work during the year so as to prevent irregularity of employment — an evil he fulminated against for the rest of his life — and this was accepted by both sides as satisfactory.[4]

---

[4]Alpheus T. Mason, *Brandeis: A Free Man's Life* (New York: Viking Press, 1946), p. 145; LDB interview, *New York Times Annualist*, January 27, 1913, p. 36, reprinted in Brandeis, *Bigness*, p. 41; Strum, *Brandeis*, pp. 96-97.

Brandeis came away from the experience with a new respect for the role of unions in protecting workers' rights. He found John Tobin, the head of the International Boot and Shoe Workers' Union, to be eminently reasonable. Moreover, he recognized that there had to be an organized voice with which the workers could counter the financially powerful voice of the employers. The McElwain and other labor situations led him to the conviction that unions were necessary to keep employers honest, and that well-intentioned union officials and employers sitting down together could solve any labor-management problem.[5]

Brandeis's entire approach to labor-management relations was an attempt to preserve capitalism while maximizing the chances of the employees' finding justice in the workplace. Seeking to insure "industrial democracy," he became adamantly opposed to socialism and to economic trusts, both of which he saw as concentrating power in the hands of the few to the detriment of the many. He was concerned about the incompatibility of great power and individual liberty, and, with Jefferson, believed that the economically dependent citizen could not be politically independent. The problem was to maintain the Jeffersonian ideal of economic independence in the industrial era.

This concern illuminated Brandeis's unionism. Speaking in 1904 to the Boston Typothetae, an organization of owners of small printing companies, he argued that if there was to be industrial peace and prosperity, "Industrial liberty must attend political liberty...Some way must be worked out by which employer and employee, each recognizing the proper sphere of the other, will each be free to work for his own and for the common good, and that the powers of the individual employee may be developed to the utmost." He did not advocate union dominance of employers any more than he favored employer dominance over employees, for the "sense of unrestricted power is just as demoralizing for the employer as it is for the employee. Neither our intelligence nor our characters can long stand the strain of unrestricted power."[6] In a sense, Brandeis was updating Acton's dictum about the corrupting effects of power and bringing it from the political into the economic sphere. But minimizing unchecked power was not the only goal: it was equally important to permit the employees' intellects and characters to be developed. This would occur only if the employees were permitted to assume responsibility over their own lives. Unionism was one step in this direction; as will be seen, Brandeis maintained this goal as his thinking developed past a belief in unionism to insistence on an eight-hour work day.

A reasonably short day was necessary because democracy, education, and self-fulfillment were inextricably intertwined. The satisfaction of workers' economic needs was important but insufficient: "The welfare of our country demands that

---

[5]Elizabeth Glendower Evans, "Mr. Justice Brandeis, The People's Tribune," *The Survey*, October 29, 1931; LDB to Clarence Darrow, December 12, 1902, BP, NMF 5-1; LDB to Henry Demarest Lloyd, November 24, 1902, BP, NMF 5-1; LDB to Frank S. Brown, June 17, 1912, BP, NMF 8-3; LDB, *Bigness*, p. 41.
[6]LDB, "The Employers and the Trade Unions," delivered to the annual banquet of the Boston Typothetae, April 21, 1904, reprinted in LDB, *Business*, pp. 13-27.

leisure be provided for...among other reasons, because with us every man is of the ruling class...Our great beneficent experiment in democracy will fail unless the people, our rulers, are developed in character and intelligence." Development was to be both physical and mental, with the former dependent upon the leisure for "outdoor recreation" and the latter requiring "free time when body and mind are sufficiently fresh to permit of mental effort." Professionals and businessmen could work more than eight-hour days because they derived joy and mental stimulation as well as money from their occupations, but the average industrial worker had to have leisure time in which to enjoy self-development.[7]

Having become a convert to unionism and the eight-hour day, Brandeis next began to wonder whether there was something basically unfair about workers not sharing the profits that their work brought to employers. He came to believe that "unions should strive to make labor share all the earnings of a business except what is required for capital and management." He told the Boston Central Labor Union that once shareholders (i.e., "capital") had received a fair return on their investment and the needs of the business itself had been met, any remaining profits should be distributed to the workers.[8] This was in 1905, long before the presidential campaign of 1912.

By 1915, Brandeis had moved beyond the idea of profit-sharing as the key to the "industrial democracy [that] must, in the end, attend political democracy."[9] Testifying before the Federal Commission on Industrial Relations, he insisted that the American system was "committed primarily to democracy...which implies the rule by the people. And therefore the end for which we must strive is that...that involves industrial democracy as well as political democracy."[10] This meant not only decent wages and hours but also that "the problems of a trade should be no longer the problems of the employer alone...The problems which exist...are the problems of employer and employee. Profit sharing, however liberal, can not meet the situation."[11] He added that labor had to have "not only a voice but a vote" in all businesses if democracy was to be achieved:

> We are striving for democracy; we are striving for the development of men. It is absolutely essential in order that men may develop that they be properly fed and properly housed, and that they have proper opportunities of education and recreation. We can not reach our goal without those things. But we may have all those things and have a nation of slaves.[12]

---

[7]LDB to Alfred Brandeis, February 23, 1906, Urofsky and Levy, *Letters*, I, 407-408; to same, June 18, 1907, BP, M 2-4; to same, February 22, 1906, *Letters*, I, 407.

[8]*Boston Post*, Feb. 6, 1905, quoted in Mason, *Brandeis*, p. 151.

[9]LDB to Maurice Barnett, May 26, 1913, BP, NMF 47-2.

[10]U.S., Congress, Senate, Commission on Industrial Relations, S. Doc. 415, 64th Cong. 1st sess. Serial 6936, pp. 7657, 7659-7660.

[11]*Ibid.*, p. 7660.

[12]*Ibid.*, p. 7663.

Brandeis was thinking in these terms at least as early as 1913, when he wrote that he viewed the "prevailing discontent" symptomized by the socialist movement as "due perhaps less to dissatisfaction with the material conditions, as to the denial of participation in management."[13] He told a social reformer that "you do not lay sufficient stress upon the importance of industrial liberty. No amount of material well-being can make up for the lack of that."[14] The "creed" that he expressed in a letter to Robert Bruère in 1922, while written after the Wilson administration had ended, reflected ideas that he had been developing for decades:

"...no remedy can be hopeful which does not devolve upon the workers' participation in, responsibility for the conduct of business; and their aim should be the eventual assumption of full responsibility — as in cooperative enterprises. This participation in and eventual control of industry is likewise an essential of obtaining justice in distributing the fruits of industry."[15] And so ultimately Brandeis came to a belief in what is known today as worker-management.

The insistent emphasis on development of the individual did not imply a belief in endless development. He told Harold Laski that "each [man] is a weak thing, despite the aids and habiliments with which science, invention and organization have surrounded him",[16] and he was fond of reminding all within hearing that every human being is but a "wee thing."[17] One of his major concerns was bigness; indeed, a book of his collected papers was aptly entitled *The Curse of Bigness*.[18] Anything that ignored the limitations of human nature had to be avoided; human beings had to be as wary of the evil of bigness in business as in government. For with their complex combination of creativity and limited intellect, human beings could create institutions that were too big to monitor for efficiency and effectiveness, too big to assess for value or liability to society, too big to control, too big to care about the policies necessary to protect individual liberties. Such were the trusts.

Brandeis's thinking about trusts — the thinking that would become part of his advice to Wilson and hence of the New Freedom — was fully developed by the time he testified in 1911 before Senator Moses Clapp's Committee on Interstate Commerce, then considering what was to become known as the La Follette-Stanley bill. The bill, for which Brandeis was largely responsible, was an attempt to give teeth to the Sherman Anti-Trust Act, the Act having recently been watered down by the Supreme Court.[19] Brandeis's testimony was based on a rejection of the belief held by many Progressives, Theodore Roosevelt among them, that trusts were inevitable. They weren't, Brandeis said; they had been created by the state and could be eliminated by the state.

---

[13]LDB to Dix W. Smith, November 5, 1913, BP, NMF 47-2.

[14]LDB to Arthur Williams, November 17, 1913, BP, NMF 4-1.

[15]LDB to Henry Bruère, February 25, 1922, BP, NMF 15.

[16]LDB to Harold Laski, September 21, 1921, *Letters*, IV, 17.

[17]Paul Freund, "Driven by Passion," in *Sunday Herald*, November 11, 1956, p. 3, Frankfurter Papers, Library of Congress, Box 128.

[18]Osmond K. Fraenkel, ed., *The Curse of Bigness* (New York: Viking Press, 1936).

[19]LDB to La Follette, July 29, 1911, BP, SC 1-2. The Court decision was *Standard Oil* v. *United States*, 221 U.S. 1 (1911).

Trusts would not have come into existence, Brandeis told the Clapp Committee, had the laws of the United States not been skewed in their favor and had the financial interests not manipulated the economy. The law had permitted seemingly unconnected businesses to agree among themselves on high prices; the state now had an obligation to undo what it had wrought, by forbidding price fixing. The tendency of the money trust was to inject money into other trusts, enabling them to conspire to set artificially low prices for their products. Once low prices had driven out competitors, the trusts raised prices. Trusts were created not by efficiency or fair competition but by manipulation of credit. "There are no natural monopolies in the industrial world," Brandeis insisted.[20]

And it was the state that permitted trusts, which by their nature were inefficient, to remain in business. As a business grew to a great size, so did the multiplicity of problems it had to confront. But because trusts were so large, "the man at the head has a diminishing knowledge of the facts" as well as "a diminishing opportunity of exercising a careful judgment upon them. Furthermore — and this is one of the most important grounds of the inefficiency of large institutions — there develops a centrifugal force greater than the centripetal force. Demoralization sets in; a condition of lessened efficiency presents itself." Efficiency was possible only when someone was firmly in charge, because while "organization can do much to make larger units possible and profitable," organization "can never supply the combined judgment, initiative, enterprise, and authority which must come from the chief executive officers."[21]

The inefficiency of trusts was to be seen in their inability to maintain incentive or produce cheap, good products. Ten years after the Steel Trust completed its takeover of the steel industry by absorbing the Carnegie Company, the United States had fallen five years behind Germany in iron and steel metallurgy, creation of updated machinery, and methods of production. The number of deaths and injuries due to the derailments of trains had led the Interstate Commerce Commission to investigate. It found that derailments due to broken rails had increased drastically since the Steel Trust had taken over. Only part of the cause was the introduction of heavier trains; the Trust was too inefficient to keep pace with the innovations in transportation, as a result of which there had been 2,059 derailments involving death and injuries to 106 people in the decade of the Trust. Similarly, when confronted with a more efficient system of shoe manufacturing, the Shoe Machinery Trust bought out the system and killed it. Trusts and rapid progress did not coexist.[22]

Because the trusts were inefficient, they inevitably would collapse if they were not artificially supported by government laws. "I am so convinced of the economic

---

[20]LDB, "Competition," in America:i Legal News, 44 (January 1913), 5-14, reprinted in LDB, Bigness, pp. 112-124. The quotation is on p. 115.

[21]LDB, "Competition," in Bigness, pp. 116-117.

[22]LDB, Bigness, pp. 119-120; LDB, "Trusts and Efficiency," Collier's Weekly, September 14, 1912, reprinted in Business, pp. 198-217; LDB, "Trusts and the Export Trade," Collier's Weekly, September 21, 1912, reprinted in Business, pp. 218-235. Also see Bigness, pp. 128-136, 236-254; LDB to Charles Crane, November 11, 1911, Letters, II, 510-511.

fallacy in a huge unit," Brandeis declared, "that if we make competition possible, if we create conditions where there could be reasonable competition, these monsters would fall to the ground." Trusts hurt consumers by monopolizing markets which they flooded with shoddy but expensive products; trusts were made possible by state laws; the state clearly was violating its mandate from the people to act in their best interests. Worse still, the state, in cooperating with trusts, was undermining democracy. Trusts destroyed unions between labor and business. Union-free, the trusts forced their workers — who, because the trusts controlled such large segments of the economy, had little choice of other employment — to work seven days a week, twelve hours a day, for minimal wages. Such schedules turned people into automatons rather than human beings with the leisure to fulfill and educate themselves and to participate in the political process. The trusts had created wage slaves in what was supposed to be a free country. They had made the United States undemocratic.[23]

The solution lay with the state: passage of the La Follette-Stanley bill, giving redress of triple damages to businesses that had been destroyed by the trusts, as well as to individuals hurt by them, and creating a rebuttable presumption that any combination controlling more than 40 percent of a trade was in restraint of it and liable under the Sherman Act.[24] Although it was not part of the proposed law, Brandeis also spoke to the Clapp Committee in favor of a federal trade commission empowered to investigate and publicize the facts about trusts, and for consumers' cooperatives. All were designed to cut things back to the proper size. In a statement as relevant to the 1980s as it was in 1911, Brandeis concluded his two and a half days of testimony with the comment that "There used to be a certain glamour about big things. Anything big, simply because it was big, seemed to be good and great. We are now coming to see that big things may be very bad and mean."[25]

The bill did not pass. Brandeis would raise his recommendations again when he became Wilson's economic advisor.

One further idea developed by Brandeis before that time entailed government ownership of land, a measure designed to keep a limited resource out of the hands of the too-powerful "interests" and insure its use for the benefit of the citizenry. Brandeis's involvement as counsel for *Collier's Weekly* in the Pinchot-Ballinger affair was directly responsible for the development of this concept. Pinchot-Ballinger, of course, revolved around the alleged "give-away" of thousands of acres of Alaskan coal and timber land to the Morgan-Guggenheim syndicate. The resultant congressional investigation was followed by the charge that President Taft had granted sole rights to Controller Bay, Alaska, one of the only two outlets from the coal fields to the sea, to the same Morgan-Guggenheim syndicate — which already controlled the second outlet. Brandeis made himself an expert on conservation,

---

23U.S., Congress, Senate, Committee on Interstate Commerce, *Hearings on Control of Corporations, Persons, and Firms Engaged in Interstate Commerce*, 62nd Cong., 2nd sess., 1911, vol. 1, pt. 16, pp. 1146-1291.
24*Ibid.*, LDB to Edwin Grozier, September 19, BP, NMF 43-4.
25*Hearings, Ibid.*

public land laws, land management, and the geography of Alaska, and came to the conclusion that not only government ownership but government-supervised development of Alaska was necessary. Alaska's wealth could not be exploited for the good of the people without a transportation system and utilities, neither of which Brandeis would trust to the kind of private ownership that had been so badly misused in New England. Brandeis could not foresee the discovery of oil in Alaska and its importance to the United States in the second half of the twentieth century, but he did realize that land and resources were finite and that control of them was a central problem for a democratic society. Land and resources meant profit, which in turn meant power; too much concentrated power was to be avoided, as was the use of land and resources for any purpose other than the enrichment of all the people. Government operation of land and resources, however, meant concentration of power, albeit public rather than private power. Its role, therefore, was to preserve land and resources for the people and to turn over decision making about the utilization of land and resources as well as about other political and economic matters to the people most immediately concerned. While the government would own transportation and utilities, it would offer leases to capitalists who would operate for the public good as well as for private gain. Government-issued public franchises "probably should not be fixed for more than a generation," so as to permit the constant experimentation and adjustments to changing necessities that characterized Brandeis's philosophy of politics and law.[26]

Thus Brandeis was not opposed to an activist state, but considered it a potential positive force to prevent illegitimate concentrations of power in the economic (and, consequently) the political sphere. But government itself had to be checked, as it would be by the constant self-interested wariness of business and by a public with the leisure time and motivation to involve itself in public affairs. Eventually, logically, Alaskan affairs would come under the control of Alaskans rather than the central government, so that federalism would provide an additional check on unbridled State (i.e., national) power.

——— ——— ——— ———

On August 17, 1912, Wilson received the delegation of Democratic Party notables who arrived at his cottage in Sea Girt, New Jersey, to notify him formally of his nomination for President. He was already prepared with a nomination speech of 6,000 words, in which he emphasized tariff reform and control of the trusts. He promised to strengthen the Sherman Anti-Trust Act; to control the combinations of banks, railroads, and other large industries united by a small group of people with vast power over credit and industry; to develop the nation's resources; and to call for legislation to protect labor and to promote education. But the program that was to become the New Freedom was not articulated; indeed, it did not yet exist in Wilson's mind. He saw the major campaign issue as tariff reform rather than the trusts. He indicated that he was not opposed to bigness as such in business, nor could he see any way of countering what he called the "world-wide economic

---

[26]Alpheus Thomas Mason, *Bureaucracy Convicts Itself* (New York: Viking, 1941), passim; Strum, *Brandeis*, pp. 132-145. Quote is in LDB to Gifford Pinchot, July 29, 1911, BP, NMF 31-1.

tendency against competition." Further, he saw no reason to attempt to counter the tendency, for he did not view the trusts as necessarily dangerous to economic freedom. Instead, he called the creation of huge businesses "normal and inevitable." The Democrats, he declared, did not mean to destroy the trusts.[27]

Had he retained these ideas throughout the campaign, Wilson and Roosevelt might well have been the Tweedledum and Tweedledee of the presidential race of 1912, which would then have been no more than a clash of personalities, styles, and political debt.[27a] But before the campaign went much further, Wilson met Brandeis.

Wilson, like Brandeis, had gone through various stages in his thinking about both the state and the economic institutions within it. In 1884, when he wrote *Congressional Government*, Wilson saw Congress as the dominant if unorganized and inefficient branch of the national government. The presidency was brushed off as relatively unimportant; Wilson did not yet consider it as the possible source of direction he felt was lacking in the American government. The model of intelligent organization of the state was the British system, which he called "perfected party government." Further, the British aristocracy played an important role in maintaining stability, and Wilson likened that role to the one performed in the American system by the Senate. While the House of Representatives was subject to the "whims of popular constituencies," to which it often paid "servile obedience," the Senate, which represented no class interests and frequently held debates of a high intellectual calibre, was able to check the worst follies of the House. Presenting the Senate as a body that should be filled by men of intelligence and merit, he found it "valuable in our democracy in proportion as it is undemocratic." What Wilson was advocating, it would appear, was less popular democracy and stronger rule by an aristocracy of men less immediately answerable to the people. The book is elitist, naive in its vision of the Senate as free of vested interests, and a far cry from the Progressivism of 1912.[28]

---

[27]Link, *Road*, pp. 472-473.

[27a]The phrase "tweedle-dum and tweedle-dee" to describe the positions of the two candidates was used by William Allen White in *Woodrow Wilson* (Boston, 1924), p. 264. White was far from the only person to lack understanding of how radical Brandeis's ideas — and Wilson, having been taught them — were. The socialists of the period, for example, made no mention of Brandeis's suggestions in their critiques of capitalism. They may have been as unaware as others were of Brandeis's cohesive approach to the state and the economy, largely because it was scattered throughout his occasional articles, speeches, and testimony before congressional committees. It was not until the New Deal period that his ideas became known, and even then they tended to be criticized primarily by "liberals" who did not fully understand them. See, e.g., Max Lerner in the *New York Herald Tribune* of March 3, 1935, quoted in Dawson, *Louis D. Brandeis, Felix Frankfurther, and the New Deal*, p. 33; A.A. Berle, "Revenue and Progress," 35 *Survey Graphic*, October 1935, p. 471; Rexford G. Tugwell, "The Rise of Business, Part I," 5 *Western Political Quarterly (1952)*, pp. 274-289; Raymond Moley, *After Seven Years* (New York: Harcourt & Brothers, 1939), p. 24. Socialist theorists of the early twentieth century advocated large-scale socialism, which presumably would have led them, had they taken note of Brandeis's approach, to disagree with his insistence that all large-scale institutions are too big to be subjected to adequate human control.

[28]Woodrow Wilson, *Congressional Government* (Boston: Houghton, Mifflin, 1885), pp. 52, 123, 226, 224, 58.

The labor unrest of the late nineteenth century was condemned by Wilson, who deplored unions as antithetical to the interest of individual laborers.[29] Yet, recognizing that new economic forces were at work, he was able to accept the idea of govenrmental control of the railroads and the concept of the Interstate Commerce Act.[30] He was concerned about the power given by the growing number of trusts and monopolies to a few men, "a control over the economic life of the country which they might abuse to the undoing of millions of men, it might even be to the permanent demoralization of society itself and of the government which was the instrument of society."[31] But he proposed no solution. He could not accept socialist government ownership of the means of production or any measures that would interfere with the country's economic growth, but he felt it "would not do to leave the economic liberty of the individual or the freedom and self-respect of the workingman unprotected."[32]

In the early years of the twentieth century, then, Wilson saw the state as necessary and with a positive role to play in the limiting of the exercise of economic power by the few over the many and in securing the well-being of individuals. He advocated a strong state, structured along the parliamentary lines that would permit it to serve as the instrument of society. But he was not ready to turn control of the state over to just any people. Although he had opposed American annexation of the Philippines, he wrote, in 1902,

> Liberty is not itself government. In the wrong hands, — in hands unpracticed, undisciplined, — it is incompatible with government. Discipline must precede it, — if necessary, the discipline of being under masters. Then will self-control make it a thing of life and not a thing of tumult...Shall we doubt, then, what the conditions precedent to liberty and self-government are, and what their invariable support and accompaniment must be [in the Philippines]?...They can have liberty no cheaper than we got it. They must first love order and instinctively yield to it.[33]

And Wilson also lacked a real understanding of the relationship between political and economic forces in the state. Link quotes one of Wilson's former students at Princeton as commenting that when speaking of the English ruling class, Wilson gave "the assumption that these public men were not moved by private gain. It was never hinted in his lecture-room that the British landed gentry, bankers, and business men enacted laws to protect their own class and group...Nor that the House of

---

[29]Woodrow Wilson, address to the graduating class at Princeton, reported in *Trenton True American*, June 14, 1909; Wilson, *A History of the American People* (New York and London: Harper and Bros., 1992), v. V, pp. 239-240.

[30]Wilson, *History of the American People*, V, pp. 184, 185.

[31]*Ibid.*, V, p. 267.

[32]*Ibid.*, V, pp. 267-268.

[33]Link, *Road*, p. 27; quotation, Wilson, "The Ideals of America," *Atlantic Monthly*, December 1902, p. 730.

Lords was in the nature of a private corporation representative of special interests even more than the United States Senate. He was not interested in economics."[34] And Norman Thomas, another former student, reported about Wilson that "If he had ever heard Harrington's dictum that the distribution of power follows the distribution of property, he never discussed it with his students in the classroom."[35]

A major alteration in his ideas was apparent by 1908, when Wilson's *Constitutional Government in the United States* was published. In a famous passage extolling presidential power, he wrote that the president can be "the political leader of the nation...His is the only national voice in affairs. Let him once win the admiration and confidence of the country, and no other single force can withstand him, no combination of forces will easily overpower him...If he rightly interpret the national thought and boldly insist upon it, he is irresistible."[36] He had also developed a higher esteem for the House of Representatives than was apparent in *Congressional Government*, and admitted that the Senate not only represented economic interests but that many Senators were dependent upon economic interests for their election. Recognizing the corruption that ran rampant in many state legislatures, he nevertheless advocated reforming them rather than transferring their powers to the national government.[37] His view of federalism and his new attitude toward presidential power would serve him well in his coming capacities as governor and president.

By 1912, Wilson's ideas had moved sufficiently close to Brandeis's for the latter to call Wilson's nomination "among the most encouraging events in American History."[38]

The two men had not yet met, but of course they were aware of each other's reputations. On August 1, Brandeis initiated a relationship by writing to compliment Wilson on the "true statesmanship" exhibited in his proposal to lower tariffs by 5 percent a year. Wilson replied that the letter had given him "a great deal of pleasure," and expressed the hope that the coming months would "give me the benefit of many conferences with you."[39] When Brandeis received a telegram from Charles Crane on August 26, saying that Wilson wanted to see him, he immediately left his vacation home in Massachusetts to go to Sea Girt. Brandeis and Wilson lunched together on August 28 and spent three hours afterward talking, primarily about trusts.[40] Link's contention that "Brandeis at once converted Wilson to the proposition that he make his campaign upon the issue of the restoration of competition

---

[34]Frederick C. Howe, quoted in Link, *Road*, p. 24.

[35]Norman Thomas, "Mr. Wilson's Tragedy and Ours," *The World Tomorrow*, March 1921, p. 82; also see Link, *Road*, p. 24.

[36]Woodrow Wilson, *Constitutional Government in the United States* (New York: Columbia University Press, 1908), p. 68.

[37]*Ibid.*, pp. 82-111, 128, 191.

[38]LDB to Norman Hapgood, July 3, 1912, BP, NMF 53-2.

[39]LDB to Woodrow Wilson, BP, NMF 35-2; WW to LDB, August 7, 1912, quoted in Mason, *Brandeis*, p. 377.

[40]*New York Times*, August 29, 1912, quoted in Melvin I. Urofsky, "Wilson, Brandeis and the Trust Issue, 1912-1914," *Mid-America*, 49 (January 1967), pp. 7-8; LDB to Alfred Brandeis, August 29, 1912, BP, M 3-3; LDB to Ray Stannard Baker, September 17, 1926, BP, NMF 86-1.

and free enterprise by means of the regulation and control of competition itself"[41] is borne out by Wilson's comment to the waiting reporters that the two men shared a joint object: "the prevention of monopoly," which is "created by unregulated competition, by competition that overwhelms all other competitions, and the only way to enjoy industrial freedom is to destroy that condition." He added that Brandeis knew more about both the economics and politics of corporations than anyone else he knew.[42]

The next day, Brandeis told *The New York Times* that Wilson was the candidate who offered the best hope of legislation for industrial freedom, whereas Roosevelt's plan to regulate monopoly and thereby legalize it was doomed to failure. Monopoly was inherently immune from regulation and could not be permitted to exist: "We must undertake to regulate competition instead of monopoly, for our industrial freedom and our civic freedom go hand in hand and there is no such thing as civic freedom in a state of industrial absolutism." He added that he had found Wilson "to be entirely in accord with my own views of what we need to do to accomplish industrial freedom."[43]

It was not quite true that Wilson was "entirely in accord" with Brandeis's ideas, for that implies that Wilson possessed those ideas before he met with Brandeis. In fact, Wilson was confused about the trusts and competition, and there is some irony in Brandeis's comment to his brother that he was "very favorably impressed" by Wilson, who struck him as "strong, simple, serious, openminded, eager to learn and deliberate."[44] Wilson certainly was openminded where Brandeis was concerned, recognizing fairly quickly that Brandeis had the clear answers Wilson lacked to what should be done about the trusts. Wilson was not only a confirmed capitalist; he was also a moral Calvinist. Good and evil were clearly defined; moral compromise was impossible. His Calvinism premeated his capitalism. Both, he believed, were based on the importance of the individual. The Calvinist sign of the chosen was morality; the reward for morality in business was prosperity. The trusts were bad, because they made it impossible for individual moral capitalists to reap the rewards that were their due. Thus, Wilson was certain that the trusts were wrong, but he did not know how to deal with them. He could not accept government regulation because he believed it inevitably would lead to government ownership, and Wilson feared big government. The state was necessary but should not be overly powerful or impinge upon economic freedom. And since he could see no way of controlling big business other than by balancing it with overly big government, he considered the cure to be fully as bad as the malady. All that could be done was for citizens to hope that goodness would triumph in the hearts of corporate leaders. Wilson could accept mandating the opening of corporate meetings to the public, directing the individuals involved away from sin and punishing them if they erred, but he was willing to do nothing about the institutions as such. Speaking in 1905, he had

---

[41] Link, *Road*, p. 488.
[42] *New York Times*, supra, n. 40.
[43] *Ibid.*
[44] LDB to Alfred Brandeis, September 17, 1926, BP, NMF 86-1.

said, "We can't abolish the trusts. We must moralize them." As late as mid-1912, his campaign speeches called only for application of the criminal provisions of the Sherman Act.[45]

In fact, Wilson was willing to move from the limited government he had advocated in the early 1900s to the beginning of an acceptance of governmental intervention in the economy — if someone could teach him *how* the government could intervene in order to create the conditions for renewal of competition. Brandeis began teaching Wilson at their first meeting. Within days, and in language that was both completely new for Wilson and thoroughly Brandeisian, the candidate was urging restriction of the kind of competition that results in monopoly. Speaking to 10,000 workers in Buffalo on Labor Day, he castigated Roosevelt and the heads of the trusts for wanting to turn workers into "wage slaves." He attacked Roosevelt's proposal to legalize monopolies, asking, rhetorically, "And what has created these monopolies? Unregulated competition. It has permitted these men to do anything they choose to do to squeeze their rivals out and crush their rivals to the earth. We know the processes by which they have done those things. We can prevent these processes through remedial legislation, and so restrict the wrong use of competition that the right use of competition will destroy monopoly. Ours is a programme of liberty; theirs a programme of regulation." He added,

> When you have thought the whole thing out, therefore, you will find that the programme of the new party legalizes monopolies and systematically subordinates workingmen to them and to plans made by the Government, both with regard to employment and with regard to wages. By what means, except open revolt, could we ever break the crust of our life again and become free men, breathing an air of our own, choosing and living lives that we wrought out for ourselves?[46]

Wilson thus differentiated himself from Roosevelt and aligned himself with Brandeis by placing a greater value on freedom as it would be achieved by individuals' control over their lives than on the wage and working conditions that might result from benevolent paternalism.

---

[45]For Wilson's thought see Alexander and Juliette George, *Woodrow Wilson and Colonel House* (New York: John Day, 1956); Arthur S. Link, *Woodrow Wilson and the Progressive Era* (New York: Harper and Brothers, 1954); William Diamond, *The Economic Thought of Woodrow Wilson* (Baltimore: Johns Hopkins University Press, 1943). Wilson and trusts: see Ray Stannard Baker, *Woodrow Wilson: Life and Letters,* 8 Vols. (Garden City, N.Y.: Doubleday, Doran, 1931-1939), III, p. 398; LDB to Alfred Brandeis, September 17, 1926, BP, NMF 86-1. Also see Link, *Progressive Era,* pp. 20-21, 28, 48; Urofsky, "Wilson, Brandeis," pp. 4-6; Link, *Road,* pp. 487-492. Wilson's 1905 speech is quoted in John Milton Cooper, Jr., *The Warrior and the Priest: Woodrow Wilson and Theodore Roosevelt* (Cambridge, Mass.: Harvard University Press, 1983), p. 120. Wilson's thinking is analyzed and contrasted with that of Roosevelt throughout the volume, but cf. particularly chapter 14, "The New Nationalism versus the New Freedom."
[46]*New York Times,* September 3, 1912.

But although from Labor Day on Wilson became a major spokesman for Brandeis's program for regulating competition,[47] and in spite of his talk of "remedial legislation," Wilson had had only his first lesson in Brandeisian theory; he still did not know how to go about creating the necessary restrictions on monopoly. Brandeis began to outline the methodology as he and Wilson drove through the streets of Boston in an open automobile on September 27, where Wilson was to give a noon address at Tremont Temple. The candidate who had insisted in August that the trusts were inevitable and that the Democratic Party would not destroy them now mocked Roosevelt's assumption that the dominance of industry by trusts was inevitable. And while he had also jeered "government by experts," as he referred to Roosevelt's proposal for establishing an industrial commission to regulate trusts, he told his Boston audience that he would establish an industrial commission to regulate business — but not trusts, which would be non-existent.[48] It was clearly no coincidence that Brandeis had been calling for a federal trade commission that would regulate competition, and that an article by him detailing his ideas, and written before Wilson's Tremont Temple appearance, was published by *Collier's Weekly* a few days after the speech.[49] Similarly, Wilson told his audience that corporations could become so big that they became inefficient. He had now learned enough to expound three Brandeisian themes: monopolies hurt economic liberty and had to be destroyed; they were inefficient; and the state had to regulate competition to protect business and workers by preventing the emergence of new trusts. Brandeis had presented Wilson with a program on which he could campaign, convincing him that the most important question confronting the American people in 1912 was that of economic freedom.[50]

Nonetheless, Wilson remained hazy about the methods to be employed. No sooner had he finished his speech and left Boston than he telegraphed Brandeis, asking him to "please set forth as explicitly as possible the actual measures by which competition can be effectively regulated. The more explicit we are on this point, the more completely will the enemies guns be spiked."[51]

The request did not surprise Brandeis, because the two men had discussed the subject during their car ride but had scarcely exhausted it. Brandeis, busy testifying before the Interstate Commerce Commission about the sins of the New Haven Railroad, could not reply immediately. In the interim he sent Wilson copies of suggestions that he had given to Norman Hapgood of *Collier's Weekly* for articles entitled "Concentration" and "Trusts and the Interstate Commssion."[52] On September 30, he sent Wilson "suggestions for the letter, about which we talked, dealing with the difference between your attitude and Roosevelt's on trusts and the remedies you propose to apply." Clearly, Wilson was uncertain about the exact

[47]Link, *Road*, p. 492.
[48]*New York Times*, September 28, 1912.
[49]LDB, "Monopoly," in *Collier's Weekly*, September 7, 1912, p. 8.
[50]Urofsky, "Wilson, Brandeis," p. 8; Link, *Progressive Era*, p. 20; Link, *Road*, pp. 509-510; Alfred Lief, *Brandeis: The Personal History of an American Ideal* (New York: Stackpole, 1936), p. 254.
[51]WW to LDB, September 27, 1912, BP, M-17.
[52]LDB to WW, September 28, 1912, *Letters*, II, p. 685.

nature of the differences and of the remedies. Brandeis went on to supply a lengthy summary of the problems with the Sherman Act and the virtues of the proposed amendments he and La Follette had tried unsuccessfully to get through Congress. He reminded Wilson that the difference between the Democrats and Roosevelt was the latter's willingness to accept monopoly as long as it was regulated, while the Democratic party insisted that monopoly had to be prevented. Again and again he emphasized that the difference between the economic policies espoused by the two parties "is the difference between industrial liberty and industrial absolutism."[53]

Link credits Brandeis's memo with being the source of "all of [the] ideas that [Wilson] expressed during the presidential campaign."[54] It was, however, too detailed for direct use in speeches, so Wilson and William Gibbs McAdoo suggested that Brandeis put the details into the form of articles.[55] Brandeis was glad to do so, and sent Norman Hapgood articles on "Trusts, Efficiency and the New Party" (Brandeis refused to call Roosevelt's party by its preferred title of "Progressive")[56] and "Trusts, the Export Trade, and the New Party," both soon published in *Collier's*. Brandeis confided to his brother, "Entre nous I have Norman supplied with editorials — through the October 19th number & shall probably add two more to make the full measure."[57] Wilson read the articles and editorials carefully and incorporated their main points in his speeches.[58] Thus Brandeis wrote both articles and editorials for *Collier's*, upon which Wilson came to rely, and which became something close to Wilson's journalistic campaign organ. Wilson utilized the magazine for such thoughts as "what this country needs above everything else is a body of laws which will look after the men who are on the make rather than the men who are already made."[59] In other words, it had become the function of the state to unclog the channels of competition so that creative businessmen would have a chance for success and so that the consumers would have access to the cheapest and best products and services American creativity could supply.

There were a number of ideas that Brandeis and Wilson had developed independently and that the close association between the men reinforced in the Wilson campaign. They were both free traders; both feared bigness in government and were strong supporters of federalism and state power; both saw the conservation of natural resources in the face of private attempts at private exploitation as a function of the state. Beyond question, however, Brandeis's major impact on Wilson lay in the area of economics, about which Wilson had known so little and about which Wilson's attitude changed fundamentally because of Brandeis.[60] Wilson moved from merely deploring the trusts to a commitment to abolish them, and there

---

[53]LDB to WW, September 30, 1912, *Letters,* pp. 686-694.

[54]Link, *Road,* pp. 491-492.

[55]LDB to Ray Stannard Baker, September 17, 1926, BP, NMF 86-1.

[56]*Collier's,* September 14, 1912, p. 14, and September 21, 1912, p. 10.

[57]Letter to Alfred Brandeis quoted in Mason, *Brandeis,* p. 378.

[58]Supra, n. 55; LDB to Baker, July 5, 1931, *Letters,* V, p. 482; Baker, *Wilson,* III, p. 366; Urofsky, "Wilson, Brandeis," p. 10.

[59]Link, *Road,* p. 489.

[60]Link, *Road,* pp. 489-490.

is every indication in Wilson's campaign speeches, communications with Brandeis, and use of Brandeis after the campaign that Wilson recognized his debt, for the alteration in Wilson's thinking and his dependence upon Brandeis outlasted the campaign. In June, 1913, three months after he moved to the White House, Wilson turned to Brandeis for advice on ways to deal with the money trust.

Wilson had written about currency reform as early as 1896 and in 1911 had called the money trust "the most pernicious of all trusts."[61] After his election he had declared, "You must put the credit of this country at the disposal of everybody upon equal terms." It was an issue of such great importance that he was prepared to overcome his distaste for big government and put banking under government supervision.[62]

The House Banking and Currency Committee (Pujo Committee) had held hearings about the money trust between May 1912 and January 1913. Unimpressed by the extent of the committee's investigation or its recommendations, Brandeis began his own inquiry. His interest was paralleled by that of Representative Carter Glass, who now chaired the Banking and Currency Committee, and Henry Parker Willis, the economist advising Glass.[63]

Glass and Willis presented Wilson with a plan to establish a reserve system that would be privately controlled and decentralized, with a maximum of twenty banks participating. Wilson added to the proposal the creation of a Federal Reserve Board that would supervise the system. When Secretary of State William Jennings Bryan learned of the plan, he quickly joined forces with Senator Robert L. Owen, a leading Progressive from Oklahoma; Samuel Untermyer, the attorney who had served as counsel to the Pujo Committee during its investigation of the money trust and who had actually orchestrated the hearings; and Secretary of the Treasury McAdoo. They regarded the Glass-Willis plan as a giveaway: the issuing of currency would still be in private hands, and the members of the proposed Federal Reserve Board would be elected by bankers. Not only would the bankers still control currency; they would now do so with the blessing of the government. McAdoo proposed a government-owned-and-operated central bank, but the Bryan faction realized this was so radical that neither the business community nor Wilson could possibly accept it. Instead, the group argued that there had to be a system that was controlled (but not owned) by the government, through government appointments of members of the Federal Reserve Board, and that its notes had to be government obligations. The banking community of course favored the Glass-Willis plan; the Progressives, with McAdoo among them, were fighting strenuously for their own plan. Wilson had to make a choice.[64]

On June 11, Wilson called Brandeis to the White House. He was inclined to support the regional reserve concept but he was unwilling to decide the two major issues — whether there should be banker representation on the Federal Reserve

---

[61]Urofsky, "Wilson, Brandeis," p. 15.
[62]Ibid.
[63]Link, Progressive Era, p. 48; Urofsky, "Wilson, Brandeis," p. 15.
[64]Ibid.

Board and who would be liable for Federal Reserve currency — without consulting Brandeis. In doing so, he was turning to an implacable foe of the money trust, who was writing a series of articles about its evils. Wilson read and annotated these articles, published in *Harper's Weekly* (and later in book form as *Other People's Money*).[65] Brandeis told Wilson firmly that he had to support the Bryan position. First, he said, "the power to issue currency should be vested exclusively in Government officials," and the bankers should be strictly limited to an advisory role. This would both minimize the bankers' influence and reassure smaller businesses that "whatever money is available, will be available for business generally, and not be subject to the control of a favored few." The people at large would have no confidence in a government financial body on which bankers served. And since only the government ought to issue currency, including that issued against commercial paper, the Federal Reserve notes had to be the obligation of the government of the United States.[66]

Wilson asked Brandeis to put his arguments in writing, and after receiving them the President announced that he was convinced. On June 18, he told all concerned that he would propose Bryan's plan: there would be a Federal Reserve Board appointed by the government, with bankers brought in as advisers; there would be regional banks, but all currency would be issued under the control of the Board. With Glass managing the bill in the House, the Federal Reserve bill passed both houses, and was sent to the White House for Wilson's signature on December 23.[67]

The experience was additional confirmation of Wilson's belief that he could rely on Brandeis's advice about money and business matters, and he did so again when faced with a decision about creating a regulatory rather than a merely investigative Federal Trade Commission.[68] Wilson was so impressed with Brandeis's statesmanship that he not only nominated him to the Supreme Court but appointed him to a commission investigating a border dispute with Mexico, asked him to chair the War Labor Policies Board (Brandeis declined the latter two offers, considering it inappropriate for a Supreme Court justice to hold other government positions), and sought his advice when rivalry between the military services and the War Department to secure labor and material during the early days of World War I began to drive up the cost of both.[69] Brandeis's suggestion of a munitions administration separate from the War Department was adopted and became the War Industries Board.[70]When the war ended and Rabbi Stephen Wise urged Wilson to

---

[65]Baker, *Wilson*, IV, p. 366.

[66]LDB to WW, June 14, 1913, *Letters*, III, pp. 113-115.

[67]*Ibid.*; H. Parker Willis, *The Federal Reserve System* (New York: Ronald Press, 1923), passim; Urofsky, "Wilson, Brandeis," p. 18; Mason, *Brandeis*, p. 399; Link, *Freedom*, pp. 211-213; Link, *Progressive Era*, p. 48; Cooper, pp. 233-234.

[68]Baker, *Wilson*, IV, p. 366; Cooper, p. 235.

[69]LDB to WW, August 14, 1916, BP, G 1-1; cf. to Justice Edward D. White, August 9 and August 14, 1916, BP, G 1-1; WW to Robert Woolley, quoted in Mason, *Brandeis*, p. 525.

[70]LDB to Colonel House, January 8, 1918, BP, WW 3-1; cf. Robert D. Cuff, *The War Industries Board* (Baltimore: Johns Hopkins, 1973), chap. 6.

name Brandeis to the Peace Commission, Wilson replied, "I need Brandeis everywhere but I must leave him somewhere," Brandeis having made it clear that he would feel constrained to resign from the Court if he accepted any other position.[71] And after Wilson left the White House and attempted to put together a progressive platform for the 1924 Democratic convention, Brandeis was one of the three men to whom he turned for ideas and comments.[72]

Wilson's post-campaign reliance upon Brandeis is mentioned only to indicate that his respect for Brandeis and the changes Brandeis made in his thinking were not passing happenstances of the campaign. Brandeis had altered Wilson's conception of the State.

Wilson had agreed, before meeting Brandeis, that human beings are both fallible and capable of great acts; that among the goals unattainable without a state is the securing of the liberty necessary to develop individual talents; that the state must respond to the will of the people, properly educated by their leaders. He believed that selfish interests could be put to good societal use; but that as still-fallible human beings would run the state, the government had to contain internal checks and disperse power. But the extent to which the state had to go, in the early twentieth century, in curbing the power of the trusts if democrary was to remain viable — indeed, the link between economic power and political power — was clear to Wilson only after he was tutored by Brandeis. The government was as responsible for economic democracy as it was for political democracy and it was as much the proper function of the state to destroy the trusts that threatened democracy as it was its function to fight an enemy abroad — this was the lesson of Brandeis. Although Wilson was a Progressive before he knew Brandeis, he was a Theodore Roosevelt Progressive by another name: he would accept and regulate trusts, not seek to abolish them. The belief that small-scale businesses and competition could be resurrected, the insistence on federalism in preference to big government (with the proviso that occasionally the central government had to take the risks attendant upon bigness when to do so might help insure individual liberty), the assumption that people given true freedom by the state could provide for themselves both economically and politically — all were part and parcel of the New Freedom; all were elements of the Brandeis credo.[73]

Wilson and Brandeis turned the campaign of 1912 into an exercise in altering the terms of political debate. They would have liked the country to ask "How can

---

[71]Quoted in Lief, *Brandeis*, p. 409.

[72]WW to LDB, June 20, November 6, and December 6, 1921, all BP, M 17-3; LDB to WW, June 25, 1921, BP, M 17-3; to same, December 28, 1921, *Letters*, V, p. 40; March 3, 1922, *Letters*, V, pp. 46-47; January 22, 1923, *Letters*, V, p. 91. Cf. Strum, *Brandeis*, p. 451 n. 50, 51; text, 219-221. The other two men were Wilson's law partner and last secretary of state, Bainbridge Colby, and Thomas Chadbourne, a lawyer and friend.

[73]Link, *Freedom*, pp. 95, 423, 433-439; Link, *Progressive Era*, pp. 70-71; Link, *Road*, pp. 488-489. Cooper credits Brandeis with "help(ing) Wilson to grasp" that "democratic government must remain self-government," and contrasts this with Roosevelt's more "aristocratic" and "paternalistic" approach to the democratic process. He also sees Wilson's view of people as essentially "optimistic." Cooper, pgs. 195, 212, 214, 219.

the state destroy trusts?" instead of "Should the state control trusts?" It was not as much as Wilson and Brandeis wanted, but persuading the electorate to question earlier unarticulated assumptions about the desirability of the trusts by insisting that they were neither good nor inevitable and that competition could be restored was a major accomplishment. Eventually, however, concerned about the 1913-1915 depression, the elections of 1916, and the war that had begun in Europe, and anxious to ensure the political support and cooperation of the business community, Wilson decided not to choose activist Progressives for the Federal Trade Commission and to appoint bankers to the Federal Reserve Board. At that point Brandeis felt that he had lost influence over his pupil and left Washington, soon to turn his attention from domestic politics to leadership of the American Zionist movement.[74]

Wilson's limited utilization of Brandeis's ideas, and his growing movement away from them, are attributable to what he viewed as political necessity. Brandeis understood politics well, and it is safe to speculate that he would have preferred to see an intensified campaign in 1916 aimed at the masses rather than big business. To Brandeis, the "masses" included not only workers but consumers and small businessmen, all of whom he regarded as the victims of big business.

But his differences with Wilson did not mean that Brandeis lost his respect for his pupil and his accomplishments. "Perhaps the most extraordinary achievement of Mr. Wilson's first administration," Brandeis wrote shortly after Wilson's death, "was dissipation of the atmosphere of materialism which had enveloped Washington for at least forty years, and probably since Lincoln's days. The rich man — the captain of industry — was distinctly at a disadvantage. One breathed the pure, rarified air of mountain tops."[75] The democratic idealism that so impressed Brandeis permeated the 1912 presidential campaign, and was as much his doing as it was that of Woodrow Wilson.

---

[74]LDB to Colonel House, December 31, 1914, *Letters,* III, p. 393; LDB to Henry French Hollis, November 4, 1914, BP, NMF 68-2; to Charles McCarthy, December 2, 1914, BP, NMF 66-3; to WW, March 6, 1915, BP, NMF 68-2; cf. additional citations in Strum, *Brandeis,* pp. 450-451 n. 40-41.
[75]LDB to Edwin Alderman, December 15, 1924, Alderman Mss., University of Virginia Library.

Business Disunity and the Progressive Movement, 1901-1914

By Robert H. Wiebe

Histories of post-Civil War America, describing the rise of an industrialized society, stress businessmen's common characteristics at the expense of their differences and seldom uncover any appreciable diversity in their response to broad economic and political issues. In the standard interpretations, the businessmen appear as a united force, determined to protect group interests against all assaults. The only common exception to this treatment is to point out the antagonism between small business and big business, although even here historians tend to reunite many of these businessmen in a community of interests. In some studies the assumption of a single business outlook seems to have served primarily as a convenience to the writer. When entrepreneurs act as a group, furnishing counterpoint for other themes, their unity helps to produce a sharper, more effective narrative.[1] In some other histories a homogeneous community develops naturally from the particular selection of business representatives — either a few prominent and verbal entrepreneurs or certain politicians, lawyers, and theorists — who presumably speak for the mass of less articulate businessmen.[2]

EDITOR'S NOTE: — This article received honorable mention in the competition for the 1957 Pelzer Award.

[1] Examples dealing with the Progressive period are George E. Mowry, *Theodore Roosevelt and the Progressive Movement* (Madison, 1946), Chap. I; Russel B. Nye, *Midwestern Progressive Politics: A Historical Study of Its Origins and Development, 1870-1950* (East Lansing, 1951), 258-59. Among the survey treatments in which business unity is assumed are Charles A. and Mary R. Beard, *The Rise of American Civilization* (2 vols., New York, 1927), II, Chaps. XX, XXV, XXVII, and XXIX; Harry J. Carman and Harold C. Syrett, *A History of the American People* (2 vols., New York, 1952), II, Chaps. IV, XI, XII, and XIV.

[2] See Chester McA. Destler, "Opposition of American Businessmen to Social Control during the 'Gilded Age'," *Mississippi Valley Historical Review* (Cedar Rapids), XXXIX (March, 1953), 641-72; Gordon Harrison, *Road to the Right: The Tradition and Hope of American Conservatism* (New York, 1954); Edward C. Kirkland, *Dream and Thought in the Business Community, 1860-1900* (Ithaca, 1956); James W. Prothro, *The Dollar Decade: Business Ideas in the 1920's* (Baton Rouge, 1954).

However valid this analysis may be for other periods of American history, an examination of businessmen's reactions to the Progressive movement indicates that far from forming a cohesive group they differed widely over the proper solution to America's problems and expended a large portion of their energies in internal conflicts.

The thirteen years between Theodore Roosevelt's ascent to the presidency and the outbreak of a general European war contained an exceptional number of public challenges to the business community's accustomed way of life.[8] Flanked by the relative complacency of the Gilded Age and the 1920's, the Progressive era stood as a period of concentrated reform. Campaigns to make government more responsive to the voters' wishes, to allow the underprivileged a larger share of the nation's benefits, and to regulate the economic system so that it would better serve the public interest were all parts of a general movement, heavy with the accumulation of past discontent, which matured in the Progressives' reform program of the early twentieth century. To integrate the several parts of this program required guidance from the federal government, now more alert to cries for change than it had been in the nineteenth century. Thus the widespread desire for reform gained respectability and momentum during the Roosevelt administrations, grew restive in the interlude of William Howard Taft's presidency, and finally culminated in Woodrow Wilson's New Freedom.

The common denominator for this mixture of campaigns was an attempt to create a more equitable balance of privilege and power in American society. Because the roots for so many Progressive problems lay in the previous half-century's rapid industrialization, businessmen, who had acted as the overseers of this economic revolution, found their interests involved or their behavior attacked in virtually all aspects of the reform process. No area caused them deeper concern or elicited a more complicated response than the attempts to supervise America's economic system. This issue raised not only the delicate problem of governmental control but also intricate questions of readjusting privilege among the entrepreneurs themselves. Three separate parts of this reform goal — the movement for banking and currency reorganization, the campaign for

---

[8] More accurately, the Progressive period should also include the last two years of Woodrow Wilson's first administration, but the material treated in this article adapts itself to the shorter time-span. The best survey of the full Progressive movement is Harold U. Faulkner, *The Quest for Social Justice* (New York, 1931).

railroad rate regulation, and the control of trusts — illustrate how the business community split into hostile factions over problems which threatened a redistribution of power among its members.

At the turn of the century, businessmen were operating within a banking and currency framework suited to the needs of a departed age. The national banking laws of 1863, 1864, and 1865 had created a system which was admirable for its uniformity at the time it passed but which became dangerously decentralized and inflexible as the economy grew increasingly national and complex.[4] These measures had tied the issuance of currency to a bank's holdings of government bonds, a regulation which made the banking structure unrelated to seasonal or exceptional fluctuations in the demand for credit. Combined with the absence of any established method of over-all co-ordination, this regulation meant that banks could neither expand their note issue to alleviate periodic currency and credit stringencies nor contract at times of overexpansion. While this arrangement was especially vulnerable to panics, it also failed annually to meet the economy's normal credit requirements. Trussed in an archaic financial system, the bankers themselves led the search for changes which would offer them greater freedom and security.

In 1902, Representative Charles N. Fowler, an outspoken Republican from New Jersey, combined two ideas then current among financiers into the first important reform program of the Progressive era. The heart of his plan was the replacement of the government-bond currency with one based upon the amount of a bank's liquid assets, an index to varying credit needs. Then, in an effort to provide more uniformity in interest rates, he advocated full legalization of branch banking, which had been prohibited by the earlier legislation.[5] Urban bankers, especially those from the Midwest, endorsed the proposal, seeing in it possibilities for flexibility and expansion.[6] Midwestern country bankers, however, formed a solid phalanx of opposition. To these smaller entrepreneurs, branch banking meant an annihilating invasion of their domains from the large

[4] For background information, see Paul Studenski and Herman E. Krooss, *Financial History of the United States* (New York, 1952), 154-55, 178-80.

[5] "Address of Hon. Charles N. Fowler of New Jersey," *Proceedings of the American Bankers' Association* (1902), 99-113. For earlier references to these ideas, see *Proceedings of the American Bankers' Association* (1901), 149-56; *Iron Age* (New York), LXVIII, No. 24 (December 12, 1901), 30.

[6] See *Proceedings of the American Bankers' Association* (1902), 132-34, 144, 175-76; (1906), 142-55, 165-99; (1907), 109-13. See also F. Cyril James, *The Growth of Chicago Banks* (2 vols., New York, 1938), II, 747.

urban centers, and the assets scheme, which did not recognize rural credits, promised a continuing city monopoly in currency. During the next few years, the country bankers, headed by Andrew J. Frame, a tireless campaigner from Waukesha, Wisconsin, remained hostile to each variation of the proposal suggested by their city colleagues. They preferred instead an emergency currency which the federal government would authorize local clearing houses to issue in times of crisis and which the government would then retire with a steeply graduated tax as conditions returned to normal.[7] While these forces battled in public, the New York money powers moved more cautiously. They frowned upon the Fowler plan as too revolutionary, with no safeguards for their dominant role in the nation's finances, and, although they gave a measure of backing to a later assets bill, they gravitated more and more to a banker-controlled central bank as the ideal solution.[8] Through 1907, recognition of a need for reform produced only dissension. With urban financiers divided East and West and their country colleagues suspicious of both, the epigram of a west coast observer summed up these early years: "[The] bankers are still divided, while the public and politicians look on, and smilingly say, 'Who shall decide when doctors disagree?' "[9]

The Panic of 1907 abruptly ended this period of leisurely debate. Warmed by the sun of prosperity, the bankers had not felt pressed to act. The chill of crisis, however, produced a new sense of urgency

[7] For examples of country banker opposition to the Fowler plan, see *Proceedings of the Minnesota Bankers' Association* (1902), 142-43; *Proceedings of the Iowa Bankers' Association* (1902), 78-84; *Commercial West* (Minneapolis), V, No. 34 (August 22, 1903), 12. Typical alternative programs which they supported are given in *Proceedings of the American Bankers' Association* (1903), 163; *Proceedings of the Kansas Bankers' Association* (1903), 138-42; *Wall Street Journal* (New York), September 29, 1905.

[8] For opposition to the Fowler plan, see James W. Stillman to Theodore Roosevelt, August 14, 1903, Papers of Theodore Roosevelt (Division of Manuscripts, Library of Congress). Their support for a 1906 assets currency bill is described in *Report of the Currency Commission to the American Bankers' Association and Remarks by Hon. A. B. Hepburn* ([New York, 1907]), 1-3; *Proceedings of the American Bankers' Association* (New York, 1907), 107-16. The growth of central bank sentiment is indicated by *Forty-ninth Annual Report of the Corporation of the Chamber of Commerce of the State of New York* (1906-1907), 15-37, 40-57; Charles A. Conant, *A History of Modern Banks of Issue* (6th ed., New York, 1927), 437-40. For further New York-Chicago differences, see James H. Eckles, *The Financial Power of the New West* (n. p., 1905); "Why Chicago Bankers Opposed Aldrich Bill," *Commercial West*, V, No. 10 (March 7, 1903), 15.

[9] Miles C. Moore, "Address of the President [of the Washington State Bankers' Association]," reprinted in *Financial Age* (New York), VIII (August 17, 1903), 265-67.

in their discussions.[10] While city financiers tried to muster strength behind a new version of their assets currency program, Congress, in an attempt to assuage public fears, passed a temporary measure, the Aldrich-Vreeland Act.[11] This expedient authorized an emergency currency which regional associations of national banks could distribute in times of special stress. Having favored this type of reform earlier, a respectable number of country bankers, with Andrew Frame again in the forefront, applauded the bill.[12] The urban financiers who demanded a general overhauling could only complain in futile opposition and base their future hopes upon the National Monetary Commission, a congressional body which the Aldrich-Vreeland Act had established to study permanent reorganization.

City bankers emerged from the Panic of 1907 with far greater unity. The crisis of that year, by underlining the constant danger of decentralized reserves, had brought leading urban financiers from East and West into agreement upon the necessity of a central bank.[13] In order to conduct a successful campaign on this principle, they needed the allegiance of businessmen generally, who had tended to favor much milder reforms, and of the country bankers, whose vocal opposition had seriously hampered them in the past.[14] Such a

[10] The Panic also accentuated the city-country split, as smaller financiers accused their city correspondents of freezing rural bank deposits when local currency needs were greatest. George W. Peltier, "President's Address," *Proceedings of the Iowa Bankers' Association* (1908), 18-25; *Transactions of the Arkansas Bankers' Association* (1908), 14.

[11] City banker efforts to replace the Aldrich-Vreeland bill with an assets plan are described in House Committee on Banking and Currency (60 Cong., 1 Sess.), *Hearings and Arguments on Proposed Currency Legislation* (Washington, 1908), 82-86; James, *Growth of Chicago Banks*, II, 775, 778. Western urban financiers, with some justification, accused big New York bankers of supporting the Aldrich-Vreeland bill despite its weaknesses, because the East monopolized the bonds upon which its currency would be based. "West against Aldrich," *Rand McNally Bankers' Monthly* (Chicago), XXXVI (February, 1908), 78-80.

[12] House Committee on Banking and Currency, *Hearings and Arguments on Proposed Currency Legislation*, 235-58; Charles E. Warren, "President's Annual Address," *Proceedings of the New York State Bankers Association* (1908), 9-17; *Proceedings of the Missouri Bankers Association* (1908), 189-90.

[13] Among the many evidences of the western city bankers' conversion, see George E. Roberts, "A Central Bank of Issue," *Proceedings of the Colorado Bankers' Association* (1908), 42-65; George M. Reynolds, "Annual Address of the President," *Proceedings of the American Bankers' Association* (1909), 69-80; Paul M. Warburg to Nelson W. Aldrich, December 24, 1909, Papers of Nelson W. Aldrich (Division of Manuscripts, Library of Congress); *Commercial West*, XIII, No. 4 (January 25, 1908), 7-8. For different interpretations of this period, see Nathaniel W. Stephenson, *Nelson W. Aldrich: A Leader in American Politics* (New York, 1930), 362-63; James, *Growth of Chicago Banks*, II, 773-74.

[14] Businessmen's suspicions of earlier city bankers' programs are shown in *Pro-*

project required tight organization behind a carefully selected plan.

After two years of preliminary propaganda, the city bankers received their concrete program early in 1911 from Senator Nelson W. Aldrich, the National Monetary Commission's chairman who had dominated its work under guidance from powerful New York financiers.[15] The Aldrich plan, while camouflaged by general and sometimes deceptive language, called for a central banking institution, with branches, which bankers would own and operate and which would regulate the issuance of assets currency.[16] By pre-arrangement, a special Business Men's Monetary Conference, sponsored by the National Board of Trade, met the day after the announcement, and, with Aldrich's chief financial mentor, Paul M. Warburg, as floor manager, the Conference gave the plan full endorsement. It also began work toward establishing the National Citizens' League, meant to serve as propaganda headquarters in the coming drive for business support.[17]

Founders of the Citizens' League tried hard to surround it with an aura of nonpartisanship. They chose Chicago as its home in order to avoid the "animosities and jealousies" associated with New York, and then announced as their open-minded goal "an improved

ceedings of the National Board of Trade (1906), 268-69; Iron Age, LXX (November 20, 1902), 30-31; New York Journal of Commerce and Commercial Bulletin, October 16, 1906. After the Panic, however, these men expressed a far livelier interest in general reform. See, for example, F. B. DeBerard to Buck's Stove and Range Co., August 1, 1908, Papers of Daniel A. Tompkins (Southern Historical Collection, University of North Carolina); also Eighteenth Annual Report of the Trades League of Philadelphia (1908), 105-108.

[15] Stephenson, Aldrich, Chap. XXIV; Thomas W. Lamont, Henry P. Davison: The Record of a Useful Life (New York, 1933), 92-102; Frank A. Vanderlip (in collaboration with Boyden Sparkes), From Farm Boy to Financier (New York, 1935), 210-19.

[16] "Suggested Plan for Monetary Legislation Submitted to the National Monetary Commission by Hon. Nelson W. Aldrich," Senate Docs., 61 Cong., 3 Sess., No. 784. Newspapers uncritically accepted Aldrich's word that his plan was not centralized. Washington Post, January 18, 1911, and New York Times, January 18, 1911. Aldrich later made some additional concessions toward banker control, described in Stephenson, Aldrich, 389-92, and Journal of the American Bankers' Association (New York), III (May, 1911), 643-48, before perfecting his plan. For its final form, see Publications of the National Monetary Commission (24 vols., Washington, 1911-1912), XXIV (Report of National Monetary Commission).

[17] Fifty-fourth Annual Report of the Corporation of the Chamber of Commerce of the State of New York (1911-1912), 146-51; Proceedings of the National Board of Trade (1911), 184-207; New York Times, January 19, 1911. For details on the establishment of the National Citizens' League, see The National Citizens' League for the Promotion of a Sound Banking System: The Origins of the League (Chicago, [1911]); Harry A. Wheeler, "From the President," Annual Report of the Chicago Association of Commerce (1911), 11-14.

banking system for the United States." [18] Beneath this veneer of impartiality, however, the Citizens' League worked diligently for the Aldrich plan, saturating the business community with speeches and literature in an effort to allay suspicions of a centralized banking system. Country bankers and other small businessmen received the most delicate handling, with constant stress placed upon the plan's supposed freedom from Wall Street domination.[19] The combination of a definite program and efficient organization achieved remarkable results during a few months of intensive campaigning. Few hazarded open criticism, while a wide assortment of approving resolutions and statements created the semblance of broad business unity behind the plan.[20]

No matter how well city bankers marshaled their business support, they could achieve final victory only by an act of Congress. In early 1912 the nation was poised on the brink of a political upheaval which would sweep reform-minded Democrats into full federal power. Democrats and progressive Republicans, crying out against privileged money powers, already controlled Congress. In such a climate no program associated with Aldrich and New York's great financiers could possibly succeed, and bills based upon the plan died one by one in committee.[21] The façade of business unity which the urban financiers had labored so hard to construct crumbled with the removal of its major prop, the Aldrich plan. Smaller

[18] *The Commercial Club of Chicago Year-Book* (1914-1915), 73; *The National Citizens' League for the Promotion of a Sound Banking System: Constitution and By-Laws* (Chicago, 1911). See also Stephenson, *Aldrich*, 381.

[19] The League's commitment is divulged by its director in "Statement by Prof. J. Laurence Laughlin" (n. d.), Papers of James Laurence Laughlin (Division of Manuscripts, Library of Congress); Laughlin to James B. Forgan, August 13, 1911, quoted in part in Laughlin, *The Federal Reserve Act: Its Origins and Problems* (New York, 1933), 48. After its first important months as propaganda co-ordinator, the League ran afoul of the old Chicago-New York hostilities, which eventually sapped its strength. Laughlin to Wallace D. Simmons, January 15, 1914, Laughlin Papers; Laughlin, *Federal Reserve Act*, 44-47; H. Parker Willis to Carter Glass, November 29, 1912, Papers of Carter Glass (Alderman Library, University of Virginia). Examples of the special treatment accorded smaller bankers and businessmen are *The National Reserve Association: Advantages It Will Give the Smaller Banks and Their Communities* ([Chicago, 1912]); "Address of Mr. Charles A. Conant," *Proceedings of the National Association of Manufacturers* (1911), 206-12; Laughlin, *Federal Reserve Act*, 79; Stephenson, *Aldrich*, 392-94.

[20] Among the rare open dissents are Daniel A. Tompkins, "Disadvantages of the Aldrich Plan," *American Industries* (New York), XI, No. 10 (May, 1911), 17-18; Andrew J. Frame, "Diagnosis of the National Monetary Bill" (Copy), Papers of William Howard Taft (Division of Manuscripts, Library of Congress).

[21] A general description of the Aldrich plan's failure in Congress is given in Stephenson, *Aldrich*, 401-404.

bankers, no longer cowed by organized pressure, now poured forth alternative proposals, most of which recommended thoroughly decentralized systems, with a sprinkling of suggestions for a government-controlled central bank.[22] In this confusion of plans and counterplans, the city financiers suddenly found themselves on the defensive, forced to wait until the Wilson administration had decided upon its choice of reform.

The Democrats' solution, gradually molded by various factions of the party, represented a compromise on the question of centralization, but it rejected banker control over the new system's policy or currency.[23] The Glass-Owen bill, through which the Federal Reserve system originated, authorized twelve regional institutions under loose supervision by a politically appointed Federal Reserve Board. It also provided for the replacement of the government-bond currency with one based upon a bank's asset structure, ultimately backed by the government. Many smaller bankers and businessmen, especially in the West and South, praised this proposal as a wise one which would satisfactorily protect their interests. "We are more willing to take our chances with the Government," explained one Wisconsin country banker.[24] On the other hand, urban financiers who believed in the banker-controlled centralization of the Aldrich plan were naturally unhappy. Yet, de-

[22] Smaller urban bankers joined in this display of opposition to centralization. The most popular plan came from a minor New York financier, James G. Cannon. See his *Clearing Houses and Currency No. 1* (Syracuse, 1913), copy in Papers of Woodrow Wilson (Division of Manuscripts, Library of Congress). See also House Subcommittee of the Committee on Banking and Currency (62 Cong., 3 Sess.), *Banking and Currency Reform, Hearings* (Washington, 1913), 337-40, 447-51; Leslie Butler, "Address of the President," *Oregon State Bankers Association Proceedings* (1913), 12-14.

[23] The details of this intraparty struggle are described in Arthur S. Link, *Wilson: The New Freedom* (Princeton, 1956), Chap. VII. It is important to point out, however, that Professor Link has ascribed too much unanimity to city banker opinion throughout the Glass-Owen bill's development, ignoring in the process the very real conflicts among those financiers who wanted to alter the measure. To the Wilson administration, these banker differences may have sounded like minor variations on a single theme of total opposition, but to the financiers they represented a clear and significant rift within the banking community, which the hostile forces found extremely difficult to reconcile.

[24] Senate Committee on Banking and Currency (63 Cong., 1 Sess.), *Hearings on H. R. 7837 (S. 2639)* (4 vols., Washington, 1913), II, 1549. See also *ibid.*, II, 2070, 2096; [D. A. Tompkins], "The Glass Currency Bill" (Copy), Papers of Daniel A. Tompkins (Division of Manuscripts, Library of Congress); "Address of W. H. Manly, President," *Proceedings of the Alabama Bankers' Association* (1913), 21-36. Excellent sources for this viewpoint are cited in Link, *Wilson: The New Freedom*, 224.

spite their common disappointment, the city bankers themselves divided sharply over the proper opposition tactics to follow.

Chicago's two strongest bankers, James B. Forgan and George M. Reynolds, led the two major factions of urban financiers. Forgan, with support from certain big New York financiers and from the officers of the American Bankers' Association, condemned the bill as "unworkable, impracticable and fundamentally unsound," and wanted to scrap it entirely.[25] Reynolds, whose followers decidedly outnumbered Forgan's irreconcilables, countered with a conciliatory plea for moderation, arguing that the bankers faced a practical, not a theoretical, situation and could win concessions only by working within the framework of the administration measure.[26] The two forces met for a test of strength in August, 1913, at a Chicago conference called by the American Bankers' Association's Currency Commission, where the conciliationists won a clear victory.[27] Joined by an equally moderate group from the infant United States Chamber of Commerce, a committee from the Chicago conference moved to Washington to negotiate the best adjustment possible with Congress.[28]

In all probability, the bankers' mission was a predestined failure. By the time the Wilson administration had mollified the diverse

[25] Quoted in *Financial Age*, XXVIII (August 30, 1913), 344. Other elements of Forgan's intransigeants are described in Senate Committee on Banking and Currency, *Hearings on H. R. 7837*, I, 680-81; Wallace D. Simmons to the Members of the Banking and Currency Committee of the United States Chamber of Commerce, January 10, 1914, Laughlin Papers; Arthur Reynolds, "Annual Address of the First Vice-President," *Proceedings of the American Bankers' Association* (1913), 54-65.

[26] The evolution of the conciliationist group can be seen from A. Barton Hepburn to Carter Glass, December 19, 1912; H. Parker Willis to Glass, December 31, 1912, January 18, 1913; George M. Reynolds to Glass, April 18, 1913; all in Glass Papers; House Subcommittee of the Committee on Banking and Currency (62 Cong., 3 Sess.), *Banking and Currency Reform, Hearings*, 357-62 and *passim*; John V. Farwell to Woodrow Wilson, July 22, 1913, Wilson Papers. Willis and Reynolds, trying to separate those bankers who would co-operate with Congress, warned Glass of the threat from intransigeants such as Forgan and officers of the American Bankers' Association.

[27] Chicago *Tribune*, August 24, 25, 1913. New York *Times*, August 23, 24, 1913. Its conclusions are given in *Report Unanimously Adopted by a Conference Held at Chicago, August 22 and 23, 1913* ([1913]), copy in Wilson Papers.

[28] For the Chamber's moderate approach, see *Nation's Business* (Washington), I, No. 13 (July 15, 1913), 4-6; No. 16 (October 15, 1913), 3; supplemented by the friendly letters of its president, Harry A. Wheeler, to J. Laurence Laughlin, August 19, 1913, Wilson Papers, and to Carter Glass, August 8, 1913, Glass Papers; also reprinted in Henry Parker Willis, *The Federal Reserve System: Legislation, Organization, and Operation* (New York, 1923), 417-21.

Democratic factions, it was in no mood to grant city financiers any major concessions.[29] But the bankers, as a fitting climax to their Progressive record, exhibited one final show of disunity. At Chicago, the urban leaders had been so involved in reconciling their own differences that they brusquely ignored their sensitive country colleagues, who now followed the conference delegation to Washington and broadcast their grievances. One irate Arkansas financier described the Chicago proceedings to amused congressmen: "That committee was stacked; that was the coldest deal I ever went against in my life. We were invited there simply and solely to set the stage, to have a crowd, to carry a spear and sing a song and dance around, so that the stage would be full while the bigwigs could have the spot lights played on them." [30] While the city financiers scurried to put their house in order, Congress applied the final touches to the Glass-Owen bill.[31] At the end as at the beginning of the Progressive period, the bankers had found their internal conflicts a more powerful force than their desire to reform the financial system.

As in the case of banking reform, the lag of legislation behind America's industrial realities provided the background for the battles of businessmen over railroad regulation. During the latter part of the nineteenth century, entrepreneurs had extended and consolidated the network of existing lines into national transportation systems, forming a skeleton for the country's remarkable commercial growth. Closely limited by court decisions, state attempts to control these private empires had proved ineffectual. Congress finally made a beginning toward regulation with the Interstate Commerce Act of 1887, but its failure to buttress the law against the weakening effect of judicial interpretations left the Interstate Commerce Com-

[29] Link, *Wilson: The New Freedom*, 226-27, shows that the distinction between intransigeants and conciliationists did not impress the Wilson administration, which viewed the Chicago conference results as proof that no co-operation with the urban bankers was possible. As tactless as they seem to have been, these resolutions were not meant to be an ultimatum, rather a complete list of ideals toward which these men hoped to move Congress.

[30] Senate Committee on Banking and Currency, *Hearings on H. R. 7837*, II, 1566. See also *ibid.*, 1539-65, and McLane Tilton, Jr., to Glass, September 3, 1913, Glass Papers.

[31] These efforts included an extraordinary country bankers' session, as well as some difficult maneuvering among full supporters and adamant opponents of the administration bill, during the regular American Bankers' Association sessions. *Proceedings of the American Bankers' Association* (1913), 75-91, 95-99, 101-16.

mission with little more power than the states to cope with major transportation problems.[32]

Few businessmen were satisfied with the rate structure which had evolved during those years of free interplay between the railroads as carriers and their customers as shippers. For the carriers, the worst abuses lay in an intricate rebate system to which a number of the bigger railroads had resorted as a result of unbridled rail competition and under pressure from giant industries. Business shippers, for their part, felt that the exorbitant transportation rates, which the railroads staunchly defended, constituted the basic evil. During the Progressive era, as the federal government experimented with various techniques of rate control, the carriers and shippers engaged in a continuous struggle, each group maneuvering to protect its special interests.

At the beginning of the century, the shippers, divided occupationally and scattered geographically throughout the nation, had no way of pressing their cause as a group. Their one national spokesman was the Interstate Commerce Law Convention, founded in 1900 by a handful of midwestern grain merchants and millers.[33] Insignificant in size, this organization gained prominence through the incessant activity of its leader, Edward P. Bacon, a politically ambitious grain dealer from Milwaukee, who set himself the task of rallying the country's diversified shippers behind a bill that would give the Interstate Commerce Commission the power to establish reasonable rates. Dubbed a "Peter the Hermit" by his enemies, Bacon began his crusade by taking his bill to Washington in hopes of attracting sufficient attention to launch a broad shippers' movement.[34] With some difficulty, he found sponsors for his measure in 1902, only to lose control of his campaign through bad strategy. Railroad leaders were simultaneously backing anti-rebate legislation, and, in a move to dull the point of Bacon's attack, they lured him into joining his proposal with theirs as the revised Elkins bill.

[32] I. L. Sharfman, *The Interstate Commerce Commission: A Study in Administrative Law and Procedure* (4 parts, New York, 1931-1937), Part I, 13-19; William Z. Ripley, *Railroads: Rates and Regulation* (New York, 1912), 456-86.

[33] *Forty-fourth Annual Report of the Chicago Board of Trade* (1901), lxxiv-lxxv; *Railway Age* (Chicago), XL (September 8, 1905), 280-82.

[34] Senate Committee on Interstate Commerce, *Regulation of Railway Rates, Hearings on Bills to Amend the Interstate Commerce Act* (*Senate Docs.*, 59 Cong., 1 Sess., No. 243; 5 vols., Washington, 1906), III, 2503. For early recognition of Bacon's importance, see *Commercial and Financial Chronicle* (New York), LXXIV (February 8, 1902), 291-92.

Bacon worked unstintingly for the combination measure, then stood impotently by as the Senate cut away his sections of the bill and passed only the Elkins Anti-Rebate Act of 1903. In defeat, Bacon grimly promised "to follow this up by vigorous effort . . . at the next session of Congress."[35]

His prospects brightened considerably as Progressive spokesmen, with the magnetic President Roosevelt prominent among them, made rate regulation a central part of their program. Shippers whom Bacon alone could never have reached now became enthusiastic members of his Interstate Commerce Law Convention.[36] Riding the crest of a Progressive wave, he decided in 1905 to call another meeting of the Convention in preparation for the final thrust. Bacon gambled everything upon the appeal of his richest asset, the Roosevelt name, requiring a pledge from each prospective delegate that he would support the President's rate reforms.[37]

This second strategic error proved fatal. While many shippers willingly responded to his call, an equally strong countermovement arose among businessmen wary of the federal powers connected with Roosevelt and reform. These dissidents had an aggressive and capable leader in David M. Parry, president of the National As-

[35] Edward P. Bacon to John C. Spooner, February 9, 1903, Papers of John C. Spooner (Division of Manuscripts, Library of Congress). For details of Bacon's labors, see Bacon to Spooner, December 2, 23, 1901, June 26, July 3, 1902, January 3, 24, 1903, and Robert Eliot (for the Milwaukee Chamber of Commerce) to Spooner, April 2, 1902, *ibid.* In rare instances a railroad executive agreed that some rate control powers should be given to the Interstate Commerce Commission. The president of the Pennsylvania Railroad, for example, explained that he supported some government control "because we believe that it is better policy to assist in framing and passing a reasonable measure now than to have a more drastic and perhaps a seriously injurious one forced upon us by public clamor." Alexander J. Cassatt to Theodore Roosevelt, April 1, 1902, Roosevelt Papers. See also Destler, "Opposition of American Businessmen to Social Control," *Mississippi Valley Historical Review,* XXXIX (March, 1953), 666-67, for corroboration in an earlier period. Hans Thorelli, *The Federal Antitrust Policy: Origination of an American Tradition* (Baltimore, 1955), 538-49, provides a broader background for the Elkins Act. Sharfman, *Interstate Commerce Commission,* I, 36-37, indicates railroad backing for the rebate portions.

[36] The best general account of this phase of the railroad regulation movement is John M. Blum, *The Republican Roosevelt* (Cambridge, 1954), Chap. VI. *Proceedings of the Interstate Commerce Law Convention* (1904), 27-38, indicates the broadening membership of the Convention while showing that its primary strength still lay in the Midwest. Although Bacon capitalized upon progressive Republican propaganda, he proved totally unable to influence the course of its policy. See Bacon to Spooner, May 4, August 5, 1904, Spooner Papers, for his failure to encourage a stronger Republican stand on regulation during the 1904 campaign; and Bacon to Roosevelt, August 15, 1904; Roosevelt to Bacon, August 19, 1904; Bacon to Roosevelt, August 23, 1904; all in Roosevelt Papers, for Roosevelt's easy mastery over his admirer.

[37] Edward P. Bacon [open letter], September 18, 1905, copy in Roosevelt Papers.

sociation of Manufacturers and a determined opponent of railroad regulation.[38] When the Interstate Commerce Law Convention met in October, 1905, Parry's followers refused to sign the necessary pledge, and Bacon, fearing that they would pack his meeting, hastily hired armed guards to bar dissenters from the Convention conference hall.[39] The rebels promptly marched a few blocks away to hold their own sessions, claiming that they were the legitimate voice of business. The farce of two meetings, approximately the same size, allegedly representing the same economic group, yet proclaiming diametrically opposed programs, ruined the effectiveness of Bacon's convention; and thus the victory went to Parry and his associates.[40]

Temporarily the shippers reverted to their earlier state of disorganization. In the final months before Congress acted upon the rate question, shippers, lacking a national representative, had to plead their cause individually or through local groups. The railroads, assisted by their own business allies, redoubled their efforts against rate regulation with a degree of success.[41] Despite the fact that the Hepburn Act of 1906 gave the Interstate Commerce Commission the right to pass judgment upon the carriers' tariffs, the railroads still retained broad use of court review before the Commission's rulings could go into effect. There matters stood until the Panic of 1907 spurred both carriers and shippers to new action. The railroads, trying to capitalize upon a measure of business sympathy for their financial plight, proposed general rate advances in the

[38] Although Parry, as a carriage and car manufacturer, was ostensibly a shipper, he had considerable railroad investments. Albert K. Steigerwalt, Jr., "The National Association of Manufacturers: Organization and Policies, 1895-1914" (Ph.D. dissertation, University of Michigan, 1952), 175.

[39] Chicago *Tribune*, October 25, 26, 1905. New York *Times*, October 27, 1905. Bacon had had ample warning of the rising opposition. See, for example, a widely circulated public letter from David M. Parry to Bacon, January 3, 1905, copy in Papers of Francis G. Newlands (Division of Manuscripts, Yale University Library).

[40] *Proceedings of the Federal Rate Regulation Association* (1905), 3-18, 22-28, 51-52; *Proceedings of the Interstate Commerce Law Convention* (1905), 11-12, 18-19, 60, 66, 99-100. Soon after this fiasco, Bacon disappeared as a factor in the regulation movement, and the Convention disintegrated.

[41] The central railroad argument was presented by railroad presidents Samuel Spencer and David Willcox in House Committee on Interstate and Foreign Commerce, *Hearings on Bills to Amend the Interstate-Commerce Act* (*House Docs.*, 58 Cong., 3 Sess., No. 422; Washington, 1905), 239-63. For other business advocacy of the carriers' arguments, see *ibid.*, 139-44, and Senate Committee on Interstate Commerce, *Regulation of Railway Rates, Hearings* (*Senate Docs.*, 59 Cong., 1 Sess., No 243), I, 169-71, 486-91.

midst of the crisis. The move backfired. Faced with loud and wide-spread denunciation from business organizations, the carriers with-drew their plan, and simultaneously the threatened shippers or-ganized once more to defend themselves.[42] This time they built their new association, the National Industrial Traffic League, upon a foundation of powerful midwestern commercial organizations, whose professional traffic managers directed the Traffic League's technical work. Firmly grounded, in contrast to the personalized Interstate Commerce Law Convention, the Traffic League pre-pared to match railroad arguments before the Interstate Commerce Commission and to encourage new legislation which would strength-en the Commission's powers.[43] The Panic period had accentuated shipper-carrier differences without satisfying either of the antago-nists.

In 1910 these strained relations produced a major crisis. The first phase involved the Mann-Elkins Act, which allowed the Inter-state Commerce Commission to suspend proposed rate changes and placed its rulings in effect before court review. Since the measure embodied two major planks in the shippers' platform, it received enthusiastic and consistent support from the Traffic League.[44] The railroads, perhaps sensing defeat, repeated their 1908 mistake by trying to slip in over-all rate advances before the bill could pass, but once again they were forced to retreat. Threatened with anti-trust prosecution if they did not comply, the carriers agreed in con-ference with President Taft to postpone the question of increases in return for tacit assurances of an Interstate Commerce Commission hearing as soon as Congress acted on the Mann-Elkins bill.[45] The railroads now centered their primary hopes for relief upon a favor-able ruling by the Commission.

[42] For examples of the national protest, see *Seventeenth Annual Report of the Trades League of Philadelphia* (1907), 53-56; *Fifty-ninth Annual Report of the Cincinnati Chamber of Commerce and Merchants' Exchange* (1907), 42; *Board of Directors Minutes of the National Association of Manufacturers* (May 18, 1908); *The Members' Annual of the Los Angeles Chamber of Commerce* (1909), 26.

[43] James C. Lincoln, *The National Industrial Traffic League* ([Chicago], 1908); Edward F. Lacey, "The National Industrial Traffic League: Organization and De-velopment" (Typed copy in Bureau of Railway Economics Library, Washington, D. C.), 5; House Committee on Interstate and Foreign Commerce (61 Cong., 1 Sess.), *Hearings on Bills Affecting Interstate Commerce* (2 vols., Washington, 1910), I, 395-98.

[44] House Committee on Interstate and Foreign Commerce, *Hearings on Bills Affect-ing Interstate Commerce, passim.*

[45] For the story of the government's action, see *Bulletin of the American Iron and Steel Association* (Philadelphia), XLIV (July 1, 1910), 59; New York *Times*, June 7, 8, 1910; "Railroad Rate Agreement" (Copy), Taft Papers; Ripley, *Railroads*, 561-62.

Once Congress passed the Mann-Elkins Act, the scene shifted to the Interstate Commerce Commission hearings and the second phase of this shipper-carrier struggle. By then, the shippers had reached their apex of organization. To accompany the midwestern strength of the Traffic League, eastern commercial associations representing shipping interests banded together to hire the brilliant Boston lawyer, Louis D. Brandeis, as their spokesman, and an assortment of local and national business groups contributed what force they could in creating a solid front of shippers to oppose the increases.[46] The railroads were not able to present sufficient evidence to counteract the combined efforts of Brandeis and well-informed traffic managers, and in February, 1911, the Commission ruled against the rate increases sought by the carriers.[47]

These defeats, as extensive as they were, did not leave the railroads helpless. At the very time shipper unity was approaching its peak of effectiveness, the carriers were in the process of undermining it. In the period of the Panic of 1907 a few alert railroad leaders had initiated a public relations movement which, after 1910, became a concerted campaign to woo the public and divide the hostile shippers. Special agents, friendly industrialists, and railroad executives canvassed the business community, probing the weakest spot in their antagonists' armor, a need for regular, efficient service. Time and again, these men warned that in a period of rising costs unchanged rates would bankrupt the roads and produce transportation chaos.[48] By 1913 the carriers were prepared to try again for rate advances.

In that year, the Interstate Commerce Commission granted the

[46] The general development and extent of shipper power can be seen from "Resolutions Unanimously Adopted by a Convention of Shippers and Representatives of Shipping and Commercial Organizations Held at Chicago, Ill., May 17, 1910," ICC Docket No. 3400; Louis D. Brandeis, *Brief on Behalf of Traffic Committee of Commercial Organizations of the Atlantic Seaboard* (Washington, 1911), ICC Investigation and Suspension No. 3; "Testimony" (August 29, 1910), 5-48, ICC Investigation and Suspension No. 4; all in Records of the Interstate Commerce Commission (National Archives, Washington).

[47] *Decisions of the Interstate Commerce Commission of the United States* (Washington), XX (1911), 243-399. See also Alpheus T. Mason, *Brandeis: A Free Man's Life* (New York, 1946), 315-51.

[48] For the development of this new diplomacy, see William W. Finley, *Addresses and Statements, 1907-1910* (Washington, n. d.), *passim*; Edward P. Ripley, "The Railroads and Public Approval," *First Annual Dinner, Railway Business Association* (1909), 30-34; J. Hampton Baumgartner, *The Railroads and Public Relations* (n. p., 1913); Eric F. Goldman, *Two-Way Street: The Emergence of the Public Relations Counsel* (Cambridge, 1948), Chap. I.

railroads a rehearing of their case for increases. This time the carriers' propaganda had neutralized or converted so many erstwhile shipper foes that there was no chance of re-creating the 1910 battle lines. On the contrary, the railroads dominated the hearings to such an extent that the Commission complained: "There appears to have been a set purpose to convince us that the people were of one mind respecting the very important questions involved in the case, and that, in order to satisfy every public requirement, there remained nothing for the Commission to do but to register this consensus of opinion by immediately entering an order permitting the carriers to make their proposed charges effective." [49] Although it first rejected the carriers' request, the Commission partially reversed itself later in 1914 and allowed the eastern roads their increases.[50] Many shippers, meanwhile, were regretting their temporary moderation. Even during the truce they had emphasized that they remained firm defenders of the existing regulatory laws and that they would scrutinize every future railroad request with critical care.[51] The earlier animosity had mellowed but had certainly not disappeared. As difficult as it was for the diversified shipping interests to achieve and maintain a working unity, their common concern over reasonable rates set them apart as the natural business antagonists of the railroads throughout the Progressive period.

The struggle over rate levels had proceeded along obvious lines of economic self-interest. The debate among businessmen over trust control, on the other hand, suffered from hazy definition and from blurred demarcation among opponents. Part of this confusion resulted from the sudden burst of business consolidation, beginning after the election of 1896, which gave the old question of supervising industrial enterprises new dimensions of complexity and

[49] *Decisions of the Interstate Commerce Commission*, XXXI (1914), 425-26. For the hard core of continuing shipper opposition, see *ibid.*, 357. Typical examples of the railroad leaders' success in neutralizing their former enemies are given in F. A. Delano to E. E. Clark, May 12, 1913, and H. C. Barlow to John H. Marble, October 22, 1913, ICC Docket No. 5860, Records of the Interstate Commerce Commission; *Report of the Boston Chamber of Commerce* (1913), 38-39; "National Industrial Traffic League," *Railway Age-Gazette* (Chicago), LV (November 21, 1913), 962-64.

[50] *Decisions of the Interstate Commerce Commission*, XXXI (1914), 351-454; XXXII (1914), 325-54.

[51] *National Industrial Traffic League: Proceedings* (July, 1912), 18; (August, 1914), 29-31; (November, 1914), 3-7. This strictly limited shipper acceptance of railroad requests is also illustrated by their unanimous refusal to allow carriers an increase in spotting charges even during the 1914 truce. See the hundreds of letters in "Protest" Files of ICC Docket No. 5860, Records of the Interstate Commerce Commission.

public concern.[52] The problem of trust control became a symbol of the Progressive period's general worry over unfamiliar bigness and the decline of competition. Into this stream of unrest flowed the specific enmity of those businessmen who felt oppressed by large enterprises because of direct competition, the price of trust products, or the uncertain future of smaller entrepreneurs in an economy of giants.[53] The exact problem was usually ill-defined, but the business conflicts were nonetheless acrimonious.

Business arguments over trust regulation remained diffuse until the Roosevelt administration dramatically placed itself in the midst of the controversy. In 1902, the government gave its basic regulatory weapon, the Sherman Antitrust Act of 1890, fresh prestige by prosecuting one of the nation's major combinations, the Northern Securities Company.[54] Then, in the wake of this surprise, came the establishment of the Bureau of Corporations as a general investigating agency within the Department of Commerce and Labor. The smaller businessmen whose hostility toward trusts had been frustrated for lack of a satisfactory outlet now flooded the administration with pleas to champion their causes, whether they be battles with the country's great corporations or conflicts with various price-fixing retail leagues.[55] Big-business leaders, on the other hand, concentrated upon coming to terms with this potential enemy, the federal government. Led by Elbert H. Gary, chairman of United States Steel's board of directors, the more discerning of these went directly to the source of their trouble and tried to negotiate private agreements with the administration, by which the corporations would co-operate in investigations in return for undefined but presumably lenient treatment.[56]

[52] For general information on this subject, see Harold U. Faulkner, *The Decline of Laissez Faire, 1897-1917* (New York, 1951), 153-63.

[53] For background concerning this sentiment, see Thorelli, *Federal Antitrust Policy*, 149, 350-51. See also *Official Proceedings of the Trans-Mississippi Commercial Congress* (1902), 244.

[54] For the legal status of the Sherman Act in 1902, see Thorelli, *Federal Antitrust Policy*, 592, 599-604.

[55] See, for examples, Sam H. Harris to James R. Garfield (concerning the American Tobacco Co.), January 7, 1905; Kelso and Anglin Correspondence (concerning a Cleveland lumber dealers' association); E. D. Beebe Correspondence (concerning the National Association of Retail Druggists); Ross E. Parks to Theodore Roosevelt (concerning a grain dealers' organization), July 13, 1906; all in Records of the Federal Trade Commission (National Archives).

[56] The arrangements are described in "Conference at White House, Evening of November 2, 1905"; "Memorandum of Interview In Re *International Harvester Company*, on January 18, 1907"; "Memorandum In Re Second Interview with In-

These efforts to commit the government to one side or the other in trust prosecution, however, did not actively involve the majority of businessmen. Although the scandals of 1905 and 1906 concerning life insurance companies and food industries shocked many business-men and quickened their reform impulses, most of them refused to endorse programs which might someday be turned upon them.[57] As a result, the popular solution among mixed business organiza-tions, such as the National Association of Manufacturers and the National Board of Trade, was a national incorporation law, elastic enough to satisfy both those desiring tighter control and those hop-ing for a relaxation of the Sherman Act's ban on restraint of trade.[58]

Out of the Panic of 1907 emerged a proposal which helped to clear the lines dividing the business community. A group of power-ful industrialists decided that their salvation lay in transforming the Sherman Act into an ally instead of a hovering threat. To achieve this, they formulated a plan whereby businessmen would submit their projects for expansion and communities of interest to the Bureau of Corporations which, after a thorough investigation, could immunize them from future prosecution by issuing a protec-tive stamp of approval.[59] With valuable help from President Roosevelt, they were able in early 1908 to bring their proposal be-fore Congress as the Hepburn amendments to the Sherman Act.[60] An opposition among lesser businessmen solidified immediately. While speaking most vigorously against certain peripheral labor

ternational Harvester Company on January 19, 1907"; all in Records of Federal Trade Commission. These loose understandings slowly deteriorated until antitrust suits against U. S. Steel and International Harvester officially terminated them. See Edgar A. Bancroft to Luther Conant, Jr., September 10, 1912, *ibid.*

[57] For examples of indignant business reactions to insurance and food scandals, see N. B. Coffman, "Some Unwise Tendencies in Banking as Viewed from the Standpoint of a Country Banker," *Proceedings of the Washington State Bankers' Association* (1905), 75; *Seventy-third Annual Report of the Philadelphia Board of Trade* (1906), 24-25; *Proceedings of the National Board of Trade* (1906), 271; *The Members' Annual of the Los Angeles Chamber of Commerce* (1906), 19.

[58] *Proceedings of the National Association of Manufacturers* (1906), 34-39; *Proceedings of the National Board of Trade* (1904), 80-93.

[59] The background to this proposal is given in *Proceedings of the National Con-ference on Trusts and Combinations under the Auspices of the National Civic Fed-eration* (1907), 454-55, 465.

[60] Roosevelt's role in this process is indicated by Roosevelt to Seth Low, April 1, 1908, in Elting E. Morison (ed.), *The Letters of Theodore Roosevelt* (8 vols., Cam-bridge, 1951-1954), VI, 986-87; and Low to Roosevelt, April 11, 1908, Records of the Federal Trade Commission. See also Gordon M. Jensen, "The National Civic Fed-eration: American Business in an Age of Social Change and Social Reform, 1900-1910" (Ph.D. dissertation, Princeton University, 1956), 277.

clauses in the bill, these smaller entrepreneurs made it patently clear to congressmen that they would not tolerate any differentiation between "reasonable" and "unreasonable" restraint of trade, no matter what else the bill might contain. To these dissenters, such a law would invite a few mammoth corporations to dominate the economy with governmental assistance.[61] The Hepburn amendments failed in an election year sensitive to big-business privileges, but its advocates did not abandon their objective.

For a time the debate waned as the nation entered an unstable transition between Roosevelt's Square Deal and Wilson's New Freedom. Businessmen tensely watched the Supreme Court for their next guidepost. In 1911 the Court issued its long-awaited decisions on the Standard Oil and American Tobacco Company antitrust suits, ruling against the legality of each but, in its famous gloss on the Sherman Act, officially separating reasonable from unreasonable restraint of trade. Once announced, these decisions somehow seemed anticlimactic. For smaller businessmen who had opposed this distinction in 1908, the Court's interpretation naturally constituted a defeat, and even for the powerful corporations, who were theoretical victors, the decisions provided little solace.[62] If each large enterprise had to undergo the ordeal of a judicial test in order to survive, who would be next? United States Steel received the unpleasant answer in October, 1911, in the form of an antitrust suit, and International Harvester followed it into court a few months later. These prosecutions underlined the big-business conviction that only a new, liberal law could offer permanent relief.

During the Progressive ferment of 1912, industrial leaders reopened the campaign which had stalled with the 1908 defeat of the

[61] For the core of smaller business opposition, see House Subcommittee of the Committee on the Judiciary (60 Cong., 1 Sess.), *An Act to Regulate Commerce, Etc., Hearings on House Bill 19745* (Washington, 1908), 153-64, 167-68; Senate Subcommittee of the Committee on the Judiciary (60 Cong., 1 Sess.), *Amendment of Sherman Antitrust Law, Hearings on the Bill (S. 6331) and the Bill (S. 6440)* (Washington, 1908), 60-62; "New York Board of Trade and Transportation Petition, April 8, 1908" (Copy), Records of the Federal Trade Commission, with an analysis in Roosevelt to Herbert Knox Smith, April 14, 1908, *ibid.*, partially reprinted in Morison (ed.), *Letters of Theodore Roosevelt,* VI, 1007-1008. The industrialists backing the Hepburn amendments would have been happy to drop the labor provisions which superficially aroused the strongest small-business opposition. Jensen, "National Civic Federation," 285-86.

[62] For smaller businessmen's continuing rejection of this viewpoint, see "Report of Mr. P. A. Peterson, President," *Reports of the Illinois Manufacturers' Association* (1911), 3-23; "Address of President Harry H. Pond," *Proceedings of the New Jersey Bankers' Association* (1912), 86-92.

Hepburn amendments. They altered their advice-and-consent formula to include an interstate trade commission, similar in status to the interstate commerce commission, as well as stricter criminal liability laws, but the goal remained government sanction for business consolidation and co-operation.[63] With this revised edition of their plan in hand, the big businessmen prepared to meet the challenge from the Wilson administration, which had been elected on a platform and in an atmosphere averse to bigness. The Democrats, too, wanted clarification of the Sherman Act, but in the Clayton bill of 1914 they chose a path opposite from the one corporation magnates followed.[64] Instead of liberalizing the anti-trust statute, the Clayton omnibus measure promised stiffer governmental control, designating specific corporate practices as destructive of competition and henceforth illegal. Although certain sections, especially those dealing with interlocking directorates and interlacing stock ownership, appealed to many entrepreneurs whose operations were more limited in scope, the measure as a whole seemed to be "a strait-jacket upon American business" which large and small businessmen joined in denouncing.[65]

The companion Democratic proposal for a Federal Trade Commission, however, contained potentially the exact solution big industrialists had sought since the days of the Hepburn amendments. Leading a far larger segment of business than before, these men concentrated their efforts upon constructing a trade commission which would serve as a business guardian. The thrust of their argument, as presented in the Chicago Association of Commerce's "Chicago Plan," by-passed the Clayton bill's approach by rejecting "further detailed definition of 'restraint of trade' or unfair practices," but at the same time embodied the contradictory complaint that "nothing hampers business like uncertainty." The reconcilia-

[63] See proposals offered by the National Civic Federation, Elbert H. Gary, and George W. Perkins, in Senate Committee on Interstate Commerce (62 Cong., 2 Sess.), *Hearings Pursuant to S. Res. 98* (3 vols., Washington, 1912), I, 515-24, 693-95, 1091-92. See also Nelson B. Gaskill, *The Regulation of Competition* (New York, 1936), 37.

[64] The best analysis of the Democrats' evolving trust program is given in Link, *Wilson: The New Freedom*, Chap. XIII.

[65] *The Cleveland Chamber of Commerce* (1915), 155. See also *Fifty-sixth Annual Report of the Corporation of the Chamber of Commerce of the State of New York* (1913-1914), 182-83; *Eighty-second Annual Report of the Philadelphia Board of Trade* (1915), 10-18. For the mixed reaction to interlocking directorates and stock ownership, see the results of a United States Chamber of Commerce referendum reported in *Nation's Business*, II, No. 7 (July 15, 1914), 3.

tion lay in a friendly Federal Trade Commission "to which we can submit business practices" and which would then "decide in advance as to the propriety, fairness and benefits of such proposed arrangements, each upon the merits of that particular case." [66]

Smaller industrialists who had steadily fought this concept recognized their old enemy in its latest disguise.[67] From their standpoint, none of the measures before Congress could benefit them, and therefore, with the National Association of Manufacturers in the vanguard, they organized a business drive to pressure Congress into immediate adjournment. "The Country Is Suffering from *Too Much Law*," they protested; let us "Free Business from Political Persecution." [68] With these notes of negativism echoing throughout the debates, Congress passed a modified Clayton Act and established the Federal Trade Commission without the advisory or directive powers outlined in the "Chicago Plan." Suspicions which had persistently kept businessmen from uniting on a trust regulation program left them neutralized in 1914 while Congress enacted legislation unsatisfactory to either of the opposing forces.

The business community had split over trust control, as it had over banking and railroad legislation, into factions shaped according to the dictates of particular economic interests. Yet, beyond motives of self-interest, these specific internal contests formed a broader pattern of business conflict. Its first thread was an urban-rural rift, most clearly shown by the battle between city and country bankers over financial reform. Another thread, in some respects similar, involved a division between businessmen of the East and those of the West and South. While the urban-rural split was related to the regional division, due to a concentration of cities in the East, special sectional characteristics separated the second as a unique strand. Thus urban bankers in Chicago and New York competed

[66] *The Chicago Plan* ([Chicago, 1914]).
[67] This hostility, now diminished because many former opponents supported a commission in order to escape the Clayton Act's controls, is indicated by another U. S. Chamber of Commerce referendum, reported in *Nation's Business*, II, No. 6 (June 18, 1914), 5-6, and analyzed in Senate Committee on Interstate Commerce (63 Cong., 2 Sess.), *Interstate Trade, Hearings on Bills Relating to Trust Legislation* (2 vols., Washington, 1914), II, 688-94.
[68] These are two samples of the stickered slogans which the National Association of Manufacturers offered in unlimited quantities to all applicants. National Association of Manufacturers to Associations, July 30, 1914, Wilson Papers. See also Simmons Hardware Company's widely distributed circular letter of June 9, 1914, *ibid.*; *Report of the Boston Chamber of Commerce* (1914), 48; John M. Glenn, *Urge Congress to Adjourn* ([Chicago, 1914]).

during this time for financial leadership and prestige; city bankers in the Democratic South more readily accepted Wilsonian reform than did their northern — and largely Republican — counterparts; and urban businessmen in the West, where shippers predominated, fought their eastern colleagues who controlled the railroads. Cleavages according to size provided a third thread, which dominated the debate over trust regulation and which also paralleled the city-country rift among bankers. Finally, functional divisions underlay the contest between shippers and carriers over rate levels and made it difficult for bankers to rally other types of businessmen, who were their customers, behind reform programs favorable to the financiers. Interwoven in various ways depending upon the time and the issue, these four strands outlined the quarrels among businessmen over the reform programs of the period. These battles, considered as a group, give consistent testimony that conflict, not co-operation, typified the business community's reaction to crisis during the Progressive era.

Cottonseed Price-Fixing in Eastern North Carolina, 1903-1907

BY LYNETTE B. WRENN*

"While we rightly emphasize our progress in textiles, in tobacco, in lumber and in furniture, we often forget the little cottonseed and its economic significance," wrote an observer of the North Carolina cottonseed industry in 1925.[1] Despite its rank as one of the most valuable classes of southern manufacturing between 1890 and 1930, cottonseed processing has received little attention from historians.[2] By transforming excess seed into useful products, cottonseed processors created so great a demand for their raw material that it became the second largest cash crop in the South.[3] Cottonseed crushers engaged in an annual frenzy of seed buying that, if not checked, caused seed prices to soar. The attempts of early twentieth-century oil mill operators in eastern North Carolina to control cottonseed prices by minimizing competition for seed is the subject of this article.

From the 1870s through the First World War owners of cottonseed oil mills in various parts of the South attempted to control volatile seed prices through cooperative agreements. Cottonseed associations in New Orleans and Memphis, the first important centers of processing, bought seed at the lowest possible prices and distributed them among participating mills according to the crushing capacity of each. Later pools set maximum seed prices that pool members agreed not to exceed. Sometimes such combinations prorated seed or assigned specific

*Dr. Wrenn is an independent scholar who is currently writing a history of the cottonseed processing industry in the United States. The author wishes to thank the following people for their assistance in the preparation of this article: Pete Daniel, Lala Steelman, Patricia Gantt, William R. Erwin, Jr., Maurice C. York, and the staff of the Manuscript Collection, East Carolina University Library, Greenville, North Carolina.

[1] W. J. Matherly, "North Carolina's Position in Cottonseed Industry," *North Carolina Commerce and Industry*, III (November, 1925), a one-page publication in the North Carolina Collection, University of North Carolina Library at Chapel Hill.

[2] Using statistics from the manufacturing schedules of the United States Census, 1890-1930, the author has ranked the cottonseed crushing industry in the former Confederate states and Oklahoma (one of the ten major cotton-producing states) according to the value of the manufacturing products produced in those states. In 1890 crude cottonseed products ranked fifth after lumber, flour-grist milling, cotton goods, and iron and steel; in 1900 fourth after lumber, cotton goods, and flour-grist milling; in 1910 third after lumber and cotton goods; in 1920 third after cotton goods and lumber; and in 1930 fifth after textiles, petroleum, tobacco, and lumber.

[3] George F. Deasy, "Geography of the United States Cottonseed Oil Industry," *Economic Geography*, XVII (October, 1941), 347; *Cotton Oil Press*, II (June, 1918), 38.

Despite the importance of cottonseed processing as one of the South's most valuable manufacturing enterprises, historians have devoted little attention to the study of that industry. This
engraving of a 200-ton cottonseed oil mill (1887) is from D. A. Tompkins, *Cotton and Cotton Oil*
(Charlotte: published by author, 1901), 223.

portions of their seed-buying territory to the mills involved.[4] Like cartels in other
sectors of American industry during the late nineteenth and early twentieth
centuries, cottonseed pools seldom lasted for more than a few months. Sooner
or later, some mills offered more than the fixed price for seed, and other crushers
had to match the higher bids or lose desirable raw materials. Nevertheless,
cottonseed pools generally enabled oil mill operators to retard seed-price
increases and even to lower seed costs when the value of cottonseed oil declined.

Because pools and other collective agreements could not be legally enforced
and competition among numerous small enterprises engaged in similar
activities seemed destructive and inefficient to entrepreneurs, many business
mergers took place during the late nineteenth and early twentieth centuries.[5]
The appearance of a number of large trusts and corporations in the 1880s
alarmed farmers, consumers, and small businessmen. Several of those corporate
giants had their greatest impact on southern farmers. The American Cotton Oil
Trust lowered cottonseed prices following its formation in the mid-1880s.[6] Sharp
increases in the cost of bagging for cotton bales resulted from the creation of the
so-called jute bag trust in 1888 and provoked a boycott by Farmers' Alliance

---

[4]Much information about early cottonseed pools and price-fixing is found in the *Oil, Paint and
Drug Reporter*, a trade journal founded in New York in 1871, and in the *Manufacturers Record*, a
journal published in Baltimore, hereinafter cited as *Manufacturers Record*.

[5]Glenn Porter, *The Rise of Big Business, 1860-1910* (New York: Thomas Y. Crowell Company,
1973), 37, 61-62.

[6]Georges Minch Weber, "The Economic Development of the American Cottonseed Oil Industry"
(unpublished doctoral dissertation, University of California, 1933), 72, hereinafter cited as Weber,
"The Economic Development of the Cottonseed Oil Industry."

members in North Carolina and other cotton-growing states.[7] Organization of the American Tobacco Company in 1890 and five years later of the Virginia-Carolina Chemical Company, known as "the fertilizer trust," intensified antitrust sentiment in the Southeast.[8] In response to the growing clamor against business combinations, both state and federal governments passed antitrust laws.

Contrary to general belief, the numerous mergers that took place around the turn of the century did not check competition in the vast majority of American industries.[9] Cottonseed oil mills, for example, increased at a more rapid rate during the three decades following the creation of the American Cotton Oil Trust than at any time in the history of cottonseed processing. The trust briefly controlled about 88 percent of all crushing facilities, but its share rapidly and steadily declined.[10] Because the merger of oil mills failed to halt competition, price-fixing persisted in the cottonseed crushing industry even after passage of antitrust legislation and a ruling against price-fixing and market division by the United States Supreme Court in 1899.[11]

Cotton growers angered by seed price conspiracies and other monopolistic practices demanded action against the trusts. Cotton belt politicians frequently used the charge of oil mill collusion to whip up popular support among their constituents.[12] Beginning in the late 1880s, cottonseed crushers faced periodic state investigations and prosecutions on charges of conspiring to depress seed prices. Antitrust proceedings against oil mills were particularly vigorous at times in Louisiana, Arkansas, Mississippi, and Texas.[13] North Carolina officials,

---

[7]Michael Schwartz, *Radical Protest and Social Structure: The Southern Farmers' Alliance and Cotton Tenancy, 1880-1890* (Chicago: University of Chicago Press, 1976), 235-246.

[8]Nannie May Tilley, *The Bright-Tobacco Industry, 1860-1929* (Chapel Hill: University of North Carolina Press, 1948), 160, 415, 422, hereinafter cited as Tilley, *The Bright-Tobacco Industry*.

[9]Gabriel Kolko, *The Triumph of Conservatism: A Reinterpretation of American History, 1900-1916* (New York: Free Press of Glencoe, 1963), 24, 29, hereinafter cited as Kolko, *The Triumph of Conservatism*.

[10]The American Cotton Oil Trust, which in 1889 had reorganized as the American Cotton Oil Company, crushed approximately 50 percent of all seed processed in 1891, 20 percent in 1901, 15 percent in 1905, and 8 percent after the First World War. Weber, "The Economic Development of the Cottonseed Oil Industry," 68-69.

[11]Kolko, *The Triumph of Conservatism*, 31.

[12]*Cotton Oil Press*, III (June, 1919), 45, IV (September, 1920), 25, V (July, 1921), 23; W. D. Shue, "The Cotton Oil Industry," *Mississippi Historical Society Publications*, VIII (1904), 289, hereinafter cited as Shue, "The Cotton Oil Industry"; *Proceedings of the Seventh Annual Session of the Texas Cotton Seed Crushers' Association, 1901* (N.p., 1901), 8; *Proceedings of the Fourteenth Annual Session of the Texas Cotton Seed Crushers' Association, 1908* (N.p., 1908), 33, hereinafter cited as *Proceedings of Texas Cotton Seed Crushers' Association*, with appropriate year.

[13]Louisiana, the state with the largest concentration of oil mills during the early years of the industry, was the first to prosecute a company for fixing the price of cottonseed. "State of Louisiana vs American Cotton Oil Trust," Arguments before the Civil District Court and the Supreme Court of Louisiana, 1889, Manuscript Department, Tulane University Library, New Orleans, Louisiana. Early cottonseed combinations are discussed in Shue, "The Cotton Oil Industry," 283-289. The state archives of Mississippi and Texas contain extensive files related to antitrust suits against cottonseed oil mills during the first decade and a half of the twentieth century. News of Arkansas and Texas antitrust suits was reported in the *Commercial and Financial Chronicle*, XCIX (August 15, 1914), 473, CXIII (July 23, 1921), 420.

on the other hand, made little effort to enforce antitrust laws passed by the General Assembly in 1889, 1899, and 1907.[14]

By the First World War price-fixing had become too risky to be practiced on a routine basis, and the crushing industry had begun to consider other methods of mitigating the harmful effects of unrestrained competition for seed. Early in the century crushers in both of the Carolinas and Texas experimented with exchanging price information.[15] Some national business leaders began to advocate full publication of financial data in conjunction with federal regulation of industry as a means of controlling competition.[16] In 1912 *The New Competition* by Arthur Jerome Eddy, a Chicago attorney who had handled cases for Standard Oil Company, promoted "open prices" as a panacea for all industries suffering from destructive competition.[17]

Although there are numerous references to price-fixing in accounts of the cottonseed industry, most provide little information about the day-to-day working of cottonseed pools. An exception is the business correspondence of Dr. Edward Victor Zoeller (1857-1944), a pharmacist and entrepreneur of Tarboro, North Carolina, which contains a detailed record of attempts to stabilize cottonseed prices in eastern North Carolina during the early years of the twentieth century. Conditions in the cottonseed crushing industry that gave rise to seed price agreements, methods used to put the agreements into effect, and results achieved by different strategies are spelled out in numerous letters

---

[14]*Laws of North Carolina, 1889,* c. 374, *1899,* c. 666, *1907,* c. 218, hereinafter cited as *N.C. Laws,* with appropriate year; Joseph F. Steelman, "The Progressive Era in North Carolina, 1884-1917" (unpublished doctoral dissertation, University of North Carolina at Chapel Hill, 1955), 86-87, 201, 286; W. Scott Morgan, *History of the Wheel and Alliance and the Impending Revolution* (Hardy, Arkansas: published by author, 1889; St. Louis: C. B. Woodward Company, 1891), 333. During the same period North Carolina fertilizer laws were strictly enforced, and some offenders were prosecuted. The timing of the North Carolina antitrust laws suggests that they had more to do with the increased price of jute bagging and low tobacco prices and distrust of the American Tobacco Company than with cottonseed prices. North Carolina tobacco farmers organized local Farmers' Alliances in 1888, and Alliance members in cotton-growing areas boycotted the jute bag cartel. Very low tobacco prices in 1899 galvanized tobacco farmers, but their greatest anger against the trust seems to have been during the years 1903-1905. Tilley, *The Bright-Tobacco Industry,* 180, 407, 421, 422.

[15]The idea of crushers' sharing information was not a new one. Industry leaders during the early 1880s had tried in vain to convince crushers to report such statistics as tonnage and prices of seed purchased, the tonnage of products manufactured, and the prices received for them. Weber, "The Economic Development of the American Cottonseed Oil Industry," 60.

[16]Some representatives of big business believed that the only solution to excessive competition was for the federal government to fix prices or collect and publicize corporate financial data. Kolko, *The Triumph of Conservatism,* 63-64, 173-174.

[17]Arthur Jerome Eddy had been organizing trade associations in highly competitive industries that fixed prices and divided markets. With monopoly under attack, Eddy in *The New Competition* promoted the idea of each manufacturer setting his own prices but with full knowledge of prices and other information in his field. Eddy encouraged firms engaged in the same economic activities to form "open price associations" for the purpose of collecting and disseminating relevant statistics. Eddy was among the strong supporters of business-government cooperation and federal regulation as a means of moderating competition. Arthur Jerome Eddy, *The New Competition: An Examination of the Conditions underlying the Radical Change That Is Taking Place in the Commercial and Industrial World—The Change from a Competitive to a Cooperative Basis* (New York: D. Appleton and Company, 1912); H. R. Tosdal, "Open Price Associations," *American Economic Review,* VII (June, 1917), 331-332; Kolko, *The Triumph of Conservatism,* 180-181, 268-269, 272.

Edward Victor Zoeller (1857-1944), a pharmacist and entrepreneur of Tarboro, was a leader in the cottonseed industry. His business correspondence provides a detailed account of efforts to stabilize cottonseed prices in eastern North Carolina. Photograph courtesy of the North Carolina Board of Pharmacy, Chapel Hill.

and telegrams to and from Zoeller, who was the secretary and treasurer of the Tar River Oil Company near Tarboro. The Zoeller Papers not only describe traditional price-fixing methods current at the turn of the century but they also reveal the beginnings of cooperative price and statistical reporting in North and South Carolina years before the practice became widespread in the cottonseed products industry.[8]

---

[8]The business correspondence of Edward Victor Zoeller—preserved in the Edward Victor Zoeller Papers, Southern Historical Collection, University of North Carolina Library at Chapel Hill, hereinafter cited as Zoeller Papers—begins in 1890. There is a gap in the papers from 1895 through 1903. After that eight-year break, price-fixing was virtually the sole subject of the letters and telegrams until 1907. Zoeller had served as secretary-treasurer of an oil mill in Shiloh, near Tarboro, since the mill's organization in 1888. That joint-stock mill, "largely owned by farmers," was incorporated as the Farmers' Cooperative Manufacturing Company in 1889, at the height of the Farmers' Alliance movement in North Carolina. Twenty-eight stockholders, including Elias Carr, a prominent planter and Alliance member soon to be elected Democratic governor of North Carolina (1893-1897), signed the articles of incorporation. In 1895 the mill's name was changed to the Tar River Oil Company, possibly because feelings between Democrats and Populists had become so inflamed that Carr and other stockholders wanted to eliminate any suggestion that the mill was an Alliance cooperative. "Articles of Incorporation of Farmers' Cooperative Manufacturing Company," Records of Incorporations, Office of the Secretary of State, Raleigh; *Farmers' Co-operative Manufacturing Company, Shiloh, Edgecombe County* (Tarboro: C. G. Bradley Book and Job Printer, 1888), 5.

Zoeller had served as secretary-treasurer of the joint-stock cottonseed oil mill (established 1888) known as the Farmers' Cooperative Manufacturing Company. In 1895 stockholders renamed the business the Tar River Oil Company, probably to avoid the implication that it was a Farmers' Alliance cooperative. Photograph of the facility—located at the community of Shiloh Mills (near Tarboro) in Edgecombe County—from the Local History Collection, Edgecombe County Library, Tarboro.

Cottonseed processing on a commercial scale began in New Orleans, Louisiana, and Providence, Rhode Island, in 1855. The primary products of the crushing process were crude oil, cake, meal, hulls, and linters. By the twentieth century those products were chiefly used in cattle feed, fertilizer, soap, vegetable oil and shortening, and in chemical cellulose employed in the manufacture of guncotton, rayon, plastics, and film.[19]

During the late nineteenth and early twentieth centuries the major cotton-growing counties of North Carolina fell into two groups: a southern tier of

---

[19]For the history of the cottonseed oil industry, see Weber, "The Economic Development of the Cottonseed Oil Industry"; H. C. Nixon, "The Rise of the American Cottonseed Oil Industry," *Journal of Political Economy*, XXXVIII (February-December, 1930), 73-85; B. F. Taylor, *Early History of the Cotton Oil Industry in America* (Columbia, S.C.: n.p., 1936); Luther A. Ransom, *The Great Cottonseed Industry of the South* (New York: Oil, Paint and Drug Reporter, 1910); Thomas R. Chaney, "The Cotton-Seed-Oil Industry" in *One Hundred Years of American Commerce*, edited by Chauncey Mitchell Depew (New York: D. O. Haynes, 1 volume, 1895; Westport, Conn.: Greenwood Press, 2 volumes, 1968), II, 451-455; William Haynes, *Cellulose: The Chemical That Grows* (New York: Southern Horizons, 1946; Garden City, N.Y.: Doubleday, 1953), 256-272. Cottonseed cake is the residue left after oil has been extracted from the seed. Meal is produced by grinding the cake. Linters are the fibers obtained when cottonseed are ginned a second or third time by oil mills. Hydraulic presses dominated the cottonseed industry until after World War II.

The major cotton-growing counties in North Carolina during the late nineteenth and early twentieth centuries are shaded on this map.

counties along the South Carolina border (Robeson, Scotland, Richmond, Anson, Union, Mecklenburg, and Cleveland) and a northeastern cluster of counties (Wake, Franklin, Johnston, Wilson, Wayne, Edgecombe, Nash, Pitt, Halifax, and Northampton). The price-fixing agreements discussed by E. V. Zoeller covered primarily the area from Raleigh to the coast and from Dunn and New Bern to the Virginia line.[20]

Wildly fluctuating cottonseed prices were a persistent problem for crushers from the earliest years of the industry. Cottonseed poured into crushing mills during September, October, and November, when most of the cotton was harvested and ginned. Prices tended to be lower during the autumn because seed supplies exceeded crushing capacity. As crushing continued, seed became scarcer, and mill operators competed more vigorously for the remaining lots of stored seed in order to ensure a large crush. Seed prices generally climbed in the middle of the crushing season and then tapered off at the end.

Because crushers bought most of their seed from cotton gins, oil mills sometimes acquired gins or gin stocks to guarantee at least a portion of the seed they needed. The Tar River Oil Company, for example, secretly helped to finance a gin in Washington, North Carolina, in 1904 that bought seed for the mill.[21] By the 1920s some states had limited gin ownership by oil mills. It then became more common for crushers to loan money to ginners, sometimes without expectation of repayment, as a way of acquiring the rights to their seed.[22]

---

[20]U.S. Census Office, *Report on the Statistics of Agriculture in the United States at the Eleventh Census, 1890* (Washington: Government Printing Office, 1891), 57; U.S. Bureau of the Census, *Thirteenth Census of the United States, 1910: Agriculture* (Washington: Government Printing Office, multivolumes and schedules, 1911), V, 231, hereinafter cited as *Census of U.S.*, with appropriate number, year, and schedule.

[21]William Bragaw to E. V. Zoeller, August 26, September 2, 1904, December 12, 1905, Zoeller Papers.

[22]Ownership of gins persisted in Oklahoma, Texas, and Tennessee in the 1920s, but some states made it illegal for oil mills to own more than one cotton gin. U.S. Congress, Senate, *Report of Federal Trade Commission on Cotton-Seed Industry*, Seventy-first Congress, Second Session, 1933, Senate Document No. 2, part 13, pp. x, xi, 6241, hereinafter cited as *Report of Federal Trade Commission on Cotton-Seed Industry*.

Because demand for seed always exceeded supply, "cutthroat competition" among seed buyers pushed up prices. Sometimes crushers paid more for raw materials than their cottonseed oil, cake, hulls, and linters were earning at the time they purchased the seed. Many operators felt compelled to gamble that product prices would rise after the peak of production passed and cottonseed products became less of a glut on the market.[23] Also, the larger the volume of seed crushed by each hydraulic press, the more likely a mill was to operate at a profit, for after fixed expenses had been paid anything earned above operating costs went into the profit column, unless a fire or other catastrophe occurred.[24]

Crushing operations went on for twenty-four hours a day, six or seven days a week as long as seed supplies lasted. Until satisfactory drying methods were developed in the late 1930s mills had to process seed as rapidly as possible in order to prevent heating and deterioration, particularly during the early weeks of the season and during a wet harvest. At its maximum, the crushing season prior to World War II ran from late August through April.[25]

Raw material costs constituted by far the major expense of production, whereas wages for the black laborers who worked in the mills required only a modest proportion of operating funds.[26] At the Tar River Oil Mill, for example, during the years 1895-1917 seed purchases absorbed from 62 percent to 81 percent of the total operating budget and labor only 4.3 percent to 6.7 percent.[27]

---

[23]The president of North Carolina's Lillington Oil Mill Company stated the seed dilemma faced by many mills when he asked the company's directors in 1915 whether the company "should go ahead and buy and take chances on finished products getting high enough for us to come out on seed bought at the prevailing prices." Minutes of Directors' Meeting, September 29, 1915, Lillington Oil Mill Company Papers, 1913-1923, Manuscript Department, Duke University Library, Durham. "We pay from week to week a higher price for raw material than we can see a profit in at the time of purchase," reported the president of the South Carolina crushers in 1908. *Proceedings of the Third Annual Session of the South Carolina Cotton Seed Crushers' Association, Held at Columbia, South Carolina, June 23, 1908* (N.p., 1908), 3, hereinafter cited as *Proceedings of South Carolina Cotton Seed Crushers' Association, 1908.*

[24]*Report of Federal Trade Commission on Cotton-Seed Industry*, 3830.

[25]Even when the presses ran only six days, hulling knives had to be sharpened and other tasks carried out on the seventh day in preparation for the next week's work. M. E. Karsten, "Fifty Years of Oil Mill Operating," *Cotton Oil Press*, XVI (July, 1932), 25. Among the Zoeller Papers is a completed census form for 1914 showing that during that year the Tar River Oil Company operated six days a week for six and a half months.

[26]North Carolina industrialist Daniel A. Tompkins estimated that four fifths of the cost of manufacturing crude cottonseed products went for the purchase of seed. D. A. Tompkins, *Cotton and Cotton Oil* (Charlotte: published by author, 1901), 220. In general, food industries spent more for raw materials and less for labor than did other manufacturers. Georges Minch Weber and C. L. Alsburg, *The American Vegetable-Shortening Industry: Its Origin and Development* (Stanford, Calif.: Stanford University Press, for Food Research Institute, 1934), 148. Southeastern oil mills had to pay even more for seed than did those in other sections. If the higher prices were not met, cotton planters simply used their whole seed as fertilizer or feed. *Manufacturers Record*, August 25, 1893.

[27]The author based these percentages on annual operating costs found in the ledgers of the Tar River Oil Company, Henry Clark Bridgers, Jr., Papers, Manuscript Collection, East Carolina University Library, Greenville, North Carolina. Other sources corroborate the Tar River Oil Company statistics. From 1914 to 1916, for example, 88 to 91 percent of the expenses of the Consumer Cotton Oil Company of Tarboro went for seed and 2.85 to 3.60 percent for labor. F. S. Royster Mercantile Company, Inc., Records, East Carolina University Manuscript Collection. Total operating expenses of North Carolina cottonseed crushing mills in 1909 were as follows: 3.3 percent for salaries, 4.1 percent for wages, 89.2 percent for materials, and 3.4 percent for miscellaneous purposes. The figure for materials included fuel, bags, press cloth, and similar items; but the major cost was for seed. *Thirteenth Census of U.S., 1910: Manufacturers*, IX, 907.

Thus, the high and variable cost of cottonseed preoccupied crushers more than any other aspect of production, and from an early date some of them turned to price-fixing as a remedy.

Cottonseed crushing mills multiplied throughout the South between 1880 and 1914 as the vegetable shortening industry expanded and cotton production increased.[28] In addition to the larger oil mills located at major railway centers, hundreds of small mills sprang up in towns along railroad lines and rivers wherever cotton flourished. Before the advent of trucks, those "cotton patch mills" saved money on freight by buying, in addition to carlots, wagon loads of seed within the ten-to-twelve-mile radius that wagons could travel in a day. From the crushed seed, mills then sold meal and hulls to local farmers or exchanged them for other seed, at a substantial saving on freight.[29]

From 45 mills in 1879, the number in the United States grew to 119 in 1889, 369 in 1899, 817 in 1909, and 882 in 1914.[30] The figures for North Carolina during the same period show a similar pattern of rapid growth.[31] In 1900 the editor of a major trade publication forecast that if mills continued to be built there would be a very "marked competition for seed."[32] Despite that prospect, 150 new mills either began operations or were under construction in 1903 alone.[33] "There seems no limit to new construction," wrote one of E. V. Zoeller's correspondents in 1904.[34]

Therefore, the price-fixing activities described in the Zoeller Papers took place during the years when the largest number of cottonseed mills in the industry's history was competing for a raw material supply whose size was determined not

---

[28]Increased cotton production during the late nineteenth and early twentieth centuries resulted from the continuous westward movement of cotton farmers into Oklahoma and Texas, the shift from corn to cotton, and the intensive use of fertilizers in the southeastern states. Gavin Wright, *Old South, New South: Revolutions in the Southern Economy since the Civil War* (New York: Basic Books, 1986), 34-35.

[29]Cottonseed meal, hulls, and waste accounted for approximately three quarters of the weight of oil mill products. By disposing of meal and hulls locally, a mill could avoid paying freight on more than 75 percent of what it produced. Most farmers transported their cotton less than ten miles to be ginned. A. B. Cox, *The Cottonseed Crushing Industry of Texas in Its National Setting* (Austin: University of Texas Press, 1949), 16.

[30]Maurice R. Cooper, "History of Cotton and the United States Cottonseed Industry," in *Cottonseed and Cottonseed Products: Their Chemistry and Chemical Technology*, edited by A. E. Bailey (New York: Interscience Publishers, 1948), 24.

[31]According to the manufacturing schedules of the U.S. Census, North Carolina had no cottonseed crushing mills in 1879, eleven mills in 1889, twenty-one in 1899, and fifty-three in 1909. The North Carolina State Board of Agriculture reported no mills in 1880 and fourteen in 1893, located in Fayetteville, Wilmington, Charlotte, Tarboro (2), Raleigh, Washington, New Bern, Elizabeth City, Kinston, Richmond County, Laurinburg, Conetoe, and Battleboro. *Hand-Book of North Carolina* (Raleigh: State Board of Agriculture, 1893), 278.

[32]Louis Bell, "Statistics of the Cottonseed Industry," a paper read at the Inter-State Cotton Seed Crushers' Association convention in 1900, in Daniel Augustus Tompkins Papers, Duke University Manuscript Department.

[33]James Curtis Ballagh (ed.), *The South in the Building of the Nation* (Richmond, Va.: Southern Publication Society, 13 volumes, 1909), VI, 291, hereinafter cited as Ballagh, *The South in the Building of the Nation.*

[34]H. E. Wells to E. V. Zoeller, June 29, 1904, Zoeller Papers. After reaching a peak on the eve of World War I, the number of mills slowly declined, although overall crushing capacity remained about the same. *Cotton Oil Press*, VII (November, 1924), 33; *Cottonseed and Its Products* (Memphis: National Cottonseed Products Association, eighth edition, 1978), 9.

Table 1
Cottonseed Oil Mills and Cotton Production, 1899 and 1909

State	Number of Mills 1899	Percentage of Total Mills 1899	Number of Mills 1909	Percentage of Total Mills 1909	Percentage of Total Cotton Bales 1899	Percentage of Total Cotton Bales 1909
Texas	103	28.0%	194	23.7%	26.3%	23.1%
S.C.	50	13.5%	103	12.6%	9.2%	12.0%
Ga.	43	11.5%	142	17.4%	13.5%	18.7%
Miss.	41	11.0%	87	10.6%	13.8%	10.6%
Ala.	28	7.5%	71	8.7%	11.6%	10.6%
La.	24	6.5%	43	5.3%	7.4%	2.5%
N.C.	21	5.7%	53	6.5%	4.8%	6.2%
Ark.*	20	5.4%	44	5.4%	7.5%	7.3%
Tenn.	17	4.6%	20	2.4%	2.5%	2.5%
Okla.	12	3.0%	39	4.8%	2.8%	5.2%
Other	10	2.7%	21	2.6%		
Total Mills	369		817			

*Much of the cottonseed produced in eastern Arkansas was crushed in western Tennessee.

SOURCES: U.S. Census Office, *Twelfth Census of the United States, 1900: Agriculture, Manufacturing* (Washington: Government Printing Office, multivolumes and schedules, 1901); U.S. Bureau of the Census, *Thirteenth Census of the United States, 1910: Agriculture, Manufacturing* (Washington: Government Printing Office, multivolumes and schedules, 1911).

by the demand for seed but by the size of the cotton crop. Although cotton production and oil mills increased at about the same rate during those years, there had never been enough seed available to satisfy the demands of crushers. With the appearance of more and more independent mills and increased railroad mileage bringing large, urban mills closer to the cotton fields, the level of competition intensified.[35]

---

[35]In 1899 North Carolina's twenty-one oil mills represented 5.7 percent of the total number of cottonseed oil mills in the United States. The state had 4.1 percent of the nation's cotton acreage and 4.8 percent of the cotton production. In that year South Carolina had 13.5 percent of the mills, 8.5 percent of the acreage, and 9.2 percent of the cotton production. Although the number of cottonseed mills increased from 21 to 53 in North Carolina and 50 to 103 in South Carolina between 1899 and 1909, cotton farmers in those states made greater productivity gains, in large part because of heavy fertilization. With 6.5 percent of the nation's cottonseed oil mills, North Carolina had 4 percent of the cotton acreage and 6.2 percent of the cotton produced in 1909. Comparable figures for South Carolina were 12.6 percent of the mills, 8 percent of the cotton acreage, and 12 percent of the cotton produced. Later, boll weevil damage reduced cotton production in the Southeast. By the 1920s, because of boll weevil infestation and the unusually large number of small mills, North Carolina mills operated at only 39 percent of capacity. *Twelfth Census of U.S., 1900: Agriculture*, II, 423, 425; *Thirteenth Census of U.S., 1910: Agriculture*, V, 681-682; George Marshall, "Cottonseed—Joint Products and Pyramidal Control," in *Price and Price Policies*, edited by Walton Hamilton (New York: McGraw Hill, 1938), 259, 264, 268, hereinafter cited as Marshall, "Cottonseed—Joint Products and Pyramidal Control."

Between 1884 and 1886, after competition from many new mills increased seed prices and depressed product values, a group of cottonseed mill owners formed the American Cotton Oil Trust. Creators of the trust hoped to acquire most of the oil mills and refineries in order to operate the industry more efficiently and to control seed and product prices. That attempt to create a monopoly did not succeed, however, because cottonseed crushing technology, unlike that of cottonseed oil refining, was not complex and expensive enough to discourage new entries.[36] Some of the men who turned over their plants to the American Cotton Oil Trust in exchange for trust certificates quickly built modern mills and began to compete with the trust.[37] Soon after the formation of the American Cotton Oil Trust, a group of capitalists also organized the Southern Cotton Oil Company, and by the early twentieth century meat-packers, soapmakers, and fertilizer manufacturers—all large users of cottonseed products—had gone into the crushing business.[38] But the majority of cottonseed crushing mills at the turn of the century were either independently owned or part of small, regional chains.

The proliferation of mills during the 1890s prompted the formation of various trade associations. Texas crushers, who owned the largest number of mills in the country and also endured fierce "cottonseed wars" between independents and the American Cotton Oil Company, formed the first state association in 1894. Three years later the Inter-State Cotton Seed Crushers' Association was born, and within a few years crushers in other southern states had created separate organizations.[39] Some of the early state associations played a role in price-stabilization operations.[40]

By 1903 most of the independent cottonseed oil mills in eastern North Carolina had formed an organization and chosen C. L. Ives of the New Bern

---

[36]Alfred Chandler has observed that profitable horizontal mergers (businesses engaged in similar manufacturing processes) attracted competitors, often from among the very businessmen who had participated in the mergers initially. Alfred Dupont Chandler, Jr., *The Visible Hand: The Managerial Revolution in American Business* (Cambridge: Harvard University Press, 1977), 334.

[37]Fred and John Oliver, for example, were New York capitalists who built a cottonseed oil mill in Charlotte, North Carolina, in 1883 and another in Columbia, South Carolina, in 1884. The American Cotton Oil Trust acquired those mills in 1886, and a year later the Olivers joined Daniel A. Tompkins and the Philadelphia meat-packing firm of Washington Butchers Sons in the formation of the Southern Cotton Oil Company. Howard B. Clay, "Daniel Augustus Tompkins and Industrial Revival in the South," *East Carolina College Publications in History*, VII (1965), 123-124.

[38]Besides owning mills outright, the Southern Cotton Oil Company encouraged communities to build mills that would affiliate with the company. In 1902 the Virginia-Carolina Chemical Company, a manufacturer of fertilizers (V-C products), acquired the Southern Cotton Oil Company. At the time of that acquisition, the Southern Cotton Oil Company owned eighty-one mills, refineries, and lard plants. *Commercial and Financial Chronicle*, LXXV (September 6, 1902), 496.

[39]The first trade association, known as the Cotton Seed Crushers' Association, had been organized in 1879, but it died in 1887. By absorbing more than 80 percent of the crushing capacity of the United States, the American Cotton Oil Trust ended the need for a cottonseed oil mill trade association. Copies of the *Proceedings of the Cotton Seed Crushers' Association* (1879-1883) are preserved in the National Agricultural Library, U.S. Department of Agriculture, Beltsville, Md.

[40]Ballagh, *The South in the Building of the Nation*, VI, 290.

VOLUME LXVII, NUMBER 4, OCTOBER, 1990

In an effort to control seed prices and products, a group of capitalists formed the Southern Cotton Oil Company. That company's mills were concentrated in the southeastern states. Shown here is the Southern Cotton Oil Company's mill in Wilson. Detail from map entitled "Bird's Eye View of Wilson, N.C., 1908," reproduced from the files of the Division of Archives and History.

Cotton Oil and Fertilizer Company as their leader.[41] At the beginning of the fall crushing season Ives informed his collaborators of the prices that the American and Southern Cotton Oil companies were quoting in eastern North Carolina for seed.[42] Small crushers counted on buying seed located as close as possible to their mills in order to save freight charges. Large companies collected seed from greater distances in order to process on a large scale and lower their operating costs. Thus, they invaded the territories of small mills whenever it seemed advantageous. Independents had to match bids made by the major chains or lose their raw material supplies.

In mid-September Ives met with Herbert E. Wells of Columbia, South Carolina, the head seed buyer for the American Cotton Oil Company in the Carolinas, to discuss the possibility of forming a pool or "compact."[43] At Wells's invitation E. V. Zoeller joined a number of North Carolina and Virginia

---

[41]The Zoeller Papers do not refer to that organization as the Eastern Carolina Cotton Seed Crushers' Association, but prior to the First World War it sent out circulars and joined the Inter-State Cotton Seed Crushers' Association under that name. See "Eastern Carolina Cotton Seed Crushers' Association," Circular No. 8, Greenville, North Carolina, September 30, 1912, in Record Group 48, volume 32, Archives, Mississippi Department of Archives and History, Jackson, Mississippi, hereinafter cited as Record Group 48, Mississippi State Archives. By 1913 H. A. White was secretary of the association. White later became secretary of the North Carolina Cottonseed Crushers' Association. *Proceedings of the Seventeenth Annual Session of the Inter-State Cotton Seed Crushers' Association, 1913* (N.p., 1913), 113, hereinafter cited as *Proceedings of the Inter-State Cotton Seed Crushers' Association*, with appropriate years.

[42]C. L. Ives to E. V. Zoeller, September 14, 1903, Zoeller Papers.

[43]C. L. Ives to E. V. Zoeller, September 14, 1903, Zoeller Papers. Herbert Ebenezer Wells (1862-1934) began working for the American Cotton Oil Company as a traveling seed buyer based in Columbia, South Carolina. He became in turn a mill manager, state supervisor, district manager, and the company's director of seed buying east of Texas. *Cotton Oil Press*, XVIII (December, 1934), 22.

Table 2
Original Members of Eastern North Carolina Cottonseed Pool
September 24, 1903

Mill Official	Mill Town(s) (if known)	Tons Allotted
F. K. Borden	Goldsboro and other Southern Cotton Oil Company mills	31,100
H. E. Wells	Columbia, S.C., and other American Cotton Oil Company mills	27,900
J. S. Cochran	Philadelphia and Norfolk	7,000 or 8,000*
C. A. Johnson	Tarboro	5,000
Fred Oliver	Norfolk and Portsmouth	5,000
C. L. Ives	New Bern	4,000
McD. Holliday		2,450
E. V. Zoeller	Tarboro	2,450
J. Havens	Washington	2,450
F. C. Dunn	Kinston	2,000
W. M. Darden	Fremont	1,500
W. W. Richardson	Spring Hope	1,500
J. D. Stewart	Scotland Neck	1,500
E. B. McCullers		1,500
M. C. Braswell	Battleboro	1,350
R. W. Brooks	Nashville	1,200

*Leaders of the pool assigned J. S. Cochran 7,000 tons of seed. Cochran insisted upon 8,000 tons, and he probably got the allocation that he requested.

SOURCES: Edward Victor Zoeller Papers, Southern Historical Collection, University of North Carolina Library at Chapel Hill; *Biennial Report of the Secretary of State ... Ending November 30, 1904* (Raleigh: State of North Carolina, 1905).

cottonseed oil men meeting in Norfolk on September 24, 1903.[44] The crushers attending that meeting agreed to fix cottonseed and meal prices and to allocate cottonseed in eastern North Carolina among pool members. Shares of seed ranged from 31,000 tons for Southern Cotton Oil Company mills and 27,900 tons for American Cotton Oil Company mills down to 1,200 tons for several of the smallest independent enterprises.[45] Representatives of the Oliver Refining Company in Portsmouth, Virginia, and of the Cotton Oil and Fibre Company in

---

[44]H. E. Wells to E. V. Zoeller, September 22, 1903, Zoeller Papers.
[45]Although the American Cotton Oil Company was the industry leader, Southern Cotton Oil Company mills were concentrated in the southeastern states. At least seven Southern Cotton Oil Company mills were included in that seed allotment. Seed shares were probably based on the number of hydraulic presses a mill operated, because that was the usual basis of allocation throughout the cottonseed crushing industry.

Norfolk refused to be parties to the pool until they had been granted larger amounts of seed than had been assigned to them initially.

The objectives of the seed pool were to curb speculation in seed by crushers and to stop them from bidding against each other for seed. Mills participating in the pool agreed to sell seed they acquired in excess of their weekly allotments to mills that lacked their full ration. Mill owners hoped that such a seed-sharing arrangement would keep the Virginia companies and other outsiders from sending their seed buyers into eastern North Carolina and bidding up prices. All seed in transactions among pool members had to be purchased at the fixed price in effect at the time of sale. Members of the compact also pledged not to store cottonseed and to sell any surplus they had on hand.[46]

Seed storage stemmed from practices that put upward pressure on prices. Mill operators tended to acquire as many seed as they could even when it meant buying at unprofitable levels. They then stored the excess, hoping for a rise in the value of cottonseed products. Later in the season they either processed the seed or sold them to other mills, depending upon which was more profitable.[47] In order to acquire large lots of seed, mills and the gins associated with them also stored seed for major growers until prices went up and then purchased the seed.

In the past, when several mills bought seed in an area, sellers traditionally had played off one buyer against another by telling each that the others had offered higher prices.[48] Because crushers were notoriously secretive about their transactions, buyers often could not verify such statements. In addition to dividing up the cottonseed produced in eastern North Carolina among members of the compact, the terms of their agreement provided for the setting of maximum seed prices in an effort to control the spiraling cost of raw materials.

Two days after the "Eastern North Carolina Compact" had been formalized at Norfolk, Zoeller received the first of many coded telegrams from "Lime," the pseudonym used by H. E. Wells for purposes of secrecy. Wells transmitted price-fixing information by codes that had been devised to protect the privacy of cottonseed transactions and to reduce the length and expense of telegrams by compressing phrases and sentences into words.[49] Wells sent standardized forms to pool members with spaces left blank for information about seed receipts and average railway freight costs. Recipients were requested to complete a form each Tuesday and return it promptly to the American Cotton Oil Company mill in Columbia, South Carolina, where the information would be compiled and

---

[46]Proceedings of the Monticello Hotel conference of September 24, 1903, were sent to the interested parties in letters from H. E. Wells dated October 2, 1903, Zoeller Papers.

[47]Jonathan Havens of Washington, North Carolina, accused E. V. Zoeller of storing cottonseed, an act that Zoeller emphatically denied. E. V. Zoeller to Jonathan Havens, September 30, 1903, Zoeller Papers.

[48]For example, see Jonathan Havens to E. V. Zoeller, November 14, 1904, and C. L. Ives to E. V. Zoeller, December 30, 1907, Zoeller Papers.

[49]Of the several codes available to cottonseed processors and brokers, the Yopp Code was the one most widely used. That code was the creation of W. I. Yopp (1855-1935), a Tennessee oil miller who became a broker of cottonseed products first in Memphis and later in Dallas. Other industries also employed codes for purposes of secrecy. *Cotton Oil Press*, IV (July, 1920), 39, X (December, 1926), 20, XIX (October, 1935), 12.

summaries sent to the individual mills for their guidance.[50] Wells asked to be notified when problems occurred and promised to work out any "kinks." He urged members not to act independently when they had complaints, because successful operation of the pool depended upon maintaining harmony among the members. Wells closed his messages by asking his correspondents to "please treat this letter as confidential."[51]

At a meeting in Norfolk during early November, 1903, pool leaders decided to offer less than the prevailing rate for seed, because the price of crude cottonseed oil had declined.[52] The Farmers' Alliance in the Tarboro area responded to the lower bids by threatening to stop the sale of seed.[53] Since that response is the only reference to the Farmers' Alliance in the voluminous Zoeller Papers, it seems reasonable to assume that the Alliance had little impact on cottonseed prices in eastern North Carolina during the early twentieth century.

Not all members of the Norfolk compact adhered to the price limit set by pool leaders. Jonathan Havens of Washington, North Carolina, claimed that he had "stuck much closer" to the agreement than many others.[54] The seed buying territories of Zoeller and Havens overlapped.[55] The two men often consulted about seed prices and seed-for-meal exchange rates, but they competed fiercely and each complained frequently about unfair practices of the other. After Havens notified Wells that Zoeller's agent in Washington had been buying more than his limit of seed and storing them for Zoeller, Wells asked Zoeller to restrain his buyer.[56]

Wells authorized an increase in cottonseed prices throughout the Carolinas in mid-December of 1903. Nonetheless, agreements that had stabilized prices for nearly three months began falling apart at year's end as some mills paid more than the fixed price in their quest for seed to extend the crushing season. Early in the new year Wells increased seed prices again.[57] About twelve mills in the Carolinas had pulled out of the pool and were paying higher prices for seed than the remaining members. Wells recommended that the eastern North Carolina mills raise their bids in order to discourage outsiders from buying in their territory.[58] Crushers in that part of the state had already been seized by the speculative mania and were paying more than the fixed price for seed.

---

[50]The Zoeller Papers contain "Consolidated Weekly Reports" of twenty pool members and indicate whether their seed receipts were over or under their assigned quotas.

[51]Form letter from Columbia, South Carolina, October 1, 1903, Zoeller Papers.

[52]"Lime" to E. V. Zoeller, October 29, 1903, Zoeller Papers.

[53]H. E. Wells to E. V. Zoeller, November 9, 1903, Zoeller Papers. Two years earlier a farmers' boycott had been averted because a rise in crude oil prices had allowed crushers to pay more for seed. See "To Cotton Farmers and Growers," clipping from unidentified newspaper, September 25, 1901, J. Bryan Grimes Papers, East Carolina University Manuscript Collection.

[54]Jonathan Havens to E. V. Zoeller, December 8, 1903, Zoeller Papers.

[55]Business papers of Jonathan Havens, Jr., founder of the Havens Oil Company of Washington, North Carolina, and a business partner of John Humphrey Small, are included in the John Humphrey Small Papers, Duke University Manuscript Department. They are primarily bills and receipts and do not touch on the issues dealt with in this study.

[56]H. E. Wells to E. V. Zoeller, November 13, 1903, Zoeller Papers.

[57]"Lime" to E. V. Zoeller, January 4, 5, 1904, Zoeller Papers.

[58]Form letter from H. E. Wells, January 5, 1904, Zoeller Papers.

Table 3
North Carolina Cottonseed Oil Mills, 1903, 1904, and 1907

Name of Mill	Town	Agent in Charge	Date of Report*
	Eastern North Carolina		
Clayton Oil Mills	Clayton	R. A. Wall	1903
		A. J. Barbour	1907
Hertford Cotton Oil Co.	Hertford	W. S. Blanchard	1903
		W. N. Gregory	1907
New Bern Cotton Oil and Fertilizer Co.	New Bern	R. F. Broaddus	1903
		C. L. Ives	1907
Chatham Cotton Oil Co.	Pittsboro	A. H. London	1904
Cotton Oil and Ginning Co.	Scotland Neck	?	1904
		J. D. Stewart	1907
Planters Cotton-Seed Oil Co.	Rocky Mount	E. L. Daughtridge	1904
			1907
Pitt County Oil Co.	Winterville	?	1904
		H. A. White	1907
Selma Oil and Fertilizer Works	Selma	dissolved (possibly acquired by Southern Cotton Oil Co.)	1904
Universal Oil and Fertilizer Co.	Wilmington	W. E. Worth	1904
Battleboro Oil Co.	Battleboro	M. C. Braswell	1904
Consumers Cotton Oil Co.	Tarboro	C. A. Johnson	1904
			1907
Dunn Oil Mill	Dunn	McD. Holliday	1904
Farmers Oil Mill Co.	Nashville	E. B. Grantham	1904
		G. N. Bissett	1907
Farmers Cotton Oil Co.	Wilson	J. R. Chamberlain	1904
			1907
Fremont Oil Mill Co.	Fremont	W. M. Darden	1904
		J. B. Lane	1907
Havens Oil Co.	Washington	Jonathan Havens	1904
			1907
Hertford Cotton Oil Co.	Hertford	W. S. Blanchard	1904
Lenoir Oil and Ice Co.	Kinston	F. C. Dunn	1907
N.C. Cotton Oil Co.	Raleigh	Garland Jones	1907
Pine Level Oil Mill Co.	Pine Level	D. B. Oliver	1907
Pinetops Oil and Guano Co.	Pinetops	W. L. Reason	1907
Spring Hope Cotton Oil Co.	Spring Hope	W. H. Taylor	1907
Tar River Oil Co.	Tarboro	E. V. Zoeller	1907
Zebulon Cotton Oil Co.	Zebulon	R. R. Creech	1907
Southern Cotton Oil Co.	Goldsboro	E. B. Borden, Jr.	1907**
Southern Cotton Oil Co.	Fayetteville	J. A. Moore	1907

Southern Cotton Oil Co.	Selma	N. E. Egleston	1907
Southern Cotton Oil Co.	Wilson	J. I. Morgan	1907
Southern Cotton Oil Co.	Tarboro	J. S. Ashburn	1907
Southern Cotton Oil Co.	Rocky Mount	J. H. Westbrook	1907
American Cotton Oil Co.	Wilmington	H. Bowden	1904***

Name of Mill	Town	Agent in Charge	Date of Report*
Southern North Carolina			
Red Springs [Morgan] Oil and Fertilizer Co.	Red Springs	Mark Morgan William Jones	1903 1907
Waxhaw Oil and Fertilizer Co.	Waxhaw	?	1903
Big Lick Cotton-Seed Mill Co.	Big Lick	?	1904
Charlotte Oil and Fertilizer Co.	Charlotte	?	1904
Kings Mountain Cotton Seed Oil Co.	Kings Mountain	W. A. Mauney G. D. Hambright	1904 1907
Lumberton Cotton Oil and Ginning Co.	Lumberton	?	1904
Concord Cotton-Seed Oil Co.	Concord	?	1904
Independent Cotton Oil Co.	Wadesboro	W. C. Hardison	1904
Cleveland Oil and Fertilizer	Cleveland	J. A. Lyerly	1907
Lorene Cotton Seed Oil Mills	Mooresville	J. W. Brown	1907
Laurinburg Oil Co.	Laurinburg	J. A. Jones	1907
Maxton Oil and Fertilizer Co.	Maxton	?	1907
Southern Cotton Oil Co.	Shelby	J. Frank Jenkins	1907
Southern Cotton Oil Co.	Monroe	T. C. Lee	1907
Southern Cotton Oil Co.	Gastonia	William King	1907
Southern Cotton Oil Co.	Davidson	C. L. Grey	1907
Southern Cotton Oil Co.	Gibson	W. E. Caldwell	1907
Southern Cotton Oil Co.	Concord	M. L. Buchanan	1907
Southern Cotton Oil Co.	Charlotte	E. W. Thompson	1907

*Dates of reports do not indicate the years that corporations were formed. For example, the Tar River Oil Co. was organized in 1888.

**Information on Southern Cotton Oil Co. mills in 1907 is from the membership list of the Inter-State Cotton Seed Crushers' Association *Proceedings* of that year.

***Information about the American Cotton Oil Co. mill at Wilmington is from the Zoeller Papers. The Raleigh mill was also part of that chain, but the date of its acquisition is uncertain. American Cotton Oil Co. mills were not identified in the membership list of the Inter-State Cotton Seed Crushers' Association around 1907.

SOURCES: *Biennial Report of the Secretary of State . . . Ending November 30, 1904* (Raleigh: State of North Carolina, 1905); *Biennial Report of the Secretary of State . . . Ending November 30, 1908* (Raleigh: State of North Carolina, 1909); Edward Victor Zoeller Papers, Southern Historical Collection, University of North Carolina Library at Chapel Hill.

The process of extracting cottonseed oil began at a mill by cleaning the seed and then ginning them a second or third time in a linter to remove lint. Drawing of a linter from Tompkins, *Cotton and Cotton Oil*, 257.

With prices continuing to rise, Wells advised eastern North Carolina crushers to make the best deals possible.[59] At the end of March prices declined rapidly as the crushing season came to an end.[60]

The scheme for allocating eastern North Carolina cottonseed among interested parties was not revived the following season, nor is there further evidence of such an arrangement. But independent mills in eastern North Carolina did seek another price agreement with the major cottonseed companies. At the beginning of the 1904 crushing season C. L. Ives approached those companies about forming another "compact" but found that the American Cotton Oil Company was not interested, at least early in the season. Wells believed that there were too many mills in eastern North Carolina. Some of them should be "made to suffer," he reportedly said, especially those that had not lived up to the agreement of the previous season.[61]

Although no formal pact existed, Ives communicated periodically with E. B. Borden, Jr., the Southern Cotton Oil Company district manager in Goldsboro, and with the manager of the large American Cotton Oil Company mill in Wilmington for the purpose of exchanging information and coordinating prices.[62]

[59]H. E. Wells to E. V. Zoeller, February 27, 1904, Zoeller Papers.
[60]H. E. Wells to E. V. Zoeller, March 11, 28, April 4, 1904, Zoeller Papers.
[61]C. L. Ives to F. C. Dunn, E. V. Zoeller, and C. A. Johnson, September 3, 1904, Zoeller Papers.
[62]C. L. Ives to E. V. Zoeller and Jonathan Havens, October 7, 8, 1904, Zoeller Papers.

Next, seed were carried to a huller, which cut them into pieces. Drawing from Tompkins, *Cotton and Cotton Oil*, 261.

Even so, Borden's agent appeared unexpectedly in Washington, North Carolina, in late October with an authorization to pay more than the going rate for seed.[63]

With seed prices increasing and crude oil prices declining, Ives, Wells, and Borden met in Goldsboro during the first week of November, 1904, to negotiate a general price agreement. Details of the compact were worked out at a conference in Norfolk, and Wells immediately notified cooperating mills of the maximum price they could pay for seed.[64] By the end of the year seed prices had

---

[63]William Bragaw to E. V. Zoeller, October 26, 27, 1904, Zoeller Papers.

[64]C. L. Ives to Jonathan Havens (Washington), E. V. Zoeller (Tarboro), M. C. Braswell (Battleboro), W. N. Gregory (Hertford), R. U. Brooks (Nashville), and W. W. Richardson (Spring Hope), November 7, 1904, form letter from Columbia, South Carolina, November 12, 1904, Zoeller Papers.

After the meats had been separated from the hulls (which could be used for fuel or sold as cattle feed), the meats were crushed, cooked, and taken to cake formers, where they were shaped into cakes. Photograph of cake former from Tompkins, *Cotton and Cotton Oil*, 303.

been lowered and might have been reduced even more had crushers in eastern North Carolina not feared that a further reduction would tempt the Oliver Refining Company and other Virginia companies to buy in the area.[65]

Despite the agreement, Jonathan Havens repeatedly charged Zoeller and his Washington agent, William Bragaw, with unfair practices and paying more than the fixed price for seed.[66] Havens complained that Bragaw had taken seed away from him by exceeding the price limit. Havens "imagines we violate," replied Bragaw, "because he does it whenever it pleases him." "I don't claim to be strictly

---

[65]Prior to the compact, seed prices in eastern North Carolina had gone as high as $16.00 per ton. After the agreement, they dropped to $14.00, then to $12.00, and finally to $11.00. Late in the crushing season, as generally happened, seed prices rose again to as high as $14.00 per ton. Form letters from H. E. Wells, November 12, December 29, 1904, C. L. Ives to E. V. Zoeller, January 12, 1905, "Lime" to E. V. Zoeller, January 13, February 21, 1905, Zoeller Papers.

[66]Jonathan Havens to E. V. Zoeller, November 16, December 22, 1904, January 12, 16, 1905, Zoeller Papers. One unfair practice that Havens complained of was Zoeller's payments to farmers for delivering their seed. That was one way of paying more for seed than the reported price, and crushers included such maneuvers in the list of unfair practices that they composed during the early New Deal. *Proposed Marketing Agreement for the Cotton Seed Industry*, November 4, 1933, p. 16, published by U.S. Department of Agriculture, copy in National Agricultural Library.

regular in all deals," wrote Havens, but "at the same time if the accounts are cast up I think there will be a big balance in my favor."[67]

The experience of rapidly rising seed prices during the early months of the 1904-1905 season convinced independent cottonseed crushers in eastern North Carolina to organize early the following year. At a meeting in Norfolk prior to the 1905-1906 crushing season they again elected C. L. Ives chairman of the group and agreed to pay his expenses at the end of the year based on the number of hydraulic presses operated by each mill.[68] Ives approached repre-sentatives of the two major companies about a general agreement. Wells explained that because of legal difficulties in Texas, the American Cotton Oil Company had instructed its officials not to attend any cottonseed meetings. He indicated to Ives, however, that he would adhere to the price limits set by the independent mills.[69] The manager of the American Cotton Oil Company mill in Wilmington and Borden of the Southern Cotton Oil Company agreed to keep Ives informed of the prices they quoted to sellers, but Borden refused to enter a tonnage agreement or a price-fixing compact because some mills "were already buying seed on a losing basis."[70] In late October, 1905, representatives of the independent mills met in Norfolk, "others agreeing to abide by the decision we made," reported Havens. "I think they are now inclined to be good, as they have not found choking the little fellows as easy as they thought. . . ."[71]

At that time some of the independent mills of Georgia and the Carolinas were exploring the possibility of buying the Oliver Refining Company at Portsmouth in order not to be "at the mercy" of the American and Southern Cotton Oil companies any longer. The small mills resented having to sell their crude oil to the two giants at the prices that those companies set when full storage tanks compelled the independents to unload their oil.[72] Several North Carolina mill men agreed to buy stock in the Portsmouth operation, but northern capitalists acquired the refinery instead.[73]

---

[67]William Bragaw to E. V. Zoeller, December 23, 1904, Jonathan Havens to E. V. Zoeller, January 14, 1905, Zoeller Papers.

[68]At the end of the season Ives sent a letter to participants reminding them of the agreement and informing each of his share of the expenses. Circular letter from C. L. Ives, March 27, 1906, Zoeller Papers.

[69]Circular letter from C. L. Ives, September 5, 1905, C. L. Ives to E. V. Zoeller, November 27, 1905, Zoeller Papers. The exact nature of the American Cotton Oil Company's legal problems in 1905 is not known, but the Texas attorney general initiated a number of antitrust prosecutions against the American Cotton Oil Company, the Standard Oil Company, and other companies prior to World War I. Texas Attorney General's Alphabetical Files (Series I), Texas State Library, Austin, Texas. In 1921 the American Cotton Oil Company was permitted to resume operations in Texas. *Commercial and Financial Chronicle*, CXIII (July 23, 1921), 420.

[70]C. L. Ives to E. B. Borden, Jr., E. V. Zoeller, Jonathan Havens, W. N. Gregory, and F. C. Dunn, September 6, 1905, C. L. Ives to C. A. Johnson, E. V. Zoeller, Jonathan Havens, and W. N. Gregory, September 15, 1905, Zoeller Papers.

[71]Jonathan Havens to W. B. Rodman, October 30, 1905, William Blount Rodman Papers, East Carolina University Manuscript Collection, hereinafter cited as Rodman Papers.

[72]F. C. Dunn to Jonathan Havens, October 28, 1905, Jonathan Havens to F. C. Dunn, October 30, 1905, Rodman Papers.

[73]John Aspergren and Louis Rosenstein acquired the Oliver facility and renamed it the Portsmouth Cotton Oil Refining Company. *Cotton Oil Press*, VI (August, 1922), 17, VIII (December, 1924), 18.

Representatives of the American and Southern Cotton Oil companies finally accepted a seed-price agreement in early December, 1905.[74] By the new year so many mills had exceeded the price limit that some independents thought the compact should be abrogated and "every man look out for self."[75] With many mills losing money because of unusually high seed prices, Ives met again with officials of the two major companies in mid-January.[76] Following this conference seed prices in eastern North Carolina fell in February and again in March.[77]

Acrimony between Havens and Zoeller reached a new level during the 1905-1906 crushing season. Havens, Zoeller, and Bragaw repeatedly accused each other of cheating. But the Oliver Refining Company may have been responsible for some of the high seed payments that the three men attributed to each other.[78] Zoeller felt so bitter that on several occasions he refused to quote prices as directed by Ives until he could be assured that other crushers in his territory were adhering to them.[79] In March when Zoeller paid his share of expenses for the eastern North Carolina compact he told Ives that he wished "the results had been as satisfactory as your zeal to make them so."[80] In reply, Ives regretted that Zoeller had experienced difficulties in his section but expressed satisfaction with the way the agreement had operated generally.

Ives urged Zoeller to attend the annual meeting of the Inter-State Cotton Seed Crushers' Association in Atlanta in May, 1906. At that time, Ives informed Zoeller, North Carolina members planned to organize a branch of the Sons of Plato, "which has been the means of doing much good in Texas during the past season."[81] South Carolina crushers already had a chapter of the Sons of Plato, which communicated with industry members in North Carolina.[82] Zoeller and his correspondents never disclosed the aims and methods of the new society, but it was an organization whose members "met in secret conclave under the guise of a fraternal order and . . . fixed prices and prorated seed among themselves."[83]

Zoeller did not attend the Inter-State Cotton Seed Crushers' convention, but his mill joined the national association. Ives next invited the Tarboro pharmacist to a meeting in Goldsboro called to organize the North Carolina Cottonseed Crushers' Association. Fifteen eastern North Carolina mills, including all of the

---

[74]Form letter from C. L. Ives, December 5, 1905, Zoeller Papers.

[75]C. L. Ives to E. V. Zoeller, January 5, 1906, Zoeller Papers.

[76]C. L. Ives to E. V. Zoeller, January 17, 1906, Zoeller Papers.

[77]Form letter from C. L. Ives, February 15, 1906, C. L. Ives to E. V. Zoeller, March 6, 8, 1906, Zoeller Papers.

[78]Jonathan Havens to E. V. Zoeller, January 30, February 1, 3, 27, 28, April 14, 1906, Zoeller to Havens, January 31, February 2, 1906, unsigned letter from Tarboro to P. Boney, February 13, 1906, unsigned letters to Havens, February 27, 28, April 16, 1906, C. L. Ives to Zoeller, February 19, 1906, letter from "W. B.," February 26, 1906, Zoeller Papers.

[79]Unsigned letters from Tarboro to C. L. Ives, February 26, March 8, 1906, Zoeller Papers.

[80]E. V. Zoeller to C. L. Ives, March 30, 1906, Zoeller Papers.

[81]C. L. Ives to E. V. Zoeller, March 31, 1906, Zoeller Papers.

[82]Form letter from the Sons of Plato, Columbia, South Carolina, signed by B. F. Taylor, April 11, 1906, Zoeller Papers.

[83]Marshall, "Cottonseed—Joint Products and Pyramidal Control," 237-238.

Cakes were placed in a press, and the oil was rendered by pressure. Hydraulic presses dominated the cottonseed industry until after World War II. Photograph of oil press from Tompkins, *Cotton and Cotton Oil*, 309.

Southern Cotton Oil Company mills in the state, had agreed to join, Ives reported.[84]

When Zoeller boycotted the Goldsboro meeting, Ives informed him that seven men had been inducted into the Sons of Plato on that occasion, bringing the total in eastern North Carolina to twenty-one members. Ives expressed the hope that when crushers met later in Norfolk Zoeller and other holdouts would join the secret society. Jonathan Havens also encouraged Zoeller to meet with them in

---

[84]C. L. Ives to E. V. Zoeller, May 21, 1906, Zoeller Papers. The number of North Carolina companies that were members of the Inter-State Cotton Seed Crushers' Association (ICCA) increased from four in 1905 to thirty-two in 1907. Not all remained members during the next few years, but Zoeller's and Havens's companies did. C. L. Ives served as president of the ICCA in 1914-1915, and E. B. Borden, Jr., F. C. Dunn, Jonathan Havens, C. A. Johnson, and W. N. Gregory all served on the governing committee of the association before 1915. *Proceedings of the Inter-State Cotton Seed Crushers' Association, 1905*, 90, *1907*, 105-106, *1909*, 111-112, *1910*, 151-152, *1911*, 116-117, *1913-1914*, 113.

Workers ground the cake remaining in an oil press in a mill to produce meal, which was used as cattle feed or as an ingredient in fertilizer. Photograph of meal mill from Tompkins, *Cotton and Cotton Oil*, 339.

Norfolk and become a member.[85] But Zoeller did not join the society, and he explained his reasons in a letter to Ives: "With Mr. Havens explanation of your aims and objects I would not care to join the organization, as I feel confident that it would be a violation of Interstate and possibly our State Laws, and in a friendly spirit I strongly suggest that none of you proceed further than you have."[86]

It is difficult to understand Zoeller's reservations about joining the Sons of Plato. He had been a party to seed pools and price-fixing agreements from 1903 through 1906, and by the early twentieth century both of those activities constituted violations of state and national laws. The antitrust law passed by the North Carolina General Assembly in 1899 had specifically prohibited pools and price-fixing and set a fine of $100 a day and forfeiture of charter as the penalties for violation.[87] In the 1899 "Addyston Pipe" decision the United States Supreme Court declared market division and price-fixing to be illegal.[88]

The relationship between the state cottonseed associations and Sons of Plato chapters and the different functions of each are not explained in the

[85]C. L. Ives to E. V. Zoeller, June 1, 1906, Jonathan Havens to E. V. Zoeller, June 20, 28, 1906, Zoeller Papers.
[86]E. V. Zoeller to C. L. Ives, June 30, 1906, Zoeller Papers.
[87]*N.C. Laws, 1899*, c. 666.
[88]Kolko, *The Triumph of Conservatism*, 31.

The extracted oil was transported to a refinery, where the impurities were removed. The oil subsequently became an ingredient in a variety of products, including vegetable oil and shortening. Drawing of refinery from Tompkins, *Cotton and Cotton Oil*, 347.

Zoeller Papers. It is clear, however, that announcements during the 1906 organizational drive of the Sons of Plato in the Carolinas came from B. F. Taylor, secretary of the South Carolina Cottonseed Crushers' Association.[89] Undoubtedly because Zoeller refused to join the North Carolina chapter, the Sons of Plato ceased to be discussed in his correspondence. How long the organization continued to function in North Carolina and what methods it used are unknown. But antitrust prosecution in several states caused the disbanding of the Sons of Plato around 1917.[90]

At the beginning of the 1906 crushing season North Carolina cotton oil men received letters from C. L. Ives in his capacity as secretary of the newly organized North Carolina Cottonseed Crushers' Association.[91] For a fee of 3 cents per ton Ives offered to inform members about the prices being paid for seed in different locations and to advise them where seed could be purchased if needed or surpluses sold. Each member of the association would receive a form to complete weekly recording his seed purchases for each week. Subsequent form letters from Ives provided Zoeller with market information and suggested cottonseed prices.[92] Secretary B. F. Taylor performed a similar service for members of the South Carolina Cottonseed Crushers' Association.

---

[89]Form letter from the Sons of Plato, Columbia, South Carolina, signed by B. F. Taylor, April 11, 1906, Zoeller Papers.

[90]For example, almost all of the Mississippi oil mill owners joined the Sons of Plato and were prosecuted by the state attorney general. Alabama and Tennessee mills also had chapters of the Sons that cooperated with the Mississippi chapter. See Record Group 48, volumes 32-35, Mississippi State Archives, and *Cotton Seed Oil Magazine*, XXVII (September, 1916), 38, copy in National Agricultural Library.

[91]A joint North and South Carolina association existed in 1905-1906. In the following year crushers in each state organized a separate association, but the two organizations held a joint convention. *Proceedings of South Carolina Cotton Seed Crushers' Association, 1908*, 2.

[92]Form letters from C. L. Ives, September 10, 22, October 6, November 14, 24, 30, December 14, 1906, January 5, March 9, 1907, Zoeller Papers.

In July, 1907, Ives notified members of the North Carolina Cottonseed Crushers' Association that they had been invited to meet with the South Carolina crushers at their convention in Asheville. At this meeting the Bureau of Information maintained by the two associations was to present aggregate statistics on the seed purchased by North and South Carolina oil mills in 1906-1907, and those present would decide whether or not to continue the bureau.[93] Following those communications, the continuous series of letters written to and by Zoeller on the subject of cottonseed crushing ended.[94]

Nevertheless, the business correspondence of E. V. Zoeller in eastern North Carolina during the early twentieth century provides a rare and valuable perspective on how strategies for stabilizing cottonseed prices evolved from seed pools and price agreements to price reporting. The movement away from fixing seed prices and toward sharing price information and other statistics characterized the cottonseed industry as a whole, although the transition occurred at a much slower pace outside the Carolinas, and possibly Texas.[95] Secret price-fixing and seed allocation schemes such as those carried out by the Sons of Plato came under increasing legal attack in several states. Those legal assaults made the adoption of other methods of moderating cottonseed prices desirable.

Statistics collected by the North and South Carolina crushers' associations in 1906-1907 were circulated among members only, according to general trade association practice at the time.[96] But shortly before World War I a new form of competition based on full publication of trade statistics won wide acceptance among businessmen as an alternative to unpopular and illegal means of lessening destructive competition. The federal government's ambivalent and sometimes hostile attitude toward statistical reporting during the postwar

---

[93]Form letter from C. L. Ives, July 10, 1907, program of the South Carolina Cottonseed Crushers' Association, 1907, circulars 47, 47a, and 48 from B. F. Taylor, July 11, 19, 1907, Zoeller Papers. B. F. Taylor, a manager for the Southern Cotton Oil Company in Columbia, South Carolina, served as president of the Inter-State Cotton Seed Crushers' Association in 1911 and authored the *Early History of the Cotton Oil Industry in America* (1936). More than any other crusher, he promoted the idea of collecting and sharing information about cottonseed and cottonseed product prices. Indeed, the gathering and reporting of cottonseed statistics by oil mills came to be known as the "South Carolina Plan" because of its enthusiastic support by B. F. Taylor, longtime secretary of the South Carolina Cottonseed Crushers' Association.

[94]Other sources document the continued existence of the information bureau that operated for the North and South Carolina associations. In 1928 the Federal Trade Commission reported that the North and South Carolina associations were the only ones that regularly collected seed-price statistics. *Cotton Oil Press*, XI (April, 1928), 21. The Inter-State Cotton Seed Crushers' Association did not create a statistics bureau.

[95]Texas crushers showed an early interest in price reporting, but no evidence has been found to show whether price reporting was practiced in Texas before the First World War. For more information on Texas, see *Proceedings of Texas Cotton Seed Crushers' Association, 1901*, 15, and *Cotton Seed Oil Magazine*, XXVII (October, 1916), 25-26, XXVIII (November, 1916), 28-29. In 1914 the North Carolina Department of Agriculture began collecting prices of cotton and cottonseed, which it sent to newspapers, county agents, and others. In 1918 the department was continuing to provide its marketing service, but it is not clear whether it still included prices of cottonseed. See *Biennial Reports of the Department of Agriculture* (Raleigh: State of North Carolina, multivolume series, 1889—), *1914*, 107, *1918*, 164.

[96]*Report of the Federal Trade Commission on Cotton-Seed Industry*, 3557-3558, 3710.

period caused cottonseed crushers to adopt a wait-and-see attitude, until the Supreme Court in 1925 ruled that gathering and publishing trade information did not in itself violate antitrust laws. In that year the general manager of the Inter-State Cotton Seed Crushers' Association gave as his first priority "a definite plan to stabilize the value of cottonseed by each day giving publicity in the widest sense to the prices paid for cottonseed all over the belt and the value of the products thereof."[97] Thus the leaders of the cottonseed processing industry came to view price reporting as a more acceptable method than price-fixing for seeking uniformity and stability of seed prices.

---

[97]*Cotton Oil Press*, IX (October, 1925), 17.

ACKNOWLEDGMENTS

Carter, John R. "From Peckham to White: Economic Welfare and the Rule of Reason." *Antitrust Bulletin* 25 (1980): 275–95. Reprinted with the permission of Federal Legal Publications, Inc. Courtesy of Yale University Law Library.

German, Jr., James C. "The Taft Administration and the Sherman Antitrust Act." *Mid-America* 54 (1972): 172–86. Reprinted with the permission of Loyola University. Courtesy of *Mid-America*.

Graebner, William. "Great Expectations: The Search for Order in Bituminous Coal, 1890–1917." *Business History Review* 48 (1974): 49–72. Reprinted with the permission of the Harvard Business School. Courtesy of Yale University Sterling Memorial Library.

Jaenicke, Douglas Walter. "Herbert Croly, Progressive Ideology, and the FTC Act." *Political Science Quarterly* 93 (1978): 471–93. Reprinted with the permission of the author and The Academy of Political Science. Courtesy of Yale University Sterling Memorial Library.

Johnson, Arthur M. "Theodore Roosevelt and the Bureau of Corporations." *Mississippi Valley Historical Review* 45 (1959): 571–90. Courtesy of Yale University Sterling Memorial Library.

Klebaner, Benjamin J. "Potential Competition and the American Antitrust Legislation of 1914." *Business History Review* 38 (1964): 163–85. Reprinted with the permission of the Harvard Business School. Courtesy of Yale University Sterling Memorial Library.

McCormick, Richard L. "The Discovery that Business Corrupts Politics: A Reappraisal of the Origins of Progressivism." *American Historical Review* 86 (1981): 247–74. Reprinted with the permission of the author. Courtesy of Yale University Sterling Memorial Library.

McCraw, Thomas K. and Forest Reinhardt. "Losing to Win: U.S. Steel's Pricing, Investment Decisions, and Market Share, 1901–1938." *Journal of Economic History* 49 (1989): 593–619. Reprinted with the permission of Cambridge University Press. Courtesy of Yale University Sterling Memorial Library.

Piott, Steven L. "Missouri and the Beef Trust: Consumer Action and Investigation, 1902." *Missouri Historical Review* 76 (1981): 31–52. Reprinted with the permission of the State Historical Society of Missouri. Courtesy of Yale University Sterling Memorial Library.

Pratt, Joseph A. "The Petroleum Industry in Transition: Antitrust and the Decline of Monopoly Control in Oil." *Journal of Economic History* 40 (1980): 815–37. Reprinted with the permission of Cambridge University Press. Courtesy of Yale University Social Science Library.

Roy, William G. "The Politics of Bureaucratization and the U.S. Bureau of Corporations." *Journal of Political & Military Sociology* 10 (1982): 183–99. Reprinted with the permission of the *Journal of Political & Military Sociology* (copyright holder). Courtesy of Yale University Sterling Memorial Library.

Seltzer, Alan L. "Woodrow Wilson as 'Corporate Liberal': Toward a Reconsideration of Left Revisionist Historiography." *Western Political Quarterly* 30 (1977): 183–212. Reprinted by permission of the University of Utah, copyright holder. Courtesy of the author.

Sklar, Martin J. "Woodrow Wilson and the Political Economy of Modern United States Liberalism." *Studies on the Left* 1 (1960): 17–47. Courtesy of Yale University Seeley G. Mudd Library.

Strum, Philippa. "Louis D. Brandeis, the New Freedom and the State." *Mid-America* 69 (1987): 105–24. Reprinted with the permission of Loyola University. Courtesy of *Mid-America*.

Wiebe, Robert H. "Business Disunity and the Progressive Movement, 1901–1914." *Mississippi Valley Historical Review* 44 (1958): 664–85. Courtesy of Yale University Sterling Memorial Library.

Wrenn, Lynette B. "Cottonseed Price-Fixing in Eastern North Carolina, 1903–1907." *North Carolina Historical Review* 67 (1990): 411–37. Reprinted with the permission of the *North Carolina Historical Review*. Courtesy of the *North Carolina Historical Review*.

For Product Safety Concerns and Information please contact our EU
representative GPSR@taylorandfrancis.com
Taylor & Francis Verlag GmbH, Kaufingerstraße 24, 80331 München, Germany